TAKING SIDES

Clashing Views in

United States History, Volume 2, Reconstruction to the Present

THIRTEENTH EDITION

D0714018

WKH1735

TAKING SIDES

Clashing Views in

United States History, Volume 2, Reconstruction to the Present

THIRTEENTH EDITION

Selected, Edited, and with Introductions by

Larry Madaras
Howard Community College

and

James M. SoRelle
Baylor University

**McGraw-Hill
Higher Education**

Boston   Burr Ridge, IL   Dubuque, IA   New York   San Francisco   St. Louis
Bangkok   Bogotá   Caracas   Kuala Lumpur   Lisbon   London   Madrid   Mexico City
Milan   Montreal   New Delhi   Santiago   Seoul   Singapore   Sydney   Taipei   Toronto

McGraw-Hill
Higher Education

TAKING SIDES: CLASHING VIEWS IN UNITED STATES HISTORY, VOLUME 2:
RECONSTRUCTION TO THE PRESENT, THIRTEENTH EDITION

Published by McGraw-Hill, a business unit of The McGraw-Hill Companies, Inc., 1221 Avenue of the Americas, New York, NY 10020. Copyright © 2009 by The McGraw-Hill Companies, Inc. All rights reserved. Previous edition(s) 1985–2007. No part of this publication may be reproduced or distributed in any form or by any means, or stored in a database or retrieval system, without the prior written consent of The McGraw-Hill Companies, Inc., including, but not limited to, in any network or other electronic storage or transmission, or broadcast for distance learning.

Some ancillaries, including electronic and print components, may not be available to customers outside the United States.

Taking Sides® is a registered trademark of the McGraw-Hill Companies, Inc.
Taking Sides is published by the **Contemporary Learning Series** group within the McGraw-Hill Higher Education division.

1 2 3 4 5 6 7 8 9 0 DOC/DOC 0 9 8

MHID: 0-07-351532-9
ISBN: 978-0-07-351532-8
ISSN: 1091-8833

Managing Editor: *Larry Loeppke*
Senior Managing Editor: *Faye Schilling*
Senior Developmental Editor: *Jill Peter*
Editorial Coordinator: *Mary Foust*
Editorial Assistant: *Nancy Meissner*
Production Service Assistant: *Rita Hingtgen*
Permissions Coordinator: *Shirley Lanners*
Senior Marketing Manager: *Julie Keck*
Marketing Communications Specialist: *Mary Klein*
Marketing Coordinator: *Alice Link*
Senior Project Manager: *Jane Mohr*
Design Specialist: *Tara McDermott*
Cover Graphics: *Kristine Jubeck*

Compositor: ICC Macmillan Inc.
Cover Image: Library of Congress

Library of Congress Cataloging-in-Publication Data
Main entry under title:
    Taking sides: clashing views on controversial issues in American history, volume ii, reconstruction to the present/selected, edited, and with introductions by Larry Madaras and James W. SoRelle—13th ed.

    Includes bibliographical references and index.
    1. United States—History—1865– I. Madaras, Larry, *comp.* II. SoRelle, James M., *comp.*
                                                                                  973

www.mhhe.com

Preface

$\mathbf{T}$he success of the past twelve editions of *Taking Sides: Clashing Views in United States History* has encouraged us to remain faithful to its original objectives, methods, and format. Our aim has been to create an effective instrument to enhance classroom learning and to foster critical thinking. Historical facts presented in a vacuum are of little value to the educational process. For students, whose search for historical truth often concentrates on *when* something happened rather than on *why*, and on specific events rather than on the *significance* of those events, *Taking Sides* is designed to offer an interesting and valuable departure. The understanding that the reader arrives at based on the evidence that emerges from the clash of views encourages the reader to view history as an *interpretive* discipline, not one of rote memorization.

As in previous editions, the issues are arranged in chronological order and can be easily incorporated into any American history survey course. Each issue has an issue *introduction*, which sets the stage for the debate that follows in the pro and con selections and provides historical and methodological background to the problem that the issue examines. Each issue concludes with a *postscript*, which ties the readings together, briefly mentions alternative interpretations, and supplies detailed *suggestions for further reading* for the student who wishes to pursue the topics raised in the issue. Also, Internet site addresses (URLs), which should prove useful as starting points for further research, have been provided on the *Internet References* page that accompanies each unit opener. At the back of the book is a listing of all the *contributors to this volume* with a brief biographical sketch of each of the prominent figures whose views are debated here.

Changes to This Edition

In this edition, we have continued our efforts to maintain a balance between the traditional political, diplomatic, and cultural issues and the new social history, which depicts a society that benefited from the presence of African Americans, women, and workers of various racial and ethnic backgrounds. With this in mind, we present nine new issues, some at the request of teachers who want some of the earlier issues revisited. These include: "Was the Wild West More Violent Than the Rest of the United States?" (Issue 2); "Were American Workers in the Gilded Age Conservative Capitalists?" (Issue 3); "Were Late-Nineteenth-Century Immigrants 'Uprooted'?" (Issue 4); "Was City Government in Late-Nineteenth-Century America a 'Conspicuous Failure'?" (Issue 5); "Was Woodrow Wilson Responsible for the Failure of the United States to Join the League of Nations?" (Issue 8); "Was Franklin Roosevelt a Reluctant Internationalist?" (Issue 11); "Was President Truman Responsible for the Cold War?" (Issue 12); "Was Rock and Roll Responsible for Dismantling America's Traditional Family, Sexual, and Racial Customs in the 1950s and 1960s?" (Issue 13); "Has the Women's Movement of the 1970s Failed to Liberate American Women?" (Issue 16); and "Were the 1980s a Decade of Affluence for the Middle Class?" (Issue 17).

A word to the instructor *An Instructor's Resource Guide With Test Questions* (multiple-choice and essay) is available through the publisher for the instructor using *Taking Sides* in the classroom. A general guidebook, *Using Taking Sides in the Classroom*, which discusses methods and techniques for integrating the pro-con approach into any classroom setting, is also available. An online version of *Using Taking Sides in the Classroom* and a correspondence service for *Taking Sides* adopters can be found at http://www.mhcls.com/usingts/.

Taking Sides: Clashing Views in United States History is only one title in the *Taking Sides* series. If you are interested in seeing the table of contents for any other titles, please visit the *Taking Sides* Web site at http://www.mhcls.com/takingsides/.

Acknowledgments Many individuals have contributed to the successful completion of past editions. We appreciate the evaluations submitted to McGraw-Hill/CLS by those who have used *Taking Sides* in the classroom. Special thanks to those who responded with specific suggestions for the previous editions:

Gary Best
University of Hawaii–Hilo
James D. Bolton
Coastline Community College
Mary Borg
University of Northern Colorado
John Whitney Evans
College of St. Scholastica
Mark Hickerson
Chaffey College
Maryann Irwin
Diablo Valley College
Tim Koerner
Oakland Community College
Gordon Lam
Sierra College
Jon Nielson
Columbia College
Andrew O'Shaugnessy
University of Wisconsin–Oshkosh

Manian Padma
DeAnza College
Elliot Pasternack
Middlesex County College (N.J.)
Robert M. Paterson
Armstrong State College
Charles Piehl
Mankato State University
Ethan S. Rafuse
University of Missouri–Kansas City
John Reid
Ohio State University–Lima
Murray Rubinstein
CUNY Baruch College
Neil Sapper
Amarillo College
Preston She
Plymouth State College
Jack Traylor
William Jennings Bryan College

We are particularly indebted to Maggie Cullen, Cindy SoRelle, the late Barry A. Crouch, Virginia Kirk, Joseph and Helen Mitchell, and Jean Soto, who shared their ideas for changes, pointed us toward potentially useful historical works, and provided significant editorial assistance. Lynn Wilder performed indispensable typing duties connected with this project.

Susan E. Myers, Ela Ciborowski, and Karen Higgins in the library at Howard Community College provided essential help in acquiring books and articles on interlibrary loan. Finally, we are sincerely grateful for the commitment, encouragement, and patience provided over the years by David Dean, former list manager for the *Taking Sides* series; David Brackley, former senior developmental editor; and the entire staff of McGraw-Hill/CLS. Indispensable to this project are Ted Knight, the former list manager, and Jill Peter, the current editor-in-charge of the *Taking Sides* series.

Larry Madaras
Howard Community College

James M. SoRelle
Baylor University

Contents In Brief

Contents

Professor of history Carl N. Degler maintains that the American labor movement accepted capitalism and reacted conservatively to the radical organizational changes brought about in the economic system by big business. Professor of history Herbert G. Gutman argues that from 1843 to 1893, American factory workers attempted to humanize the system through the maintenance of their traditional, artesian, preindustrial work habits.

Issue 4. Were Late-Nineteenth-Century Immigrants "Uprooted"? 78

Oscar Handlin asserts that immigrants to the United States in the late nineteenth century were alienated from the cultural traditions of the homeland they had left as well as from those of their adopted country. Mark Wyman argues that as many as four million immigrants to the United States between 1880 and 1930 viewed their trip as temporary and remained tied psychologically to their homeland to which they returned once they had accumulated enough wealth to enable them to improve their status back home.

Issue 5. Was City Government in Late-Nineteenth-Century America a "Conspicuous Failure"? 100

Professor of political science and political economy Ernest S. Griffith (1896–1981) focuses upon illegal and unethical operations of the political machine and concludes that the governments controlled by the bosses represented a betrayal of the public trust. Professor of history Jon C. Teaford argues that scholars traditionally have overlooked the remarkable success that municipal governments in the late nineteenth century achieved in dealing with the challenges presented by rapid urbanization.

UNIT 2 THE RESPONSE TO INDUSTRIALISM AND REFORM, WAR, AND DEPRESSION 125

Issue 6. Did Booker T. Washington's Philosophy and Actions Betray the Interests of African Americans? 126

Donald Spivey contends that Booker T. Washington alienated both students and faculty at Tuskegee Institute by establishing an authoritarian system that failed to provide an adequate academic curriculum to prepare students for the industrial workplace. Robert J. Norrell insists that Booker T. Washington, while limited in what he could accomplish by the racial climate of the day, nevertheless spoke up for political and civil rights, decried mob violence, and defended black education as a means of promoting a more positive image for African Americans in an era dominated by the doctrine of white supremacy.

Issue 7. Did the Progressives Fail? 150

Professor of history Richard M. Abrams maintains that progressivism was a failure because it tried to impose a uniform set of values upon a culturally diverse people and never seriously confronted the inequalities that still exist in American society. Professors of history Arthur S. Link and Richard L. McCormick argue that the Progressives were a diverse group of reformers who confronted and ameliorated the worst abuses that emerged in urban industrial America during the early 1900s.

Issue 8. Was Woodrow Wilson Responsible for the Failure of the United States to Join the League of Nations? 174

The late Thomas A. Bailey, argues that a physically infirm Woodrow Wilson was unable to make the necessary compromises with the U.S. Senate to join the League of Nations and convince America that the United States should play a major role in world affairs. William G. Carleton believed that Woodrow Wilson understood the role that the United States would play in world affairs.

Issue 9. Was Prohibition a Failure? 196

David E. Kyvig admits that alcohol consumption declined sharply in the prohibition era but that federal actions failed to impose abstinence among an increasingly urban and heterogeneous populace that resented and resisted restraints on their individual behavior. J. C. Burnham states that the prohibition experiment was more a success than a failure and contributed to a substantial decrease in liquor consumption, reduced arrests for alcoholism, fewer alcohol-related diseases and hospitalizations, and destroyed the old-fashioned saloon that was a major target of the law's proponents.

Professor of history Roger Biles contends that, in spite of its minimal reforms and non-revolutionary programs, the New Deal created a limited welfare state that implemented economic stabilizers to avert another depression. Professor of history Gary Dean Best argues that Roosevelt established an antibusiness environment with the creation of the New Deal regulatory programs, which retarded the nation's economic recovery from the Great Depression until World War II.

Diplomatic historian Robert A. Divine argues that even after France fell to Nazi Germany in June 1940, Franklin D. Roosevelt remained a reluctant internationalist who spoke belligerently but acted timidly because he sincerely hated war. Pulitzer Prize–winning historian Arthur M. Schlesinger, Jr., maintains that from a 1990s perspective, Roosevelt—not Stalin, Churchill, or anyone else—was the only wartime leader who saw clearly the direction and shape of the new world that the leaders were trying to create.

UNIT 3　THE COLD WAR AND BEYOND　273

Arnold A. Offner argues that President Harry S. Truman was a parochial nationalist whose limited vision of foreign affairs precluded negotiations with the Russians over cold war issues. John Lewis Gaddis argues that after a half century of scholarship, Joseph Stalin was uncompromising and primarily responsible for the cold war.

Professor Glenn C. Altschuler maintains that rock and roll's "switchblade" beat opened wide divisions in American society along the fault lines of family, sexuality, and race. Writer J. Ronald Oakley argues that although the lifestyles of youth departed from their parents, their basic ideas and attitudes were still the conservative ones that mirrored the conservativism of the affluent age in which they grew up.

Peter Irons argues that, despite evidence that integration improves the status of African Americans, the school integration prescribed by the *Brown* decision was never seriously tried, with the consequence that major gaps between white and black achievement persist and contribute to many of the social problems confronting African Americans today. Richard Kluger concludes that fifty years after the *Brown* decision, African Americans are better educated, better housed, and better employed than they were before 1954 in large part because the Supreme Court's ruling spawned the modern civil rights movement that culminated in the Civil Rights Act of 1964, the 1965 Voting Rights Act, and many programs of Lyndon Johnson's Great Society that were designed to improve the status of African Americans.

Professor of history Brian VanDeMark argues that President Lyndon Johnson failed to question the viability of increasing U.S. involvement in the Vietnam War because he was a prisoner of America's global containment policy and because he did not want his opponents to accuse him of being soft on communism or endanger support for his Great Society reforms. H. R. McMaster, an active-duty army tanker, maintains that the Vietnam disaster was not inevitable but a uniquely human failure whose responsibility was shared by President Johnson and his principal military and civilian advisers.

Writer and lecturer F. Carolyn Graglia argues that women should stay at home and practice the values of "true motherhood" because contemporary feminists have discredited marriage, devalued traditional homemaking, and encouraged sexual promiscuity. According to Professor Sara M. Evans, despite class, racial, religious, ethnic and regional differences, women in America experienced major transformations in their private and public lives in the twentieth century.

According to Professor J. David Woodard, supply-side economics unleashed a wave of entrepreneurial and technological innovation that transformed the economy and restored America's confidence in the Golden Age from 1983 to 1992. Political journalist Thomas B. Edsall argues that the Reagan revolution brought about a policy realignment that reversed the New Deal and redistributed political power and economic wealth to the top 20 percent of Americans.

Correlation Guide

The *Taking Sides* series presents current issues in a debate-style format designed to stimulate student interest and develop critical thinking skills. Each issue is thoughtfully framed with an issue summary, an issue introduction, and a postscript. The pro and con essays—selected for their liveliness and substance—represent the arguments of leading scholars and commentators in their fields.

Taking Sides: Clashing Views in United States History, Volume 2: Reconstruction to the Present, 13/e is an easy-to-use reader that presents issues on important topics such as *immigration, racial equality, the Great Depression, the Vietnam War,* and *the Cold War.* For more information on *Taking Sides* and other *McGraw-Hill Contemporary Learning Series* titles, visit www.mhcls.com.

This convenient guide matches the issues in **Taking Sides: United States History, Volume 2, 13/e** with the corresponding chapters in three of our best-selling McGraw-Hill History textbooks by Davidson et al. and Brinkley.

Taking Sides: United States History, Volume 2, 13/e	Nation of Nations: A Narrative History of the American Republic, Volume II: Since 1865, 6/e by Davidson et al.	The Unfinished Nation: A Concise History of the American People, Volume 2: From 1865, 5/e by Brinkley	American History: A Survey, Volume II: Since 1865, 13/e by Brinkley
Issue 1: Is History True?			
Issue 2: Was the Wild West More Violent than the Rest of the Nation?	**Chapter 18:** The New South and the Trans-Mississippi West (1870–1914)	**Chapter 16:** The Conquest of the Far West **Chapter 18:** The Age of the City	**Chapter 16:** The Conquest of the Far West
Issue 3: Were American Workers in the Gilded Age Conservative Capitalists?	**Chapter 19:** The New Industrial Order (1870–1914)	**Chapter 17:** Industrial Supremacy	**Chapter 17:** Industrial Supremacy
Issue 4: Were Late-Nineteenth-Century Immigrants "Uprooted"?	**Chapter 20:** The Rise of an Urban Order (1870–1914)	**Chapter 18:** The Age of the City	**Chapter 17:** Industrial Supremacy **Chapter 18:** The Age of the City **Chapter 21:** The Rise of Progressivism
Issue 5: Was City Government in Late-Nineteenth-Century America a "Conspicuous Failure"?	**Chapter 20:** The Rise of an Urban Order (1870–1914) **Chapter 22:** The Progressive Era (1890–1920)	**Chapter 21:** The Rise of Progressivism	**Chapter 21:** The Rise of Progressivism
Issue 6: Did Booker T. Washington's Philosophy and Actions Betray the Interests of African Americans?	**Chapter 21:** The Political System under Strain at Home and Abroad (1877–1900) **Chapter 22:** The Progressive Era (1890–1920) **Chapter 24:** The New Era (1920–1929)	**Chapter 15:** Reconstruction and the New South **Chapter 21:** The Rise of Progressivism	**Chapter 15:** Reconstruction and the New South **Chapter 21:** The Rise of Progressivism

Taking Sides: United States History, Volume 2, 13/e	Nation of Nations: A Narrative History of the American Republic, Volume II: Since 1865, 6/e by Davidson et al.	The Unfinished Nation: A Concise History of the American People, Volume 2: From 1865, 5/e by Brinkley	American History: A Survey, Volume II: Since 1865, 13/e by Brinkley
Issue 7: Did the Progressives Fail?	**Chapter 22:** The Progressive Era (1890–1920)	**Chapter 21:** The Rise of Progressivism	**Chapter 21:** The Rise of Progressivism **Chapter 22:** The Battle for National Reform **Chapter 24:** "The New Era"
Issue 8: Was Woodrow Wilson Responsible for the Failure of the United States to Join the League of Nations?	**Chapter 23:** The United States and the Collapse of the Old World Order (1901–1920) **Chapter 24:** The New Era (1920–1929)	**Chapter 23:** America and the Great War	**Chapter 23:** America and the Great War
Issue 9: Was Prohibition a Failure?	**Chapter 24:** The New Era (1920–1929)	**Chapter 21:** The Rise of Progressivism **Chapter 24:** The New Era **Chapter 26:** The New Deal	**Chapter 24:** "The New Era" **Chapter 26:** The New Deal
Issue 10: Was the New Deal an Effective Answer to the Great Depression?	**Chapter 25:** The Great Depression and the New Deal (1929–1939)	**Chapter 25:** The Great Depression **Chapter 26:** The New Deal **Chapter 28:** America in a World at War	**Chapter 25:** The Great Depression **Chapter 26:** The New Deal
Issue 11: Was Franklin Roosevelt a Reluctant Internationalist?	**Chapter 25:** The Great Depression and the New Deal (1929–1939) **Chapter 26:** America's Rise to Globalism (1927–1945)	**Chapter 27:** The Global Crisis, 1921–1941 **Chapter 28:** America in a World at War	**Chapter 23:** America and the Great War **Chapter 27:** The Global Crisis, 1921–1941 **Chapter 28:** America in a World at War
Issue 12: Was President Truman Responsible for the Cold War?	**Chapter 27:** Cold War America (1945–1954)	**Chapter 28:** America in a World at War **Chapter 29:** The Cold War	**Chapter 28:** America in a World at War **Chapter 29:** The Cold War
Issue 13: Was Rock and Roll Responsible for Dismantling America's Traditional Family, Sexual, and Racial Customs in the 1950s and 1960s?	**Chapter 28:** The Suburban Era (1945–1963) **Chapter 29:** Civil Rights and Uncivil Liberties (1947–1969)	**Chapter 30:** The Affluent Society **Chapter 32:** The Crisis of Authority	**Chapter 30:** The Affluent Society **Chapter 32:** The Crisis of Authority
Issue 14: Did the Brown Decision Fail to Desegregate and Improve the Status of African Americans?	**Chapter 29:** Civil Rights and Uncivil Liberties (1947–1969)	**Chapter 30:** The Affluent Society **Chapter 31:** The Ordeal of Liberalism	**Chapter 31:** The Ordeal of Liberalism
Issue 15: Was the Americanization of the War in Vietnam Inevitable?	**Chapter 30:** Vietnam and the End of the Liberal Era (1963–1976)	**Chapter 31:** The Ordeal of Liberalism **Chapter 32:** The Crisis of Authority	**Chapter 31:** The Ordeal of Liberalism **Chapter 32:** The Crisis of Authority
Issue 16: Has the Women's Movement of the 1970s Failed to Liberate American Women?	**Chapter 30:** Vietnam and the End of the Liberal Era (1963–1976) **Chapter 31:** The Conservative Challenge (1976–1992)	**Chapter 32:** The Crisis of Authority	**Chapter 32:** The Crisis of Authority
Issue 17: Were the 1980s a Decade of Affluence for the Middle Class?	**Chapter 31:** The Conservative Challenge (1976–1992) **Chapter 32:** Nation of Nations in a Global Community (1980–2007)	**Chapter 33:** From "The Age of Limits" to the Age of Reagan	**Chapter 33:** From "The Age of Limits" to the Age of Reagan

Introduction

The Study of History

Larry Madaras

James M. SoRelle

In a pluralistic society such as ours, the study of history is bound to be a complex process. How an event is interpreted depends not only on existing evidence but also on the perspective of the interpreter. Consequently, understanding history presupposes the evaluation of information, a task that often leads to conflicting conclusions. An understanding of history, then, requires the acceptance of the idea of historical relativism. Relativism means the redefinition of our past is always possible and desirable. History shifts, changes, and grows with new and different evidence and interpretations. As is the case with the law and even with medicine, beliefs that were unquestioned 100 or 200 years ago have been discredited or discarded since.

Relativism then encourages revisionism. There is a maxim that says, "The past must remain useful to the present." Historian Carl Becker argued that every generation should examine history for itself, thus ensuring constant scrutiny of our collective experience through new perspectives. History, consequently, does not remain static, in part because historians cannot avoid being influenced by the times in which they live. Almost all historians commit themselves to revising the views of other historians by either disagreeing with earlier interpretations or creating new frameworks that pose different questions.

Schools of Thought

Three predominant schools of thought have emerged in American history since the first graduate seminars in history were given at the Johns Hopkins University in Baltimore, Maryland, in the 1870s. The *progressive* school dominated the professional field in the first half of the twentieth century. Influenced by the reform currents of populism, progressivism, and the New Deal, these historians explored the social and economic forces that energized America. The progressive scholars tended to view the past in terms of conflicts between groups, and they sympathized with the underdog.

The post–World War II period witnessed the emergence of a new group of historians who viewed the conflict thesis as overly simplistic. Writing against the backdrop of the Cold War, these *neoconservative* and *consensus* historians argued that Americans possess a shared set of values and that the areas of agreement within the nation's basic democratic and capitalistic framework are more important than the areas of disagreement.

In the 1960s, however, the civil rights movement, women's liberation, and the student rebellion (with its condemnation of the war in Vietnam) fragmented the consensus of values upon which historians of the 1950s centered their interpretations. This turmoil set the stage for the emergence of another group of scholars. *New Left* historians began to reinterpret the past once again. They emphasized the significance of conflict in American history, and they resurrected interest in those groups ignored by the consensus school. New Left history is still being written.

The most recent generation of scholars focuses upon social history. Their primary concern is to discover what the lives of "ordinary Americans" were really like. These new social historians employ previously overlooked court and church documents, house deeds and tax records, letters and diaries, photographs, and census data to reconstruct the everyday lives of average Americans. Some employ new methodologies, such as quantification (enhanced by advanced computer technology) and oral history, while others borrow from the disciplines of political science, economics, sociology, anthropology, and psychology for their historical investigations.

The proliferation of historical approaches, which are reflected in the issues debated in this book, has had mixed results. On the one hand, historians have become so specialized in their respective time periods and methodological styles that it is difficult to synthesize the recent scholarship into a comprehensive text for the general reader. On the other hand, historians now know more about new questions or ones that previously were considered to be germane only to scholars in other social sciences. Although there is little agreement about the answers to these questions, the methods employed and the issues explored make the "new history" a very exciting field to study.

The topics that follow represent a variety of perspectives and approaches. Each of these controversial issues can be studied for its individual importance to American history. Taken as a group, they interact with one another to illustrate larger historical themes. When grouped thematically, the issues reveal continuing motifs in the development of American history.

Intellectual and Economic Questions

Issue 1 explores the big question that historians face. Is history true? Two prize-winning historians who write from a macro-perspective disagree. Oscar Handlin argues that "truth is absolute; it is as absolute as the world is real . . . truth is knowable and will out if earnestly pursued and science is the procedure or set of procedures for approximating it." But William H. McNeill disagrees. "[W]hat seems true to one historian will seem false to another, so one historian's truth becomes another's myth, even at the moment of utterance."

Issue 3 explores the dynamics of the modern American economy through investigations of the nineteenth-century entrepreneurs. Were these industrial leaders robber barons, as portrayed by contemporary critics and many history texts? Or were they industrial statesmen and organizational geniuses? John Tipple believes that industrialists like Corneluics Vanderbilt and John D. Rockefeller undermined American institutions and individualistic values by rendering them impotant in their pursuit of wealth. In contrast, Alfred D. Chandler, Jr., characteries those businessmen as organizational and marketing innovators who created huge corporations that stimulated the rise of a national urban economy.

The Outsiders: Laborers, Immigrants, African Americans, and Farm Workers

In the wake of industrialization during the late 1800s, the rapid pace of change created new working conditions for the labor class. How did laborers react to these new changes? Did they lose their autonomy in large corporations? Did they accept or reject the wage system? Were they pawns of the economic cycles of boom and bust, to be hired and fired at will? Did they look for an alternative to capitalism by encaging in strikes, establishing labor unions, or creating a socialist movement? In Issue 3, Carl N. Degler maintains that American workers accepted capitalism and the changes that it brought forth. Herbert G. Gutman, however, argues that in the years 1843–1893, American factory workers attempted to humanize the system by maintaining their traditional artisan values. By the beginning of the twentieth century, however, the organizational innovations of Rockefeller and the assembly-line techniques pioneered by Henry Ford had revolutionized American capitalism.

The vast majority of these factory workers came from the farms and cities of Europe. Massive immigration to the United States in the late nineteenth and early twentieth centuries introduced widespread changes in American society. Moreover, the presence of increasing numbers of immigrants from southern and eastern Europe, many of them Catholics and Jews, seemed to threaten native-born citizens, most of whom were Protestant and of northern and western European ancestry. Asian immigrants, mainly from China or Japan, added to nativist fears. In Issue 4, Oscar Handlin argues that the immigrants were alienated from their Old World cultures as they adjusted to an unfamiliar and often hostile environment. But Professor Mark Wyman argues that immigrants never gave up the fight for their personal autonomy. Mark Wyman points out that many immigrants to the United States believed that their stay in America would be temporary, a fact that limited their efforts at assimilation and reinforced ties to their original homelands to which many of them returned once they had acquired some wealth.

One of the most controversial figures in American history was the early-twentieth-century African American leader Booker T. Washington. Was Washington too accommodating toward white values and goals and too accepting of the political disfranchisement and social segregation that took away the basic freedoms that African Americans earned after their emancipation from slavery? In Issue 6, Donald Spivey argues that Washington not only subordinated political, social, and civil rights to economic goals, but also failed to provide the training necessary to allow students to become capable, skilled artisans. Robert J. Norrell, on the other hand, insists that Washington frequently challenged the political, economic, and social status quo of African Americans both publicly and behind the scenes.

No group seemed further away from urban-industrial America than the cowboys, farmers, miners, and lumberjacks who worked on America's last frontier. Issue 2 asks whether the Wild West was real or a mythical image created by novelists, movies, radio, television, and Wild West shows. Professor of history David T. Courtright argues that the cattle, mining, and lumbering western frontiers were extremely violent because these regions were populated by young, single, and transient males who frequented saloons and prostitutes, and engaged in fights with the local Indians and Chinese, as well as with each other. Professor Robert R. Dykstra argues that Dodge City had a low crime rate in the decade 1876—1885, and in the murder case of *Kansas V. Gill*, it conducted a jury trial "according to conventions nurtured through a thousand years of Anglo-American judicial traditions."

Political and Social Successes and Failure, 1880–1945

Issue 6 assesses the nature of urban government in the late nineteenth century. Ernest S. Griffith views these governments as "conspicuous failures" because they were unable to cope effectively with the numerous problems associated with the evolution of the industrial city. Jon C. Teaford takes a more positive look at the late-nineteenth-century city. He argues that scholars traditionally have overlooked the remarkable accomplishments of municipal governments. While admitting numerous shortcomings, Teaford argues that American city dwellers enjoyed a higher standard of public services than any other urban residents in the world.

The Progressive movement is examined in Issue 8. Richard M. Abrams attributes the failure of the movement to its limited scope. He maintains that it imposed a uniform set of values on a diverse people and did not address the inequalities that prevailed in American society. Arthur S. Link and Richard L. McCormick, however, emphasize the reforms introduced by the Progressives that checked the abuses of industrialization and urbanization during the early 1900s.

Issue 10 discusses one of the major progressive "social control" reforms—Prohibition. The "noble experiment" to prohibit the manufacture, sale, and transportation of alcoholic beverages had a rather short life. Originally passed in 1919, the Prohibition amendment was repealed fourteen years later. To this day, it remains the only amendment ever to have been removed from the Constitution. John C. Burnham revises the traditional image of the decade of the 1920s as the "lawless years." He points out that when the "Prohibition experiment" was passed, two-thirds of the states, which encompassed over half of the population, were already dry. The purpose of the legislation, he argues, was to control the political and social practices of the immigrant working classes who lived in the cities. He denies that crime increased dramatically in the decade, attributing the so-called crime waves to the overblown accounts in the newspapers and newsreels. Gambling, rather than the sale of illegal liquor, remained the major source of revenue for organized crime. Burnham also marshals statistical evidence to document a decline in per capita drinking in the early 1920s as well as in the diseases and deaths related to alcohol. David Kyvig concedes that Prohibition "sharply reduced the consumption of alcohol in the United States." But images of lawbreaking through Hollywood films and newsreels and the inability of law enforcement officials in all levels of government to enforce a law, especially unpopular in American cities, "disenchanted many Americans and moved some to an active effort to bring an end to the dry law."

The Great Depression of the 1930s remains one of the most traumatic events in U.S. history. The characteristics of that decade are deeply etched in American folk memory, but the remedies that were applied to these social and economic ills—known collectively as the New Deal—are not easy to evaluate. In Issue 11, Roger Biles contents that the economic stabilizers created by the New Deal programs prevented the recurrence of the Great Depression. Gary Dean Best, on the other hand, criticizes the New Deal from a 1990s conservative perspective. In his view, because New Deal agencies were antibusiness, they overregulated the economy and did not allow the free enterprise system to work out the depression that FDR's programs prolonged.

The United States and the World

As the United States developed a preeminent position in world affairs, the nation's politicians were forced to consider the proper relationship between their country and the rest of the world. To what extent, many asked, should the United States seek to expand its political, economic, and moral influence around the world? This was a particularly intriguing question for the Progressives of the early twentieth century, most of whom were more interested in domestic reforms than foreign policy.

The United States became a major participant in two world wars in the twentieth century. At the end of the First World War, President Wilson tried to enlarge the United States' role in the world by brokering the peace and establishing a League of Nations to prevent the outbreak of another war. Why did he fail? In Issue 8, the long-time leader of diplomatic history, the late Thomas A. Bailey, argues that a physically infirm Woodrow Wilson was unable to make the necessary compromises with the U.S. Senate to join the League of Nations and convince an ill-informed, isolationist, disillusioned American public that the United States should play a major role in world affairs. But William G. Carleton believed that Woodrow Wilson understood better than his nationalistic opponents the new internationalist role that the United States would play in world affairs.

Whether the Second World War could have been prevented if the United States had joined the League of Nations and abandoned its traditional isolationist foreign policy is a subject of debate for historians. Issue 11 wonders if Franklin Delano Roosevelt was a reluctant internationalist even when faced with the expansionist policies of Adolph Hitler. Diplomatic historian Robert A. Divine argues that even after France fell to Nazi Germany in June 1940, Franklin D. Roosevelt remained a reluctant internationalist who spoke belligerently but acted timidly because he sincerely hated war. Pulitzer Prize–winning historian Arthur M. Schlesinger, Jr., maintains that from a 1990s perspective, Roosevelt—not Stalin, Churchill, or anyone else—was the only wartime leader who saw clearly the direction and shape of the new world that the leaders were trying to create.

World War II brought the end of Nazi Germany and imperial Japan. It was the war that was really supposed to end all wars. FDR, haunted by the ghost of Woodrow Wilson, hoped that the United Nations could resolve national conflicts. Unfortunately, an unintended consequence was the reemergence of the rivalry between the United States and the Soviet Union. Who started the cold war? Was it inevitable, or should one side take more of the blame? In Issue 12, Professor Arnold A. Offner argues that President Harry S. Truman was a parochial nationalist whose limited vision of foreign affairs precluded negotiations with the Russians over cold war issues. But John Gaddis, the most important American scholar of the cold war, argues that after a half century of scholarship, Joseph Stalin was uncompromising and primarily responsible for the cold war.

No discussion of American foreign policy is complete without some consideration of the Vietnam War. Was America's escalation of the war inevitable in 1965? In Issue 16, Brian VanDeMark argues that President Lyndon Johnson was a prisoner of America's global "containment" policy and was afraid to pull out of Vietnam because he feared that his opponents would accuse him of being soft on communism and that they would also destroy his Great Society reforms. H. R. McMaster blames Johnson and his civilian and military advisers for failing to develop a coherent policy in Vietnam.

Social, Cultural, and Economic Changes Since 1945

Carl N. Degler has labeled the years from 1945 to 1963 as the age of "anxiety and affluence." Issue 13 deals with this unique period in U.S. history. The population explosion that took place after World War II led to a youth culture who challenged the value system of their parents. Tensions between parents and children have always existed in America. Do different tastes in dress and music reflect revolutionary or surface changes? Professor Glen C. Altschuler maintains that rock and roll's "switchblade beat" opened wide division in American society along the fault lines of family, sexuality, and race. But writer J. Ronald Oakley argues that although the lifestyles of youth departed from their parents, their basic ideas and attitudes were still the conservative ones that mirrored the conservatism of the affluent age in which they grew up.

The situation for African Americans has vastly improved since the civil rights revolution of the 1950s and 1960s. But did it improve educational opportunities for minorities? The *Brown* case of 1954 was a landmark Supreme Court decision because it overthrew the "separate but equal" principle of the *Plessy* case of 1896, which had legally sanctioned school desegregation. But did *Brown* really desegregate schools and, more importantly, improve the status of African Americans? In Issue 14, Peter Irons argues that the majority of African Americans still attend segregated and inferior schools because of "resegregation" based on housing patterns and that the two generations of "desegregation" cannot erase the educational harm of five generations of segregation. But Richard Kluger argues that *Brown* delegitimized the caste system and by about every measurable standard in housing, jobs, income, and education, African Americans were significantly better off in 2004 than they had been in 1954.

A direct lineage of the civil rights revolution was the Women's Liberation Movement of the 1970s. Did it help or harm women? In Issue 16, writer and lecturer F. Carolyn Garglia argues that women should stay at home and practice the values of "true motherhood" because contemporary feminists have discredited marriage, devalued traditional homemaking, and encouraged sexual promiscuity. But feminist and activist scholar Sara M. Evans takes a much more positive view of the women's movements for suffrage and liberation in the past 100 years. Despite their class, racial, religious, ethnic, and regional differences, Evans argues that women in America experienced major transformations in their private and public lives in the twentieth century.

The American public experienced a shock in the late 1970s due to the normal expectations of constant growth. Rising oil prices, foreign economic competition, and double-digit interest and inflation rates created an economic recession. Issue 17 debates whether the 1970s was a decade of affluence or decline for middle-class Americans. According to Professor J. David Woodard, supply-side economics unleashed a wave of entrepreneurial and technological innovation that transformed the economy and restored America's confidence in the Golden Age from 1983 to 1992. Political journalist Thomas Byrne Edsall argues that the Reagan revolution brought about a policy realignment that reversed the New Deal and redistributed political power and economic wealth to the top 20 percent of Americans.

Conclusion

The process of historical study should rely more on thinking than on memorizing data. Once the basics of who, what, when, and where are determined, historical thinking shifts to a higher gear. Explanation, analysis, evaluation, comparison, and contrast take command. These skills not only increase our knowledge of the past, but they also provide general tools for the comprehension of all the topics about which human beings think.

The diversity of a pluralistic society, however, creates some obstacles to comprehending the past. The spectrum of differing opinions on any particular subject eliminates the possibility of quick and easy answers. In the final analysis, conclusions are often built through a synthesis of several different interpretations, but even then they may be partial and tentative.

The study of history in a pluralistic society allows each citizen the opportunity to teach independent conclusions about the past. Since most, if not all, historical issues affect the present and future, understanding the past becomes necessary if society is to progress. Many of today's problems have a direct connection with the past. Additionally, other contemporary issues may lack obvious direct antecedents, but historical investigation can provide illuminating analogies. At first, it may appear confusing to read and to think about opposing historical views, but the survival of our democratic society depends on such critical thinking by acute and discerning minds.

Internet References . . .

Internet Web sites containing historical material relevant to the subjects discussed in all the issues can be reached through the McGraw-Hill history site.

http://www.mhhe.comsocscience/history/usa/link/linktop.html

Important journal articles and book reviews that reflect the most recent scholarship on all the issues can be found on the following site:

http://H-NE.msu.edu

John D. Rockefeller and the Standard Oil Company

This site, created by Swiss entrepreneur Francois Micheloud, provides a highly detailed history of the American oil industry, with John D. Rockefeller as a main focus.

http://www.micheloud.com./FXM/SO/rock.htm

Industrial Revolution

This site provides an extensive list of links to pages on the Industrial Revolution grouped into categories, including Child Labor, Disparity of Wealth, Unions, and Urban Planning.

http://members.aol.com/TeacherNet/Industrial.html

World Wide Web Virtual Library

This site focuses on labor and business history. As an index site, this is a good place to start exploring these two vast topics.

http://www.iisg.nl/~w3vl/

International Channel

Immigrants helped to create modern America. Visit this interesting site to experience "the memories, sounds, even tastes of Ellis Island. Hear immigrants describe in their own words their experiences upon entering the gateway to America."

http://www.i-channel.com/

American Immigration Resources on the Internet

This site contains many links to American immigration resources on the Internet. It includes a site on children's immigration issues, the Immigration and Naturalization Service home page, and a forum on immigration.

http://www.immigration-usa.com/resource.html

(Gene) Autry National Center

4700 Western Heritage Way, Los Angeles, CA 90027; phone (323) 667-2000
This site contains information about one of the most important museums and collections of Western and Indian history. The center is massive, fabulous and deserves a visit.

http://www.autrynationalcenter.org

The Last West, Cities, Immigrants, and the Industrial Revolution

*E*conomic expansion and the seemingly unlimited resources available in postbellum America offered great opportunity and created new political, social, and economic challenges. Political freedom and economic opportunity provided incentives for immigration to America. The need for cheap labor to run the machinery of the Industrial Revolution created an atmosphere for potential exploitation that was intensified by the concentration of wealth in the hands of a few capitalists. The labor movement took root, with some elements calling for an overthrow of the capitalist system, while others sought to establish political power within the existing system. Strains began to develop between immigrant and native-born workers as well as between workers and owners, husbands and wives, and parents and their children.

With the growth of industry, urban problems became more acute. Improvements in water and sewage, street cleaning, housing, mass transit, and fire and crime prevention developed slowly because incredible population growth strained municipal services. Urban governments had limited powers, which often fell under the control of political bosses. Historians disagree as to whether or not attempts to remedy these problems through a brokered political system were successful. Meanwhile, the last frontier had been reached with the end of the Indian wars. Were the western communities more violent than the large industrial cities of the 1890s? Or have radio, television, and the movies portrayed a mythical West?

- Is History True?

- Was the Wild West More Violent than the Rest of the Country?

- Were American Workers in the Gilded Age Conservative Capitalists?

- Did Late-Nineteenth Century Immigrants "Uprooted"?

- Was City Government in Late-Nineteenth-Century America a "Conspicuous Failure"?

ISSUE 1

Is History True?

YES: Oscar Handlin, from *Truth in History* (The Belknap Press of Harvard University Press, 1979)

NO: William H. McNeill, from "Mythistory, or Truth, Myth, History, and Historians," *American Historical Review* (February 1986)

ISSUE SUMMARY

YES: Oscar Handlin insists that historical truth is absolute and knowable by historians who adopt the scientific method of research to discover factual evidence that provides both a chronology and context for their findings.

NO: William McNeill argues that historical truth is general and evolutionary and is discerned by different groups at different times and in different places in a subjective manner that has little to do with a scientifically absolute methodology.

The basic premise of this volume of readings is that the study of history is a complex process that combines historical facts and the historian's interpretation of those facts. Underlying this premise is the assumption that the historian is committed to employing evidence that advances an accurate, truthful picture of the past. Unfortunately, the historical profession in the last several years has been held up to close public scrutiny as a result of charges that a few scholars, some quite prominent, have been careless in their research methods, have cited sources that do not exist, and have reached conclusions that were not borne out by the facts. The result has been soiled or ruined reputations and the revocation of degrees, book awards, and tenure. Certainly, this is not the end to which most historians aspire, and the failures of a few should not cast a net of suspicion on the manner in which the vast majority of historians practice their craft.

In reflecting upon her role as a historian, the late Barbara Tuchman commented, "To write history so as to enthrall the reader and make the subject as captivating and exciting to him as it is to me has been my goal. . . . A prerequisite . . . is to be enthralled one's self and to feel a compulsion to communicate the magic." For Tuchman, it was the historian's responsibility to the reader to conduct thorough research on a particular topic, sort through the mass of facts to determine what was essential and what was not, and to formulate what remained into a dramatic narrative. Tuchman and most practicing historians also agree with the nineteenth-century German historian Leopold von Ranke that the task of the historian is to discover what really happened. In most instances, however, historians write about events at which they were not present. According to Tuchman, "We can never be certain that we have recaptured [the past] as it really was. But the least we can do is to stay within the evidence."

David Hackett Fischer has written about the difficulties confronting historians as they attempt to report a truthful past, and he is particularly critical of what he terms the "absurd and pernicious doctrine" of historical relativism as it developed in the United States in the 1930s under the direction of Charles Beard and Carl Becker. Becker's suggestion that each historian will write a history based upon his or her own values or the climate of opinion in a particular generation strikes Fischer as a slippery slope leading to the loss of historical accuracy. In conclusion, Fischer writes, "The factual errors which academic historians make today are rarely deliberate. The real danger is not that a scholar will delude his readers, but that he will delude himself."

The selections that follow explore the topic of historical truth. In the late 1970s, Oscar Handlin, like Fischer, became extremely concerned about the impact of the historical and cultural relativism of postmodern and deconstructionist approaches to the study of history. For Handlin, historical truth is absolute and knowable if pursued by the historian adopting the scientific method of research. The value of history, he believes, lies in the capacity to advance toward the truth by locating discrete events, phenomena, and expressions in the historical record.

In contrast, William McNeill recognizes a very thin line between fact and fiction. He claims that historians distinguish between the truth of their conclusions and the myth of those conclusions they reject. The result is what he terms "mythistory." Moreover, the arrangement of historical facts involves subjective judgments and intellectual choices that have little to do with the scientific method. Historical truth, McNeill proposes, is evolutionary, not absolute.

The Uses of History

Why resist the temptation to be relevant? The question nags historians in 1978 as it does other scholars. The world is turning; it needs knowledge; and possession of learning carries an obligation to attempt to shape events. Every crisis lends weight to the plea: transform the library from an ivory tower into a fortress armed to make peace (or war), to end (or extend) social inequality, to alter (or preserve) the existing economic system. The thought boosts the ego, as it has ever since Francis Bacon's suggestion that knowledge is power. Perhaps authority really does lie in command of the contents of books!

In the 1960s the plea became an order, sometimes earnest, sometimes surly, always insistent. Tell us what we need to know—straight answers. Thus, students to teachers, readers to authors. The penalties for refusal ranged from mere unpopularity to organized boycotts and angry confrontations—in a few cases even to burning manuscripts and research notes. Fear added to the inducements for pleasing the audience, whether in the classroom or on the printed page.

To aim to please is a blunder, however. Sincere as the supplicants generally are, it is not knowledge they wish. Having already reached their conclusions, they seek only reassuring confirmation as they prepare to act. They already know that a unilateral act of will could stop wars, that the United States is racist, and that capitalism condemns the masses to poverty. The history of American foreign policy, of the failure of post-Civil War Reconstruction, and of industrial development would only clutter the mind with disturbing ambiguities and complexities.

At best, the usable past demanded of history consists of the data to flesh out a formula. We must do something about the war, the cities, pollution, poverty, and population. Our moral sense, group interest, and political affiliation define the goals; let the historian join the other social scientists in telling us how to reach them. At worst, the demand made of the past is for a credible myth that will identify the forces of good and evil and inspire those who fight with slogans or fire on one side of the barricades or the other.

The effort to meet either demand will frustrate the historian true to his or her craft. Those nimble enough to catch the swings of the market in the classroom or in print necessarily leave behind interior standards of what is important and drop by the wayside the burden of scrupulous investigation and rigorous judgment. Demands for relevance distort the story of ethnicity as they corrupt the historical novel.

Whoever yields, forgoes the opportunity to do what scholars are best qualified to do. Those who chase from one disaster to another lose sight of the long-term trend; busy with the bandaids, they have no time to treat the patient's illness. The family did not originate yesterday, or the city, or addiction to narcotics; a student might well pick up some thoughts on those subjects by shifting his sights from the 1970s to Hellenistic society.

Above all, obsession with the events of the moment prevents the historian from exercising the faculty of empathy, the faculty of describing how people, like us, but different, felt and behaved as they did in times and places similar to, but different, from our own. The writer or teacher interested only in passing judgment on the good guys and the bad will never know what it meant to be an Irish peasant during a famine, or the landlord; an Alabama slave in the 1850s, or the master; a soldier at Antietam, or a general.

⋅◈⋅

The uses of history arise neither from its relevance nor from its help in preparing for careers—nor from its availability as a subject which teachers pass on to students who become teachers and in turn teach others to teach.

Nevertheless, again and again former pupils who come back for reunions after twenty-five years or more spontaneously testify to the utility of what they had learned at college in the various pursuits to which life's journey had taken them. Probing usually reveals not bits of information, not a general interpretation, but a vague sense that those old transactions of classroom and library had somehow expanded their knowledge of self. The discipline of history had located them in time and space and had thereby helped them know themselves, not as physicians or attorneys or bureaucrats or executives, but as persons.

These reassuring comments leave in suspense the question of why study of the past should thus help the individuals understand himself or herself. How do those who learn this subject catch a glimpse of the process of which they are part, discover places in it?

Not by relevance, in the competition for which the other, more pliable, social sciences can always outbid history. Nor by the power of myth, in the peddling of which the advantage lies with novelists. To turn accurate knowledge to those ends is, as C. S. Peirce noted, "like running a steam engine by burning diamonds."

The use of history lies in its capacity for advancing the approach to truth.

The historian's vocation depends on this minimal operational article of faith: Truth is absolute; it is as absolute as the world is real. It does not exist because individuals wish it to anymore than the world exists for their convenience. Although observers have more or less partial views of the truth, its actuality is unrelated to the desires or the particular angles of vision of the viewers. Truth is knowable and will out if earnestly pursued; and science is the procedure or set of procedures for approximating it.

⌑

What is truth? Mighty above all things, it resides in the small pieces which together form the record.

History is not the past, any more than biology is life, or physics, matter. History is the distillation of evidence surviving from the past. Where there is no evidence, there is no history. Much of the past is not knowable in this way, and about those areas the historian must learn to confess ignorance.

No one can relive the past; but everyone can seek truth in the record. Simple, durable discoveries await the explorer. So chronology—the sequential order of events reaching back beyond time's horizon—informs the viewer of the long distance traversed and of the immutable course of occurrences: no reversal of a step taken; no after ever before. The historian cannot soar with the anthropologists, who swoop across all time and space. Give or take a thousand years, it is all one to them in pronouncements about whether irrigation systems succeeded or followed despotisms, or in linking technology, population, food, and climatic changes. In the end they pick what they need to prop up theory. The discipline of dates rails off the historian and guards against such perilous plunges. No abstraction, no general interpretation, no wish or preference can challenge chronology's dominion, unless among those peoples who, lacking a sense of time, lack also a sense of history. And whoever learns to know the tyranny of the passing hours, the irrecoverable nature of days passed, learns also the vanity of all aspirations to halt the clock or slow its speed, of all irridentisms, all efforts to recapture, turn back, redeem the moments gone by.

Another use of history is in teaching about vocabulary, the basic component of human communication. Words, singularly elusive, sometimes flutter out of reach, hide in mists of ambiguity, or lodge themselves among inaccessible logical structures, yet form the very stuff of evidence. The historian captures the little syllabic clusters only by knowing who inscribed or spoke them—a feat made possible by understanding the minds and hearts and hands of the men and women for whom they once had meaning. Words released by comprehension wing their messages across the centuries. A use of history is to instruct in the reading of a word, in the comprehension of speakers, writers different from the listener, viewer.

And context. Every survival bespeaks a context. Who graved or wrote or built did so for the eyes of others. Each line or shape denotes a relation to people, things, or concepts—knowable. The identities of sender and recipient explain the content of the letter; the mode of transmission explains the developing idea, the passions of employers and laborers, the organization of the factory. A use of history is its aid in locating discrete events, phenomena, and expressions in their universes.

The limits of those universes were often subjects of dispute. Early in the nineteenth century Henry Thomas Buckle complained, in terms still applicable decades thereafter, of "the singular spectacle of one historian being ignorant of political economy; another knowing nothing of law; another nothing of ecclesiastical affairs and changes of opinion; another neglecting the philosophy of statistics, another physical science," so that those important pursuits, being cultivated, "some by one man, and some by another, have been isolated rather than united," with no disposition to concentrate them upon history. He thus echoed Gibbon's earlier injunction to value all facts. A Montesquieu, "from the meanest of them, will draw conclusions unknown to ordinary men" and arrive at "philosophical history."

On the other hand, a distinguished scholar fifty years later pooh-poohed the very idea that there might be a relation among the Gothic style, feudalism, and scholasticism, or a link between the Baroque and Jesuitism. Nevertheless, the dominant thrust of twentieth-century historians has been toward recognition of the broader contexts; in a variety of fashions they have searched for a totality denominated civilization, culture, or spirit of an epoch, and which they have hoped would permit examination of enlightening linkages and reciprocal relations. Even those who deny that history is a single discipline and assert that it is only "congeries of related disciplines" would, no doubt, expect each branch to look beyond its own borders.

In the final analysis, all the uses of history depend upon the integrity of the record, without which there could be no counting of time, no reading of words, no perception of the context, no utility of the subject. No concern could be deeper than assaults upon the record, upon the very idea of a record.

≈⟨◉⟩≈

Although history is an ancient discipline, it rests upon foundations laid in the seventeenth century, when a century of blood shed in religious and dynastic warfare persuaded those who wrote and read history to accept a vital difference in tolerance between facts and interpretation. The text of a charter or statute was subject to proof of authenticity and validity, whatever the meanings lawyers or theologians imparted to its terms. The correct date, the precise phrasing, the seal were facts which might present difficulties of verification, but which, nevertheless, admitted of answers that were right or wrong. On the other hand, discussion of opinions and meanings often called for tolerance among diverse points of view, tolerance possible so long as disputants distinguished interpretation from the fact, from the thing in itself. Scholars could disagree on large matters of interpretation; they had a common interest in agreeing on the small ones of fact which provided them grounds of peaceful discourse.

From that seminal insight developed the scientific mechanisms that enabled historians to separate fact from opinion. From that basis came the Enlightenment achievements which recognized the worth of objectivity and asserted the possibility of reconstructing the whole record of the human past.

True, historians as well as philosophers often thereafter worried about the problems of bias and perspective; and some despaired of attaining the ideal of ultimate objectivity. None were ever totally free of bias, not even those like Ranke who most specifically insisted on the integrity of the fact which he struggled to make the foundation of a truly universal body of knowledge. But, however fallible the individual scholar, the historian's, task, Wilhelm von Humboldt explained, was "to present what actually happened." It may have been a dream to imagine that history would become a science meaningful to all people, everywhere. If so, it was a noble dream.

By contrast, historians in the 1970s and increasingly other scientists regarded the fact itself as malleable. As the distinction between fact and interpretation faded, all became faction—a combination of fact and fiction. The passive acceptance of that illegitimate genre—whatever mixes with fiction ceases to be fact—revealed the erosion of scholarly commitment. More and more often, the factual elements in an account were instrumental to the purpose the author-manipulator wished them to serve. It followed that different writers addressing different readers for different purposes could arrange matters as convenient. In the end, the primacy of the fact vanished and only the authority of the author, the receptivity of the audience, and the purpose intended remained.

Whence came this desertion, this rejection of allegiance to the fact?

Chroniclers of the past always suffered from external pressure to make their findings relevant, that is, to demonstrate or deny the wisdom, correctness, or appropriateness of current policies. They resisted out of dedication to maintaining the integrity of the record; and long succeeded in doing so. In the 1970s, however, the pressures toward falsification became more compelling than ever before.

Although the full fruits of the change appeared only in that decade, its origins reached back a half-century. It was one of Stalin's most impressive achievements to have converted Marxism from its nineteenth-century scientific base to an instrument of state purpose, and it was not by coincidence that history was the first discipline to suffer in the process. The Soviet Union did more than impose an official party line on interpretations of Trotsky's role in the revolution of 1917; it actually expunged the name Trotsky from the record, so that the fact of the commissar's existence disappeared. What started in the domain of history led in time to Lysenko's invasion of the natural sciences. The Nazis, once in power, burned the nonconforming books; and after 1945 the assault spread to all countries subject to totalitarian control. Those developments were neither surprising nor difficult to comprehend; they followed from the nature of the regimes which fostered them.

More surprising, more difficult to comprehend, was the acquiescence by the scholars of free societies in the attack on history, first, insofar as it affected colleagues less fortunately situated, then as it insinuated itself in their own ranks. External and internal circumstances were responsible.

In a sensate society the commercial standards of the media governed the dissemination of information. Since whatever sold was news, the salient consideration was one of attracting attention; factual accuracy receded to the remote background. An affluent and indulgent society also mistook flaccid permissiveness for tolerance. Everything went because nothing was worth defending, and the legitimate right to err became the disastrous obliteration of the difference between error and truth.

Difficult critical issues tempted the weak-minded to tailor fact to convenience. In the United States, but also in other parts of the world, the spread of a kind of tribalism demanded a history unique to and written for the specifications of particular groups. Since knowledge was relative to the knowers, it was subject to manipulation to suit their convenience. The process by which blacks, white ethnics, and women alone were conceded the capability of understanding and writing their own histories wiped out the line between truth and myth.

That much was comprehensible; these forces operated outside the academy walls and were not subject to very much control. More important, more susceptible to control, and less explicable was the betrayal by the intellectuals of their own group interests and the subsequent loss of the will to resist. A variety of elements contributed to this most recent *trahison des clercs*. Exaggerated concern with the problems of bias and objectivity drove some earnest scholars to despair. Perhaps they reacted against the excessive claims of the nineteenth century, perhaps against the inability of historians, any more than other scholars, to withstand the pressures of nationalism in the early decades of the twentieth century. In any case, not a few followed the deceptive path from acknowledgment that no person was entirely free of prejudice or capable of attaining a totally objective view of the past to the conclusion that all efforts to do so were vain and that, in the end, the past was entirely a recreation emanating from the mind of the historian. Support from this point of view came from the philosophers Benedetto Croce in Italy and, later, R. G. Collingwood in England. Support also came from a misreading of anthropological relativism, which drew from the undeniable circumstances that different cultures evolved differently, the erroneous conclusion that judgments among them were impossible.

Perhaps playfully, perhaps seriously, Carl L. Becker suggested that the historical fact was in someone's mind or it was nowhere, because it was "not the past event," only a symbol which enabled later writers to recreate it imaginatively. His charmingly put illustrations deceived many a reader unaware that serious thinkers since Bayle and Hume had wrestled with the problem. "No one could ever object to the factual truth that Caesar defeated

Pompey; and whatever the principles one wishes to use in dispute, one will find nothing less questionable than this proposition—Caesar and Pompey existed and were not just simple modification of the minds of those who wrote their lives"—thus Bayle.

The starting point in Becker's wandering toward relativism, as for others among his contemporaries, was the desire to be useful in solving "the everlasting riddle of human experience." Less subtle successors attacked neutrality "toward the main issues of life" and demanded that society organize all its forces in support of its ideals. "Total war, whether it be hot or cold, enlists everyone and calls upon everyone to assume his part. The historian is no freer from this obligation than the physicists." Those too timid to go the whole way suggested that there might be two kinds of history, variously defined: one, for instance, to treat the positive side of slavery to nurture black pride; another, the negative, to support claims for compensation."

Historians who caved in to pressure and ordered the past to please the present neglected the future, the needs of which would certainly change and in unpredictable ways. Scholarship could no more provide the future than the present with faith, justification, self-confidence, or sense of purpose unless it first preserved the record, intact and inviolable.

History does not recreate the past. The historian does not recapture the bygone event. No amount of imagination will enable the scholar to describe exactly what happened to Caesar in the Senate or to decide whether Mrs. Williams actually lost two hundred pounds by an act of faith. History deals only with evidence from the past, with the residues of bygone events. But it can pass judgment upon documentation and upon observers' reports of what they thought they saw.

Disregarding these constraints, Becker concluded that, since objectivity was a dream, everyman could be his own historian and contrive his own view of the past, valid for himself, if for no one else. He thus breached the line between interpretation, which was subjective and pliable, and fact, which was not.

Internal specialization allowed historians to slip farther in the same direction. The knowledge explosion after 1900 made specialization an essential, unavoidable circumstance of every form of scholarly endeavor. No individual could presume to competence in more than a sector of the whole field; and the scope of the manageable sector steadily shrank. One result was the dissolution of common standards; each area created its own criteria and claimed immunity from the criticism of outsiders. The occupants of each little island fortress sustained the illusion that the dangers to one would not apply to others. Lines of communication, even within a single faculty or department, broke down so that, increasingly, specialists in one area depended upon the common mass media for knowledge about what transpired in another.

The dangers inherent in these trends became critical as scholarship lost its autonomy. Increasingly reliance on support from external sources—whether governments or foundations—circumscribed the freedom of researchers and writers to choose their own subjects and to arrive at their own conclusions. More generally, the loss of autonomy involved a state of mind which regarded the fruits of scholarship as dependent and instrumental—that is, not as worthy of pursuit for their own sake, not for the extent to which they brought the inquirer closer to the truth, but for other, extrinsic reasons. Ever more often, scholars justified their activity by its external results—peace, training for citizenship, economic development, cure of illness, and the like—in other words, by its usefulness. The choice of topics revealed the extent to which emphasis had shifted from the subject and its relation to the truth to its instrumental utility measured by reference to some external standard.

The plea from utility was dangerous. In the 1930s it blinded well-intentioned social scientists and historians to the excesses of totalitarianism. It was inevitable in creating the omelette of a great social experiment that the shells of a few eggs of truth would be broken, so the argument ran. So, too, in the avid desire for peace, in the praiseworthy wish to avoid a second world war, Charles A. Beard abandoned all effort at factual accuracy. Yet the errors to which the plea for utility led in the past have not prevented others from proceeding along the same treacherous path in pursuit of no less worthy, but equally deceptive utilitarian goals.

Finally, the reluctance to insist upon the worth of truth for its own sake stemmed from a decline of faith by intellectuals in their own role as intellectuals. Not many have, in any conscious or deliberate sense, foresworn their allegiance to the pursuit of truth and the life of the spirit. But power tempted them as it tempts other men and women. The twentieth-century intellectual had unparalleled access to those who actually wielded political or military influence. And few could resist the temptation of being listened to by presidents and ministers, of seeing ideas translated into action. Moreover, a more subtle, more insidious temptation nested in the possibility that possession of knowledge may itself become a significant source of power. The idea that a name on the letterhead of an activist organization or in the endorsement of a political advertisement might advance some worthy cause gives a heady feeling of sudden consequence to the no-longer-humble professor. Most important of all is the consciousness that knowledge can indeed do good, that it is a usable commodity, not only capable of bringing fame to its possessor but actually capable of causing beneficent changes in the external world.

All too few scholars are conscious that in reducing truth to an instrument, even an instrument for doing good, they necessarily blunt its edge and expose themselves to the danger of its misuse. For, when truth ceases to be an end in itself and becomes but a means toward an end, it also becomes malleable and manageable and is in danger of losing its character—not necessarily, not inevitably, but seriously. There may be ways of avoiding the extreme choices of the ivory tower and the marketplace, but they are far from easy and call for extreme caution.

◦◦◦

In 1679 Jacques Bossuet wrote for his pupil the Dauphin, heir apparent to the throne of France, a discourse on universal history. Here certainly was an opportunity to influence the mind of the future monarch of Europe's most powerful kingdom. Bossuet understood that the greatest service he could render was to tell, not what would be pleasant to hear, but the truth about the past, detached and whole, so that in later years his pupil could make what use he wished of it.

Therein Bossuet reverted to an ancient tradition. The first law for the historian, Cicero had written, "is never to dare utter an untruth and the second, never to suppress anything true." And, earlier still, Polybius had noted that no one was exempt from mistakes made out of ignorance. But "deliberate misstatements in the interest of country or of friends or for favour" reduced the scholar to the level of those who gained "their living by their pens" and weighed "everything by the standard of profit."

In sum, the use of history is to learn from the study of it and not to carry preconceived notions or external objectives into it.

◦◦◦

The times, it may be, will remain hostile to the enterprise of truth. There have been such periods in the past. Historians would do well to regard the example of those clerks in the Dark Ages who knew the worth of the task. By retiring from an alien world to a hidden monastic refuge, now and again one of them at least was able to maintain a true record, a chronicle that survived the destructive passage of armies and the erosion of doctrinal disputes and informed the future of what had transpired in their day. That task is ever worthy. Scholars should ponder its significance.

William H. McNeill  **NO**

Mythistory, or Truth, Myth, History, and Historians

Myth and history are close kin inasmuch as both explain how things got to be the way they are by telling some sort of story. But our common parlance reckons myth to be false while history is, or aspires to be, true. Accordingly, a historian who rejects someone else's conclusions calls them mythical, while claiming that his own views are true. But what seems true to one historian will seem false to another, so one historian's truth becomes another's myth, even at the moment of utterance.

A century and more ago, when history was first established as an academic discipline, our predecessors recognized this dilemma and believed they had a remedy. Scientific source criticism would get the facts straight, whereupon a conscientious and careful historian needed only to arrange the facts into a readable narrative to produce genuinely scientific history. And science, of course, like the stars above, was true and eternal, as Newton and Laplace had demonstrated to the satisfaction of all reasonable persons everywhere.

Yet, in practice, revisionism continued to prevail within the newly constituted historical profession, as it had since the time of Herodotus. For a generation or two, this continued volatility could be attributed to scholarly success in discovering new facts by diligent work in the archives; but early in this century thoughtful historians began to realize that the arrangement of facts to make a history involved subjective judgments and intellectual choices that had little or nothing to do with source criticism, scientific or otherwise.

In reacting against an almost mechanical vision of scientific method, it is easy to underestimate actual achievements. For the ideal of scientific history did allow our predecessors to put some forms of bias behind them. In particular, academic historians of the nineteenth century came close to transcending older religious controversies. Protestant and Catholic histories of post-Reformation Europe ceased to be separate and distinct traditions of learning—a transformation nicely illustrated in the Anglo-American world by the career of Lord Acton, a Roman Catholic who became Regius Professor of History at Cambridge and editor of the first *Cambridge Modern History.* This was a great accomplishment. So was the accumulation of an

As seen in *The American Historical Review*, vol. 91, no. 1, February 1986, pp. 1–10; adapted from *Mythistory and other Essays* (University of Chicago Press, 1986). Copyright © 1986 by William H. McNeill. Reprinted by permission of the author.

enormous fund of exact and reliable data through painstaking source criticism that allowed the writing of history in the western world to assume a new depth, scope, range, and precision as compared to anything possible in earlier times. No heir of that scholarly tradition should scoff at the faith of our predecessors, which inspired so much toiling in archives.

Yet the limits of scientific history were far more constricting than its devotees believed. Facts that could be established beyond all reasonable doubt remained trivial in the sense that they did not, in and of themselves, give meaning or intelligibility to the record of the past. A catalogue of undoubted and indubitable information, even if arranged chronologically, remains a catalogue. To become a history, facts have to be put together into a pattern that is understandable and credible; and when that has been achieved, the resulting portrait of the past may become useful as well—a font of practical wisdom upon which people may draw when making decisions and taking action.

Pattern recognition of the sort historians engage in is the chef d'oeuvre of human intelligence. It is achieved by paying selective attention to the total input of stimuli that perpetually swarm in upon our consciousness. Only by leaving things out, that is, relegating them to the status of background noise deserving only to be disregarded, can what matters most in a given situation become recognizable. Suitable action follows. Here is the great secret of human power over nature and over ourselves as well. Pattern recognition is what natural scientists are up to; it is what historians have always done, whether they knew it or not.

Only some facts matter for any given pattern. Otherwise, useless clutter will obscure what we are after: perceptible relationships among important facts. That and that alone constitutes an intelligible pattern, giving meaning to the world, whether it be the world of physics and chemistry or the world of interacting human groups through time, which historians take as their special domain. Natural scientists are ruthless in selecting aspects of available sensory inputs to pay attention to, disregarding all else. They call their patterns theories and inherit most of them from predecessors. But, as we now know, even Newton's truths needed adjustment. Natural science is neither eternal nor universal; it is instead historical and evolutionary, because scientists accept a new theory only when the new embraces a wider range of phenomena or achieves a more elegant explanation of (selectively observed) facts than its predecessor was able to do.

No comparably firm consensus prevails among historians. Yet we need not despair. The great and obvious difference between natural scientists and historians is the greater complexity of the behavior historians seek to understand. The principal source of historical complexity lies in the fact that human beings react both to the natural world and to one another chiefly through the mediation of symbols. This means, among other things, that any theory about human life, if widely believed, will alter actual behavior, usually by inducing people to act as if the theory were true. Ideas and ideals thus become self-validating within remarkably elastic limits. An extraordinary behavioral motility results. Resort to symbols, in effect, loosened up the connection between external reality and human responses, freeing us from instinct by setting us adrift on a sea of uncertainty. Human beings thereby acquired a new capacity to err, but also to change, adapt, and learn new ways of doing things. Innumerable errors, corrected by experience, eventually made us lords of creation as no other species on earth has ever been before.

The price of this achievement is the elastic, inexact character of truth, and especially of truths about human conduct. What a particular group of persons understands, believes, and acts upon, even if quite absurd to outsiders, may nonetheless cement social relations and allow the members of the group to act together and accomplish feats otherwise impossible. Moreover, membership in such a group and participation in its sufferings and triumphs give meaning and value to individual human lives. Any other sort of life is not worth living, for we are social creatures. As such we need to share truths with one another, and not just truths about atoms, stars, and molecules but about human relations and the people around us.

Shared truths that provide a sanction for common effort have obvious survival value. Without such social cement no group can long preserve itself. Yet to outsiders, truths of this kind are likely to seem myths, save in those (relatively rare) cases when the outsider is susceptible to conversion and finds a welcome within the particular group in question.

The historic record available to us consists of an unending appearance and dissolution of human groups, each united by its own beliefs, ideals, and traditions. Sects, religions, tribes, and states, from ancient Sumer and Pharaonic Egypt to modern times, have based their cohesion upon shared truths—truths that differed from time to time and place to place with a rich and reckless variety. Today the human community remains divided among an enormous number of different groups, each espousing its own version of truth about itself and about those excluded from its fellowship. Everything suggests that this sort of social and ideological fragmentation will continue indefinitely.

Where, in such a maelstrom of conflicting opinions, can we hope to locate historical truth? Where indeed?

Before modern communications thrust familiarity with the variety of human idea-systems upon our consciousness, this question was not particularly acute. Individuals nearly always grew up in relatively isolated communities to a more or less homogeneous world view. Important questions had been settled long ago by prophets and sages, so there was little reason to challenge or modify traditional wisdom. Indeed there were strong positive restraints upon any would-be innovator who threatened to upset the inherited consensus.

To be sure, climates of opinion fluctuated, but changes came surreptitiously, usually disguised as commentary upon old texts and purporting merely to explicate the original meanings. Flexibility was considerable, as the modern practice of the U.S. Supreme Court should convince us; but in this traditional ordering of intellect, all the same, outsiders who did not share the prevailing orthodoxy were shunned and disregarded when they could not be converted. Our predecessors' faith in a scientific method that would make written history absolutely and universally true was no more than a recent example of such a belief system. Those who embraced it felt no need to pay attention to ignoramuses who had not accepted the truths of "modern science." Like other true believers, they were therefore spared the task of taking others' viewpoints seriously or wondering about the limits of their own vision of historical truth.

But we are denied the luxury of such parochialism. We must reckon with multiplex, competing faiths—secular as well as transcendental, revolutionary as well as traditional—that resound amongst us. In addition, partially autonomous professional idea-systems have proliferated in the past century or so. Those most important to historians are the so-called social sciences—anthropology, sociology, political science, psychology, and economics—together with the newer disciplines of ecology and semeiology. But law, theology, and philosophy also pervade the field of knowledge with which historians may be expected to deal. On top of all this, innumerable individual authors, each with his own assortment of ideas and assumptions, compete for attention. Choice is everywhere; dissent turns into cacaphonous confusion; my truth dissolves into your myth even before I can put words on paper.

The liberal faith, of course, holds that in a free marketplace of ideas, Truth will eventually prevail. I am not ready to abandon that faith, however dismaying our present confusion may be. The liberal experiment, after all, is only about two hundred and fifty years old, and on the appropriate world-historical time scale that is too soon to be sure. Still, confusion is undoubted. Whether the resulting uncertainty will be bearable for large numbers of people in difficult times ahead is a question worth asking. Iranian Muslims, Russian communists, and American sectarians (religious and otherwise) all exhibit symptoms of acute distress in face of moral uncertainties, generated by exposure to competing truths. Clearly, the will to believe is as strong today as at any time in the past; and true believers nearly always wish to create a community of the faithful, so as to be able to live more comfortably, insulated from troublesome dissent.

The prevailing response to an increasingly cosmopolitan confusion has been intensified personal attachment, first to national and then to subnational groups, each with its own distinct ideals and practices. As one would expect, the historical profession faithfully reflected and helped to forward these shifts of sentiment. Thus, the founding fathers of the American Historical Association and their immediate successors were intent on facilitating the consolidation of a new American nation by writing national history in a WASPish mold, while also claiming affiliation with a tradition of Western civilization that ran back through modern and medieval Europe to the ancient Greeks and Hebrews. This version of our past was very widely repudiated in the 1960s, but iconoclastic revisionists felt no need to replace what they attacked with any architectonic vision of their own. Instead, scholarly energy concentrated on discovering the history of various segments of the population that had been left out or ill-treated by older historians: most notably women, blacks, and other ethnic minorities within the United States and the ex-colonial peoples of the world beyond the national borders.

Such activity conformed to our traditional professional role of helping to define collective identities in ambiguous situations. Consciousness of a common past, after all, is a powerful supplement to other ways of defining who "we" are. An oral tradition, sometimes almost undifferentiated from the practical wisdom embodied in language itself, is all people need in a stable social universe where in-group boundaries are self-evident. But with civilization, ambiguities multi pled, and formal written history became useful in defining "us" versus "them." At first, the central ambiguity ran between rulers and ruled. Alien conquerors who lived on taxes collected from their subjects were at best a necessary evil when looked at from the bottom of civilized society. Yet in some situations, especially when confronting natural disaster or external attack, a case could be made for commonality, even between taxpayers and tax consumers. At any rate, histories began as king lists, royal genealogies, and boasts of divine favor—obvious ways of consolidating rulers' morale and asserting their legitimacy vis-à-vis their subjects.

Jewish history emphasized God's power over human affairs, narrowing the gap between rulers and ruled by subjecting everybody to divine Providence. The Greeks declared all free men equal, subject to no one, but bound by a common obedience to law. The survival value of both these visions of the human condition is fairly obvious. A people united by their fear and love of God have an ever-present help in time of trouble, as Jewish history surely proves. Morale can survive disaster, time and again; internal disputes and differences diminish beneath the weight of a shared subjection to God. The Greek ideal of freedom under law is no less practical in the sense that willing cooperation is likely to elicit maximal collective effort, whether in war or peace.

Interplay between these two ideals runs throughout the history of Western civilization, but this is not the place to enter into a detailed historiographical analysis. Let me merely remark that our professional heritage from the liberal and nationalist historiography of the nineteenth century drew mainly on the Greek, Herodotean model, emphasizing the supreme value of political freedom within a territorially defined state.

World War I constituted a catastrophe for that liberal and nationalist vision of human affairs, since freedom that permitted such costly and lethal combat no longer seemed a plausible culmination of all historic experience. Boom, bust, and World War II did nothing to clarify the issue, and the multiplication of subnational historiographies since the 1950s merely increased our professional confusion.

What about truth amidst all this weakening of old certainties, florescence of new themes, and widening of sensibilities? What really and truly matters? What should we pay attention to? What must we neglect?

All human groups like to be flattered. Historians are therefore under perpetual temptation to conform to expectation by portraying the people they write about as they wish to be. A mingling of truth and falsehood, blending history with ideology, results. Historians are likely to select facts to show that we—whoever "we" may be—conform to our cherished principles: that we are free with Herodotus, or saved with Augustine, or oppressed with Marx, as the case may be. Grubby details indicating that the group fell short of its ideals can be skated over or omitted entirely. The result is mythical: the past as we want it to be, safely simplified into a contest between good guys and bad guys, "us" and "them." Most national history and most group history is of this kind, though the intensity of chiaroscuro varies greatly, and sometimes an historian turns traitor to the group he studies by setting out to unmask its pretensions. Groups struggling toward self-consciousness and groups whose accustomed status seems threatened are likely to demand (and get) vivid, simplified portraits of their admirable virtues and undeserved sufferings. Groups accustomed to power and surer of their internal cohesion can afford to accept more subtly modulated portraits of their successes and failures in bringing practice into conformity with principles.

Historians respond to this sort of market by expressing varying degrees of commitment to, and detachment from, the causes they chronicle and by infusing varying degrees of emotional intensity into their pages through particular choices of words. Truth, persuasiveness, intelligibility rest far more on this level of the historians' art than on source criticism. But, as I said at the beginning, one person's truth is another's myth, and the fact that a group of people accepts a given version of the past does not make that version any truer for outsiders.

Yet we cannot afford to reject collective self-flattery as silly, contemptible error. Myths are, after all, often self-validating. A nation or any other human group that knows how to behave in crisis situations because it has inherited a heroic historiographical tradition that tells how ancestors resisted their enemies successfully is more likely to act together effectively than a group lacking such a tradition. Great Britain's conduct in 1940 shows how world politics can be redirected by such a heritage. Flattering historiography does more than assist a given group to survive by affecting the balance of power among warring peoples, for an appropriately idealized version of the past may also allow a group of human beings to come closer to living up to its noblest ideals. What is can move toward what ought to be, given collective commitment to a flattering self-image. The American civil rights movement of the fifties and sixties illustrates this phenomenon amongst us.

These collective manifestations are of very great importance. Belief in the virtue and righteousness of one's cause is a necessary sort of self-delusion for human beings, singly and collectively. A corrosive version of history that emphasizes all the recurrent discrepancies between ideal and reality in a given group's behavior makes it harder for members of the group in question to act cohesively and in good conscience. That sort of history is very costly indeed. No group can afford it for long.

On the other hand, myths may mislead disastrously. A portrait of the past that denigrates others and praises the ideals and practice of a given group naively and without restraint can distort a people's image of outsiders so that foreign relations begin to consist of nothing but nasty surprises. Confidence in one's own high principles and good intentions may simply provoke others to resist duly accredited missionaries of the true faith, whatever that faith may be. Both the United States and the Soviet Union have encountered their share of this sort of surprise and disappointment ever since 1917, when Wilson and Lenin proclaimed their respective recipes for curing the world's ills. In more extreme cases, mythical, self-flattering versions of the past may push a people toward suicidal behavior, as Hitler's last days may remind us.

More generally, it is obvious that mythical, self-flattering versions of rival groups' pasts simply serve to intensify their capacity for conflict. With the recent quantum jump in the destructive power of weaponry, hardening of group cohesion at the sovereign state level clearly threatens the survival of humanity; while, within national borders, the civic order experiences new strains when subnational groups acquire a historiography replete with oppressors living next door and, perchance, still enjoying the fruits of past injustices.

The great historians have always responded to these difficulties by expanding their sympathies beyond narrow in-group boundaries. Herodotus set out to award a due meed of glory both to Hellenes and to the barbarians; Ranke inquired into what really happened to Protestant and Catholic, Latin and German nations alike. And other pioneers of our profession have likewise expanded the range of their sympathies and sensibilities beyond previously recognized limits without ever entirely escaping, or even wishing to escape, from the sort of partisanship involved in accepting the general assumptions and beliefs of a particular time and place.

Where to fix one's loyalties is the supreme question of human life and is especially acute in a cosmopolitan age like ours when choices abound. Belonging to a tightly knit group makes life worth living by giving individuals something beyond the self to serve and to rely on for personal guidance, companionship, and aid. But the stronger such bonds, the sharper the break with the rest of humanity. Group solidarity is always maintained, at least partly, by exporting psychic frictions across the frontiers, projecting animosities onto an outside foe in order to enhance collective cohesion within the group itself. Indeed, something to fear, hate, and attack is probably necessary for the full expression of human emotions; and ever since animal predators ceased to threaten, human beings have feared, hated, and fought one another.

Historians, by helping to define "us" and "them," play a considerable part in focusing love and hate, the two principal cements of collective behavior known to humanity. But myth making for rival groups has become a dangerous game in the atomic age, and we may well ask whether there is any alternative open to us.

In principle the answer is obvious. Humanity entire possesses a commonality which historians may hope to understand just as firmly as they can comprehend what unites any lesser group. Instead of enhancing conflicts, as parochial historiography inevitably does, an intelligible world history might be expected to diminish the lethality of group encounters by cultivating a sense of individual identification with the triumphs and tribulations of humanity as a whole. This, indeed, strikes me as the moral duty of the historical profession in our time. We need to develop an ecumenical history, with plenty of room for human diversity in all its complexity.

Yet a wise historian will not denigrate intense attachment to small groups. That is essential to personal happiness. In all civilized societies, a tangle of overlapping social groupings lays claim to human loyalties. Anyone person may therefore be expected to have multiple commitments and plural public identities, up to and including membership in the human race and the wider DNA community of life on planet Earth. What we need to do as historians and as human beings is to recognize this complexity and balance our loyalties so that no one group will be able to command total commitment. Only so can we hope to make the world safer for all the different human groups that now exist and may come into existence.

The historical profession has, however, shied away from an ecumenical view of the human adventure. Professional career patterns reward specialization; and in all the well-trodden fields, where pervasive consensus on important matters has already been achieved, research and innovation necessarily concentrate upon minutiae. Residual faith that truth somehow resides in original documents confirms this direction of our energies. An easy and commonly unexamined corollary is the assumption that world history is too vague and too general to be true, that is, accurate to the sources. Truth, according to this view, is only attainable on a tiny scale when the diligent historian succeeds in exhausting the relevant documents before they exhaust the historian. But as my previous remarks have made clear, this does not strike me as a valid view of historical method. On the contrary, I call it naive and erroneous.

All truths are general. All truths abstract from the available assortment of data simply by using words, which in their very nature generalize so as to bring order to the incessantly fluctuating flow of messages in and messages out that constitutes human consciousness. Total reproduction of experience is impossible and undesirable. It would merely perpetuate the confusion we seek to escape. Historiography that aspires to get closer and closer to the documents—all the documents: and nothing but the documents—is merely moving closer and closer to incoherence, chaos, and meaninglessness. That is a dead end for sure. No society will long support a profession that produces arcane trivia and calls it truth.

Fortunately for the profession, historians' practice has been better than their epistemology. Instead of replicating confusion by paraphrasing the totality of relevant and available documents, we have used our sources to discern, support, and reinforce group identities at national, transnational, and subnational levels and, once in a while, to attack or pick apart a group identity to which a school of revisionists has taken a scunner.

If we can now realize that our practice already shows how truths may be discerned at different levels of generality with equal precision simply because different patterns emerge on different time-space scales, then, perhaps, repugnance for world history might diminish and a juster proportion between parochial and ecumenical historiography might begin to emerge. It is our professional duty to move toward ecumenicity, however real the risks may seem to timid and unenterprising minds.

With a more rigorous and reflective epistemology, we might also attain a better historiographical balance between Truth, truths, and myth. Eternal and universal Truth about human behavior is an unattainable goal, however delectable as an ideal. Truths are what historians achieve when they bend their minds as critically and carefully as they can to the task of making their account of public affairs credible as well as intelligible to an audience that shares enough of their particular outlook and assumptions to accept what they say. The result might best be called mythistory perhaps (though I do not expect the term to catch on in professional circles), for the same words that constitute truth for some are, and always will be, myth for others, who inherit or embrace different assumptions and organizing concepts about the world.

This does not mean that there is no difference between one mythistory and another. Some clearly are more adequate to the facts than others. Some embrace more time and space and make sense of a wider variety of human behavior than others. And some, undoubtedly, offer a less treacherous basis for collective action than others. I actually believe that historians' truths, like those of scientists, evolve across the generations, so that versions of the past acceptable today are superior in scope, range, and accuracy to versions available in earlier times. But such evolution is slow, and observable only on an extended time scale, owing to the self-validating character of myth. Effective common action can rest on quite fantastic beliefs. *Credo quia absurdum may* even become a criterion for group membership, requiring initiates to surrender their critical faculties as a sign of full commitment to the common cause. Many sects have prospered on this principle and have served their members well for many generations while doing so.

But faiths, absurd or not, also face a long-run test of survival in a world where not everyone accepts anyone set of beliefs and where human beings must interact with external objects and nonhuman forms of life, as well as with one another. Such "foreign relations" impose limits on what any group of people can safely believe and act on, since actions that fail to secure expected and desired results are always costly and often disastrous. Beliefs that mislead action are likely to be amended; too stubborn an adherence to a faith that encourages or demands hurtful behavior is likely to lead to the disintegration and disappearance of any group that refuses to learn from experience.

Thus one may, as an act of faith, believe that our historiographical myth making and myth breaking is bound to cumulate across time, propagating mythistories that fit experience better and allow human survival more often, sustaining in-groups in ways that are less destructive to themselves and to their neighbors than was once the case or is the case today. If so, ever-evolving mythistories will indeed become truer and more adequate to public life, emphasizing the really important aspects of human encounters and omitting irrelevant background noise more efficiently so that men and women will know how to act more wisely than is possible for us today.

This is not a groundless hope. Future historians are unlikely to leave out blacks and women from any future mythistory of the United States, and we are unlikely to exclude Asians, Africans, and Amerindians from any future mythistory of the world. One hundred years ago this was not so. The scope and range of historiography has widened, and that change looks as irreversible to me as the widening of physics that occurred when Einstein's equations proved capable of explaining phenomena that Newton's could not.

It is far less clear whether in widening the range of our sensibilities and taking a broader range of phenomena into account we also see deeper into the reality we seek to understand. But we may. Anyone who reads historians of the sixteenth and seventeenth centuries and those of our own time will notice a new awareness of social process that we have attained. As one who shares that awareness, I find it impossible not to believe that it represents an advance on older notions that focused attention exclusively, or almost exclusively, on human intentions and individual actions, subject only to God or to a no less inscrutable Fortune, while leaving out the social and material context within which individual actions took place simply because that context was assumed to be uniform and unchanging.

Still, what seems wise and true to me seems irrelevant obfuscation to others. Only time can settle the issue, presumably by outmoding my ideas and my critics' as well. Unalterable and eternal Truth remains like the Kingdom of Heaven, an eschatological hope. Mythistory is what we actually have—a useful instrument for piloting human groups in their encounters with one another and with the natural environment.

To be a truth-seeking mythographer is therefore a high and serious calling, for what a group of people knows and believes about the past channels expectations and affects the decisions on which their lives, their fortunes, and their sacred honor all depend. Formal written histories are not the only shapers of a people's notions about the past; but they are sporadically powerful, since even the most abstract and academic historiographical ideas do trickle down to the level of the commonplace, if they fit both what a people want to hear and what a people need to know well enough to be useful.

As members of society and sharers in the historical process, historians can only expect to be heard if they say what the people around them want to hear—in some degree. They can only be useful if they also tell the people some things they are reluctant to hear—in some degree. Piloting between this Scylla and Charybdis is the art of the serious historian, helping the group he or she addresses and celebrates to survive and prosper in a treacherous and changing world by knowing more about itself and others.

Academic historians have pursued that art with extraordinary energy and considerable success during the past century. May our heirs and successors persevere and do even better!

POSTSCRIPT

Is History True?

Closely associated to the question of historical truth is the matter of historical objectivi0ty. Frequently, we hear people begin statements with the phrase "History tells us . . ." or "History shows that . . . ," followed by a conclusion that reflects the speaker or writer's point of view. In fact, history does not directly tell or show us anything. That is the job of historians, and as William McNeill argues, much of what historians tell us, despite their best intentions, often represents a blending of historical evidence and myth.

Is there such a thing as a truly objective history? Historian Paul Conkin agrees with McNeill that objectivity is possible only if the meaning of that term is sharply restricted and is not used as a synonym for certain truth. History, Conkin writes, "is a story about the past; it is not the past itself. . . . Whether one draws a history from the guidance of memory or of monuments, it cannot exactly mirror some directly experienced past nor the feelings and perceptions of people in the past." He concludes, "In this sense, much of history is a stab into partial darkness, a matter of informed but inconclusive conjecture. . . . Obviously, in such areas of interpretation, there is no one demonstrably correct 'explanation,' but very often competing, equally unfalsifiable, theories. Here, on issues that endlessly fascinate the historian, the controversies rage, and no one expects, short of a great wealth of unexpected evidence, to find a conclusive answer. An undesired, abstractive precision of the subject might so narrow it as to permit more conclusive evidence. But this would spoil all the fun." For more discussion on this and other topics related to the study of history, see Paul K. Conkin and Roland N. Stromberg, *The Heritage and Challenge of History* (Dodd, Mead & Company, 1971).

The most thorough discussion of historical objectivity in the United States is Peter Novick, *That Noble Dream: The 'Objectivity Question' and the American Historical Profession* (Cambridge University Press, 1988), which draws its title from Charles A. Beard's article in the *American Historical Review* (October 1935) in which Beard reinforced the views expressed in his 1933 presidential address to the American Historical Association. [See "Written History as an Act of Faith," *American Historical Review* (January 1934).] Novick's thorough analysis generated a great deal of attention, the results of which can be followed in James T. Kloppenberg, "Objectivity and Historicism: A Century of American Historical Writing," *American Historical Review* (October 1989), Thomas L. Haskell, "Objectivity Is Not Neutrality: Rhetoric vs. Practice in Peter Novick's *That Noble Dream*," *History & Theory* (1990), and the scholarly forum "Peter Novick's *That Noble Dream:* The

Objectivity Question and the Future of the Historical Profession," *American Historical Review* (June 1991). A critique of recent historical writing that closely follows the concerns expressed by Handlin can be found in Keith Windschuttle, *The Killing of History: How Literary Critics and Social Theorists Are Murdering Our Past* (The Free Press, 1996).

Readers interested in this subject will also find the analyses in Barbara W. Tuchman, *Practicing History: Selected Essays* (Alfred A. Knopf, 1981) and David Hackett Fischer, *Historians' Fallacies: Toward a Logic of Historical Thought* (Harper & Row, 1970) to be quite stimulating. Earlier, though equally rewarding, volumes include Harvey Wish, *The American Historian: A Social-Intellectual History of the Writing of the American Past* (Oxford University Press, 1960); John Higham, with Leonard Krieger and Felix Gilbert, *History: The Development of Historical Studies in the United States* (Prentice-Hall, 1965); and Marcus Cunliffe and Robin Winks, eds., *Pastmasters: Some Essays on American Historians* (Harper & Row, 1969).

ISSUE 2

Was the Wild West More Violent than the Rest of the United States?

YES: David T. Courtright, from "Frontiers" in Ronald Gottesman and Richard Maxwell Brown, eds., *Violence in America: An Encyclopedia, vol. 1* (Charles Scribner's Sons, 1999)

NO: Robert R. Dykstra, from "To Live and Die in Dodge City: Body Counts, Law and Order and the Case of Kansas V. Gill," in Michael A. Bellesiles, ed., *Lethal Imagination, Violence and Brutality in American History* (New York University Press, 1999)

ISSUE SUMMARY

YES: Professor of history David T. Courtwright argues that the cattle, mining, and lumbering Western frontiers were extremely violent because these regions were populated by young, single, and transient males who frequented saloons and prostitutes, and engaged in fights.

NO: Professor Robert R. Dykstra argues that Dodge City had a low crime rate in the decade 1876–1885, and in the murder case of *Kansas V. Gill,* it conducted a jury trial "according to conventions nurtured through a thousand years of Anglo-American judicial traditions."

In 1893, the young historian Frederick Jackson Turner (1861–1932) delivered an address before the American Historical Association entitled *The Significance of the Frontier in American History.* Turner's essay not only sent him from Wisconsin to Harvard University, but also became one of the most important essays ever written in American history. According to Turner's thesis, American civilization was different from European civilization because the continent contained an abundance of land that was settled in four waves of migration from 1607 through 1890. During this process, the European heritage was shed, and the American characteristics of individualism, mobility, nationalism, and democracy developed.

This frontier theory of American history did not go unchallenged. Some historians argued that Turner's definition of the frontier was too vague and imprecise; he underestimated the cultural forces that came to the West from Europe and the eastern states; he neglected the forces of urbanization and industrialization in opening the West; he placed an undue emphasis on sectional development and neglected class struggles for power; finally, his provincial view of American history prolonged the isolationist views of a nation that became involved in world affairs in the twentieth century.

Younger historians have begun to question the traditional interpretation of Western expansion. For example, older historians believed that growth was good and automatically brought forth progress. New historians such as William Cronin, Patricia Limerick, and others, however, have questioned this assumption in examining the disastrous ecological effects of American expansionism, such as the elimination of the American buffalo and the depletion of forests.

Turner's romantic view of the frontier became popularized in the literature of the West from the 1860s through modern times. As America went through its Industrial Revolution with factories manned by immigrants pouring in from Europe and Asia and second- and third-generation farmers diminishing in numbers, a mythic view of the frontier developed. The publishing house of Beadle and Adams had five million of its dime novels in circulation. Its most prolific hero was William F. Cody, a real person glamorized as "Buffalo Bill, the King of the Border Men." Buffalo Bill or his ghostwriters produced 121 novels—all with the same formula. Cody's Wild West shows toured the United States and Europe and featured reenactments of such famous episodes as Custer's Last Stand "at the battle of Little Bighorn in 1876." Buffalo Bill even hired the aged Sitting Bull one season to ride around the arena once per show. The rest of the time, Sitting Bull sat in his tent signing autographs in the fashion of today's retired athletes.

The prototype Western for the twentieth century and beyond is found in Owen Wister's novel *The Virginian*. Written in 1902, it went through six printings its first year and remains in print today. The hero, a southerner gone to Wyoming, is forced at the end to kill his former best friend and his rustling partner. *The Virginian* legitimized the use of violence on the frontier. The good guys would use force only when necessary against the bad. Since Wister, novelists such as Louis L'Amour (whose 80-plus novels have sold over 100 million copies), motion pictures, radio, and television have perpetuated the mythical West.

"The United States," says Richard Hofstadter, "has a history but not a tradition of domestic violence" for two reasons. First, it lacks an ideological and geographical center; second, "we have a remarkable lack of memory where violence is concerned and left most of our excesses apart of our buried history. . . . What is most exceptional about the Americans is not the voluminous record of their violence, but their extraordinary ability, in the face of that record, to persuade themselves that they are among the best-behaved and best-regulated of peoples."

Since Professor Hofstadter wrote those words in 1971, a number of studies have attempted to systematically study the American history of violence. One major question is whether or not the late-nineteenth-century West was more violent than other parts of the country.

YES

David T. Courtright

Frontiers

The Two Types of Frontiers

Type I	Type II
farming, farm building	mining, ranching, other extraction
families, usually nuclear	individuals
balanced gender distribution	80 to 90 percent (or more) male
a few over forty-five years old	almost none over forty-five years old
many children	few children
high birthrate	low birthrate
women less highly valued	women more highly valued
relatively permanent	transient
limited vice	widespread commercialized vice
peaceful	violent
colonizing	imperialist, exploitative

Source: An elaboration of Walter Nugent, "Frontiers and Empires in the Late Nineteenth Century." *Western Historical Quarterly* 20 (1989): 401.

A Stabbing in Idaho

Don Maguire was a Rocky Mountain trader who made his money selling guns, knives, dice, cards, and various other items at a 1,000 percent profit. He kept a journal, which has been edited by the historian Gary Topping. This entry, composed in a hurried, stream-of-consciousness style, was written in the course of an 1877 trip to the mining town of Atlanta, Idaho:

> The two noted characters of the town Coyote Smith and Poker Smith. My attention was first drawn to Coyote Smith. While he was engaged in a quarrel with two carpenters who were working lumber in front of a saloon, he being drunk made much disturbance and at the same time vowing to whip the two carpenters whereupon one of them gave him a kick in the hip. This set him wild. He snarled for a revolver swearing to kill the two. A revolver he could not procure. Midway up the street entered into a second altercation with Poker Smith and seizing a

carving knife from the counter of a restaurant he made a stroke [passage obliterated] to sever the jugular vein for Poker Smith but missing his aim the knife struck the collar bone broke and his hand running down the blade he received a horrible wound cutting his hand from the hollow between the thumb and forefinger nearly to the wrist blood flowed freely from both parties but neither was fatally injured. There were no arrests made.

"No arrests made" was the outcome of many a similar confrontation. This sort of affray kept the local surgeon busy, not necessarily the sheriff or vigilance committee. One of the busiest surgeons was George Kenny of Salmon City, Idaho. Before he was through, he managed to fill half a coffee mug with bullets dug from miners.

Source: "A Trader in the Rocky Mountains: Don Maguire's 1877 Diary."
Idaho Yesterdays 27 (summer 1983): 2–4, 7 (quotation). Where indicated by Maguire's capitalization, periods have been inserted; the spelling of one word, "seizing" for "siezing," has been corrected.

In the last decades of the twentieth century the concept of the frontier had become for many U.S. historians the equivalent of an insult in a crowded saloon: an invitation to fight. Many a blow had been leveled at Frederick Jackson Turner's famous account of European-descended whites "advancing" into "free lands" along an "empty" frontier, a notion of national progress that was condemned as oblivious to the existence of the native peoples. Some indignant historians refrained from using the word *frontier* altogether, an extreme reaction that jettisoned a useful analytical concept. Properly understood in a neutral, ecological sense as a shifting, generally westward-moving zone of interaction between indigenous and nonindigenous populations, the idea of the frontier is useful in making sense of the historical pattern of violence in the United States. In fact, it is indispensable.

Peaceful and Not-So-Peaceful Frontiers

The frontier violence of fact and legend was mostly a product of developing regions with an excess of young single males. The historian Walter Nugent calls these type II frontiers and contrasts them with type I farming frontiers, which were generally peaceful, not to say dull. The people of the farming frontiers were the "colorless many, . . . too busy trying to raise families and eke out a living to become legendary." The denizens of the cattle towns and mining camps were the "colorful few," whose lives were more often cut short by accidents, drunken violence, or hygienic neglect.

Type II frontiers were most common in ranching country and in the mining and lumbering regions of the cordillera, the vast elevated region from the eastern Rocky Mountains to the western foothills of the Sierra Nevada and Cascade ranges. With the exception of Mormon-settled Utah, type I frontiers were found in rainier areas with good soil and readier access to the East. In their very earliest stages, they were pioneered by men who came ahead of their families to scout the land, build primitive shelters, and pave the way for agriculture. As soon as they judged conditions to be satisfactory, these men brought their fiancées or wives and children to join them. Though raids by Native Americans or outlaws might bring moments of terror (and retreat to safer lands), populations consisting mostly of young farming families enjoyed relatively stable social lives.

Type II frontiers were far more volatile. In any society young men in their late teens and twenties are responsible for a disproportionate amount of violence and disorder. Statistically, populations that consist mostly of young men have shown a tendency toward violent crime. This is not only because the young men are so numerous or brimful of testosterone, but also because so many of them are unattached. In type II frontiers there simply were not enough eligible women.

In normal circumstances, marriage acts as a brake on rambunctious male behavior: the boys get hitched and settle down. The cliché is grounded in both sociology and evolutionary psychology. When men acquire wives and families, they have more to lose and so behave more cautiously. Other things being equal, a married frontiersman thought twice before wading into the thick of a barroom fray. A married frontiersman was less likely to be in a barroom in the first place.

Vice, another prominent characteristic of type II frontier towns, was linked to violence in several ways. Unattached laborers—cowboys, miners, lumberjacks, fur trappers, navvies, teamsters—were the natural prey of gamblers, pimps, prostitutes, and whiskey peddlers, all of whom followed the frontier. Many vice figures were armed and hardened criminals who used violence or its threat to settle disputes over poker stakes and dance-hall girls. Vice institutions were flash points for trouble.

Nowhere was this clearer than in the China-towns of western cities and towns. Chinatowns were, among other things, recreational vice districts for the overwhelmingly male Cantonese laborers who poured into California and other western states and territories after the discovery of gold. They featured gambling parlors, brothels, and opium dens that were controlled by organized gangs called tongs. Tong enforcers (called highbinders or hatchet men) used muscle to collect gambling debts and prevent indentured prostitutes ("slave girls") from running away with customers. They waged pitched battles with other tongs to maintain control of the vice operations, much as rival gangs of bootleggers would later do during Prohibition. The homicide arrest rate for the Chinese in Portland, Oregon, in the 1870s was roughly four times that of the general population, a reflection of the abnormally high ratio of Chinese men to women and the consequent flourishing of vice and organized crime. The Chinese were also preyed upon by white robbers, extortionists, and bullies who found them easy and politically popular targets. The *English-Chinese Phrase Book* (1875, revised 1877) distributed by Wells, Fargo and Company included grimly useful sentences such as "He came to his death by homicide," "He was choked to death with a lasso, by a robber," "He was killed by an assassin," and "He was smothered in his room."

Outside Chinatown the saloon was the central establishment of vice. Spree drinking was common, particularly among workers who had just been paid. When they drank too much, they became careless and clumsy, likelier to give or take offense in dangerous circumstances. Clare McKanna, who studied nearly one thousand homicide cases in three western counties from 1880 to 1920, found that seven in ten of the perpetrators had been drinking, as had about six in ten of the victims. More than one-third of the male victims died in saloons or in the streets in front of them. Thirty-two of them had been shot by bartenders (mostly with pistols, not, according to legend, with a shotgun from behind the counter), while sixteen of the dead were themselves bartenders. Most of the killings took place in the evening or on the weekend, that is, the times when tipsy men were apt to be congregating in saloons and other places of bibulous recreation.

Drunken brawls were not necessarily homicidal. What made them so lethal was the frontier habit of carrying knives or especially guns. Handguns were responsible for 63 percent of the homicides in McKanna's sample; handguns, rifles, and shotguns were responsible for 75 percent. Ready access to deadly (and often concealed) weapons greatly increased the odds that a simple assault would escalate to homicide. Most frontier killings and maimings were sordid, unpremeditated affairs that arose from jostling or insults among touchy men who had had too much to drink.

Gun toting also carried the risk of accidental death. The *Caldwell Post,* a cattle-town newspaper, estimated that five cowboys were killed by accidental gun discharges for every one who was shot intentionally. An unjacketed .44- or .45-caliber bullet did tremendous damage. Many of those who survived gun mishaps had to live with terrible injuries: blasted groins, shot-away knees, missing faces, and the like.

Measuring the Violence

The most frequently studied measure of frontier violence is the homicide rate. Killings usually made it into newspapers and official documents and thus into the historical record, while lesser crimes such as assaults were often unremarked or unprosecuted. As Robert Dykstra has argued, even in legendary places like Dodge City the number of murders was actually small, owing to the smallness of their populations. Men did not duel in the streets every noon, nor was killing, criminal or otherwise, a common event.

In proportional terms, however, frontier killings were much more frequent than in the East. When homicide is expressed as a ratio (conventionally the number of cases per 100,000 people per year), type II frontier communities had rates that were at least an order of magnitude greater than those prevailing in eastern cities or midwestern agricultural regions. The homicide rate of Fort Griffin, a central Texas frontier town frequented by cowboys, buffalo hunters, and soldiers, was 229 per 100,000 in the 1870s. That of Boston, a long-settled eastern city whose population included proportionately more women, children, and old people, was only about 6.

Some of the most clear-cut evidence comes from California. Roger McGrath has calculated that the homicide rate for the mining town of Bodie (90 percent male) was 116 per 100,000 from 1878 to 1882, years when eastern homicide rates rarely exceeded single digits. (By contrast, the robbery rates in Bodie and nearby Aurora, Nevada, were comparable to, and burglary rates lower than, those of eastern cities—a reflection, perhaps, of the fear of armed retaliation by potential victims.) Kevin Mullen has estimated that the San Francisco homicide rate ranged from 28 to 80 per 100,000, with an average of about 49, during the city's tumultuous early years (1849–1856). The rate thereafter subsided to a range of 4 to 13 per 100,000 during the 1860s. The main reason for the shift was that the disproportionately youthful and male population characteristic of the early gold rush gradually gave way to a more balanced population that included more women, children, and old people.

This was in fact a universal pattern. Type II settlements did not retain their unbalanced populations forever. Within a decade or two the surplus men moved on to new frontiers, died prematurely, or married and settled down. Women, who were initially scarce, married and began bearing children at an early age, often in their teens. These children were roughly divided between boys and girls. Eventually the children married and further normalized the population. With the increasing numbers of women and children came institutions—schools, churches, and the Woman's Christian Temperance Union—that militated against vice and violence and improved the moral climate of the once-raucous frontier towns.

Frontier violence is thus best understood as a passing migratory anomaly. The nature of the labor demand drew youthful male workers to ranching, mining, and other type II frontier regions. These young men found themselves thrown together in competitive masculine company, isolated from familial influences, tempted by predaceous vice and payday sprees, and at least temporarily unable to find women to marry. When these circumstances changed—when the type II frontiers came to resemble more nearly the type I frontiers—the propensity toward public violence abated or at least stabilized at a lower level.

Cultural Influences

There is more to the story of frontier violence than population structure. Cultural factors also help to explain why men were so quick to fight other men and why there was so much conflict with Native Americans.

Men who come from cultures that stress personal honor are more likely to become involved in fights than those who do not. Such cultures emphasize the importance of responding to any perceived insult or slight, however trivial, lest a man lose face in the eyes of others who determine his social worth. The approved response is to display physical courage, to fight the offender, or, in certain upper-class contexts, to challenge him to a duel. The addition of deadly weapons to the honor imperative, epitomized by a Colorado grave marker, "He called Bill Smith a liar," explains why hotheaded killings were common on the frontier.

Those portions of the frontier settled or traversed by southerners were especially prone to hotheaded killings. The religiously motivated European immigrants who first journeyed to New England and the littoral regions of the middle colonies—Puritans, Quakers, German Pietists, and the like—were not particularly concerned about honor. However, the Cavaliers who settled in the Chesapeake colonies were. (Maryland's homicide rate from 1657 to 1680 was more than twice that of Massachusetts, though this probably reflects excess males as well as cultural differences.) The Scots, Scots-Irish, border English, and Finns who settled along the backwoods frontier were also highly honor-conscious. They were accustomed to weapons and warfare, because they or their ancestors had come from remote and often violent rural areas on the hardscrabble periphery of northern and western Europe.

As the frontier moved westward, most new settlers situated themselves in places climatically similar to those whence they came. New Englanders moved to Ohio, southerners to the Gulf Plain, and so on. Until the twentieth century, migration tended to follow lines of latitude, as did cultural attitudes toward honor. Frontier regions settled by northerners were less violent than those settled by migrants from the South or Midlands. "All old-timers who know the West will tell you that they did not have so many killings and shooting scrapes after they got up North as they did in Texas," recalled E. C. "Teddy Blue" Abbott in his cowboy memoir, *We Pointed Them North: Recollections of a Cowpuncher* (1939; p. 231). The figures back him up. The statewide homicide rate in Texas was 32 per 100,000 in 1878, far higher than in northern climes.

Conflict with Native Americans

Many frontiersmen, northern as well as southern, had definite ideas about Anglo-Saxon racial superiority and the self-evident correctness of manifest destiny. At best, Native Americans were objects of suspicion; at worst, they were savages, disgusting, incorrigible, and even diabolical obstacles to the advance of civilization. Such extreme ethnocentrism naturally made it easier to justify killing them and appropriating their lands. The classic case was California, where miners enslaved, raped, or simply shot down Native Americans for no better reason, wrote one French missionary, than "to try their pistols." Miners, ranchers, and militiamen—the latter much more lethal to Native Americans than the better-disciplined regular soldiers—together accounted for more than forty-five hundred killings of Native Americans in California between 1848 and 1880.

Of course, the Native Americans in California and elsewhere fought back, often matching and surpassing whites in the ferocity of their attacks. Apaches were known to kindle slow fires under the heads of suspended captives. Tales of such atrocities confirmed the whites' conviction that the elimination of hostile Native Americans was in principle no different from hunting predatory animals. Even when Native Americans were accorded the formalities of a trial, bias against them practically guaranteed convictions. For example, every Apache accused of killing a white in Gila County, Arizona, in the late 1880s was convicted. The only Apaches who were acquitted or had their cases dismissed were those accused of killing other Apaches. For those found guilty, a long sentence was often tantamount to the death penalty. Well over one-third of all Native Americans sent off to prison in Arizona and California were dead within five years.

Native Americans were at a marked demographic disadvantage in their conflict with whites. Their numbers progressively dwindled because of their vulnerability to imported Old World diseases such as smallpox. Too many women and dependents were another military handicap. Braves were in short supply, a legacy of intertribal warfare and, more speculatively, of the greater susceptibility of males to infectious disease. Native American women and dependents were less mobile than the braves and therefore easier to attack. The tactic of destroying villages rather than going after elusive bands of warriors, which emerged in Massachusetts and Virginia as early as the 1620s and 1630s, was used repeatedly in the eighteenth and nineteenth centuries and led to such notorious and lopsided Native American defeats as Sand Creek (1864), Washita (1868), and Wounded Knee (1890).

Ecological violence by Europeans brought further hardship to Native Americans. Hunting was a popular pastime among frontiersmen, particularly during the nineteenth century. Competitive in masculine company and keen on proving their prowess, Europeans often killed more than was necessary to feed their families or sell to others. The rotting carcasses of thousands of Plains buffalo were a stark reminder of the excess slaughter and a signal source of Native American distress. Give the hunters bronze medals with a dead buffalo on one side and a discouraged Native American on the other, General Philip Sheridan admonished the Texas legislature. "Let them kill, skin, and sell until the buffalo are exterminated," he declared. "Then your prairies can be covered with speckled cattle, and the festive cowboy, who follows the hunter as a second forerunner of an advanced civilization."

Native Americans themselves were drawn into overhunting so they could barter meat and skins for European trade goods, thus heightening conflict with other tribes. One of those trade goods, alcohol, had horrific consequences. European memoirs are full of accounts of drunken Native Americans selling their squaws into prostitution, going on wild binges, stumbling into fires, cutting one another to pieces. One theory to account for this extreme behavior is that Native Americans had no knowledge of distilled alcohol before contact with Europeans and thus no store of social knowledge about drinking. Native Americans learned to drink hard liquor from the worst possible tutors: fur trappers, traders, mule skinners, and other denizens of the type II frontier. When they saw white men swill whiskey and become dangerously, obstreperously drunk, they did likewise and suffered the same consequences.

Government's Failure to Control Frontier Violence

Selling liquor to Native Americans was illegal in most places from colonial times on. Neither the British nor the American government was able to suppress the trade, however. The U.S. government, nominally responsible for policing the western territories, was seldom able adequately to enforce any policy to protect Native Americans. The frontier was vast, the settlers numerous and greedy, and the resources of the federal government limited. The army was spread too thin to control the movements of frontiersmen or to prevent them from trespassing on treaty lands. Local courts and juries were invariably sympathetic toward white defendants and hostile toward Native Americans.

In the early stages of frontier expansion, legal institutions were either lacking or inadequate. One response to this situation, patterned after the Regulator movement in South Carolina in 1767–1769 (in which backcountry settlers organized to restore law and order and establish institutions of local government), was vigilantism, or organized extralegal movements against robbers, rustlers, counterfeiters, and other outlaws. The historian Richard Maxwell Brown counted 326 such movements in the country between 1767 and 1904, the majority of which were in southern and southwestern territories and states, the single most important of which was Texas.

When vigilante actions were limited in scope and controlled by local elites, they often served socially constructive purposes. Selected malefactors were whipped, branded, banished, or sometimes hanged in public dramas that affirmed the values of property and order. But vigilantism could also miscarry. In California, racial minorities, particularly Hispanics, made up a disproportionate percentage of those subjected to lynch courts, which were especially swift and merciless if the victims were white. Vigilantism also ran the risk of triggering private warfare, when friends and relatives of the lynch victims sought revenge against the vigilante faction, or of miscarriages of justice, when personal enemies were killed under the guise of the popular will. Vigilantism, in short, was a poor substitute for professional police and regular courts and had been widely superseded by the close of the nineteenth century.

Frontier Violence After 1900

Frontier violence is not entirely a thing of the past. The night, for example, is a present-day frontier where colonization has been made possible by cars and electric lights. Charles Lindbergh wrote in his autobiography that the most spectacular change he had seen in the earth's surface in all his decades of flying was the sprinkling of myriad lights across the United States on a clear night. These lights were signs of "conquest," of human movement into the frontier of darkness. But that movement is highly selective. Midnight finds mostly young men on the streets—and higher rates of drunkenness, accidents, assault, rape, and murder than in the daylight hours. Nighttime, in brief, resembles a type II frontier.

In some respects, inner cities also resemble a type II frontier. Urban women are hardly outnumbered by men, as they were on the nineteenth-century frontier. Nevertheless, many young innercity males, for economic, subcultural, and demographic reasons, delay marriage or avoid the institution altogether. An increasing number of them have grown up in single-parent households and so have experienced little parental guidance and supervision. Those who have joined gangs, acquired weapons, and become involved with drug traffic and other forms of organized vice are statistically among the most violence-prone members of society, just like their type II frontier counterparts. Indeed, urban ghettos can be thought of as artificial and unusually violent frontier societies: vice-ridden combat zones in which groups of armed, unsupervised touchy bachelors, high on alcohol and other drugs, menace one another and the local citizenry.

Some historians have also seen analogies between twentieth-century U.S. involvement in Pacific wars—particularly against Filipino rebels, Japanese soldiers, and Vietnamese communists—and the earlier frontier campaigns against Native Americans. In all these cases, young American men, remote from what they called civilization, were pitted against enemies they deemed treacherous and racially inferior. The conflicts quickly assumed a ferocious quality reminiscent of the worst episodes of the wars against Native Americans. Indeed, the parallel was made explicit in the language of the Vietnam War, when young GIs spoke of forays into "Indian country" and code-named their operations Texas Star and Cochise Green (a reference to the chief of the Chiricahua Apache who waged relentless war against the U.S. Army).

These GIs has grown up in the golden age of the Western, a hugely successful genre in the publishing, film, radio, and television industries (also advertising: a square-jawed cowboy beat out a crusty taxi driver as the emblem of Philip Morris's legendary Marlboro cigarette campaign). That whole generation had been saturated with images of stylized violence and morally simplistic frontier stories of cowboys, Indians, desperadoes, and six-shooters. Did the public's fascination with these stories of frontier violence contribute to the high rates of violence in the United States relative to other industrial democracies? Did it matter that America's mythic hero was a man with a gun, an attitude, and a Stetson hat?

The answer is a qualified yes. We become who we are by emulating other figures in our environment, including the electronic environment with its celebrities and "action figures." Communications researchers have discovered that, for many people, these figures become role models: people act like them, dress like them, talk like them, even talk *to* them. Insofar as larger-than-life frontier figures, played by the likes of John Wayne and James Arness, entered and shaped mass consciousness, they reinforced the belief that gun violence was an appropriate means for resolving conflicts. It is doubtful, however, that their influence was greater than more fundamental social and economic factors—racism, ghetto isolation, subcultures of poverty, deindustrialization, secularization, family decline, homicidal sensitivity about honor, lax gun control laws, drug abuse, and drug trafficking—that have contributed to the ongoing reputation of the United States as a violent land.

Colonel House Nearly Gets Himself Killed

Edward Mandell House (1858–1938) is best known as Woodrow Wilson's adviser and confidant, a man so close to the president that Wilson once called him "my second personality . . . my independent self." But House, who came of age in Texas's most violent era and who counted it nothing to carry a gun, almost did not make it to Washington. In 1879 he was visiting a mining camp near Como, Colorado:

> It was like all other camps of that sort–rough men and rougher women, gambling, drinking, and killing. I was in a saloon, talking to a man whom I had known in Texas, when . . . a big, brawny individual came into the room and began to abuse me in violent terms. I had never seen the man before and could not imagine why he was doing this. I retreated, and he followed. I had my overcoat on at the time and had my hand on my six-shooter in my pocket and cocked it. The owner of the saloon jumped over the bar between us. In five seconds more, I would have killed him. An explanation followed which cleared up the mystery. He had taken me for some one else against whom he had a grudge, and whom he had seen but once. I learned later that he was a popular ex-sheriff of Summit county and that if I had killed him I should have been lynched within the hour.
>
> It always amuses me when I see the bad men in plays depicted as big, rough fellows with their trousers in their boots and six-shooters buckled around their waists. As a matter of fact, the bad men I have been used to in southern Texas were as unlike this as daylight from dark. They were usually gentle, mild-mannered, mild-spoken, and often delicate-looking men. They were invariably polite, and one not knowing the species would be apt to misjudge them to such an extent that a rough word or an insult would sometimes be offered. This mistake of judgment was one that could never be remedied, for a second opportunity was never given.

Source: Charles Seymour, ed., *The Intimate Papers of Colonel House.* New York: Houghton Mifflin, 1926, pp. 24–25.

Robert R. Dykstra  **NO**

To Live and Die in Dodge City: Body Counts, Law and Order, and the Case of Kansas v. Gill

Never mind that during its celebrated decade as a tough cattle town only fifteen persons died violently in Dodge City, 1876–1885, for an average of just 1.5 killings per cowboy season. Today, three decades after the first release of the homicide data, frontier Dodge City remains a universal metaphor for slaughter and civic anarchy.

Professional historians of the American West are, of course, presumed to know better. And yet there have been recent hints of scholarly skepticism about Dodge City's modest body count. In 1994, for instance, a very prominent essay on frontier violence discussed Dodge and the other Kansas cattle towns without so much as noting in passing their low absolute numbers of killings.

This odd disregard is puzzling. One explanation might be that the homicide data are deemed irrelevant to the question of frontier violence. This is simply hard to credit. A second might be that the data do not conform to the New Western History paradigm, which tends to insist that things were always worse than we thought. That notion can be argued either way. A third possibility is that the data are somehow suspect, and thus better left unmentioned until the question can somehow be settled once and for all. This last possibility, more than the persistence of the Dodge City metaphor among those who learned their Western history in darkened theaters, suggests the value of a revisit to the real, if legendary, town in question.

All the Homicide News Fit to Print

Dodge City was indeed a legend in its own time. It was where livestock herded up from Texas to the railroad tracks in Kansas would be sold, shipped east to market, or walked onward to the ranges of the northern Great Plains. The summertime influx of transients—well-heeled drovers and cattle brokers, festive cowboys, predatory gamblers, and sporting women—more than equaled the town's resident population. But a police

From *Lethal Imagination: Violence and Brutality in American History* by Michael A. Bellesiles, ed. (New York University Press, 1999), pp. 211–224 (notes omitted). Copyright © 1999 by New York University Press. Reprinted by permission.

force of multiple officers, their salaries totaling nearly half of Dodge City's entire municipal budget, closely supervised the behavior of these itinerants by enforcing strict gun-control laws.

The richest man in town, merchant Robert M. Wright, had been present in the bad old days when, in its unorganized first year of existence, Dodge had been the scene of several violent deaths. Wright and his entrepreneurial colleagues had not feared for their lives; they feared for their pocketbooks—that is, their local property values—as the newspapers of eastern Kansas delighted in such energetic headlines as "HOMICIDE AT DODGE CITY. A Notorious Desperado Killed" or "SHOT DEAD. Another Tragedy at Dodge City," or in such sly one-liners as "Only two men killed at Dodge City last week."

But with an expectation of the Texas cattle trade's coming to Dodge, local businessmen foresaw that the influx of new transients would only magnify all problems related to law and order. They therefore established a municipal government late in 1875, levied taxes to pay for it, and criminalized gun toting by private citizens. A photograph taken a few years later shows the town's busiest corner, downtown Front Street at its intersection with Bridge Street, the main thoroughfare in and out of Dodge. In the left background stand R. M. Wright's brick store and the facade of the celebrated Long Branch Saloon. In the middle foreground the superstructure of a town well displays a prominent sign: "The Carrying of Fire Arms Strictly PROHIBITED." As this proximity suggests handgun violence was considered bad for business, an emphatic collective belief of Dodge City's business and professional elite that ultimately explains the low body count.

Scholars' attempts to dilute the significance of such body counts first appeared in the 1980s. "These statistics seem to indicate that the cattle towns were not particularly violent," wrote Roger McGrath. "However, a note of caution is appropriate. Dykstra compiled his statistics exclusively from the local newspapers." The subtext here: How can we be sure that more murders and justifiable homicides than reported did not occur?

There is no known official list of violent deaths at Dodge. Pending discovery of any such compendium, we must depend on a few reasonable assumptions about those reported by the press. The first is the absolute and primal newsworthiness of violent death. However enthusiastically they might conspire in cover-ups and damage control regarding local social conflict, Dodge City's journalists seemed no more able to resist a good homicide story than any circulation-chasing New York or Chicago city editor.

A second assumption involves the substantial array of local weekly newspapers that offer a fairly intimate summary of life in Dodge during the trail-driving era. The *Dodge City Times* began publishing in May 1876, just in time for the town's first cattle-trading season. The *Ford County Globe* joined it in January 1878. The *Dodge City Democrat* appeared in December 1883. And the *Kansas Cowboy* moved to Dodge from Ness County in June 1884. True enough, the first ten months of the *Times*, save for a single issue, are not extant. For 1876, one must extrapolate from the absence of murderous dispatches about Dodge in the press of eastern Kansas; so far, none has been discovered. But certainly from March 1877 to the close of the Texas cattle trade at Dodge City late in 1885, all newspaper runs are virtually complete. Every nineteenth-century village should be so well documented.

A third guiding assumption seems equally reasonable. Cattle-town homicides, when they occasionally occur, are almost always reported in some detail, as the story of Henry Heck's demise will show. This attention lends weight to the notion that news concerning violent death tended to be revealed rather than suppressed.

Deadly Competition: Miami (1980) versus Dodge (1880)

A rather more comprehensive criticism of the cattle-town death statistics also appeared in the 1980s. This critique questioned the significance of the absolute numbers themselves, and argued for replacing them with homicide rates of the type annually devised by the FBI to measure urban violence. For today's metropolitan areas, each case of "murder and non-negligent manslaughter" (excluding justifiable homicides by the police) is calculated as a proportion of every 100,000 of population. The simple formula is

$$hr = (100,000/N_p)N_h,$$

where *hr* equals homicide rate, N_p equals population, and N_h equals number of homicides. Since the 1940s the FBI has used this formula in running a kind of annual negative sweepstakes in which the losing city becomes America's most violent community, the murder capital of the world. In 1980, for example, greater Mami's homicide rate soared to 32.7—the nation's highest that year.

But, as a few scholars began to note, a murder rate of 32.7 is not very high when contrasted with similarly calculated homicide rates back in time. That for late-thirteenth-century London, noted James Given, was about the same as the yearly average for Miami, 1948–1952. Barbara Hanawalt similarly discovered that the rate for London in the early fourteenth century soared even higher, to something between 36.0 and 51.3. Then, uncritically borrowing the two medievalists' methodology, Roger McGrath discovered that the average annual homicide rate at nineteenth-century Bodie, California, a mining camp, was a stratospheric 116.0.

These historians have been compromised by the statistical fallacy of small numbers. In 1980, Miami's absolute number of homicides exceeded 500, while Hanawalt's yearly average for London was only 18 and McGrath's body count for Bodie over several years was a measly 29. It was London's modest population (an estimated 35,000 to 50,000) and Bodie's small population (no more than 5,000 in any year) that caused their homicide rates to surpass modern Miami's.

As to tiny Dodge City—population 1,275 in 1880—its FBI homicide rate calculates out at an enormous 78.4 for that year, compared with Miami's 32.7 exactly a century later. Yet, the absolute numbers of murders on which these ratios are based are these: Dodge, 1; Miami, 515. In other words, if a bullet fired by John ("Concho") Gill had missed Henry C. Heck instead of striking him in the chest, Dodge City's 1880 murder rate would have been zero instead of soaring to more than twice that of the 1980 murder capital of the world.

But one may argue that a single killing in a village like frontier Dodge may have had more traumatic psychological impact on its residents than Miami's 515 homicides must have had on its citizens in 1980. This proposition is supported by such personal testaments as Elizabeth Salamon's account of a double murder in her quiet New Jersey town in 1997 ("a killing has occurred in our midst and we will never be the same"), the emotional agony in awaiting identification of the shooter ("at night, my husband and I try to sleep, but sleep does not come easily"), and her guilty elation when she learns that the killer himself has died violently ("when murder hits this close to home, a dark heart is a regrettable residual"). And the general idea accords with what scholars have occasionally noted about the sociological equivalence of small and large places concerning such things as population fertility and rural-urban value conflicts.

But how does the argument fare in any specific contrast between 1980s Miami and 1880s Dodge? The *Miami Herald* for late December of 1980 is studded with allusions to the "record 555 homicides in Dade County this year," as reported by the local medical examiner's office—a figure that evidently includes 40 justifiable homicides by the police that would not be included in the FBI calculation. The newspaper reported that things are much worse in California, where Los Angeles County's homicides had reached a record 2,130 for the year. (Unfortunately for the *Herald*, however, greater Miami's smaller population imposed a 32.7 murder rate as against only 23.3 for Los Angeles.)

In any event, such defensive finger-pointing did not help much. The mood of urgency within Miami's political and economic leadership was palpable. Announcing itself "very concerned about the high incidence of homicides and other acts of violence occurring in certain liquor establishments," Miami's city council urged that they be put out of business, and a special police task force convened to identify these evil influences. "It will help when we get sufficient manpower aboard," complained the chief of Miami's patrol division. As if in anticipation, a federation of local homeowner associations formed a blue-ribbon Citizens Action Council "to pressure state and local legislators to bolster programs to counter Dade's rising crime rate." At the behest of the Citizens Crime Commission of Greater Miami, the Dade County Metro Council endorsed the new group, which planned to meet with judges, state legislators, and Governor Bob Graham. One of the commissioners set the agenda by demanding that Graham convene a special legislative session to appropriate a hundred million dollars for Dade's "war on crime." "For too long," he conceded, "the word 'war' has been overworked. . . . Nevertheless, our city can quite accurately be described at this moment as a battleground of war." Such was the local response to Miami's 32.7 murder rate for 1980.

In contrast, the public mood of Dodge City in late 1880 in the wake of its 78.4 homicide rate is much less alarmist. True enough, Concho Gill's killing of Henry Heck of November 17 caused a sensation, especially in view of the fact that nobody had died violently at Dodge in more than a year. Both weekly newspaper expressed considerable indignation. N. B. Klaine, the dour and moralistic editor of the Times who moonlighted as Ford County's probate judge, broke the story on Saturday, November 20, complete with sinister overtones:

> **MURDER IN DODGE CITY.**
> On Tuesday night a murder was committed in this city, in that part of town south of the railroad track. . . . It has been some time since a murder has been committed in Dodge City, but the shooting Tuesday night offers no parallel to any of the crimes committed here. There was no provocation, and it is hinted that the unfortunate Heck was the victim of a conspiracy, the facts of which may be developed upon the trial of the murderer.

On November 23, in its turn, the *Globe* ran a much more forthcoming account that contained most of what we know of the killing's background. The paper was managed by D.M. Frost, a practicing attorney, and his journalistic associate Lloyd Shinn, who doubled as Dodge Township justice of he peace. From the breezy vernacular tone of the article, we may be almost certain that its author was Shinn rather than the more earnest Frost. The piece opens as follows:

> **HENRY C. HECK KILLED.**
> John Gill, Alias Concho, Establishes
> Himself as a Killer
>
> On last Wednesday morning the report that a killing had taken place in the city the night previous, was rife on the streets at an early hour. The report was soon confirmed and everybod[y] felt that Dodge had still some of the bloody instinct for which she was so famous in the lawless days of her infancy, when money was as dross and whisky four bits a drink.

But to the locals, as to any reasonably sensitive historian, the death of Henry Heck was much more than just a blemish on Dodge City's 1880 crime-control statistics. A human life had been taken, an industrious citizen was gone, the community diminished.

The Unredeemed Lover

Where does the story begin?

In southwestern Kansas. In the year 1876 or 1877.

Henry C. Heck arrived in Dodge. We know that he was single, the Ohio-born son of German immigrants, twenty-four or twenty-five years old. In fairly short order he became the trusted employee of H. B. ("Ham") Bell, the owner of a popular livery stable, a man not much older than himself. The two evidently become close friends. Heck, according to Lloyd Shinn's account, was often "left in charge of the extensive livery and other business, whenever Mr. Bell was absent from the city." Bell's "other business" increased considerably in June 1978, when he had a local contractor build him a dance hall, the Varieties Theatre, on Locust Street in the "notorious" south side of town. The establishment was a success from the start, and a month after its opening the *Globe* reported that "the Texas boys and visitors generally still continue to throng the Varieties nightly."

Ham Bell placed Heck in charge of this enterprise. In a legal deposition of early 1879, in which he adroitly distanced himself from entrepreneurial proximity, Bell described the place as "kept by Henry Heck." It is, he wrote," a long frame building with a hall and bar in front and sleeping rooms in the rear." A contemporary photograph shows a low room with dark, wood-paneled ceiling and large side windows. In the foreground a bar extends along the right wall, three gaming tables stand beyond the bar, and a dance floor lies beyond the tables. Presumably the bedrooms are behind the wall in the back.

Management of the Varieties naturally brought Henry into close— not to say intimate—association with several young women (one as young as fourteen) identified by Ham Bell as "prostitutes, who belonged to the house and for the benefit of it solicited the male visitors to dance." And, Bell added, "The rooms in the rear [are] occupied, both during the dancing hours and after, both day and night[,] by the women for the purpose of prostitution."

In short, Heck's was not a particularly savory occupation, although it entailed much responsibility. Overseeing the bar and kitchen; tallying receipts; dispensing payments to liquor and grocery wholesalers, to the cook and bartenders and musicians, and (of course) to the young women. And keeping order, a task that brought him several close acquaintanceships among the police—successive marshals Ed Masterson and Charlie Bassett, the various assistant marshals (Wyatt Earp, for one), and the rank-and-file officers—who kept a watchful eye on the Varieties and its two competitors, the Lady Gay and the Comique, especially during the wee hours when spirits were high and inhibitions low.

There soon arose a complication. One of the young women, a violet-eyed blonde named Caroline ("Callie") Moore, had captured Henry's affections. "Nearly ever since Mr. Heck has resided in this county," wrote Shinn," . . . this woman has been his faithful companion, according to the approved method of this class of Dodge City lotus eaters." Read: Henry and Callie lived together. And in time they planned a joint future beyond the confines of Dodge south of the tracks. Ham Bell had acquired a ranch twelve miles below town where the Camp Supply trail toward Texas intersected Mulberry Creek. Later, when trying to sell it, Bell laconically described

Mulberry Ranch as "good range, good water running by the place, a well of good water at the door, good corral 100 feet square, good house 22 × 35." But better still was its situation: "a No. 1 location for keeping passersby, and cattle or sheep." Heck agreed to lease Mulberry Ranch. In the latter part of 1879 Heck and Callie Moore quit Ham Bell's employ and settled at the ranch. Here, as Lloyd Shinn puts it in words that suggest strong community approval, Heck "was raising a little stock which was being steadily accumulated by his industry and prudence." And "for nearly a year," wrote Shinn, Moore "performed the duties which usually fall to the lot of a rural housewife." Her life seemed a model of common-law domesticity.

But, we may guess, bright prairie flowers and frisky colts and wonderful sunsets and a convivial parade of teamsters stopping for dinner cannot forever compensate for the relative isolation of agricultural pioneering, which had defeated many a woman of stronger psychological construction than Callie Moore. Ranch life may have begun to pall. In any event, in September 1880, while on a shopping trip to town that no doubt included a visit to old friends and old haunts, she met Concho Gill, an unemployed cowboy whom the newspapers refer to as a gambler—a common cattle-town usage for any man who frequents saloons to play cards for money.

Gill, aged twenty-three, was the Texas-born son of an Irish immigrant father and a mother from Mississippi. The father must have died, for the mother was married to James D. Young, a Mississippi-born preacher. Gill's nickname probably refered to an adolescence in frontier Concho County of west-central Texas. Gill stood a half inch short of six feet, had a fair complexion, hazel eyes, and black hair. He could read and write, and "was a quiet man," said Shinn, "and not considered quarrelsome or dangerous." When visited in June 1880 by the Dodge City census taker, Gill was sharing a Front Street building with four other unattached males, each in his own apartment: two sheep raisers, another unemployed cowboy, and the manager of the local stockyard.

On that same day Gill also said he was sick, suffering from scurvy. This is not as unlikely an illness for a cowboy as it might seem today, when the disease is occasionally encountered among infants and the very elderly. But scurvy had been diagnosed as recently as the 1850s among frontier settlers lacking sustained access to foods rich in vitamin C—citrus fruits, tomatoes, vegetables. Adult symptoms include swollen, bleeding gums and loose teeth, bleeding under the skin and into the joints, mental depression, fatigue, and increased susceptibility to infection. Unless treated, the disease is fatal. Yet, as physicians of the time well knew, scurvy is easily cured; since the early sixteenth century lime juice was the infallible remedy, and fresh vegetables—especially potatoes and wild salad greens—were by the 1860s prescribed as effective preventives.

So why was Concho Gill sick in June and again in November? In a community blessed with doctors and druggists and grocery stores? Perhaps he suffered from some more serious malady than just a vitamin C deficiency. It is possible that he had a misdiagnosed case of gonorrhea or secondary-stage syphilis (not uncommon among cowboys), some of whose symptoms—joint pain, skin blotches, depression, lassitude—resemble those of scurvy.

Concho's illness, whatever it was, did not diminish his attractiveness to Callie Moore; in fact, a touch of chronic illness possibly added a certain Byronic allure, prompting some maternal impulse, perhaps. In any event, according to Shinn, Moore was immediately smitten. "His dark brown eyes, classic features, and complexion bronzed by a southern sun, together with [a prospect of] the indolent life of a gambler's paramour, were too dazzling to be resisted, when compared with kitchen drudgery, and the society of her more homely lover." Soon the young woman bid a permanent farewell to Mulberry Ranch, moving back to Dodge and in with Gill.

Moore's betrayal devastated Heck. He turned to drink, but it did not good. He at last resorted to an ultimatum. On Saturday, November 13, Heck told Moore that she had three days to return to him or leave Dodge City forever. Or else.

Late in the evening of November 16 Henry Heck came to Dodge City to separate Callie Moore from Concho Gill. But some things, as John Demos reminds us, we have to imagine. We know nothing of how Heck managed his wait. But wait he did, as an unseasonably early winter gripped the village. Perhaps he had proposed their old workplace, the Varieties Theatre, as a rendezvous, where he now lingered, occasionally greeting friends, but moody, on edge, drinking too much. At last she arrived, accompanied by a companion, Sallie Frazier, a middle-aged woman of color who, we can imagine, hovered protectively as a tearful Moore faced her former lover. The young woman reaffirmed that she would neither get out of Dodge nor leave Gill. She and Frazier turned to go. Heck says that if she does not return to him by midnight he will, as both women later remember his words, kill Concho Gill "before morning."

At midnight, Heck gathered himself into his coat and stepped out into the night, somewhat unsteadily perhaps, his mood as bitter as the weather. He trudged through fallen snow, crossing the railroad track toward Front Street and the intermittent glow of its all-night saloons. He made his way to Gill's apartment and, without announcing himself, began kicking in the front door.

Inside, Gill had been sick for the past ten days. Moore was building a fire in the stove. A friend, one Charlie Milde, was also present in the room. Aroused from bed, Gill grabbed a pistol and went to the door. It flew open and he fired twice.

One bullet struck Henry Heck in the right breast just below the nipple, perforating the lung.

Heck retreated back into the darkness. We do not know how he spent the next half hour—perhaps dazed, bewildered by shock. Probably there was no pain: his neural synapses have shut down. Perhaps he rested, leaning upright in an alleyway, out of the wind, uncontrollably trembling. Perhaps he collapsed unconscious until the snow against his cheek finally brought him around. He roused himself and stumbled toward a lamp-lit saloon. He entered, and after calling for a drink told the night bartender that Gill had shot him. He left the saloon for a moment, returned, dropped to the floor, and expired "without a groan." It had taken him forty-five minutes to die.

This love story from early Dodge City is over. But the consequences were not, and they provide us with an important cultural reading of frontier justice in Dodge City.

The Judgment of Concho Gill

As the dying Henry Heck silently stumbled along Front Street, Assistant Marshal Neil Brown, alerted by the gunshots, arrived at Gill's apartment. He confiscated the fatal pistol, ordered Gill to dress, and escorted him to jail.

Later that morning of November 17, a coroner's inquest convened, as required for any death happening by violence or under suspicious circumstances. The coroner's jury was heavy with law-enforcement types characteristically impatient with troublemakers. The county coroner himself, Col. John W. Straughn, doubled as a deputy sheriff. The six jurors included Ham Bell, now the deputy U.S. marshal in Dodge; blacksmith Pat Sughrue, a former Dodge Township constable and future Ford County sheriff; and merchant A. B. Webster, soon to run for mayor on a law-and-order platform. W. J. Miller, a local cattle raiser; James Mufty, an unemployed carpenter; and Fred Berg, a baker, rounded out the jury. They presumably viewed the body and then took testimony from bartender A. J. Tuttle, Officer Brown, Charlie Milde, and Callie Moore.

Although the victim literally broke into Gill's domicile, he may not have been armed. Tuttle testified that Heck was not carrying a weapon when he took his last drink. The jurors returned a verdict of felonious homicide, thereby asserting that the killing had been done without justification or excuse and signaling that Gill was in very serious trouble indeed. The following day editor N. B. Klaine, in his role as probate judge, appointed Under-Sheriff Fred Singer as administrator of the deceased's estate. As for Callie Moore, she "is still true to her imprisoned lover," noted Lloyd Shinn, "and supplies him daily with tempting viands."

The excitement subsided, life resumed its normal rhythms. Cattle continued loading down at the freight yard, and wagons bearing livestock feed, hay, and millet, arrived daily from outlying farms. U.S. Senator P. B. Plumb was in town several hours on his way home from Colorado. Saloon-owner Chaulk Beeson's sojourning parents departed for Iowa "well pleased with their visit" The respectable "dancing people" of the town announced plans to organize a social club. "Professor" W. H. LyBrand, hotel proprietor and former bandmaster, was recruiting an orchestra "to supply music for the holidays." On Thanksgiving Day churchgoers held interdenominational services and the Methodists hosted an oyster supper. The following afternoon children presented "literary exercises" at the grammar school. A baby was born to businessman A. J. Anthony and his wife. "Mother and son *drastic = evil*

proposition

are doing well," it was reported. All of which suggests that frontier Dodge had more in common with fictional Grover's Corners, New Hampshire ("nice town, y'know what I mean?"), than with modern Miami.

And in contrast to Miami's plea for more cash for cops late in 1980, Dodge City's municipal council late in 1880 continued pressing the mayor to cut police expenditures. The reason was liquor prohibition, adopted as a constitutional amendment in November's general election, ending the legal sale of intoxicants in Kansas. With saloon license fees far and away the most important source of municipal income, citizens did not view the loss of revenue with equanimity. By mid-December 1880 the village found itself more than $2,200 in debt, with unpaid bills shortly hiking the total to $3,239. More than a hundred taxpayers panicked, petitioning the council for a referendum on dissolving the municipal corporation entirely. The council scheduled a vote for New Year's Eve. The *Ford County Globe* approved this drastic proposition, warning that saloon closings would leave Dodge City "without resources except such as might be derived from direct taxation. . . . This would swell the total tax upon the property owners of the city to about eight cents on the dollar." But cooler heads prevailed, and on December 31 a low voter turnout doomed this solution to the crisis.

Meanwhile, Concho Gill's fate was being decided. On December 1, Gill appeared at a preliminary examination before Lloyd Shinn, in his role as justice of the peace, to determine if sufficient evidence existed to warrant his trial by a higher court. Col. Thomas S. Jones appeared for the accused, County Attorney Mike Sutton, Dodge City's most prominent attorney, for the people. Owing to the absence of one witness, the defense requested a continuance, which Shinn granted. The hearing resumed on the fourth. We lack details; both newspapers evidently considered the testimony old news. On December 7, Shinn ruled that the evidence merited binding Gill over for trial at the January 1881 term of district court. Shinn set bail at $3,000. The charge was first-degree manslaughter, meaning that Gill allegedly killed Heck, in the words of the law, "without a design to effect death," at a moment when Heck was "engaged in the perpetration or [the] attempt to perpetrate [a] crime or misdemeanor, not amounting to a felony."

Justice Shinn's reasoning is discernible. Heck's death clearly had not been murder: provocating circumstances closely preceding the shooting— the unlawful attack by Heck on the defendant's door—had caused Gill to react on impulse, in the heat of the moment. Yet it also seemed to Shinn not to be a case of justifiable homicide, although Kansas law gave as one definition a killing "committed by any person . . . in resisting any attempt to murder such person, or to commit any felony upon him or her, or in any dwelling house in which such person shall be."

Gill probably assumed that Heck had a gun. But—and this was a major qualifier—whether Heck was or was not armed, Gill had had an obligation to "retreat to the wall," to avail himself of any reasonable avenue of escape, even if that was only a few feet of floor space, before employing deadly force. That Concho may have failed to understand this virtually universal responsibility was simply his bad luck. As it happened, Texas was unlike most other states. Where Gill came from, the law said a man did not have to retreat from an attacker any farther than "the air at his back." Unfortunately for Gill, Kansas was not Texas.

State of Kansas v. John Gill alias Concho opened at the courthouse in Dodge on January 17, 1881—two months to the day after the shooting. Again we lack details, although Judge Samuel R. Peters's summary for the record preserves the essential procedural facts. Again Mike Sutton prosecuted, Colonel Jones defended. As late as December 21 the charge was still first-degree manslaughter, punishable by "confinement and hard labor for a term not less than five years nor more than twenty-one years." But since then Mike Sutton, for some reason, had upped the charge to first-degree murder, punishable by death. The accusation Sutton filed with the court asserted that Gill "feloniously, willfully and of his deliberate and premeditated malice did kill and murder one Henry Heck contrary to law." Gill pleaded not guilty, he and Jones still probably confident that his act could be seen as self-defense.

A jury was empaneled, consisting of twelve men from outside the corporate boundaries of Dodge, the most prominent of them being the prosperous sheep rancher R. W. Tarbox. After hearing the evidence and arguments of counsel and being instructed in writing by the court, the jury retired to deliberate. The next day it rendered its verdict: Gill was guilty not of first-degree murder but of murder in the second degree—a killing "committed purposely and maliciously, but without deliberation and premeditation," and punishable by "confinement and hard labor for not less than ten years."

The jurors evidently concluded that Gill had killed Heck with no set design to take life but that, nevertheless, there was a purpose to kill (or at least a purpose to inflict injury without caring whether it caused death or not) formed instantaneously in Gill's mind. And they must have been unimpressed by testimony suggesting that Gill had been so provoked by Heck's behavior as to reduce the crime to manslaughter.

Colonel Jones immediately moved for a new trial on the ground that the verdict was "contrary to evidence"—that is, the jurors had mistakenly interpreted the weight of the testimony in the case. Judge Peters pondered that for three days, then brought attorneys and defendant together again on January 21. He denied the motion to retry, and sentenced Gill to fifteen years' hard labor in the Kansas State Penitentiary. Concho was taken into custody, and the next day Sheriff George Hinkle and Under-Sheriff Singer took him off to Lansing.

The Rest of the Story

In March 1884, somebody—presumably Mike Sutton, the man who had successfully prosecuted Concho Gill three years earlier—addressed a petition to Governor George W. Glick. "We the undersigned Citizens of Ford County

Kansas respectfully ask your excellency to commute the sentence of John Gill now confined in the penitentiary of the State of Kansas, under a sentence for fifteen years," Sutton wrote. "Since his incarceration his health has failed, and there is strong probability that . . . he will not live until the expiration of his term." But, the petition added, "The crime for which said John Gill was convicted was committed by him under a misapprehension . . . that the man he killed was hunting him [in order] to kill him."

This document resulted from a visit to Dodge City by Gill's stepfather, the Reverend Young. Probably after conferring with Callie Moore (now Mrs. C. F. Lane) and Sallie Frazier, he brought them to Sutton. The former county attorney took depositions from the two women, and then had these sworn to before E. D. Swan, a notary public. Incredibly enough, it seems, the knowledge that Heck had specifically threatened Gill's life, and that Gill knew it, had not been presented at the trial; apparently this was the first Sutton learned of it. Thus he drafted the petition, which the Rev. Mr. Young then circulated.

Soon thirty-six names graced the document. The signatories included Dodge City's mayor and its city clerk; *Times* editor and now postmaster N. B. Klaine; W. F. Petillon, Ford County's registrar of deeds; Sheriff Pat Sughrue, who had been a member of the coroner's jury that had initiated the case against Gill; Assistant City Marshal David ("Mysterious Dave") Mather; merchants R. M. Wright, H. M. Beverley, and a scattering of other commercial men; lawyers Sutton, Swan, and T. S. Jones, who had defended Gill; baker Fred Berg, who also had sat on the coroner's jury; plus a butcher, a druggist, two hoteliers, a bookkeeper, and two of the town's more respectable saloon owners. Although admitting that "I was not here at the time," Police Judge R. E. Burns added a note that "from Statements of Responsible citizens I believe this petition should be granted." In addition, Jones and Petillon each wrote supporting letters to Governor Glick.

"Everyone here seems to sympathize with him," said Petillon of the Reverend Young, and journalist Klaine agreed. "Time seems to efface unpleasant memories," he philosophized, "as well as to soften prejudices and produce sympathy." The tendency of cattle-town people to find excuses for leniency in cases of shooting homicides was belatedly asserting itself.

In his letter, Colonel Jones added an interesting interpretation of the trial. Gill "would have been promptly acquitted," he told the governor, "had a it not been for the evidence of a personal enemy." The identity of this enemy is unknown. One may guess that it was Heck's friend Ham Bell, who may have been responsible for the severe stance taken by the coroner's jury, who then had less influence over the more lenient Shinn decision but who later yet may have convinced Mike Sutton to escalate the charge against Gill to first-degree murder. What testimony Bell may have offered is also unknown; perhaps it maintained that Heck's killing was the result of a conspiracy, as suggested in the first news report of the death. In any event, Mike Sutton's implicit repudiation of his role in Gill's conviction included the suggestion that he, as county attorney, had been duped by somebody into wholly discounting Gill's claim of self-defense. For him, the two women's affidavits now proved definitive.

Gill's stepfather evidently hand carried the petition, the two affidavits, and the two supporting letters to Topeka, delivering them to Governor Glick. The governor said that prior to any formal application to commute, Young must give public notice in plenty of time for those with objections to make them known. On April 3 and 10, therefore, the *Dodge City Times* printed the required notice, editor Klaine certified its publication, and lawyer Swan sent copies of both to the governor. Formal application to commute his stepson's sentence would be made by Young on April 16, 1884.

But in the end the governor refused the request for unknown reasons. Concho did not die in prison, but he did stay for another seven years. On August 19, 1891, his sentence at last commuted, he emerged from the Kansas penitentiary after having served ten and one-half years for the murder of Henry Heck.

Body Counts or Murder Rates?

The point of the story of *Kansas v. Gill* is that the people of Dodge City took Heck's death seriously, and instituted deliberate legal action against his slayer according to conventions nurtured through a thousand years of Anglo-American judicial tradition. The judgment of Concho Gill was, as it was meant to be, a series of civic rituals assuring villagers that although situated on the geographic extremity of civilization, theirs was a fully domesticated society, culturally located well within the larger American community.

As for public fear, neither in Miami in December 1980 nor in Dodge in December 1880 did any important number of citizens cower behind locked doors. But Miami's business community clearly had been terrified by how its spiraling homicides would affect property values and tourism; Dodge City's businessmen, although attuned to the need to attract new residents and capital investment, were not. The important cause of these different responses was hardly the contrast between homicide rates of 32.7 and 78.4 but between body counts of 515 (or 555) and 1.

Let anthropologist Lawrence Keeley have the penultimate word on murder rates versus body counts. Keeley's recent book criticizing the "peaceful-savage" myth displays a wealth of evidence on the lethal nature of tribal life. Its relevance to the present discussion is that its author employs death rates somewhat similar to those calculated for the FBI crime reports, leading him to relish a number of absurd comparisons. For example, he judges a chance Blackfoot massacre of a 52-man Assiniboine raiding party more lethal (100.0 percent killed) than the loss of 21,392 British soldiers on the horrifying first day of the Battle of the Somme (only 13.5 percent killed). Obviously, the statistical fallacy of small numbers is in full flower here.

But Keeley has a ready reply. The unsophisticated, he says, are always "more impressed by absolute numbers than ratios." And he asks if, consistent with such views, any reader would rather undergo a critical medical operation at a "small, rural, Third-World clinic"—where the number of inadvertent deaths from surgery is numerically small but the death rate high—than at a large American "university or urban hospital" where such deaths are more frequent but the rate low. According to the same reasoning, would anyone prefer to fly regularly on small planes rather than airliners? And would one prefer to live on an Indian reservation than in a large city, "since the annual absolute number of deaths from homicide, drug abuse, alcoholism, cancer, heart disease, and automobile accidents will always be far fewer on the reservations than in major cities and their suburbs"?

There are, for the sake of argument, answers. Most health insurance would not pay for elective surgery in a jungle hospital, so that point is moot. But yes, those wealthy enough to own airplanes regularly and routinely defy the odds. And yes again, many persons would rather live in Navaho country than in parts of Manhattan.

But more to the point of this essay, a great majority of fully informed time-travelers surely would feel safer cruising the all-night saloons of Dodge City in 1880 than barhopping in Little Havana, Coconut Grove, or downtown Miami a hundred years later. And that is a ratio beyond dispute.

POSTSCRIPT

Was the Wild West More Violent than the Rest of the United States?

David T. Courtwright believes that the frontier was a very violent place. He qualifies his answer by accepting the distinction of Professor Walter Nugent, who distinguishes between the two types of frontiers: type one, which centered on farming, and type two, which focused on mining, ranching, and other extractive industries. The author argues that type one had minimal violence because of its concentration of large nuclear families engaged in farming. On the other hand, the more volatile type-two frontiers of mining and cattle raising were manned by young, single males who often brawled in bar fights that were caused by excessive drinking, gambling, and womanizing.

Courtwright also takes a quick look at the violence that occurred on the multicultural West stressed in the writings of the new Western historians. He argues that Native Americans and whites engaged in some serious atrocities committed by both sides. He also discusses high crime rates among the Chinese in San Francisco because of tong (gang) battles.

Justice was limited in type-two frontier communities. The army was spread too thin, and local governments concentrated on property claims. Consequently, vigilante movements or quasi-legal groups emerged to enforce the law. Professor Richard Maxwell Brown, who has spent a lifetime writing books and articles about these movements, has calculated that 326 such movements emerged in the country between 1767 and 1904. Most of these movements occurred in the southern and southwestern territories and states, with Texas being the most violent.

Richard Maxwell Brown divides Western violence into roughly three periods. Period one, which is what this issue is concerned with, extends from 1850 to 1910. It parallels the tumult brought about by the Industrial Revolution. Brown employs the concept Western Civil War of Incorporation (WCWI) to interpret the feuds between Yankees and ex-Confederates, cattlemen and land barons, and Republicans and Democrats who use violence to gain power in the last American frontier. See Brown's summative article on "Violence" in Clyde A. Milner, II, et al., eds., *The Oxford History of the American West* (Oxford University Press, 1994).

Ironically, in recent years, historians have tried to lay to rest the myths about gunfighters. Writers such as Joseph Rosa have argued the term "gunfight" did not come into popular usage until the 1890s. The number of killings by Wild Bill Hickok was really seven or eight, not between 30 and 85. Even psychopathic killers like John Wesley Hardin and Billy the Kid had the numbers of killings inflated over the years by pop writers and the movie industry. The bar-room brawl, not "the stereotypical walkdown of motion picture frame," was responsible for most of the violence. And when gunfights took place, the most famous killers were often outnumbered and ambushed. See Joseph G. Rosa, *The Gunfighter: Man or Myth* (University of Oklahoma Press, 1969), and Gary L. Roberts, "The West's Gunmen," *American West* (January 1972, 10–15, 64; March 1972, 18–23, 61–62), and "Gunfighters and Outlaws, Western," in Ronald Gottesman and Richard Maxwell Brown, eds., *Violence in America: An Encyclopedia, vol. 1* (Charles Scribner's Sons, 1999).

Robert R. Dykstra was one of the first historians to challenge the image of the West as a section more violent than the rest of the country. His study of *The Cattletowns* (Knopf, 1968, 1983) rejected the view that the five towns of Abilene, Caldwell, Dodge City, Ellsworth, and Wichita were hellholes. In fact, from 1870 to 1885 only a total of 45 killings took place. The homicides varied widely from accidental deaths to those that involved law officers, cowboys, and gamblers, among others. Of the shootings that took place, "less than a third of them returned the fire."

Dykstra has been criticized on numerous grounds. First of all, he did not count the 17-plus murders committed in three of the five towns in the years prior to his study, a point the author concedes. Secondly, he has been challenged by studies of other communities whose authors compare the high crime rates of some of these Western counties and communities with the lower crime rates of nineteenth- and twentieth-century cities. Finally, Dykstra has been taken to task for relying on contemporary newspaper accounts for his main sources.

The author has responded vigorously to these charges. He challenges writers who use the FBI statistical rate of crimes per 100,000 by claiming the samples of a town or county are too small and, therefore, one less murder can radically skew the homicide ratio downward. In addition, the comparisons may be between apples and oranges. As Harold J. Weiss, Jr., points out in his valuable article, "Overdosing and Underestimating: A Look at a Violent and Not-So-Violent American West," *Quarterly of the National Association for Outlaw and Lawman History* (April–June 2003), "Have western historical writers used the same data base? Information about criminal homicides can be collected in several ways; those committed; those reported to the police; those cleared by police arrests; those that resulted in an indictment by a Grand Jury; those that came to trial; those that ended in a court conviction; and those that involve prison time."

Dykstra also believes that contemporary newspapers reported every homicide in as much detail as possible. Would a nineteenth-century newspaper miss a major crime any more than the nightly local news broadcasts, which comb the police blotter for every gruesome homicide?

Dykstra's most recent assessments of the newest literature on Western violence are (1) "Overdosing on Dodge City," *Western Historical Quarterly* (Winter 1996); (2) "Violence, Gender and Methodology in the 'New' Western History," *Reviews in American History* (March 1999); and (3) "Body

Counts and Murder Rates: The Contested Statistics of Western Violence," *Reviews in American History* (December 2003).

The most recent assessment, "Guns, Murder, and Probability: How Can We Decide Which Figures to Trust," *Reviews in American History* (June 2007) by Randolph Roth, challenges Dykstra's theory of the statistical fallacy of small numbers. A recent study by Clare V. McKanna, Jr., *Race and Homicide in Nineteenth Century California* (University of Nevada Press, 2002), examines seven counties in California and the one by David Peterson Del Mar, *Beaten Down: A History of Interpersonal Violence in the West* (University of Washington Press, 2002), studies all of Oregon. These figures, says Roth, constitute representative samples similar to contemporary pollsters who use small numbers to predict elections. Both books argue that very high crime rates existed in the nineteenth-century West.

Students interested in pursuing the subject further should consult the following bibliographical articles and books: Indispensable and balanced are Harold J. Weiss, Jr., "Overdosing and Underestimating: A Look at a Violent and Not-So-Violent American West," *Quarterly of the National Association for Outlaw and Lawman History, Inc.* (April–June 2003) and Michael A. Bellesiles, "Western Violence," in William Deverell, ed., *A Companion to the American West* (Blackwell Publishing, 2004), which plays down Western violence, while Robert McGrath is ambivalent in *Gunfighters, Highwaymen and Vigilantes: Violence in the Frontier* (University of California Press, 1984). Giles Vandal's *Rethinking Southern Violence: Homicides in Post–Civil War Louisiana, 1866–1884* (Ohio State University Press, 2000) offers a comprehensive look at the 4,986 recorded homicides in a southern state mostly against African Americans committed collectively by whites who refused to accept the new political order of the Reconstruction era.

More general are Michael A. Bellesiles, ed., *Lethal Imagination: Violence and Brutality in American History* (New York University Press, 1999), and the three-volume reference work in alphabetical order by Ronald Gottesman and Richard M. Brown, eds., *Violence in America: An Encyclopedia* (Charles Scribner's Sons, 1999). Easier to locate are two anthologies written in the shadow of the violent 1960s: Hugh Davis Graham and Ted Robert Gurrs, eds., *Violence in America: Historical and Comparative Perspectives* (New American Library, 1969) and Richard Hofstadter and Michael Wallace, eds., *American Violence: A Documentary History* (Random House, 1971), which argues that America has a history, but not a tradition, of violence.

ISSUE 3

Were American Workers in the Gilded Age Conservative Capitalists?

YES: Carl N. Degler, from *Out of Our Past: The Forces That Shaped Modern America,* 3rd ed. (Harper & Row, 1984)

NO: Herbert G. Gutman, from *Work, Culture, and Society in Industrializing America: Essays in American Working-Class and Social History* (Alfred A. Knopf, 1976)

ISSUE SUMMARY

YES: Professor of history Carl N. Degler maintains that the American labor movement accepted capitalism and reacted conservatively to the radical organizational changes brought about in the economic system by big business.

NO: Professor of history Herbert G. Gutman argues that from 1843 to 1893, American factory workers attempted to humanize the system through the maintenance of their traditional, artisan, preindustrial work habits.

T he two major labor unions that developed in the late nineteenth century were the Knights of Labor and the American Federation of Labor. Because of hostility toward labor unions, the Knights of Labor functioned for 12 years as a secret organization. Between 1879 and 1886 the Knights of Labor grew from 10,000 to 700,000 members. Idealistic in many of its aims, the union supported social reforms such as equal pay for men and women, the prohibition of alcohol, and the abolition of convict and child labor. Economic reforms included the development of workers' cooperatives, public ownership of utilities, and a more moderate, eight-hour workday. The Knights declined after 1886 for several reasons. Although it was opposed to strikes, the union received a black eye (as did the whole labor movement) when it was blamed for the bombs that were thrown at the police during the 1886 Haymarket Square riot in Chicago. According to most historians, other reasons that are usually associated with the decline of the Knights include the failure of some cooperative businesses, conflict between skilled and unskilled workers, and, most important, competition from the American Federation of Labor. By 1890 the Knight's membership had dropped to 100,000. It died in 1917.

A number of skilled unions got together in 1896 and formed the American Federation of Labor (AFL). Samuel Gompers was elected its first president, and his philosophy permeated the AFL during his 37 years in office. He pushed for practical reforms—better hours, wages, and working conditions. Unlike the Knights, the AFL avoided associations with political parties, workers' cooperatives, unskilled workers, immigrants, and women. Decision-making power was in the hands of locals rather than the central board. Gompers was heavily criticized by his contemporaries, and later by historians, for his narrow craft unionism. But despite the depression of the 1890s, membership increased from 190,000 to 500,000 by 1900, to 1,500,000 by 1904, and to 2,000,000 by the eve of World War I.

Gompers's cautiousness is best understood in the context of his times. The national and local governments were in the hands of men who were sympathetic to the rise of big business and hostile to the attempts of labor to organize. Whether it was the railroad strike of 1877, the Homestead steel strike of 1892, or the Pullman car strike of 1894, the pattern of repression was always the same. Companies would cut wages, workers would go out on strike, scab workers would be brought in, fights would break out, companies would receive court injunctions, and the police and state and federal militia would beat up the unionized workers. After a strike was broken, workers would lose their jobs or would accept pay cuts and longer workdays.

On the national level, Theodore Roosevelt became the first president to show any sympathy for the workers. As a police commissioner in New York City and later as governor of New York, Roosevelt observed firsthand the deplorable occupational and living conditions of the workers. Although he avoided recognition of the collective bargaining rights of labor unions, Roosevelt forced the anthracite coal owners in Pennsylvania to mediate before an arbitration board for an equitable settlement of a strike with the mine workers.

In 1905 a coalition of socialists and industrial unionists formed America's most radical labor union: the Industrial Workers of the World (IWW). There were frequent splits within this union and much talk of violence. But in practice, the IWW was more interested in organizing workers into industrial unions than in fighting, as were the earlier Knights of Labor and the later Congress of Industrial Organizations. Strikes were encouraged to improve the daily conditions of the workers through long-range goals, which included reducing the power of the capitalists by increasing the power of the workers.

Were the American workers of the Gilded Age conservative supporters of American capitalism? In the following selection, Carl N. Degler argues in the affirmative. He concludes that, led by the bread-and-butter leader of the American Federation of Labor, Samuel Gompers, the American worker sought a larger slice of the profits in the form of better hours, wages, and benefits. In the second selection, however, Herbert G. Gutman argues that in the Gilded Age, the American worker tried to humanize the factory system through the maintenance of traditional, cultural, artisan, preindustrial work habits.

YES

Carl N. Degler

Out of Our Past

The Workers' Response

To say that the labor movement was affected by the industrialization of the postwar years is an understatement; the fact is, industrial capitalism created the labor movement. Not deliberately, to be sure, but in the same way that a blister is the consequence of a rubbing shoe. Unions were labor's protection against the forces of industrialization as the blister is the body's against the irritation of the shoe. The factory and all it implied confronted the workingman with a challenge to his existence as a man, and the worker's response was the labor union.

There were labor unions in America before 1865, but, as industry was only emerging in those years, so the organizations of workers were correspondingly weak. In the course of years after Appomattox, however, when industry began to hit a new and giant stride, the tempo of unionization also stepped up. It was in these decades, after many years of false starts and utopian ambitions, that the American labor movement assumed its modern shape.

Perhaps the outstanding and enduring characteristic of organized labor in the United States has been its elemental conservatism, the fantasies of some employers to the contrary notwithstanding. Indeed, it might be said that all labor unions, at bottom, are conservative by virtue of their being essentially reactions against a developing capitalism. Though an established capitalist society views itself as anything but subversive, in the days of its becoming and seen against the perspective of the previous age, capitalism as an ideology is radically subversive, undermining and destroying many of the cherished institutions of the functioning society. This dissolving process of capitalism is seen more clearly in Europe than in America because there the time span is greater. But, as will appear later, organized labor in the United States was as much a conservative response to the challenge of capitalism as was the European trade union movement.

Viewed very broadly, the history of modern capitalism might be summarized as the freeing of the three factors of production—land, labor, and capital—from the web of tradition in which medieval society held them. If capitalism was to function, it was necessary that this liberating process take place. Only when these basic factors are free to be bought and sold according to the dictates of the profit motive can the immense production which capitalism promises be realized. An employer, for example, had to be free to dismiss labor when the balance sheet required it, without being compelled to retain workers because society or custom demanded it. Serfdom, with its requirement that the peasant could not be taken from the land, was an anachronistic institution if capitalism was to become the economic ideology of society. Conversely, an employer needed to be unrestricted in his freedom to hire labor or else production could not expand in accordance with the market. Guild restrictions which limited apprenticeships were therefore obstacles to the achievement of a free capitalism.

The alienability of the three factors of production was achieved slowly and unevenly after the close of the Middle Ages. By the nineteenth century in most nations of the West, land had become absolutely alienable—it could be bought and sold at will. With the growth of banking, the development of trustworthy monetary standards, and finally the gold standard in the nineteenth century, money or capital also became freely exchangeable. Gradually, over the span of some two centuries, the innovating demands of capitalism stripped from labor the social controls in which medieval and mercantilistic government had clothed it. Serfdom as an obstacle to the free movement of labor was gradually done away with; statutes of laborers and apprenticeships which fixed wages, hours, and terms of employment also fell into disuse or suffered outright repeal. To avoid government interference in the setting of wage rates, the English Poor Law of 1834 made it clear that the dole to the unemployed was always to be lower than the going rate for unskilled labor. Thus supply and demand would be the determinant of wage levels. Both the common law and the Combination Acts in the early nineteenth century in England sought to ensure the operation of a free market in labor by declaring trade unions to be restraints on trade.

Like land and capital, then, labor was being reduced to a commodity, freely accessible, freely alienable, free to flow where demand was high. The classical economists of the nineteenth century analyzed this long historical process, neatly put it together, and called it the natural laws of economics.

To a large extent, this historical development constituted an improvement in the worker's status, since medieval and mercantilist controls over labor had been more onerous than protective. Nevertheless, something was lost by the dissolution of the ancient social ties which fitted the worker into a larger social matrix. Under the old relationship, the worker belonged in society; he enjoyed a definite if not a high status; he had a place. Now he was an individual, alone; his status was up to him to establish; his urge for community with society at large had no definite avenue of expression. Society and labor alike had been atomized in pursuit of an individualist economy. Herein lay the radical character of the capitalist ideology.

That the workingman sensed the radical change and objected to it is evident from what some American labor leaders said about their unions.

Without rejecting the new freedom which labor enjoyed, John Mitchell, of the Mine Workers, pointed out that the union "stands for fraternity, complete and absolute." Samuel Gompers' eulogy of the social microcosm which was the trade union has the same ring. "A hundred times we have said it," he wrote, "and we say it again, that trade unionism contains within itself the potentialities of working class regeneration." The union is a training ground for democracy and provides "daily object lessons in ideal justice; it breathes into the working classes the spirit of unity"; but above all, it affords that needed sense of community. The labor union "provides a field for noble comradeship, for deeds of loyalty, for self-sacrifice beneficial to one's fellow-workers." In the trade union, in short, the workers could obtain another variety of that sense of community, of comradeship, as Gompers put it, which the acid of individualistic capitalism had dissolved.

And there was another objection to the transformation of labor into an exchangeable commodity. The theoretical justification for the conversion of the factors of production into commodities is that the maximum amount of goods can be produced under such a regime. The increased production is deemed desirable because it would insure greater amounts of goods for human consumption and therefore a better life for all. Unfortunately for the theory, however, labor cannot be separated from the men who provide it. To make labor a commodity is to make the men who provide labor commodities also. Thus one is left with the absurdity of turning men into commodities in order to give men a better life! . . .

Seen in this light, the trade union movement stands out as a truly conservative force. Almost instinctively, the workers joined labor unions in order to preserve their humanity and social character against the excessively individualistic doctrines of industrial capitalism. Eventually, the workers' organizations succeeded in halting the drive to the atomized society which capitalism demanded, and in doing so, far from destroying the system, compelled it to be humane as well as productive.

The essential conservatism of the labor movement is to be seen in particular as well as in general. The organizations of American labor that triumphed or at least survived in the course of industrialization were conspicuous for their acceptance of the private property, profit-oriented society. They evinced little of the radical, anticapitalist ideology and rhetoric so common among European trade unions. Part of the reason for this was the simple fact that all Americans—including workers—were incipient capitalists waiting for "the break." But at bottom it would seem that the conservatism of American labor in this sense is the result of the same forces which inhibited the growth of socialism and other radical anticapitalist ideologies. . . .

"The overshadowing problem of the American labor movement," an eminent labor historian has written, "has always been the problem of staying organized. No other labor movement has ever had to contend with the fragility so characteristic of American labor organizations." So true has this been that even today the United States ranks below Italy and Austria in percentage of workers organized (about 25 per cent as compared, for instance, with Sweden's 90 per cent). In such an atmosphere, the history of organized labor in America has been both painful and conservative. Of the two major national organizations of workers which developed in the latter half of the nineteenth century, only the cautious, restrictive, pragmatic American Federation of Labor [A.F. of L.] lived into the twentieth century. The other, the Knights of Labor, once the more powerful and promising, as well as the less accommodating in goals and aspirations, succumbed to Selig Perlman's disease of fragility.

Founded in 1869, the Noble Order of the Knights of Labor recorded its greatest successes in the 1880's, when its membership rolls carried 700,000 names. As the A.F. of L. was later to define the term for Americans, the Knights did not seem to constitute a legitimate trade union at all. Anyone who worked, except liquor dealers, bankers, lawyers, and physicians, could join, and some thousands of women workers and Negroes were members in good standing of this brotherhood of toilers. But the crucial deviation of the Knights from the more orthodox approach to labor organization was its belief in worker-owned producers' co-operatives, which were intended to make each worker his own employer. In this way, the order felt, the degrading dependence of the worker upon the employer would be eliminated. "There is no good reason," Terence V. Powderly, Grand Master Workman of the order, told his followers, "why labor cannot, through co-operation, own and operate mines, factories and railroads."

In this respect the order repudiated the direction in which the America of its time was moving. It expressed the small-shopkeeper mentality which dominated the thinking of many American workers, despite the obvious trend in the economy toward the big and the impersonal. As the General Assembly of 1884 put it, "our Order contemplates a radical change, while Trades' Unions . . . accept the industrial system as it is, and endeavor to adapt themselves to it. The attitude of our Order to the existing industrial system is necessarily one of war." Though the order called this attitude "radical," a more accurate term, in view of the times, would have been "conservative" or "reactionary."

In practice, however, the Knights presented no more of a threat to capitalism than any other trade union. Indeed, their avowed opposition to the strike meant that labor's most potent weapon was only reluctantly drawn from the scabbard. The Constitution of 1884 said, "Strikes at best afford only temporary relief"; members should learn to depend on education, co-operation, and political action to attain "the abolition of the wage system."

Though the order officially joined in political activity and Grand Master Workman Powderly was at one time mayor of Scranton, its forays into politics accomplished little. The experience was not lost on shrewd Samuel Gompers, whose American Federation of Labor studiously eschewed any alignments with political parties, practicing instead the more neutral course of "rewarding friends and punishing enemies."

In a farewell letter in 1893, Powderly realistically diagnosed the ills of his moribund order, but offered no cure: "Teacher of important and much-needed reforms, she has been obliged to practice differently from her teachings. Advocating arbitration and conciliation as first steps in labor disputes she has been forced to take upon her shoulders the responsibilities of the aggressor first and, when hope of arbitrating and conciliation failed, to beg of the opposing side to do what we should have applied for in the first instance. Advising against strikes we have been in the midst of them. While not a political party we have been forced into the attitude of taking political action."

For all its fumblings, ineptitude, and excessive idealism, the Knights did organize more workers on a national scale than had ever been done before. At once premature and reactionary, it nonetheless planted the seeds of industrial unionism which, while temporarily overshadowed by the successful craft organization of the A.F. of L., ultimately bore fruit in the C.I.O. [Committee for Industrial Organization]. Moreover, its idealism, symbolized in its admission of Negroes and women, and more in tune with the mid-twentieth century than the late nineteenth, signified its commitment to the ideals of the democratic tradition. For these reasons the Knights were a transitional type of unionism somewhere between the utopianism of the 1830's and the pragmatism of the A.F. of L. It seemed to take time for labor institutions to fit the American temper.

In the course of his long leadership of the American Federation of Labor, Samuel Gompers welcomed many opportunities to define the purposes of his beloved organization. . . .

"The trade unions are the business organizations of the wage-earners," Gompers explained in 1906, "to attend to the business of the wage-earners." Later he expressed it more tersely: "The trade union is not a Sunday school. It is an organization of wage-earners, dealing with economic, social, political and moral questions." As Gompers' crossing of swords with Hillquit demonstrated, there was no need or place for theories. "I saw," the labor leader wrote years later, in looking back on his early life in the labor movement, "the danger of entangling alliances with intellectuals who did not understand that to experiment with the labor movement was to experiment with human life. . . . I saw that the betterment of workingmen must come primarily through workingmen."

In an age of big business, Samuel Gompers made trade unionism a business, and his reward was the survival of his Federation. In a country with a heterogeneous population of unskilled immigrants, reviled and feared Negroes, and native workers, he cautiously confined his fragile organization to the more skilled workers and the more acceptable elements in the population. The result was a narrow but lasting structure.

Though never ceasing to ask for "more," the A.F. of L. presented no threat to capitalism. "Labor Unions are *for* the workingman, but against no one," John Mitchell of the United Mine Workers pointed out. "They are not hostile to employers, not inimical to the interests of the general public. . . . There is no necessary hostility between labor and capital," he concluded. Remorselessly pressed by Morris Hillquit as Gompers was, he still refused to admit that the labor movement was, as Hillquit put it, "conducted against the interests of the employing people." Rather, Gompers insisted, "It is conducted for the interests of the employing people." And the rapid expansion of the American economy bore witness to the fact that the Federation was a friend and not an enemy of industrial capitalism. Its very adaptability to the American scene—its conservative ideology, if it was an ideology at all—as Selig Perlman has observed, contained the key to its success. "The unionism of the American Federation of Labor 'fitted' . . . because it recognized the virtually inalterable conservatism of the American community as regards private property and private initiative in economic life."

This narrow conception of the proper character of trade unionism—job consciousness, craft unionism, lack of interest in organizing the unskilled, the eschewing of political activity—which Gompers and his Federation worked out for the American worker continued to dominate organized labor until the earthquake of the depression cracked the mold and the Committee for Industrial Organization issued forth.

Nobody Here But Us Capitalists

"By any simple interpretation of the Marxist formula," commented Socialist Norman Thomas in 1950, "the United States, by all odds the greatest industrial nation and that in which capitalism is most advanced, should have had long ere this is a very strong socialist movement if not a socialist revolution. Actually," he correctly observed, "in no advanced western nation is organized socialism so weak." Nor was this the first time Socialists had wondered about this. Over eighty years ago, in the high noon of European socialism, Marxist theoretician Werner Sombart impatiently put a similar question: *"Warum gibt es in den Vereinigten Staaten keinen Sozialismus?"*

The failure of the American working class to become seriously interested in socialism in this period or later is one of the prominent signs of the political and economic conservatism of American labor and, by extension, of the American people as a whole. This failure is especially noteworthy when one recalls that in industrialized countries the world over—Japan, Italy, Germany, Belgium, to mention only a few—a Socialist movement has been a "normal" concomitant of industrialization. Even newly opened countries like Australia and New Zealand have Labour parties. Rather than ask, as Americans are wont to do, why these countries have nurtured such frank repudiators of traditional capitalism, it is the American deviation from the general pattern which demands explanation.

In large part, the explanation lies in the relative weakness of class consciousness among Americans. Historically, socialism is the gospel of the *class-conscious* working class, of the workingmen who feel themselves bound to their status for life and their children after them. It is not accidental, therefore, that the major successes of modern socialism are in Europe, where class lines have been clearly and tightly drawn since time immemorial, and where the possibility of upward social movement has been severely restricted in practice if not in law. Americans may from time to time have exhibited class consciousness and even class hatred, but such attitudes have not persisted, nor have they been typical. As Matthew Arnold observed in 1888, "it is indubitable that rich men are regarded" in America "with less envy and hatred than rich men in Europe." A labor leader like Terence Powderly was convinced that America was without classes. "No matter how much we may say about classes and class distinction, there are no classes in the United States. . . . I have always refused to admit that we have classes in our country just as I have refused to admit that the labor of a man's hand or brain is a commodity." And there was a long line of commentators on American society, running back at least to Crèvecoeur, to illustrate the prevalence of Powderly's belief.

The weakness of American class consciousness is doubtless to be attributed, at least in part, to the fluidity of the social structure. Matthew Arnold, for example, accounted for the relative absence of class hatred on such grounds, as did such very different foreign observers as Werner Sombart and Lord Bryce. The British union officials of the Mosely Commission, it will be recalled, were convinced of the superior opportunities for success enjoyed by American Workers. Stephan Thernstrom in his study of Newburyport gave some measure of the opportunities for economic improvement among the working class when he reported that all but 5 per cent of those unskilled workers who persisted from 1850 to 1900 ended the period with either property or an improvement in occupational status.

Men who are hoping to move upward on the social scale, and for whom there is some chance that they can do so, do not identify themselves with their present class. "In worn-out, king-ridden Europe, men stay where they are born," immigrant Charles O'Conor, who became an ornament of the New York bar, contended in 1869. "But in America a man is accounted a failure, and certainly ought to be, who has not risen about his father's station in life." So long as Horatio Alger means anything to Americans, Karl Marx will be just another German philosopher.

The political history of the United States also contributed to the failure of socialism. In Europe, because the franchise came slowly and late to the worker, he often found himself first an industrial worker and only later a voter. It was perfectly natural, in such a context, for him to vote according to his economic interests and to join a political party avowedly dedicated to those class interests. The situation was quite different in America, however, for political democracy came to America prior to the Industrial Revolution. By the time the industrial transformation was getting under way after 1865, all adult males could vote and, for the most part, they had already chosen their political affiliations without reference to their economic class; they were Republicans or Democrats first and workers only second—a separation between politics and economics which has become traditional in America. "In the main," wrote Lord Bryce about the United States of the 1880's, "political questions proper have held the first place in a voter's mind and questions affecting his class second." Thus, when it came to voting, workers registered their convictions as citizens, not as workingmen. (In our own day, there have been several notable failures of labor leaders to swing their labor vote, such as John L. Lewis' attempt in 1940 and the C.I.O.'s in 1950 against Senator Taft and the inability of union leaders to be sure they could hold their members to support Hubert Humphrey in the Presidential election of 1968.) To most workers, the Socialist party appeared as merely a third party in a country where such parties are political last resorts.

Nor did socialism in America gain much support from the great influx of immigration. It is true that many Germans came to this country as convinced Socialists and thus swelled the party's numbers, but they also served to pin the stigma of "alien" upon the movement. Even more important was the fact that the very heterogeneity of the labor force, as a result of immigration, often made animosities between ethnic groups more important to the worker than class antagonism. It must have seemed to many workers that socialism, with its central concern for class and its denial of ethnic antagonism, was not dealing with the realities of economic life.

In the final reckoning, however, the failure of socialism in America is to be attributed to the success of capitalism. The expanding economy provided opportunities for all, no matter how meager they might appear or actually be at times. Though the rich certainly seemed to get richer at a prodigious rate, the poor, at least, did not get poorer—and often got richer. Studies of real wages between 1865 and 1900 bear this out. Though prices rose, wages generally rose faster, so that there was a net gain in average income for workers during the last decades of the century. The increase in real wages in the first fifteen years of the twentieth century was negligible—but, significantly, there was no decline. The high wages and relatively good standard of living of the American worker were patent as far as the twenty-three British labor leaders of the Mosely Commission were concerned. The American is a "better educated, better housed, better clothed and more energetic man than his British brother," concluded the sponsor, Alfred Mosely, a businessman himself.

But America challenged socialism on other grounds than mere material things. Some years ago an obscure Socialist, Leon Samson, undertook to account for the failure of socialism to win the allegiance of the American working class; his psychological explanation merits attention because it illuminates the influence exercised by the American Dream. Americanism, Samson observes, is not so much a tradition as it is a doctrine; it is "what socialism is to a socialist." Americanism to the American is a body of ideas like "democracy, liberty, opportunity, to all of which the American adheres rationalistically much as a socialist adheres to his socialism—because it does him good, because it gives him work, because, so he thinks, it guarantees him happiness. America has thus served as a substitute for socialism."

Socialism has been unable to make headway with Americans, Samson goes on, because "every concept in socialism has its substitutive counterconcept in Americanism." As Marxism holds out the prospect of a classless society, so does Americanism. The opportunities for talent and the better material life which socialism promised for the future were already available in America and constituted the image in which America was beheld throughout the world. The freedom and equality which the oppressed proletariat of Europe craved were a reality in America—or at least sufficiently so to blunt the cutting edge of the Socialist appeal. Even the sense of mission, of being in step with the processes of history, which unquestionably was one of the appeals of socialism, was also a part of the American Dream. Have not all Americans cherished their country as a model for the world? Was not this the "last, best hope of earth"? Was not God on the side of America, as history, according to Marx, was on the side of socialism and the proletariat?

Over a century ago, Alexis de Tocqueville predicted a mighty struggle for the minds of men between two giants of Russia and the United States. In the ideologies of socialism and the American Dream, his forecast has been unexpectedly fulfilled.

Herbert G. Gutman

 **NO**

Work, Culture, and Society in Industrializing America

The traditional imperial boundaries (a function, perhaps, of the professional subdivision of labor) that have fixed the territory open to American labor historians for exploration have closed off to them the study of such important subjects as changing work habits and the culture of work. Neither the questions American labor historians usually ask nor the methods they use encourage such inquiry. With a few significant exceptions, for more than half a century American labor history has continued to reflect both the strengths and the weaknesses of the conceptual scheme sketched by its founding fathers, John R. Commons and others of the so-called Wisconsin school of labor history. Even their most severe critics, including the orthodox "Marxist" labor historians of the 1930s, 1940s, and 1950s and the few New Left historians who have devoted attention to American labor history, rarely questioned that conceptual framework. Commons and his colleagues asked large questions, gathered important source materials, and put forth impressive ideas. Together with able disciples, they studied the development of the trade union as an institution and explained its place in a changing labor market. But they gave attention primarily to those few workers who belonged to trade unions and neglected much else of importance about the American working population. Two flaws especially marred this older labor history. Because so few workers belonged to permanent trade unions before 1940, its overall conceptualization excluded most working people from detailed and serious study. More than this, its methods encouraged labor historians to spin a cocoon around American workers, isolating them from their own particular subcultures and from the larger national culture. An increasingly narrow "economic" analysis caused the study of American working-class history to grow more constricted and become more detached from larger developments in American social and cultural history and from the writing of American social and cultural history itself. After 1945 American working-class history remained imprisoned by self-imposed limitations and therefore fell far behind the more imaginative and innovative British and Continental European work in the field. . . .

[T]he focus in these pages is on free white labor in quite different time periods: 1815–1843, 1843–1893, 1893–1919. The precise years serve only as guideposts to mark the fact that American society differed greatly in each period. Between 1815 and 1843, the United States remained a predominantly preindustrial society and most workers drawn to its few factories were the products of rural and village preindustrial culture. Preindustrial American society was not premodern in the same way that European peasant societies were, but it was, nevertheless, premodern. In the half-century after 1843 industrial development radically transformed the earlier American social structure, and during this Middle Period (an era not framed around the coming and the aftermath of the Civil War) a profound tension existed between the older American preindustrial social structure and the modernizing institutions that accompanied the development of industrial capitalism. After 1893 the United States ranked as a mature industrial society. In each of these distinctive stages of change in American society, a recurrent tension also existed between native and immigrant men and women fresh to the factory and the demands imposed upon them by the regularities and disciplines of factory labor. That state of tension was regularly revitalized by the migration of diverse premodern native and foreign peoples into an industrializing or a fully industrialized society. The British economic historian Sidney Pollard has described well this process whereby "a society of peasants, craftsmen, and versatile labourers became a society of modern industrial workers." "There was more to overcome," Pollard writes of industrializing England,

> than the change of employment or the new rhythm of work: there was a whole new culture to be absorbed and an old one to be traduced and spurned, there were new surroundings, often in a different part of the country, new relations with employers, and new uncertainties of livelihood, new friends and neighbors, new marriage patterns and behavior patterns of children within the family and without.

That same process occurred in the United States. Just as in all modernizing countries, the United States faced the difficult task of industrializing whole cultures, but in this country the process was regularly repeated, each stage of American economic growth and development involving different first-generation factory workers. The social transformation Pollard described occurred in England between 1770 and 1850, and in those decades premodern British cultures and the modernizing institutions associated primarily with factory and machine labor collided and interacted. A painful transition occurred, dominated the ethos of an entire era, and then faded in relative importance. After 1850 and until quite recently, the British working class reproduced itself and retained a relative national homogeneity. New tensions emerged but not those of a society continually busy (and worried about) industrializing persons born out of that society and often alien in birth and color and in work habits, customary values, and behavior. "Traditional social habits and customs," J. F. C. Harrison reminds us, "seldom fitted into the patterns of industrial life, and they had . . . to be discredited as hindrances to progress." That happened regularly in the United States after 1815 as the nation absorbed and worked to transform new groups of preindustrial peoples, native whites among them. The result however, was neither a static tension nor the mere recurrence of similar cycles, because American society itself changed as did the composition of its laboring population. But the source of the tension remained the same, and conflict often resulted. It was neither the conflict emphasized by the older Progressive historians (agrarianism versus capitalism, or sectional disagreement) nor that emphasized by recent critics of that early twentieth-century synthesis (conflict between competing elites). It resulted instead from the fact that the American working class was continually altered in its composition by infusions, from within and without the nation, of peasants, farmers, skilled artisans, and casual day laborers who brought into industrial society ways of work and other habits and values not associated with industrial necessities and the industrial ethos. Some shed these older ways to conform to new imperatives. Others fell victim or fled, moving from place to place. Some sought to extend and adapt older patterns of work and life to a new society. Others challenged the social system through varieties of collective associations. But for all—at different historical moments—the transition to industrial society, as E. P. Thompson has written, "entailed a severe restructuring of working habits—new disciplines, new incentives, and a new human nature upon which these incentives could bite effectively."

Much in the following pages depends upon a particular definition of culture and an analytic distinction between culture and society. Both deserve brief comment. "Culture" as used here has little to do with Oscar Lewis's inadequate "culture of poverty" construct and has even less to do with the currently fashionable but nevertheless quite crude behavioral social history that defines class by mere occupation and culture as some kind of a magical mix between ethnic and religious affiliations. Instead this [selection] has profited from the analytic distinctions between culture and society made by the anthropologists Eric Wolf and Sidney W. Mintz and the exiled Polish sociologist Zygmunt Bauman. Mintz finds in culture "a kind of resource" and in society "a kind of arena," the distinction being "between sets of historically available alternatives or forms on the one hand, and the societal circumstances or settings within which these forms may be employed on the other." "Culture," he writes, "is *used;* and any analysis of its use immediately brings into view the arrangements of persons in societal groups for whom cultural forms confirm, reinforce, maintain, change, or deny particular arrangements of status, power, and identity.". . .

Despite the profound economic changes that followed the American Civil War, Gilded Age artisans did not easily shed stubborn and time-honored work habits. Such work habits and the life-styles and subcultures related to them retained a vitality long into these industrializing decades. Not all artisans worked in factories, but some that did retained traditional craft skills. Mechanization came in different ways and at different times to diverse industries. Samuel Gompers recollected that New York City cigarmakers paid a fellow craftsman to read a newspaper to them while they worked, and Milwaukee cigarmakers struck in 1882 to retain such privileges as keeping (and then selling) damaged cigars and leaving the shop without a foreman's permission. "The difficulty with many cigar-makers," complained a New York City manufacturer in 1877, "is this. They come down to the shop in the morning; roll a few cigars and then go to a beer saloon and play pinnocio or some other game, . . . working probably only two or three hours a day." Coopers felt new machinery "hard and insensate," not a blessing but an evil that "took a great deal of joy out of life" because machine-made barrels undercut a subculture of work and leisure. Skilled coopers "lounged about" on Saturday (the regular payday), a "lost day" to their employers. A historian of American cooperage explained:

> Early on Saturday morning, the big brewery wagon would drive up to the shop. Several of the coopers would club together, each paying his proper share, and one of them would call out the window to the driver, "Bring me a Goose Egg," meaning a half-barrel of beer. Then others would buy "Goose Eggs," and there would be a merry time all around. . . . Little groups of jolly fellows would often sit around upturned barrels playing poker, using rivets for chips, until they had received their pay and the "Goose Egg" was dry.
>
> Saturday night was a big night for the old-time cooper. It meant going out, strolling around the town, meeting friends, usually at a favorite saloon, and having a good time generally, after a week of hard work. Usually the good time continued over into Sunday, so that on the following day he usually was not in the best of condition to settle down to the regular day's work.
>
> Many coopers used to spend this day [Monday] sharpening up their tools, carrying in stock, discussing current events, and in getting things in shape for the big day of work on the morrow. Thus, "Blue Monday" was something of a tradition with the coopers, and the day was also more or less lost as far as production was concerned.
>
> "Can't do much today, but I'll give her hell tomorrow," seemed to be the Monday slogan. But bright and early Tuesday morning, "Give her hell" they would, banging away lustily for the rest of the week until Saturday which was pay day again, and its thoughts of the "Goose Eggs."

Such traditions of work and leisure—in this case, a four-day work week and a three-day weekend—angered manufacturers anxious to ship goods as much as worried Sabbatarians and temperance reformers. Conflicts over life- and work-styles occurred frequently and often involved control over the work process and over time. The immigrant Staffordshire potters in Trenton, New Jersey, worked in "bursts of great activity" and then quit for "several days at a time." "Monday," said a manufacturer, "was given up to debauchery." After the potters lost a bitter lockout in 1877 that included torchlight parades and effigy burnings, *Crockery and Glass Journal* mockingly advised:

> Run your factories to please the crowd. . . . Don't expect work to begin before 9 a.m. or to continue after 3 p.m. Every employee should be served hot coffee and a bouquet at 7 a.m. and allowed the two hours to take a free perfumed bath. . . . During the summer, ice cream and fruit should be served at 12 p.m. to the accompaniment of witching music.

Hand coopers (and potters and cigarmakers, among others) worked hard but in distinctly preindustrial styles. Machine-made barrels pitted modernizing technology and modern habits against traditional ways. To the owners of competitive firms struggling to improve efficiency and cut labor costs, the Goose Egg and Blue Monday proved the laziness and obstinacy of craftsmen as well as the tyranny of craft unions that upheld venerable traditions. To the skilled cooper the long weekend symbolized a way of work and life filled with almost ritualistic meanings. Between 1843 and 1893, compromise between such conflicting interests was hardly possible.

Settled premodern work habits existed among others than those employed in nonfactory crafts. Owners of already partially mechanized industries complained of them, too. "Saturday night debauches and Sunday carousels though they be few and far between," lamented the *Age of Steel* in 1882, "are destructive of modest hoardings, and he who indulges in them will in time become a striker for higher wages." In 1880 a British steelworker boasted that native Americans never would match immigrants in their skills: "adn't the 'ops, you know." Manufacturers, when able, did not hesitate to act decisively to end such troubles. In Fall River new technology allowed a print cloth manufacturer to settle a long-standing grievance against his stubborn mule spinners. "On Saturday afternoon after they had gone home," a boastful mill superintendent later recollected, "we started right in and smashed a room full of mules with sledge hammers. . . . On Monday morning, they were astonished to find that there was not work for them. That room is now full of ring frames run by girls." Woolen manufacturers also displaced hand-jack spinners with improved machinery and did so because of "the disorderly habits of English workmen. Often on a Monday morning, half of them would be absent from the mill in consequence of the Sunday's dissipation." Blue Monday, however, did not entirely disappear. Paterson artisans and factory hands held a May festival on a Monday each year ("Labor Monday") and that popular holiday soon became state law, the American Labor Day. It had its roots in earlier premodern work habits.

The persistence of such traditional artisan work habits well into the nineteenth century deserves notice from others besides labor historians, because those work habits did not exist in a cultural or social vacuum. If modernizing technology threatened and even displaced such work patterns, diverse nineteenth-century subcultures sustained and nourished them. "The old nations of the earth creep on at a snail's pace," boasted Andrew Carnegie in *Triumphant Democracy* (1886), "the Republic thunders past with the rush of an express." The articulate steelmaster, however, had missed the point. The very rapidity of the economic changes occurring in Carnegie's lifetime meant that many, unlike him, lacked the time, historically, culturally, and psychologically, to be separated or alienated from settled ways of work and life and from relatively fixed beliefs. Continuity not consensus counted for much in explaining working-class and especially artisan behavior in those decades that witnessed the coming of the factory and the radical transformation of American society. Persistent work habits were one example of that significant continuity. But these elements of continuity were often revealed among nineteenth-century American workers cut off by birth from direct contact with the preindustrial American past, a fact that has been ignored or blurred by the artificial separation between labor history and immigration history. In Gilded Age America (and afterward in the Progressive Era despite the radical change in patterns of immigration), working-class and immigration history regularly intersected, and that intermingling made for powerful continuities. In 1880, for example, 63 of every 100 Londoners were native to that city, 94 coming from England and Wales, and 98 from Great Britain and Ireland. Foreign countries together contributed only 1.6 percent to London's massive population. At that same moment, more than 70 of every 100 persons in San Francisco (78), St. Louis (78), Cleveland (80), New York (80), Detroit (84), Milwaukee (84), and Chicago (87) were immigrants or the children of immigrants, and the percentage was just as high in many smaller American industrial towns and cities. "Not every foreigner is a workingman," noticed the clergyman Samuel Lane Loomis in 1887, "but in the cities, at least, it may almost be said that every workingman is a foreigner." And until the 1890s most immigrants came from Northern and Western Europe, French- and English-speaking Canada, and China. In 1890, only 3 percent of the nation's foreign-born residents—290,000 of 9,200,000 immigrants—had been born in Eastern or Southern Europe. (It is a little recognized fact that most North and West European immigrants migrated to the United States after, not before, the American Civil War.) When so much else changed in the industrializing decades, tenacious traditions flourished among immigrants in ethnic subcultures that varied greatly among particular groups and according to the size, age, and location of different cities and industries. ("The Irish," Henry George insisted, "burn like chips, the English like logs.") Class and occupational distinctions within a particular ethnic group also made for different patterns of cultural adaptation, but powerful subcultures thrived among them all.

Suffering and plain poverty cut deeply into these ethnic working-class worlds. In reconstructing their everyday texture there is no reason to neglect or idealize such suffering, but it is time to discard the notion that the large-scale uprooting and exploitative processes that accompanied industrialization caused little more than cultural breakdown and social anomie. Family, class, and ethnic ties did not dissolve easily. "Almost as a matter of definition," the sociologist Neil Smelzer has written, "we associate the factory system with the decline of the family and the onset of anonymity."

Smelzer criticized such a view of early industrializing England, and it has just as little validity for nineteenth-century industrializing America. Family roles changed in important ways, and strain was widespread, but the immigrant working-class family held together. Examination of household composition in sixteen census enumeration districts in Paterson in 1880 makes that clear for this predominantly working-class immigrant city, and while research on other ethnic working-class communities will reveal significant variations, the overall patterns should not differ greatly. The Paterson immigrant (and native white) communities were predominantly working class, and most families among them were intact in their composition. For this population, at least (and without accounting for age and sex ratio differences between the ethnic groups), a greater percentage of immigrant than native white households included two parents. Ethnic and predominantly working-class communities in industrial towns like Paterson and in larger cities, too, built on these strained but hardly broken familial and kin ties. Migration to another country, life in the city, and labor in cost-conscious and ill-equipped factories and workshops tested but did not shatter what the anthropologist Clifford Geertz has described as primordial (as contrasted to civic) attachments, "the 'assumed' givens . . . of social existence: immediate contiguity and kin connections mainly, but beyond them, the givenness that stems from being born into a particular religious community, speaking a particular language, and following particular social patterns." Tough familial and kin ties made possible that transmission and adaptation of European working-class cultural patterns and beliefs to industrializing America. As late as 1888, residents in some Rhode Island mill villages figured their wages in British currency. Common rituals and festivals bound together such communities. Paterson silk weavers had their Macclesfield wakes, and Fall River cotton mill workers their Ashton wakes. British immigrants "banded together to uphold the popular culture of the homeland" and celebrated saints' days: St. George's Day, St. Andrew's Day, and St. David's Day. Even funerals retained an archaic flavor. Samuel Sigley, a Chartist house painter, had fled Ashton-under-Lyne in 1848, and built American trade unions. When his wife died in the late 1890s a significant ritual occurred during the funeral: some friends placed a chaff of wheat on her grave. Mythic beliefs also cemented ethnic and class solidarities. The Irish-American press, for example, gave Martin O'Brennan much space to argue that Celtic had been spoken in the Garden of Eden, and in Paterson Irish-born silk, cotton, and iron workers believed in the magical powers of that town's "Dublin Spring." An old resident remembered:

> There is a legend that an Irish fairy brought over the water in her apron from the Lakes of Killarney and planted it in the humble part of that town. . . . There were dozens of legends connected with the Dublin Spring and if a man drank from its precious depository. . . he could never leave Paterson [but] only under the fairy influence, and the wand of the nymph would be sure to bring him back again some time or other.

When a "fairy" appeared in Paterson in human form, some believed she walked the streets "as a tottering old woman begging with a cane." Here was a way to assure concern for the elderly and the disabled.

Much remains to be studied about these cross-class but predominantly working-class ethnic subcultures common to industrializing America. Relations within them between skilled and unskilled workers, for example, remain unclear. But the larger shape of these diverse immigrant communities can be sketched. More than mythic beliefs and common work habits sustained them. Such worlds had in them what Thompson has called "working-class intellectual traditions, working-class community patterns, and a working-class structure of feeling," and men with artisan skills powerfully affected the everyday texture of such communities. A model subculture included friendly and benevolent societies as well as friendly local politicians, community-wide holiday celebrations, an occasional library (the Baltimore Journeymen Bricklayer's Union taxed members one dollar a year in the 1880s to sustain a library that included the collected works of William Shakespeare and Sir Walter Scott's *Waverley* novels), participant sports, churches sometimes headed by a sympathetic clergy, saloons, beer gardens, and concert halls or music halls and, depending upon circumstances, trade unionists, labor reformers, and radicals. The Massachusetts cleric Jonathan Baxter Harrison published in 1880 an unusually detailed description of one such ethnic, working-class institution, a Fall River music hall and saloon. About fifty persons were there when he visited it, nearly one-fourth of them young women. "Most of those present," he noticed, were "persons whom I had met before, in the mills and on the streets. They were nearly all operatives, or had at some time belonged to that class." An Englishman sang first, and then a black whose songs "were of many kinds, comic, sentimental, pathetic, and silly. . . . When he sang 'I got a mammy in the promised land,' with a strange, wailing refrain, the English waiter-girl, who was sitting at my table, wiped her eyes with her apron, and everybody was very quiet." Harrison said of such places in Fall River:

> All the attendants. . . had worked in the mills. The young man who plays the piano is usually paid four or five dollars per week, besides his board. The young men who sing receive one dollar per night, but most of them board themselves. . . . The most usual course for a man who for any reason falls out of the ranks of mill workers (if he loses his place by sickness or is discharged) is the opening of a liquor saloon or drinking place.

Ethnic ties with particular class dimensions sometimes stretched far beyond local boundaries and even revealed themselves in the behavior of the most successful practitioners of Gilded Age popular culture. In 1884, for example, the pugilist John L. Sullivan and the music-hall entertainers Harrigan and Hart promised support to striking Irish coal miners in the Ohio Hocking Valley. Local ties, however, counted for much more and had their roots inside and outside of the factory and workshop. Soon after Cyrus H. McCormick, then twenty-one, took over the management of his father's great Chicago iron machinery factory (which in the early 1880s employed twelve hundred men and boys), a petition signed by "Many Employees" reached his hands:

> It only pains us to relate to you. . . that a good many of our old hands is not here this season and if Mr. Evarts is kept another season a good many more will leave. . . . We pray for you. . . to remove this man. . . . We are treated as though we were dogs. . . . He has cut wages down so low they are living on nothing but bread. . . . We can't talk to him about wages if we do he will tell us to go out side the gate. . . . He discharged old John the other day he has been here seventeen years. . . . There is Mr. Church who left us last Saturday he went about and shook hands with every old hand in the shop . . . this brought tears to many men's eyes. He has been here nineteen years and has got along well with them all until he came to Mr. Evarts the present superintendent.

Artisans, themselves among those later displaced by new technology, signed this petition, and self-educated artisans (or professionals and petty enterprisers who had themselves usually risen from the artisan class) often emerged as civic and community leaders. "Intellectually," Jennie Collins noticed in Boston in the early 1870s, "the journeymen tailors . . . are ever discussing among themselves questions of local and national politics, points of law, philosophy, physics, and religion."

Such life-styles and subcultures adapted and changed over time. In the Gilded Age piece-rates in nearly all manufacturing industries helped reshape traditional work habits. "Two generations ago," said the Connecticut Bureau of Labor Statistics in 1885, "time-work was the universal rule." "Piece-work" had all but replaced it, and the Connecticut Bureau called it "a moral force which corresponds to machinery as a physical force." Additional pressures came in traditional industries such as shoe, cigar, furniture, barrel, and clothing manufacture, which significantly mechanized in these years. Strain also resulted where factories employed large numbers of children and young women (in the 1880 manuscript census 49.3 percent of all Paterson boys and 52.1 percent of all girls aged eleven to fourteen had occupations listed by their names) and was especially common among the as yet little-studied pools of casual male laborers found everywhere. More than this, mobility patterns significantly affected the structure and the behavior of these predominantly working-class communities. A good deal of geographic mobility, property mobility (home ownership), and occupational mobility (skilled status in new industries or in the expanding building trades, petty retail enterprise, the professions, and public employment counted as the most important ways to advance occupationally) reshaped these ethnic communities as Stephan Thernstrom and others have shown. But so little is yet known about the society in which such men and women lived and about the cultures which had produced them that it is entirely premature to infer "consciousness" (beliefs and values) only from mobility rates. Such patterns and rates of mobility, for example, did not entirely shatter working-class capacities for self-protection. The fifty-year period between 1843 and 1893 was not conducive to permanent, stable trade unions, but these decades were a time of frequent strikes and lockouts and other forms of sustained conflict.

Not all strikes and lockouts resulted in the defeat of poorly organized workers. For the years 1881 to 1887, for example, the New Jersey Bureau of Labor Statistics collected information on 890 New Jersey industrial disputes involving mostly workers in the textile, glass, metal, transportation, and building trades: 6 percent ended in compromise settlements; employers gained the advantage in 40 percent; strikers won the rest (54 percent). In four of five disputes concerning higher wages and shorter hours, New Jersey workers, not their employers, were victorious. Large numbers of such workers there and elsewhere were foreign-born or the children of immigrants. More than this, immigrant workers in the mid-1880s joined trade unions in numbers far out of proportion to their place in the labor force. Statistical inquiries by the Bureau of Labor Statistics in Illinois in 1886 and in New Jersey in 1887 make this clear. Even these data may not have fully reflected the proclivity of immigrants to seek self-protection. (Such a distortion would occur if, for example, the children of immigrants apparently counted by the bureaus as native-born had remained a part of the ethnic subcultures into which they had been born and joined trade unions as regularly as the foreign-born). Such information from Illinois and New Jersey suggests the need to treat the meaning of social mobility with some care. So does the sketchy outline of Hugh O'Donnell's career. By 1892, when he was twenty-nine years old, he had already improved his social status a great deal. Before the dispute with Andrew Carnegie and Henry Clay Frick culminated in the bitter Homestead lockout that year, O'Donnell had voted Republican, owned a home, and had in it a Brussels carpet and even a piano. Nevertheless this Irish-American skilled worker led the Homestead workers and was even indicted under a Civil War treason statute never before used. The material improvements O'Donnell had experienced mattered greatly to him and suggested significant mobility, but culture and tradition together with the way in which men like O'Donnell interpreted the transformation of Old America defined the value of those material improvements and their meaning to him.

Other continuities between 1843 and 1893 besides those rooted in artisan work habits and diverse ethnic working-class subcultures deserve brief attention as important considerations in understanding the behavior of artisans and other workers in these decades. I have suggested in other writings that significant patterns of opposition to the ways in which industrial capitalism developed will remain baffling until historians re-examine the relationship between the premodern American political system and the coming of the factory along with the strains in premodern popular American ideology shared by workers and large numbers of successful self-made Americans (policemen, clergymen, politicians, small businessmen, and even some "traditional" manufacturers) that rejected the legitimacy of the modern factory system and its owners. One strain of thought common to the rhetoric of nineteenth-century immigrant and native-born artisans is considered here. It helps explain their recurrent enthusiasm for land and currency reform, cooperatives, and trade unions. It was the fear of dependence, "proletarianization," and centralization, and the worry that industrial capitalism threatened to transform "the Great Republic of the West" into a "European" country. In 1869, the same year that saw the completion of the transcontinental railroad, the chartering of the Standard Oil Company, the founding of the Knights of Labor, and the dedication of a New York City statue to Cornelius Vanderbilt, some London workers from Westbourne Park and Notting Hill petitioned the American ambassador for help to emigrate. "Dependence," they said of Great Britain, "not independence, is inculcated. Hon. Sir, this state of things we wish to fly from . . . to become citizens of that great Republican country, which has no parallels in the world's history." Such men had a vision of Old America, but it was not a new vision. Industrial transformation between 1840 and 1890 tested and redefined that vision. Seven years after their visit, the New York *Labor Standard,* then edited by an Irish socialist, bemoaned what had come over the country: "There was a time when the United States was the workingman's country, . . . the land of promise for the workingman. . . . We are now in an *old country.*" This theme recurred frequently as disaffected workers, usually self-educated artisans, described the transformation of premodern America. "America," said the Detroit *Labor Leaf* "used to be the land of promise to the poor. . . . The Golden Age is indeed over—the Age of Iron has taken its place. The iron law of necessity has taken the place of the golden rule." We need not join in mythicizing preindustrial American society in order to suggest that this tension between the old and the new helps give a coherence to the decades between 1843 and 1893 that even the trauma of the Civil War does not disturb.

POSTSCRIPT

Were American Workers in the Gilded Age Conservative Capitalists?

Degler agrees with the traditional labor historians that the American worker accepted capitalism and wanted a bigger piece of the pie. But he reverses the radical-conservative dichotomy as applied to the conflict between the worker and the businessman. In his view, the real radicals were the industrialists who created a more mature system of capitalism. Labor merely fashioned a conservative response to the radical changes brought about by big business. The system led to its demise. Its place was taken by the American Federation of Labor, whose long-time leader Samuel Gompers was famous for his acceptance of the wage system and American capitalism. The American Federation of Labor adopted practical goals; it strove to improve the lot of the worker by negotiating for better hours, wages, and working conditions. "In an age of big business," says Degler, "Samuel Gompers made trade unionism a business, and his reward was the survival of his Federation."

In explaining the failure of socialism in America, Degler argues that Americans lacked a working-class consciousness because they believed in real mobility. Also, a labor party failed to emerge because Americans developed their commitment to the two-party system before the issues of the industrial revolution came to the forefront. The influx of immigrants from a variety of countries created the heterogeneous labor force, and animosities between rival ethnic groups appeared more real than class antagonisms. "In the final reckoning," says Degler, "the failure of socialism in America is to be attributed to the success of capitalism."

For the past 25 years historians have been studying the social and cultural environment of the American working class. The approach is modeled after Edward P. Thompson's highly influential and sophisticated Marxist analysis *The Making of the English Working Class* (Vintage Books, 1966), which is the capstone of an earlier generation of British and French social historians. The father of the "new labor history" in the United States is Gutman, who was the first to discuss American workers as a group separate from the organized union movement. Gutman's distinction between preindustrial and industrial values laid the groundwork for a whole generation of scholars who have performed case studies of both union and nonunion workers in both urban and rural areas of America. Such works have proliferated in recent years but should be sampled first in the following collections of articles: Daniel J. Leab and Richard B. Morris, eds., *The Labor History Reader* (University of Illinois Press, 1985); Charles Stephenson and Robert Asher, eds., *Life and Labor: Dimensions of American Working-Class History* (State University of New York

Press, 1986); and Milton Cantor, ed., *American Working Class Culture: Explorations in American Labor and Social History* (Greenwood, 1979).

Gutman's essay differs from Degler's more traditional approach in several ways. Gutman abandons the division of American history at the Civil War/Reconstruction fault line. He proposes a threefold division for free, white workers: (1) the premodern early industrial period from 1815 to 1843; (2) the transition to capitalism, which encompasses the years 1843–1893; and (3) the development of a full-blown industrial system, which took place from the late 1890s through World War I. Gutman's unique periodization enables us to view the evolution of the free, white nonunion worker, whose traditional values withstood the onslaughts of an increasingly large-scale dehumanized factory system that emphasized productivity and efficiency until the depression of 1893.

Gutman also challenges the view that workers were helpless pawns of the owners and that they were forced to cave in every time a strike took place. He shows that on a local level in the 1880s, immigrant workers not only joined unions but also usually won their strikes. This is because small shopkeepers and workers in other industries often supported those who were out on strike. Gutman also argues from census data of the 1880s that immigrant families were more stable and less prone to divorce and desertion than native-born families. Gutman applied many of these insights to slaves in his prizewinning book *The Black Family in Slavery and Freedom* (Pantheon, 1976).

To learn more about the rise and fall of the Knights of Labor, see the case studies in Leon Fink's *Workingmen's Democracy: The Knights of Labor and American Politics* (University of Illinois Press, 1983). See also Fink's collection of articles *In Search of the Working Class* (University of Illinois Press, 1994). Two other noteworthy books on the Knights of Labor are Robert E. Weir, *Beyond Labor's Veil: The Culture of the Knights of Labor* (Penn State University Press, 1996) and Kim Voss, *The Making of American Exceptionalism: The Knights of Labor and Class Formation in the Nineteenth Century* (Cornell University Press, 1993).

Two journals have devoted entire issues to the American labor movement: the fall 1989 issue of *The Public Historian* and the February 1982 issue of *Social Education*. Students who wish to sample the diverse scholarships on the American worker should consult "A Round Table: Labor, Historical Pessimism, and Hegemony," *Journal of American History* (June 1988).

The question of why the United States never developed a major socialist movement or labor party has been the subject of much speculation. A good starting point is John H. Laslett and Seymour Martin Lipset, eds., *Failure of a Dream? Essays in the History of American Socialism* (University of California Press, 1984). Political scientist Theodore J. Lowi argues that the U.S. political system of federalism prevented a socialist movement in "Why Is There No Socialism in the United States?" *Society* (January/February 1985). Finally, see Rick Halpern and Jonathan Morris, eds., *American Exceptionalism? U.S. Working-Class Formation in an International Context* (St. Martin's Press, 1997).

ISSUE 4

Were Late-Nineteenth-Century Immigrants "Uprooted"?

YES: Oscar Handlin, from *The Uprooted: The Epic Story of the Great Migrations That Made the American People,* 2nd ed. (Little Brown and Company, 1973)

NO: Mark Wyman, from *Round-Trip to America: The Immigrants Return to Europe, 1880–1930* (Cornell University Press, 1993)

ISSUE SUMMARY

YES: Oscar Handlin asserts that immigrants to the United States in the late nineteenth century were alienated from the cultural traditions of the homeland they had left as well as from those of their adopted country.

NO: Mark Wyman argues that as many as four million immigrants to the United States between 1880 and 1930 viewed their trip as temporary and remained tied psychologically to their homeland to which they returned once they had accumulated enough wealth to enable them to improve their status back home.

Immigration has been one of the most powerful forces shaping the development of the United States since at least the early seventeenth century. In fact, it should not be overlooked that even the ancestors of the country's Native American population were migrants to this "New World" some 37,000 years ago. There can be little doubt that the United States is a nation of immigrants, a reality reinforced by the motto "E Pluribus Unum" (one from many), which is used on the Great Seal of the United States and on several U.S. coins.

The history of immigration to the United States can be organized into four major periods of activity: 1607–1830, 1830–1890, 1890–1924, and 1968 to the present. During the first period, the seventeenth and eighteenth centuries, there were a growing number of European migrants who arrived in North America, mostly from the British Isles, as well as several million Africans who were forced to migrate to colonial America as a consequence of the Atlantic slave trade. While increased numbers of non-English immigrants arrived in America in the eighteenth century, it was not until the nineteenth century that large numbers of immigrants from other northern and western European countries, as well as from China, arrived and created significant population diversity. Two European groups predominated during this second major period: As a result of the potato famine, large numbers of Irish Catholics emigrated in the 1850s, and for a variety of religious, political, and economic reasons, so did many Germans. Chinese immigration increased, and these immigrants found work in low-paying service industries, such as laundries and restaurants, and as railroad construction workers.

The Industrial Revolution of the late nineteenth century sparked a third wave of immigration. Immigrants by the millions began pouring into the United States attracted by the unskilled factory jobs that were becoming more abundant. Migration was encouraged by various companies whose agents distributed handbills throughout Europe, advertising the ready availability of good-paying jobs in America. This phase of immigration, however, represented something of a departure from previous ones as most of these "new immigrants" came from southern and eastern Europe. This flood continued until World War I, after which mounting xenophobia culminated in the passage by Congress in 1924 of the National Origins Act, which restricted the number of immigrants into the country to 150,000 annually, and which placed quotas on the numbers of immigrants permitted from each foreign country.

In the aftermath of World War II, restrictions were eased for several groups, especially those who survived the Nazi death camps or who sought asylum in the United States in the wake of the aggressive movement into Eastern Europe by the Soviet Union after the war. But restrictions against Asians and Africans were not lifted until the Immigration Reform Act of 1965, which set in motion a fourth phase of immigration history. In contrast to earlier migrations, the newest groups have come from Latin America and Asia.

Efforts to curb immigration to the United States reflect an anxiety and ambivalence that many Americans have long held with regard to "foreigners." Anxious to benefit from the labor of these newcomers but still hesitant to accept the immigrants as full-fledged citizens entitled to the same rights and privileges as native-born residents, Americans have on a number of occasions discovered that they had an "immigrant problem." Harsh anti-immigrant sentiment based on prejudicial attitudes toward race, ethnicity, or religion has periodically boiled over into violence and calls for legislation to restrict immigration.

What effect did these kinds of attitudes have on those who migrated to the United States in search of a life better than the one they experienced in their native lands? What happened to their Old World customs and traditions? How fully did immigrants assimilate into the new culture they encountered in the United States? Was the United States, in fact, a melting pot for immigrants, as some have suggested?

In the following readings, Oscar Handlin argues that the immigrants were uprooted from their Old World cultures as they attempted to adjust to an unfamiliar and often hostile environment in the United States. Mark Wyman points out that many immigrants to the United States believed that their stay in America would be temporary, a fact that limited their efforts at assimilation and reinforced ties to their original homelands.

YES

Oscar Handlin

The Shock of Alienation

. . . As the passing years widened the distance, the land the immigrants had left acquired charm and beauty. Present problems blurred those they had left unsolved behind; and in the haze of memory it seemed to these people they had formerly been free of present dissatisfactions. It was as if the Old World became a great mirror into which they looked to see right all that was wrong with the New. The landscape was prettier, the neighbors more friendly, and religion more efficacious; in the frequent crises when they reached the limits of their capacities, the wistful reflection came: *This would not have happened there.*

The real contacts were, however, disappointing. The requests—that back there a mass be said, or a wise one consulted, or a religious medal be sent over—those were gestures full of hope. But the responses were inadequate; like all else they shrank in the crossing. The immigrants wrote, but the replies, when they came, were dull, even trite in their mechanical phrases, or so it seemed to those who somehow expected these messages to evoke the emotions that had gone into their own painfully composed letters. Too often the eagerly attended envelopes proved to be only empty husks, the inner contents valueless. After the long wait before the postman came, the sheets of garbled writing were inevitably below expectations. There was a trying sameness to the complaints of hard times, to the repetitious petty quarrels; and before long there was impatience with the directness with which the formal greeting led into the everlasting requests for aid.

This last was a sore point with the immigrants. The friends and relatives who had stayed behind could not get it out of their heads that in America the streets were paved with gold. *Send me for a coat . . . There is a piece of land here and if only you would send, we could buy it . . . Our daughter could be married, but we have not enough for a dowry . . . We are ashamed, everyone else gets . . . much more frequently than we.* Implicit in these solicitations was the judgment that the going-away had been a desertion, that unfulfilled obligations still remained, and that the village could claim assistance as a right from its departed members.

From the United States it seemed there was no comprehension, back there, of the difficulties of settlement. It was exasperating by sacrifices to scrape together the remittances and to receive in return a catalogue of new

From *The Uprooted: The Epic Story of the Great Migrations That Made the American People, 2nd ed.*, by Oscar Handlin (Little Brown & Company, 1951, 1973), excerpts from pp. 260–266, 270–274, 279–285. Copyright © 1951, 1973 by Oscar Handlin. Reprinted by permission of Little, Brown & Company/Hachette Book Group USA.

needs, as if there were not needs enough in the New World too. The immigrants never shook off the sense of obligation to help; but they did come to regard their Old Countrymen as the kind of people who depended on help. The trouble with the Europeans was, they could not stand on their own feet.

The cousin green off the boat earned the same negative appraisal. Though he be a product of the homeland, yet here he cut a pitiable figure; awkward manners, rude clothes, and a thoroughgoing ineptitude in the new situation were his most prominent characteristics. The older settler found the welcome almost frozen on his lips in the face of such backwardness.

In every real contact the grandeur of the village faded; it did not match the immigrants' vision of it and it did not stand up in a comparison with America. When the picture came, the assembled family looked at it beneath the light. This was indeed the church, but it had not been remembered so; and the depressing contrast took some of the joy out of remembering.

The photograph did not lie. There it was, a low building set against the dusty road, weather-beaten and making a candid display of its ill-repair. But the recollections did not lie either. As if it had been yesterday that they passed through those doors, they could recall the sense of spaciousness and elevation that sight of the structure had always aroused.

Both impressions were true, but irreconcilable. The mental image and the paper representation did not jibe because the one had been formed out of the standards and values of the Old Country, while the other was viewed in the light of the standards and values of the New. And it was the same with every other retrospective contact. Eagerly the immigrants continued to look back across the Atlantic in search of the satisfactions of fellowship. But the search was not rewarded. Having become Americans, they were no longer villagers. Though they might willingly assume the former obligations and recognize the former responsibilities, they could not recapture the former points of view or hold to the former judgments. They had seen too much, experienced too much to be again members of the community. It was a vain mission on which they continued to dispatch the letters; these people, once separated, would never belong again.

⟡

Their home now was a country in which they had not been born. Their place in society they had established for themselves through the hardships of crossing and settlement. The process had changed them, had altered the most intimate aspects of their lives. Every effort to cling to inherited ways of acting and thinking had led into a subtle adjustment by which those ways were given a new American form. No longer Europeans, could the immigrants then say that they belonged in America? The answer depended upon the conceptions held by other citizens of the United States of the character of the nation and of the role of the newcomers within it.

In the early nineteenth century, those already established on this side of the ocean regarded immigration as a positive good. When travel by sea became safe after the general peace of 1815 and the first fresh arrivals trickled in, there was a general disposition to welcome the movement. The favorable attitude persisted even when the tide mounted to the flood levels of the 1840's and 1850's. The man off the boat was then accepted without question or condition.

The approval of unlimited additions to the original population came easily to Americans who were conscious of the youth of their country. Standing at the edge of an immense continent, they were moved by the challenge of empty land almost endless in its extension. Here was room enough, and more, for all who would bend their energies to its exploitation. The shortage was of labor and not of acres; every pair of extra hands increased the value of the abundant resources and widened opportunities for everyone.

The youth of the nation also justified the indiscriminate admission of whatever foreigners came to these shores. There was high faith in the destiny of the Republic, assurance that its future history would justify the Revolution and the separation from Great Britain. The society and the culture that would emerge in this territory would surpass those of the Old World because they would not slavishly imitate the outmoded forms and the anachronistic traditions that constricted men in Europe. The United States would move in new directions of its own because its people were a new people.

There was consequently a vigorous insistence that this country was not simply an English colony become independent. It was a nation unique in its origins, produced by the mixture of many different types out of which had come an altogether fresh amalgam, the American. The ebullient citizens who believed and argued that their language, their literature, their art, and their polity were distinctive and original also believed and argued that their population had not been derived from a single source but had rather acquired its peculiar characteristics from the blending of a variety of strains.

There was confidence that the process would continue. The national type had not been fixed by its given antecedents; it was emerging from the experience of life on a new continent. Since the quality of men was determined not by the conditions surrounding their birth, but by the environment within which they passed their lives, it was pointless to select among them. All would come with minds and spirits fresh for new impressions; and being in America would make Americans of them. Therefore it was best to admit freely everyone who wished to make a home here. The United States would then be a great smelting pot, great enough so that there was room for all who voluntarily entered; and the nation that would ultimately be cast from that crucible would be all the richer for the diversity of the elements that went into the molten mixture.

The legislation of most of the nineteenth century reflected this receptive attitude. The United States made no effort actively to induce anyone to immigrate, but neither did it put any bars in the way of their coming. Occasional laws in the four decades after 1819 set up shipping regulations in the hope of improving the conditions of the passage. In practice, the provisions that specified the minimum quantities of food and the maximum number of passengers each vessel could carry were easily evaded. Yet the intent of those statutes was to protect the travelers and to remove harsh conditions that might discourage the newcomers.

Nor were state laws any more restrictive in design. The seaports, troubled by the burdens of poor relief, secured the enactment of measures to safeguard their treasuries against such charges. Sometimes the form was a bond to guarantee that the immigrant would not become at once dependent upon public support; sometimes it was a small tax applied to defray the costs of charity. In either case there was no desire to limit entry into the country; and none of these steps had any discernible effect upon the volume of admissions.

Once landed, the newcomer found himself equal in condition to the natives. Within a short period he could be naturalized and acquire all the privileges of a citizen. In some places, indeed, he could vote before the oath in court so transformed his status. In the eyes of society, even earlier than in the eyes of the law, he was an American. . . .

As the nineteenth century moved into its last quarter, a note of petulance crept into the comments of some Americans who thought about this aspect of the development of their culture. It was a long time now that the melting pot had been simmering, but the end product seemed no closer than before. The experience of life in the United States had not broken down the separateness of the elements mixed into it; each seemed to retain its own identity. Almost a half-century after the great immigration of Irish and Germans, these people had not become indistinguishable from other Americans; they were still recognizably Irish and German. Yet even then, newer waves of newcomers were beating against the Atlantic shore. Was there any prospect that all these multitudes would ever be assimilated, would ever be Americanized?

A generation earlier such questions would not have been asked. Americans of the first half of the century had assumed that any man who subjected himself to the American environment was being Americanized. Since the New World was ultimately to be occupied by a New Man, no mere derivative of any extant stock, but different from and superior to all, there had been no fixed standards of national character against which to measure the behavior of newcomers. The nationality of the new Republic had been supposed fluid, only just evolving; there had been room for infinite variation because diversity rather than uniformity had been normal.

The expression of doubts that some parts of the population might not become fully American implied the existence of a settled criterion of what was American. There had been a time when the society had recognized no distinction among citizens but that between the native and the foreign-born, and that distinction had carried no imputation of superiority or inferiority. Now there were attempts to distinguish among the natives between those who really belonged and those who did not, to separate out those who were born in the United States but whose immigrant parentage cut them off from the truly indigenous folk.

It was difficult to draw the line, however. The census differentiated after 1880 between natives and native-born of foreign parents. But that was an inadequate line of division; it provided no means of social recognition and offered no basis on which the *true Americans* could draw together, identify themselves as such.

Through these years there was a half-conscious quest among some Americans for a term that would describe those whose ancestors were in the United States before the great migrations. Where the New Englanders were, they called themselves Yankees, a word that often came to mean non-Irish or non-Canadian. But Yankee was simply a local designation and did not take in the whole of the old stock. In any case, there was no satisfaction to such a title. Its holders were one group among many, without any distinctive claim to Americanism, cut off from other desirable peoples prominent in the country's past. Only the discovery of common antecedents could eliminate the separations among the really American.

But to find a common denominator, it was necessary to go back a long way. Actually no single discovery was completely satisfactory. Some writers, in time, referred to the civilization of the United States as Anglo-Saxon. By projecting its origins back to early Britain, they implied that their own culture was always English in derivation, and made foreigners of the descendants of Irishmen and Germans, to say nothing of the later arrivals. Other men preferred a variant and achieved the same exclusion by referring to themselves as "the English-speaking people," a title which assumed there was a unity and uniqueness to the clan which settled the home island, the Dominions, and the United States. Still others relied upon a somewhat broader appellation. They talked of themselves as Teutonic and argued that what was distinctively American originated in the forests of Germany; in this view, only the folk whose ancestors had experienced the freedom of tribal self-government and the liberation of the Protestant Reformation were fully American.

These terms had absolutely no historical justification. They nevertheless achieved a wide currency in the thinking of the last decades of the nineteenth century. Whatever particular phrase might serve the purpose of a particular author or speaker, all expressed the conviction that some hereditary element had given form to American culture. The conclusion was inescapable: to be Americanized, the immigrants must conform to the American way of life completely defined in advance of their landing.

There were two counts to the indictment that the immigrants were not so conforming. They were, first, accused of their poverty. Many benevolent citizens, distressed by the miserable conditions in the districts inhabited by the laboring people, were reluctant to believe that such social flaws were indigenous to the New World. It was tempting, rather, to ascribe them to

the defects of the newcomers, to improvidence, slovenliness, and ignorance rather than to inability to earn a living wage.

Indeed to those whose homes were uptown the ghettos were altogether
alien territory associated with filth and vice and crime. It did not seem possible that men could lead a decent existence in such quarters. The good vicar
on a philanthropic tour was shocked by the moral dangers of the dark un-
lighted hallway. His mind rushed to the defense of the respectable young girl:
*Whatever her wishes may be, she can do nothing—shame prevents her from crying
out.* The intention of the reformer was to improve housing, but the summa-
tion nevertheless was, *You cannot make an American citizen out of a slum.*

The newcomers were also accused of congregating together in their
own groups and of an unwillingness to mix with outsiders. The foreign-
born flocked to the great cities and stubbornly refused to spread out as
farmers over the countryside; that alone was offensive to a society which
still retained an ideal of rusticity. But even the Germans in Wisconsin and
the Scandinavians in Minnesota held aloofly to themselves. Everywhere,
the strangers persisted in their strangeness and willfully stood apart from
American life. A prominent educator sounded the warning: *Our task is to
break up their settlements, to assimilate and amalgamate these people and to
implant in them the Anglo-Saxon conception of righteousness, law, and order.*

It was no simple matter to meet this challenge. The older residents
were quick to criticize the separateness of the immigrant but hesitant when
he made a move to narrow the distance. The householders of Fifth Avenue
or Beacon Street or Nob Hill could readily perceive the evils of the slums but
they were not inclined to welcome as a neighbor the former denizen of the
East Side or the North End or the Latin Quarter who had acquired the means
to get away. Among Protestants there was much concern over the growth
of Catholic, Jewish, and Orthodox religious organizations, but there was no
eagerness at all to provoke a mass conversion that might crowd the earlier
churches with a host of poor foreigners. When the population of its neighborhood changed, the parish was less likely to try to attract the newcomers
than to close or sell its building and move to some other section.

Indeed there was a fundamental ambiguity to the thinking of those
who talked about "assimilation" in these years. They had arrived at their
own view that American culture was fixed, formed from its origins, by
shutting out the great mass of immigrants who were not English or at least
not Teutonic. Now it was expected that those excluded people would alter
themselves to earn their portion in Americanism. That process could only
come about by increasing the contacts between the older and the newer
inhabitants, by sharing jobs, churches, residences. Yet in practice, the
man who thought himself an Anglo-Saxon found proximity to the other
folk just come to the United States uncomfortable and distasteful and, in
his own life, sought to increase rather than to lessen the gap between his
position and theirs.

There was an escape from the horns of this unpleasant dilemma.
It was tempting to resolve the difficulty by arguing that the differences
between Americans on the one hand and Italians or Jews or Poles on the

other were so deep as to admit of no conciliation. If these other stocks were cut off by their own innate nature, by the qualities of their heredity, then the original breed was justified both in asserting the fixity of its own character and in holding off from contact with the aliens. . . .

The fear of everything alien instilled by the First World War brought to fullest flower the seeds of racist thinking. Three enormously popular books by an anthropologist, a eugenist, and a historian revealed to hundreds of thousands of horrified Nordics how their great race had been contaminated by contact with lesser breeds, dwarfed in stature, twisted in mentality, and ruthless in the pursuit of their own self-interest.

These ideas passed commonly in the language of the time. No doubt many Americans who spoke in the bitter terms of race used the words in a figurative sense or in some other way qualified their acceptance of the harsh doctrine. After all, they still recognized the validity of the American tradition of equal and open opportunities, of the Christian tradition of the brotherhood of man. Yet, if they were sometimes troubled by the contradiction, nevertheless enough of them believed fully the racist conceptions so that five million could become members of the Ku Klux Klan in the early 1920's. . . .

⚹

The activities of the Klan were an immediate threat to the immigrants and were resisted as such. But there was also a wider import to the movement. This was evidence, at last become visible, that the newcomers were among the excluded. The judgment at which the proponents of assimilation had only hinted, about which the racist thinkers had written obliquely, the Klan brought to the open. The hurt came from the fact that the mouthings of the Kleagle were not eccentricities, but only extreme statements of beliefs long on the margin of acceptance by many Americans. To the foreign-born this was demonstration of what they already suspected, that they would remain as alienated from the New World as they had become from the Old.

Much earlier the pressure of their separateness had begun to disturb the immigrants. As soon as the conception of Americanization had acquired the connotation of conformity with existing patterns, the whole way of group life of the newcomers was questioned. Their adjustment had depended upon their ability as individuals in a free society to adapt themselves to their environment through what forms they chose. The demand by their critics that the adjustment take a predetermined course seemed to question their right, as they were, to a place in American society.

Not that these people concerned themselves with theories of nationalism, but in practice the hostility of the "natives" provoked unsettling doubts about the propriety of the most innocent actions. The peasant who had become a Polish Falcon or a Son of Italy, in his own view, was acting as an American; this was not a step he could have taken at home. To subscribe to a newspaper was the act of a citizen of the New World, not of the Old, even if the journal was one of the thousand published by 1920 in languages other than English. When the immigrants heard their societies and their press described as un-American they could only conclude that they had somehow become involved in an existence that belonged neither in the old land nor in the new.

Yet the road of conformity was also barred to them. There were matters in which they wished to be like others, undistinguished from anyone else, but they never hit upon the means of becoming so. There was no pride in the surname, which in Europe had been little used, and many a new arrival was willing enough to make a change, suitable to the new country. But August Björkegren was not much better off when he called himself Burke, nor the Blumberg who became Kelly. The Lithuanians and Slovenes who moved into the Pennsylvania mining fields often endowed themselves with nomenclature of the older settlers, of the Irish and Italians there before them. In truth, these people found it difficult to know what were the "American" forms they were expected to take on.

What they did know was that they had not succeeded, that they had not established themselves to the extent that they could expect to be treated as if they belonged where they were.

If he was an alien, and poor, and in many ways helpless, still he was human, and it rankled when his dignity as a person was disregarded. He felt an undertone of acrimony in every contact with an official. Men in uniform always found him unworthy of respect; the bullying police made capital of his fear of the law; the postmen made sport of the foreign writing on his letters; the streetcar conductors laughed at his groping requests for directions. Always he was patronized as an object of charity, or almost so.

His particular enemies were the officials charged with his special oversight When misfortune drove him to seek assistance or when government regulations brought them to inspect his home, he encountered the social workers, made ruthless in the disregard of his sentiments by the certainty of their own benevolent intentions. Confident of their personal and social superiority and armed with the ideology of the sociologists who had trained them, the emissaries of the public and private agencies were bent on improving the immigrant to a point at which he would no longer recognize himself.

The man who had dealings with the social workers was often sullen and unco-operative; he disliked the necessity of becoming a case, of revealing his dependence to strangers. He was also suspicious, feared there would be no understanding of his own way of life or of his problems; and he was resentful, because the powerful outsiders were judging him by superficial standards of their own. The starched young gentleman from the settlement house took stock from the middle of the kitchen. Were there framed pictures on the walls? Was there a piano, books? He made a note for the report: *This family is not yet Americanized; they are still eating Italian food.*

The services are valuable, but taking them is degrading. It is a fine thing to learn the language of the country; but one must be treated as a child to do so. *We keep saying all the time, This is a desk, this is a door. I know it is a desk and a door. What for keep saying it all the time? My teacher is a very nice young lady, very young. She does not understand what I want to talk about or know about.*

The most anguished conflicts come from the refusal of the immigrants to see the logic of their poverty. In the office it seems reasonable enough: people incapable of supporting themselves would be better off with someone to take care of them. It is more efficient to institutionalize the destitute than to allow them, with the aid of charity, to mismanage their homes. But the ignorant poor insist on clinging to their families, threaten suicide at the mention of the Society's refuge, or even of the hospital. What help the woman gets, she is still not satisfied. Back comes the ungrateful letter. *I don't ask you to put me in a poorhouse where I have to cry for my children. I don't ask you to put them in a home and eat somebody else's bread. I can't live here without them. I am so sick for them. I could live at home and spare good eats for them. What good did you give me to send me to the poorhouse? You only want people to live like you but I will not listen to you no more.*

A few dedicated social workers, mostly women, learned to understand the values in the immigrants' own lives. In some states, as the second generation became prominent in politics, government agencies came to co-operate with and protect the newcomers. But these were rare exceptions. They scarcely softened the rule experience everywhere taught the foreign-born, that they were expected to do what they could not do—to live like others.

For the children it was not so difficult. They at least were natives and could learn how to conform; to them the settlement house was not always a threat, but sometimes an opportunity. Indeed they could adopt entire the assumption that national character was long since fixed, only seek for their own group a special place within it. Some justified their Americanism by discovery of a colonial past; within the educated second generation there began a tortuous quest for eighteenth-century antecedents that might give them a portion in American civilization in its narrower connotation. Others sought to gain a sense of participation by separating themselves from later or lower elements in the population; they became involved in agitation against the Orientals, the Negroes, and the newest immigrants, as if thus to draw closer to the truly native. Either course implied a rejection of their parents who had themselves once been green off the boat and could boast of no New World antecedents.

◦◦◦

The old folk knew then they would not come to belong, not through their own experience nor through their offspring. The only adjustment they had been able to make to life in the United States had been one that involved the separateness of their group, one that increased their awareness of the differences between themselves and the rest of the society. In that adjustment they had always suffered from the consciousness they were strangers. The demand that they assimilate, that they surrender their separateness, condemned them always to be outsiders. In practice, the free structure of American life permitted them with few restraints to go their own way, but under the shadow of a consciousness that they would never belong. They had thus completed their alienation from the culture to which they had come, as from that which they had left.

The America Trunk Comes Home

T he emigrant who once boarded a ship for America was returning, and with him came the "America trunk" that had been loaded so carefully for the outgoing voyage. In Finland, this *American arkku* was filled when it came home with everything from glass dishes to locks from a baby's first haircut to such prized American objects as a phonograph player or double-bitted axe. Its contents were the talk of the neighborhood, valued for decades as mementos.

The America trunk is an apt symbol of both emigration and remigration, of immigrants coming to America and returning to their homelands. The symbol persists, for the trunk occupies hallowed positions today in homes of third-generation Americans who cling to an image of their ancestral saga; in many European homes, similarly, the chest that came back is still revered as a remnant, a piece of that dream which once drew an emigrant across the seas.

But there was more, much more, symbolized in the America trunk. Within its recesses were tools or clothes that carried memories of hard struggles abroad. It provided a continuing connection with America, and because the United States increasingly played a leading role in international affairs, remigrants would be called on to interpret that role. They became *americani* and "Yanks"; America's importance raised their importance. And the items they valued enough to carry back in trunks would provide clues to what America's impact would be: was it tools the returners brought? or books on political theory, nationalist aspirations, labor organization, new churches? Or were the contents of the America trunk to be used to impress neighbors, perhaps to be sold to help purchase a shop or an extra piece of land? Modern students of immigration who seek answers to such questions are no different than Charles Dickens, who gazed at the emigrants returning home to Europe on his ship in 1842 and admitted that he was "curious to know their histories, and with what expectations they had gone out to America, and on what errands they were going home, and what their circumstances were.". . .

The Ubiquitous Remigrant

The trunks were but one small part, like the tip of an iceberg, of the enormity of the movement of people, objects, and ideas back to Europe.

From *Round Trip to America: The Immigrants' Return to Europe, 1880–1930* by Mark Wyman (Cornell University Press, 1993), excerpts from pp. 189, 191–197, 204–209 . Copyright © 1993 by Cornell University Press. Reprinted by permission.

Percentage rates of return ranged from 30 to 40 percent for such groups as the Italians, down to 10 percent among the Irish. Using these as a rough guide, it is possible to estimate that the total return to Europe may have been as high as four million repatriated emigrants during the 1880–1930 era of mass immigration into North America.

Examined within individual countries, these massive totals mean that one in twenty residents of Italy was a returned emigrant at the time of World War I, and shortly thereafter in a Norwegian county of heavy emigration it was found that one-fourth of all males over age fifteen had lived at least two years in America. Such high numbers signify that for the next sixty years visitors to European villages would encounter former residents of Scranton or Cleveland or Detroit, happy to describe their American experiences, wanting to know how the baseball pennant race was shaping up. . . .

A More-Reachable America

The years 1880–1930 stand out in the immigrant experience. Europeans crossed to North America in ever-increasing numbers as major improvements appeared in transportation. For generations before, however, an extensive pattern of short-term, work-seeking migration had existed in most areas of Europe, from Macedonians heading out to jobs around the Mediterranean to Irishmen and women crossing to England and Scotland for farm work. These nearby treks continued into the era of mass transatlantic emigration, as was evident in Polish totals: at the peak of Polish emigration to the United States in 1912–13, 130,000 left for America—compared to 800,000 heading for seasonal work elsewhere in Europe. It is true that development of the oceangoing steamship, coupled with an increasing flow of news and publicity about American jobs, helped shift the destinations of many short-term migrants to the West, across the Atlantic. North and South America were becoming more closely fitted into the Atlantic economy and, if this meant that midwestern pork could now be packed for consumers in Germany, it also signified that Germans from those same consuming areas, and Poles, Italians, and Finns, could easily travel to find employment in those same U.S. packing plants.

These developments welded mass migration closely to the variations, booms, and busts of American industry. To these immigrants, America became basically the site of factory employment, gang labor on a railroad section, a job underground following a coal seam. One Italian could talk of his American experiences only in terms of trains, rails, and crossties, "as if all of America was nothing but a braid of tracks," a countryman reported.

As the trio of concerns of *journey, job bunt,* and *employment* became more predictable, less dangerous, the trip to America could then be viewed as something other than a lifetime change. Like short-term labor migration within Europe, it became a means to improve life at home, through earning enough to achieve a higher status or more solid position in the village. It was not so much the start of a new life as another step in the process of social mobility. These factors in turn dictated that life in the American "workshop" would be temporary for many.

. . . In all, it is impossible to know what percentage of immigrants planned to return home, but it is not reaching far beyond the evidence to estimate that a majority in the 1880–1930 period initially expected to turn their backs on life and labor overseas once they had accumulated some wealth. Various things caused most to change their minds: in the United States these included realizing that opportunities in America outstripped those at home, gaining a better job, becoming accustomed to a higher standard of living, the arrival of news from abroad that removed the necessity for return, or gradual Americanization through learning the language, acquiring American friends, falling in love with a local girl.

Sometimes the shifts in expectations could be traced through a progression of names, as in the case of a Lithuanian immigrant couple who lived in coal towns in Pennsylvania and Illinois, always planning to return to Lithuania until they moved on to Oklahoma and decided to settle down. Their first two children were born in 1896 and 1900, when they still expected to go back to Europe, and were accordingly named Gediminas and Juozas. The third arrived in 1912, when they had become Americans. They named him Edwin.

But until that decision was made, until the carefully plotted return plans were finally abandoned, then every act, every expenditure had to be undertaken with an eye toward repatriation. This fact dawned gradually on an American in 1903 as he traveled about Italy and found that returned emigrants were much different, better persons at home; they had lived in brutal conditions in the United States because of "a feeling among them that they were merely temporizing . . .; that they had come to America to make a few hundred dollars to send or take back to Italy; and that it did not make much difference what they ate, wore or did, just so long as they got the money and got back." Their day-to-day existence in the United States would not improve until they were "drawn into the real American life" and changed their minds about going back to Europe.

Dreams of the village were especially strong among such persons; their thoughts were directed eastward toward home, even while they lived and worked in the West. This longing made assimilation difficult, and ethnic identities were further maintained by life in immigrant enclaves, blocking or discouraging connections with American institutions. Such isolation drew the fire of many Americans and settled members of the Old Immigration. Angered at the spectacle of U.S. dollars being carried overseas, they were also appalled by living conditions among those expecting to return. Labor unions suffered from the influx of these low-wage immigrants who often rejected invitations to join their fight for better wages and conditions. For years the unions approached the newcomers from two directions, often at the same time: seeking to organize the aliens while attacking them as strikebreakers and cheap competition. And the continued exodus of remigrants added to the pressure on union leaders to side with the restrictionist movement. . . .

As these immigrants held back from identifying with their new country of residence, many became part of a subculture within their own immigrant culture; that is, the temporary immigrant did even less than other immigrants to learn English, adapt to American ways, join American organizations. This reluctance further stimulated nativist attacks, which reached a climax with the restriction legislation of the postwar 1920s. Remigrants were not the only cause of the nativist surge, but their life-styles in America helped fuel the restrictionist drive and they became one of the nativists' easiest targets.

Praise and Scorn at Home

As they returned to Europe the remigrants found a mixed welcome. Con-structing new-style houses of brick rather than wood, many wore fancy clothes and endeavored to climb the social ladder. But villagers often looked askance at these people who seemed all too often to be putting on airs. One critic was the father of later emigrant Stoyan Christowe, who observed the well-dressed remigrants parading around their Bulgarian village and spat out, "An ox is an ox even if you put golden horns on him."

Their stories were often too fantastic, too farfetched. Norwegians began referring to them as *Amerikaskroner*—"tall tales from America." One man recalled his uncle's return to Norway in 1929 and his strange revelations about the things he had seen: "He told us about the Christmas trees that went round and round, he talked about streetcars, he talked of electric lights, he told of huge buildings, skyscrapers, he told us how they built them, he talked about the communications, railroads that went to every corner in the land, he told us about an industrial society which was so dif-ferent from what we knew that it was like a completely different world." Was it all believable? Perhaps not. More recently, a returned emigrant showed his Norwegian grade school pupils a U.S. postcard with a photo-graph of a giant Pacific Northwest log on a logging truck, the driver stand-ing proudly on top. When he translated the postcard's legend, "Oregon Toothpick," one child retorted, "I've always heard that Americans have big mouths."

Their money was a reality that could not be denied, however. The cash carried home, together with the vast sums mailed back by those still toiling across the ocean, helped stabilize the economies of Europe and served as a stimulus for local booms. Business experience and connections became the most obvious gains from remigration in many districts, espe-cially in Germany. Land, apartment houses, taverns, shops, and other firms were purchased by those coming home with "golden horns." For a time in Bydgoszcz, a Polish city in Pomerania, seventy agencies worked primarily to help remigrants obtain or sell properties. Two generations later the flow of retirees back from America would stimulate similar activities through their Social Security checks and factory pensions.

Most who returned in the 1880–1930 era went into agriculture, and this activity was at the center of much of the debate over their impact. Certainly agriculture was extremely backward in many areas; one estimate by returning Norwegians was that farming in Norway was fifty years behind that in the United States. But would returned emigrants be the ones to launch the required changes? Remigrants rushed to buy farmland, and large-scale commercialization of land became one of the most noted results of the vast emigration and return. But early evidence indicated that remigrants then continued or even expanded traditional and backward farming practices.

In contrast, areas such as Prussia and the English Midlands, where farm progress was extensive in the late nineteenth century, featured either the growth of larger land units with major investments of capital or the contrary development of smaller but more specialized farms that used the latest in farm technology and benefited from growing consumer demand. A student of the transformation of British agriculture notes increased farming complexity through use of artificial manures and new seeds and livestock breeds and adds that this "no doubt . . . also required flexibility of mind." But flexibility of mind regarding agricultural improvements may have been missing among many remigrants coming back to traditional farming in such, areas as southern Italy or Poland. Few had worked on American farms, and this fact alone predicted that their impact on the Continent's agriculture would be minimal. Sporadic improvements and changes were widely publicized, but these were unusual, like the tomatoes planted by some Finns or the new flowers appearing in Polish gardens. Only in certain areas, such as parts of Scandinavia, could it be said that the remigrants were a definite mainstay of drives to modernize agriculture.

But in other occupations and situations, where emigrants had been able to learn American methods, improvements were obvious. To begin with, more vigorous work habits were widely noted. Also, many carried home sewing machines, which led to improvements in clothing, and holiday garb began to be worn more regularly. Homemaking benefited: when Irish women returned, they refused to continue traditional hearth cooking because it only permitted meat to be boiled; soon they installed grates or bought ranges. Personal hygiene improved, and a Hungarian report indicated that remigrants even kept their windows open at night, rejecting the traditional belief that night air held evils.

Many threw themselves into various campaigns for government change: Irish Home Rulers sought to throw off British control, Slovaks and Croatians pushed for separate nations, some Finns who had attended the Duluth Work People's College wanted to destroy capitalism. Others agitated for the development of public schools, and the remigrants' presence helped spread English through Gaelic-speaking areas of Ireland and in many other districts across Europe. Returned emigrants began to appear as members of village councils, school boards, even national legislatures; three of them became prime ministers, of Norway, Latvia, and Finland. . . .

Conclusions

In an examination of the remigrant from 1880 to 1930, before leaving Europe, at work in America, and after the return home, nine broad conclusions emerge:

1. The temporary immigrant was in truth far different from the immigrant who planned to stay. The expectations of any immigrant were all-important in directing his or her job-seeking, assimilation, and adjustment to American life, and the immigrant who stepped onto American sail planning permanent residence saw these goals differently than did the short-term industrial migrant. The latter was basically a *sojourner,* defined by sociologists as a deviant form of the stranger, who remains psychologically in his homeland while living somewhere else, culturally isolated, tied physically but not mentally to a job. He may have changed his mind eventually, but until that point he lived the life of one who saw his future back in Europe.

Employment became the critical part of the remigrant's American existence. Like a New England girl arriving to work briefly in the Lowell mills in the 1830s, or a Turkish *Gastarbeiter* in Germany today, the temporary industrial migrant in the 1880–1930 period saw the world through different eyes than did (or does) the worker planning to remain. To ignore this fact and its implications is to miss a major facet of immigration's impact and an important explanation of immigrants' failure to assimilate despite lengthy residence abroad. Failing to take it into account would also make it difficult to understand why so many who returned home took up farming rather than the industrial occupations they had known overseas. If one task of the historian is to see the past from different angles, then following the contrary path of the temporary immigrant can provide an important new perspective.

2. The American immigration story becomes less unified, more diverse, when remigrants are considered within the broad picture of the peopling of a continent. There was little in common between the Bohemian family settling the Nebraska prairies in the 1890s and Bohemian men arriving for a year's work in a Chicago stockyard. Assimilation was soon forced on those farming in Nebraska; it was not even a remote goal of most of those lining up for their wages each fortnight in Chicago. One immigrant is not always equal to another—an obvious fact, but one made both more apparent and more significant when the remigrant experience is considered. . . .

3. There were many Americas contained within the broad vision of the United States by the 1880s, but America as the symbol of economic opportunity increasingly became uppermost for immigrants, especially those planning a temporary stay. Democracy was of little importance to a sojourner dreaming of adding to his piece of earth in the Mezzogiorno. When economic opportunity and democracy were seen as two branches of the same trunk, however, one could buttress the other in forming an image of the nation. But a remigrant who had witnessed few examples of democracy in his twelve-hour days in a steel mill would consider America

in a different light than would another new resident escaping from religious unrest and finding herself in the competitive free-for-all of U.S. church denominations. Economic opportunity became the representative American symbol to millions.

4. The basis of American nativism was not opposition to return migration, but it gained several major arguments in the course of reacting to temporary immigrants. Nativists began to erupt in anger as thousands and thousands of short-term residents avoided assimilation and escaped abroad with their American earnings. The exodus goaded many Americans into ever stronger condemnations of immigration in general, and the identification of European remigrants with Chinese sojourners became complete. This provided an opening for earlier, permanent immigrants to condemn later arrivals and to become in effect immigrant nativists. Anti-foreign sentiment among U.S. labor groups leaned especially hard on the temporary immigrant.

5. The striving for status—to hold onto a vanishing position, or even to climb higher—emerges as one of the main forces behind remigration as well as emigration. Remigrants often left Europe to seek a higher status at home; they did not seek a permanent existence and better status in America. The New World may have represented a horn of plenty, but its wealth would be more useful back in Europe. Basic subsistence could be met, and after that the possibility of becoming landowners of importance in the village. Immigrants knew enough about life in the United States to understand the saying, "America for the oxen, Europe for the peasant." It was in Europe, not America, that the opportunity to reach a new level of existence waited.

6. The remigrant's importance in stimulating further immigration may have eclipsed even that of the much-maligned steamship agent. A large-scale exodus developed mainly from European areas where there had been an earlier emigration, which had produced a return flow of successes with money to purchase land and to construct "American houses." These acts promoted America with more impact than did handbills posted on village walls. There is also evidence of what might be called "emigration families," providing members from each generation who spent time in the United States and then returned, their tales handed down to stimulate others to try America later. The process was then repeated, generation after generation, and the remigrant ancestors became long-term role models. Their example competed with the emigrant letter as the chief propagandist of emigration. And the picture of America as a horn of plenty became indelibly fastened on a people who grew up hearing American stories around the winter hearth.

7. The return flow must be counted as a major reason that Europe's enormous exodus to America did not result in a net loss for the home society. Some form of general decline might have been expected for a continent that lost 36 million of its most active and future-oriented citizens to the United States from 1820 to 1975. The same could have been predicted for other regions that sent their people to America; one might even apply

it to Mexico and the Caribbean nations today. But instead of causing a deterioration, the era of mass emigration proved overall to be one of general advance and progress for the people of many nations. This pattern continues. Certainly many things, tangible and intangible, have contributed to this result, but one is the extensive return flow of people, money, and ideas. As a Polish priest concluded from his study of the emigration from Miejsce parish in 1883, the returns from America meant that the exodus was "not a loss but a gain for this province." It could be said for most of Europe.

The Continent benefited as well from the return of organizational and political skills, as men and women of all ideologies and aspirations came back to launch labor unions and community organizations and to become involved in political affairs. Churches were challenged and new philosophies began to circulate. When Finland and Latvia achieved independence amid scenes of enormous chaos, leadership in each new country fell to those already experienced in labor and political struggles in America. Norway also chose a remigrant as its prime minister to lead the country through the dark days of depression and World War II. Many others coming back occupied government posts in municipalities as well as in national regimes.

The remigrants brought change in many forms. New words were carried home: modern Finnish has been enriched by many remigrant words and phrases, according to recent studies. Beyond this, many of those returning to Europe displayed an openness, an attitude that shook off the old and helped transform the peasant world. And remigration contributed further to a mingling of cultures which encouraged change as well as helping bring a gradual integration of the cultures of Europe and America.

The United States is more than just people transferred from Europe; Europe is guided by more than influences from America. But the two-way exchange was one crucial factor in the historical development of both, and the remigrant helped in both directions, a continuing link between two cultures.

8. American "exceptionalism," the view that the American experience has been unique and that developments in the United States were basically different from those elsewhere, is dealt a further blow by the remigration story. The United States was not a land where every immigrant came to stay; it was a country seen by many foreigners as a means rather than an end. As such, the American immigration pageant contained many scenes known elsewhere, for temporary stays as well as permanent moves have long been part of human migrations.

Parallels are numerous. Just as was often the case in the United States, temporary migrants were unpopular in the Ruhr, where German unions fought Poles, employers put aliens in the dirtiest jobs, and officials sought their removal. Swiss workers assaulted Italians in 1896, the government meanwhile blocked their naturalization, and welfare groups refused to give aid. This was nativism run wild. Riots erupted against Italian workers in France from the 1880s on; in 1893, fifty Italians were killed and 150 wounded during an attack by French miners at the Aigues-Mortes salt-works. There was physical violence in the United States, but as in Europe the opposition to those planning to return usually took other forms: unions sought their dismissal, politicians argued for bans on their employment, and editorial writers aimed darts at those who carried off national wealth. . . .

9. Finally, the story of the returned immigrant brings the historian face to face with the importance of human feelings, human emotions, in world events. Scholars often stress impersonal forces when discussing developments involving masses of people. But the fact that several million immigrants could turn around and leave a land with a higher standard of living and all the glitter of modernization, to cross the ocean again and return to a backward peasant village, with its distinctive culture and traditions, stands as supreme testimony to the pull of kin and home.

The Psalmist cried, "How shall we sing the Lord's song in a strange land?" And the longing to be within the family circle, in the familiar pathways and fields of home, has always been part of the human condition. The human heart must be given equal rank here with cold economic statistics and the pleadings of steamship agents. For the sense of being lost, away from moorings, left thousands of immigrants with the feeling that nothing seemed right in the New World—not holidays, not religious rites, not even the summer sunrise. They like the Psalmist felt lost in a strange land. The Swedish novelist of emigration, Vilhelm Moberg, reflected on these feelings in his autobiographical novel *A Time on Earth;*

> Man must have a root in the world; he must belong somewhere. He cannot abandon the land where he was born and adopt another country as his birthplace. Prattle about old and new mother countries is prattle only, and a lie. Either I have a country of my own, or I have not. Mother country is singular, never plural.
>
> The country you knew as child and young man was the country you left. That was your fate; you could never find another homeland.

In the final analysis, the story of the returned immigrants is a record of the endurance of home and family ties. It provides further evidence that, for many, immigration demonstrated the strength and unity of the family—both in going to America and in returning—rather than the family's weakening or destruction. For it was to rejoin their people, to walk again on their own land, to sit in the parish church once more, that the temporary immigrants repacked their America trunks and booked passage again, this time for home. The journey to America had been round-trip. And as they had helped shape life in the United States, its world of work, its image of itself and of foreigners, now they would affect the lives of their own families, their villages, their homelands. It would be a different future on both continents because of the returned immigrants.

POSTSCRIPT

Were Late-Nineteenth-Century Immigrants "Uprooted"?

Oscar Handlin has been recognized as the most influential scholar on immigration history since his doctoral dissertation won the Dunning Prize when he was only twenty-six years old. Published as *Boston's Immigrants: A Study in Acculturation* (Harvard University Press, 1941), this was the first study of immigration to integrate sociological concepts within a historical framework. A decade later, Handlin published *The Uprooted*, in which he combined the interdisciplinary framework with a personal narrative of the immigrants' history. Although many historians criticized this approach, the book earned Handlin a Pulitzer Prize.

John Bodnar's *The Transplanted*, while offering a contrasting metaphor for the immigration experience to the United States, shares with Handlin's work an attempt to present a general account of that experience, to portray the immigrants in a sympathetic light and to employ an interdisciplinary approach by borrowing concepts from the social sciences. Handlin and Bodnar, however, differ in their perspectives about America's ethnic past. Handlin views the immigrants as people who were removed from their particular Old World cultures and who assimilated into the New World value system within two generations. In contrast, Bodnar argues that some first-generation immigrants may have shed their traditional culture quickly upon arrival in the United States, but more continued to maintain a viable lifestyle in their adopted homeland that focused upon the family household and the neighboring ethnic community. "Not solely traditional, modern or working class," says Bodnar, "it was a dynamic culture, constantly responding to changing needs and opportunities and grounded in a deep sense of pragmatism and mutual assistance."

The Harvard Encyclopedia of American Ethnic Groups (Harvard University Press, 1980), edited by Stephan Thernstrom and Oscar Handlin, is a valuable collection of articles on every ethnic group in the United States. It also contains twenty-nine thematic essays on such subjects as prejudice, assimilation, and folklore. Also useful and more manageable is Stephanie Bernardo, *The Ethnic Almanac* (Doubleday, 1981), whose purpose is to "amuse, inform and entertain you with facts about your heritage and that of your friends, neighbors and relatives." Leonard Dinnerstein and David Reimers's *Ethnic Americans: A History of Immigration and Assimilation,* 2nd ed. (Harper & Row, 1982), is a short but accurate text, while Joe R. Feagan's *Racial and Ethnic Relations,* 2nd ed. (Prentice Hall, 1985), is a useful sociological text that examines the major ethnic groups through assimilationist and power-conflict models.

In the last generation, dozens of studies have focused on the experiences of particular immigrant groups in the United States. See, for example, Moses Rischin, *The Promised City: New York's Jews, 1870–1914* (Harvard University Press, 1962); Jack Chen, *The Chinese in America* (Harper & Row, 1980); Matt S. Meier and Feliciano Rivera, *The Chicanos: A History of Mexican Americans* (Hill and Wang, 1972); Humbert Nelli, *Italians in Chicago, 1880–1930: A Study of Ethnic Mobility* (Oxford University Press, 1970); and Thomas Kessner, *The Golden Door: Italian and Jewish Immigrant Mobility in New York City, 1880–1915* (Oxford University Press, 1977). The reaction to the immigration of the late nineteenth century can be observed in Jacob Riis's contemporary account of New York City, *How the Other Half Lives* (1890; reprint, Hill and Wang, 1970), and in John Higham's *Strangers in the Land: Patterns of American Nativism, 1860–1925* (Rutgers University Press, 1955), which is considered the best work on anti-immigrant prejudice in this time period.

ISSUE 5

Was City Government in Late-Nineteenth-Century America a "Conspicuous Failure"?

YES: Ernest S. Griffith, from *A History of American City Government: The Conspicuous Failure, 1870–1900* (National Civic League Press, 1974)

NO: Jon C. Teaford, from *The Unheralded Triumph: City Government in America, 1860–1900* (Johns Hopkins University Press, 1984)

ISSUE SUMMARY

YES: Professor of political science and political economy Ernest S. Griffith (1896–1981) focuses upon illegal and unethical operations of the political machine and concludes that the governments controlled by the bosses represented a betrayal of the public trust.

NO: Professor of history Jon C. Teaford argues that scholars traditionally have overlooked the remarkable success that municipal governments in the late nineteenth century achieved in dealing with the challenges presented by rapid urbanization.

During the late nineteenth century, American farmers based their grievances on revolutionary changes that had occurred in the post–Civil War United States. Specifically, they saw themselves as victims of an industrial wave that had swept over the nation and submerged their rural, agricultural world in the undertow. Indeed, the values, attitudes, and interests of all Americans were affected dramatically by the rapid urbanization that accompanied industrial growth. The result was the creation of the modern city, with its coordinated network of economic development, which emphasized mass production and mass consumption.

In the years from 1860 to 1920, the number of urban residents in the United States increased much more rapidly than the national population as a whole. For example, the Census Bureau reported in 1920 that the United States housed 105,711,000 people, three times the number living in the country on the eve of the Civil War. Urban dwellers, however, increased ninefold during the same period. The number of "urban" places (incorporated towns with 2,500 or more residents, or unincorporated areas with at least 2,500 people per square mile) increased from 392 in 1860 to 2,722 in 1920. Cities with populations in excess of 100,000 increased from 9 in 1860 to 68 in 1920.

Reflecting many of the characteristics of "modern" America, these industrial cities produced a number of problems for the people who lived in them—problems associated with fire and police protection, sanitation, utilities, and a wide range of social services. These coincided with increased concerns over employment opportunities and demands for transportation and housing improvements. Typically, municipal government became the clearinghouse for such demands. What was the nature of city government in the late-nineteenth-century United States? How effectively were American cities governed? To what extent did municipal leaders listen to and redress the grievances of urban dwellers? In light of James Lord Bryce's blunt statement in 1888 that city government in the United States was a "conspicuous failure," it is worthwhile to explore scholarly assessments of Bryce's conclusion.

In the following selection, Ernest S. Griffith surveys the nature of municipal government in the last three decades of the nineteenth century and concludes that city politics was consumed by a "cancer of corruption" that predominated in the years from 1880 to 1893. He identifies numerous factors that contributed to this unethical environment, as well as the disreputable and illegal lengths gone to that perpetuated the power of the bosses but prevented city government from operating in the true interest of the people.

In the second selection, Jon C. Teaford contends that scholars like Griffith are too eager to condemn the activities of late-nineteenth-century municipal governments without recognizing their accomplishments. Teaford argues that, although there were numerous shortcomings, American city dwellers enjoyed a higher standard of public services than any other urban residents in the world. Also, in contrast to the portrait of boss dominance presented by Griffith and others, Teaford maintains that authority was widely distributed among various groups that peacefully coexisted with one another. For Teaford, nineteenth-century cities failed to develop a political image but succeeded to a remarkable degree in meeting the needs of those who were dependent upon them.

YES

Ernest S. Griffith

The Cancer of Corruption

Introduction

Corruption may be defined as personal profit at the expense of the public—stealing and use of office for private gain, including the giving and taking of bribes outside of the law. More broadly defined, it is any antisocial conduct that uses government as an instrument. Its twilight zone is never the same from age to age, from community to community, or even from person to person. . . .

Historically, the motivations of the electorate, the uses to which tax money and campaign contributions were put, the pressures of reward and punishment to which candidates and officeholders were subjected, were never very far from the gray zone in which the line between the corrupt and the ethical—or even the legal—had somehow to be drawn. Votes were "coin of the realm" in a democracy; office holding or power-wielding was secured by votes. They might be freely and intelligently given; they might be the result of propaganda, friendship, or pressure; they might be purchased by money or otherwise; they might be manufactured out of election frauds. Those who were members of the government, visible or invisible, were ultimately dependent on the voters for their opportunity to serve, for their livelihood, for the chance to steal or betray. These conditions existed in the late nineteenth century; with differing emphases they still exist today.

What, then, determined whether a late-nineteenth-century city government was corrupt or ethical, or something in between? Ethically speaking, the nadir of American city government was probably reached in the years between 1880 and 1893. Why and how? There was obviously no one answer. The time has long since passed when municipal reformers, not to mention historians, believed there was a single answer. There was present a highly complex situation—a *Gestalt*, or pattern—never identical in any two places, but bearing a family resemblance in most respects. The path to better municipal governance was long and difficult because of this very complexity. The story of the 1890's and of the Progressive Era of the first twelve or fifteen years of the twentieth century was the story of a thousand battles on a thousand fronts—the unraveling of a refractory network of unsuitable charters and procedures, of a human nature that at times led to despair, of an economic order that put a premium on greed, of a social order of class and ethnic divisions reflected often in incompatible value systems—all infinitely complicated by rapidity of growth and population mobility. . . .

Patronage

. . . [H]ow are we to account for the corrupt machine in the first place, and for what came to be its endemic character in American cities for two or three decades? This is part of a broader analysis, and will be undertaken presently. As always, in the end the legacy of a corrupt and corrupting regime was a malaise of suspicion, discouragement, and blunted ideals in society as a whole.

In examining the fact of corruption, it was obvious that the city—any city, good or bad—provided livelihood for scores, hundreds, even thousands of people directly employed. They would fight if their livelihood were threatened. There were also large numbers dependent upon the city for contracts, privileges, and immunities. Not as sharply defined, and often overlapping one or both of these categories, were persons who served as organizers, brokers, or instruments of these other two groups, and whose livelihoods therefore also depended upon the city. They, too, would fight to attain, keep, or augment this livelihood, and probably the sense of power (and occasionally the constructive achievements) that their positions carried with them. They were the "machine," the "ring," the "boss," the professional politician, the political lawyer. This is to say, for many people (as regards the city) employment, power, and access to those with power were matters of economic life or death for themselves and their families—and, if these same people were wholly self-seeking, to them the end justified the means.

First, consider the municipal employees. "To the victors belong the spoils"—the party faction and machine rewarded their own and punished the others. In 1889 the mayor of Los Angeles appointed all of his six sons to the police force, but this helped to defeat him in the next election. In the smaller cities, and in the larger ones before skills seemed essential, a change of administration or party was the signal for wholesale dismissals and wholesale patronage. This fact created the strongest incentive for those currently employed to work for the retention in power of those influential in their employment; that they had so worked constituted a logical basis for their dismissal; given the success of the opposing candidates. That the city might suffer in both processes was unimportant to those whose livelihood was at stake in the outcome of the struggle. Those involved, in many instances, would not even respect the position of school teacher, and could usually find ways and means to subvert the civil service laws when they emerged, in intent if not in formal ritual. In Brooklyn, for example, during the Daniel Whitney administration of 1885, only favored candidates were informed of the dates of the examinations in time to apply. Examinations were then leniently graded, to put it mildly. One illiterate received a grade of 97.5 per cent on a written test. About 1890, each member of the Boston city council received a certain number of tickets corresponding to his quota of men employed by the city. No one was eligible without such a ticket, and existing employees were discharged to make room if necessary.

Sale of Privileges and Immunities

As regards the sale for cash of privileges and immunities, many politicians and officials did not stop with the twilight zone of liquor violations, gambling, and prostitution, but went on to exploit what would be regarded as crime in any language or society. Denver (incidentally, at least until the 1960's) was one of the worst. From the late 1880's until 1922, Lou Blonger, king of the city's underworld, held the police department in his grasp. For many of these years he had a direct line to the chief of police, and his orders were "law." Criminals were never molested if they operated outside the city limits, and often not within the limits, either. He contributed liberally to the campaign funds of both parties, those of the district attorneys being especially favored. Blonger was sent to jail in 1922 by Philip Van Cise, a district attorney who had refused his conditional campaign contribution of $25,000.

Yet, it was the insatiable appetite of men for liquor, sex, and the excitement and eternal hope of gambling that proved by all the odds the most refractory and the most corrupting day-to-day element. . . .

The police of most cities, and the politicians and officials, took graft or campaign contributions from the liquor interests so that they would overlook violations of the law. Judging from extant material of the period, corruption by the liquor trade occurred more frequently than any other. Over and over again the question of enforcement of whatever laws existed was an issue at the polls. The fact was that, at this time, the trade did not want *any* regulation and resented all but the most nominal license fee, unless the license in effect granted a neighborhood semimonopoly, and increased profitability accordingly. It was prepared to fight and pay for its privileges. Council membership was literally jammed with saloon keepers, and Buffalo (1880) was not too exceptional in having a brewer as mayor. Apparently in one instance (in Nebraska), the liquor interests resorted to assassination of the clerk of the U.S. Federal Circuit Court in revenge for his part in the fight against them.

More clearly illegal, because here it was not a question of hours of sale but of its right to exist, was commercial gambling. State laws and even municipal ordinances were fairly usual in prohibiting it, but these laws were sustained neither by enforcement nor by public opinion. If the public opinion calling for enforcement was present, the requisite ethical standard was not there that would preclude the offering and accepting of the bribes that made the continuance of gambling possible—except for an occasional spasm of raids and reform.

Oklahoma City will serve as a case study. At one point gambling houses regularly paid one fine a month. Four-fifths of the businessmen refused to answer whether they would favor closing such joints; going on record either way would hurt their business. Citing District Attorney William T. Jerome's views of attempts to secure enforcement of this type of law, one writer commented: "The corrupt politician welcomes the puritan as an ally. He sees in laws that cannot and will not be permanently enforced a yearly revenue in money and in power."

The situation regarding commercialized vice was similar. Laws and ordinances forbidding brothels were on the statute books. Brothels existed in every large city and most of the smaller ones. Especially in the Western cities where men greatly outnumbered women, they appeared in large numbers, and the same might be said of the commercial centers and the seaport towns. A boss like Boies Penrose of Philadelphia patronized them. So, in fact, did a number of presumably otherwise respectable citizens. Many of this last group also drew rent from the brothels.

What this meant to the city government of a place like Seattle may be illustrated by an episode in 1892:

> The police department thought it had a vested property right in the collections from prostitutes and gamblers. The new mayor, Ronald, was waited on almost immediately by a group of high ranking police officers who asked him how much of a cut he wanted out of the monthly "pay off" for gambling and prostitution. "Not a cent! Moreover, there isn't going to be any collection or places that pay protection money," he said as he pounded the table. The committee patiently explained that it was "unofficial licensing," a very effective way to control crime. The mayor exploded again and one of the captains took out a revolver and dropped it on the table. "Somebody is going to get hurt—maybe." The mayor tried as hard as ever anyone could to clean up, but found it impossible. He was powerless because he had no real support. He resigned in less than a year.

For the depths of degradation into which the combination of lust and greed can sink a city government, one can only cite the example of Kansas City, where girls at the municipal farm were sold by the politicians (who of course pocketed the money) and sent to brothels in New Orleans. . . .

Each city, as the pressures of urban living forced regulation, found itself under conflicting demands. The people as a whole probably wanted "nuisances" cleared up—unsanitary dwellings, cattle in the streets, sign encroachments, garbage left around, and a hundred other annoying matters—the counterpart in today's world of illegal parking. But to the particular person involved, there was an interest in leaving things as they were—an interest for which he was prepared to pay by a tip or a vote. Compulsory education laws ran up against parents who regarded them as a violation of their God-given right to employ their children as they wished. Political revenge might well await the enforcer—the truant officer, health officer, inspector of meat, dairies, or housing, or policeman. Political and often pecuniary rewards awaited those who would overlook matters of this type. There were other favors, tips on the location of a proposed public improvement or on the location of a road or a park relevant to real estate value. These were advantageous to the official and his friends to know and to control for their own personal profit. Real estate profit through advance notice or an actual share in the decision on a municipal improvement or purchase was one of the most lucrative perquisites of councilors or the "ring" members. A special instance of this was the desire of many members of Congress for seats on the low-status District of Columbia Committee so as to secure advance information as to what would be profitable real estate purchases in the District. In general, these examples came under the heading of "honest graft" in those days, as not necessarily costing the city treasury an undue amount. The term was invented by George W. Plunkett of Tammany as a rationalization.

Graft From Contracts and Franchises

Quite otherwise were the profits, direct and indirect, from lucrative city contracts. Probably in the majority of cities there was a tacit understanding that a favored contractor would "kick back" a substantial amount (10 per cent or more being quite usual) either to party campaign funds for which accounting was rare, as fees to a "political lawyer," with the ultimate distribution uncertain, or as out-and-out bribes to those with the power to make the decisions. There were always any number of devices to evade the intent of the law, even in situations where the law called for competitive bidding. Pittsburgh for years found that William Flinn, one of its two bosses, was always the lowest "responsible" bidder for contracts. In other instances, specifications were such that only the favored one could meet them. In New Orleans, around 1890, in spite of the protests of the property owners, almost all paving was with rosetta gravel (in which one man had a monopoly). In other cases, the lowest bid was accepted, but there would be advance assurance (private and arranged) that the inspectors would not insist that the contractor meet the specifications. Contractors in Portland (Oregon) in 1893 whose men voted "right" were laxly supervised. In still other instances, the bidders themselves formed rings, bid high, and arranged for distribution of the contracts among themselves. This practice seems to have been a particular bent among paving contractors. William Gabriel of Cleveland, high in Republican circles, will serve as an example. This was not incompatible with generous bribes to municipal officials or rings as well. Graft in contracts extended to the schools—to their construction and to the textbooks purchased. Things were probably not so flagrant in Cleveland, where campaign contributions and not bribes were the favored means of business.

Franchises and privileges for the railroads and the various utilities came to be special sources of demoralization, particularly for the councils that usually had the responsibility for granting them. Initially, a community welcomed the railroad and even subsidized its coming. With growing urbanization, it looked forward to waterworks, lighting (gas or electricity), street cars (horse or cable), and eventually electricity and the telephone. The earliest of the franchises were likely to be most liberal with respect to rate allowed, duration, and service rendered. The cities wanted the utilities and often urged their coming. Later, as the latter proved enormously profitable, the stakes grew high, and betrayal of the public interest probably took place in the majority of cases. Power to grant franchises greatly increased the desirability of membership on the council. Hazen Pingree, mayor of Detroit in the early 1890's wrote:

> My experiences in fighting monopolistic corporations as mayor of Detroit, and in endeavoring to save to the people some of their right as against their greed, have further convinced me that they, the corporations, are responsible for nearly all the thieving and boodling with which cities are made to suffer from their servants. They seek almost uniformly to secure what they want by means of bribes, and in this way they corrupt our councils and commissions.

Providence, in the 1890's allowed only property owners to vote. They elected businessmen to the city council. This council then awarded Nelson Aldrich, the state boss, a perpetual franchise, which he sold out at an enormous profit. He went to the Senate through wholesale bribery of rural voters, with money contributed by the sugar magnates for whom as congressman he had arranged a protective tariff. The city of Pawtucket, which sought to block a franchise, was overridden by the rurally dominated state legislature.

It was Lincoln Steffens who later dramatized beyond any forgetting the unholy link between the protected underworld, the city governments, and the portion of the business community in search of contracts and franchises—a link found in city after city. The story of his exposures belongs to the Progressive Era. At the time, these betrayals of the public interest were either not known or, if known, were enjoyed and shared, shrugged off and rationalized, or endured in futile fury.

Two or three further examples of documented franchise bribery might be cited. In 1884, in New York City, the Broadway Surface Railroad paid $25,000 to each of eighteen alderman and received the franchise. The rival company had offered the *city* $1 million. Another corporation set aside $100,000 to buy the council. The street-car companies of Indianapolis contributed to both political parties. So it went in city after city.

Some other examples of business corruption might be cited. Governor John P. Altgeld of Illinois sent a message (1895) to the state legislature, calling attention to the fantastically low rents paid by newspapers for school lands. In a most complex arrangement involving shipping companies, boarding-house keepers, "crimps" (recruiters of seamen), and the city authorities, the San Francisco waterfront instituted a reign of near-peonage, in which seamen were grossly overcharged for their lodging and shore "amenities," prevented from organized resistance, and virtually terrorized and blackmailed into signing on the ships again. In the early 1870's, local speculators of Dubuque, including two former mayors, bought up city bonds for a small amount and held out for redemption at par. Favored banks (that is, those contributing through appropriate channels to the city treasurer, the party, or the boss) received city deposits without having to pay interest thereon, or, as in Pittsburgh, paying the interest to the politicians. Finally, the employer power structure threw its weight and its funds in support of almost any administration that would protect strikebreakers, break up "radical" gatherings, and otherwise preserve the "American system" against alien ideas—this, without reference to the extent of the known corruption of the administration.

Theft, Assessment Favoritism, "Kickbacks," "Rake-Offs"

As might be expected, there were a number of examples of actual theft, most frequently by a city treasurer. Judges would occasionally keep fines. A certain amount of this was to be expected in an age of ruthless money-making when business ethics condoned all kinds of sharp practices in the private sector. What was more discouraging was that many of these thieves remained unpunished, as the machine with its frequent control over the courts protected its own. City officials of Spokane even stole funds contributed for relief after its great fire (1889).

How widespread was political favoritism in tax assessment would be extraordinarily difficult to determine. The practice of underassessment across the board to avoid litigation was almost universal, and in some communities it had a statutory base. Certainly many corporations were favored, in part because they were deemed an asset to the community's economic life. What was more probable was the widespread fear that, if a person were to criticize the city administration, he would find his underassessment raised. This particular form of blackmail took place in blatant fashion at one time in Jersey City. It also occurred under Park Board administration in the Bronx in 1874. From time to time, there would be exposures in the local press of assessment anomalies, but the press was itself vulnerable to punitive retaliation of this type because of its frequent underassessment.

The practice of compensating certain employees by fees instead of fixed salaries lingered on, in spite of or often because of the large amounts of money involved. Such employees were usually expected, by virtue of their election or appointment, to "kick back" a substantial portion to the party organization. Such "kickbacks" from the receiver of taxes amounted in Philadelphia to $200,000 in one of the years after 1873—divided among the small number who constituted the gas-house ring. Other compensations by the fee system were abandoned in 1873, and the employees were put on salaries. Some nominations and appointments were sold, with the receipts going, it was hoped, to the party campaign funds, concerning the use of which there was rarely in these days any effective accounting.

Political assessments of city employees probably ruled in the majority of the cities.

How much graft in fact found its way into the pockets of the city employees for their betrayal of trust or, for that matter, for services they should have rendered in any event, how much "rake-off" the ring or the boss took, will never be known. What was graft and what was "rake-off" shaded into a gray zone after a while. The amount must have been colossal in the cities—certainly enough, had it been dedicated to municipal administration, to have enhanced efficiency and service enormously, or to have cut the tax rate drastically. Utility rates would have tumbled and service improved. . . .

Extortion and Blackmail

Extortion and blackmail, if not standard practice, were frequent enough to call for comment. Once in a while, as in Fort Worth (1877), they were used in an intriguing and perhaps constructive fashion. It was proposed that the sale of intoxicants be forbidden at the theaters. The ordinance was tabled, with the notation that it would be passed unless one of the theater owners paid his taxes.

In Brooklyn during the Whitney administration, the head of the fire department blocked an electric franchise until he was given one-fifth of the company's stock and several other politicians had taken a cut.

The newspapers were particularly vulnerable to blackmail. A threat of loss of the city's advertising was a marvelous silencer. In Tacoma (1889), enough businessmen believed a particular gambling house was a community asset that the newspaper that had denounced its protected status as a result lost heavily in both advertising and circulation.

The gangs of Detroit seemed to be immune in the 1880's and able to bring about the promotion or dismissal of a policeman. Sailors, tugmen, longshoremen made up the bulk of their personnel. In the early 1880's in Indianapolis, citizens were arrested on trumped-up charges and fined by judges who at that time were paid by the fines.

Police and the Courts

. . . [D]ifficulties stemmed from the key role played by the police in the electoral process, the graft from the under-world, and the desire on the part of the allegedly more respectable for immunities. In Tacoma, the mayor reprimanded the chief of police for raiding a brothel in which a number of the city's influential men were found. All these factors meant that in city after city the police force was really regarded as an adjunct of the political party or machine. In some of the smaller cities, the patronage aspect was expressed in extreme form. For example, until 1891 each new mayor of Wilmington (Delaware) appointed a new set of policemen, usually of his own party.

Nor were the courts immune as adjuncts to corruption. The district attorney and the judges, especially the local ones, were usually elected, and by the same processes as the mayors and councils. The same network of political and corrupt immunities that pervaded the police and stemmed from the rings and other politicians was present in the courts. Four hazards to justice were thus in a sense vulnerable to pressure and purchase—the stages of arrest, prosecution, the verdicts (and delays) of the judge, and the possibilities of a packed or bribed jury. William Howard Taft commented at a later date as follows:

> [The] administration of criminal law is a disgrace to our civilization, and the prevalence of crime and fraud, which here is greatly in excess of that in European countries, is due largely to the failure of the law to bring criminals to justice.

Quite apart from overt corruption, there were numerous ways in which courts could reward the party faithful, such as by appointment as favored bondsmen, stenographers, or auctioneers.

It was not surprising that an exasperated and otherwise respectable public occasionally fought back by violent means. In Cincinnati (1884), so flagrant had been the court delays and acquittals that a mass meeting, held to protest the situation, evolved into a mob bent on direct action. They burned the courthouse and attempted to storm the jail. For days the mob ruled. Police and militia failed, and only federal troops finally restored order. There were over fifty deaths. In Dallas, in the early 1880's, the "respectable" element, despairing of action by the city government in closing some of the worst resorts, took to burning them. Acquittal of the murderers of the chief of police of New Orleans by a probably corrupted jury was followed by lynchings. . . .

Summary Scenario

This in general was the scenario of most American cities about 1890: fitful reforms, usually not lasting; charters hopelessly tangled, with no agreement on remedies; civil service laws circumvented in the mad search for patronage opportunities; election frauds virtually normal; an underworld capitalizing on man's appetites and finding it easy to purchase allies in the police and the politician; countless opportunities for actual theft; business carrying over its disgraceful private ethics into subverting city government for its own ends, and city officials competing to obtain the opportunity to be lucratively subverted; citizens who might be expected to lead reforms generally indifferent, discouraged, frightened, and without the time necessary to give to the effort; a community with conflicting value systems into which the exploiter entered, albeit with an understanding and a sympathy denied to those from another class; ballots complicated; a nomination process seemingly built to invite control by the self-seeking; sinecures used to provide fulltime workers for the party machine; state governments ready to step in to aid in the corruption if local effort proved inadequate; confusion over the claims of party loyalty; a press often intimidated and frequently venal; countless opportunities to make decisions that would favor certain real estate over other locations; a burgeoning population rapidly urbanizing and dragging in its train innumerable problems of municipal services and aspirations.

For the unraveling of this tangled mess, the reformer and the career administrator had no acceptable philosophy.

Jon C. Teaford  **NO**

Trumpeted Failures and Unheralded Triumphs

In 1888 the British observer James Bryce proclaimed that "there is no denying that the government of cities is the one conspicuous failure of the United States." With this pronouncement he summed up the feelings of a host of Americans. In New York City, residents along mansion-lined Fifth Avenue, parishioners in the churches of then-sedate Brooklyn, even petty politicos at party headquarters in Tammany Hall, all perceived serious flaws in the structure of urban government. Some complained, for example, of the tyranny of upstate Republican legislators, others attacked the domination of ward bosses, and still others criticized the greed of public utility companies franchised by the municipality. Mugwump reformer Theodore Roosevelt decried government by Irish political machine hacks, the moralist Reverend Charles Henry Parkhurst lambasted the reign of rum sellers, and that pariah of good-government advocates, New York City ward boss George Washington Plunkitt, also found fault, attacking the evils of civil service. For each, the status quo in urban government was defective. For each, the structure of municipal rule needed some revision. By the close of the 1880s the litany of criticism was mounting, with one voice after another adding a shrill comment on the misrule of the cities.

During the following two decades urban reformers repeated Bryce's words with ritualistic regularity, and his observation proved one of the most-quoted lines in the history of American government. Time and again latter-day Jeremiahs damned American municipal rule of the late nineteenth century, denouncing it as a national blight, a disgrace that by its example threatened the survival of democracy throughout the world. In 1890 Andrew D. White, then-president of Cornell University, wrote that "without the slightest exaggeration . . . the city governments of the United States are the worst in Christendom—the most expensive, the most inefficient, and the most corrupt." Four years later the reform journalist Edwin Godkin claimed that "the present condition of city governments in the United States is bringing democratic institutions into contempt the world over, and imperiling some of the best things in our civilization." Such preachers as the Reverend Washington Gladden denounced the American city as the "smut of civilization," while his clerical colleague Reverend Parkhurst said of the nation's municipalities: "Virtue is at the bottom and knavery on top. The rascals are out of jail and standing guard over men who aim to be honorable and law-abiding." And in 1904 journalist Lincoln Steffens stamped American urban rule with an indelible badge of opprobrium in the corruption-sated pages of his popular muckraking exposé *The Shame of the Cities*. Books, magazines, and newspapers all recited the catalog of municipal sins.

Likewise, many twentieth-century scholars passing judgment on the development of American city government have handed down a guilty verdict and sentenced American urban rule to a place of shame in the annals of the nation. In 1933 a leading student of municipal home rule claimed that "the conduct of municipal business has almost universally been inept and inefficient" and "at its worst it has been unspeakable, almost incredible." That same year the distinguished historian Arthur Schlesinger, Sr., in his seminal study *The Rise of the City*, described the development of municipal services during the last decades of the nineteenth century and found the achievements "distinctly creditable to a generation . . . confronted with the phenomenon of a great population everywhere clotting into towns." Yet later in his study he returned to the more traditional position, recounting tales of corruption and describing municipal rule during the last two decades of the century as "the worst city government the country had ever known." Writing in the 1950s, Bessie Louise Pierce, author of the finest biography to date of an American city, a multivolume history of Chicago, described that city's long list of municipal achievements but closed with a ritual admission of urban shortcomings, citing her approval of Bryce's condemnation. Similarly, that lifelong student of American municipal history, Ernest Griffith, subtitled his volume on late-nineteenth-century urban rule "the conspicuous failure," though he questioned whether municipal government was a greater failure than state government.

Historians such as Schlesinger and Griffith were born in the late nineteenth century, were raised during the Progressive era, and early imbibed the ideas of such critics as Bryce and White. Younger historians of the second half of the twentieth century were further removed from the scene of the supposed municipal debacle and could evaluate it more dispassionately. By the 1960s and 1970s, negative summations such as "unspeakable" and "incredible" were no longer common in accounts of nineteenth-century city government, and historians professing to the objectivity of the social sciences often refused to pronounce judgment on the quality of past rule. Yet recent general histories of urban America have continued both to describe the "deterioration" of city government during the Gilded Age and to focus on political bosses and good-government reformers who were forced to struggle with a decentralized, fragmented municipal structure supposedly unsuited to fast-growing metropolises of the 1880s and 1890s. Some chronicles of the American city have recognized the material advantages in public services during the late nineteenth century, but a number speak of the failure of the municipality to adapt to changing realities and of the shortcomings of an outmoded and ineffectual municipal framework. Sam Bass Warner, Jr., one of the leading new urban historians of the 1960s, has characterized the pattern of urban rule as one of "weak, corrupt, unimaginative municipal government." Almost one hundred years after Bryce's original declaration, the story of American city government remains at best a tale of fragmentation and confusion and at worst one of weakness and corruption.

If modern scholars have not handed down such damning verdicts as the contemporary critics of the 1880s and 1890s, they have nevertheless issued evaluations critical of the American framework of urban rule. As yet, hindsight has not cast a golden glow over the municipal institutions of the late nineteenth century, and few historians or political scientists have written noble tributes to the achievements of American municipal government. Praise for the nation's municipal officials has been rare and grudging. Though many have recognized the elitist predilections of Bryce and his American informants, the influence of Bryce's words still persists, and the image of nineteenth-century city government remains tarnished. Historians have softened the harsh stereotype of the political boss, transforming him from a venal parasite into a necessary component of a makeshift, decentralized structure. Conversely, the boss's good-government foes have fallen somewhat from historical grace and are now typified as crusaders for the supremacy of an upper-middle-class business culture. But historians continue to aim their attention at these two elements of municipal rule, to the neglect of the formal, legal structure. They write more of the boss than of the mayor, more on the civic leagues than on the sober but significant city comptroller. Moreover they continue to stage the drama of bosses and reformers against a roughly sketched backdrop of municipal disarray. The white and black hats of the players may have shaded to gray, but the setting of the historian's pageant remains a ramshackle municipal structure.

Nevertheless, certain nagging realities stand in stark contrast to the traditional tableau of municipal rule. One need not look far to discover the monuments of nineteenth-century municipal achievement that still grace the nation's cities, surviving as concrete rebuttals to Bryce's words. In 1979 the architecture critic for the *New York Times* declared Central Park and the Brooklyn Bridge as "the two greatest works of architecture in New York . . . each . . . a magnificent object in its own right; each . . . the result of a brilliant synthesis of art and engineering after which the world was never quite the same." Each was also a product of municipal enterprise, the creation of a city government said to be the worst in Christendom. Moreover, can one visit San Francisco's Golden Gate Park or enter McKim, Mead, and White's palatial Boston Public Library and pronounce these landmarks evidence of weakness or failure? Indeed, can those city fathers be deemed "unimaginative" who hired the great landscape architect Frederick Law Olmsted to design the first public park systems in human history? And were the vast nineteenth-century water and drainage schemes that still serve the cities the handiwork of bumbling incompetents unable to cope with the demands of expanding industrial metropolises? The aqueducts of Rome were among the glories of ancient civilization; the grander water systems of nineteenth-century New York City are often overlooked by those preoccupied with the more lurid aspects of city rule.

A bright side of municipal endeavor did, then, exist. American city governments could claim grand achievements, and as Arthur Schlesinger, Sr., was willing to admit in 1933, urban leaders won some creditable victories in the struggle for improved services. Certainly there were manifold shortcomings: Crime and poverty persisted; fires raged and pavements buckled; garbage and street rubbish sometimes seemed insurmountable problems. Yet no government has ever claimed total success in coping with the problems of society; to some degree all have failed to service their populations adequately. If government ever actually succeeded, political scientists would have to retool and apply themselves to more intractable problems, and political philosophers would have to turn to less contemplative pursuits. Those with a negative propensity can always find ample evidence of "bad government," and late-nineteenth-century critics such as Bryce, White, and Godkin displayed that propensity. In their writings the good side of the municipal structure was as visible as the dark side of the moon.

Thus, observers of the late-nineteenth-century American municipality have usually focused microscopic attention on its failures while overlooking its achievements. Scoundrels have won much greater coverage than conscientious officials. Volumes have appeared, for example, on that champion among municipal thieves, New York City's political boss William M. Tweed, but not one book exists on the life and work of a perhaps more significant figure in nineteenth-century city government, Ellis Chesbrough the engineer who served both Boston and Chicago and who transformed the public works of the latter city. Only recently has an admirable group of studies begun to explore the work of such municipal technicians who were vital to the formulation and implementation of public policy. But prior to the 1970s accounts of dualistic conflicts between political bosses and good-government reformers predominated, obscuring the complexities of municipal rule and the diversity of elements actually vying for power and participating in city government. And such traditional accounts accepted as axiomatic the inadequacy of the formal municipal structure. Critics have trumpeted its failures, while its triumphs have gone unheralded.

If one recognizes some of the challenges that municipal leaders faced during the period 1870 to 1900, the magnitude of their achievements becomes clear. The leaders of the late nineteenth century inherited an urban scene of great tumult and stress and an urban population of increasing diversity and diversion. . . . The melting pot was coming to a boil, and yet throughout the 1870s, 1880s, and 1890s, waves of newcomers continued to enter the country, including more and more representatives of the alien cultures of southern and eastern Europe. To many in 1870, social and ethnic diversity seemed to endanger the very foundation of order and security in the nation, and municipal leaders faced the need to maintain a truce between Protestants and Catholics, old stock and new, the native business elite and immigrant workers.

The rush of migrants from both Europe and rural America combined with a high birth rate to produce another source of municipal problems, a soaring urban population. . . . During the last thirty years of the century, the nation's chief cities absorbed thousands of acres of new territory to accommodate this booming population, and once-compact cities sprawled outward from the urban core. This expansion sprawl produced demands for the extension of services and the construction of municipal facilities. The newly annexed peripheral wards needed sewer lines and water mains; they required fire and police protection; and residents of outlying districts expected the city to provide paved streets and lighting. Municipal governments could not simply maintain their services at existing levels; instead, they had to guarantee the extension of those services to thousands of new urban dwellers.

Improved and expanded municipal services, however, required funding, and revenue therefore posed another challenge for city rulers. . . . Inflation in the 1860s and economic depression in the 1870s exacerbated the financial problems of the city, leading to heightened cries for retrenchment. And throughout the 1880s and 1890s city governments faced the difficult problem of meeting rising expectations for services while at the same time satisfying demands for moderate taxes and fiscal conservatism. This was perhaps the toughest task confronting the late-nineteenth-century municipality.

During the last three decades of the century, American city government did, however, meet these challenges of diversity, growth, and financing with remarkable success. By century's close, American city dwellers enjoyed, on the average, as high a standard of public services as any urban residents in the world. Problems persisted, and there were ample grounds for complaint. But in America's cities, the supply of water was the most abundant, the street lights were the most brilliant, the parks the grandest, the libraries the largest, and the public transportation the fastest of any place in the world. American city fathers rapidly adapted to advances in technology, and New York City, Chicago, and Boston were usually in the forefront of efforts to apply new inventions and engineering breakthroughs to municipal problems. Moreover, America's cities achieved this level of modern service while remaining solvent and financially sound. No major American municipality defaulted on its debts payments during the 1890s, and by the end of the century all of the leading municipalities were able to sell their bonds at premium and pay record-low interest. Any wise financier would have testified that the bonds of those purported strongholds of inefficiency and speculation, the municipal corporations, were far safer investments than were the bonds of those quintessential products of American business ingenuity: the railroad corporations.

Not only did the city governments serve their residents without suffering financial collapse, but municipal leaders also achieved an uneasy balance of the conflicting forces within the city, accommodating each through a distribution of authority. Though commentators often claimed that the "better elements" of the urban populace had surrendered municipal administration to the hands of "low-bred" Irish saloonkeepers, such observations were misleading. Similarly incorrect is the claim that the business and professional elite abandoned city government during the late nineteenth century to decentralized lower-class ward leaders. The patrician, the plutocrat, the plebeian, and the professional bureaucrat all had their place in late-nineteenth-century municipal government; each staked an informal but definite claim to a particular domain within the municipal structure.

Upper-middle-class business figures presided over the executive branch and the independent park, library, and sinking-fund commissions. Throughout the last decades of the nineteenth century the mayor's office was generally in the hands of solid businessmen or professionals who were native-born Protestants. The leading executive officers were persons of citywide reputation and prestige, and during the period 1870 to 1900 their formal authority was increasing. Meanwhile, the legislative branch—the board of aldermen or city council—became the stronghold of small neighborhood retailers, often of immigrant background, who won their aldermanic seats because of their neighborhood reputation as good fellows willing to gain favors for their constituents. In some cities men of metropolitan standing virtually abandoned the city council, and in every major city this body was the chief forum for lower-middle-class and working-class ward politicians.

At the same time, an emerging body of trained experts was also securing a barony of power within city government. Even before the effective application of formal civil service laws, mayors and commissioners deferred to the judgment and expertise of professional engineers, landscape architects, educators, physicians, and fire chiefs, and a number of such figures served decade after decade in municipal posts, despite political upheavals in the executive and legislative branches. By the close of the century these professional civil servants were securing a place of permanent authority in city government. Their loyalty was not to downtown business interests nor to ward or ethnic particularism, but to their profession and their department. And they were gradually transforming those departments into strongholds of expertise.

The municipal professional, the downtown business leader, and the neighborhood shopkeeper and small-time politico each had differing concepts of city government and differing policy priorities. They thus represented potentially conflicting interests that could serve to divide the municipal polity and render it impotent. Yet, during the period 1870 to 1900, these elements remained in a state of peaceful, if contemptuous, coexistence. Hostilities broke out, especially if any element felt the boundaries of its domain were violated. But city governments could operate effectively if the truce between these elements was respected; in other words, if ward business remained the primary concern of ward alderman, citywide policy was in the hands of the business elite, and technical questions were decided by experts relatively undisturbed by party politics. This was the informal détente that was gradually developing amid the conflict and complaints.

Such extralegal participants as political parties and civic leagues also exerted their influence over municipal government, attempting to tip the uneasy balance of forces in their direction. The political party organization with its ward-based neighborhood bosses was one lever that the immigrants and less affluent could pull to affect the course of government. Civic organizations and reform leagues, in contrast, bolstered the so-called better element in government, the respected businessmen who usually dominated the leading executive offices and the independent commissions. Emerging professional groups such as engineering clubs and medical societies often lent their support to the rising ambitions and growing authority of the expert bureaucracy and permanent civil servants. And special-interest lobbyists like the fire insurance underwriters also urged professionalism in such municipal services as the fire department. Municipal government was no simple dualistic struggle between a citywide party boss with a diamond shirt stud and malodorous cigar and a good-government reformer with a Harvard degree and kid gloves. Various forces were pushing and pulling the municipal corporations, demanding a response to petitions and seeking a larger voice in the chambers of city government.

State legislatures provided the structural flexibility to respond to these demands. The state legislatures enjoyed the sovereign authority to bestow municipal powers and to determine the municipal structure, but when considering local measures, state lawmakers generally deferred to the judgment of the legislative delegation from the affected locality. If the local delegation favored a bill solely affecting its constituents, the legislature usually ratified the bill without opposition or debate. This rule of deference to the locality no longer applied, however, if the bill became a partisan issue, as it occasionally did. But in most cases authorization for new powers or for structural reforms depended on the city's representatives in the state legislature, and each session the state assemblies and senates rubber-stamped hundreds of local bills. Thus, indulgent legislators provided the vital elasticity that allowed urban governments to expand readily to meet new challenges and assume new responsibilities. . . .

Even so, this process of perpetual adjustment resulted in a mechanism that succeeded in performing the job of city government. Municipal leaders adapted to the need for experts trained in the new technologies and hired such technicians. Moreover, downtown businessmen and ward politicos, the native-born and the immigrants, Protestants and Catholics, loosened the lid on the melting pot and reduced the boiling hostility of the midcentury to a simmer. The cities provided services; they backed off from the brink of bankruptcy; and the municipal structure guaranteed a voice to the various elements of society in both immigrant wards and elite downtown clubs.

Why, then, all the complaints? Why did so many critics of the 1880s and 1890s indulge in a rhetoric of failure, focusing on municipal shortcomings to the neglect of municipal successes? Why was municipal government so much abused? The answer lies in a fundamental irony: The late-nineteenth-century municipal structure accommodated everyone but satisfied no one. It was a system of compromise among parties discontented with compromise. It was a marriage of convenience, with the spouses providing a reasonably comfortable home for America's urban inhabitants. But it was not a happy home. The parties to the nuptials tolerated one another because they had to. Nevertheless, the businessman-mayors and plutocrat park commissioners disliked their dependence on ward politicians, whom they frequently regarded as petty grafters, and they frowned upon the power of the immigrant voters. Likewise, the emerging corps of civil servants was irked by interference from laypersons of both high and law status. And the plebeian party boss opposed efforts to extend the realm of the civil servants who had performed no partisan duties and thus merited no power. None liked their interdependence with persons they felt to be unworthy, incompetent, or hostile.

Enhancing this dissatisfaction was the cultural absolutism of the Victorian era. The late nineteenth century was an age when the business elite could refer to itself as the "best element" of society and take for granted its "God-given" superiority. It was an age when professional engineers, landscape architects, public health experts, librarians, educators, and fire fighters were first becoming aware of themselves as professionals, and with the zeal of converts they defended their newly exalted state of grace. It was also an age when most Protestants viewed Catholics as papal pawns and devotees of Italian idolatry, while most Catholics believed Protestants were little better than heathens and doomed to a quick trip to hell with no stops in purgatory. The late nineteenth century was not an age of cultural relativism but one of cultural absolutes, an age when people still definitely knew right from wrong, the correct from the erroneous. The American municipality, however, was a heterogeneous polyarchy, a network of accommodation and compromise in an era when accommodation and compromise smacked of unmanly dishonor and unprincipled pragmatism. Municipal government of the 1870s, 1880s, and 1890s rested on a system of broker politics, of bargaining and dealing. . . .

Late-nineteenth-century urban government was a failure not of structure but of image. The system proved reasonably successful in providing services, but there was no prevailing ideology to validate its operation. In fact, the beliefs of the various participants were at odds with the structure of rule that governed them. The respectable elements believed in sobriety and government by persons of character. But the system of accommodation permitted whiskey taps to flow on the Sabbath for the Irish and for Germans, just as it allowed men in shiny suits with questionable reputations to occupy seats on the city council and in the municipal party conventions. The ward-based party devotees accepted the notions of Jacksonian democracy and believed quite literally in the maxim To the victor belong the spoils. But by the 1890s they faced a growing corps of civil servants more devoted to their profession than to any party. Although new professional bureaucrats preached a gospel of expertise, they still had to compromise with party-worshiping hacks and the supposedly diabolical forces of politics. Likewise, special-interest lobbyists such as the fire insurance underwriters were forced to cajole or coerce political leaders whom they deemed ignorant and unworthy of public office. Each of these groups worked together, but only from necessity and not because they believed in such a compromise of honor. There was no ideology of heterogeneous polyarchy, no system of beliefs to bolster the existing government structure. Thus late-nineteenth-century city government survived without moral support, and to many urban dwellers it seemed a bargain with the devil.

Twentieth-century historians also had reasons for focusing on urban failure rather than urban success. Some chroniclers in the early decades accepted rhetoric as reality and simply repeated the condemnations of critics such as Bryce, White, and Godkin. By the midcentury greater skepticism prevailed, but so did serious ills. In fact, the urban crisis of the 1960s provided the impetus for a great upsurge of interest in the history of the city, inspiring a search for the historical roots of urban breakdown and collapse. Urban problems were the scholars' preoccupation. Not until the much-ballyhooed "back-to-the-city" movement of the 1970s did the city become less an object of pity or contempt and more a treasured relic. By the late 1970s a new rhetoric was developing, in which sidewalks and streets assumed a nostalgic significance formerly reserved to babbling brooks and bucolic pastures.

The 1980s, then, seem an appropriate time to reevaluate the much-maligned municipality of the late nineteenth century. Back-to-the-city euphoria, however, should not distort one's judgment of the past. Instead, it is time to understand the system of city government from 1870 to 1900 complete with blemishes and beauty marks. One should not quickly dismiss the formal mechanisms of municipal rule as inadequate and outdated, requiring the unifying grasp of party bosses. Nor should one mindlessly laud municipal rule as a triumph of urban democracy. A serious appreciation of the municipal structure is necessary.

POSTSCRIPT

Was City Government in Late-Nineteenth-Century America a "Conspicuous Failure"?

The opposing viewpoints expressed by Griffith and Teaford represent a longstanding scholarly debate about the consequences of boss politics in the United States. James Bryce, *The American Commonwealth,* 2 vols. (Macmillan, 1888); Moisei Ostrogorski, *Democracy and the Organization of Political Parties* (1902; Anchor Books, 1964); and Lincoln Steffens, *The Shame of the Cities* (McClure, Phillips, 1904), present a litany of misdeeds associated with those who controlled municipal government. Political bosses, these authors charge, were guilty of malfeasance in office and all forms of graft and corruption.

Efforts to rehabilitate the sullied reputations of the machine politicians can be dated to the comments of one of Boss Tweed's henchmen, George Washington Plunkitt, a New York City ward heeler whose turn-of-the-century observations included a subtle distinction between "honest" and "dishonest" graft. A more scholarly effort was presented by Robert K. Merton, a political scientist who identified numerous "latent functions" of the political machine. According to Merton, city bosses created effective political organizations that humanized the dispensation of assistance, offered valuable political privileges for businessmen, and created alternative routes of social mobility for citizens, many of them immigrants, who typically were excluded from conventional means of personal advancement.

There are several excellent urban history texts that devote space to the development of municipal government in the late nineteenth century. Among these are David R. Goldfield and Blaine A. Brownell, *Urban America: From Downtown to No Town* (Houghton Mifflin, 1979); Howard P. Chudacoff and Judith E. Smith, *The Evolution of American Urban Society,* 3rd ed. (Prentice Hall, 1981); and Charles N. Glaab and A. Theodore Brown, *A History of Urban America,* 3rd ed. (Macmillan, 1983). Various developments in the industrial period are discussed in Blake McKelvey, *The Urbanization of America, 1860–1915* (Rutgers University Press, 1963) and Raymond A. Mohl, *The New City: Urban America in the Industrial Age, 1860–1920* (Harlan Davidson, 1985). Boss politics is analyzed in William L. Riordon, *Plunkitt of Tammany Hall* (E. P. Dutton, 1963); Robert K. Merton, *Social Theory and Social Structure* (Free Press, 1957); and John M. Allswang, *Bosses, Machines, and Urban Voters: An American Symbiosis* (Kennikat Press, 1977). The most famous urban boss is analyzed in Alexander B. Callow, Jr., *The Tweed Ring*

(Oxford University Press, 1966) and Leo Hershkowitz, *Tweed's New York: Another Look* (Anchor Press, 1977). Scott Greer, ed., *Ethnics, Machines, and the American Future* (Harvard University Press, 1981) and Bruce M. Stave and Sondra Astor Stave, eds., *Urban Bosses, Machines, and Progressive Reformers*, 2d ed. (D. C. Heath, 1984) are excellent collections of essays on urban political machinery. Significant contributions to urban historiography are Sam Bass Warner, Jr., *Streetcar Suburbs: The Process of Growth in Boston, 1870–1900 (Harvard University Press, 1962);* Stephan Thernstrom, *Poverty and Progress: Social Mobility in the Nineteenth-Century City* (Harvard University Press, 1964); Gunther Barth, *City People: The Rise of Modern City Culture in Nineteenth-Century America* (Oxford University Press, 1980); and Martin V. Melosi, *Garbage in the Cities: Refuse, Reform, and the Environment, 1880–1980* (Texas A & M University Press, 1982).

Internet References . . .

National Center for Policy Analysis

This site contains links on an array of topics that are of major interest in the study of American history.

http://www.public-policy.org/web.public-policy.org/index.php

Gilded Age and Progressive Era Resources

General Resources on the Gilded Age and Progressive Era.

http://www.tntech.edu:8080/www/acad/hist/gilprog.html

Prohibition

The National Archives offers visitors the chance to view "The Volstead Act and Related Prohibition Documents."

http://www.archives.gov/

The 1920s

This site aims to raise awareness about an amazing time in history.

http://www.louisville.edu/~kprayb01/1920s.html

New Deal Network

Launched by the Frank and Eleanor Roosevelt Institute (FERI) in October 1996, the New Deal Network (NDN) is a research and teaching resource on the World Wide Web devoted to the public works and arts project of the New Deal.

http://www.newdeal.feri.org

World War I—Trenches on the Web

Mike Lawrence's interesting site supplies extensive resources about the Great War and is the appropriate place to begin exploration of this topic as regards to the American experience in World War I. There are "virtual tours" on certain topics, such as "Life on the Homefront."

http://www.worldwar1.com/

World War II WWW Sites

Visit this site as a starting point to find research links for World War II, including topics specific to the United States' participation and the impact on the country.

http://www.lib.muohio.edu/inet/subj/history/wwii/general.html

The Response to Industrialism and Reform, War, and Depression

*T*he maturing of the industrial system, a major economic depression, agrarian unrest, and labor violence all came to a head in 1898 with the Spanish–American War. The Progressives brought about major domestic reforms to ameliorate the worst abuses of rapid industrial growth and urbanization. American presidents advanced a proactive foreign policy, but the nation's role as a mediator of global conflicts was pushed to the limit when Woodrow Wilson tried to get the United States to join the League of Nations at the end of World War I.

The most serious problems of inequality were never addressed by the Progressives. African Americans began fighting for civil and political rights. Spokespersons for blacks emerged, but their programs for advancement frequently touched off controversy among both black and white people. There was controversy over whether the prohibition movement curbed drinking or whether it created a climate of lawlessness in the 1920s.

The onset of a more activist federal government accelerated with the Great Depression. In the midst of widespread unemployment, Franklin D. Roosevelt was elected on a promise to give Americans a "New Deal." Every sector of the economy was affected by the proliferation of the alphabet soup New Deal agencies, and historians continue to debate whether the New Deal measures ameliorated or prolonged the Great Depression.

The impending World War killed the New Deal by 1939. With the fall of France to the Germans in 1940, FDR tried to abandon the traditional foreign policy of isolationism by aiding allies in Europe and Asia without becoming involved in the war. The effort failed, and the Japanese attacked Pearl Harbor and destroyed most of the Pacific fleet.

- Did Booker T. Washington's Philosophy and Actions Betray the Interests of African Americans?

- Did the Progressives Fail?

- Was Woodrow Wilson Responsible for the Failure of the United States to Join the League of Nations?

- Was Prohibition a Failure?

- Was the New Deal an Effective Answer to the Great Depression?

- Was Franklin Roosevelt a Reluctant Internationalist?

ISSUE 6

Did Booker T. Washington's Philosophy and Actions Betray the Interests of African Americans?

YES: Donald Spivey, from *Schooling for the New Slavery: Black Industrial Education, 1868–1915* (Greenwood Press, 1978)

NO: Robert J. Norrell, from "Understanding the Wizard: Another Look at the Age of Booker T. Washington," in W. Fitzhugh Brundage, ed., *Booker T. Washington and Black Progress: Up From Slavery 100 Years Later* (University of Florida Press, 2003)

ISSUE SUMMARY

YES: Donald Spivey contends that Booker T. Washington alienated both students and faculty at Tuskegee Institute by establishing an authoritarian system that failed to provide an adequate academic curriculum to prepare students for the industrial workplace.

NO: Robert J. Norrell insists that Booker T. Washington, while limited in what he could accomplish by the racial climate of the day, nevertheless spoke up for political and civil rights, decried mob violence, and defended black education as a means of promoting a more positive image for African Americans in an era dominated by the doctrine of white supremacy.

In the late nineteenth and early twentieth centuries, most black Americans' lives were characterized by increased inequality and powerlessness. Although the Thirteenth Amendment had fueled a partial social revolution by emancipating approximately four million southern slaves, the efforts of the Fourteenth and Fifteenth Amendments to provide all African Americans with the protections and privileges of full citizenship had been undermined by the U. S. Supreme Court.

Seventy-five percent of all African Americans resided in rural areas by 1910. Ninety percent lived in the South, where they suffered from abuses associated with the sharecropping and crop-lien systems, political disfranchisement, and antagonistic race relations, which often boiled over into acts of violence, including race riots and lynchings. Black southerners who moved north in the decades preceding World War I to escape the ravages of racism instead discovered a society in which the color line was drawn more rigidly to limit black opportunities. Residential segregation led to the emergence of racial ghettos. Jim Crow also affected northern education, and competition for jobs produced frequent clashes between black and white workers. By the early twentieth century, then, most African Americans endured a second-class citizenship reinforced by segregation laws (both customary and legal) in the "age of Jim Crow."

Prior to 1895, the foremost spokesman for the nation's African American population was former slave and abolitionist Frederick Douglass, whose crusade for blacks emphasized the importance of civil rights, political power, and immediate integration. August Meier has called Douglass "the greatest living symbol of the protest tradition during the 1880s and 1890s." At the time of Douglass's death in 1895, however, this tradition was largely replaced by the emergence of Booker T. Washington. Born into slavery in Virginia in 1856, Washington became the most prominent black spokesman in the United States as a result of a speech delivered in the year of Douglass's death at the Cotton States Exposition in Atlanta, Georgia. Known as the "Atlanta Compromise," this address, with its conciliatory tone, found favor among whites and gave Washington, who was the president of Tuskegee Institute in Alabama, a reputation as a "responsible" spokesman for black America.

What did Booker T. Washington really want for African Americans? Did his programs realistically address the difficulties confronted by blacks in a society where the doctrine of white supremacy was prominent? Is it fair to describe Washington simply as a conservative whose accommodationist philosophy betrayed his own people? Did the "Sage of Tuskegee" consistently adhere to his publicly stated philosophy of patience, self-help, and economic advancement?

One of the earliest and most outspoken critics of Washington's program was his contemporary, W. E. B. Du Bois. In a famous essay in *The Souls of Black Folk* (1903), Du Bois leveled an assault upon Washington's narrow educational philosophy for blacks and his apparent acceptance of segregation. By submitting to disfranchisement and segregation, Du Bois charged, Washington had become an apologist for racial injustice in the United States. He also claimed that Washington's national prominence had been bought at the expense of black interests throughout the nation.

In the first of the following selections, Donald Spivey offers a more recent interpretation that follows the critical assessment of Du Bois. He portrays Booker T. Washington as an authoritarian "overseer" who imposed a militaristic system at Tuskegee and who alienated students and faculty by insisting upon a program that not only subordinated political, social, and civil rights to economic goals but also failed to provide the training necessary to allow students to become capable, skilled artisans.

In the second selection, Robert J. Norrell concludes that Washington never stopped trying to act on behalf of African American interests. He denies that Washington was simply an accommodationist and claims that there was a fundamental similarity between Washington's direct and indirect challenges to white supremacy on the one hand and the substance of the protests sponsored by the National Association for the Advancement of Colored People (NAACP) on the other.

YES

Donald Spivey

Shine, Booker, Shine: The Black Overseer of Tuskegee

Perhaps Paulo Freire had Booker T. Washington in mind when he wrote in his classic study on education, "The oppressed have been destroyed precisely because their situation has reduced them to things. In order to regain their humanity they must cease to be things and fight as men. . . . They cannot enter the struggle as objects in order later to become men." To Booker T. Washington the sensible thing for blacks to do was to fashion a coalition with whites in power to make themselves indispensable "objects" to the prosperity of the nation. His conception of the proper course for blacks rested upon the blacks' own exploitability. He believed that the profit motive dictated American thought and action. Those who proved themselves antagonistic would remain powerless or be annihilated; those who proved themselves of value would be rewarded. Thus, he contended that social, political, and civil rights were secondary issues for blacks—subordinate to and dependent upon the race's economic importance. This philosophy of uplift through submission drew heated criticism from many black leaders. What is not a familiar story is that in his championing of these ideas, Washington alienated many of his Tuskegee students and faculty members and never gained the full support of the white South. . . .

Like the good overseer, and like his mentor, Samuel Chapman Armstrong, Booker T. sought to make his students superb laborers, that is, totally reliable. He criticized Tuskegee students who showed any signs of being unreliable. "Young men come here [Tuskegee Institute] and want to work at this industry or that, for a while, and then get tired and want to change to something else." To be a good worker, Washington professed, one must understand "the Importance of Being Reliable."

Booker Washington worked diligently to please the dominant white society, to make his blacks "the best labor in the world." He watched his students' every move. He was a stickler for precision and detail. The Founder emphasized such things to the Tuskegee student body and teachers as the proper positioning of brooms. Washington sent a notice to three department heads: "Will you kindly see that all brooms in your department are kept on their proper end. I notice that this is not done now." One faculty member responded on top of the Founder's memo: "This must be a mistake." It was not. Booker Washington demanded that everyone, including Mrs. Washington, place and store brooms with the brush end up.

The Founder placed every aspect of the student's life at Tuskegee under a strict regime of rules and regulations. Committees were formed that conducted daily examinations of the students' rooms and personal belongings. Careful attention was given to whether or not all had toothbrushes. One committee reported that it had noted some "absence of tooth brushes and tooth mugs." The Founder received other reports on the toothbrush situation. "There is a very large number of students that use the tooth brush only to adorn the washstand," one of Washington's student informers reported.

The slightest trace of dirt or grime was call for alarm and disciplinary action at Tuskegee. A committee appointed to inspect one of the dorms noted, "The wood work needs scrubbing and dusting thoroughly." The committee also reported that beds were not properly made in military fashion and some of the linen needed ironing and was improperly folded. Students who left their beds unmade were often punished by not receiving dinner.

When Tuskegee students did dine, they did so under stringent rules and regulations. Talking during meals was permitted only at precise intervals designated by the ringing of bells.

The list of regulations ended with Rule Number 15: "For the violation of the above rules you will be severely punished."

Naturally, students sometimes fell short of the mark. Captain Austin, a stickler for detail, noted that student discipline during meals needed improvement. And no detail escaped his military eye: "Students continue to eat after bell rings and this together with the noise made by the knives and forks tinkling against the plates make it very difficult to hear the adjutant read the notices." In Austin's report to Booker Washington, which contained dining violations, he stated that the men students had become "careless in dress." He complained also about the behavior of women students in the dining hall. "The girls," Austin reported, "are exceedingly boisterous and rough when rising from their tables."

Search and seizure comprised part of the everyday life at Tuskegee. Men and women alike were searched for liquor, obscene materials, or anything else that in some way might contribute to the breakdown of rules or affect the school's "reputation." Searching of students' rooms and personal belongings became official policy at Tuskegee in 1906, when it was written into the School Code.

Booker Washington gave the students' social life the closest scrutiny. The institute forbade male and female students from associating after classes. The woman students received constant reminders from the Dean of Women to remain "moral and pure." This same advice was given to the men students by the Commandant of Cadets. Separate walkways across campus were designated for male and female to guarantee the two kept separated. Male students were forbidden to walk around or near the girls' dormitory after dusk. This was done, as one school official put it, to "prevent the promiscuous mingling of boys and girls."

Washington was working to make Tuskegee students into the type of blacks that the white South relished. Their training was primarily in "how to behave" rather than in how to become skilled tradesmen. To be a skilled craftsman requires proficiency in mathematical and verbal skills. The school's curriculum, however, was industrial almost to the total exclusion of the academic. What academic studies that did exist were secondary and often optional. That the school would commit itself to this type of program was clear from the staff that Washington employed at the school. Most of the faculty members were Hampton graduates, and they knew more about discipline than trades.

The *Southern Workman* reported that Hampton graduates held most of the key posts at Tuskegee Institute, noting the fact that the school's principal was "Hampton's most distinguished graduate." Washington issued a directive in 1908 to his departmental heads in which he stated that he wanted the school to "employ each year a reasonable number of Hampton graduates." He added that he "did not want the number of Hampton graduates decreased on the teaching force at Tuskegee."

The Founder was not completely closeminded in hiring personnel for teaching positions at Tuskegee, but instructors he hired from academic institutions often failed to fit well into his educational scheme because he subordinated every aspect of Tuskegee's educational program to the industrial schooling idea of producing tractable blacks. Blacks from academic universities like Howard, Fisk, and Atlanta were employed at the school. Roscoe Conkling Bruce, a product of Harvard University who headed the so-called academic curriculum at Tuskegee, found that the institute's commitment to preparing students as common laborers was total. Bruce thought that perhaps some of the students might be material for professional careers. He complained about educating students "chiefly in accordance with the demands for labor."

Another thorn in Washington's side was a young instructor in the academic department named Leslie P. Hill, who had been hired by Bruce. Hill obviously failed to adjust to the second-class status of academic studies at Tuskegee. He initiated innovative approaches to his teaching of educational theory, history, and philosophy. However, the Founder regarded Hill as hostile to the educational philosophy of the school. Washington, in his explanation for firing Hill, remarked that the young Harvard graduate seemed to feel that the methods employed at Tuskegee were "either wrong or dangerous."

If he had many of the school's instructors in mind, Hill was absolutely right. Higher education at Tuskegee was a sad joke. Hill recognized that the general atmosphere discouraged serious effort among the industrial faculty. He noted that courses lacked outlines, instructors failed to use facilities properly, and that many of them lacked the competence to teach the skills for which they were hired.

Roscoe Bruce found the entire Tuskegee situation quite perplexing. He understood that Tuskegee was an industrial school—a fact, Bruce remarked, that he was "often reminded of." But he said that he failed to see how students who received little to no academic training would be able to carry on up-to-date craft positions. He wrote to the principal, "You see, the truth is that the carpenter is not taught enough mathematics, the machinist enough physics, or the farmer enough chemistry for the purpose of his particular work." Bruce also found it discouraging that there was no distinction made in the school's curriculum between those students who were going to be teachers and the ones "who plan to make horseshoes or to paint houses."

Washington conceded that some difficulties existed with the industrial idea of education, but that he had said so in his book, *Up From Slavery.*

> I told those who doubted the wisdom of the plan [industrial education] that I knew our first buildings would not be so comfortable or so complete in their finish as buildings erected by the experienced hands of outside workmen, but that in the teaching of civilization, self-help, and self-reliance, the erection of the buildings by the students themselves would more than compensate for any lack of comfort or fine finish.

His point, no doubt, was that problems are to be expected but they will be solved in time.

Regardless of what Booker T. said, Tuskegee was not preparing its students to take their place as skilled artisans in the industrial world. The school maintained a general policy of allowing students to graduate without even having finished a trade course. One report indicated that some positions calling for manual skills had become open to blacks in the South and that the opportunities for the Tuskegee graduates were "greater than ever," but that the students were not properly prepared for these jobs.

Roscoe C. Bruce reported to Washington on another separate occasion in which he complained that upon visiting the Girls' Laundry Department he was struck by the lack of any real skills training. Bruce said that the students did not seem to be receiving instruction in the art of the task but in fact simply performed menial chores.

W.T.B. Williams of the General Education Board conducted a survey of Tuskegee in 1906 and concluded that the student who completed the course of studies had what might be equivalent to a ninth grade education in the public school system. He considered there to be a general lack of training and preparation at the school. In addition, said Williams, "the majority of the students are barely able to read the Bible." He said in conclusion, "Considering the elementary nature of much of this work and the maturity of the students, the daily requirements seem pretty light."

The lack of quality in instruction and academic training at Tuskegee drove Roscoe Bruce to resign in 1906. Washington replaced him with J.R.E. Lee, who fit well into the Tuskegee idea. But Lee's own correspondence reveals the lack of serious academic or skills education at the school. Lee noted that the students who had attended one or two years of education at the general education schools, such as Fisk or Atlanta, were able to go immediately to the senior ranks at Tuskegee. Lee admitted that the work required of students at those schools was "far above the work required here [at Tuskegee]."

The lack of a positive, achievement-oriented atmosphere at Tuskegee had a negative effect on students and teachers. In 1912, one Tuskegee instructor openly admitted that the students they produced were ill-equipped to pursue a skilled occupation in industry. He thought that perhaps the problem lay with the teachers. He begged that they "give more time and attention" to their duties.

Instructors, on the other hand, blamed the problem on the students. Teachers in the industrial classes claimed that the students lacked the necessary attitude to become tradesmen, that they took their assignments lightly and performed them poorly. The instructor in basic construction and design accused the students of not following floor plans and of being sloppy and lazy in the performance of their tasks.

However, the teachers seemed more preoccupied with social matters than with correcting their students' deficiencies. "The young women teachers engage in frivolities hardly in keeping with their calling," W.T.B. Williams reported. "They are good women but not seriously concerned about the work in hand. They seem to give far more attention to dress rather than to almost anything else. . . ."

The female instructors were not alone. The men could stand on their own in terms of being frivolous. They repeatedly hosted gala social outings. One example was the going away party for Booker T. Washington, Jr., given in his honor by the faculty men. It was an elaborate and extravagant affair with orchestra, "seating arrangements patterned after that in the Cabinet Room of the White House," and dinner crowned with "Fried Chicken, Booker T. Washington, Jr. Style."

After a visit to Tuskegee in 1904, Robert Curtis Ogden commented on the "peculiar" social attitude of the school's faculty. He and his other white companions had been guests of honor at a faculty-hosted concert of classical music. Ogden, commenting later to Booker Washington about the concert, said that he believed his guests appreciated the entertainment, but that they would have enjoyed seeing more of the teachers and students at work rather than watching their hosts do their "level best to be like white folks and not natural."

Tuskegee's faculty was imitative of whites, but they were black and not the omnipotent authority symbol that, for example, Hampton's all-white staff was to its students. Tuskegee students, justifiably, found faults with the faculty, the education they received, and the conditions of campus life. They voiced their displeasure. The class in agricultural science at Tuskegee was taught by the renowned George Washington Carver, and he could not escape the growing discontent among students. One student complained that he had come to Tuskegee to learn the most advanced techniques in farming from George Washington Carver but found that the professor seemed to be more interested in producing "hired hands." The student remarked that overall he felt that he was "not receiving progressive instruction."

In addition, students challenged the strict discipline of the school in subtle ways. Julio Despaigne, Washington's key informant in the dorms, reported, "The students have the habit of making their beds at the morning good for when the inspector comes that he can find it well, and in the afternoon they disorder them and put clean and dirty clothes on them."

The rebellion of the students against the oppressive social restrictions of the institute manifested itself in different subtle ways. Some students began skipping chapel to meet with members of the opposite sex. Others volunteered for duties that held a high likelihood of putting them in contact with the opposite sex; a favorite assignment among male and female students was night duty at the school's hospital. Those fortunate enough to draw that duty were on their honor not to fraternize. The administration, however, soon found out the hospital was being used as a place for social carousing. Walter McFadden and Katie Paterson received an official reprimand from the administration "for questionable socializing while on night duty together at the hospital."

Some male students placed latches on their doors to keep night inspectors from entering while they, allegedly, broke school rules. This was met with quick action on the part of the administration. The Executive Council decided that because of

> the misconduct, gambling and so forth, which is indulged in on the part of certain young men who place night latches on their doors and lock themselves into their rooms from teachers' and officers' attempts to get into the room and who jump out of the windows before they can be detected in their mischief: because of this it has been found necessary to remove all the night latches from the doors.

The women students of the laundry class asserted themselves against unfair practices. They could not understand why they should be paid less than their labor was worth. They objected to the hard work with low pay. The young women said that they had the work of both students and teachers to do including that of the summer teachers and that on one occasion they had remained until five o'clock on Saturday evening in order to supply the boys with their week's laundry. "We hope you will not think of us as complainers," they closed in their letter to Booker Washington, "but, simply as children striving to perform their duty; and, at the same time receive some recompense in return. We are asking for higher wages. May we have it?" The Founder's answer was to appoint a committee to investigate their complaint, with the quiet result that nothing ever came of it.

The students' discontent gradually gave way to outright hostility against the school. Students stole from the institution, broke windows, wrecked dormitories, defaced walls, and on several occasions debased the school chapel. Some tried to avoid school and work by pretending to be ill. The institute's physician reported to Booker Washington, "I wish you also to bear in mind that a large number of the students who come to the hospital are not calling because they are ill, but are simply giving way to some imaginary ills, or else taking advantage of the easy method of losing an hour or two from work." One student spoke bluntly to Washington about the feeling among many of the students that to be successful at the school it was required to become "slaves of you [Mr. Washington] and Tuskegee." A group of native-born African students, accused of challenging the authority of one of their instructors and later brought before Washington for discipline, criticized the education they were receiving at Tuskegee and the attitude of teachers, including the Founder himself, who they said "acted as a master ordering his slaves." They concluded: "We do not intend no longer to remain in your institution. . . ."

Students openly rebelled against the school's disciplinary practices. Charles H. Washington, a member of the senior class, considered the prying eyes of the faculty into every aspect of the individual student's private life to be too much for him. He told a faculty member point-blank to pass on the word that they "are to cease meddling with his affairs."

During the last ten years of Washington's reign at Tuskegee, from 1905 to his death in 1915, faculty members alluded to a growing student hostility against them. They became fearful for their personal safety, believing that students were carrying weapons and ready to use them. The situation at Tuskegee became more tense with the passing of each day. Students acted discourteously to instructors in and out of class. A group of faculty members reported to Washington that pupils had become so rebellious that they "never felt safe in appearing before the students."

In the tradition of the overseer whose position is dependent upon his ability to keep those under his charge in line, Washington met student discontent each step of the way with a tightening of rules and regulations. But student unrest continued. The result was that discipline at Tuskegee during the latter part of his administration approached absurdity. Students were suspended for talking without permission, failing to dress according to standards, or even for "failing to take a napkin to the dining hall." Young men students were chastised for "putting their hands in their pockets," and failing to obey that rule, the administration sought to offer "such inducements as will make them do so."

That the punishment students received outweighed the offense is clearly indicated in the case of Lewis Smith, whom a fellow student accused of "over indiscrete conduct with Emma Penny of the same class." Smith, a senior and slated to graduate as class salutatorian, was brought before the administration for allegedly attempting to hug and kiss Miss Penny. Although he denied the charges and his testimony was substantiated by a fellow classmate, the administration saw fit to punish Smith. He was denied the distinction of graduating as class salutatorian.

Smith was lucky. He could have been suspended or expelled—favorite disciplinary measures during the latter years of Booker T.'s rule over Tuskegee Institute. A case in point is the 1912 flag incident. A few members of the senior class of that year decided to celebrate by flying their class flag over Tompkins Hall. They made the unpardonable mistake, however, of not obtaining the administration's permission. School officials considered the students' act a conspiracy against the institute's authority, an "organized movement on the part of some of the members of the senior class . . . and that this was not carried out on the spur of the moment." The accused students begged for mercy and swore that they acted out of no intent to challenge school authority or embarrass the administration. One of the accused vowed they would rather have had their "heads severed from their bodies" than to do anything against Tuskegee. The young men were suspended.

The slightest infraction on the part of the student, or even suspicion of having broken a rule, was reason enough for the Washington administration to notify parents. This had near disastrous results in the case of Charles Bell, a senior who was brought before the administration on the suspicion of having engaged in "sexual misconduct" with a young woman named Varner of the same class. Both denied the charges. There was no eyewitness testimony or other "proof" that Bell and Varner had done anything wrong, except the fact that they were often seen together. The administration, nevertheless, passed its suspicions on to Miss Varner's father. He showed up later on campus with his gun, saying that he would shoot Bell on sight. Bell was forced to leave the institute until the situation quieted.

When Tuskegee students did pose a real threat to the sovereignty of Booker Washington, he showed no mercy. In 1903, a group of Tuskegee students launched a strike against the school. The material on the strike, and it is extremely sketchy, does indicate that the participants objected to the entire Tuskegee order of things. They wanted more academic training, better instruction, more opportunity to learn trades, and an easing of rules and regulations. Washington's response was undiluted: "No concessions."

In an official but insubstantial report on the strike to the school's white financial backers, Booker T. contended that a few malcontents had occupied one of the school's buildings, thinking that this was the way to be heard. The students were not upset with the institute, he said, "nor were they in opposition to any industrial work," but "objected to being required to devote too much time to both industrial work and studies with too little time for preparation." The strike apparently ended as quickly as it had begun once the administration served notice that all those who failed to return to work immediately would be expelled.

Those who obtained an "education" at Tuskegee did so in accordance with the industrial schooling idea and under the watchful eyes of Booker Taliaferro Washington. Student dissatisfaction did nothing to change the Founder's mind about the rightness of the type of educational philosophy he professed and protected. His administration practiced a stiff brand of discipline that it never backed down from. But students, on occasion, continued to try and voice their complaints. Perhaps it is understandable, then, why the Washington administration felt it might be necessary to establish a "guard house" for the purpose of confining its student incorrigibles. It did just that in 1912.

Booker T.'s educational practices were based on his desire to please whites and gain their support. The Founder worked to make whites more a part of the school's operations. He invited them to visit the institute on every occasion. He believed that the school's annual commencement exercises afforded an excellent opportunity to win goodwill from the local whites. "I think it would be well for you to spend a week in Montgomery among the white and colored people," Washington advised a fellow faculty member. "I am very anxious that in addition to the colored people we have a large representative class of whites to attend Commencement." In fact, the Founder considered paying the fares of white visitors to the commencement exercises. The school advertised the commencement of 1904 in the *Tuskegee News.*

Washington did everything possible to bring in more local white support. When Washington received advice from a "reliable source" that if he kept the number of Jews down in attendance at commencement, more local whites would probably come, he responded: "Of course I do not want to keep the Jews away, but I think it would be a good plan to increase the number of Gentiles if possible."

The Founder received unsolicited advice on how to gain more local and national support. One Northerner wrote him suggesting that the school would gain more support if it devoted itself exclusively to the production of domestic servants. The writer suggested that the program should stress "cooking, waiting on table, cleaning silver and washing windows, sewing, dusting, washing and ironing."

In his response, Washington made it clear that Tuskegee did this and more:

> At this institution we give training in every line of domestic work, hence any girl who finishes our course should be able to perform any of the usual duties connected with a servant's life, but one of the most important things to be accomplished for the colored people now is the getting of them to have correct ideas concerning labor, that is to get them to feel that all classes of labor, whether of the head or hand, are dignified. This lesson I think Tuskegee, in connection with Hampton, has been successful in teaching the race.

And, like Hampton, Tuskegee aimed to do more than serve as an agency to place individual domestics. Washington in conclusion said that the most economical thing to be done was to send out a set of people not only trained in hand but thoroughly equipped in mind and heart so that they themselves could go out and start smaller centers or training schools. He believed that it would be of greater service to the whole country "if we can train at Tuskegee one girl who could go out and start a domestic training school in Atlanta, Baltimore, or elsewhere, than we would be doing by trying to put servants directly into individual houses which would be a never ending task." . . .

Booker T. Washington never intentionally did anything to upset or anger Southern whites. He repledged his love for the South and his obedience to its traditions in *My Larger Education,* published four years before his death. The Founder said in that work, "I understand thoroughly the prejudices, the customs, the traditions of the South—and, strange as it may seem to those who do not wholly understand the situation, I love the South." The philosophy of "uplift" for blacks that he preached across the nation and taught at Tuskegee Institute was in accordance with that love and the prevailing racial, economic order. His role was like that of the black overseer during slavery who, given the position of authority over his fellow slaves, worked diligently to keep intact the very system under which they both were enslaved.

Understanding the Wizard Another Look at the Age of Booker T. Washington

From his day to ours, Booker T. Washington has been viewed as a symbol of the age in which he lived, but he has proved to be an elastic emblem, one pulled and stretched to mean different things to different people. Washington clearly recognized his symbolic role and acted always to shape its meaning, but often he failed to persuade his audience of the object lessons he meant to teach. When Washington's autobiography *Up From Slavery* appeared in 1901, William Edward Burghardt Du Bois began to critique the Tuskegee principal as a black leader chosen by whites. Du Bois wrote that Washington had taken the idea of industrial training for blacks and "broadened it from a by-path into a veritable Way of Life." Washington thought the older black schools that offered a liberal education were "wholly failures, or worthy of ridicule," which was partly why, Du Bois claimed, other blacks had "deep suspicion and dislike" for the Tuskegeean. "Among the Negroes, Mr. Washington is still far from a popular leader." In *The Souls of Black Folk* in 1903, Du Bois perfected his critique, asserting that Washington's program "practically accepts the alleged inferiority of the Negro races." In the 1895 Atlanta Exposition speech—Du Bois dubbed it the "Atlanta Compromise," a pejorative that would prove enduring—Washington had, he insisted, accepted the denial of black citizenship rights. Washington was "striving nobly to make Negro artisans, business men, and property-owners; but it is utterly impossible, under modern competitive methods, for the workingmen and property-owners to defend their rights and exist without the right of suffrage."

In the years after Washington's death in 1915, many readers of *Up From Slavery* would come to a more positive evaluation of the book and its author, and little was added to Du Bois's critique of Washington until 1951, when C. Vann Woodward's sharp irony in *Origins of the New South* seconded Du Bois's criticism of Washington's materialist values: "The businessman's gospel of free enterprise, competition, and *laissez faire* never had a more loyal exponent than the master of Tuskegee." Louis R. Harlan, a Woodward student, stepped forward as the most influential interpreter of Washington with the publication in 1972 of the first installments of both his two-volume biography of Washington and the fourteen-volume *Booker T. Washington Papers.* Professor Harlan criticized Washington's failure to protest the wrongs he witnessed against African Americans, writing that he "acquiesced in segregation," accepted "complacently" the denial of equal rights after Reconstruction, rose to power only because whites chose him to lead blacks, and offered leadership that amounted to a "setback of his race." Professor Harlan emphasized the hypocrisy of Washington's public disavowal of politics at the same time he was working constantly to influence federal appointments in the South. Precisely because Harlan drove his thesis so well and paraded a variety of vivid symbols before the readers about the "faustian" Wizard, he shaped almost all the writing on post-Reconstruction race relations published after 1972. Still, Harlan mainly put Washington in two contexts: the conflict with Do Bois, and Washington's influence in Republican politics. Placing Washington in other historical contexts, however, can yield different understandings. What follows is an attempt to broaden the contextual framework in which Washington's life and work are judged.

⁕

One crucial context for understanding Booker T. Washington was the thinking of whites in the 1880s and 1890s about the future of race relations. Intellectuals and politicians writing to shape public opinion, from both North and South, had turned increasingly hostile toward African Americans. . . .

These intensely hostile views toward African Americans found their way to the average person in the South through the white-owned newspapers in that region, which gave the suggestion of the all-encompassing nature of race trouble in the United States. In his study of shall-town newspapers in the South, Thomas D. Clark found that most papers in the 1880s and 1890s clearly reflected the "Negro-as-beast" thinking of the time. The editors revealed "a general fear of the Negro," whom they often depicted as uncivilized, a "wild, ignorant animal . . . [a] black sensual fiend, whose intense hatred of the white race would cause him to strike with wild demoniacal fury at an unguarded moment.". . .

In his 1895 Atlanta Exposition speech, Washington challenged the images then current in white intellectual and cultural presentations of African Americans, insisting that blacks were a people of "love and fidelity" to whites, a "faithful, law-abiding, and unresentful" people. In its larger thrust, the Atlanta speech represented Washington's attempt to counter the presumption on the part of the white South, and much of the rest of the nation, that African Americans had declined in character and morality in freedom. The overarching message that Washington intended was not acceptance of disfranchisement and segregation but rather a message of progress, of movement forward and upward. In Atlanta, Washington began to offer Americans a new point of view in order to challenge the ideology of white supremacy.

In the years after the Atlanta speech, Washington often spoke up for civil and political rights. This is contrary to Professor Harlan's contention that "his public utterances were limited to what whites approved" and that Washington's actions on behalf of civil and political rights were exclusively part of his "secret life" of arranging court challenges and organizing protests but taking no public part. In fact, in 1896 Washington told the *Washington Post* that forcing blacks "to ride in a 'Jim Crow' car that is far inferior to that used by the white people is a matter that cannot stand much longer against the increasing intelligence and prosperity of the colored people." In a speech at a Spanish-American War Peace jubilee in Chicago before 16,000 people, Washington asserted that the United States had won all its battles but one, "the effort to conquer ourselves in the blotting out of racial prejudice. . . . Until we thus conquer ourselves. I make no empty statement when I say that we shall have, especially in the Southern part of our country, a cancer gnawing at the heart of the Republic, that shall one day prove as dangerous as an attack from an army without or within." In 1899, in response to the horrific Sam Hose lynching in Newnan, Georgia, Washington wrote to the *Birmingham Age-Herald* that he opposed "mob violence under all circumstances. Those guilty of crime should be surely, swiftly and terribly punished, but by legal methods." In June of that year, he published a long article on lynching that appeared in many southern and northern newspapers in which he offered statistics to show that only a small portion of those lynched were even charged with rape. Lynching did not deter crime, Washington insisted; it degraded whites who participated, and it gave the South a bad name throughout the world.

As he became recognized after 1895 as the most prominent African American—and as he consciously accepted the role as leader of his race—Washington constantly gave speeches and interviews and wrote to try to improve the image of African Americans. In practice, creating an ideology to challenge white supremacy usually amounted to influencing what the public media reported about blacks. By the late 1890s Washington frequently sent press releases to both black and white newspapers that either pointed to black achievements that contradicted the "Negro-as-beast" image by showing black success or suggesting actions that contradicted blacks' negative image. Washington seemed always to know what modern-day publicists teach public figures in a critical spotlight: Answering criticism often only fuels the public-relations crisis. He quoted Oliver Wendell Holmes: "Controversy equalizes wise men and fools, and the fools know it." Thus, whether the criticism came from whites or blacks, Washington's first instinct was to keep his response to himself.

Running through all Washington's public efforts to counter the intensely anti-black feeling in the South in the late 1890s was a defense of black education. In virtually every speech, magazine article, or newspaper interview, and in many of the press releases sent out from Tuskegee, Washington dwelt on the great and growing value of African American

education, and only some of his emphases promoted industrial education. Having observed the removal of blacks from politics in Mississippi
and South Carolina and having fought disfranchisement in Louisiana and
lost, Washington by 1900 privately doubted that anything could halt the
powerful momentum of the movement to take away black suffrage. The
attack on black education that intensified over the course of the 1890s,
however, represented an even more fundamental assault, one that Washington had to turn back, or the purpose of his life was defeated. Senator
Benjamin R. Tillman of South Carolina constantly declared that "it is fool-
ish to my mind to disfranchise the Negro on account of illiteracy and turn
right around and compel him to become literate.

Up From Slavery represented Washington's ultimate statement of black
progress. "No one can come into contact with the race for twenty years as I
have done in the heart of the South," he wrote, "without being convinced
that the race is constantly making slow but sure progress materially, edu-
cationally, and morally." Washington had made himself, and he clearly
understood that his life personified the progress that he wanted whites
to believe about African Americans in general. Tuskegee Institute was to
be seen as an objective demonstration of black progress. From the time
that he emerged as a national figure and the leader of his race at Atlanta
in 1895, through the publication of *Up From Slavery* in 1901, Washington
held fast to the idea that African Americans were going up, not down.

⋅⊙⋅

The local context in which Booker T. Washington worked always circumscribed his options. Like many Black Belt towns during Reconstruction,
Tuskegee had been the scene of violent racial conflict over political power.
The founding of Tuskegee Institute in 1881 represented an effort for peaceful accommodation between the dominant local whites and a defeated
and unhappy black community. The white leaders mainly responsible for
helping blacks obtain the initial state support for the new school had earlier helped to direct the vigilantes terrorizing Republican voters and officeholders. The message of the local history was clear: Washington's school,
the object lesson of black progress, could only survive if it had the support,
or at least the toleration, of the white community. . . .

White hostility to black education was growing more intense in the
South at the turn of the century. By 1903, when James K. Vardaman was
elected governor of Mississippi, Booker T. Washington was alarmed about
what might happen to black education, because the election had demonstrated that "the majority of white people in Mississippi oppose Negro
education of any character." Industrial education was growing increasingly
controversial. In 1901 the governor of Georgia expressed his view that
while Washington was a "good negro . . . I am opposed to putting negroes
in factories and offices. When you do that you will cause dissatisfaction
between the two races and such things might lead to a race war. The field of
agriculture is the proper one for the negro." In *The Leopard's Spots*, Dixon's

all-knowing white minister claims that industrial education increases the Negro's danger to white society. "Industrial training gives power. If the Negro ever becomes a serious competitor of the white labourer in the industries of the South, the white man will kill him."

◆◎◆

Booker T. Washington's presence at a White House dinner in October 1901 drastically and permanently undermined his acceptance in the white South. There, he would never return to the level of popularity that he had achieved prior to the dinner. The dinner caused leading figures to erupt in outrage. . . .

Although threatening letters poured into Tuskegee and rumors of Washington's impending assassination circulated for years, Tuskegee's principal forged ahead with the purpose that had taken him to the White House in the first place, the naming of federal appointments in the South. Washington had already prevailed on Roosevelt to name Thomas Goode Jones, his ally and the former Democratic governor of Alabama, to the federal judiciary because Jones had, Washington wrote Roosevelt, "stood up in the constitutional convention and elsewhere for a fair election law, opposed lynching, and has been outspoken for the education of both races." In 1903 Washington began a protracted defense of Roosevelt's appointment of William Crum, a black Republican, to be collector of the port of Charleston, South Carolina, against the determined opposition of Senator Tillman. That same year, after Vardaman had ridiculed whites in Indianola, Mississippi, for "tolerating a nigger wench" as postmistress, which caused the woman in question to resign, Washington encouraged Roosevelt not to accept her resignation. All the while he was leading a vigorous, South-wide campaign against the spreading "lily-white" movement in the Republican party, an effort of southern white Republicans to become as "white" as the Democrats. From Roosevelt's entry into the White House at least through the 1908 presidential election, Washington worked constantly to get and maintain black political influence in the Republican party.

Washington's determination to retain African American political influence has earned him the scorn of historians who have seen hypocrisy in his defense of black officeholding while seeming to disavow the importance of suffrage for African Americans. But it may also be understood as the resolve of a man who believed that it was only just that African Americans get some political positions. Washington believed that those few appointments encouraged blacks to feel that they were not entirely removed from American democracy. It also possibly represented the actions of a man who viewed himself as a race leader in competition with other race leaders—Tillman and Vardaman, for example—and he wanted his race to win occasionally. . . .

Throughout 1903 and 1904, Washington continued to push for black appointments, especially a permanent position for Dr. Crum. From 1901 to 1908, southern newspapers focused on no public issue more consistently than Roosevelt's patronage appointments, and there was virtually no support for his position from white-owned newspapers. In Alabama in 1903, judge Jones presided over criminal trials of men charged with peonage, which occasioned condemnation of Jones, Roosevelt, and Booker T. Washington in the southern press. Time and again, editorials and articles referred back to the White House dinner, a perfect symbol of the way that black political influence led to demands for social equality. Further agitating white concerns about political participation during these years was the proposal of the Indiana congressman Edgar Crumpacker, starting in 1901, to reduce the congressional representation of the southern states that had disfranchised black voters. Booker T. Washington opposed the reduction because he thought it would validate and further encourage disfranchisement, and it was not passed in the Congress, but "Crumpackerism" provided southern politicians and editorialists with evidence of continuing northern "meddling" in whites' control of politics in the South. As such it fueled southern whites' hypersensitivity about protecting white supremacy. . . .

◆

After 1905 Washington continued on all the same lines, but his intensity waned as events relentlessly buried his optimism. Although the constitutional limits on funding black education had been defeated, Washington worried about the decimation of black primary schools as local school districts across the South discriminated against black children in the allocation of money for teachers, buildings, and books. "In the country districts I am quite sure that matters are going backward," he wrote privately in 1906. "In many cases in Alabama teachers are being paid as little as Ten dollars per month. This of course means no school." Catastrophic events in 1906 further damaged the person viewed as the leader of the race. The Atlanta riot in September and Roosevelt's wholesale dismissal of black soldiers charged with rioting at Brownsville, Texas, in November represented such injustice that African Americans and sympathetic whites in the North questioned the leadership of the man presumably in charge of protecting black rights. Roosevelt added insult to injury in a presidential address in December that grossly exaggerated black criminality and pandered to the common stereotype. Kelly Miller of Howard University wrote to Washington that Roosevelt's speech did "more to damn the Negro to everlasting infamy than all the maledictions of Tillman, Vardaman, [and] Dixon" and predicted that Washington would be held responsible for Roosevelt's behavior. "When Mr. Roosevelt requested you to act as his adviser and when you accepted that delicate responsibility, the world may be expected to believe that he is guided by the advice of his own seeking." With the symbolism of equality that the White House dinner had represented to African Americans now exploded by Roosevelt's bigotry, Washington lost authority as the leader of his race at the same time that the Niagara Movement solidified northern black opposition to him. He never recovered from these reverses, though typically he never acknowledged his defeat.

❧

The contextual evidence presented herein suggests that Booker T. Washington had great obstacles before him as he tried to lead his race in the 1890s and early twentieth century, and by no honest measure can he be seen as an overall success. His most basic goal was to demonstrate a trajectory of progress among African Americans at a time when the thoroughly white-supremacist society believed that blacks were declining into criminality and even oblivion. He faced a public discourse and a popular culture that were relentlessly set against him. He confronted personal and political enemies in the South who fought to keep him from projecting an ideology of black progress and who, starting in 1901, stirred race hate by attacking Washington for his defense of black officeholders and education. Those attacks undermined his ability to pursue his symbolic action on behalf of black progress, though he never stopped trying.

These reconsiderations of Washington's reputation should make historians think again about how this period of American history is presented. Washington often has been portrayed as the symbol of the age of segregation, he of course standing for acquiescence in Jim Crow. In light of evidence presented herein of Washington's active challenges, direct and indirect, to white supremacy, that understanding seems wrong. So do those views, including ones expressed by Professors Woodward and Harlan, which characterize Washington as "conservative." At the least they represent an unacceptably imprecise meaning for the term. Washington clearly was set against "conserving" the white-supremacist society and culture in which he lived. His purpose was to change things for African Americans. He could only be considered a conservative in his support of the capitalist system.

The designation of Washington as an "accommodationist" also has to be questioned in the light of the evidence herein. He worked too hard to resist and to overcome white supremacy to call him an accommodationist, even if some of his white-supremacist southern neighbors so construed some of his statements. Having conditions forced on him, with threat of destruction clearly the cost of resistance, does not constitute a fair definition of accommodation. The protest-versus-accommodation dichotomy has functioned as virtually a Manichaean divide in writing about African American leadership. The tendency to make protest leaders the good guys and accommodators the bad guys reflects the sentiments at large in society since the Civil Rights Movement. If Booker T. Washington has been the main historical antecedent for accommodationism as the misguided opposite of protest, and if in fact "accommodationism" misrepresents much of his real work, then writing about American race relations must be reevaluated. Indeed, there have been few if any black "leaders" in American history who were not protest leaders in some measure. It is only by comparing degrees of protest commitment, or preferring certain styles of protest to others, that distinctions are drawn (and often overdrawn). This divide has also been understood as between "idealism" and "realism," and historians have favored idealists in writing about black leaders, perhaps because of their self-identity with Washington's critics. In the early 1920s, Kelly Miller noted that "there always existed a small group of assertive Negroes . . . composed mainly of college bred men of liberal culture who were unwilling to compromise their intellectual integrity by surrendering the abstract claim of political rights. They could not tolerate the suggestion of inferiority which Washington's program implied. . . . The man with the theory always has the advantage of the man with the thing, in abstract disquisition. Since Mr. Washington's death, this group has gained the ascendancy in dominating the thought and opinion of the race, but has not been able to realize to the least degree the rights and recognition so vehemently demanded."

The protest-accommodation dichotomy has obscured the fundamental similarity of the substance of Washington's action to the protests agenda put forward starting in 1909 by the National Association for the Advancement of Colored People (NAACP). Washington made public protests against discrimination on railroads, lynching, unfair voting qualifications, discriminatory funding in education, segregated housing legislation, and discrimination by labor unions—the latter two protests coming after 1910. He arranged and personally provided partial funding for lawsuits challenging disfranchisement, jury discrimination, and peonage. And he campaigned constantly against the pernicious images projected in the media and popular culture about blacks, including the 1915 protest against *Birth of a Nation*. He attempted to organize a national black newspaper. The NAACP would have the same protest concerns about segregated public accommodations, lynching, the criminal justice system, and economic discrimination, and it would bring legal challenges to protect blacks' right to vote, get an education, and have fair access to housing. It would also condemn regularly the ugly stereotypes prevalent in American life, starting with *Birth of a Nation* and continuing through *Amos 'n' Andy* on radio in the early 1930s, Hollywood films in the 1940s, and *Amos 'n' Andy* on television in the 1950s. The NAACP did, of course, establish a national publication, Crisis, that accomplished much of what Washington had in mind. Washington's anticipation of virtually all the NAACP protest agenda suggests that a consensus of what needed to be done to protect black rights had been identified as early as 1900, and he and the NAACP had in turn pursued it.

It seems that much common ground lay beneath the two men slugging it out for leadership of the race. Beyond the civil rights strategies that they both embraced in one way or another, they shared a similar despair at the inability of whites to see the achievement of so much decency and intelligence among African Americans. Although Du Bois held the African past in higher regard than Washington did, they both were convinced that people of African descent had been readily civilized. Both were deeply dismayed by the disjuncture between their own achievements and the awful reputation of African Americans as a group among whites. Although Washington did not voice it openly, he and Du Bois understood in similar ways the downward trajectory of black prospects between 1900 and 1908. They agreed that intelligence among African Americans had to be manifest in order to overcome the race's reputation for weakness and poor character, and they also believed that the development of a cadre of black leaders and achievers was necessary to accomplish that. To be sure, they had somewhat different ideas of how to develop African American exemplars, but the nurturing of "human capital" clearly was the first goal of each as a race leader. It is partly because each man distrusted the other so much personally and was so determined to see the other as a major obstruction to his own purposes that their similarities of thought and strategy have been overlooked.

Led by Du Bois, however, historians confused the style with the substance of Booker T. Washington. Many historians have shown a narrowmindedness about black leaders' styles: African American leaders must always be "lions" like Frederick Douglass, Du Bois, Martin Luther King Jr., or Jesse Jackson. They cannot be "foxes" or "rabbits," else they will be accused of lacking manhood. On the level of sound logic, historians must be honest in recognizing that protest has yielded the desired results more episodically than consistently. Other strategies for change have worked better at other times, and external influences have also been the prime determinant of change at some points. It is misleading to teach that change is the result exclusively, or even predominantly, of protest.

But then Washington also misled when he taught that economic uplift would ultimately bring the return of political rights. In a hundred different ways he expressed his faith that a black person who acquired economic independence would command the respect of white neighbors and ultimately with it would come the full rights of citizenship. But he never seems to have acknowledged, not even privately, what was clear from the anti-industrial-education arguments made by Dixon and others at the turn of the century—that most whites objected fundamentally to the rise in status represented by a black skilled worker, business proprietor, or landowner. To concede that would have undermined his economic strategy. And there was no other realistic avenue for progress; certainly, neither politics nor protest would work in the South of 1901. Instead, he did what any good public-relations man does—he ignored the facts that did not fit his presentation of reality. He insisted that blacks would rise in status through education and economic success. To a certain extent, events after his death vindicated his faith: World wars, great migrations, and a vastly expanded national government did bring enough economic opportunity to free many African Americans from the South's hostility to all black economic progress. But those events also brought a greater chance for political solutions, and it would be political action in the 1960s that ended segregation and disfranchisement.

Notwithstanding the sympathetic attitude toward Booker T. Washington herein, let it be understood that he failed in his larger purpose of persuading whites that African Americans were progressing rather than degenerating. His public relations campaign simply could not overcome the intense political and cultural authority of white supremacy that mounted in the 1890s and held sway in the early twentieth century. But neither did the efforts of the NAACP in that regard succeed until World War II, when the national resolve to defeat racist enemies resulted in a commitment, some of it based in government propaganda, to the rejection of racial stereotypes in American culture. The removal of anti-black stereotypes from mass culture that began during World War II enabled the acceptance of African American equality in the 1950s and 1960s. Washington did not succeed in remaking the black image in the American mind, but he identified it as a necessary challenge that others did meet. He should be credited with anticipating the "modern" world in which image was more readily manipulated, and sometimes more important, than reality. His efforts to shape his own symbolism, and that of African Americans as a group, should be marked as a shrewd and valiant effort to lift his people.

POSTSCRIPT

Did Booker T. Washington's Philosophy and Actions Betray the Interests of African Americans?

Discussions of race relations in the late-nineteenth- and early twentieth-century United States invariably focus on the ascendancy of Booker T. Washington, his apparent accommodation to existing patterns of racial segregation, and the conflicting traditions within black thought, epitomized by the clash between Washington and Du Bois. Seldom, however, is attention given to black nationalist thought in the "Age of Booker T. Washington."

Black nationalism, centered on the concept of racial solidarity, has been a persistent theme in African American history, and it reached one of its most important stages of development between 1880 and 1920. In the late 1800s Henry McNeal Turner and Edward Wilmot Blyden encouraged greater interest in the repatriation of black Americans to Africa, especially Liberia. This goal continued into the twentieth century and culminated in the "Back-to-Africa" program of Marcus Garvey and his Universal Negro Improvement Association. Interestingly, Booker T. Washington also exhibited nationalist sentiment by encouraging blacks to withdraw from white society, develop their own institutions and businesses, and engage in economic and moral uplift. Washington's nationalism concentrated on economic self-help and manifested itself in 1900 with the establishment of the National Negro Business League.

A thorough assessment of the protest and accommodation views of black Americans is presented in August Meier, *Negro Thought in America, 1880–1915* (University of Michigan Press, 1963). Rayford Logan, in *The Betrayal of the Negro: From Rutherford B. Hayes to Woodrow Wilson* (Macmillan, 1965), describes the last quarter of the nineteenth century as "the nadir" for black life. By far the best studies on Booker T. Washington are two volumes by Louis R. Harlan: *Booker T. Washington: The Making of a Black Leader, 1856–1901* (Oxford University Press, 1972) and *Booker T. Washington: The Wizard of Tuskegee, 1901–1915* (Oxford University Press, 1983). In addition, Harlan has edited the 13-volume *Booker T. Washington Papers* (University of Illinois Press, 1972–1984). For assessments of two of Booker T. Washington's harshest critics, see Stephen R. Fox's *The Guardian of Boston: William Monroe Trotter* (Atheneum, 1970) and David Levering Lewis's two Pulitzer Prize winning volumes, *W. E. B. Du Bois: Biography of a Race, 1868–1919* (Henry Holt, 1993) and *W. E. B. Du Bois: The Fight for Equality and the American Century, 1919–1963* (Henry Holt, 2000).

John H. Bracey, Jr., August Meier, and Elliott Rudwick, in *Black Nationalism in America* (Bobbs-Merrill, 1970), provide an invaluable collection of documents pertaining to black nationalism. See also Edwin S. Redkey, *Black Exodus: Black Nationalist and Back-to-Africa Movements, 1890–1910* (Yale University Press, 1969), and Hollis R. Lynch, *Edward Wilmot Blyden: Pan-Negro Patriot, 1832–1912* (Oxford University Press, 1967). Diverse views of Marcus Garvey, who credited Booker T. Washington with inspiring him to seek a leadership role on behalf of African Americans, are found in Edmund David Cronon, *Black Moses: The Story of Marcus Garvey and the Universal Negro Improvement Association* (University of Wisconsin Press, 1955), Tony Martin, *Race First: The Ideological and Organizational Struggles of Marcus Garvey and the UNIA* (Greenwood Press, 1976) and Judith Stein, *The World of Marcus Garvey: Race and Class in Modern Society* (Louisiana State University Press, 1986). Some of Garvey's own writings are collected in Amy Jacques-Garvey, ed., *Philosophy and Opinions of Marcus Garvey* (1925; reprint; Atheneum, 1969).

Race relations in the late-nineteenth century are explored in C. Vann Woodward, *The Strange Career of Jim Crow*, 2nd rev. ed. (Oxford University Press, 1966), a volume that sparked a lively historiographical debate concerning the origins of segregation. Of the numerous challenges to the Woodward thesis that a full-blown pattern of racial segregation did not emerge until 1890, Howard N. Rabinowitz's *Race Relations in the Urban South, 1865–1890* (Oxford University Press, 1978) is one of the most insightful. Robert J Norrell provides the most recent overview of American race relations in *The House I Live In: Race in the American Century* (Oxford University Press, 2005). In addition, a number of monographs have appeared over the past four decades, which explore the development of the African American presence in the nation's major cities. Among the best of these urban studies are Gilbert Osofsky, *Harlem: the Making of a Ghetto: Negro New York, 1890–1930* (Harper & Row, 1966); Allan H. Spear, *Black Chicago: the Making of a Negro Ghetto, 1890–1920* (University of Chicago Press, 1967); Kenneth L. Kusmer, *A Ghetto Takes Shape: Black Cleveland, 1870–1930* (University of Illinois Press, 1976); and George C. Wright, *Life Behind a Veil: Blacks in Louisville, Kentucky, 1865–1930* (Louisiana State University Press, 1985).

ISSUE 7

Did the Progressives Fail?

YES: Richard M. Abrams, from "The Failure of Progressivism," in Richard Abrams and Lawrence Levine, eds., *The Shaping of the Twentieth Century*, 2d ed. (Little, Brown, 1971)

NO: Arthur S. Link and Richard L. McCormick, from *Progressivism* (Harlan Davidson, 1983)

ISSUE SUMMARY

YES: Professor of history Richard M. Abrams maintains that progressivism was a failure because it tried to impose a uniform set of values upon a culturally diverse people and never seriously confronted the inequalities that still exist in American society.

NO: Professors of history Arthur S. Link and Richard L. McCormick argue that the Progressives were a diverse group of reformers who confronted and ameliorated the worst abuses that emerged in urban industrial America during the early 1900s.

*P*rogressivism is a word used by historians to define the reform currents in the years between the end of the Spanish-American War and America's entrance into the Great War in Europe in 1917. The so-called Progressive movement had been in operation for over a decade before the label was first used in the 1919 electoral campaigns. Former president Theodore Roosevelt ran as a third-party candidate in the 1912 election on the Progressive party ticket, but in truth the party had no real organization outside of the imposing figure of Theodore Roosevelt. Therefore, as a label, "progressivism" was rarely used as a term of self-identification for its supporters. Even after 1912, it was more frequently used by journalists and historians to distinguish the reformers of the period from socialists and old-fashioned conservatives.

The 1890s was a crucial decade for many Americans. From 1893 until almost the turn of the century, the nation went through a terrible economic depression. With the forces of industrialization, urbanization, and immigration wreaking havoc upon the traditional political, social, and economic structures of American life, changes were demanded. The reformers responded in a variety of ways. The proponents of good government believed that democracy was threatened because the cities were ruled by corrupt political machines while the state legislatures were dominated by corporate interests. The cure was to purify democracy and place government directly in the hands of the people through such devices as the initiative, referendum, recall, and the direct election of local school board officials, judges, and U.S. senators.

Social justice proponents saw the problem from a different perspective. Settlement workers moved into cities and tried to change the urban environment. They pushed for sanitation improvements, tenement house reforms, factory inspection laws, regulation of the hours and wages of women, and the abolition of child labor.

A third group of reformers considered the major problem to be the trusts. They argued for controls over the power of big business and for the preservation of the free enterprise system. Progressives disagreed on whether the issue was size or conduct and on whether the remedy was trust-busting or the regulation of big business. But none could deny the basic question: How was the relationship between big business and the U.S. government to be defined?

How successful was the Progressive movement? What triggered the reform impulse? Who were its leaders? How much support did it attract? More important, did the laws that resulted from the various movements fulfill the intentions of its leaders and supporters?

In the following selections, Richard M. Abrams distinguishes the Progressives from other reformers of the era, such as the Populists, the Socialists, the mainstream labor unions, and the corporate reorganization movement. He then argues that the Progressive movement failed because it tried to impose a uniform set of middle-class Protestant moral values upon a nation that was growing more culturally diverse, and because the reformers supported movements that brought about no actual changes or only superficial ones at best. The real inequalities in American society, says Abrams, were never addressed.

In contrast, Arthur S. Link and Richard L. McCormick view progressivism from the point of view of the reformers and rank it as a qualified success. They survey the criticisms of the movement made by historians since the 1950s and generally find them unconvincing. They maintain that the Progressives made the first real attempts to change the destructive direction in which modern urban-industrial society was moving.

YES

Richard M. Abrams

The Failure of Progressivism

Our first task is definitional, because clearly it would be possible to beg the whole question of "failure" by means of semantical niceties. I have no intention of being caught in that kind of critics' trap. I hope to establish that there was a distinctive major reform movement that took place during most of the first two decades of this century, that it had a mostly coherent set of characteristics and long-term objectives, and that, measured by its own criteria—not criteria I should wish, through hindsight and preference, to impose on it—it fell drastically short of its chief goals.

One can, of course, define a reform movement so broadly that merely to acknowledge that we are where we are and that we enjoy some advantages over where we were would be to prove the "success" of the movement. In many respects, Arthur Link does this sort of thing, both in his and William B. Catton's popular textbook, *American Epoch,* and in his article, "What Happened to the Progressive Movement in the 1920's?" In the latter, Link defines "progressivism" as a movement that "began convulsively in the 1890's and waxed and waned afterward to our own time, to insure the survival of democracy in the United States by the enlargement of governmental power to control and offset the power of private economic groups over the nation's institutions and life." Such a definition may be useful to classify data gathered to show the liberal sources of the enlargement of governmental power since the 1890's; but such data would not be finely classified enough to tell us much about the *non*liberal sources of governmental power (which were numerous and important), about the distinctive styles of different generations of reformers concerned with a liberal society, or even about vital distinctions among divergent reform groups in the era that contemporaries and the conventional historical wisdom have designed as progressive. . . .

Now, without going any further into the problem of historians' definitions which are too broad or too narrow—there is no space here for such an effort—I shall attempt a definition of my own, beginning with the problem that contemporaries set themselves to solve and that gave the era its cognomen, "progressive." That problem was *progress*—or more specifically, how American society was to continue to enjoy the fruits of material progress without the accompanying assault upon human dignity and the

From *The Shaping of the Twentieth Century,* 2nd ed., by Richard M. Abrams. Copyright © 1971 by Richard M. Abrams. Reprinted by permission of the author, who is a Professor of History and Associate Dean of International & Area Studies, University of California in Berkeley.

erosion of the conventional values and moral assumptions on which the social order appeared to rest. . . .

To put it briefly and yet more specifically, a very large body of men and women entered into reform activities at the end of the nineteenth century to translate "the national credo" (as Henry May calls it) into a general program for social action. Their actions, according to Richard Hofstadter, were "founded upon the indigenous Yankee-Protestant political tradition [that] assumed and demanded the constant disinterested activity of the citizen in public affairs, argued that political life ought to be run, to a greater degree than it was, in accordance with general principles and abstract laws apart from and superior to personal needs, and expressed a common feeling that government should be in good part an effort to moralize the lives of individuals while economic life should be intimately related to the stimulation and development of individual character."

The most consistently important reform impulse, among many reform impulses, during the progressive era grew directly from these considerations. It is this reform thrust that we should properly call "the progressive movement." We should distinguish it carefully from reform movements in the era committed primarily to other considerations.

The progressive movement drew its strength from the old mugwump reform impulse, civil service reform, female emancipationists, prohibitionists, the social gospel, the settlement-house movement, some national expansionists, some world peace advocates, conservation advocates, technical efficiency experts, and a wide variety of intellectuals who helped cut through the stifling, obstructionist smokescreen of systematized ignorance. It gained powerful allies from many disadvantaged business interests that appealed to politics to redress unfavorable trade positions; from some ascendant business interests seeking institutional protection; from publishers who discovered the promotional value of exposes; and from politicians-on-the-make who sought issues with which to dislodge long-lived incumbents from their place. Objectively it focused on or expressed (1) a concern for responsive, honest, and efficient government, on the local and state levels especially; (2) recognition of the obligations of society—particularly of an affluent society—to its underprivileged; (3) a desire for more rational use of the nation's resources and economic energies; (4) a rejection, on at least intellectual grounds, of certain social principles that had long obstructed social remedies for what had traditionally been regarded as irremediable evils, such as poverty; and, above all, (5) a concern for the maintenance or restoration of a consensus on what conventionally had been regarded as *fixed moral* principles. "The first and central faith in the national credo," writes Professor May, "was, as it always had been, the reality, certainty, and eternity of moral values. . . . A few thought and said that ultimate values and goals were unnecessary, but in most cases this meant that they believed so deeply in a consensus on these matters that they could not imagine a serious challenge." Progressives shared this faith with most of the rest of the country, but they also conceived of themselves, with a grand sense of stewardship, as its heralds, and its agents.

The progressive movement was (and is) distinguishable from other Contemporary reform movements not only by its devotion to social conditions regarded, by those within it as well as by much of the generality, as *normative*, but also by its definition of what forces threatened that order. More specifically, progressivism directed its shafts at five principal enemies, each in its own way representing reform:

1. The socialist *reform movement*—because, despite socialism's usually praiseworthy concern for human dignity, it represented the subordination of the rights of private property and of individualistic options to objectives that often explicitly threatened common religious beliefs and conventional standards of justice and excellence.
2. The corporate reorganization of American business, which I should call the *corporate reform movement* (its consequence has, after all, been called "the corporate revolution")—because it challenged the traditional relationship of ownership and control of private property, because it represented a shift from production to profits in the entrepreneurial definition of efficiency, because it threatened the proprietary small-business character of the American social structure, because it had already demonstrated a capacity for highly concentrated and socially irresponsible power, and because it sanctioned practices that strained the limits of conventionality and even legality.
3. *The labor union movement*—because despite the virtues of unionized labor as a source of countervailing force against the corporations and as a basis for a more orderly labor force, unionism (like corporate capitalism and socialism) suggested a reduction of individualistic options (at least for wage-earners and especially for small employers), and a demand for a partnership with business management in the decision-making process by a class that convention excluded from such a role.
4. *Agrarian radicalism,* and populism in particular—because it, too, represented (at least in appearance) the insurgency of a class conventionally believed to be properly excluded from a policy-making role in the society, a class graphically represented by the "Pitchfork" Bens and "Sockless" Jerrys, the "Cyclone" Davises and "Alfalfa" Bills, the wool hat brigade and the rednecks.
5. *The ethnic movement*—the demand for specific political and social recognition of ethnic or ex-national affiliations—because accession to the demand meant acknowledgment of the fragmentation of American society as well as a retreat from official standards of integrity, honesty, and efficiency in government in favor of standards based on personal loyalty, partisanship, and sectarian provincialism.

Probably no two progressives opposed all of these forces with equal animus, and most had a noteworthy sympathy for one or more of them. . . .

So much for what progressivism was not. Let me sum it up by noting that what it rejected and sought to oppose necessarily says much about what it was—perhaps even more than can be ascertained by the more direct approach.

My thesis is that progressivism failed. It failed in what it—or what those who shaped it—conceived to be its principal objective. And that was, over and above everything else, to restore or maintain the conventional consensus on a particular view of the universe, a particular set of values, and a particular constellation of behavioral modes in the country's commerce, its industry, its social relations, and its politics. Such a view, such values, such modes were challenged by the influx of diverse religious and ethnic elements into the nation's social and intellectual stream, by the overwhelming economic success and power of the corporate form of business organization, by the subordination of the work-ethic bound up within the old proprietary and craft enterprise system, and by the increasing centrality of a growing proportion of low-income, unskilled, wage-earning classes in the nation's economy and social structure. Ironically, the *coup de grâce* would be struck by the emergence of a philosophical and scientific rationale for the existence of cultural diversity within a single social system, a rationale that largely grew out of the very intellectual ferment to which progressivism so substantially contributed.

Progressivism sought to save the old view, and the old values and modes, by educating the immigrants and the poor so as to facilitate their acceptance of and absorption into the Anglo-American mode of life, or by excluding the "unassimilable" altogether; by instituting antitrust legislation or, at the least, by imposing regulations upon corporate practices in order to preserve a minimal base for small proprietary business enterprise; by making legislative accommodations to the newly important wage-earning classes—accommodations that might provide some measure of wealth and income redistribution, on-the-job safety, occupational security, and the like—so as to forestall a forcible transfer of policy-making power away from the groups that had conventionally exercised that power; and by broadening the political selection process, through direct elections, direct nominations, and direct legislation, in order to reduce tensions caused unnecessarily by excessively narrow and provincial cliques of policymakers. When the economic and political reforms failed to restore the consensus by giving the previously unprivileged an ostensible stake in it, progressive energies turned increasingly toward using the force of the state to proscribe or restrict specifically opprobrious modes of social behavior, such as gaming habits, drinking habits, sexual habits, and Sabbatarian habits. In the ultimate resort, with the proliferation of sedition and criminal syndicalist laws, it sought to constrict political discourse itself. And (except perhaps for the disintegration of the socialist movement) *that* failed, too.

One measure of progressivism's failure lies in the xenophobic racism that reappeared on a large scale even by 1910. In many parts of the country, for example, in the far west and the south, racism and nativism had been fully blended with reform movements even at the height of progressive activities there. The alleged threats of "coolie labor" to American living standards, and of "venal" immigrant and Negro voting to republican institutions generally, underlay the alliance of racism and reform in this period. By and large, however, for the early progressive era the alliance was conspicuous only in the south and on the west coast. By 1910, signs of heightening ethnic animosities, most notably anti-Catholicism, began appearing in other areas of the country as well. As John Higham has written, "It is hard to explain the rebirth of anti-Catholic ferment [at this time] except as an outlet for expectations which progressivism raised and then failed to fulfill." The failure here was in part the inability of reform to deliver a meaningful share of the social surplus to the groups left out of the general national progress, and in part the inability of reform to achieve its objective of assimilation and consensus.

The growing ethnic animus, moreover, operated to compound the difficulty of achieving assimilation. By the second decade of the century, the objects of the antagonism were beginning to adopt a frankly assertive posture. The World War, and the ethnic cleavages it accentuated and aggravated, represented only the final blow to the assimilationist idea; "hyphenate" tendencies had already been growing during the years before 1914. It had only been in 1905 that the Louisvilleborn and secular-minded Louis Brandeis had branded as "disloyal" all who "keep alive" their differences of origin or religion. By 1912, by now a victim of anti-Semitism and aware of a rising hostility toward Jews in the country, Brandeis had become an active Zionist; before a Jewish audience in 1913, he remarked how "practical experience" had convinced him that "to be good Americans, we must be better Jews, and to be better Jews, we must become Zionists."

Similarly, American Negroes also began to adopt a more aggressive public stance after having been subdued for more than a decade by antiblack violence and the accommodationist tactics suggested in 1895 by Booker T. Washington. As early as 1905, many black leaders had broken with Washington in founding the Niagara Movement for a more vigorous assertion of Negro demands for equality. But most historians seem to agree that it was probably the Springfield race riot of 1908 that ended illusions that black people could gain an equitable share in the rewards of American culture by accommodationist or assimilationist methods. The organization of the NAACP in 1909 gave substantive force for the first time to the three-year-old Niagara Movement. The year 1915 symbolically concluded the demise of accommodationism. That year, the Negro-baiting movie, "The Birth of a Nation," played to massive, enthusiastic audiences that included notably the president of the United States and the chief justice of the Supreme Court; the KKK was revived; and Booker T. Washington died. The next year, black nationalist Marcus Garvey arrived in New York from Jamaica.

Meanwhile, scientific knowledge about race and culture was undergoing a crucial revision. At least in small part stimulated by a keen self-consciousness of his own "outsider" status in American culture, the German-Jewish immigrant Franz Boas was pioneering in the new anthropological concept of "cultures," based on the idea that human behavioral traits are conditioned by historical traditions. The new view of culture was in time to undermine completely the prevailing evolutionary view that ethnic differences must mean racial inequality. The significance of Boas's work after 1910, and that of his students A. L. Kroeber and Clyde Kluckhohn in particular, rests on the fact that the racist thought of the progressive era had founded its intellectual rationale on the monistic, evolutionary view of culture; and indeed much of the progressives' anxiety over the threatened demise of "the American culture" had been founded on that view.

Other intellectual developments as well had for a long time been whittling away at the notion that American society had to stand or fall on the unimpaired coherence of its cultural consensus. Yet the new work in anthropology, law, philosophy, physics, psychology, and literature only unwittingly undermined that assumption. Rather, it was only as the ethnic hostilities grew, and especially as the power of the state came increasingly to be invoked against dissenting groups whose ethnic "peculiarities" provided an excuse for repression, that the new intelligence came to be developed. "The world has thought that it must have its culture and its political unity coincide," wrote Randolph Bourne in 1916 while chauvinism, nativism, and antiradicalism were mounting; now it was seeing that cultural diversity might yet be the salvation of the liberal society—that it might even serve to provide the necessary countervailing force to the power of the state that private property had once served (in the schema of Locke, Harrington, and Smith) before the interests of private property became so highly concentrated and so well blended with the state itself.

The telltale sign of progressivism's failure was the violent crusade against dissent that took place in the closing years of the Wilson administration. It is too easy to ascribe the literal hysteria of the postwar years to the dislocations of the War alone. Incidents of violent repression of labor and radical activities had been growing remarkably, often in step with xenophobic outbreaks, for several years before America's intervention in the War. To quote Professor Higham once more. "The seemingly unpropitious circumstances under which antiradicalism and anti-Catholicism came to life [after 1910] make their renewal a subject of moment." It seems clear that they both arose out of the sources of the reform ferment itself. When reform failed to enlarge the consensus, or to make it more relevant to the needs of the still disadvantaged and disaffected, and when in fact reform seemed to be encouraging more radical challenges to the social order, the old anxieties of the 1890's returned.

The postwar hysteria represented a reaction to a confluence of anxietyladen developments, including the high cost of living, the physical and social dislocations of war mobilization and the recruitment of women and Negroes into war production jobs in the big northern cities, the Bolshevik Revolution, a series of labor strikes, and a flood of radical literature that exaggerated the capabilities of radical action. "One Hundred Per Cent Americanism" seemed the only effective way of meeting all these challenges at once. As Stanley Coben has written, making use of recent psychological studies and anthropological work on cultural "revitalization movements"; "Citizens who joined the crusade for one hundred per cent Americanism sought, primarily, a unifying forte which would halt the apparent disintegration of their culture. . . . The slight evidence of danger from radical organizations aroused such wild fear only because Americans had already encountered other threats to cultural stability."

Now, certainly during the progressive era a lot of reform legislation was passed, much that contributed genuinely to a more liberal society, though more that contributed to the more absolutistic moral objectives of progressivism. Progressivism indeed had real, lasting effects for the blunting of the sharper edges of self-interest in American life, and for the reduction of the harsher cruelties suffered by the society's underprivileged. These achievements deserve emphasis, not least because they derived directly from the progressive habit of looking to standards of conventional morality and human decency for the solution of diverse social conflicts. But the deeper nature of the problem confronting American society required more than the invocation of conventional standards; the conventions themselves were at stake, especially as they bore upon the allocation of privileges and rewards. Because most of the progressives never confronted that problem, in a way their efforts were doomed to failure.

In sum, the overall effect of the period's legislation is not so impressive. For example, all the popular government measures put together have not conspicuously raised the quality of American political life. Direct nominations and elections have tended to make political campaigns so expensive as to reduce the number of eligible candidates for public office to (1) the independently wealthy; (2) the ideologues, especially on the right, who can raise the needed campaign money from independently wealthy ideologues like themselves, or from the organizations set up to promote a particular ideology; and (3) party hacks who payoff their debt to the party treasury by whistle-stopping and chicken dinner speeches. Direct legislation through the Initiative and Referendum device has made cities and states prey to the best-financed and organized special-interest group pressures, as have so-called nonpartisan elections. Which is not to say that things are worse than before, but only that they are not conspicuously better. The popular government measures did have the effect of shaking up the established political organizations of the day, and that may well have been their only real purpose.

But as Arthur Link has said, in his text, *The American Epoch*, the popular government measures "were merely instruments to facilitate the capture of political machinery. . . . They must be judged for what they accomplished or failed to accomplish on the higher level of substantive reform." Without disparaging the long list of reform measures that passed during the progressive era, the question remains whether all the "substantive reforms" together accomplished what the progressives wanted them to accomplish.

Certain social and economic advantages were indeed shuffled about, but this must be regarded as a short-term achievement for special groups at best. Certain commercial interests, for example, achieved greater political leverage in railroad policy-making than they had had in 1900 through measures such as the Hepburn and Mann-Elkins Acts—though it was not until the 1940's that any real change occurred in the general rate structure, as some broad regional interests had been demanding at the beginning of the century. Warehouse, farm credits, and land-bank acts gave the diminishing numbers of farm owners enhanced opportunities to mortgage their property, and some business groups had persuaded the federal government to use national revenues to educate farmers on how to increase their productivity (Smith-Lever Act, 1914); but most farmers remained as dependent as ever upon forces beyond their control—the bankers, the middlemen, the international market. The FTC, and the Tariff Commission established in 1916, extended the principle of using government agencies to adjudicate intra-industrial conflicts ostensibly in the national interest, but these agencies would develop a lamentable tendency of deferring to and even confirming rather than moderating the power of each industry's dominant interests. The Federal Reserve Act made the currency more flexible, and that certainly made more sense than the old system, as even the bankers agreed. But depositers would be as prey to defaulting banks as they had been in the days of the Pharaoh—bank deposit insurance somehow was "socialism" to even the best of men in this generation. And despite Woodrow Wilson's brave promise to end the banker's stifling hold on innovative small business, one searches in vain for some provision in the FRA designed specifically to encourage small or new businesses. In fact, the only constraints on the bankers' power that emerged from the era came primarily from the ability of the larger corporations to finance their own expansion out of capital surpluses they had accumulated from extortionate profits during the War.

A major change almost occurred during the war years when organized labor and the principle of collective bargaining received official recognition and a handful of labor leaders was taken, temporarily, into policy-making councils (e.g., in the War Labor Board). But actually, as already indicated, such a development, if it had been made permanent, would have represented a defeat, not a triumph, for progressivism. The progressives may have fought for improved labor conditions, but they jealously fought against the enlargement of union power. It was no aberration that once the need for wartime productive efficiency evaporated, leading progressives such as A. Mitchell Palmer, Miles Poindexter, and Woodrow Wilson himself helped civic and employer organizations to bludgeon the labor movement into disunity and docility. (It is possible, I suppose, to argue that such progressives were simply inconsistent, but if we understand progressivism in the terms I have outlined above I think the consistency is more evident.) Nevertheless, a double irony is worth noting with respect to progressivism's objectives and the wartime labor developments. On the one hand, the progressives' hostility to labor unions defeated their own objectives of (1) counterbalancing the power of collectivized capital (i.e., corporations), and (2) enhancing workers' share of the nation's wealth. On the other hand, under wartime duress, the progressives did grant concessions to organized labor (e.g., the Adamson Eight-Hour Railway

Labor Act, as well as the WLB) that would later serve as precedents for the very "collectivization" of the economic situation that they were dedicated to oppose.

Meanwhile, the distribution of advantages in the society did not change much at all. In some cases, from the progressive reformers' viewpoint at least, it may even have changed for the worse. According to the figures of the National Industrial Conference Board, even income was as badly distributed at the end of the era as before. In 1921, the highest 10 percent of income recipients received 38 percent of total personal income, and that figure was only 34 percent in 1910. (Since the share of the top S percent of income recipients probably declined in the 1910–20 period, the figures for the top 10 percent group suggest a certain improvement in income distribution at the top. But the fact that the share of the lowest 60 percent also declined in that period, from 35 percent to 30 percent, confirms the view that no meaningful improvement can be shown.) Maldistribution was to grow worse until after 1929.

American farmers on the whole and in particular seemed to suffer increasing disadvantages. Farm life was one of the institutional bulwarks of the mode of life the progressives ostensibly cherished. "The farmer who owns his land" averred Gifford Pinchot, "is still the backbone of the Nation; and one of the things we want most is more of him, . . . [for] he is the first of home-makers." If only in the sense that there were relatively fewer farmers in the total population at the end of the progressive era, one would have to say farm life in the United States had suffered. But, moreover, fewer owned their own farms. The number of farm tenants increased by 21 percent from 1900 to 1920; 38.1 percent of all farm operators in 1921 were tenants; and the figures look even worse when one notices that tenancy *declined* in the most *impoverished* areas during this period, suggesting that the family farm was surviving mostly in the more marginal agricultural areas. Finally, although agriculture had enjoyed some of its most prosperous years in history in the 1910–20 period, the 21 percent of the nation's gainfully employed who were in agriculture in 1919 (a peak year) earned only 16 percent of the national income.

While progressivism failed to restore vitality to American farming, it failed also to stop the vigorous ascendancy of corporate capitalism, the most conspicuous challenge to conventional values and modes that the society faced at the beginning of the era. The corporation had drastically undermined the very basis of the traditional rationale that had supported the nation's freewheeling system of resource allocation and had underwritten the permissiveness of the laws governing economic activities in the nineteenth century. The new capitalism by-passed the privately-owned proprietary firm, it featured a separation of ownership and control, it subordinated the profit motive to varied and variable other objectives such as empire-building, and, in many of the techniques developed by financial brokers and investment bankers, it appeared to create a great gulf between the making of money and the producing of useful goods and services. Through a remarkable series of judicial sophistries, this nonconventional form of business enterprise had become, in law, a person, and had won privileges and liberties once entrusted only to men, who were presumed to be conditioned and restrained by the moral qualities that inhere in human nature. Although gaining legal dispensations from an obliging Supreme Court, the corporation could claim no theoretical legitimacy beyond the fact of its power and its apparent inextricable entanglement in the business order that had produced America's seemingly unbounded material success.

Although much has been written about the supposed continuing vitality of small proprietary business enterprise in the United States, there is no gainsaying the continued ascendancy of the big corporation nor the fact that it still lacks legitimation. The fact that in the last sixty years the number of small proprietary businesses has grown at a rate that slightly exceeds the rate of population growth says little about the character of small business enterprise today as compared with that of the era of the American industrial revolution; it does nothing to disparage the apprehensions expressed in the antitrust campaigns of the progressives. To focus on the vast numbers of automobile dealers and gasoline service station owners, for example, is to miss completely their truly humble dependence upon the very few giant automobile and oil companies, a foretold dependence that was the very point of progressives' anticorporation, antitrust sentiments. The progressive movement must indeed be credited with placing real restraints upon monopolistic tendencies in the United States, for most statistics indicate that at least until the 1950's business concentration showed no substantial increase from the turn of the century (though it may be pertinent to note that concentration ratios did increase significantly in the decade immediately following the progressive era). But the statistics of concentration remain impressive—just as they were when John Moody wrote *The Truth About the Trusts* in 1904 and Louis Brandeis followed it with *Other People's Money* in 1914. That two hundred corporations (many of them interrelated) held almost one-quarter of all business assets, and more than 40 percent of all corporate assets in the country in 1948; that the fifty largest manufacturing corporations held 35 percent of all industrial assets in 1948, and 38 percent by 1962; and that a mere twenty-eight corporations or one one-thousandth of a percentage of all nonfinancial firms in 1956 employed 10 percent of all those employed in the nonfinancial industries, should be sufficient statistical support for the apprehensions of the progressive era—*just as it is testimony to the failure of the progressive movement to achieve anything substantial to alter the situation.*

Perhaps the crowning failure of progressivism was the American role in World War I. It is true that many progressives opposed America's intervention, but it is also true that a great many more supported it. The failure in progressivism lies not in the decision to intervene but in the futility of intervention measured by progressive expectations.

Arthur S. Link and
Richard L. McCormick

 **NO**

Progressivism in History

Convulsive reform movements swept across the American landscape from the 1890s to 1917. Angry farmers demanded better prices for their products, regulation of the railroads, and the destruction of what they thought was the evil power of bankers, middlemen, and corrupt politicians. Urban residents crusaded for better city services and more efficient municipal government. Members of various professions, such as social workers and doctors, tried to improve the dangerous and unhealthy conditions in which many people lived and worked. Businessmen, too, lobbied incessantly for goals which they defined as reform. Never before had the people of the United States engaged in so many diverse movements for the improvement of their political system, economy, were calling themselves *progressives*. Ever since, historians have used the term *progessivism* to describe the many reform movements of the early twentieth century.

Yet in the goals they sought and the remedies they tried, the reformers were a varied and contradictory lot. Some progressives wanted to increase the political influence and control of ordinary people, while other progressives wanted to concentrate authority in experts. Many reformers tried to curtail the growth of large corporations; others accepted bigness in industry on account of its supposed economic benefits. Some progressives were genuinely concerned about the welfare of the "new" immigrants from southern and eastern Europe; other progressives sought, sometimes frantically, to "Americanize" the newcomers or to keep them out altogether. In general, progressives sought to improve the conditions of life and labor and to create as much social stability as possible. But each group of progressives had its own definitions of improvement and stability. In the face of such diversity, one historian, Peter G. Filene, has even argued that what has been called the progressive movement never existed as a historical phenomenon ("An Obituary for 'The Progressive Movement,'" *American Quarterly*, 1970).

Certainly there was no *unified* movement, but, like most students of the period, we consider progessivism to have been a real, vital, and significant phenomenon, one which contemporaries recognized and talked and fought about. Properly conceptualized, progressivism provides a useful framework for the history of the United States in the late nineteenth and early twentieth centuries.

One source of confusion and controversy about progressives and progressivism is the words themselves. They are often used judgmentally to describe people and changes which historians have deemed to be "good," "enlightened," and "farsighted." The progressives themselves naturally intended the words to convey such positive qualities, but we should not accept their usage uncritically. It might be better to avoid the terms progressive and progressivism altogether, but they are too deeply embedded in the language of contemporaries and historians to be ignored. Besides, we think that the terms have real meaning. In this [selection] the words will be used neutrally, without any implicit judgment about the value of reform.

In the broadest sense, progressivism was the way in which a whole generation of Americans defined themselves politically and responded to the nation's problems at the turn of the century. The progressives made the first comprehensive efforts to grapple with the ills of a modern urban-industrial society. Hence the record of their achievements and failures has considerable relevance for our own time.

Who Were the Progressives?

Ever since the early twentieth century, people have argued about who the progressives were and what they stood for. This may seem to be a strange topic of debate, but it really is not. Progressivism engaged many different groups of Americans, and each group of progressives naturally considered themselves to be the key reformers and thought that their own programs were the most important ones. Not surprisingly, historians ever since have had trouble agreeing on who really shaped progressivism and its goals. Scholars who have written about the period have variously identified farmers, the old middle classes, professionals, businessmen, and urban immigrants and ethnic groups as the core group of progressives. But these historians have succeeded in identifying *their* reformers only by defining progressivism narrowly, by excluding other reformers and reforms when they do not fall within some specific definition, and by resorting to such vague, catch-all adjectives as "middle class." . . .

The advocates of the middle-class view might reply that they intended to study the leaders of reform, not its supporters, to identify and describe the men and women who imparted the dominant character to progressivism, not its mass base. The study of leadership is surely a valid subject in its own right and is particularly useful for an understanding of progressivism. But too much focus on leadership conceals more than it discloses about early twentieth-century reform. The dynamics of progressivism were crucially generated by ordinary people—by the sometimes frenzied mass supporters of progressive leaders, by rank-and-file voters willing to trust a reform candidate. The chronology of progressivism can be traced by events which aroused large numbers of people—a sensational muckraking article, an outrageous political scandal, an eye-opening legislative investigation, or a tragic social calamity. Events such as these gave reform its rhythm and its power.

Progressivism cannot be understood without seeing how the masses of Americans perceived and responded to such events. Widely circulated magazines gave people everywhere the sordid facts of corruption and carried the clamor for reform into every city, village, and county. State and national election campaigns enabled progressive candidates to trumpet their programs. Almost no literate person in the United States in, say, 1906 could have been unaware that ten-year-old children worked through the night in dangerous factories, or that many United States senators served big business. Progressivism was the only reform movement ever experienced by the whole American nation. Its national appeal and mass base vastly exceeded that of Jacksonian reform. And progressivism's dependence on the people for its objectives and timing has no comparison in the executive-dominated New Deal of Franklin D. Roosevelt or the Great Society of Lyndon B. Johnson. Wars and depressions had previously engaged the whole nation, but never reform. And so we are back to the problem of how to explain and define the outpouring of progressive reform which excited and involved so many different kinds of people.

A little more than a decade ago, Buenker and Thelen recognized the immense diversity of progressivism and suggested ways in which to reorient the study of early twentieth-century reform. Buenker observed that divergent groups often came together on one issue and then changed alliances on the next ("The Progressive Era: A Search for a Synthesis," *Mid-America*, 1969). Indeed, different reformers sometimes favored the same measure for distinctive, even opposite, reasons. Progressivism could be understood only in the light of these shifting coalitions. Thelen, in his study of Wisconsin's legislature, also emphasized the importance of cooperation between different reform groups. "The basic riddle in Progressivism," he concluded, "is not what drove groups apart but what made them seek common cause."

There is a great deal of wisdom in these articles, particularly in their recognition of the diversity of progressivism and in the concept of shifting coalitions of reformers. A two-pronged approach is necessary to carry forward this way of looking at early twentieth-century reform. First, we should study, not an imaginary unified progressive movement, but individual reforms and give particular attention to the goals of their diverse supporters, the public rationales given for them, and the results which they achieved. Second, we should try to identify the features which were more or less common to different progressive reforms.

The first task—distinguishing the goals of a reform from its rhetoric and its results—is more difficult than it might appear to be. Older interpretations of progressivism implicitly assumed that the rhetoric explained the goals and that, if a proposed reform became law, the results fulfilled the intentions behind it. Neither assumption is a sound one: purposes, rationale, and results are three different things. Samuel P. Hays' influential article, "The Politics of Reform in Municipal Government in the Progressive Era" (*Pacific Northwest Quarterly*, 1964), exposed the fallacy of automatically equating the democratic rhetoric of the reformers with their true purposes. The two may have coincided, but the historian has to demonstrate that fact, not take it for granted. The unexamined identification of either intentions or rhetoric with results is also invalid, although it is still a common feature of the scholarship on progressivism. Only within the last decade have historians begun to examine the actual achievements of the reformers. To carry out this first task, in the following . . . we will distinguish between the goals and rhetoric of individual reforms and will discuss the results of reform whenever the current literature permits. To do so is to observe the ironies, complexities, and disappointments of progressivism.

The second task—that of identifying the common characteristics of progressivism—is even more difficult than the first but is an essential base on which to build an understanding of progressivism. The rest of this [selection] focuses on identifying such characteristics. The place to begin that effort is the origins of progressivism. . . .

The Character and Spirit of Progressivism

Progressivism was characterized, in the first place, by a distinctive set of attitudes toward industrialism. By the turn of the century, the overwhelming majority of Americans had accepted the permanence of large-scale industrial, commercial, and financial enterprises and of the wage and factory systems. The progressives shared this attitude. Most were not socialists, and they undertook reform, not to dismantle modern economic institutions, but rather to ameliorate and improve the conditions of industrial life. Yet progressivism was infused with a deep outrage against the worst consequences of industrialism. Outpourings of anger at corporate wrongdoing and of hatred for industry's callous pursuit of profit frequently punctuated the course of reform in the early twentieth century. Indeed, antibusiness emotion was a prime mover of progressivism. That the acceptance of industrialism *and* the outrage against it were intrinsic to early twentieth-century reform does not mean that progressivism was mindless or that it has to be considered indefinable. But it does suggest that there was a powerful irony in progressivism: reforms which gained support from a people angry with the oppressive aspects of industrialism also assisted the same persons to accommodate to it, albeit to an industrialism which was to some degree socially responsible.

The progressives' ameliorative reforms also reflected their faith in progress—in mankind's ability, through purposeful action, to improve the environment and the conditions of life. The late nineteenth-century dissidents had not lacked this faith, but their espousal of panaceas bespoke a deep pessimism: "Unless this one great change is made, things will get worse." Progressive reforms were grounded on a broader assumption. In particular, reforms could protect the people hurt by industrialization, and make the environment more humane. For intellectuals of the era, the achievement of such goals meant that they had to meet Herbert Spencer head on and confute his absolute "truths." Progressive thinkers, led by Lester Frank Ward, Richard T. Ely, and, most important, John Dewey, demolished social Darwinism with what Goldman has called "reform Darwinism." They asserted that human adaptation to the environment did not interfere with the evolutionary process, but was, rather, part and parcel of the law of natural change. Progressive intellectuals and their popularizers produced a vast literature to condemn laissez faire and to promote the concept of the active state.

To improve the environment meant, above all, to intervene in economic and social affairs in order to control natural forces and impose a measure of order upon them. This belief in interventionism was a third component of progressivism. It was visible in almost every reform of the era, from the supervision of business to the prohibition of alcohol John W. Chambers II, *The Tyranny of Change: America in the Progressive Era, 1900–1917*, 1980). Interventionism could be both private and public. Given their choice, most progressives preferred to work noncoercively through voluntary organizations for economic and social changes. However, as time passed, it became evident that most progressive reforms could be achieved only by legislation and public control. Such an extension of public authority made many progressives uneasy, and few of them went so far as Herbert Croly in glorifying the state in his *The Promise of American Life* (1909) and *Progressive Democracy* (1914). Even so, the intervention necessary for their reforms inevitably propelled progressives toward an advocacy of the use of governmental power. A familiar scenario during the period was one in which progressives called upon public authorities to assume responsibility for interventions which voluntary organizations had begun.

The foregoing describes the basic characteristics of progressivism but says little about its ideals. Progressivism was inspired by two bodies of belief and knowledge—evangelical Protestantism and the natural and social sciences. These sources of reform may appear at first glance antagonistic to one another. Actually, they were complementary, and each imparted distinctive qualities to progressivism.

Ever since the religious revivals from about 1820 to 1840, evangelical Protestantism had spurred reform in the United States. Basic to the reform mentality was an all-consuming urge to purge the world of sin, such as the sins of slavery and intemperance, against which nineteenth-century reformers had crusaded. Now the progressives carried the struggle into the modern citadels of sin—the teeming cities of the nation. No one can read their writings and speeches without being struck by the fact that many of them believed that it was their Christian duty to right the wrongs created by the processes of industrialization. Such belief was the motive force behind the Social Gospel, a movement which swept through the Protestant churches in the 1890s and 1900s. Its goal was to align churches, frankly and aggressively, on the side of the downtrodden, the poor, and working people—in other words, to make Christianity relevant to this world, not the next. It is difficult to measure the influence of the Social Gospel, but it seared the consciences of millions of Americans, particularly in urban areas. And it triumphed in the organization in 1908 of the Federal Council of Churches of Christ in America, with its platform which condemned exploitative capitalism and proclaimed the right of workers to organize and to enjoy a decent standard of living. Observers at the Progressive party's national convention of 1912 should not have been surprised to hear the delegates sing, spontaneously and emotionally, the Christian call to arms, "Onward, Christian Solders!"

The faith which inspired the singing of "Onward, Christian Soldiers!" had significant implications for progressive reforms. Progressives used moralistic appeals to make people feel the awful weight of wrong in the world and to exhort them to accept personal responsibility for its eradication. The resultant reforms could be generous in spirit, but they could also seem intolerant to the people who were "reformed." Progressivism sometimes seemed to envision life in a small town Protestant community or an urban drawing room—a vision sharply different from that of Catholic or Jewish immigrants. Not every progressive shared the evangelical ethos, much less its intolerance, but few of the era's reforms were untouched by the spirit and techniques of Protestant revivalism.

Science also had a pervasive impact on the methods and objectives of progressivism. Many leading reformers were specialists in the new disciplines of statistics, economics, sociology, and psychology. These new social scientists set out to gather data on human behavior as it actually was and to discover the laws which governed it. Since social scientists accepted environmentalist and interventionist assumptions implicitly, they believed that knowledge of natural laws would make it possible to devise and apply solutions to improve the human condition. This faith underpinned the optimism of most progressives and predetermined the methods used by almost all reformers of the time: investigation of the facts and application of social-science knowledge to their analysis; entrusting trained experts to decide what should be done; and, finally, mandating government to execute reform.

These methods may have been rational, but they were also compatible with progressive moralism. In its formative period, American social science was heavily infused with ethical concerns. An essential purpose of statistics, economics, sociology, and psychology was to improve and uplift. Leading practitioners of these disciplines, for example, Richard T. Ely, an economist at the University of Wisconsin, were often in the vanguard of the Social Gospel. Progressives blended science and religion into a view of human behavior which was unique to their generation, which had grown up in an age of revivals and come to maturity at the birth of social science.

All of progressivism's distinctive features found expression in muckraking—the literary spearhead of early twentieth-century reform. Through the medium of such new ten-cent magazines as *McClure's, Everybody's and Cosmopolitan,* the muckrakers exposed every dark aspect and corner of American life. Nothing escaped the probe of writers such as Ida M. Tarbell, Lincoln Steffens, Ray Stannard Baker, and Burton J. Hendrick—not big business, politics, prostitution, race relations, or even the churches. Behind the exposes of the muckrakers lay the progressive attitude toward industrialism: it was here to stay, but many of its aspects seemed to be deplorable. These could be improved, however, if only people became aware of conditions and determined to ameliorate them. To bring about such awareness, the muckrakers appealed to their readers' consciences. Steffens' famous series, published in book form as *The Shame of the Cities* in 1904, was frankly intended to make people feel guilty for the corruption which riddled their cities. The muckrakers also used the social scientists' method of careful and painstaking gathering of data—and with devastating effects. The investigative function—which was later largely taken over by governmental agencies—proved absolutely vital to educating and arousing Americans.

All progressive crusades shared the spirit and used the techniques discussed here, but they did so to different degrees and in different ways. Some voiced a greater willingness to accept industrialism and even to extol its potential benefits; others expressed more strongly the outrage against its darker aspects. Some intervened through voluntary organizations; others relied on government to achieve changes. Each reform reflected a distinctive balance between the claims of Protestant moralism and of scientific rationalism. Progressives fought among themselves over these questions even while they set to the common task of applying their new methods and ideas to the problems of a modern society. . . .

In this analysis we have frequently pointed to the differences between the rhetoric, intentions, and results of progressive reform. The failure of reform always to fulfill the expectations of its advocates was not, of course, unique to the progressive era. Jacksonian reform, Reconstruction, and the New Deal all exhibited similar ironies and disappointments. In each case, the clash between reformers with divergent purposes, the inability to predict how given methods of reform would work in practice, and the ultimate waning of popular zeal for change all contributed to the disjuncture of rationale, purpose, and achievement. Yet the gap between these things seems more obvious in the progressive era because so many diverse movements for reform took place in a brief span of time and were accompanied by resounding rhetoric and by high expectations for the improvement of the American social and political environment. The effort to change so many things all at once, and the grandiose claims made for the moral and material betterment which would result, meant that disappointments were bound to occur.

Yet even the great number of reforms and the uncommonly high expectations for them cannot fully account for the consistent gaps which we have observed between the stated purposes, real intentions, and actual results of progressivism. Several additional factors, intrinsic to the nature of early twentieth-century reform, help to explain the ironies and contradictions.

One of these was the progressives' confident reliance on modern methods of reform. Heirs of recent advances in natural science and social science, they enthusiastically devised and applied new techniques to improve American government and society. Their methods often worked; on the other hand, progressive programs often simply did not prove capable of accomplishing what had been expected of them. This was not necessarily the reformers' fault. They hopefully used untried methods even while they lacked a science of society which was capable of solving all the great problems which they attacked. At the same time, the progressives' scientific methods made it possible to know just how far short of success their programs had sometimes fallen. The evidence of their failures thus was more visible than in any previous era of reform. To the progressives' credit, they usually published that evidence—for contemporaries and historians alike to see.

A second aspect of early twentieth-century reform which helps to account for the gaps between aims and achievements was the deep ambivalence of the progressives about industrialism and its consequences. Individual reformers were divided, and so was their movement as a whole. Compared to many Americans of the late 1800s, the progressives fundamentally accepted an industrial society and sought mainly to control and ameliorate it. Even reformers who were intellectually committed to socialist ideas often acted the part of reformers, not radicals.

Yet progressivism was infused and vitalized, as we have seen, by people truly angry with their industrial society. Few of them wanted to tear down the modern institutions of business and commerce, but their anger was real, their moralism was genuine, and their passions were essential to the reforms of their time.

The reform movement never resolved this ambivalence about industrialism. Much of its rhetoric and popular passion pointed in one direction—toward some form of social democracy—while its leaders and their programs went in another. Often the result was confusion and bitterness. Reforms frequently did not measure up to popular, antibusiness expectations, indeed, never were expected to do so by those who designed and implemented them. Even conservative, ameliorative reformers like Theodore Roosevelt often used radical rhetoric. In doing so, they misled their followers and contributed to the ironies of progressivism.

Perhaps most significant, progressives failed to achieve all their goals because, despite their efforts, they never fully came to terms with the divisions and conflicts in American society. Again and again, they acknowledged the existence of social disharmony more fully and frankly than had nineteenth-century Americans. Nearly every social and economic reform of the era was predicated on the progressive recognition that diverse cultural and occupational groups had conflicting interests, and that the responsibility for mitigating and adjusting those differences lay with the whole society, usually the government. Such recognition was one of the progressives' most significant achievements. Indeed, it stands among the most important accomplishments of liberal reform in all of American history. For, by frankly acknowledging the existence of social disharmony, the progressives committed the twentieth-century United States to recognizing—and to lessening—the inevitable conflicts of a heterogeneous industrial society.

Yet the significance of the progressives' recognition of diversity was compromised by the methods and institutions which they adopted to diminish or eliminate social and economic conflict. Expert administrative government turned out to be less neutral than the progressives believed that it would be. No scientific reform could be any more impartial than the experts who gathered the data or than the bureaucrats who implemented the programs. In practice, as we have seen, administrative government often succumbed to the domination of special interests.

It would be pointless to blame the progressives for the failure of their new methods and programs to eradicate all the conflicts of an industrial society, but it is perhaps fair to ask why the progressives adopted measures which tended to disguise and obscure economic and social conflict almost as soon as they had uncovered it. For one thing, they honestly believed in the almost unlimited potentialities of science and administration. Our late twentieth-century skepticism of these wonders should not blind us to the faith with which the progressives embraced them and imbued them with what now seem magical properties. For another, the progressives were reformers, not radicals. It was one thing to recognize the existence of economic and social conflict, but quite another thing to admit that it was permanent. By and large, these men and women were personally and ideologically inclined to believe that the American society was, in the final analysis, harmonious, and that such conflicts as did exist could be resolved. Finally, the class and cultural backgrounds of the leading progressives often made them insensitive to lowerclass immigrant Americans and their cultures. Attempts to reduce divisions sometimes came down to imposing middle-class Protestant ways on the urban masses. In consequence, the progressives never fulfilled their hope of eliminating social conflict. Reformers of the early twentieth century saw the problem more fully than had their predecessors, but they nonetheless tended to consider conflicts resolved when, in fact, they only had been papered over. Later twentieth-century Americans have also frequently deceived themselves in this way.

Thus progressivism inevitably fell short of its rhetoric and intentions. Lest this seem an unfairly critical evaluation, it is important to recall how terribly ambitious were the stated aims and true goals of the reformers. They missed some of their marks because they sought to do so much. And, despite all their shortcomings, they accomplished an enormous part of what they set out to achieve.

Progressivism brought major innovations to almost every facet of public and private life in the United States. The political and governmental systems particularly felt the effects of reform. Indeed, the nature of political participation and the uses to which it was put went through transitions as momentous as those of any era in American history. These developments were complex, as we have seen, and it is no easy matter to sort out who was helped and who was hurt by each of them or by the entire body of reforms. At the very least, the political changes of the progressive era significantly accommodated American public life to an urban-industrial society. On balance, the polity probably emerged neither more nor less democratic than before, but it did become better suited to address, or at least recognize, the questions and problems which arose from the cities and factories of the nation. After the progressive era, just as before, wealthier elements in American society had a disproportionate share of political power, but we can hardly conclude that this was the fault of the progressives.

The personal and social life of the American people was also deeply affected by progressivism. Like the era's political changes, the economic and social reforms of the early twentieth century were enormously complicated and are difficult to summarize without doing violence to their diversity. In the broadest sense, the progressives sought to mitigate the injustice and the disorder of a society now dominated by its industries and cities. Usually, as we have observed, the quests for social justice and social control were extricably bound together in the reformers' programs, with each group of progressives having different interpretations of these dual ends. Justice sometimes took second place to control. However, before one judges the reformers too harshly for that, it is well to remember how bad urban social conditions were in the late nineteenth century and the odds against which the reformers fought. It is also well to remember that they often succeeded in mitigating the harshness of urban-industrial life.

The problems with which the progressives struggled have, by and large, continued to challenge Americans ever since. And, although the assumptions and techniques of progressivism no longer command the confidence which early twentieth-century Americans had in them, no equally comprehensive body of reforms has ever been adopted in their place. Throughout this study, we have criticized the progressives for having too much faith in their untried methods. Yet if this was a failing, it was also a source of strength, one now missing from reform in America. For the essence of progressivism lay in the hopefulness and optimism which the reformers brought to the tasks of applying science and administration to the high moral purposes in which they believed. The historical record of their aims and achievements leaves no doubt that there were many men and women in the United States in the early 1900s who were not afraid to confront the problems of a modern industrial society with vigor, imagination, and hope. They of course failed to solve all those problems, but no other generation of Americans has done conspicuously better in addressing the political, economic, and social conditions which it faced.

POSTSCRIPT

Did the Progressives Fail?

In spite of their differences, both Abrams's and Link and McCormick's interpretations make concessions to their respective critics. Link and McCormick, for example, admit that the intended reforms did not necessarily produce the desired results. Furthermore, the authors concede that many reformers were insensitive to the cultural values of the lower classes and attempted to impose middle-class Protestant ways on the urban masses. Nevertheless, Link and McCormick argue that in spite of the failure to curb the growth of big business, the progressive reforms did ameliorate the worst abuses of the new urban industrial society. Although the Progressives failed to solve all the major problems of their times, they did set the agenda that still challenges the reformers of today.

Abrams also makes a concession to his critics when he admits that "progressivism had real lasting effects for the blunting of the sharper edges of selfinterest in American life, and for the reduction of the harsher cruelties suffered by the society's underprivileged." Yet the thrust of his argument is that the progressive reformers accomplished little of value. While Abrams probably agrees with Link and McCormick that the Progressives were the first group to confront the problems of modern America, he considers their intended reforms inadequate by their very nature. Because the reformers never really challenged the inequalities brought about by the rise of the industrial state, maintains Abrams, the same problems have persisted to the present day.

Historians have generally been sympathetic to the aims and achievements of the progressive historians. Many, like Charles Beard and Frederick Jackson Turner, came from the Midwest and lived in model progressive states like Wisconsin. Their view of history was based on a conflict between groups competing for power, so it was easy for them to portray progressivism as a struggle between the people and entrenched interests.

It was not until after World War II that a more complex view of progressivism emerged. Richard Hofstadter's *Age of Reform* (Alfred A. Knopf, 1955) was exceptionally critical of the reformist view of history as well as of the reformers in general. Born of Jewish immigrant parents and raised in cities in New York, the Columbia University professor argued that progressivism was a moral crusade undertaken by WASP families in an effort to restore older Protestant and individualistic values and to regain political power and status. Both Hofstadter's "status revolution" theory of progressivism and his profile of the typical Progressive have been heavily criticized by historians. Nevertheless, he changed the dimensions of the debate and made progressivism appear to be a much more complex issue than had previously been thought.

Most of the writing on progressivism for the past 20 years has centered around the "organizational" model. Writers of this school have stressed the role of the "expert" and the ideals of scientific management as basic to an understanding of the Progressive Era. This fascination with how the city manager plan worked in Dayton or railroad regulation in Wisconsin or the public schools laws in New York City makes sense to a generation surrounded by bureaucracies on all sides. Two books that deserve careful reading are Robert Wiebe's *The Search for Order, 1877–1920* (Hill & Wang, 1967) and the wonderful collection of essays by Samuel P. Hayes, *American Political History as Social Analysis* (Knoxville, 1980), which brings together two decades' worth of articles from diverse journals that were seminal in exploring ethnocultural approaches to politics within the organizational model.

In a highly influential article written for the *American Quarterly* in spring 1970, Professor Peter G. Filene proclaimed "An Obituary for the 'Progressive Movement.'" After an extensive review of the literature, Filene concluded that since historians cannot agree on its programs, values, geographical location, members, and supporters, there was no such thing as a Progressive movement. Few historians were bold enough to write progressivism out of the pantheon of American reform movements. But Filene put the proponents of the early-twentieth-century reform movement on the defensive. Students who want to see how professional historians directly confronted Filene in their refusal to attend the funeral of the Progressive movement should read the essays by John D. Buenker, John C. Burnham, and Robert M. Crunden in *Progressivism* (Schenkman, 1977).

Three works provide an indispensable review of the literature of progressivism in the 1980s. Link and McCormick's *Progressivism* (Harlan Davidson, 1983) deserves to be read in its entirety for its comprehensive yet concise coverage. More scholarly but still readable are the essays on the new political history in McCormick's *The Party Period and Public Policy: American Politics From the Age of Jackson to the Progressive Era* (Oxford University Press, 1986). The more advanced student should consult Daniel T. Rodgers, "In Search of Progressivism," *Reviews in American History* (December 1982). While admitting that Progressives shared no common creed or values, Rodgers nevertheless feels that they were able "to articulate their discontents and their social visions" around three distinct clusters of ideas: "The first was the rhetoric of antimonopolism, the second was an emphasis on social bonds and the social nature of human beings, and the third was the language of social efficiency."

ISSUE 8

Was Woodrow Wilson Responsible for the Failure of the United States to Join the League of Nations?

YES: Thomas A. Bailey, from "Woodrow Wilson Wouldn't Yield," in *Alexander De Conde and Armin Rappaport, eds., Essays Diplomatic and Undiplomatic of Thomas A. Bailey* (Appleton-Century-Crofts, 1969)

NO: William G. Carleton, from "A New Look at Woodrow Wilson," *The Virginia Quarterly Review* (Autumn 1962)

ISSUE SUMMARY

YES: The late Thomas A. Bailey, argues that a physically infirm Woodrow Wilson was unable to make the necessary compromises with the U.S. Senate to join the League of Nations and convince America that the United States should play a major role in world affairs.

NO: William G. Carleton believed that Woodrow Wilson understood the role that the United States would play in world affairs.

The presidential polls of Arthur Schlesinger in 1948 and 1962 as well as the 1983 Murray-Blessing poll have ranked Wilson among the top 10 presidents. William Carleton considers him the greatest twentieth-century president, only two notches below Jefferson and Lincoln. Yet, among his biographers, Wilson has been treated ungenerously. They carp at him for being naïve, overly idealistic, and too inflexible. It appears that Wilson's biographers respect the man but do not like the person.

Why the nagging pettiness? Part of the reason may have been Wilson's own introspective personality. He was, along with Jefferson and to some extent Theodore Roosevelt, America's most intellectual president. He spent nearly 20 years as a history and political science teacher and scholar at Bryn Mawr, Wesleyan, and at his alma mater, Princeton University. While his multi-volume *History of the United States* appears dated as it gathers dust on musty library shelves, his Ph.D. dissertation on *Congressional Government,* written as a graduate student at Johns Hopkins, remains a classic statement of the weakness of leadership in the American constitutional system.

There is one other reason why Wilson has been so critically analyzed by his biographers. Certainly, no president before or since has had less formal political experience than Wilson. Apparently, academic work does not constitute the proper training for the presidency. Yet, in addition to working many years as a college professor and a short stint as a lawyer, Wilson served eight distinguished years as the president of Princeton University. He turned it into one of the outstanding universities in the country. He introduced the preceptorial system, widely copied today, which supplemented course lectures with discussion conferences led by young instructors. He took the lead in reorganizing the university's curriculum. He lost two key battles. The alumni became upset when he tried to replace the class-ridden eating clubs with his "Quadrangle Plan," which would have established smaller colleges within the university system. What historians most remember about his Princeton career, however, was his losing fight with the Board of Trustees and Dean Andrew West concerning the location and eventual control over the new graduate school. Wilson resigned when it was decided to build a separate campus for the graduate school.

Shortly after Wilson left Princeton in 1910, he ran for governor of New Jersey and won his only political office before he became the president. As a governor, he gained control over the state Democratic Party and pushed through the legislature a litany of progressive measures—a primary and elections law, a corrupt practices act, workmen's compensation, utilities regulation, school reforms, and an enabling act that allowed certain cities to adopt the commission form of government. When he was nominated on the 46th ballot at the Democratic convention in 1912, Wilson had enlarged the power of the governor's office in New Jersey and foreshadowed the way in which he would manage the presidency.

If one uses the standard categories of the late Professor Clinton Rossiter, Wilson ranks very high as a textbook president. No one with the exception of Franklin Roosevelt and perhaps Ronald Reagan performed the *ceremonial* role of the presidency as well as Wilson. His speeches rang with oratorical brilliance and substance. No wonder he abandoned the practice of Jefferson and his successors by delivering the president's annual State of the Union address to Congress in person rather than in writing.

During his first four years, he also fashioned a legislative program rivaled only by FDR's later "New Deal." The "New Freedom" pulled together conservative and progressive, rural and urban, as well as southern and northern Democrats in passing such measures as the Underwood-Simmons Tariff, the first bill to significantly lower tariff rates since the Civil War, and the Owens–Keating Child Labor Act. It was through Wilson's adroit maneuvering that the Federal Reserve System was established. This banking measure, the most significant in American history, established the major agency that regulates money supply in the country today. Finally, President Wilson revealed his flexibility when he abandoned his initial policy of rigid and indiscriminate trust busting for one of regulating big business through the creation of the Federal Trade Commission.

In the first essay, Professor Thomas A. Bailey believes that Wilson's inability to rally an indifferent American public and his unwillingness to compromise with Senator Lodge caused the treaty to die in the Senate. But Professor William G. Carleton gives a spirited defense of Wilson's domestic and foreign policies in the second essay. He believes that narrow-minded nationalists, like Senator Henry Cabot Lodge, destroyed the international peace of the post-war world by blocking America's entrance into the League of Nations.

YES    **Thomas A. Bailey**

Woodrow Wilson Wouldn't Yield

"As a friend of the President . . . I solemnly declare to him this morning: If you want to kill your own child [League of Nations] because the Senate straightens out its crooked limbs, you must take the responsibility and accept the verdict of history."

—Senator Henry F. Ashurst, in Senate, 1920

I

The story of America's rejection of the League of Nations revolves largely around the personality and character of Thomas Woodrow Wilson.

Born in Virginia and reared in Yankee-gutted Georgia and the Carolinas, Wilson early developed a burning hatred of war and a passionate attachment to the Confederate-embraced principle of self-determination for minority peoples. From the writings of Thomas Jefferson he derived much of his democratic idealism and his invincible faith in the judgment of the masses, if properly informed. From his stiff-backed Scotch-Presbyterian forebears, he inherited a high degree of inflexibility; from his father, a dedicated Presbyterian minister, he learned a stern moral code that would tolerate no compromise with wrong—as defined by Woodrow Wilson.

As a leading academician who had first failed at law, he betrayed a contempt for "money-grubbing" lawyers, many of whom sat in the Senate, and an arrogance toward lesser intellects, including those of the "pygmy-minded" senators. As a devout Christian keenly aware of the wickedness of this world, he emerged as a fighting reformer, whether as president of Princeton, governor of New Jersey, or President of the United States.

As a war leader, Wilson was superb. Holding aloft the torch of idealism in one hand and the flaming sword of righteousness in the other, he aroused the masses to a holy crusade. We would fight a war to end wars; we would make the world safe for democracy. The phrase was not a mockery then. The American people, with an amazing display of self-sacrifice, supported the war effort unswervingly.

The noblest expression of Wilson's idealism was his Fourteen Points address to Congress in January, 1918. It compressed his war aims into

From *Essays Diplomatic and Undiplomatic of Thomas A. Bailey* (Appleton-Century-Crofts, 1969); original to *American Heritage,* June 1957, pp. 20–25, 105–106. Copyright © 1957 by American Heritage Publishing Co. Reprinted by permission.

punchy, placard-like paragraphs, expressly designed for propaganda purposes. It appealed tremendously to oppressed peoples everywhere by promising such goals as the end of secret treaties, freedom of the seas, the removal of economic barriers, a reduction of arms burdens, a fair adjustment of colonial claims, and self-determination for oppressed minorities. In Poland, university men would meet on the streets of Warsaw, clasp hands, and soulfully utter one word, "Wilson." In remote regions of Italy peasants burned candles before poster portraits of the mighty new prophet arisen in the West.

The fourteenth and capstone point was a league of nations, designed to avert future wars. The basic idea was not original with Wilson; numerous thinkers, including Frenchmen and Britons, had been working on the concept long before he embraced it. Even Henry Cabot Lodge, the Republican senator from Massachusetts, had already spoken publicly in favor of a league of nations. But the more he heard about the Wilsonian League of Nations, the more critical of it he became.

A knowledge of the Wilson–Lodge feud is basic to an understanding of the tragedy that unfolded. Tall, slender, aristocratically bewhiskered, Dr. Henry Cabot Lodge (Ph.D., Harvard), had published a number of books and had been known as "the scholar in politics" before the appearance of Dr. Woodrow Wilson (Ph.D., Johns Hopkins). The Presbyterian professor had gone further in both scholarship and politics than the Boston Brahmin, whose mind was once described as resembling the soil of his native New England: "naturally barren but highly cultivated." Wilson and Lodge, two stubborn men, developed a mutual antipathy which soon turned into freezing hatred.

II

The German armies, reeling under the blows of the Allies, were ready to surrender November, 1918. The formal armistice terms stipulated that Germany was to be guaranteed a peace based on the Fourteen Points, with two reservations concerning freedom of the seas and reparations.

Meanwhile the American people had keyed themselves up for the long-awaited march on Berlin; eager voices clamored to hang the Kaiser. Thus the sudden end of the shooting left inflamed patriots with a sense of frustration and letdown that boded ill for Wilson's policies. The red-faced Theodore Roosevelt, Lodge's intimate of long standing, cried that peace should be dictated by the chatter of machine guns and not "the clicking of typewriters."

Wilson now towered at the dizzy pinnacle of his popularity and power. He had emerged as the moral arbiter of the world and the hope of all peoples for a better tomorrow. But regrettably his wartime sureness of touch began to desert him, and he made a series of costly fumbles. He was so preoccupied with reordering the world, someone has said, that he reminded one of the baseball player who knocks the ball into the bleachers and then forgets to touch home plate.

First came his tactlessly direct appeal for a Democratic Congress in October, 1918. The voters trooped to the polls the next month and, by a narrow margin, returned a Republican Congress. Wilson had not only goaded his partisan foes to fresh outbursts of fury, but he had unnecessarily staked his prestige on the outcome—and lost. When the Allied leaders met at the Paris peace table, he was the only one not entitled to be there—on the European basis of a parliamentary majority.

Wilson next announced that he was sailing for France, presumably to use his still enormous prestige to fashion an enduring peace. At that time no President had ever gone abroad, and Republicans condemned the decision as evidence of a dangerous Messiah complex—of a desire, as former President Taft put it, "to hog the whole show."

The naming of the remaining four men to the peace delegation caused partisans further anguish. Only one, Henry White, was a Republican, and he was a minor figure at that. The Republicans, now the majority party, complained that they had been good enough to die on the battlefield; they ought to have at least an equal voice at the peace table. Nor were any United States senators included, even though they would have a final whack at the treaty. Wilson did not have much respect for the "bungalow-minded" senators, and if he took one, the logical choice would be Henry Cabot Lodge. There were already enough feuds brewing at Paris without taking one along.

Doubtless some of the Big Business Republicans were out to "get" the President who had been responsible for the hated reformist legislation of 1913–14. If he managed to put over the League of Nations, his prestige would soar to new heights. He might even arrange—unspeakable thought!—to be elected again and again and again. Much of the partisan smog that finally suffocated the League would have been cleared away if Wilson had publicly declared, as he was urged to do, that in no circumstances would he run again. But he spurned such counsel, partly because he was actually receptive to the idea of a third term.

III

The American President, hysterically hailed by European crowds as "Voovro Veelson," came to the Paris peace table in January, 1919, to meet with Lloyd George of Britain, Clemenceau of France, and Orlando of Italy. To his dismay, he soon discovered that they were far more interested in imperialism than in idealism. When they sought to carve up the territorial booty without regard for the colonials, contrary to the Fourteen Points, the stern-jawed Presbyterian moralist interposed a ringing veto. The end result was the mandate system—a compromise between idealism and imperialism that turned out to be more imperialistic than idealistic.

Wilson's overriding concern was the League of Nations. He feared that if he did not get it completed and embedded in the treaty, the imperialistic powers might sidetrack it. Working at an incredible pace after hours, Wilson headed the commission that drafted the League Covenant in ten meetings and some thirty hours. He then persuaded the conference not only to approve the hastily constructed Covenant but to incorporate it bodily in the peace treaty. In support of his adopted brain child he spoke so movingly on one occasion that even the hard-boiled reporters forgot to take notes.

Wilson now had to return hurriedly to the United States to sign bills and take care of other pressing business. Shortly after his arrival the mounting Republican opposition in the Senate flared up angrily. On March 4, 1919, 39 senators or senators-elect—more than enough to defeat the treaty—published a round robin to the effect that they would not approve the League in its existing form. This meant that Wilson had to return to Paris, hat in hand, and there weaken his position by having to seek modifications.

Stung to the quick, he struck back at his senatorial foes in an indiscreet speech in New York just before his departure. He boasted that when he brought the treaty back from Paris, the League Covenant would not only be tied in but so thoroughly tied in that it could not be cut out without killing the entire pact. The Senate, he assumed, would not dare to kill the treaty of peace outright.

IV

At Paris the battle was now joined in deadly earnest. Clemenceau, the French realist, had little use for Wilson, the American idealist. "God gave us the ten commandments and we broke them," he reportedly sneered. "Wilson gave us the Fourteen Points—we shall see." Clemenceau's most disruptive demand was for the German Rhineland; but Wilson, the champion of self-determination, would never consent to handing several million Germans over to the tender mercies of the French. After a furious struggle, during which Wilson was stricken with influenza, Clemenceau was finally persuaded to yield the Rhineland and other demands in return for a security treaty. Under it, Britain and America agreed to come to the aid of France in the event of another unprovoked aggression. The United States Senate shortsightedly pigeonholed the pact, and France was left with neither the Rhineland nor security.

Two other deadlocks almost broke up the conference. Italy claimed the Adriatic port of Fiume, an area inhabited chiefly by Yugoslavs. In his battle for self-determination, Wilson dramatically appealed over the head of the Italian delegation to the Italian people, whereupon the delegates went home in a huff to receive popular endorsement. The final adjustment was a hollow victory for self-determination.

The politely bowing Japanese now stepped forward to press their economic claims to China's Shantung, which they had captured from the Germans early in the war. But to submit 30,000,000 Chinese to the influence of the Japanese would be another glaring violation of self-determination. The Japanese threatened to bolt the conference, as the Italians had already done, with consequent jeopardy to the League. In the end, Wilson reluctantly consented to a compromise that left the Japanese temporarily in possession of Shantung.

The Treaty of Versailles, as finally signed in June, 1919, included only about four of the Fourteen Points essentially intact. The Germans, with considerable justification, gave vent to loud cries of betrayal. But the iron hand of circumstance had forced Wilson to compromise away many of his points in order to salvage his fourteenth point, the League of Nations, which he hoped would iron out the injustices that had crept into the treaty. He was like the mother who throws her younger children to the pursuing wolves in order to save her sturdy first born son.

V

Bitter opposition to the completed treaty had already begun to form in America. Tens of thousands of homesick and disillusioned soldiers were pouring home, determined to let Europe "stew in its own juice." The wartime idealism, inevitably doomed to slump, was now plunging to alarming depths. The beloved Allies had apparently turned out to be greedy imperialists. The war to make the world safe for democracy had obviously fallen dismally short of the goal. And at the end of the war to end wars there were about twenty conflicts of varying intensity being waged all over the globe.

The critics increased their clamor. Various foreign groups, including the Irish-Americans and the Italian-Americans, were complaining that the interests of the "old country" had been neglected. Professional liberals, notaby the editors of the *New Republic,* were denouncing the treaty as too harsh. The illiberals, far more numerous, were denouncing it as not harsh enough. The Britain-haters, like the buzz-saw Senator James Reed of Missouri and the acid-penned William R. Hearst, were proclaiming that the British had emerged with undue influence. Such ultra-nationalists as the isolationist Senator William E. Borah of Idaho were insisting that the flag of no superstate should be hoisted above the glorious Stars and Stripes.

When the treaty came back from Paris, with the League firmly riveted in, Senator Lodge despaired of stopping it. "What are you going to do? It's hopeless," he complained to Borah. "All the newspapers in my state are for it." The best that he could hope for was to add a few reservations. The Republicans had been given little opportunity to help write the treaty in Paris; they now felt that they were entitled to do a little rewriting in Washington.

Lodge deliberately adopted the technique of delay. As chairman of the powerful Senate Committee on Foreign Relations, he consumed two weeks by reading aloud the entire pact of 264 pages, even though it had already been printed. He then held time-consuming public hearings, during which persons with unpronounceable foreign names aired their grievances against the pact.

Lodge finally adopted the strategy of tacking reservations onto the treaty, and he was able to achieve his goal because of the peculiar composition of the Senate. There were 49 Republicans and 47 Democrats. The Republicans consisted of about twenty "strong reservationists" like Lodge, about twelve "mild reservationists" like future Secretary of State Kellogg, and about a dozen "irreconcilables." This last group was headed by Senator

Borah and the no less isolationist Senator Hiram Johnson of California, a fiery spellbinder.

The Lodge reservations finally broke the back of the treaty. They were all added by a simple majority vote, even though the entire pact would have to be approved by a two-thirds vote. The dozen or so Republican mild reservationists were not happy over the strong Lodge reservations, and if Wilson had deferred sufficiently to these men, he might have persuaded them to vote with the Democrats. Had they done so, the Lodge reservations could have all been voted down, and a milder version, perhaps acceptable to Wilson, could have been substituted.

VI

As the hot summer of 1919 wore on, Wilson became increasingly impatient with the deadlock in the Senate. Finally he decided to take his case to the country, as he had so often done in response to his ingrained "appeal habit." He had never been robust, and his friends urged him not to risk breaking himself down in a strenuous barnstorming campaign. But Wilson, having made up his mind, was unyielding. He had sent American boys into battle in a war to end wars; why should he not risk his life in a battle for a League to end wars?

Wilson's spectacular tour met with limited enthusiasm in the Middle West, the home of several million German-Americans. After him, like baying bloodhounds, trailed Senators Borah and Johnson, sometimes speaking in the same halls a day or so later, to the accompaniment of cries of "Impeach him, impeach him!" But on the Pacific Coast and in the Rocky Mountain area the enthusiasm for Wilson and the League was overwhelming. The high point—and the breaking point—of the trip came at Pueblo, Colorado, where Wilson, with tears streaming down his cheeks, pleaded for his beloved League of Nations.

That night Wilson's weary body rebelled. He was whisked back to Washington, where he suffered a stroke that paralyzed the left side of his body. For weeks he lay in bed, a desperately sick man. The Democrats, who had no first-rate leader in the Senate, were left rudderless. With the wisdom of hindsight, we may say that Wilson might better have stayed in Washington, providing the necessary leadership and compromising with the opposition, insofar as compromise was possible. A good deal of compromise had already gone into the treaty, and a little more might have saved it.

Senator Lodge, cold and decisive, was now in the driver's seat. His Fourteen Reservations, a sardonic parallel to Wilson's Fourteen Points, had been whipped into shape. Most of them now seem either irrelevant, inconsequential, or unnecessary; some of them merely reaffirmed principles and policies, including the Monroe Doctrine, already guaranteed by the treaty or by the Constitution.

But Wilson, who hated the sound of Lodge's name, would have no part of the Lodge reservations. They would, he insisted, emasculate the entire treaty. Yet the curious fact is that he had privately worked out his own set of reservations with the Democratic leader in the Senate, Gilbert M. Hitchcock, and these differed only in slight degree from those of Senator Lodge.

VII

As the hour approached for the crucial vote in the Senate, it appeared that public opinion had evidently veered considerably. Although confused by the angry debate, it still favored the treaty—but with some safeguarding reservations. A stubborn Wilson was unwilling to accept this disheartening fact, or perhaps he was not made aware of it. Mrs. Wilson, backed by the President's personal physician, Dr. Cary Grayson, kept vigil at his bedside to warn the few visitors that disagreeable news might shock the invalid into a relapse.

In this highly unfavorable atmosphere, Senator Hitchcock had two conferences with Wilson on the eve of the Senate ballot. He suggested compromise on a certain point, but Wilson shot back, "Let Lodge compromise!" Hitchcock conceded that the Senator would have to give ground but suggested that the White House might also hold out the olive branch. "Let Lodge hold out the olive branch," came the stern reply. On this inflexible note, and with Mrs. Wilson's anxiety mounting, the interview ended.

The Senate was ready for final action on November 19, 1919. At the critical moment Wilson sent a fateful letter to the Democratic minority in the Senate, urging them to vote down the treaty with the hated Lodge reservations so that a true ratification could be achieved. The Democrats, with more than the necessary one-third veto, heeded the voice of their crippled leader and rejected the treaty with reservations. The Republicans, with more than the necessary one-third veto, rejected the treaty without reservations.

The country was shocked by this exhibition of legislative paralysis. About four-fifths of the senators professed to favor the treaty in some form, yet they were unable to agree on anything. An aroused public opinion forced the Senate to reconsider, and Lodge secretly entered into negotiations with the Democrats in an effort to work out acceptable reservations. He was making promising progress when Senator Borah got wind of his maneuvers through an anonymous telephone call. The leading irreconcilables hastily summoned a council of war, hauled Lodge before them, and bluntly accused him of treachery. Deeply disturbed, the Massachusetts Senator said: "Well, I suppose I'll have to resign as majority leader."

"No, by God!" burst out Borah. "You won't have a chance to resign! On Monday, I'll move for the election of a new majority leader and give the reasons for my action." Faced with an upheaval within his party such as had insured Wilson's election in 1912, Lodge agreed to drop his backstage negotiations.

VIII

The second-chance vote in the Senate came on March 19, 1920. Wilson again directed his loyal Democratic following to reject the treaty, disfigured as it was by the Lodge reservations. But by this time there was no

other form in which the pact could possibly be ratified. Twenty-one realistic Democrats turned their backs on Wilson and voted Yea; 23 loyal
Democrats, mostly from the rock-ribbed South, joined with the irreconcilables to do the bidding of the White House. The treaty, though commanding a simple majority this time of 49 Yeas to 35 Nays, failed of the
necessary two-thirds vote.

Wilson, struggling desperately against the Lodge reservation trap,
had already called upon the nation, in a "solemn referendum," to give
him a vote in favor of the League in the forthcoming Presidential election
of 1920. His hope was that he could then get the treaty approved without
reservations. But this course was plainly futile. Even if all the anti-League
senators up for reelection in 1920 had been replaced by the pro-League
senators, Wilson would still have lacked the necessary two-thirds majority
for an unreserved treaty.

The American people were never given a chance to express their
views directly on the League of Nations. All they could do was vote either
for the voluble Democratic candidate, Cox, who stood for the League, or
the stuffed-shirt Republican candidate, Harding, who wobbled all over the
evasive Republican platform. If the electorate had been given an opportunity to express itself, a powerful majority probably would have favored
the world organization, with at least some reservations. But wearied of
Wilsonism, idealism, and self-denial, and confused by the wordy fight over
the treaty, the voters rose up and swept Harding into the White House on
a tidal wave of votes. The winner had been more anti-League than pro-
League, and his prodigious plurality of 7,000,000 votes condemned the
League to death in America.

IX

What caused this costly failure of American statesmanship?

Wilson's physical collapse intensified his native stubbornness. A
judicious compromise here and there no doubt would have secured Senate
approval of the treaty, though of course with qualifications. Wilson believed that in any event the Allies would reject the Lodge reservations.
The probabilities are that the Allies would have worked out some kind
of acceptance, so dire was their need of America's economic support, but
Wilson never gave them a chance to act.

Senator Lodge was also inflexible, but prior to the second rejection
he was evidently trying to get the treaty through—on his own terms. As
majority leader of the Republicans, his primary task was to avoid another
fatal split in his party. Wilson's primary task was to get the pact approved.
From a narrowly political point of view, the Republicans had little to gain
by engineering ratification of a Democratic treaty.

The two-thirds rule in the Senate, often singled out as the culprit,
is of little relevance. Wilson almost certainly would have pigeonholed
the treaty, as he threatened, if it had passed with the Lodge reservations
appended.

Wilson's insistence that the League be wedded to the treaty actually contributed to the final defeat of both. Either would have had a better chance if it had not been burdened by the enemies of the other. The United Nations, one should note, was set up in 1945 independently of any peace treaty.

Finally, the American public in 1919–20 was not yet ready for the onerous new world responsibilities that had suddenly been forced upon it. The isolationist tradition was still potent, and it was fortified by postwar disillusionment. If the sovereign people had cried out for the League with one voice, they almost certainly would have had their way. A treaty without reservations, or with a few reservations acceptable to Wilson, doubtless would have slipped through the Senate. But the American people were one war short of accepting that leadership in a world organization for peace which, as Wilson's vision perceived, had become a necessity for the safety and the welfare of mankind.

The blame for this failure of statesmanship cannot fall solely on the excessive partisanship of both parties, the shortsighted outlook of Lodge, or the rigidity of a sick and ill-informed President. Much of the responsibility must be placed at the door of a provincial population anxious to escape overseas responsibilities while basking in the sunshine of normalcy and prosperity.

William G. Carleton

 **NO**

A New Look at Woodrow Wilson

All high-placed statesmen crave historical immortality. Woodrow Wilson craved it more than most. Thus far the fates have not been kind to Wilson; there is a reluctance to admit him to as great a place in history as he will have.

Congress has just gotten around to planning a national memorial for Wilson, several years after it had done this for Theodore Roosevelt and Franklin D. Roosevelt. Wilson is gradually being accepted as one of the nation's five or six greatest Presidents. However, the heroic mold of the man on the large stage of world history is still generally unrecognized.

There is a uniquely carping, hypercritical approach to Wilson. Much more than other historical figures he is being judged by personality traits, many of them distorted or even fancied. Wilson is not being measured by the yardstick used for other famous characters of history. There is a double standard at work here.

What are the common errors and misrepresentations with respect to Wilson? In what ways is he being judged more rigorously? What are the reasons for this? Why will Wilson eventually achieve giant stature in world history?

⁂

There are two criticisms of Wilson that go to the heart of his fame and place in history. One is an alleged inflexibility and intransigence, an inability to compromise. The other is that he had no real understanding of world politics, that he was a naïve idealist. Neither is true.

If Wilson were indeed as stubborn and adamant as he is often portrayed he would have been a bungler at his work, for the practice and art of politics consist in a feeling for the possible, a sense of timing, a capacity for give-and-take compromise. In reality, Wilson's leadership of his party and the legislative accomplishments of his first term were magnificent. His performance was brilliantly characterized by the very qualities he is said to have lacked: flexibility, accommodation, a sense of timing, and a willingness to compromise. In the struggles to win the Federal Reserve Act, the Clayton Anti-Trust Law, the Federal Trade Commission, and other major measures of his domestic program, Wilson repeatedly mediated between

From *Virginia Quarterly Review*, vol. 38, no. 4 (Autumn 1962), pp. 545–566. Copyright © 1962 by University of Virginia. Reprinted by permission.

the agrarian liberals and the conservatives of his party, moving now a little to the left, now to the right, now back to the left. He learned by experience, cast aside pride of opinion, accepted and maneuvered for regulatory commissions after having warned of their danger during the campaign of 1912, and constantly acted as a catalyst of the opposing factions of his party and of shifting opinion.

The cautious way Wilson led the country to military preparedness and to war demonstrated resiliency and a sense of timing of a high order. At the Paris Conference Wilson impressed thoughtful observers with his skill as a negotiator; many European diplomats were surprised that an "amateur" could do so well. Here the criticism is not that Wilson was without compromise but that he compromised too much.

Actually, the charge that Wilson was incapable of compromise must stand or fall on his conduct during the fight in the Senate over the ratification of the League of Nations, particularly his refusal to give the word to the Democratic Senators from the South to vote for the Treaty with the Lodge Reservations, which, it is claimed, would have assured ratification. Wilson, say the critics, murdered his own brain child. It is Wilson, and not Lodge, who has now become the villain of this high tragedy.

Now, would a Wilsonian call to the Southerners to change their position have resulted in ratification? Can we really by sure? In order to give Southerners time to readjust to a new position, the call from the White House would have had to have been made several weeks before that final vote. During that time what would have prevented Lodge from hobbling the League with still more reservations? Would the mild reservationists, all Republicans, have prevented this? The record shows, I think, that in the final analysis the mild reservationists could always be bamboozled by Lodge in the name of party loyalty. As the fight on the League had progressed, the reservations had become more numerous and more crippling. Wilson, it seems, had come to feel that there simply was no appeasing Lodge.

During the Peace Conference, in response to the Senatorial Round Robin engineered by Lodge, Wilson had reopened the whole League question and obtained the inclusion of American "safeguards" he felt would satisfy Lodge. This had been done at great cost, for it had forced Wilson to abandon his position as a negotiator above the battles for national advantages and to become a suppliant for national concessions. This had resulted in his having to yield points in other parts of the Treaty to national-minded delegations from other countries. When Wilson returned from Paris with the completed Treaty, Lodge had "raised the ante," the Lodge Reservations requiring the consent of other signatory nations were attached to the Treaty, and these had multiplied and become more restrictive in nature as the months went by. Would not then a "final" yielding by Wilson have resulted in even stiffer reservations being added? Was not Lodge using the Reservations to effect not ratification but rejection, knowing that there was a point beyond which Wilson could not yield?

Wilson seems honestly to have believed that the Lodge Reservations emasculated the League. Those who read them for the first time will be surprised, I think, to discover how nationally self-centered they were. If taken seriously, they surely must have impaired the functioning of the League. However, Wilson was never opposed to clarifying or interpretative reservations which would not require the consent of the other signatories. Indeed, he himself wrote the Hitchcock Reservations.

Even had the League with the Lodge Reservations been ratified, how certain can we really be that this would have meant American entrance into the League? Under the Lodge Reservations, every signatory nation had to accept them before the United States could become a member. Would all the signatories have accepted every one of the fifteen Lodge Reservations? The United States had no monopoly on chauvinism, and would not other nations have interposed reservations of their own as a condition to their acceptance of the Lodge Reservations?

At Paris, Wilson had personally experienced great difficulty getting his own mild "reservations" incorporated into the Covenant. Now, at this late date, would Brit ain have accepted the Lodge Reservation on Irish self-determination? In all probability. Would Japan have accepted the Reservation on Shantung? This is more doubtful. Would the Latin American states have accepted the stronger Reservation on the Monroe Doctrine? This is also doubtful. Chile had already shown concern, and little Costa Rica had the temerity to ask for a definition of the Doctrine. Would the British Dominions have accepted the Reservation calling for one vote for the British Empire or six votes for the United States? Even Lord Grey, who earlier had predicted that the signatories would accept the Lodge Reservations, found that he could not guarantee acceptance by the Dominions, and Canada's President of the Privy Council and Acting Secretary for External Affairs, Newton W. Rowell, declared that if this Reservation were accepted by the other powers Canada would withdraw from the League.

By the spring of 1920, Wilson seems to have believed that making the League of Nations the issue in the campaign of 1920 would afford a better opportunity for American participation in an effective League than would further concessions to Lodge. To Wilson, converting the Presidential election into a solemn referendum on the League was a reality. For months, because of his illness, he had lived secluded in the White House, and the memories of his highly emotional reception in New York on his return from Paris and of the enthusiasm of the Western audiences during his last speaking trip burned vividly bright. He still believed that the American people, if given the chance, would vote for the League without emasculating reservations. Does this, then, make Wilson naïve? It is well to remember that in the spring of 1920 not even the most sanguine Republican envisaged the Republican sweep that would develop in the fall of that year.

If the strategy of Wilson in the spring of 1920 was of debatable wisdom, the motives of Lodge can no longer be open to doubt. After the landslide of 1920, which gave the Republicans the Presidency and an overwhelming majority in a Senate dominated by Lodge in foreign policy, the Treaty was never resurrected. The Lodge Reservations, representing months of gruelling legislative labor, were cavalierly jettisoned, and a separate peace was made with Germany.

What, then, becomes of the stock charge that Wilson was intolerant of opposition and incapable of bending? If the truth of this accusation must rest on Wilson's attitude during the Treaty fight, and I think it must, for he showed remarkable adaptability in other phases of his Presidency, then it must fall. The situation surrounding the Treaty fight was intricately tangled, and there is certainly as much evidence on the side of Wilson's forbearance as on the side of his obstinacy.

A far more serious charge against Wilson is that he had no realistic understanding of world politics, that he was an impractical idealist whose policies intensified rather than alleviated international problems. Now what American statesman of the period understood world politics better than Wilson—or indeed in any way as well as he? Elihu Root, with his arid legalism? Philander Knox, with his dollar diplomacy? Theodore Roosevelt or Henry Cabot Lodge? Roosevelt and Lodge had some feel for power politics, and they understood the traditional balance of power, at least until their emotions for a dictated Allied victory got the better of their judgment: but was either of them aware of the implications for world politics of the technological revolution in war and the disintegration of the old balance of power? And were not both of them blind to a new force in world politics just then rising to a place of importance—the anti-imperialist revolutions, which even before World War I were getting under way with the Mexican Revolution and the Chinese Revolution of Sun Yat-sen?

Wilson is charged with having no understanding of the balance of power, but who among world statesmen of the twentieth century better sated the classic doctrine of the traditional balance of power than Wilson in his famous Peace Without Victory speech? And was it not Theodore Roosevelt who derided him for stating it? With perfectly straight faces Wilson critics, and a good many historians, tell us that TR, who wanted to march to Berlin and saddle Germany with a harsh peace, and FDR, who sponsored unconditional surrender, "understood" the balance of power, but that Wilson, who fought to salvage a power balance by preserving Germany from partition, was a simple simon in world politics—an illustration of the double standard at work in evaluating Wilson's place in history.

Wilson not only understood the old, but with amazing clarity he saw the new, elements in world politics. He recognized the emergence of the anti-imperialist revolutions and the importance of social politics in the international relations of the future. He recognized, too, the implications for future world politics of the technological revolution in war, of total war, and of the disintegration of the old balance of power—for World War I had decisively weakened the effective brakes on Japan in Asia, disrupted the Turkish Empire in the Middle East and the Austro-Hungarian Empire in Europe, and removed Russia as a make-weight for the foreseeable future. Wilson believed that a truncated Germany and an attempted French hegemony would only add to the chaos, but he saw too that merely preserving Germany as a power unit would not restore the old balance of power. To Wilson, even in its prime the traditional balance of power had worked only indifferently and collective security would have been preferable, but in his mind the revolutionary changes in the world of 1919 made a collective-security system indispensable.

Just what is realism in world politics? Is it not the ability to use purposefully many factors, even theoretically contradictory ones, and to use them not singly and consecutively but interdependently and simultaneously, shifting the emphasis as conditions change? If so, was not Wilson a very great realist in world politics? He used the old balance-of-power factors, as evidenced by his fight to save Germany as a power unit and his sponsoring of a tripartite alliance of the United States, Britain, and France to guarantee France from any German aggression until such time as collective security would become effective. But he labored to introduce into international relations the new collective-security factors to supplement and gradually supersede in importance the older factors, now increasingly outmoded by historical developments. To label as doctrinaire idealist one who envisaged world politics in so broad and flexible a way is to pervert the meaning of words. . . .

＊＊＊

Ranking the Presidents has become a popular game, and even Presidents like to play it, notably Truman and Kennedy. In my own evaluation, I place Wilson along with Jefferson and Lincoln as the nation's three greatest Presidents, which makes Wilson our greatest twentieth-century President. If rated solely on the basis of long-range impact on international relations, Wilson is the most influential of all our Presidents.

What are the achievements which entitle Wilson to so high a place? Let us consider the major ones, although of course some of these are more important than others.

. . . [B]etter than any responsible statesman of his day, Wilson understood and sympathized with the anti-imperialist revolutions and their aspirations for basic internal reforms. He withdrew American support for the Bankers' Consortium in China, and the United States under Wilson was the first of the great powers to recognize the Revolution of Sun Yat-sen. Early in his term he had to wrestle with the Mexican Revolution. He saw the need for social reform; avoided the general war with Mexico that many American investors, Catholics, and professional patriots wanted; and by refusing to recognize the counter-revolution of Huerta and cutting Huerta off from trade and arms while allowing the flow of arms to Carranza, Villa, and Zapata, he made possible the overthrow of the counter-revolution and the triumph of the Revolution. What merciless criticism was heaped on Wilson for insisting that Latin Americans should be positively encouraged to institute reforms and develop democratic practices. Yet today Americans applaud their government's denial of Alliance-for-Progress funds to Latin American countries which refuse to undertake fundamental economic and social reforms and flout democracy.

. . . [C]onfronted with the stupendous and completely novel challenge of having to mobilize not only America's military strength but also its civilian resources and energies in America's first total war, the Wilson Administration set up a huge network of administrative agencies, exemplifying the highest imagination and creativity in the art of practical administration. FDR, in his New Deal and in his World War II agencies, was to borrow heavily from the Wilson innovations.

. . . Wilson's Fourteen Points and his other peace aims constituted war propaganda of perhaps unparalleled brilliance. They thrilled the world. They gave high purpose to the peoples of the Allied countries and stirred their war efforts. Directed over the heads of the governments to the enemy peoples themselves, they produced unrest, helped bring about the revolutions that overthrew the Sultan, the Hapsburgs, and the Hohenzollerns, and hastened the end of the war.

. . . [T]he Treaty of Versailles, of which Wilson was the chief architect, was a better peace than it would have been (considering, among other things, the imperialist secret treaties of the Allies) because of Wilson's labors for a just peace. The League of Nations was founded, and this was to be the forerunner of the United Nations. To the League was assigned the work of general disarmament. The mandate system of the League, designed to prepare colonial peoples for self-government and national independence, was a revolutionary step away from the old imperialism. The aspirations of many peoples in Europe for national independence were fulfilled. (If the disruption of the Austro-Hungarian Empire helped destroy the old balance of power, it must be said that in this particular situation Wilson's doctrine of national autonomy only exploited an existing fact in the interest of Allied victory, and even had there been no Wilsonian self-determination the nationalities of this area were already so well developed that they could not have been denied independence after the defeat of the Hapsburgs. Wilson's self-determination was to be a far more *creative* force among the colonial peoples than among the Europeans.) The Treaty restrained the chauvinism of the Italians, though not as much as Wilson would have liked. It prevented the truncating of Germany by preserving to her the Left Bank of the Rhine. The war-guilt clause and the enormous reparations saddled on Germany were mistakes, but Wilson succeeded in confining German responsibility to civilian damage and the expenses of Allied military pensions rather than the whole cost of the war; and had the United States ratified the Treaty and participated in post-war world affairs, as Wilson expected, the United States would have been in a position to join Britain in scaling down the actual reparations bill and in preventing any such adventure as the French seizure of the Ruhr in 1923, from which flowed Germany's disastrous inflation and the ugly forces of German nihilism. (There is poignancy in the broken Wilson's coming out of retirement momentarily in 1923 to denounce France for making "waste paper" of the Treaty of Versailles.) Finally, if Shantung was Wilson's Yalta, he paid the kind of price FDR paid and for precisely the same reason—the collapse of the balance of power in the immediate area involved.

. . . [T]he chief claim of Wilson to a superlative place in history—and it will not be denied him merely because he was turned down by the United States Senate—is that he, more than any other, formulated and articulated the ideology which was the polestar of the Western democracies in World War I, in World War II, and in the decades of Cold War against the Communists. Today, well past the middle of the twentieth century, the long-time program of America is still a Wilsonian program: international collective security, disarmament, the lowering of economic barriers between nations (as in America's support for the developing West European community today), anti-colonialism, self-determination of nations, and democratic social politics as an alternative to Communism. And this was the program critics of Wilson called "anachronistic," a mere "throw-back" to nineteenth-century liberalism!

America today is still grappling with the same world problems Wilson grappled with in 1917, 1918, and 1919, and the programs and policies designed to meet them are still largely Wilsonian. But events since Wilson's time have made his solutions more and more prophetic and urgent. The sweep of the anti-imperialist revolutions propels us to wider self-determination and social politics. The elimination of space, the increasing interdependence of the world, the further disintegration of the balance of power in World War II, and the nuclear revolution in war compel us to more effective collective security and to arms control supervised by an agency of the United Nations.

There will be more unwillingness to identify Wilson with social politics abroad than with the other policies with which he is more clearly identified. Historians like to quote George L. Record's letter to Wilson in which he told Wilson that there was no longer any glory in merely standing for political democracy, that political democracy had arrived, that the great issues of the future would revolve around economic and social democracy. But Wilson stood in no need of advice on this score. Earlier than any other responsible statesman, Wilson had seen the significance of the Chinese Revolution of Sun Yat-sen and of the Mexican Revolution, and he had officially encouraged both. Wilson believed that economic and social reform was implicit in the doctrine of self-determination, especially when applied to the colonial peoples. He recognized, too, that the Bolshevist Revolution had given economic and social reform a new urgency in all parts of the world. He was also well aware that those who most opposed his program for a world settlement were the conservative and imperialist elements in Western Europe and Japan, that socialist and labor groups were his most effective supporters. He pondered deeply how closely and openly he could work with labor and socialist parties in Europe without cutting off necessary support at home. (This—how to use social democracy and the democratic left to counter Communism abroad and still carry American opinion—was to be a central problem for every discerning American statesman after 1945.) Months before he had received Record's letter, Wilson himself had expressed almost the same views as Record. In a long conversation with Professor Stockton Axson at the White House, Wilson acknowledged that his best support was coming from labor people, that they were in touch with world movements and were international-minded, that government ownership of some basic resources and industries was coming, even in the United States, and that it was by a program of social democracy that Communism could be defeated.

In 1918 two gigantic figures—Wilson and Lenin—faced each other and articulated the contesting ideologies which would shake the world during the century. Since then, the lesser leaders who have succeeded them have added little to the ideology of either side. We are now far enough into the century to see in what direction the world is headed, provided there is no third world war. It is not headed for Communist domination. It is not headed for an American hegemony. And it is not headed for a duality with half the world Communist and the other half capitalist. Instead, it is headed for a new pluralism. The emerging new national societies are adjusting their new industrialism to their own conditions and cultures; and their developing economies will be varying mixtures of privatism, collectivism, and welfarism. Even the Communist states differ from one another in conditions, cultures, stages of revolutionary development, and degrees of Marxist "orthodoxy" or "revisionism." And today, all national states, old and new, Communist and non-Communist, join the United Nations as a matter of course.

There will be "victory" for neither "side," but instead a world which has been historically affected by both. Lenin's international proletarian state failed to materialize, but the evolving economies of the underdeveloped peoples are being influenced by his collectivism. However, the facts that most of the emerging economies are mixed ones, that they are working themselves out within autonomous national frameworks, and that the multiplying national states are operating internationally through the United Nations all point to a world which will be closer to the vision of Wilson than to that of Lenin. For this reason Wilson is likely to become a world figure of heroic proportions, with an acknowledged impact on world history more direct and far-reaching than that of any other American.

POSTSCRIPT

Was Woodrow Wilson Responsible for the Failure of the United States to Join the League of Nations?

Professor Thomas A. Bailey was a popular professor and an outstanding scholar of diplomatic history for five decades at Stanford University. His two books on *Woodrow Wilson and the Lost Peace* (The Macmillan Co., 1944) and *Woodrow Wilson and the Great Betrayal* (The Macmillan Co., 1945) were written during World War II as guidance for President Franklin Roosevelt to avoid the mistakes that Wilson made at home and abroad in his failure to gain ratification of the Treaty of Versailles.

Among the mistakes at home include Wilson's attempt to politicize the issue by asking voters to elect a Democratic Congress in the off-year elections in 1918. The public responded by restoring the Republicans to power in the Senate. Wilson also failed to name any prominent Republicans to the peace delegation he took to Paris. This was the first time a president was going outside the United States to conduct foreign affairs. Had he brought any prominent Senate Republicans with him, including Henry Cabot Lodge, he might have successfully negotiated a treaty acceptable to Senate ratification?

During the negotiations at Paris, Wilson was forced to compromise on issues of self-determination for settling territorial disputes, parceling out "mandates" to the winners over former German clinical possessions, and saddling Germany with a high reparations bill.

Bailey mentions but does not dwell on the attempts by Senator Lodge to privately negotiate a compromise treaty with the Democrats. Might the real villain have been the irreconcilable isolationist Senator William Borah who threatened to remove Lodge as Senate majority leader? Was Lodge afraid that an open fight with Borah could have split the Republican Party as had occurred in 1912 when ex-President Theodore Roosevelt walked out of the convention and ran as a third-party candidate? Wilson, who hated the sound of Lodge's name, had also privately worked out his own set of reservations with Democratic Senate minority leader Gilbert M. Hitchcock. Bailey maintains the compromise reservations differed only slightly in degree from those of Senator Lodge. If this was the case, would Wilson have been better off staying at home negotiating a compromise with the Senate instead of delivering emotional appeals to the American public on the ill-fated tour where he suffered a paralyzing stroke to the left side of his body?

In the second selection, William G. Carleton presents an impassioned defense of both Wilson's policies at Versailles as well as their implication for the future of American foreign policy. Carleton responds to the two main charges historians continue to level against Wilson: his inability to compromise and his naïve idealism. Unlike Professor Thomas A. Bailey, who in *Woodrow Wilson and the Great Betrayal* (Macmillan, 1945) blames Wilson for failing to compromise with Senator Henry Cabot Lodge, Carleton excoriates the chairman of the Senate Foreign Relations Committee for adding "nationally self-centered" reservations that he knew would emasculate the League of Nations and most likely cause other nations to add reservations to the Treaty of Versailles. Wilson, says Carleton, was a true realist when he rejected the Lodge reservations.

Professor Carleton's article was in many ways a response to the realist critique of traditional American foreign policy put forth during the height of the cold war. Most influential were the series of lectures on *American Diplomacy, 1900–1950* (Mentor Books, 1951) by former diplomat George F. Kennan who protested vehemently about the "legalistic-moralistic" streak that permeated American foreign policy. Other realistic critics included influential journalist Walter Lippman and political scientist Robert Endicott Osgood and Hans Morgenthau. Osgood's study of *Ideals and Self-Interest in American Foreign Relations* (University of Chicago Press, 1953) established the realist/idealist dichotomy later utilized by former Secretary of State Henry Kissinger in his scholarly history of *Diplomacy* (Simon & Schuster, 1994). According to Kissinger, Wilson was reflective of an excessive moralism and naïveté, which Americans hold about the world even today. Rejecting the fact that the United States had a basic national interest in preserving the balance of power of Europe, Wilson told the American people that they were entering the war to "bring peace and safety to all nations and make the world itself at last free." Kissinger believes that Theodore Roosevelt, the realist, had a firmer handle on foreign policy than did Wilson, the idealist. But in the long run, Wilsonianism triumphed and has influenced every modern-day president's foreign policy.

Scholars have criticized the realist approach to Wilson for a number of reasons. Some say that it is "unrealistic" to expect an American president to ask for a declaration of war to defend abstract principles such as the balance of power or the American national interest. Presidents and other elected officials must have a moral reason if they expect the American public to support a foreign war in which American servicemen might be killed.

Many recent historians agree with David F. Trask that Wilson developed realistic and clearly articulated goals and coordinated his larger diplomatic aims with the use of force better than any other wartime U.S. president. See "Woodrow Wilson and the Reconciliation of Force and Diplomacy, 1917–1918," *Naval War College Review* (January/February 1975). Arthur S. Link, coeditor of the *Papers of Woodrow Wilson*, 69 vols. (Princeton, 1966–1993), gave a blow-by-blow response to Kennan in revised lectures given at Johns Hopkins University in *Woodrow Wilson: Revolution, War and Peace* (Harlan Davidson, 1979) nicely summarized in "The Higher Realism of Woodrow Wilson," in a book of essays with the same title (Vanderbilt University Press, 1971). John Milton Cooper, Jr., in *The Warrior and the Priest: Woodrow Wilson and Theodore Roosevelt* (Harvard University Press, 1984), presents Wilson as the realist and Theodore Roosevelt as the idealist. Finally, George Kennan acknowledges that his earlier criticism of Wilson had to be viewed within the context of the cold war. "I now view Wilson," he wrote in 1991, "as a man who, like so many other people of broad vision and acute sensitivities, was ahead of his time, and did not live long enough to know what great and commanding relevance his ideas would acquire before this century was out." See "Comments on the Paper, Entitled 'Kennan Versus Wilson'" by Thomas J. Knock in John Milton Cooper et al., eds., *The Wilson Era: Essays in Honor of Arthur S. Link* (Harlan Davidson, 1991).

In his article, Professor Carleton advanced many of the arguments that historians Trask, Link, and Kennan later used defending Wilson's "higher realism." Rejecting the view of Wilson as a naïve idealist, Carleton maintains: "He recognized the emergence of the anti-imperialist revolutions . . . the importance of social politics in the international relations of the future . . . the implications for future world politics of the technological revolutions in war, of total war, and of the disintegration of the old balance of power."

Wilson's health has received serious scrutiny from scholars. In the early 1930s, Sigmund Freud and William C. Bullitt, a former diplomat, wrote a scathing and highly inaccurate biography of *Thomas Woodrow Wilson* (Houghton Mifflin, 1967) published posthumously in 1967. The book was poorly received and scathingly reviewed by Arthur S. Link, "The Case for Woodrow Wilson," in *The Higher Realism. . . .* The major controversy seems to be those who stress psychological difficulties—see Alexander and Juliette George, *Woodrow Wilson and Colonel House: A Personality Study* (Dover Press, 1956, 1964)—versus medical illnesses—see Edwin A. Weinstein, *Woodrow Wilson: A Medical and Psychological Biography* (Princeton University, 1981). For the best summaries of the controversy, see Thomas T. Lewis, "Alternative Psychological Interpretations of Woodrow Wilson," *Mid-America* (vol. 45, 1983), and Lloyd E. Ambrosius, "Woodrow Wilson's Health and the Treaty Fight, 1919–1920," *The International History Review* (February 1987). Phyllis Lee Levin, *Edith and Woodrow: The White House Years* (Scribners, 2001), and Robert J. Maddox, "Mrs. Wilson and the Presidency," *American History* (February 1973), make the case that we have already had America's first woman president.

The four best bibliographies of Wilson are as follows: the introduction to Lloyd E. Ambrosius's *Wilsonianism: Woodrow Wilson and His Legacy in American Foreign Relations* (Palgrave Macmillan, 2002), which is a collection of his articles from the leading realist Wilsonian scholar. John A. Thompson, a British scholar, has an up-to-date analysis of the Wilson scholarship in *Woodrow Wilson* (Pearson Education, 2002), a short, scholarly sympathetic study in the "Profiles in Power" series designed for student use. Advanced undergraduates should consult David Steigerwald, "The Reclamation of Woodrow Wilson," *Diplomatic History* (Winter 1999). Political science majors should consult Francis J. Gavin, "The Wilsonian Legacy in the Twentieth Century," *Orbis* (Fall 1997).

ISSUE 9

Was Prohibition a Failure?

YES: David E. Kyvig, from *Repealing National Prohibition*, 2d ed. (The University of Chicago Press, 1979, 2000)

NO: J. C. Burnham, from "New Perspectives on the Prohibition 'Experiment' of the 1920s," *Journal of Social History*, Volume 2 (Fall 1968)

ISSUE SUMMARY

YES: David E. Kyvig admits that alcohol consumption declined sharply in the prohibition era but that federal actions failed to impose abstinence among an increasingly urban and heterogeneous populace that resented and resisted restraints on their individual behavior.

NO: J. C. Burnham states that the prohibition experiment was more a success than a failure and contributed to a substantial decrease in liquor consumption, reduced arrests for alcoholism, fewer alcohol-related diseases and hospitalizations, and destroyed the old-fashioned saloon that was a major target of the law's proponents.

Americans, including many journalists and scholars, have never been shy about attaching labels to their history, and frequently they do so to characterize particular years or decades in their distant or recent past. It is doubtful, however, that any period in our nation's history has received as many catchy appellations as has the decade of the 1920s. Described at various times as the "Jazz Age," the "Roaring Twenties," the "prosperity decade," the "age of normalcy," or simply the "New Era," these are years that obviously have captured the imagination of the American public, including the chroniclers of the nation's past.

In 1920, the Great War was over, and President Woodrow Wilson received the Nobel Peace Prize despite his failure to persuade the Senate to adopt the Covenant of the League of Nations. The "Red Scare," culminating in the Palmer raids conducted by the Justice Department, came to an embarrassingly fruitless halt, and Republican Warren Harding won a landslide victory in the campaign for the presidency, an election in which women, buoyed by the ratification of the Nineteenth Amendment, exercised their suffrage rights for the first time in national politics. In Pittsburgh, the advent of the radio age was symbolized by the broadcast of election results by KDKA, the nation's first commercial radio station. F. Scott Fitzgerald and Sinclair Lewis each published their first important novels and thereby helped to usher in the most significant American literary renaissance since the early nineteenth century.

During the next nine years, Americans witnessed a number of amazing events: the rise and fall of the Ku Klux Klan; the trial, conviction, and execution of anarchists Nicola Sacco and Bartolomeo Vanzetti on murder charges and the subsequent legislative restrictions on immigration into the United States; battles over the teaching of evolution in the schools epitomized by the rhetorical clashes between William Jennings Bryan and Clarence Darrow during the Scopes trial in Dayton, Tennessee; the Harding scandals; "talking" motion pictures; and, in 1929, the collapse of the New York Stock Exchange, symbolizing the beginning of the Great Depression and bringing a startling end to the euphoric claims of business prosperity that had dominated the decade.

The 1920s are also remembered as the "dry decade," as a consequence of the ratification of the Eighteenth Amendment and the passage by Congress of the Volstead Act that prohibited the manufacture, sale, or transportation of alcoholic beverages. The implementation of national prohibition represented a continuation of the types of reforms designed by Progressives to improve the quality of life for the American citizenry; however, the illicit manufacture and trade of alcohol and the proliferation of speakeasies, where patrons seemed to flaunt the law with impunity, raise questions about the effectiveness of such legislation. Did prohibition work, or was it a noble, but failed, experiment? The selections that follow address this matter from different perspectives.

David Kyvig points out that the Volstead Act did not specifically prohibit the use or purchase of alcoholic beverages and that liquor continued to be provided by various sources, including gangland bootleggers, to meet consumer demand. Despite efforts to enforce the law, the federal government failed to create an adequate institutional network to insure compliance. Hence, although the consumption of alcohol did drop during the decade of the 1920s, legislation failed to eliminate drinking or to produce a feeling that such a goal was even within reach.

J. C. Burnham, on the other hand, argues that enforcement of the prohibition laws was quite effective in many places. Moreover, in addition to reducing the per capita consumption of alcohol, the enactment of prohibition legislation led to several positive social consequences. For example, during the 1920s, fewer people were arrested for public drunkenness, and there were substantially fewer Americans treated for alcohol-related diseases. All in all, he concludes, prohibition was more of a success than a failure.

YES

David E. Kyvig

America Sobers Up

When the Eighteenth Amendment took effect on January 17, 1920, most observers assumed that liquor would quickly disappear from the American scene. The possibility that a constitutional mandate would be ignored simply did not occur to them. "Confidence in the law to achieve a moral revolution was unbounded," one scholar of rural America has pointed out, explaining that "this was, after all, no mere statute, it was the Constitution." The assistant commissioner of the Internal Revenue Service, the agency charged with overseeing the new federal law, predicted that it would take six years to make the nation absolutely dry but that prohibition would be generally effective from the outset. Existing state and federal law enforcement agencies were expected to be able to police the new law. Initial plans called for only a modest special enforcement program, its attention directed to large cities where the principal resistance was anticipated. Wayne Wheeler of the Anti-Saloon League confidently anticipated that national prohibition would be respected, and estimated that an annual federal appropriation of five million dollars would be ample to implement it. The popular evangelist Billy Sunday replaced his prohibition sermon with one entitled "Crooks, Corkscrews, Bootleggers, and Whiskey Politicians—They Shall Not Pass." Wartime prohibition, which only banned further manufacture of distilled spirits and strong beer (with an alcohol content exceeding 2.75 percent) had already significantly reduced consumption. Few questioned the Volstead Act's capacity to eliminate intoxicants altogether. Americans accustomed to a society in which observation and pressure from other members of a community encouraged a high degree of conformity did not foresee that there would be difficulties in obtaining compliance with the law. They did not realize that the law would be resented and resisted by sizable elements in an increasingly urban and heterogeneous society where restraints on the individual were becoming far less compelling.

Within a few months it became apparent that not every American felt obliged to stop drinking the moment constitutional prohibition began. In response to consumer demand, a variety of sources provided at first a trickle and later a growing torrent of forbidden beverages. Physicians could legally prescribe "medicinal" spirits or beer for their patients, and before prohibition was six months old, more than fifteen thousand, along with over fifty-seven thousand pharmacists, obtained licenses to dispense

From *Repealing National Prohibition* by David E. Kyvig, (University of Chicago Press, 1979, 2000) pp. 20–32, 35. Copyright © 1979 by David E. Kyvig. Reprinted by permission of the author.

liquor. Grape juice or concentrates could be legitimately shipped and sold and, if the individual purchaser chose, allowed to ferment. Distributors learned to attach "warning" labels, reporting that United States Department of Agriculture tests had determined that, for instance, if permitted to sit for sixty days the juice would turn into wine of twelve percent alcohol content. The quadrupled output and rising prices of the California grape industry during the decade showed that many people took such warnings to heart.

Other methods of obtaining alcoholic beverages were more devious. Some "near-beer," which was legally produced by manufacturing genuine beer, then removing the three to five percent alcohol in excess of the approved one-half percent, was diverted to consumers before the alcohol was removed. In other instances, following government inspection, alcohol was reinjected into near-beer, making what was often called "needle beer." Vast amounts of alcohol produced for industrial purposes were diverted, watered down, and flavored for beverage purposes. To discourage this practice, the government directed that industrial alcohol be rendered unfit to drink by the addition of denaturants. Bootleggers did not always bother to remove such poisons, which cost some unsuspecting customers their eyesight or their lives.

Theft of perhaps twenty million gallons of good preprohibition liquor from bonded warehouses in the course of the decade, as well as an undeterminable amount of home brewing and distilling, provided more palatable and dependable beverages. By 1930 illegal stills provided the main supply of liquor, generally a high quality product. The best liquor available was that smuggled in from Canada and from ships anchored on "Rum Row" in the Atlantic beyond the twelve-mile limit of United States jurisdiction. By the late 1920s, one million gallons of Canadian liquor per year, eighty percent of that nation's greatly expanded output, made its way into the United States. British shipment of liquor to islands which provisioned Rum Row increased dramatically. Exports to the Bahamas, for example, went from 944 gallons in 1918 to 386,000 gallons in 1922. The tiny French islands of St. Pierre and Miguelon off the coast of Newfoundland imported 118,600 gallons of British liquor in 1922, "quite a respectable quantity," a British official observed, "for an island population of 6,000." Bootlegging, the illicit commercial system for distributing liquor, solved most problems of bringing together supply and demand. Government appeared unable—some claimed even unwilling—to halt a rising flood of intoxicants. Therefore, many observers at time, and increasing numbers since the law's repeal, assumed that prohibition simply did not work. . . .

The Volstead Act specified how the constitutional ban on "intoxicating liquors . . . for beverage purposes" was to be enforced. What the statute did not say had perhaps the greatest importance. While the law barred manufacture, transport, sale, import, or export of intoxicants, it did not specifically make their purchase or use a crime. This allowed continued possession of intoxicants obtained prior to prohibition, provided that such beverages were only for personal use in one's own home. Not only did the failure outlaw use render prohibition harder to enforce by eliminating possession as *de facto* evidence of crime, but also it allowed the purchaser and consumer of alcoholic beverages to defend his own behavior. Although the distinction was obviously artificial, the consumer could and did insist that there was nothing illegal about his drinking, while at the same time complaining that failure of government efforts to suppress bootlegging represented a break down of law and order.

Adopting the extreme, prohibitionist view that any alcohol whatsoever was intoxicating, the Volstead Act outlawed all beverages with an alcoholic content of .5 percent or more. The .5 percent limitation followed a traditional standard used to distinguish between alcoholic and nonalcoholic beverages for purposes of taxation, but that standard was considered by many to be unrealistic in terms of the amount of alcohol needed to produce intoxication. Wartime prohibition, after all, only banned beer with an alcohol content of 2.75 percent or more. Many did not associate intoxication with beer or wine at all but rather with distilled spirits. Nevertheless, the only exception to the .5 percent standard granted by the Volstead Act, which had been drafted by the Anti-Saloon League, involved cider and fruit juices; these subjects of natural fermentation were to be illegal only if declared by a jury to be intoxicating in fact. The Volstead Act, furthermore, did permit the use of intoxicants for medicinal purposes and religious sacraments; denatured industrial alcohol was exempted as well.

The Eighteenth Amendment specified that federal and state governments would have concurrent power to enforce the ban on intoxicating beverages. Therefore the system which evolved to implement prohibition had a dual nature. Congress, anticipating general compliance with the liquor ban as well as cooperation from state and local policing agencies in dealing with those violations which did occur, created a modest enforcement program at first. Two million dollars was appropriated to administer the law for its first five months of operation, followed by $4,750,000 for the fiscal year beginning July 1, 1920. The Prohibition Bureau of the Treasury Department recruited a force of only about fifteen hundred enforcement agents. Every state except Maryland adopted its own antiliquor statute. Most state laws were modeled after the Volstead Act, though some dated from the days of state prohibition and several imposed stricter regulations or harsher penalties than did the federal statute. State and local police forces were expected to enforce these laws as part of their normal duties. Critics at the time and later who claimed that no real effort was made to enforce national prohibition because no large enforcement appropriations were forthcoming need to consider the assumptions and police practices of the day. No general national police force, only specialized customs and treasury units, existed. Furthermore, neither federal nor state officials initially felt a need for a large special force to carry out this one task. The creators of national prohibition anticipated only a modest increase in the task facing law-enforcement officials.

Most Americans obeyed the national prohibition law. Many, at least a third to two-fifths of the adult population if Gallup poll surveys in the

1930s are any indication, had not used alcohol previously and simply continued to abstain. Others ceased to drink beer, wine, or spirits when to do so became illegal. The precise degree of compliance with the law is difficult to determine because violation levels cannot be accurately measured. The best index of the extent to which the law was accepted comes from a somewhat indirect indicator.

Consumption of beer, wine, and spirits prior to and following national prohibition was accurately reflected in the payment of federal excise taxes on alcoholic beverages. The tax figures appear reliable because bootlegging lacked sufficient profitability to be widespread when liquor was legally and conveniently obtainable. The amount of drinking during prohibition can be inferred from consumption rates once alcoholic beverages were again legalized. Drinking may have increased after repeal; it almost certainly did not decline. During the period 1911 through 1915, the last years before widespread state prohibition and the Webb-Kenyon Act began to significantly inhibit the flow of legal liquor, the per capita consumption by Americans of drinking age (15 years and older) amounted to 2.56 gallons of absolute alcohol. This was actually imbibed as 2.09 gallons of distilled spirits (45 percent alcohol), 0.79 gallons of wine (18 percent alcohol), and 29.53 gallons of beer (5 percent alcohol). In 1934, the year immediately following repeal of prohibition, the per capita consumption measured 0.97 gallons of alcohol distributed as 0.64 gallons of spirits, 0.36 gallons of wine, and 13.58 gallons of beer (4.5 percent alcohol after repeal). Total alcohol consumption, by this measure, fell by more than 60 percent because of national prohibition. Granting a generous margin of error, it seems certain that the flow of liquor in the United States was at least cut in half. It is difficult to know whether the same number of drinkers each consumed less or, as seems more likely, fewer persons drank. The crucial factor for this discussion is that national prohibition caused a substantial drop in aggregate alcohol consumption. Though the figures began to rise almost immediately after repeal, not until 1970 did the annual per capita consumption of absolute alcohol reach the level of 1911–15. In other words, not only did Americans drink significantly less as a result of national prohibition, but also the effect of the law in depressing liquor usage apparently lingered for several decades after repeal.

Other evidence confirms this statistical picture of sharply reduced liquor consumption under prohibition. After the Volstead Act had been in force for a half dozen years, social worker Martha Bensley Bruere conducted a nationwide survey of drinking for the National Federation of Settlements. Her admittedly impressionistic study, based upon 193 reports from social workers across the country, focused on lower-class, urban America. Social workers, who generally favored prohibition, perhaps overrated the law's effectiveness. Nevertheless, Bruere's book provided probably the most objective picture of prohibition in practice in the mid-1920s.

The Bruere survey reported that adherence to the dry law varied from place to place. The Scandinavians of Minneapolis and St. Paul continued to drink. On the other hand, prohibition seemed effective in Sioux Falls, South

Dakota. In Butte, Montana, the use of intoxicants had declined, though bootleggers actively plied their trade. Idaho, Oregon, and Washington had generally accepted prohibition, and even in the West Coast wet bastion, San Francisco, working-class drinking appeared much reduced. The Southwest from Texas to Los Angeles was reported to be quite dry. The survey cited New Orleans as America's wettest city, with bootlegging and a general disregard of the law evident everywhere. In the old South, prohibition was said to be effectively enforced for Negroes but not whites. Throughout the Midwest, with some exceptions, residents of rural areas generally observed prohibition, but city dwellers appeared to ignore it. In the great metropolises of the North and East, with their large ethnic communities—Chicago, Detroit, Cleveland, Pittsburgh, Boston, New York, and Philadelphia—the evidence was overwhelming that the law was neither respected nor observed.

Throughout the country, Bruere suggested, less drinking was taking place than before prohibition. Significantly, she reported the more prosperous upper and middle classes violated the alcoholic beverage ban far more frequently than did the working class. Illicitly obtained liquor was expensive. Yale economist Irving Fisher, himself an advocate of prohibition, claimed that in 1928 on the average a quart of beer cost 80¢ (up 600 percent from 1916), gin $5.90 (up 520 percent), and corn whiskey $3.95 (up 150 percent) while average annual income per family was about $2,600. If nothing else, the economics of prohibition substantially reduced drinking by lower-class groups. Thus prohibition succeeded to a considerable degree in restraining drinking by the very social groups with whom many advocates of the law had been concerned. The Bruere study, therefore, offered cheer to drys. Yet her report also demonstrated that acceptance of prohibition varied with ethnic background and local custom as well as economics. Community opinion appeared more influential than federal or state laws or police activity. People in many parts of the United States voluntarily obeyed the Eighteenth Amendment, but elsewhere citizens chose to ignore it. In the latter part of the decade, violations apparently increased, both in small towns and large cities. In Detroit it reportedly became impossible to get a drink "unless you walked at least ten feet and told the busy bartender what you wanted in a voice loud enough for him to hear you above the uproar."

Any evidence to the contrary notwithstanding, national prohibition rapidly acquired an image, not as a law which significantly reduced the use of alcoholic beverages, but rather as a law that was widely flouted. One Wisconsin congressmen, writing to a constituent after a year of national prohibition, asserted, "I believe that there is more bad whiskey consumed in the country today than there was good whiskey before we had prohibition and of course we have made a vast number of liars and law violators through the Volstead Act." In part this commonly held impression stemmed from the substantial amount of drinking which actually did continue. Even given a 60 percent drop in total national alcohol consumption, a considerable amount of imbibing still took place. Yet the image also derived in part from the unusually visible character of those prohibition violations which did occur.

Drinking by its very nature attracted more notice than many other forms of law-breaking. It was, in the first place, generally a social, or group, activity. Moreover, most drinking took place, Bruere and others acknowledged, in urban areas where practically any activity was more likely to witnessed. Bootleggers had to advertise their availability, albeit carefully, in order to attract customers. The fact that the upper classes were doing much of the imbibing further heightened its visibility. Several additional factors insured that many Americans would have a full, perhaps even exaggerated, awareness of the extent to which the prohibition law was being broken.

The behavior of those who sought to profit by meeting the demand for alcoholic beverages created an indelible image of rampant lawlessness. National prohibition provided a potentially very profitable opportunity for persons willing to take certain risks. "Prohibition is a business," maintained the best known and most successful bootlegger of all, Al Capone of Chicago. "All I do is supply a public demand." Obtaining a supply of a commodity, transporting it to a marketplace, and selling it for an appropriate price were commonplace commercial activities; carrying out these functions in the face of government opposition and without the protections of facilities, goods, and transactions normally provided by government made bootlegging an unusual business. Indeed bootleggers faced the problem—or the opportunity that hijacking a competitor's shipment of liquor often presented the easiest and certainly the cheapest way of obtaining a supply of goods, and the victim of such a theft had no recourse to regular law enforcement agencies. Nor, for better or worse, could bootleggers expect government to restrain monopolistic practices, regulate prices, or otherwise monitor business practices. Consequently, participants in the prohibition-era liquor business had to develop their own techniques for dealing with competition and the pressures of the marketplace. The bootlegging wars and gangland killings, so vividly reported in the nation's press, represented, on one level, a response to a business problem. . . .

Violence was commonplace in establishing exclusive sales territories, in obtaining liquor, or in defending a supply. In Chicago, for instance, rival gangs competed intensely. Between September 1923 and October 1926, the peak period of struggle for control of the large Chicago market, an estimated 215 criminals died at the hands of rivals. In comparison, police killed 160 gangsters during the same period. Although by conventional business standards the violence level in bootlegging remained high, it declined over the course of the 1920s. Consolidation, agreement on markets, regularizing of supply and delivery all served to reduce turbulence. John Torrio and Al Capone in Chicago, Charles Solomon in Boston, Max Hoff in Philadelphia, Purple Gang in Detroit, the Mayfield Road Mob in Cleveland, and Joseph Roma in Denver imposed some order on the bootlegging business in their cities. The more than a thousand gangland murders in New York during prohibition reflect the inability of Arnold Rothstein, Lucky Luciano, Dutch Schultz, Frank Costello, or any other criminal leader to gain control and put an end to (literally) cut-throat competition in the largest market of all. . . .

Ironically, the federal government in its efforts to enforce national prohibition often contributed to the image of a heavily violated law. Six months after the Eighteenth Amendment took effect, for example, Jouett Shouse, an Assistant Secretary of the Treasury whose duties included supervising prohibition enforcement, announced that liquor smuggling had reached such (portions that it could no longer be handled by the 6,000 agents of the Customs Bureau. Shouse estimated that 35,000 men would be required to guard the coasts and borders against the flood of liquor pouring into the country. The Assistant Secretary attributed the problem to an unlimited market for smuggled whiskey and the 1,000 percent profits which could be realized from its sale.

During the 1920 presidential campaign, Republican nominee Warren G. Harding pledged to enforce the Volstead Act "as a fundamental principle of the American conscience," implying that the Wilson administration had neglected its duty. Despite his known fondness for drink, Harding attracted dry support with such statements while his opponent, the avowedly wet James A. Cox, floundered. Once inaugurated, President Harding tried to fulfill his campaign promise but met with little success. He explained to his wet Senate friend, Walter Edge of New Jersey, "Prohibition is a constitutional mandate and I hold it to be absolutely necessary to give it a fair and thorough trial." The president appointed the Anti-Saloon league's candidate, Roy A. Haynes, as commissioner of prohibition and gave the corpulent, eternally optimistic Haynes a generally free hand in selecting personnel to wage battle against bootlegging. Harding began to receive considerable mail from across the country complaining about the failure of the dry law. As reports of prohibition violations increased, Harding became more and more disturbed. Never much of a believer in prohibition himself, Harding had, nevertheless, been willing as a senator to let the country decide whether it wanted the Eighteenth Amendment, and now as president he deplored the wholesale breaking of the law. In early 1923, having gradually realized the importance of personal example, Harding gave up his own clandestine drinking. In a speech in Denver just prior to his death, Harding appealed rigorously for observance of prohibition in the interest of preventing lawlessness, corruption, and collapse of national moral fiber. "Whatever satisfaction there may be in indulgence, whatever objection there is to the so-called invasion of personal liberty," the president asserted, "neither counts when the supremacy of law and the stability of our institutions are menaced." Harding's rhetoric, although intended to encourage compliance with prohibition, furthered the image of a law breaking down.

A report by Attorney General Harry Daugherty to President Calvin Coolidge shortly after Harding's death suggested the extent to which the Volstead Act was being violated in its early years of operation. Daugherty indicated that in the first forty-one months of national prohibition, the federal government had initiated 90,330 prosecutions under the law. The number of cases had been rising: 5,636 were settled in April 1923, 541 than in the initial six months of prohibition. The number of new cases doubled between fiscal 1922 and fiscal 1923. The government obtained convictions in 80 percent of the terminated cases. These figures showed, the attorney general argued, that prohibition enforcement was becoming increasingly effective. They could just as well be seen, however, as an indication of an enormous and increasing number of violations.

The prohibition cases brought into federal court most certainly represented only a small fraction of actual offenses. They nevertheless seemed to be more than the court and prison system could handle. In 1920, 5,095 of the 34,230 cases terminated in the federal courts involved prohibition violation; during 1929, 75,298 prohibition cases alone were concluded. In 1920, federal prisons contained just over 5,000 inmates; ten years later they contained over 12,000, more than 4,000 of whom were serving time for liquor violations. The courts were so overworked that they frequently resorted to the expedient of "bargain days." Under this system, on set days large numbers of prohibition violators would plead guilty after being given prior assurance that they would not receive jail sentences or heavy fines. By 1925, pleas of guilty, without jury trials, accounted for over 90 percent of the convictions obtained in federal courts. The legal system appeared overwhelmed by national prohibition.

As president, Calvin Coolidge found prohibition enforcement to be the same headache it had been for his predecessor. Like Harding, Coolidge was constantly under pressure from Wayne Wheeler and other dry leaders to improve enforcement. He received hundreds of letters deploring the rate of Volstead Act violations and urging forceful action. Coolidge merely acknowledged receipt of letters on the subject, avoiding any substantial response. As it did with many other issues, the Coolidge administration sought to avoid the prohibition question as much as possible. Other than seeking Canadian and British cooperation in halting smuggling, and holding White House breakfasts for prestigious drys, few federal initiatives were taken while Coolidge remained in office. The picture of rampant prohibition violation stood unchallenged.

Congress, once having adopted the Volstead Act and appropriated funds for its enforcement, assumed its job was done and avoided all mention of prohibition during the law's first year of operation. Evidence of violations, however, quickly provoked dry demands that Congress strengthen the prohibition law. Whenever Congress acted, it drew attention to the difficulties of abolishing liquor. When it failed to respond, as was more frequently the case, drys charged it with indifference to law breaking. Whatever it did, Congress proved unable to significantly alter prohibition's image.

After Harding's inauguration, Congress learned that retiring Attorney General A. Mitchell Palmer had ruled that the Volstead Act placed no limit on the authority of physicians to prescribe beer and wine for medicinal purposes." Senator Frank B. Willis of Ohio and Representative Robert S. Campbell of Kansas moved quickly to correct this oversight by introducing a bill that would forbid the prescription of beer and rigidly limit physicians' authority to prescribe wine and spirits. Only one pint of liquor would be permitted to be dispensed for a patient during any ten-day period, under their plan. Well-prepared dry spokesmen completely dominated the hearings on the Willis-Campbell bill, insisting that this substantial source of intoxicants be eliminated. Physicians and pharmacists protested that beer possessed therapeutic value and that Congress had no right to restrict doctors in their practice of medicine. Nevertheless, in the summer of 1921 the bill passed the House by a vote of 250 to 93, and the Senate by 39 to 20. The Willis-Campbell Act reflected congressional determination to shut off the liquor supply, but like the Volstead Act, it did not resolve the problem of imposing abstinence on those willing to ignore the law in order to have a drink.

For years, Congress continued to wrestle with the problem of creating and staffing an effective federal enforcement organization. The Volstead Act delegated responsibility for implementing national prohibition to an agency of the Bureau of Internal Revenue in the Department of the Treasury. The act exempted enforcement agents from civil service regulations, making them political appointees. The Anti-Saloon League, through its general counsel, Wayne B. Wheeler, relentlessly pressed Harding and Coolidge to name its candidates to positions in the enforcement agency. The prohibition unit, beset by patronage demands and inadequate salaries, attracted a low caliber of appointee and a high rate of corruption. By 1926 one out of twelve agents had been dismissed for such offenses as bribery, extortion, solicitation of money, conspiracy to violate the law, embezzlement, and submission of false reports. A senator who supported prohibition argued lamely that this record was no worse than that of the twelve apostles, but he could not disguise the enforcement unit's very tarnished reputation.

Even if the agency had been staffed with personnel of better quality, its task would have been overwhelming. It received little cooperation from the Department of Justice, with which it shared responsibility for prosecuting violators. Furthermore, the prohibition unit lacked both the manpower and the money to deal with the thousands of miles of unpatrolled coastline, the millions of lawbreaking citizens, and the uncountable hordes of liquor suppliers. The agency focused its efforts on raiding speakeasies and apprehending bootleggers, but this task alone proved beyond its capacity and discouraged a series of prohibition commissioners.

Congress steadily increased enforcement appropriations but never enough to accomplish the goal. In 1927 prohibition agents were finally placed under civil service, and in 1930 the Prohibition Bureau was at last transferred to the Justice Department. As useful as these congressional steps may have been, they came long after the enforcement effort had acquired a dismal reputation and doubts as to whether prohibition could possibly be effective had become deeply ingrained.

Early in 1929 Congress made a determined effort to compel greater adherence to national prohibition. A bill introduced by Washington senator Wesley L. Jones drastically increased penalties for violation of the liquor ban. Maximum prison terms for first offenders were raised from six months to five years, and fines were raised from $1,000 to $10,000. The Jones "Five-and-Ten" Bill, as it was called, passed by lopsided majorities in

Congress and signed into law by Coolidge days before he left office, did not improve prohibition's effectiveness but strengthened its reputation as a harsh and unreasonable statute.

During the 1920s the Supreme Court did more than either the Congress or the president to define the manner in which national prohibition would be enforced and thereby to sharpen the law's image. As a Yale law professor and earlier as president, William Howard Taft had opposed a prohibition amendment because he preferred local option, disliked any changes in the Constitution, and felt national prohibition would be unenforceable. But when the Eighteenth Amendment was ratified, Taft, a constant defender the sanctity of democratically adopted law, accepted it completely and even became an advocate of temperance by law. He condemned critics of national prohibition, saying, "There isn't the slightest chance that the constitutional amendment will be repealed. You know that and I know it." As chief justice from 1921 until 1930, he sought to have the prohibition laws strictly enforced and took upon himself the writing of prohibition decisions. The opinions handed down by the Taft Court during the 1920s greatly influenced conceptions of the larger implications of the new law as well as the actual course of prohibition enforcement. . . .

While in reality national prohibition sharply reduced the consumption of alcohol in the United States, the law fell considerably short of expectations. It neither eliminated drinking nor produced a sense that such a goal was within reach. So long as the purchaser of liquor, the supposed victim of a prohibition violation, participated in the illegal act rather than complained about it, the normal law enforcement process simply did not function. As a result, policing agencies bore a much heavier burden. The various images of lawbreaking, from contacts with the local bootlegger to Hollywood films to overloaded court dockets, generated a widespread belief that violations were taking place with unacceptable frequency. Furthermore, attempts at enforcing the law created an impression that government, unable to cope with lawbreakers by using traditional policing methods, was assuming new powers in order to accomplish its task. The picture of national prohibition which emerged over the course of the 1920s disenchanted many Americans and moved some to an active effort to bring an end to the dry law.

J. C. Burnham  **NO**

New Perspectives on the Prohibition "Experiment" of the 1920's

Recently a number of historians have shown that the temperance movement that culminated in national prohibition was central to the American reform tradition. Such writers as James H. Timberlake have demonstrated in detail how the Eighteenth Amendment was an integral part of the reforms of the Progressive movement. Yet we commonly refer to the "prohibition experiment" rather than the "prohibition reform." This characterization deserves some exploration. The question can be raised, for example, why we do not refer to the "workmen's compensation law experiment."

One explanation may be that of all of the major reforms enacted into law in the Progressive period, only prohibition was decisively and deliberately repealed. The Sixteenth and Seventeenth Amendments are still on the books; the Eighteenth is not. For historians who emphasize the theme of reform, referring to prohibition as an experiment gives them the option of suggesting that its repeal involved no loss to society. To characterize the repeal of prohibition as a major reversal of social reform would seriously impair the view that most of us have of the cumulative nature of social legislation in the twentieth century.

We have been comfortable for many decades now with the idea that prohibition was a great social experiment. The image of prohibition as an experiment has even been used to draw lessons from history: to argue, for example, that certain types of laws—especially those restricting or forbidding the use of liquor and narcotics—are futile and probably pernicious. Recently, however, some new literature has appeared on prohibition, whose total effect is to demand a re-examination of our customary view.

The idea that prohibition was an experiment may not survive this renaissance of scholarship in which the reform and especially Progressive elements in the temperance movement are emphasized. But it is profitable, at least for the purposes of this article, to maintain the image of an experiment, for the perspectives available now permit a fresh evaluation of the experiment's outcome.

Specifically, the prohibition experiment, as the evidence stands today, can more easily be considered a success than a failure. While far from clear-cut, the balance of scholarly evidence has shifted the burden of proof to those who would characterize the experiment a failure. . . .

From *Journal of Social History,* Autumn 1968/1969, pp. 51–52, 55–68. Copyright © 1969 by Journal of Social Histtory, George Mason University. Reprinted by permission via Copyright Clearance Center.

The American prohibition experiment grew out of the transformation that the combination of Progressive reformers and businessmen wrought in the temperance movement. Beginning in 1907 a large number of state and local governments enacted laws or adopted constitutional provisions that dried up—as far as alcoholic beverages were concerned—a substantial part of the United States. The success of the anti-liquor forces, led by the Anti-Saloon League, was so impressive that they were prepared to strike for a national prohibition constitutional amendment. This issue was decided in the 1916 Congressional elections, although the Amendment itself was not passed by Congress until December 22, 1917. A sufficient number of states ratified it by January 16, 1919, and it took effect on January 16, 1920.

In actuality, however, prohibition began well before January, 1920. In addition to the widespread local prohibition laws, federal laws greatly restricted the production and sale of alcoholic beverages, mostly, beginning in 1917, in the guise of war legislation. The manufacture of distilled spirits beverages, for example, had been forbidden for more than three months when Congress passed the Eighteenth Amendment late in 1917. The Volstead Act of 1919, passed to implement the Amendment, provided by law that wartime prohibition would remain in effect until the Amendment came into force.

The Eighteenth Amendment prohibited the manufacturing, selling, importing, or transporting of "intoxicating liquors." It was designed to kill off the liquor business in general and the saloon in particular; but at the same time the Amendment was not designed to prohibit either the possession or drinking of alcoholic beverages. At a later time the courts held even the act of buying liquor to be legal and not part of a conspiracy. Most of the local and state prohibition laws were similar in their provisions and intent. The very limited nature of the prohibition experiment must, therefore, be understood from the beginning.

At the time, a number of union leaders and social critics pointed out that the Eighteenth Amendment constituted class legislation; that is, the political strength of the drys lay among middle class Progressives who wanted, essentially, to remove the saloon from American life. The Amendment permitted those who had enough money to lay in all the liquor they pleased, but the impecunious workingman was to be deprived of his day-to-day or week-to-week liquor supply. The class aspect of prohibition later turned out to have great importance. Most of the recent revisionist writers have concentrated upon the interplay between prohibition and social role and status.

The primary difficulty that has stood in the way of properly assessing the prohibition experiment has been methods of generalization. Evidence gathered from different sections of the country varies so radically as to make weighing of evidence difficult. In addition, there has been a great deal of confusion about time: When did prohibition begin? What period of its operation should be the basis for judgment? The difficulties of time and place are particularly relevant to the fundamental question of enforcement.

As the country looked forward to prohibition after the elections of 1916, widespread public support, outside of a few urban areas, was expected to make prohibition a success both initially and later on. It was reasonable to expect that enforcement would be strict and that society both institutionally and informally would deal severely with any actions tending to revive the liquor trade. These expectations were realistic through the years of the war, when prohibition and patriotism were closely connected in the public mind. Only some years after the passage of the Volstead Act did hopes for unquestionably effective enforcement fade away. In these early years, when public opinion generally supported enforcement, the various public officials responsible for enforcement were the ones who most contributed to its breakdown. This breakdown in many areas in turn led to the evaporation of much public support in the country as a whole.

Successive Congresses refused to appropriate enough money to enforce the laws. Through its influence in Congress the Anti-Saloon League helped to perpetuate the starvation of the Prohibition Bureau and its predecessors in the name of political expediency. Huge sums spent on prohibition, the drys feared, would alienate many voters—and fearful Congressmen—more or less indifferent to prohibition. The prohibitionists therefore made the claim that prohibition was effective so that they would not have to admit the necessity of large appropriations for enforcement. A second act of irresponsibility of the Congresses was acquiescing in exempting the enforcement officers from Civil Service and so making the Prohibition Bureau part of the political spoils system. League officials who had written this provision into the Volstead Act hoped by using their political power to dictate friendly appointments, but the record shows that politics, not the League, dominated federal enforcement efforts. Not until 1927 did the Prohibition Bureau finally come under Civil Service.

The men charged with enforcement, the Presidents of the 1920's, were, until Hoover, indifferent to prohibition except as it affected politics. Wilson, although not a wet, vetoed the Volstead Act, and it was passed over his veto. Harding and Coolidge were notoriously uninterested in enforcing prohibition. When Hoover took office in 1929 he reorganized the administration of enforcement, and his effectiveness in cutting down well established channels of supply helped give final impetus to the movement for a re-evaluation of prohibition.

In some areas prosecutors and even judges were so unsympathetic that enforcement was impossible. Elsewhere local juries refused to convict in bootlegging cases. These local factors contributed greatly to the notable disparities in the effectiveness of prohibition from place to place.

By a unique concurrent enforcement provision of the Eighteenth Amendment, state and local officials were as responsible for enforcement as federal authorities. The Anti-Saloon League, because of its power in the states, expected to use existing law enforcement agencies and avoid huge federal appropriations for enforcement. Contrary to the expectations of the League, local officials were the weakest point in enforcement. Most of the states—but not all—enacted "little Volstead" acts; yet in 1927 only eighteen of the forty-eight states were appropriating money for the enforcement of such acts. Local enforcement in many Southern and Western areas was both severe and effective; in other areas local enforcement was even more unlikely than federal enforcement. For years the entire government of New Jersey openly defied the Eighteenth Amendment, and it was clear that the governor was not troubled a bit about his oath of office. Some states that had enforced their own prohibition laws before 1919 afterward made no attempt to continue enforcement.

With such extreme variations in the enforcement of prohibition over the United States, judging the over-all success of the experiment on the basis of enforcement records is hazardous. Bootlegging in New York, Chicago, and San Francisco clearly was not necessarily representative of the intervening territory, and vice versa.

An easier basis for generalizing about the effectiveness of enforcement is the impact that prohibition had on consumption of alcohol. Here the second major complication mentioned crops up: the availability of liquor varied greatly from time to time and specifically from an initial period of effectiveness in 1919–1922 to a later period of widespread violation of the law, typically 1925–1927.

In the early years of national prohibition, liquor was very difficult to obtain. In the later years when the laws were being defied by well-organized bootleggers operating through established channels, the supply increased. By the late 1920's, for example, the domestic supply of hard liquor in northern California was so great that the price fell below the point at which it was profitable to run beverages in from Canada by ship. In the last years of prohibition it became very easy—at least in some areas with large populations—to obtain relatively good liquor. Many people, relying on their memories, have generalized from this later period, after about 1925, to all of the prohibition years and have come, falsely, to the conclusion that enforcement was neither real nor practical. Overall one can say that considering the relatively slight amount of effort put into it, enforcement was surprisingly effective in many places, and particularly in the early years.

Both so-called wet and dry sources agree that the amount of liquor consumed per capita decreased substantially because of prohibition. The best figures available show that the gallons of pure alcohol ingested per person varied widely over four different periods. In the period 1911–1914, the amount was 1.69 gallons. Under the wartime restrictions, 1918–1919, the amount decreased to .97. In the early years of national prohibition, 1921–1922, there was still further decrease to .73 gallons. In the later years of prohibition, 1927–1930, the amount rose to 1.14 gallons.

These figures suggest that great care must be used in making comparisons between "before" prohibition and "after." Statistics and memories that use 1920 as the beginning of prohibition are misleading, since not only were federal laws in force before then but there was also extensive state prohibition. The peak of absolute consumption of beer, for example, was reached in the years 1911–1914, not 1916–1918, much less 1919. The real "before" was sometime around 1910.

The best independent evidence of the impact of prohibition can be found in the available figures for certain direct and measurable social effects of alcohol consumption. The decrease from about 1915 to 1920–1922 in arrests for drunkenness, in hospitalization for alcoholism, and in the incidence of other diseases, such as cirrhosis of the liver, specifically related to drinking was remarkable. The low point of these indexes came in 1918–1921, and then they climbed again until the late 1920's. Because of confusion about when prohibition began, the significance of these well known statistics has seldom been appreciated: there is clear evidence that in the early years of prohibition not only did the use of alcohol decrease but American society enjoyed some of the direct benefits promised by proponents of prohibition.

Undoubtedly the most convincing evidence of the success of prohibition is to be found in the mental hospital admission rates. There is no question of a sudden change in physicians' diagnoses, and the people who had to deal with alcohol-related mental diseases were obviously impressed by what they saw. After reviewing recent hospital admission rates for alcoholic psychoses, James V. May, one of the most eminent American psychiatrists, wrote in 1922: "With the advent of prohibition the alcoholic psychoses as far as this country is concerned have become a matter of little more than historical interest. The admission rate in the New York state hospitals for 1920 was only 1.9 percent [as compared with ten percent in 1909–1912]." For many years articles on alcoholism literally disappeared from American medical literature.

In other words, after World War I and until sometime in the early 1920's, say, 1922 or 1923, when enforcement was clearly breaking down, prohibition was generally a success. Certainly there is no basis for the conclusion that prohibition was inherently doomed to failure. The emasculation of enforcement grew out of specific factors that were not organically related to the Eighteenth Amendment.

Nor is most of this analysis either new or controversial. Indeed, most of the criticism of prohibition has centered around assertions not so much that the experiment failed but that it had two more or less unexpected consequences that clearly show it to have been undesirable. The critics claim, first, that the Eighteenth Amendment caused dangerous criminal behavior; and, second, that in spite of prohibition more people drank alcohol than before. If a candid examination fails to confirm these commonly accepted allegations, the interpretation of prohibition as a failure loses most of its validity. Such is precisely the case.

During the 1920's there was almost universal public belief that a "crime wave" existed in the United States. In spite of the literary output on the subject, dealing largely with a local situation in Chicago, there is no firm evidence of this supposed upsurge in lawlessness. Two criminologists, Edwin H. Sutherland and C. H. Gehlke, at the end of the decade reviewed the available crime statistics, and the most that they could conclude was that "there is no evidence here of a 'crime wave,' but only of a slowly rising level" These admittedly inadequate statistics emphasized large urban areas and were, it should be emphasized, *not* corrected to reflect the increase in population. Actually no statistics from this period dealing with crime are of any value whatsoever in generalizing about crime rates. Apparently what happened was that in the 1920's the long existent "underworld" first became publicized and romanticized. The crime wave, in other words, was the invention of enterprising journalists feeding on some sensational crimes and situations and catering to a public to whom the newly discovered "racketeer" was a covert folk hero.

Even though there was no crime wave, there was a connection between crime and prohibition, as Frederick Lewis Allen suggested in his alliterative coupling of "Alcohol and Al Capone." Because of the large profits involved in bootlegging and the inability of the producers and customers to obtain police protection, criminal elements organized and exploited the liquor business just as they did all other illegal activities. It would be a serious distortion even of racketeering, however, to emphasize bootlegging at the expense of the central criminal-directed activity, gambling. Since liquor-related activities were not recognized as essentially criminal in nature by substantial parts of the population, it is difficult to argue that widespread violation of the Volstead Act constituted a true increase of crime. Nevertheless, concern over growing federal "crime" statistics, that is, bootlegging cases, along with fears based on hysterical journalism, helped to bring about repeal.

We are left, then, with the question of whether national prohibition led to more drinking than before. It should first be pointed out not only that the use of 1920 as the beginning of prohibition is misleading but that much of the drinking during the 1920's was not relevant to the prohibition of the Eighteenth Amendment and Volstead Act. Private drinking was perfectly legal all of the time, and possession of liquor that had been accumulated by the foresighted before prohibition was entirely lawful. The continued production of cider and wine at home was specifically provided for also. Indeed, the demand for wine grapes was so great that many grape growers who in 1919 faced ruin made a fortune selling their grapes in the first years of the Amendment. Ironically, many an old lady who made her own wine believed that she was defying prohibition when in fact the law protected her.

We still face the problem of reconciling the statistics quoted above that show that alcohol consumption was substantially reduced, at one point to about half of the pre-prohibition consumption, with the common observation of the 1920's that as many or more people were drinking than before.

What happened, one can say with hindsight, was predictable. When liquor became unavailable except at some risk and considerable cost, it became a luxury item, that is, a symbol of affluence and, eventually, status. Where before men of good families tended not to drink and women certainly did not, during the 1920's it was precisely the sons and daughters of the "nice" people who were patronizing the bootleggers and speakeasies, neither of which for some years was very effectively available to the lower classes. This utilization of drinking as conspicuous consumption was accompanied by the so-called revolution in manners and morals that began among the rebellious intellectuals around 1912 and reached a high point of popularization in the 1920's when the adults of the business class began adopting the "lower" social standards of their children.

We can now understand why the fact was universally reported by journalists of the era that "everyone drank, including many who never did before." Drinking, and often new drinking, was common among the upper classes, especially among the types of people likely to consort with the writers of the day. The journalists and other observers did indeed report honestly that they saw "everyone" drinking. They seldom saw the lower classes and almost never knew about the previous drinking habits of the masses. The situation was summed up by an unusually well-qualified witness, Whiting Williams, testifying before the Wickersham Commission. A vice-president of a Cleveland steel company, he had for many years gone in disguise among the working people of several areas in connection with handling labor problems. He concluded:

> . . . very much of the misconception with respect to the liquor problem comes from the fact that most of the people who are writing and talking most actively about the prohibition problem are people who, in the nature of things, have never had any contact with the liquor problem in its earlier pre-prohibition form and who are, therefore, unduly impressed with the changes with respect to drinking that they see on their own level; their own level, however, representing an extremely small proportion of the population.
>
> The great mass who, I think, are enormously more involved in the whole problem, of course, in the nature of things are not articulate and are not writing in the newspapers.

The important point is that the "everyone" who was reported to be drinking did not include working-class families, i.e., the pre-ponderant part of the population. Clark Warburton, in a study initiated with the help of the Association Against the Prohibition Amendment, is explicit on this point: "The working class is consuming not more than half as much alcohol per capita as formerly." The classic study is Martha Bensley Bruère's. She surveyed social workers across the country, and the overwhelming impression (even taking account of urban immigrant areas where prohibition laws were flouted) was that working people drank very much less than before and further, as predicted, that prohibition had, on the balance, substantially improved conditions among low-income Americans.

Even in its last years the law, with all of its leaks, was still effective in cutting down drinking among the workers, which was one of the primary aims of prohibition. Here, then, is more evidence of the success of the prohibition experiment. Certainly the Anti-Saloon League did succeed in destroying the old-fashioned saloon, the explicit target of its campaign.

Taking together all of this evidence of the success of prohibition, especially in its class differential aspects, we are still left with the question of why the law was repealed.

The story of repeal is contained largely in the growth of the idea that prohibition was a failure. From the beginning, a number of contemporary observers (particularly in the largest cities) saw many violations of the law and concluded that prohibition was not working. These observers were in the minority, and for a long time most people believed that by and large prohibition was effective. Even for those who did not, the question of repeal—once appeals to the Supreme Court had been settled—simply never arose. Bartlett C. Jones has observed, "A peculiarity of the Prohibition debate was the fact that repeal, called an absolute impossibility for much of the period, became irresistibly popular in 1932 and 1933. Not even enemies of prohibition considered absolute repeal as an alternative until quite late, although they upheld through all of these years their side of the vigorous public debate about the effectiveness and desirability of the prohibition laws.

In the early days of prohibition, the predominant attitudes toward the experiment manifested in the chief magazines and newspapers of the country were either ambivalent acceptance or, more rarely, impotent hostility. In 1923–1924 a major shift in the attitudes of the mass circulation information media occurred so that acceptance was replaced by nearly universal outright criticism accompanied by a demand for modification of the Volstead Act. The criticism was based on the assumption that Volsteadism, at least, was a failure. The suggested solution was legalizing light wines and beers.

The effectiveness of the shift of "public opinion" is reflected in the vigorous counterattack launched by the dry forces who too often denied real evils and asserted that prohibition was effective and was benefitting the nation. By claiming too much, especially in the late 1920's, the drys discredited that which was really true, and the literate public apparently discounted all statements that might show that prohibition was at least a partial success, partly on the rigidly idealistic basis that if it was a partial failure, it was a total failure.

Great impetus was given to sentiment hostile to prohibition by the concern of respectable people about the "crime wave." They argued, plausibly enough given the assumptions that there was a crime wave and that prohibition was a failure, that universal disregard for the Eighteenth Amendment was damaging to general respect for law. If the most respectable elements of society, so the argument went, openly showed contempt for the Constitution, how could anyone be expected to honor a mere statute? Much of the leadership of the "anti's" soon came from the bar associations rather than the bar patrons.

Coincident with this shift in opinion came the beginning of one of the most effective publicity campaigns of modern times, led by the Association Against the Prohibition Amendment. At first largely independent of liquor money, in the last years of prohibition the AAPA used all it could command. By providing journalists with reliable information, the AAPA developed a virtual monopoly on liquor and prohibition press coverage." In the late 1920's and early 1930's it was unusual to find a story about prohibition in small local papers that did not have its origin-free of charge, of course—with the AAPA.

The AAPA had as its announced goal the modification of the Volstead Act to legalize light wines and beers. The organization also headed up campaigns to repeal the "little Volstead" acts most states had enacted. By the late 1920's the AAPA beat the Anti-Saloon League at its own game, chipping away at the state level. State after state, often by popular vote, did away with the concurrent enforcement acts. Both the wets and the drys viewed state repeals and any modification of the Volstead Act as only steps toward full repeal. Perhaps they were correct; but another possibility does need examination.

Andrew Sinclair, in the most recent and thorough examination of the question, contends that modification of the Volstead Act to legalize light wines and beers would have saved the rest of the prohibition experiment. It is difficult to differ with Sinclair's contention that complete repeal of the Eighteenth Amendment was unprovoked and undesirable.

When President Hoover appointed the Wickersham Commission, public opinion was almost unanimous in expecting that the solution to the prohibition problem would be modification. The Commission's report strengthened the expectation. Not even the Association Against the Prohibition Amendment hoped for more than that, much less repeal. But suddenly an overwhelming surge of public sentiment brought about the Twenty-First Amendment denouement.

The cause of this second sudden shift in opinion was the Great Depression that began about 1929. Jones has shown convincingly that every argument used to bring about repeal in 1932–1933 had been well known since the beginning of prohibition. The class aspect of the legislation, which had been so callously accepted in 1920, was suddenly undesirable. The main depression-related argument, that legalization of liquor manufacture would produce a badly needed additional tax revenue, was well known in the 1910's and even earlier. These rationalizations of repeal were masks for the fact that the general public, baffled by the economic catastrophe, found a convenient scapegoat: prohibition. (The drys had, after all, tried to credit prohibition for the prosperity of the 1920's.) The grouns well of public feeling was irresistible and the entire "experiment, noble in motive and far-reaching in purpose," was not modified but thrown out with Volsteadism, bathwater, baby, and all.

Because the AAPA won, its explanations of what happened were accepted at face value. One of the lasting results of prohibition, therefore, was perpetuation of the stereotypes of the wet propaganda of the 1920's and the myth that the American experiment in prohibition (usually misunderstood to have outlawed personal drinking as well as the liquor business) was a failure. Blanketed together here indiscriminately were all of the years from 1918 to 1933.

More than thirty years have passed since the repeal of the Eighteenth Amendment. Surely the AAPA has now had its full measure of victory and it is no longer necessary for historians to perpetuate a myth that grew up in another era. For decades there has been no realistic possibility of a resurgence of prohibition in its Progressive form—or probably any other form.

The concern now is not so much the destruction of myth, however; the concern is that our acceptance of the myth of the failure of prohibition has prevented us from exploring in depth social and especially sociological aspects of the prohibition experiment. Recent scholarship, by treating prohibition more as a reform than an experiment, has shown that we have been missing one of the most interesting incidents of twentieth-century history.

POSTSCRIPT

Was Prohibition a Failure?

For many historians, the 1920s marked an era of change in the United States, from international involvement and war to isolationism and peace, from the feverish reform of the Progressive era to the conservative political retrenchment of "Republican ascendancy," from the entrenched values of Victorian America to the cultural rebellion identified with the proliferation of "flivvers," "flappers," and hip flasks. In 1931, Frederick Lewis Allen focused on these changes in his popular account of the decade, *Only Yesterday*. In a chapter entitled "The Revolution of Morals and Manners," Allen established a widely accepted image of the 1920s as a period of significant social and cultural rebellion. An excellent collection of essays that explores this issue is John Braeman, Robert H. Bremner, and David Brody, eds., *Change and Continuity in Twentieth Century America: The 1920s* (Ohio State University Press, 1968).

The history of the temperance and prohibition movements in the United States is effectively presented in Andrew Sinclair, *Prohibition: The Era of Excess* (Harper & Row, 1962), Joseph R. Gusfield, *Symbolic Crusade: Status Politics and the American Temperance Movement* (University of Illinois Press, 1963), James H. Timberlake, *Prohibition and the Progressive Movement* (1963), Norman H. Clark, *Deliver Us from Evil: An Interpretation of American Prohibition* (W. W. Norton, 1976), and Thomas R. Pegram, *Battling Demon Rum: The Struggle for a Dry America, 1800–1933* (Ivan R. Dee, 1998). Mark E. Lender and James Kirby Martin provide an excellent survey that includes a chapter on the rise and fall of the prohibition amendment in *Drinking in America* (The Free Press, 1982).

There are a number of important overviews of the 1920s. Among the more useful are John D. Hicks, *Republican Ascendancy, 1921–1933* (Harper & Row, 1960), a volume in The New American Nation Series; Roderick Nash, *The Nervous Generation: American Thought, 1917–1930* (Rand McNally, 1970); and two volumes by Paul Carter, *The Twenties in America*, 2d ed. (Harlan Davidson, 1975) and *Another Part of the Twenties* (Columbia University Press, 1977). The classic sociological study by Robert and Helen Lynd, *Middletown: A Study in Contemporary American Culture* (Harcourt, Brace, 1929) explores the values of a group of "typical" Americans of the 1920s.

The economic history of the decade is discussed in George Soule, *Prosperity Decade: From War to Depression, 1917–1929* (Holt, Rinehart & Winston, 1947); Peter Fearon, *War, Prosperity, and Depression* (University of Kansas Press, 1987); and John Kenneth Galbraith, *The Great Crash, 1929*, rev. ed. (Houghton Mifflin, 1989). For a critical biography of the decade's most notable business leader, see Keith Sward, *The Legend of Henry Ford* (Rinehart, 1948).

The status of women in the decade after suffrage receives general treatment in William H. Chafe, *The Paradox of Change: American Women in the 20th Century* (Oxford University Press, 1991) and, more thoroughly, in Dorothy M. Brown, *Setting a Course: American Women in the 1920s* (Twayne, 1987). Discussions of feminism in the 1920s are competently presented in William L. O'Neill, *Everyone Was Brave: The Rise and Fall of Feminism in America* (University of Illinois Press, 1973); Susan D. Baker, *The Origins of the Equal Rights Amendment: Feminism Between the Wars* (Greenwood Press, 1981); and Nancy F. Cott, *The Grounding of Feminism* (Yale University Press, 1987). David M. Kennedy, *Birth Control in America: The Career of Margaret Sanger* (Yale University Press, 1970) examines an important issue that attracted the interest of many women's groups in the 1920s, while Jacqueline Dowd Hall, *Revolt Against Chivalry: Jessie Daniel Ames and the Women's Campaign Against Lynching* (Columbia University Press, 1979) explores the role of women in the area of race relations.

Race is also the focal point of several studies of the Harlem Renaissance. The best of these works include Nathan Irvin Huggins, *Harlem Renaissance* (Oxford University Press, 1971); David Levering Lewis, *When Harlem Was in Vogue* (Alfred A. Knopf, 1981); and Cary D. Wintz, *Black Culture and the Harlem Renaissance* (Rice University Press, 1988).

Recent scholarship on the Ku Klux Klan in the 1920s has focused on its grassroots participation in local and state politics. Klan members are viewed less as extremists and more as political pressure groups whose aims were to gain control of various state and local governmental offices. The best overview of this perspective is Shawn Lay, ed., *The Invisible Empire in the West: Toward a New Historical Appraisal of the Ku Klux Klan of the 1920s* (University of Illinois Press, 1992). For additional approaches to the KKK's activities in the "Roaring Twenties," see Charles C. Alexander, *The Ku Klux Klan in the Southwest* (University of Kentucky Press, 1965); Kenneth T. Jackson, *The Ku Klux Klan in the City, 1915–1930* (Oxford University Press, 1967); Kathleen M. Blee, *Women of the Klan: Racism and Gender in the 1920s* (University of California Press, 1991); and Nancy MacLean, *Behind the Mask of Chivalry: The Making of the Second Ku Klux Klan* (Oxford University Press, 1994).

ISSUE 10

Was the New Deal an Effective Answer to the Great Depression?

YES: Roger Biles, from *A New Deal for the American People* (Northern Illinois University Press, 1991)

NO: Gary Dean Best, from *Pride, Prejudice, and Politics: Roosevelt Versus Recovery, 1933–1938* (Praeger, 1990)

ISSUE SUMMARY

YES: Professor of history Roger Biles contends that, in spite of its minimal reforms and non-revolutionary programs, the New Deal created a limited welfare state that implemented economic stabilizers to avert another depression.

NO: Professor of history Gary Dean Best argues that Roosevelt established an antibusiness environment with the creation of the New Deal regulatory programs, which retarded the nation's economic recovery from the Great Depression until World War II.

The catastrophe triggered by the 1929 Wall Street debacle crippled the American economy, deflated the optimistic future most Americans assumed to be their birthright, and ripped apart the values by which the country's businesses, farms, and governments were run. During the next decade, the inertia of the Great Depression stifled their attempts to make ends meet.

The world depression of the 1930s began in the United States. The United States had suffered periodic economic setbacks—in 1873, 1893, 1907, and 1920—but those slumps had been limited and temporary. The omnipotence of American productivity, the ebullient American spirit, and the self-deluding thought "it can't happen here" blocked out any consideration of an economic collapse that might devastate the capitalist economy and threaten U.S. democratic government.

All aspects of American society trembled from successive jolts; there were 4 million unemployed people in 1930 and 9 million more by 1932. Those who had not lost their jobs took pay cuts or worked for scrip. There was no security for those whose savings were lost forever when banks failed or stocks declined.

Manufacturing halted, industry shut down, and farmers destroyed wheat, corn, and milk rather than sell them at a loss. Worse, there were millions of homeless Americans—refugees from the cities roaming the nation on freight trains, victims of the drought or the Dust Bowl seeking a new life farther west, and hobo children estranged from their parents.

Business and government leaders alike seemed immobilized by the economic giant that had fallen to its knees. Herbert Hoover, the incumbent president at the start of the Great Depression, attempted some relief programs. However, they were ineffective considering the magnitude of the unemployment, hunger, and distress.

As governor of New York, Franklin D. Roosevelt (who was elected president in 1932) had introduced some relief measures, such as industrial welfare and a comprehensive system of unemployment remedies, to alleviate the social and economic problems facing the citizens of the state. Yet his campaign did little to reassure his critics that he was more than a "Little Lord Fauntleroy" rich boy who wanted to be the president. In light of later developments, Roosevelt may have been the only presidential candidate to deliver more programs than he actually promised.

The first "hundred days" of the New Deal attempted to jump-start the economy with dozens of recovery and relief measures. On inauguration day, FDR told the nation "the only thing we have to fear is fear itself." A bank holiday was immediately declared. Congress passed the Emergency Banking Act, which pumped Federal Reserve notes into the major banks and stopped the wave of bank failures. Later banking acts separated commercial and investment institutions, and the Federal Deposit Insurance Corporation (FDIC) guaranteed people's savings from a loss of up to $2,500 in member banks. A number of relief agencies were set up that provided work for youth and able-bodied men on various state and local building projects. Finally the Tennessee Valley Administration (TVA) was created to provide electricity in rural areas not serviced by private power companies.

In 1935 the Supreme Court ended the First New Deal by declaring both the Agriculture Adjustment Administration and National Recovery Act unconstitutional. In response to critics on the left who felt that the New Deal was favoring the large banks, big agriculture, and big business, FDR shifted his approach in 1935. The Second New Deal created the Works Project Administration (WPA), which became the nation's largest employer in its eight years of operation. Social Security was passed, and the government guaranteed monthly stipends for the aged, the unemployed, and dependent children. Labor pressured the administration for a collective bargaining bill. The Wagner Act established a National Labor Relations Board to supervise industry-wide elections. The steel, coal, automobile and some garment industries were unionized as membership tripled from 3 million in 1933 to 9 million in 1939.

With the immediate crisis over, entrenched conservatives in Congress blocking new legislation and World War II looming, the New Deal ended by 1938. In the first selection, historian Gary Dean Best argues that with its swollen government agencies, promotion of cartels, confiscatory taxes, and dubious antitrust lawsuits, the New Deal prolonged the depression. But historian Roger Biles contends that, in spite of its minimal reform programs, the New Deal created a limited welfare state that implemented economic stabilizers to avert another depression.

YES

Roger Biles

A New Deal for the American People

At the close of the Hundred Days, Franklin D. Roosevelt said, "All of the proposals and all of the legislation since the fourth day of March have not been just a collection of haphazard schemes, but rather the orderly component parts of a connected and logical whole." Yet the president later described his approach quite differently. "Take a method and try it. If it fails admit it frankly and try another. But above all, try something." The impetus for New Deal legislation came from a variety of sources, and Roosevelt relied heavily at various times on an ideologically diverse group of aides and allies. His initiatives reflected the contributions of, among others, Robert Wagner, Rexford Tugwell, Raymond Moley, George Norris, Robert LaFollette, Henry Morgenthau, Marriner Eccles, Felix Frankfurter, Henry Wallace, Harry Hopkins, and Eleanor Roosevelt. An initial emphasis on recovery for agriculture and industry gave way within two years to a broader-based program for social reform; entente with the business community yielded to populist rhetoric and a more ambiguous economic program. Roosevelt suffered the opprobrium of both the conservatives, who vilified "that man" in the White House who was leading the country down the sordid road to socialism, and the radicals, who saw the Hyde Park aristocrat as a confidence man peddling piecemeal reform to forestall capitalism's demise. Out of so many contradictory and confusing circumstances, how does one make sense of the five years of legislative reform known as the New Deal? And what has been its impact on a half century of American life?[1]

A better understanding begins with the recognition that little of the New Deal was new, including the use of federal power to effect change. Nor, for all of Roosevelt's famed willingness to experiment, did New Deal programs usually originate from vernal ideas. Governmental aid to increase farmers' income, propounded in the late nineteenth century by the Populists, surfaced in Woodrow Wilson's farm credit acts. The prolonged debates over McNary-Haugenism in the 1920s kept the issue alive, and Herbert Hoover's Agricultural Marketing Act set the stage for further federal involvement. Centralized economic planning, as embodied in the National Industrial Recovery Act, flowed directly from the experiences of Wilson's War Industries Board; not surprisingly, Roosevelt chose Hugh Johnson, a veteran of the board, to head the National Recovery Administration. Well established in England and Germany before the First World War, social insurance appeared in a handful of states—notably Wisconsin—before the federal government became involved. Similarly, New Deal labor reform took its cues from the path-breaking work of state legislatures. Virtually alone in its originality, compensatory fiscal policy seemed revolutionary in the 1930s. Significantly, however, Roosevelt embraced deficit spending quite late after other disappointing economic policies and never to the extent Keynesian economists advised. Congress and the public supported the New Deal, in part, because of its origins in successful initiatives attempted earlier under different conditions.

Innovative or not, the New Deal clearly failed to restore economic prosperity. As late as 1938 unemployment stood at 19.1 percent and two years later at 14.6 percent. Only the Second World War, which generated massive industrial production, put the majority of the American people back to work. To be sure, partial economic recovery occurred. From a high of 13 million unemployed in 1933, the number under Roosevelt's administration fell to 11.4 million in 1934, 10.6 million in 1935, and 9 million in 1936. Farm income and manufacturing wages also rose, and as limited as these achievements may seem in retrospect, they provided sustenance for millions of people and hope for many more. Yet Roosevelt's resistance to Keynesian formulas for pump priming placed immutable barriers in the way of recovery that only war could demolish. At a time calling for drastic inflationary methods, Roosevelt introduced programs effecting the opposite result. The NRA restricted production, elevated prices, and reduced purchasing power, all of which were deflationary in effect. The Social Security Act's payroll taxes took money from consumers and out of circulation. The federal government's $4.43 billion deficit in fiscal year 1936, impressive as it seemed, was not so much greater than Hoover's $2.6 billion shortfall during his last year in office. As economist Robert Lekachman noted, "The 'great spender' was in his heart a true descendant of thrifty Dutch Calvinist forebears." It is not certain that the application of Keynesian formulas would have sufficed by the mid-1930s to restore prosperity, but the president's cautious deflationary policies clearly retarded recovery.[2]

Although New Deal economic policies came up short in the 1930s, they implanted several "stabilizers" that have been more successful in averting another such depression. The Securities and Exchange Act of 1934 established government supervision of the stock market, and the Wheeler-Rayburn Act allowed the Securities and Exchange Commission to do the same with public utilities. Severely embroiled in controversy when adopted, these measures have become mainstays of the American financial system. The Glass-Steagall Banking Act forced the separation of commercial and investment banking and broadened the powers of the Federal Reserve Board to change interest rates and limit loans for speculation. The creation of the Federal Deposit Insurance Corporation (FDIC) increased government supervision of state banks and significantly lowered the number of bank failures. Such safeguards restored confidence in the discredited banking system and established a firm economic foundation that performed well for decades thereafter.

The New Deal was also responsible for numerous other notable changes in American life. Section 7(a) of the NIRA, the Wagner Act, and the Fair Labor Standards Act transformed the relationship between workers and business and breathed life into a troubled labor movement on the verge of total extinction. In the space of a decade government laws eliminated sweatshops, severely curtailed child labor, and established enforceable standards for hours, wages and working conditions. Further, federal action eliminated the vast majority of company towns in such industries as coal mining. Although Robert Wagner and Frances Perkins dragged Roosevelt into labor's corner, the New Deal made the unions a dynamic force in American society. Moreover, as Nelson Lichtenstein has noted, "by giving so much of the working class an institutional voice, the union movement provided one of the main political bulwarks of the Roosevelt Democratic party and became part of the social bedrock in which the New Deal welfare state was anchored."[3]

Roosevelt's avowed goal of "cradle-to-grave" security for the American people proved elusive, but his administration achieved unprecedented advances in the field of social welfare. In 1938 the president told Congress: "Government has a final responsibility for the well-being of its citizenship. If private co-operative endeavor fails to provide work for willing hands and relief for the unfortunate, those suffering hardship from no fault of their own have a right to call upon the Government for aid; and a government worthy of its name must make fitting response." The New Deal's safety net included low-cost housing; old-age pensions; unemployment insurance; and aid for dependent mothers and children, the disabled, the blind, and public health services. Sometimes disappointing because of limiting eligibility requirements and low benefit levels, these social welfare programs nevertheless firmly established the principle that the government had an obligation to assist the needy. As one scholar wrote of the New Deal, "More progress was made in public welfare and relief than in the three hundred years after this country was first settled."[4]

More and more government programs, inevitably resulting in an enlarged administrative apparatus and requiring additional revenue, added up to a much greater role for the national government in American life. Coming at a time when the only Washington bureaucracy most of the people encountered with any frequency was the U.S. Postal Service, the change seemed all the more remarkable. Although many New Deal programs were temporary emergency measures, others lingered long after the return of prosperity. Suddenly, the national government was supporting farmers, monitoring the economy, operating a welfare system, subsidizing housing, adjudicating labor disputes, managing natural resources, and providing electricity to a growing number of consumers. "What Roosevelt did in a period of a little over 12 years was to change the form of government," argued journalist Richard L. Strout. "Washington had been largely run by big business, by Wall Street. He brought the government to Washington." Not surprisingly, popular attitudes toward government also changed. No longer willing to accept economic deprivation and social dislocation as the vagaries of an uncertain existence, Americans tolerated—indeed, came to expect—the national government's involvement in the problems of everyday life. No longer did "government" mean just "city hall."[5]

The operation of the national government changed as well. For one thing, Roosevelt's strong leadership expanded presidential power, contributing to what historian Arthur Schlesinger, Jr., called the "imperial presidency." Whereas Americans had in previous years instinctively looked first to Capitol Hill, after Roosevelt the White House took center stage in Washington. At the same time, Congress and the president looked at the nation differently. Traditionally attentive only to one group (big business), policymakers in Washington began responding to other constituencies such as labor, farmers, the unemployed, the aged, and to a lesser extent, women, blacks, and other disadvantaged groups. This new "broker state" became more accessible and acted on a growing number of problems, but equity did not always result. The ablest, richest, and most experienced groups fared best during the New Deal. NRA codes favored big business, and AAA benefits aided large landholders; blacks received relief and government jobs but not to the extent their circumstances merited. The long-term result, according to historian John Braeman, has been "a balkanized political system in which private interests scramble, largely successfully, to harness governmental authority and/or draw upon the public treasury to advance their private agendas."[6]

Another legacy of the New Deal has been the Roosevelt revolution in politics. Urbanization and immigration changed the American electorate, and a new generation of voters who resided in the cities during the Great Depression opted for Franklin D. Roosevelt and his party. Before the 1930s the Democrats of the northern big-city machines and the solid South uneasily coexisted and surrendered primacy to the unified Republican party. The New Deal coalition that elected Roosevelt united behind common economic interests. Both urban northerners and rural southerners, as well as blacks, women, and ethnic immigrants, found common cause in government action to shield them from an economic system gone haywire. By the end of the decade the increasing importance of the urban North in the Democratic party had already become apparent. After the economy recovered from the disastrous depression, members of the Roosevelt coalition shared fewer compelling interests. Beginning in the 1960s, tensions mounted within the party as such issues as race, patriotism, and abortion loomed larger. Even so, the Roosevelt coalition retained enough commitment to New Deal principles to keep the Democrats the nation's majority party into the 1980s.[7]

Yet for all the alterations in politics, government, and the economy, the New Deal fell far short of a revolution. The two-party system survived intact, and neither fascism, which attracted so many followers in European states suffering from the same international depression, nor communism attracted much of a following in the United States. Vital government institutions functioned without interruption and if the balance of powers shifted, the national dremained capitalistic; free enterprise and private ownership, not socialism, emerged from the 1930s. A limited welfare state changed the meld of the public and private but left them separate. Roosevelt could be likened to the British conservative Edmund Burke, who advocated measured change to offset drastic alterations—"reform to preserve." The New Deal's great achievement was the application of just enough change to preserve the American political economy.

Indications of Roosevelt's restraint emerged from the very beginning of the New Deal. Rather than assume extraordinary executive powers as Abraham Lincoln had done in the 1861 crisis, the president called Congress into special session. Whatever changes ensued would come through normal governmental activity. Roosevelt declined to assume direct control of the economy, leaving the nation's resources in the hands of private enterprise. Resisting the blandishments of radicals calling for the nationalization of the banks, he provided the means for their rehabilitation and ignored the call for national health insurance and federal contributions to Social Security retirement benefits. The creation of such regulatory agencies as the SEC confirmed his intention to revitalize rather than remake economic institutions. Repeatedly during his presidency Roosevelt responded to congressional pressure to enact bolder reforms, as in the case of the National Labor Relations Act, the Wagner-Steagall Housing Act, and the FDIC. The administration forwarded the NIRA only after Senator Hugo Black's recovery bill mandating 30-hour workweeks seemed on the verge of passage.

As impressive as New Deal relief and social welfare programs were, they never went as far as conditions demanded or many liberals recommended. Fluctuating congressional appropriations, oscillating economic conditions, and Roosevelt's own hesitancy to do too much violence to the federal budget left Harry Hopkins, Harold Ickes, and others only partially equipped to meet the staggering need. The president justified the creation of the costly WPA in 1935 by "ending this business of relief." Unskilled workers, who constituted the greatest number of WPA employees, obtained but 60 to 80 percent of the minimal family income as determined by the government. Roosevelt and Hopkins continued to emphasize work at less than existing wage scales so that the WPA or PWA never competed with free labor, and they allowed local authorities to modify pay rates. They also continued to make the critical distinction between the "deserving" and "undeserving" poor, making sure that government aided only the former. The New Deal never challenged the values underlying this distinction, instead seeking to provide for the growing number of "deserving" poor created by the Great Depression. Government assumed an expanded role in caring for the disadvantaged, but not at variance with existing societal norms regarding social welfare.

The New Deal effected no substantial redistribution of income. The Wealth Tax Act of 1935 (the famous soak-the-rich tax) produced scant revenue and affected very few taxpayers. Tax alterations in 1936 and 1937 imposed no additional burdens on the rich; the 1938 and 1939 tax laws actually removed a few. By the end of the 1930s less than 5 percent of

Americans paid income taxes, and the share of taxes taken from personal and corporate income levies fell below the amount raised in the 1920s. The great change in American taxation policy came during World War II, when the number of income tax payers grew to 74 percent of the population. In 1942 Treasury Secretary Henry Morgenthau noted that "for the first time in our history, the income tax is becoming a people's tax." This the New Deal declined to do.[8]

Finally, the increased importance of the national government exerted remarkably little influence on local institutions. The New Deal seldom dictated and almost always deferred to state and local governments—encouraging, cajoling, bargaining, and wheedling to bring parochial interests in line with national objectives. As Harry Hopkins discovered, governors and mayors angled to obtain as many federal dollars as possible for their constituents but with no strings attached. Community control and local autonomy, conditions thought to be central to American democracy, remained strong, and Roosevelt understood the need for firm ties with politicians at all levels. In his study of the New Deal's impact on federalism, James T. Patterson concludes: "For all the supposed power of the New Deal, it was unable to impose all its guidelines on the autonomous forty-eight states. . . . What could the Roosevelt administration have done to ensure a more profound and lasting impression on state policy and politics? Very little."[9]

Liberal New Dealers longed for more sweeping change and lamented their inability to goad the president into additional action. They envisioned a wholesale purge of the Democratic party and the creation of a new organization embodying fully the principles of liberalism. They could not abide Roosevelt's toleration of the political conservatives and unethical bosses who composed part of the New Deal coalition. They sought racial equality, constraints upon the southern landholding class, and federal intrusion to curb the power of urban real estate interests on behalf of the inveterate poor. Yet to do these things would be to attempt changes well beyond the desires of most Americans. People pursuing remunerative jobs and the economic security of the middle class approved of government aiding the victims of an unfortunate economic crisis but had no interest in an economic system that would limit opportunity. The fear that the New Deal would lead to such thoroughgoing change explains the seemingly irrational hatred of Roosevelt by the economic elite. But, as historian Barry Karl has noted, "it was characteristic of Roosevelt's presidency that he never went as far as his detractors feared or his followers hoped."[10]

The New Deal achieved much that was good and left much undone. Roosevelt's programs were defined by the confluence of forces that circumscribed his admittedly limited reform agenda—hostile judiciary; powerful congressional opponents, some of whom entered into alliances of convenience with New Dealers and some of whom awaited the opportunity to build on their opposition; the political impotence of much of the populace; the pugnacious independence of local and state authorities; the strength of people's attachment to traditional values and institutions; and the basic conservatism of American culture. Obeisance to local custom and the decision to avoid tampering with the fabric of American society allowed much injustice to survive while shortchanging blacks, women, small farmers, and the "unworthy" poor. Those who criticized Franklin Roosevelt for an unwillingness to challenge racial, economic, and gender inequality misunderstood either the nature of his electoral mandate or the difference between reform and revolution—or both.

If the New Deal preserved more than it changed, that is understandable in a society whose people have consistently chosen freedom over equality. Americans traditionally have eschewed expanded government, no matter how efficiently managed or honestly administered, that imposed restraints on personal success—even though such limitations redressed legitimate grievances or righted imbalances. Parity, most Americans believed, should not be purchased with the loss of liberty. But although the American dream has always entailed individual success with a minimum of state interference, the profound shock of capitalism's near demise in the 1930s undermined numerous previously unquestioned beliefs. The inability of capitalism's "invisible hand" to stabilize the market and the failure of the private sector to restore prosperity enhanced the consideration of stronger executive leadership and centralized planning. Yet with the collapse of democratic governments and their replacement by totalitarian regimes, Americans were keenly sensitive to any threats to liberty. New Deal programs, frequently path breaking in their delivery of federal resources outside normal channels, also retained a strong commitment to local government and community control while promising only temporary disruptions prior to the return of economic stability. Reconciling the necessary authority at the federal level to meet nationwide crises with the local autonomy desirable to safeguard freedom has always been one of the salient challenges to American democracy. Even after New Deal refinements, the search for the proper balance continues.

Notes

1. Otis L. Graham Jr., and Meghan Robinson Wander, eds., *Franklin D. Roosevelt, His Life and Times: An Encyclopedic View* (Boston: G. K. Hall, 1985), p. 285 (first quotation); Harvard Sitkoff, "Introduction," in Sitkoff, *Fifty Years Later*, p. 5 (second quotation).

2. Richard S. Kirkendall, "The New Deal as Watershed: The Recent Literature," *Journal of American History* 54 (March 1968), p. 847 (quotation).

3. Graham and Wander, *Franklin D. Roosevelt, His Life and Times*, p. 228 (quotation).

4. Leuchtenburg, "The Achievement of the New Deal," p. 220 (first quotation); Patterson, *America's Struggle against Poverty, 1900–1980*, p. 56 (second quotation).

5. Louchheim, *The Making of the New Deal: The Insiders Speak*, p. 15 (quotation).

6. John Braeman, "The New Deal: The Collapse of the Liberal Consensus," *Canadian Review of American Studies* 20 (Summer 1989), p. 77.

7. David Burner, *The Politics of Provincialism: The Democratic Party in Transition, 1918–1932* (New York: Alfred A. Knopf, 1968).

8. Mark Leff, *The Limits of Symbolic Reform,* p. 287 (quotation).

9. James T. Patterson, *The New Deal and the States: Federalism in Transition* (Princeton: Princeton University Press, 1969), p. 202.

10. Barry D. Karl, *The Uneasy State: The United States from 1915 to 1945* (Chicago: University of Chicago Press, 1983), p. 124.

NO

Pride, Prejudice and Politics: Roosevelt Versus Recovery, 1933–1938

This book had its genesis in the fact that I have for a long time felt uncomfortable with the standard works written about Franklin Delano Roosevelt and the New Deal, and with the influence those works have exerted on others writing about and teaching U.S. history. Although I approach the subject from a very different perspective, Paul K. Conkin's preface to the second edition of *The New Deal* (1975) expressed many of my own misgivings about writings on the subject. Conkin wrote that "pervading even the most scholarly revelations was a monotonous, often almost reflexive, and in my estimation a very smug or superficial valuative perspective—approval, even glowing approval, of most enduring New Deal policies, or at least of the underlying goals that a sympathetic observer could always find behind policies and programs."

Studies of the New Deal such as Conkin described seemed to me to be examples of a genre relatively rare in U.S. historiography—that of "court histories." . . .

But, like most historians teaching courses dealing with the Roosevelt period, I was captive to the published works unless I was willing and able to devote the time to pursue extensive research in the period myself. After some years that became possible, and this book is the result.

My principal problem with Roosevelt and the New Deal was not over his specific reforms or his social programs, but with the failure of the United States to recover from the depression during the eight peacetime years that he and his policies governed the nation. I consider that failure tragic, not only for the 14.6 percent of the labor force that remained unemployed as late as 1940, and for the millions of others who subsisted on government welfare because of the prolonged depression, but also because of the image that the depression-plagued United States projected to the world at a crucial time in international affairs. In the late 1930s and early 1940s, when U.S. economic strength might have given pause to potential aggressors in the world, our economic weakness furnished encouragement to them instead.

From the standpoint, then, not only of our domestic history, but also of the tragic events and results of World War II, it has seemed to me that Roosevelt's failure to generate economic recovery during this critical period deserved more attention than historians have given it.

From *Pride, Prejudice, and Politics: Roosevelt versus Recovery, 1933–1938* (Praeger 1990), pp. ix–xv, xvii, 217–223. Copyright © 1990 by Gary Dean Best. Reprinted by permission of Greenwood Publishing Group, Inc., Westport, CT.

Most historians of the New Deal period leave the impression that the failure of the United States to recover during those eight years resulted from Roosevelt's unwillingness to embrace Keynesian spending. According to this thesis, recovery came during World War II because the war at last forced Roosevelt to spend at the level required all along for recovery. This, however, seemed to me more an advocacy of Keynes' theories by the historians involved that an explanation for the U.S. failure to recover during those years. Great Britain, for example, managed to recover by the late 1930s without recourse to deficit spending. By that time the United States was, by contrast, near the bottom of the list of industrial nations as measured in progress toward recovery, with most others having reached the predepression levels and many having exceeded them. The recovered countries represented a variety of economic systems, from state ownership to private enterprise. The common denominator in their success was not a reliance on deficit spending, but rather the stimulus they furnished to industrial enterprise.

What went wrong in the United States? Simplistic answers such as the reference to Keynesianism seemed to me only a means of avoiding a real answer to the question. A wise president, entering the White House in the midst of a crippling depression, should do everything possible to stimulate enterprise. In a free economy, economic recovery means *business* recovery. It follows, therefore, that a wise chief executive should do everything possible to create the conditions and psychology most conducive to business recovery—to encourage business to expand production, and lenders and investors to furnish the financing and capital that are required. An administration seeking economic recovery will do as little as possible that might inhibit recovery, will weigh all its actions with the necessity for economic recovery in mind, and will consult with competent business and financial leaders, as well as economists, to determine the best policies to follow. Such a president will seek to promote cooperation between the federal government and business, rather than conflict, and will seek to introduce as much consistency and stability as possible into government economic policies so that businessmen and investors can plan ahead. While obviously the destitute must be cared for, ultimately the most humane contribution a liberal government can make to the victims of a depression is the restoration of prosperity and the reemployment of the idle in genuine jobs.

In measuring the Roosevelt policies and programs during the New Deal years against such standards, I was struck by the air of unreality that hung over Washington in general and the White House in particular during this period. Business and financial leaders who questioned the wisdom of New Deal policies were disregarded and deprecated because of their "greed" and "self-interest," while economists and business academicians who persisted in calling attention to the collision between New Deal policies and simple economic realities were dismissed for their "orthodoxy." As one "orthodox" economist pointed out early in the New Deal years,

> economic realism . . . insists that policies aiming to promote recovery will, in fact, ratard recovery if and where they fail to take into account

correctly of stubborn facts in the existing economic situation and of the arithmetic of business as it must be carried out in the economic situation we are trying to revive. The antithesis of this economic realism is the vaguely hopeful or optimistic idealism in the field of economic policy, as such, which feels that good intentions, enough cleverness, and the right appeal to the emotions of the people ought to insure good results in spite of inconvenient facts.

Those "inconvenient facts" dogged the New Deal throughout these years, only to be stubbornly resisted by a president whose pride, prejudices, and politics would rarely permit an accommodation with them.

Most studies of the New Deal years approach the period largely from the perspective of the New Dealers themselves. Critics and opponents of Roosevelt's policies and programs are given scant attention in such works except to point up the "reactionary" and "unenlightened" opposition with which Roosevelt was forced to contend in seeking to provide Americans with "a more abundant life." The few studies that have concentrated on critics and opponents of the New Deal in the business community have been by unsympathetic historians who have tended to distort the opposition to fit the caricature drawn by the New Dealers, so that they offer little to explain the impact of Roosevelt's policies in delaying recovery from the depression.

The issue of *why* businessmen and bankers were so critical of the New Deal has been for too long swept under the rug, together with the question of *how* Roosevelt and his advisers could possibly expect to produce an economic recovery while a state of war existed between his administration and the employers and investors who, alone, could produce such a recovery. Even a Keynesian response to economic depression is ultimately dependent on the positive reactions of businessmen and investors for its success, as Keynes well knew, and those reactions were not likely to be as widespread as necessary under such a state of warfare between government and business. Businessmen, bankers, and investors may have been "greedy" and "self-interested." They may have been guilty of wrong perceptions and unfounded fears. But they are also the ones, in a free economy, upon whose decisions and actions economic recovery must depend. To understand their opposition to the New Deal requires an immersion in the public and private comments of critics of Roosevelt's policies. The degree and nature of business, banking, and investor concern about the direction and consequences of New Deal policies can be gleaned from the hundreds of banking and business periodicals representative of every branch of U.S. business and finance in the 1930s, and from the letters and diaries of the New Deal's business and other critics during the decade.

⋯✦⋯

Statistics are useful in understanding the history of any period, but particularly periods of economic growth or depression. Statistics for the Roosevelt years may easily be found in *Historical Statistics of the United States* published by the

Bureau of the Census, U.S. Department of Commerce (1975). Some of the trauma of the depression years may be inferred from the fact that the population of the United States grew by over 17 million between 1920 and 1930, but by only about half of that (8.9 million) between 1930 and 1940.

Historical Statistics gives the figures . . . for unemployment, 1929–1940. These figures are, however, only estimates. The federal government did not monitor the number of unemployed during those years. Even so, these figures are shocking, indicating as they do that even after the war had begun in Europe, with the increased orders that it provided for U.S. mines, factories, and farms, unemployment remained at 14.6 percent.

One characteristic of the depression, to which attention was frequently called during the Roosevelt years, was the contrast between its effects on the durable goods and consumer goods industries. Between 1929 and 1933, expenditures on personal durable goods dropped by nearly 50 percent, and in 1938 they were still nearly 25 percent below the 1929 figures. Producers' durable goods suffered even more, failing by nearly two-thirds between 1929 and 1933, and remaining more than 50 percent below the 1929 figure in 1938. At the same time, expenditures on nondurable, or consumer, goods showed much less effect. Between 1929 and 1933 they fell only about 14.5 percent, and by 1938 they exceeded the 1929 level. These figures indicate that the worst effects of the depression, and resultant unemployment, were being felt in the durable goods industries. Roosevelt's policies, however, served mainly to stimulate the consumer goods industries where the depression and unemployment were far less seriously felt.

One consequence of Roosevelt's policies can be seen in the U.S. balance of trade during the New Deal years. By a variety of devices, Roosevelt drove up the prices of U.S. industrial and agricultural products, making it difficult for these goods to compete in the world market, and opening U.S. markets to cheaper foreign products. . . . With the exception of a $41 million deficit in 1888, these were the only deficits in U.S. trade for a century, from the 1870s to the 1970s.

. . . [W]hile suicides during the Roosevelt years remained about the same as during the Hoover years, the death rate by "accidental falls" increased significantly. In fact, according to *Historical Statistics,* the death rate by "accidental falls" was higher in the period 1934–1938 than at any other time between 1910 and 1970 (the years for which figures are given).

Interestingly, the number of persons arrested grew steadily during the depression years. In 1938 nearly twice as many (554,000) were arrested as in 1932 (278,000), and the number continued to increase until 1941. And, while the number of telephones declined after 1930 and did not regain the 1930 level until 1939, the number of households with radios increased steadily during the depression years. And Americans continued to travel. Even in the lowest year, 1933, 300,000 Americans visited foreign countries (down from 517,000 in 1929), while the number visiting national parks, monuments, and such, steadily increased during the depression—in 1938 nearly five times as many (16,331,000) did so as in 1929 (3,248,000).

Comparisons of the recovery of the United States with that of other nations may be found in the volumes of the League of Nations' *World Economic Survey* for the depression years. [A] table (from the volume of 1938/39) shows comparisons of unemployment rates. From this it can be seen that in 1929 the United States had the lowest unemployment rate of the countries listed; by 1932 the United States was midway on the list, with seven nations reporting higher unemployment rates and seven reporting lower unemployment. By mid-1938, however, after over five years of the New Deal, only three nations had higher unemployment rates, while twelve had lower unemployment. The United States, then, had lost ground in comparison with the other nations between 1932 and 1938.

The *World Economic Survey* for 1937/38 compared the levels of industrial production for 23 nations in 1937, expressed as a percentage of their industrial production in 1929. . . . It must be remembered that the figures for the United States reflect the level of industrial production reached just before the collapse of the economy later that year. Of the 22 other nations listed, 19 showed a higher rate of recovery in industrial production that the United States, while only 3 lagged behind. One of these, France, had followed policies similar to those of the New Deal in the United States. As the *World Economic Survey* put it, both the Roosevelt administration and the Blum government in France had "adopted far-reaching social and economic policies which combined recovery measures with measures of social reform." It added: "The consequent doubt regarding the prospects of profit and the uneasy relations between businessmen and the Government have in the opinion of many, been an important factor in delaying recovery," and the two countries had, "unlike the United Kingdom and Germany," failed to "regain the 1929 level of employment and production." The *World Economic Survey* the following year (1939) pointed out that industrial production in the United States had fallen from the 92.2 to 65 by June 1938, and hovered between 77 and 85 throughout 1939. Thus, by the end of 1938 the U.S. record was even sorrier than revealed by the [data].

⚜

Every survey of American historians consistently finds Franklin Delano Roosevelt ranked as one of this nation's greatest presidents. Certainly, exposure to even a sampling of the literature on Roosevelt and the New Deal can lead one to no other conclusion. Conventional wisdom has it that Roosevelt was an opportune choice to lead the United States through the midst of the Great Depression, that his cheerful and buoyant disposition uplifted the American spirit in the midst of despair and perhaps even forestalled a radical change in the direction of American politics toward the right or the left. Roosevelt's landslide reelection victory in 1936, and the congressional successes in 1934, are cited as evidence of the popularity of both the president and the New Deal among the American people. Polls by both Gallup and the Democratic National Committee early in the 1936 campaign, however, give a very different picture, and suggest that the electoral victories can be as accurately accounted for in terms of the vast outpourings of federal money in 1934 and 1936, and the inability or unwillingness of Landon to offer a genuine alternative to the New Deal in the latter year. To this must be added the fact that after early 1936 two of the most unpopular New Deal programs—the NRA and the AAA—had been removed as issues by the Supreme Court.

Conventional wisdom, in fact, suffers many setbacks when the Roosevelt years are examined from any other perspective than through a pro–New Deal Prism—from the banking crisis of 1933 and the first inaugural address, through the reasons for the renewed downturn in 1937, to the end of the New Deal in 1937–1938. The American present has been ill-served by the inaccurate picture that has too often been presented of this chapter in the American past by biographers and historians. Roosevelt's achievements in alleviating the hardship of the depression are deservedly well known, his responsibility for prolonging the hardship is not. His role in providing long-overdue and sorely needed social and economic legislation is in every high school American history textbook, but the costs for the United States of his eight-year-long war against business recovery are mentioned in none.

Such textbooks (and those in college, too) frequently contain a chapter on the Great Depression, followed by one on the New Deal, the implication being that somewhere early in the second of the chapters the depression was ended by Roosevelt's policies. Only careful reading reveals that despite Roosevelt's immense labors to feed the unemployed, only modest recovery from the lowest depths of the depression was attained before the outbreak of World War II. Roosevelt, readers are told, was too old-fashioned, too conservative, to embrace the massive compensatory spending and unbalanced budgets that might have produced a Keynesian recovery sooner. But World War II, the books tell us, made such spending necessary and the recovery that might have occurred earlier was at last achieved.

Generations of Americans have been brought up on this version of the New Deal years. Other presidential administrations have been reevaluated over the years, and have risen or fallen in grace as a result, but not the Roosevelt administration. The conventional wisdom concerning the Roosevelt administration remains the product of the "court historians," assessments of the New Deal period that could not have been better written by the New Dealers themselves. The facts, however, are considerably at variance with this conventional wisdom concerning the course of the depression, the reasons for the delay of recovery, and the causes of the recovery when it came, finally, during World War II.

From the uncertainty among businessmen and investors about the new president-elect that aborted a promising upturn in the fall of 1932, to the panic over the prospect of inflationary policies that was a major factor in the banking crisis that virtually paralyzed the nation's economy by the date of his inauguration, Roosevelt's entry into the White House was not an auspicious beginning toward recovery. The prejudices that were to guide the policies and programs of the New Deal for the next six years were revealed in

Roosevelt's inaugural address, although the message was largely overlooked until it had become more apparent in the actions of the administration later. It was an attitude of hostility toward business and finance, of contempt for the profit motive of capitalism, and of willingness to foment class antagonism for political benefit. This was not an attitude that was conducive to business recovery, and the programs and policies that would flow from those prejudices would prove, in fact, to be destructive of the possibility of recovery.

There followed the "hundred days," when Roosevelt rammed through Congress a variety of legislation that only depressed business confidence more. The new laws were served up on attractive platters, with tempting descriptions—truth in securities, aid for the farmer, industrial self-regulation—but when the covers were removed the contents were neither attractive nor did they match the labels. By broad grants of power to the executive branch of the government, the legislation passed regulation of the U.S. economy into the hands of New Dealers whose aim was not to promote recovery but to carry out their own agendas for radical change of the economic system even at the expense of delaying recovery. Thus, truth in securities turned to paralysis of the securities markets, aid for the farmer became a war against profits by processors of agricultural goods, and industrial self-regulation became government control and labor-management strife. International economic cooperation as a device for ending the depression was abandoned for an isolationist approach, and throughout 1933 the threat of inflation added further uncertainty for businessmen and investors.

The grant of such unprecedented peacetime authority to an American president aroused concern, but these after all were only "emergency" powers, to be given up once recovery was on its way. Or were they? Gradually the evidence accumulated that the Tugwells and the Brandeisians intended to institutionalize the "emergency" powers as permanent features of American economic life. By the end of 1933, opposition to the New Deal was already sizable. Business alternated between the paralysis of uncertainty and a modest "recovery" born of purchases and production inspired by fear of higher costs owing to inflation and the effects of the AAA and NRA. The implementation of the latter two agencies in the fall of 1933 brought a renewed downturn that improved only slightly during the winter and spring. A renewed legislative onslaught by the New Deal in the 1934 congress, combined with labor strife encouraged by the provisions of the NIRA, brought a new collapse of the economy in the fall of 1934, which lowered economic indices once again to near the lowest levels they had reached in the depression.

The pattern had been established. The war against business and finance was under way, and there would be neither retreat nor cessation. Roosevelt's pride and prejudices, and the perceived political advantages to be gained from the war, dictated that his administration must ever be on the offensive and never in retreat. But the administration suffered defeats, nevertheless, and embarrassment. The Supreme Court proved a formidable foe, striking down both the NRA and the AAA. Dire predictions from the administration about the implications for the economy of the loss of the NRA proved embarrassing when the economy began to show gradual improvement after its departure. But defeat did not mean retreat. Under the goading of Felix Frankfurter and his disciples, Roosevelt became even more extreme in his verbal and legislative assault against business. Their attempts to cooperate with the Roosevelt administration having been spurned, businessmen and bankers awakened to the existence of the war being waged upon them and moved into opposition. Roosevelt gloried in their opposition and escalated the war against them in the 1936 reelection campaign.

Reelected in 1936 on a tidal wave of government spending, and against a lackluster Republican campaigner who offered no alternative to the New Deal, Roosevelt appeared at the apogee of his power and prestige. His triumph was, however, to be short-lived, despite an enhanced Democratic majority in Congress. A combination of factors was about to bring the New Deal war against business to a stalemate and eventual retreat. One of these was his ill-advised attempt to pack the Supreme Court with subservient justices, which aroused so much opposition even in his own party that he lost control of the Democrat-controlled Congress. More important, perhaps, was the growing economic crisis that the Roosevelt administration faced in 1937, largely as a result of its own past policies. The massive spending of 1936, including the payment of the veterans' bonus, had generated a speculative recovery during that year from concern about inflationary consequences. Fears of a "boom" were increased as a result of the millions of dollars in dividends, bonuses, and pay raises dispensed by businesses late in 1936 as a result of the undistributed profits tax. The pay raises, especially, were passed on in the form of higher prices, as were the social security taxes that were imposed on businesses beginning with 1937. Labor disturbances, encouraged by the Wagner Labor Act and the Roosevelt alliance with John L. Lewis' Congress of Industrial Organizations in the 1936 campaign, added further to the wage-price spiral that threatened as 1937 unfolded. Massive liquidations of low-interest government bonds, and sagging prices of the bonds, fueled concern among bankers and economists, and within the Treasury, that a "boom" would imperil the credit of the federal government and the solvency of the nation's banks whose portfolios consisted mainly of low-interest government bonds.

In considering the two principal options for cooling the "boom"— raising interest rates or cutting federal spending—the Roosevelt administration chose to move toward a balanced budget. It was a cruel dilemma that the New Dealers faced. All knew that the economy had not yet recovered from the depression, yet they were faced with the necessity to apply brakes to an economy that was becoming overheated as a consequence of their policies. Moreover, the reduction in consumer purchasing power caused by the cuts in federal spending was occurring at the same time that purchasing power was already being eroded as a result of the higher prices that worried the administration. Private industry, it should have been obvious, could not "take up the slack," since the Roosevelt administration had done nothing to prepare for the transition from government to private spending that John Maynard Keynes and others had warned them was necessary. The New Dealers had been far too busy waging war against business to allow it the opportunity to prepare for any such transition.

In fact, far from confronting the emergency of 1937 by making long-overdue attempts to cooperate with business in generating recovery, Roosevelt was busy pressing a new legislative assault against them. Denied passage of his legislative package by Congress during its regular 1937 session, Roosevelt called a special session for November despite evidence that the economy had begun a new downturn. Even the collapse of the stock market, within days after his announcement of the special session, and the growing unemployment that soon followed, did not deter Roosevelt from his determination to drive the legislative assault through it. With the nation in the grips of a full-blown economic collapse, Roosevelt offered nothing to the special session but the package of antibusiness legislation it had turned down in the regular session. Once again he was rebuffed by Congress. The nation drifted, its economic indices falling, with its president unwilling to admit the severity of the situation or unable to come to grips with what it said about the bankruptcy of the New Deal policies and programs.

By early 1938, Roosevelt was faced with problems similar to those he had faced when he first entered the White House five years earlier, but without the political capital he had possessed earlier. In 1933 the Hoover administration could be blamed for the depression. In 1938 the American people blamed the Roosevelt administration for retarding recovery. Five years of failure could not be brushed aside. Five years of warfare against business and disregard of criticism and offers of cooperation had converted supporters of 1933 into cynics or opponents by 1938. Even now, however, pride, prejudice, and politics dominated Roosevelt, making it impossible for him to extend the needed olive branch to business. The best that he could offer in 1938 was a renewal of federal spending and more of the same New Deal that had brought the nation renewed misery. In the 1938 congressional session he continued to press for passage of the antibusiness legislation that had been rejected by both sessions of 1937.

But Congress was no longer the pliant body it had been in 1933, and in the 1938 congressional elections the people's reaction was registered when the Republicans gained 81 new seats in the House and 8 in the Senate—far more than even the most optimistic Republican had predicted. If the message was lost on Roosevelt, it was obvious to some in his administration, notably his new Secretary of Commerce Harry Hopkins and his Secretary of the Treasury Henry Morgenthau. Two of the earliest business-baiters in the circle of Roosevelt advisers, they now recognized the bankruptcy of that course and the necessity for the administration to at last strive for recovery by removing the obstacles to normal and profitable business operation that the New Deal had erected. This was not what Roosevelt wanted to hear, nor was it what his Frankfurter disciples wanted him to hear. These latter knew, as Hopkins and Morgenthau had learned earlier, just which Rooseveltian buttons could be pushed to trigger his antibusiness prejudices and spite. A battle raged within the New Deal between the Frankfurter radicals and the "new conservatives," Hopkins and Morgenthau, amid growing public suspicion that the former were not interested in economic recovery.

It was not a fair battle. Hopkins and Morgenthau knew how to play the game, including use of the press, and had too many allies. They did not hesitate to talk bluntly to Roosevelt, perhaps the bluntest talk he had heard since the death of Louis McHenry Howe. Moreover, Roosevelt could afford the loss of a Corcoran and/or a Cohen, against whom there was already a great deal of congressional opposition, but a break with both Hopkins and Morgenthau would have been devastating for an administration already on the defensive. Gradually the Frankfurter radicals moved into eclipse, along with their policies, to be replaced increasingly by recovery and preparedness advocates, including many from the business and financial world.

Conventional wisdom has it that the massive government spending of World War II finally brought a Keynesian recovery from the depression. Of more significance, in comparisons of the prewar and wartime economic policies of the Roosevelt administration, is the fact that the war against business that characterized the former was abandoned in the latter. Both the attitude and policies of the Roosevelt administration toward business during the New Deal years were reversed when the president found new, foreign enemies to engage his attention and energies. Antibusiness advisers were replaced by businessmen, pro-labor policies became pro-business policies, cooperation replaced confrontation in relations between the federal government and business, and even the increased spending of the war years "trickled down" rather than "bubbling up." Probably no American president since, perhaps, Thomas Jefferson ever so thoroughly repudiated the early policies of his administration as Roosevelt did between 1939 and 1942. This, and not the emphasis on spending alone, is the lesson that needs to be learned from Roosevelt's experience with the depression, and of the legacy of the New Deal economic policies.

The judgment of historians concerning Roosevelt's presidential stature is curiously at odds with that of contemporary observers. One wonders how scholars of the Roosevelt presidency are able so blithely to ignore the negative assessments of journalists, for example, of the stature of Raymond Clapper, Walter Lippmann, Dorothy Thompson, and Arthur Krock, to name only a few. Can their observations concerning Roosevelt's pettiness and spitefulness, their criticism of the obstacles to recovery created by his anticapitalist bias, and their genuine concern over his apparent grasp for dictatorial power be dismissed so cavalierly? Is there any other example in U.S. history of an incumbent president running for reelection against the open opposition of the two previous nominees of his own party? Will a public opinion poll ever again find 45 percent of its respondents foreseeing the likelihood of dictatorship arising from a president's policies? Will a future president ever act in such a fashion that the question will again even suggest itself to a pollster? One certainly hopes not.

Perhaps the positive assessment of Roosevelt by American historians rests upon a perceived liberalism of his administration. If so, one must wonder at their definition of liberalism. Surely a president who would pit class against class for political purposes, who was fundamentally hostile to the very basis of a free economy, who believed that his ends could justify very illiberal means, who was intolerant of criticism and critics, and who grasped for dictatorial power does not merit description as a liberal. Nor are the results of the Gallup poll mentioned above consistent with the actions of a liberal president. If the perception is based on Roosevelt's support for the less fortunate "one-third" of the nation, and his program of social legislation, then historians need to be reminded that such actions do not, in themselves, add up to liberalism, they having been used by an assortment of political realists and demagogues—of the left and the right—to gain and hold power.

There were certainly positive contributions under the New Deal, but they may not have outweighed the negative aspects of the period. The weight of the negative aspects would, moreover, have been much heavier except for the existence of a free and alert press, and for the actions of the Supreme Court and Congress in nullifying, modifying, and rejecting many of the New Deal measures. When one examines the full range of New Deal proposals and considers the implications of their passage in the original form, the outline emerges of a form of government alien to any definition of liberalism except that of the New Dealers themselves. Historians need to weigh more thoroughly and objectively the implications for the United States if Roosevelt's programs had been fully implemented. They need also to assess the costs in human misery of the delay in recovery, and of reduced U.S. influence abroad at a critical time in world affairs owing to its economic prostration. We can only speculate concerning the possible alteration of events from 1937 onward had the United States faced the world with the economic strength and military potential it might have displayed had wiser economic policies prevailed from 1933 to 1938. There is, in short, much about Roosevelt and the New Deal that historians need to reevaluate.

POSTSCRIPT

Was the New Deal an Effective Answer to the Great Depression?

Both Biles and Best agree that the New Deal concentrated a tremendous amount of power in the executive branch of the government. They also acknowledge that it was World War II—not the New Deal's reform programs—that pulled the United States out of the depression. But the two historians disagree with each other in their assumptions and assessments of the New Deal.

Best argues that the New Deal was radical in its anti-business assumptions. His conservative critique is similar to Jim Powell's *FDR's Folly: How Roosevelt and His New Deal Prolonged the Great Depression* (Crown Forum, 2003). Powell has been a senior fellow since 1988 at the Cato Institute in Washington, D.C., a well-known conservative and libertarian think tank that has produced a number of policymakers who have staffed the Reagan and two Bush presidential administrations. Powell argues that the New Deal itself with its short-sighted programs increased the size and power of the federal government, which prevented the country from ending the depression more quickly. Powell's critique is based on the conservative assumptions of the well-known free-market advocates Milton Friedman and Anna Jacobson Schwartz, who argue in *A Monetary History of the United States, 1867–1960* (Princeton University Press, 1963) that the Great Depression was a government failure, brought on primarily by Federal Reserve policies that abruptly cut the money supply. This view runs counter to those of Peter Temin, *Did Monetary Forces Cause the Depression?* (Norton, 1976), Michael A. Bernstein, *The Great Depression: Delayed Recovery and Economic Change in America* (Cambridge University Press, 1987), and the readable and lively account of John Kenneth Galbraith, *The Great Crash* (Houghton Mifflin, 1955), which argue that the crash exposed various structural weaknesses in the economy that caused the depression.

Both Best's and Powell's analysis can be faulted on several grounds. For example, they underestimate the enormity of the economic crisis facing the country on the eve of Roosevelt's inauguration. Bank failures were rampant, farmers declared "farm holidays" and destroyed crops to keep up prices, and an assassin tried to kill the president-elect in Miami. As Roosevelt often quipped, "People don't eat in the long run, they eat every day." His immediate response to the crisis was the "100 days" New Deal recovery programs.

Best and Powell agree with other liberal and radical New Deal analysts that it was World War II and not the New Deal that brought us out of the Great Depression. If this is true, didn't the recovery take place because of the enormous sums of money that the government pumped into the defense industries and the armed services that reduced the unemployment rate to almost 0 percent?

Historian Roger Biles argues that the New Deal was a non-revolution compared to the economic and political changes that were taking place in communist Russia, fascist Italy, and Nazi Germany. The New Deal, in his view, was not so new. Social insurance appeared earlier in several states, notably Wisconsin. The economic planning embodied in the National Industrial Recovery Act extends back to President Wilson's World War I War Industries Board. The use of the federal government to aid farmers was begun with President Wilson's Farm Credit Act and continued during the Harding, Collidge, and Hoover administrations.

Although the recovery doesn't come about until World War II, Biles admits that the New Deal changed the relationship between the federal government and the people. The New Deal stabilized the banking industry and stock exchange. It ameliorated the relationship of workers with business with its support of the Wagner Act and the Fair Standard Labor Act. Social Security provided a safety net for the aged, the unemployed, and the disabled. In politics, urbanization and immigration cemented a new Democratic coalition in 1936 with the conservative South around common economic interests until the 1980s when racial issues and the maturing of a new suburban middle class fractured the Democratic majority.

Biles' analysis basically agrees with the British historian Anthony J. Badger who argues in *The New Deal* (Hill and Wang, 1989) that the New Deal was a "holding operation" until the Second World War created the "political economy of modern America." Both Biles and Badger argue that once the immediate crisis of 1933 subsided, opposition to the New Deal came from big business, conservative congressmen, and local governments who resisted the increasing power of the federal government. As the Office of War Information told Roosevelt, the American people's post-war aspirations were "compounded largely of 1929 values and the economics of the 1920s, levend with a handover from the makeshift controls of the war."

The most recent annotated bibliography is Robert F. Himmelberg, *The Great Depression and the New Deal* (Greenwood Press, 2001). The conservative case with full bibliographical references is contained in Powell's *FDR's Folly.* See also Robert Eden's edited *The New Deal and Its Legacy: Critique and Reappraisal* (Greenwood Press, 1989). Two important collections of recent writings are David E. Hamilton, ed., *The New Deal* (Houghton Mifflin, 1999) and Colin Gordon, ed., *Major Problems in American History 1920–1945* (Houghton Mifflin, 1999). Finally Steve Fraser and Gary Gerstle edited a series of social and economic essays, which they present in *The Rise and Fall of the New Deal Order, 1930–1980* (Princeton University Press, 1989).

Out of vogue but still worth reading are the sympathetic studies of the New Deal by William Leuchtenburg, *Franklin D. Roosevelt and the New Deal*

(Harper and Row, 1963) and his interpretative essays written over 30 years in *The FDR Years: On Roosevelt and His Legacy* (Columbia University Press, 1985). See also the beautifully written but never to be completed second and third volumes of Arthur M. Schlesinger, Jr.'s *The Coming of the New Deal* (Houghton Mifflin, 1959) and *The Politics of Upheaval* (Houghton Mifflin, 1960), which advances the interpretation of the first and second New Deal, found in most American history survey textbooks.

ISSUE 11

Was Franklin Roosevelt a Reluctant Internationalist?

YES: Robert A. Divine, from *Roosevelt and World War II* (Johns Hopkins University Press, 1969)

NO: Arthur M. Schlesinger, Jr., from "The Man of the Century," *American Heritage* (May/June 1994)

ISSUE SUMMARY

YES: Diplomatic historian Robert A. Divine argues that even after France fell to Nazi Germany in June 1940, Franklin D. Roosevelt remained a reluctant internationalist who spoke belligerently but acted timidly because he sincerely hated war.

NO: Pulitzer Prize–winning historian Arthur M. Schlesinger, Jr., maintains that from a 1990s perspective, Roosevelt—not Stalin, Churchill, or anyone else—was the only wartime leader who saw clearly the direction and shape of the new world that the leaders were trying to create.

By the end of World War I, the United States had become the world's most powerful nation. Because of its loans to the Allies during the war and its growing international trade in agricultural products, manufactured goods, and armaments, the United States became a creditor nation for the first time in its history. Militarily, the United States had become the world's dominant power.

In order to prevent the reoccurrence of another world war, the United States initiated a series of arms limitation conferences. The most successful conference took place in Washington, D.C., in 1921. In spite of its participation in world trade and its attempts to restore financial solvency in Europe, however, the United States followed a policy that Professor Thomas Paterson has called "independent internationalism." For example, the United States refused to ratify the Treats of Versailles because by doing so it would have to become a member of the League of Nations. In 1928 the United States and France, along with just about every other nation in the world, signed the Kellogg-Briand Pact outlawing war as an instrument of national policy. But none of the agreements signed by the United States in the 1920s had any enforcement provisions that would have bound the nation to share security responsibilities in Europe or Asia or to punish violators.

The Great Depression of the 1930s destroyed the balance of power in Europe and Asia. When Japan attacked China's province of Manchuria in 1931 it violated the Kellogg-Briand Pact and the Nine-Power Treaty signed at the Washington conference. Meanwhile, events took an ugly turn in Europe. Five weeks before Franklin Roosevelt became president, Adolf Hitler was installed as chancellor of Germany. Hitler hated democracy and communism, but most of all he despised Jews. In 1936 his soldiers marched into the Rhineland and continued making annexations until 1939, when he overran Poland. England and France had no recourse but to declare war. A little more than 20 years after World War I ended, World War II began.

How did the United States respond to the aggressive actions of Germany and Japan? Most of the American public agreed that the drive for profits in the arms industry was one (though not the only one) of the major causes of America's entrance into World War I. Therefore, the American public concluded that they should isolate themselves from the political turmoil in the rest of the world.

President Franklin Roosevelt himself took a nationalist approach, preferring to concentrate on his own domestic New Deal solutions. The Johnson Act of 1934 specified that governments that defaulted on war debt payments to the United States were not permitted to borrow from private American citizens or firms. Congress also passed three Neutrality Acts from 1935 to 1937 that were designed to keep the country from repeating the mistakes that dragged the United States into World War I.

When World War II broke out in September 1939, the cash-and-carry provision of the permanent Neutrality Law had expired the previous May. Roosevelt failed to revise the neutrality laws in the spring and summer of 1939, but in November, after the European war began, he convinced Congress to repeal the arms embargo. Now England and France could purchase munitions from the United States—still on a cash-and-carry basis—to aid their fight against the Nazis.

Did Roosevelt acquiesce in neutrality legislation that he did not like during his first six years in office because he had to concentrate on his domestic reforms? Or did he follow a policy of appeasement, like his English and French counterparts did, at the Munich Conference of 1938? Were there other alternatives?

In the following selections, Robert A. Divine argues that until 1938 Roosevelt was a sincere isolationist like most of the American public because he truly hated war. He remained a reluctant internationalist who spoke belligerently but acted timidly until he was reelected for a third term in 1940. Arthur M. Schlesinger, Jr., argues that Roosevelt saw the dangers of Nazism sooner than his contemporaries did and that he also understood better than anyone the direction and shape of the new world that the Allies were trying to create.

YES

Robert A. Divine

Roosevelt and World War II

[B]y the end of 1938, Roosevelt was no longer the confirmed isolationist he had been earlier in the decade. The brutal conquests by Italy; Japan, and Germany had aroused him to their ultimate threat to the United States. But he was still haunted by the fear of war that he voiced so often and so eloquently. His political opponents and subsequent historians have too readily dismissed his constant reiteration of the horrors of war as a politician's gesture toward public opinion. I contend that he was acting out of a deep and sincere belief when he declared that he hated war, and it was precisely this intense conviction that prevented him from embracing an interventionist foreign policy in the late 1930's. In the Munich crisis, he reveals himself in painful transition from the isolationist of the mid-1930's who wanted peace at almost any price to the reluctant internationalist of the early 1940's who leads his country into war in order to preserve its security.

No aspect of Roosevelt's foreign policy has been more controversial than his role in American entry into World War II. Although much of the discussion centers on the events leading to Pearl Harbor, I do not intend to enter into that labyrinth. The careful and well-researched studies by Herbert Feis, Roberta Wohlstetter, and Paul Schroeder demonstrate that while the administration made many errors in judgment, Roosevelt did not deliberately expose the fleet to a Japanese attack at Pearl Harbor in order to enter the war in Europe by a back door in the Pacific. This revisionist charge has already received far more attention than it deserves and has distracted historians from more significant issues.

What is more intriguing is the nature of Roosevelt's policy toward the war in Europe. There are a number of tantalizing questions that historians have not answered satisfactorily. Why was Roosevelt so devious and indirect in his policy toward the European conflict? When, if ever, did F.D.R. decide that the United States would have to enter the war in Europe to protect its own security? And finally, would Roosevelt have asked Congress for a declaration of war against Germany if Japan had not attacked Pearl Harbor?

In the months that followed the Munich Conference, President Roosevelt gradually realized that appeasement had served only to postpone, not to prevent, a major European war. In January, 1939, he sought to impart this fact in his annual message to Congress. He warned the representatives and senators that "philosophies of force" were loose in the world that threatened "the tenets of faith and humanity" on which the American way of life was founded. "The world has grown so small and weapons of attack so swift," the President declared, "that no nation can be safe" when aggression occurs anywhere on earth. He went on to say that the United States had "rightly" decided not to intervene militarily to prevent acts of aggression abroad and then added, somewhat cryptically, "There are many methods short of war, but stronger and more effective than mere words, of bringing home to aggressor governments the aggregate sentiments of our own people." Roosevelt did not spell out these "methods short of war," but he did criticize the existing neutrality legislation, which be suggested had the effect of encouraging aggressor nations. "We have learned," he continued, "that when we deliberately try to legislate neutrality, our neutrality laws may operate unevenly and unfairly—may actually give aid to an aggressor and deny it to the victim. The instinct of self-preservation should warn us that we ought not to let that happen any more."

Most commentators interpreted the President's speech as a call to Congress to revise the existing neutrality legislation, and in particular the arms embargo. Yet for the next two months, Roosevelt procrastinated. Finally, after Hitler's armies overran the remainder of Czechoslovakia in mid-March, Senator Key Pittman came forward with an administration proposal to repeal the arms embargo and permit American citizens to trade with nations at war on a cash-and-carry basis. The Pittman bill obviously favored England and France, since if these nations were at war with Nazi Germany, they alone would possess the sea power and financial resources to secure arms and supplies from a neutral United States. At the same time, the cash-and-carry restrictions would guard against the loss of American lives and property on the high seas and thus minimize the risk of American involvement.

Although the Pittman bill seemed to be a perfect expression of Roosevelt's desire to bolster the European democracies yet not commit the United States, the President scrupulously avoided any public endorsement in the spring of 1939. His own political stock was at an all-time low as a result of the court-packing dispute, a sharp economic recession, and an unsuccessful effort to purge dissident Democrats in the 1938 primaries. By May, Roosevelt's silence and Pittman's inept handling had led to a deadlock in the Senate. The President then turned to the House of Representatives, meeting with the leaders of the lower chamber on May 19 and telling them that passage of the cash-and-carry measure was necessary to prevent the outbreak of war in Europe. Yet despite this display of concern, Roosevelt refused to take the issue to the people, asking instead that Cordell Hull champion neutrality revision. The presidential silence proved fatal. In late June, a rebellious House of Representatives voted to retain the arms embargo and thus sabotage the administration's effort to align the United States with Britain and France.

Belatedly, Roosevelt decided to intervene. He asked the Senate Foreign Relations Committee to reconsider the Pittman bill, but in early July the Committee rebuffed the President by voting 12 to 11 to postpone action until the next session of Congress. Roosevelt was furious. He prepared a draft of a public statement in which he denounced congressional isolationists "who scream from the housetops that this nation is being led into a world war" as individuals who "deserve only the utmost contempt and pity of the American people." Hull finally persuaded him not to release this inflammatory statement. Instead, Roosevelt invited a small bipartisan group of senators to meet with him and Cordell Hull at the White House. The senators listened politely while the President and Secretary of State warned of the imminence of war in Europe and the urgent need of the United States to do something to prevent it. Senator William Borah, a leading Republican isolationist, then stunned Roosevelt and Hull by announcing categorically that there would be no war in Europe in the near future, that he had access to information from abroad that was far more reliable than the cables arriving daily at the State Department. When the other senators expressed their belief that Congress was not in the mood to revise the Neutrality Act, the meeting broke up. In a press release the next day, Roosevelt stated that the administration would accept the verdict of Congress, but he made it clear that he and Hull still believed that its failure to revise the neutrality legislation "would weaken the leadership of the United States . . . in the event of a new crisis in Europe." In a press conference three days later, Roosevelt was even blunter, accusing the Republicans of depriving him of the only chance he had to prevent the outbreak of war in Europe.

When the German invasion of Poland on September 1, 1939, touched off World War II, Roosevelt immediately proclaimed American neutrality and put the arms embargo and other restrictions into effect. In a radio talk to the American people on the evening of September 3, he voiced his determination to keep the country out of the conflict. "We seek to keep war from our firesides," he declared, "by keeping war from coming to the Americas." Though he deliberately refrained from asking the people to remain neutral in thought as Wilson had done in 1914, he closed by reiterating his personal hatred of war and pledging that, "as long as it remains within my power to prevent, there will be no blackout of peace in the United States."

President Roosevelt did not give up his quest for revision of the Neutrality Act, however. After a careful telephone canvass indicated that a majority of the Senate would now support repeal of the arms embargo, the President called Congress into special session. On September 21, Roosevelt urged the senators and representatives to repeal the arms embargo and thereby return to the traditional American adherence to international law. Calling Jefferson's embargo and the neutrality legislation of the 1930's the sole exceptions to this historic policy, he argued that the removal of the arms embargo was a way to insure that the United States would not be involved in the European conflict, and he promised that the government would also insist that American citizens and American ships be barred from entering the war zones. Denying that repeal was a step toward war, Roosevelt asserted that his proposal "offers far greater safeguards than we now passes or have ever possessed to protect American lives and property from danger. . . . There lies the road to peace." He then closed by declaring that America must stand aloof from the conflict so that it could preserve the culture of Western Europe. "Fate seems now to compel us to assume the task of helping to maintain in the western world a citadel wherein that civilization may be kept alive," he concluded.

It was an amazing speech. No less than four times the President declared that his Policy was aimed at keeping the United States out of the war. Yet the whole intent of arms embargo repeal was to permit England and France to purchase arms and munitions from the United States. By basing his appeal on a return to international law and a desire to keep out of the war, Roosevelt was deliberately misleading the American people. The result was a long and essentially irrelevant debate in Congress over the administration bill to repeal the arms embargo and to place all trade with belligerents on a cash-and-carry basis. Advocates of the bill followed the President's cue, repeatedly denying that the legislation was aimed at helping Britain and France and insisting that the sole motive was to preserve American neutrality. Isolationist opponents quite logically asked, if the purpose was to insure neutrality, why did not the administration simply retain the arms embargo and add cash-and-carry for all other trade with countries at war. With heavy majorities already lines up in both houses, administration spokesman refused to answer this query. They infuriated the isolationist by repeating with parrot-like precision the party line that the substitution of cash-and-carry for the arms embargo would keep the nation out of war.

The result was an overwhelming victory for Roosevelt. In late October the Senate, thought to be the center of isolationist strength, voted for the administration bill by more than two to one; in early November the House concurred after a closer ballot. Now Britain and France could purchase from the United States anything they needed for their war effort, including guns, tanks, and airplanes, provided only that they paid cash and carried away these supplies in their own ships.

Roosevelt expressed his thoughts most clearly in a letter to William Allen White a month later. "Things move with such terrific speed, these days," he wrote, "that it really is essential to us to think in broader terms and, in effect, to warn the American people that they, too, should think of possible ultimate results in Europe. . . . Therefore, my sage old friend, my problem is to get the American people to think of conceivable consequences without scaring the American people into thinking that they are going to be dragged into this war." In 1939, Roosevelt evidently decided that candor was still too risky, and thus he chose to pursue devious tactics in aligning the United States indirectly on the side of England and France.

The blitzkrieg that Adolf Hitler launched in Europe in the spring of 1940 aroused Americans to their danger in a way that Roosevelt never could. Norway and Denmark fell in April, and then on May 10 Germany launched an offensive thrust through the low countries into northern France that drove Holland and Belgium out of the war in less than a week and forced the British into a humiliating retreat from the continent at Dunkirk before the month was over. The sense of physical security from foreign danger that the United States had enjoyed for over a century was shattered in a matter of days. The debate over policy would continue, but from May, 1940, on, virtually all Americans recognized that the German victories in Europe imperiled the United States. . . .

In early June, the news from Europe became even worse. As he sat in his White House study one evening reading the latest dispatches, Roosevelt remarked to his wife, "All bad, all bad." He realized that a vigorous defense program was not enough—that American security depended on the successful resistance of England and France to German aggression. As Hitler's armies swept toward Paris and Mussolini moved his troops toward the exposed French frontier on the Mediterranean, Roosevelt sought to throw American influence into the balance. On June 10, he was scheduled to deliver a commencement speech at the University of Virginia in Charlottesville. Going over the State Department draft, he stiffened the language, telling a diplomat who called at the White House that morning that his speech would be a "'tough' one—one in which the issue between the democracies and the Fascist powers would be drawn as never before." News that Italy had attacked France reached the President just before he boarded the train to Charlottesville and reinforced his determination to speak out boldly.

Addressing the graduates that evening, President Roosevelt condemned the concept of isolationism that he himself had held so strongly only a few years before. He termed the idea that the United States could exist as a lone island of peace in a world of brute force "a delusion." "Such an island," he declared, "represents to me and to the overwhelming majority of Americans today a helpless nightmare of a people without freedom— the nightmare of a people lodged in prison, handcuffed, hungry, and fed through the bars from day to day by the contemptuous, unpitying masters of other continents." In clear and unambiguous words, he declared that his sympathies lay wholly on the side of "those nations that are giving their life blood in combat" against Fascist aggression. Then, in his most significant policy statement, he announced that his administration would follow a twofold course of increasing the American defense effort and extending to England and France "the material resources of this nation."

The Charlottesville speech marks a decisive turn in Roosevelt's policy. At the time, most commentators focused on one dramatic sentence, written in at the last moment, in which he condemned the Italian attack on France by saying, "the hand that held the dagger has struck it into the back of its neighbor." But far more important was the President's pledge to defend American security by giving all-out aid to England and France. By promising to share American supplies with these two belligerents, Roosevelt was gambling that they could successfully contain Germany on the European continent and thus end the threat to American security. Given the German military advantages, the risks were enormous. If Roosevelt diverted a large portion of the nation's limited supply of weapons to England and France and then they surrendered to Hitler, the President would be responsible for leaving this country unprepared to meet a future German onslaught.

At the same time, the President's admirers have read too much into the Charlottesville speech. Basil Rauch argues that the speech ended America's status as a neutral. Robert Sherwood goes even further, claiming that at Charlottesville Roosevelt committed the United States "to the assumption of responsibility for nothing less than the leadership of the world." Samuel Rosenman is more moderate, labeling this address as "the beginning of all-out aid to the democracies," but noting that it stopped short of war. But is it even accurate to say that the speech signified all-out aid short of war? An examination of Roosevelt's subsequent steps to help France and England reveals that the President was still extremely reluctant to do anything that would directly involve the United States in the European conflict.

The French quickly discovered the limitations of the President's new policy. Heartened by Roosevelt's words at Charlottesville, Paul Reynaud, the French Premier, immediately tried to secure American military intervention to save his country. In a personal appeal to Roosevelt on June 14, Reynaud asked him to send American troops as well as American supplies in France's hour of greatest need. The next day, the President replied. The United States admired the stubborn and heroic French resistance to German aggression, Roosevelt wrote, and he promised to do all he could to increase the flow of arms and munitions to France. But there he drew the line. "I know that you will understand that these statements carry with them no implication of military commitments," the President concluded. "Only the Congress can make such commitments." On June 17, the French, now fully aware that American military involvement was out of the question, surrendered to Germany.

The British, left waging the fight alone against Germany, also discovered that Roosevelt's actions failed to live up to the promise of his words. On May 15, five days after he replaced Neville Chamberlain as Prime Minister, Winston Churchill sent an urgent message to President Roosevelt. Churchill eloquently expressed his determination to fight Hitler to the bitter end, but he warned that Britain had to have extensive aid from the United States. Above all else, England needed forty or fifty American destroyers to protect the Atlantic supply line from German submarine attacks. Churchill pointed out that England had lost thirty-two destroyers since the war began, and she needed most of her remaining sixty-eight in home waters to guard against a German invasion. "We must ask, therefore," Churchill concluded, "as a matter of life or death, to be reinforced with these destroyers."

Despite the urgency of the British request, Roosevelt procrastinated. On June 5, the President told Secretary of the Interior Harold Ickes that it would require an act of Congress to transfer the destroyers to Great Britain. Even pressure from several other cabinet members, including Henry

Morgenthau and the two new Republicans Roosevelt appointed in June, Secretary of War Henry Stimson and Secretary of the Navy Frank Knox, failed to move Roosevelt. His reluctance was increased when Congress decreed on June 28 that the President could not transfer any warships to a belligerent until the Chief of Naval Operations certified that they were "not essential to the defense of the United States."

Roosevelt's inaction caused deep concern among members of the Committee to Defend America by Aiding the Allies, the pro-British pressure group headed by William Allen White. A few of the more interventionist members of White's committee developed the idea in mid-July of arranging a trade whereby the United States would give Britain the needed destroyers in return for the right to build naval and air bases on British islands in the Western Hemisphere. On August 1, a three-man delegation called at the White House to present this idea to the President, who received it noncommittally. Lord Lothian, the British ambassador, had suggested as far back as May 24 that England grant the United States the rights for bases on Newfoundland, Bermuda, and Trinidad, and in July, in talks with Secretary of the Navy Frank Knox, Lothian linked the possibility of these bases with the transfer of destroyers. Knox liked the idea, but he could not act without the President's consent. And Roosevelt remained deaf to all pleas, including one by Churchill on July 21 in which the British Prime Minister said, "Mr. President, with great respect I must tell you that in the long history of the world this is a thing to do NOW."

Churchill's appeal and the possibility of justifying the transfer of the destroyers as a trade for bases evidently persuaded Roosevelt to act. On August 2, when Frank Knox raised the issue in a cabinet meeting, Roosevelt approved the idea of giving Britain the destroyers in return for the right to build bases on British islands in the Atlantic and Caribbean, and, in addition, in return for a British pledge to send its fleet to the New World if Germany defeated England. Roosevelt still believed that the destroyer transfer would require an act of Congress, and the cabinet advised him to secure the support of Wendell Willkie, the Republican candidate for the presidency in the forthcoming campaign, to insure favorable Congressional action. Through William Allen White, who acted as an intermediary, Roosevelt received word that while Willkie refused to work actively to line up Republican support in Congress, he did agree not to make the destroyer deal a campaign issue.

Roosevelt called his advisers together on August 13 to make a final decision. With the help of Morgenthau, Knoxi, Stimson, and Undersecretary of State Sumner Welles, Roosevelt drafted a cable to Churchill proposing the transfer of fifty destroyers in return for eight bases and a private pledge in regard to the British fleet. The next day a joyous Churchill cabled back his acceptance of these terms, saying that "each destroyer you can spare to us is measured in rubies." But Churchill realized that the deal meant more than just help at sea. "The moral value of this fresh aid from your Government and your people at this critical time," he cabled the President, "will be very great and widely felt."

It took two more weeks to work out the details of the transaction, and during that period a group of distinguished international lawyers convinced the Attorney General that the administration could transfer the destroyers without the approval of Congress. One final hitch developed when Churchill insisted that the bases be considered free gifts from the British; Roosevelt finally agreed that two of the sites would be gifts, but that the remaining six would have to be considered a *quid pro quo* for the destroyers. On September 3, the President made the transaction public in a message to Congress in which he bore down heavily on the advantages to be gained by the United States. Barely mentioning the transfer of the destroyers, the President called the acquisition of eight naval and air bases stretching in an arc from Newfoundland to British Guiana "an epochal and far-reaching act of preparation for continental defense in the face of grave danger." Searching desperately for a historical precedent, Roosevelt described the trade as "the most important action in the reinforcement of our national defense that has been taken since the Louisiana Purchase."

What is most striking about the destroyer-for-bases deal is the caution and reluctance with which the President acted. In June he announced a policy of all-out aid to Britain, yet he delayed for nearly four months after receiving Churchill's desperate plea for destroyers. He acted only after interventionists had created strong public support, only after the transfer could be disguised as an act in support of the American defense program, only after the leader of the opposition party had agreed not to challenge him politically on this issue, and only after his legal advisers found a way to bypass Congress. What may have appeared on the surface to be a bold and courageous act by the President was in reality a carefully calculated and virtually foolproof maneuver.

It would be easy to dismiss the destroyer-for-bases deal as just another example of Roosevelt's tendency to permit political expediency to dictate his foreign policy. Certainly Roosevelt acted in this case with a careful eye on the political realities. This was an election year, and he was not going to hand Wendell Willkie and the Republicans a ready-made issue. But I believe that Roosevelt's hesitation and caution stem as much from his own uncertainty as from political calculation. He realized that the gift of vessels of war to a belligerent was a serious departure from traditional neutrality, and one that might well give Germany the grounds on which to declare war against the United States. He wanted to give England all-out aid short of war, but he was not at all sure that this step would not be an act of war. Only when he convinced himself that the destroyer-for-bases deal could be construed as a step to defend the nation's security did he give his consent. Thus his rather extravagant public defense of his action was not just a political move to quiet isolationist critics; rather it was his own deeply felt rationalization for a policy step of great importance that undoubtedly moved the United States closer to participation in the European conflict.

Perhaps even more significant is the pattern that emerges from this review of Roosevelt's policy in the spring and summer of 1940, for it is one that recurs again and again in his conduct of foreign policy. Confronted by a major crisis, he makes a bold and forthright call at Charlottesville for a policy of all-out aid short of war. But then, having pleased the interventionists with his rhetoric, he immediately retreats, turning down the French appeal for intervention and delaying on the British plea for destroyers, thus reassuring his isolationist critics. Then, as a consensus begins to form, he finally enters into the destroyer-for-bases deal and thus redeems the pledge he had made months before at Charlottesville. Like a child playing a game of giant steps, Roosevelt moved two steps forward and one back before he took the giant step ahead. Movement in a straight and unbroken line seems to have been alien to his nature—he could not go forward until he had tested the ground, studied all the reactions, and weighed all the risks. . . .

After his triumphant election to a third term, Roosevelt relaxed on a Caribbean cruise. But after only a week, a navy sea-plane arrived with an urgent dispatch from Winston Churchill. The Prime Minister gave a lengthy and bleak description of the situation in Europe and then informed the President that England was rapidly running out of money for continued purchases of American goods. "The moment approaches when we shall no longer be able to pay cash for shipping and other supplies," Churchill wrote, concluding with the confident assertion that Roosevelt would find "ways and means" to continue the flow of munitions and goods across the Atlantic.

When the President returned to Washington in mid-December, he called in the press, and in his breeziest and most informal manner began to outline the British dilemma and his solution to it. His advisers were working on several plans, he said, but the one that interested him most was simply to lend or lease to England the supplies she needed, in the belief that "the best defense of Great Britain is the best defense of the United States." Saying that he wanted to get rid of the dollar sign, Roosevelt compared his scheme to the idea of lending a garden hose to a neighbor whose house was on fire. When the fire is out, the neighbor either returns the hose or, if it is damaged, replaces it with a new one. So it would be, Roosevelt concluded, with the munitions the United States would provide Britain in the war against Nazi Germany.

In a fireside chat to the American people a few days later, Roosevelt justified this lend-lease concept on grounds of national security. Asserting that Hitler aimed not just at victory in Europe but at world domination, Roosevelt repeated his belief that the United States was in grave peril. If England fell, he declared, "all of us in the Americas would be living at the point of a gun." He admitted that the transfer of arms and munitions to Britain risked American involvement in the conflict, but he argued that "there is far less chance of the United States getting into war if we do all we can now to support the nations defending themselves against attack by the Axis that if we acquiesce in their defeat, submit tamely to an Axis victory, and wait our turn to be the object of attack in another war later on." He declared that he had no intention of sending American troops to Europe; his sole purpose was to "keep war away from our country and our people."

Then, in a famous phrase, he called upon the United States to become "the great arsenal of democracy."

Congress deliberated over the lend-lease bill for the next two months, and a strong consensus soon emerged in favor of the measure. Leading Republicans; including Wendell Willkie, endorsed the bill, and most opponents objected only to the leasing provision, suggesting instead an outright loan to Britain. The House acted quickly, approving lend-lease by nearly 100 votes in February; the Senate took longer but finally gave its approval by a margin of almost two to one in early March. After the President signed the legislation into law, Congress granted an initial appropriation of seven billion dollars to guarantee the continued flow of vital war supplies to Great Britain.

Roosevelt had thus taken another giant step forward, and this time without any hesitation. His election victory made him bolder than usual, and Churchill's candid plea had convinced him that speed was essential. The granting of lend-lease aid was very nearly an act of war, for it gave Britain unrestricted access to America's enormous industrial resources. But the President felt with great sincerity that this policy would lead not to American involvement but to a British victory that alone could keep the nation out of war. . . .

In the six months preceding Pearl Harbor, Franklin Roosevelt moved slowly but steadily toward war with Germany. On July 7, he announced that he had sent 4,000 American marines to Iceland to prevent that strategic island from falling into German hands. Secretary of War Stimson, though pleased with this action, expressed disappointment over the President's insistence on describing it solely as a measure of hemispheric self-defense. Iceland was the key to defending the supply route across the Atlantic, and Stimson believed that the President should have frankly told Congress that the United States was occupying the island to insure the delivery of goods to Britain.

Once American forces landed in Iceland, Roosevelt authorized the Navy to convoy American ships supplying the marines on the island. In addition, he at first approved a naval operations plan which permitted British ships to join these convoys and thus receive an American escort halfway across the Atlantic, but in late July he reversed himself, ordering the Navy to restrict its convoys to American and Icelandic vessels. In August, at the famous Atlantic Conference with Churchill, Roosevelt once again committed himself to the principle of convoying British ships halfway across the Atlantic, but he failed to give the necessary order to the Navy after his return to Washington.

Roosevelt's hesitancy and indecision finally ended in early September when a German submarine fired a torpedo at the American destroyer *Greer.* Though subsequent reports revealed that the *Greer* had been following the U-boat for more than three hours and had been broadcasting its position to nearby British naval units, Roosevelt interpreted this incident as a clear-cut case of German aggression. In a press release on September 5, he called the attack on the *Greer* deliberate, and on the same day he told Samuel

Rosenman to begin drafting a statement that would express his determination "to use any means necessary to get the goods to England." Rosenman and Harry Hopkins prepared a strongly worded speech, and after a few revisions the President delivered it over a worldwide radio network on the evening of September 11.

In biting phrases, Roosevelt lashed out against Hitler and Nazi Germany. He described the attack on the *Greer* as part of a concerted German effort to "acquire absolute control and domination of the seas for themselves." Such control, he warned, would lead inevitably to a Nazi effort to dominate the Western Hemisphere and "create a permanent world system based on force, terror, and murder." The attack on the *Greer* was an act of piracy, Roosevelt declared; German submarines had become the "rattlesnakes of the Atlantic." Then, implying but never openly saying that American ships would shoot German submarines on sight, Roosevelt declared that henceforth the United States Navy would escort "all merchant ships—not only American ships but ships of any flag—engaged in commerce in our defensive waters."

Contemporary observers and many historians labeled this the "shoot-on-sight" speech, seeing its significance primarily in the orders to American naval officers to fire at German submarines in the western Atlantic. "The undeclared war" speech would be a better label, for its real importance was that Roosevelt had finally made a firm decision on the convoy issue on which he had been hedging ever since the passage of lend-lease by Congress. Branding the Germans as "pirates" and their U-boats as "rattlesnakes" distracted the American people from the fact that the President was now putting into practice the policy of convoying British ships halfway across the ocean, and thereby assuming a significant share of the responsibility for the Battle of the Atlantic. The immediate effect was to permit the British to transfer forty destroyers from the western Atlantic to the submarine-infested waters surrounding the British Isles. In the long run, the President's decision meant war with Germany, since from this time forward there would inevitably be more and more U-boat attacks on American destroyers, increasingly heavy loss of life, and a direct challenge to the nation's honor and prestige. Only Hitler's reluctance to engage in war with the United States while he was still absorbed in the assault on Russia prevented an immediate outbreak of hostilities.

With the convoy issue now resolved, Roosevelt moved to revise the Neutrality Act. In mid-October he asked the House to permit the arming of American merchant ships with deck guns, and then later in the month he urged the Senate to remove the "carry" provision of the law so that American merchantmen could take supplies all the way across the Atlantic to British ports. When a German submarine torpedoed the destroyer *Kearney* near Iceland, Roosevelt seized on the incident to speed up action in Congress.

"America has been attacked," the President declared in a speech on October 27. "The U.S.S. *Kearney* is not just a Navy ship. She belongs to every man, woman, and child in this Nation." Describing Nazi efforts at infiltration in South America, the President bluntly charged that Germany was bent on the conquest of "the United States itself." Then, coming very close to a call for war, he asserted, "The forward march of Hitlerism can be stopped—and it will be stopped. Very simply and very bluntly—we are pledged to pull our own oar in the destruction of Hitlerism." Although he called only for the revision of the Neutrality Act, the tone of the entire address was one of unrelieved belligerency, culminating in the following peroration: "Today in the face of this newest and greatest challenge, we Americans have cleared our decks and taken our battle stations. We stand ready in the defense of our Nation and the faith of our fathers to do what God has given us the power to see as our full duty."

Two weeks later, by quite slim majorities, Congress removed nearly all restrictions on American commerce from the Neutrality Act. For the first time since the war began in 1939, American merchant vessels could carry supplies all the way across the Atlantic to British ports. The significance of this action was obscured by the Japanese attack on Pearl Harbor which triggered American entry into the war in December and gave rise to the subsequent charge that Roosevelt led the nation into the conflict via the back door. Revision of the Neutrality Act was bound to lead to war with Germany within a matter of months. Hitler could be forbearing when it was only a question of American escort vessels operating in the western Atlantic. He could not have permitted American ships to carry a major portion of lend-lease supplies to Britain without giving up the Battle of the Atlantic. With the German offensive halting before Leningrad and Moscow in December, Hitler would have been compelled to order his submarine commanders to torpedo American ships as the only effective way to hold Britain in check. And once Germany began sinking American ships regularly, Roosevelt would have had to ask Congress for a declaration of war.

The crucial question, of course, is why Roosevelt chose such an oblique policy which left the decision for peace or war in the hands of Hitler. His apologists, notably Robert Sherwood and Basil Rauch, insist that he had to choice. The isolationists were so powerful that the President could not lay the issue squarely before Congress and ask for a declaration of war. If he had, writes Basil Rauch, he would have "invited a prolonged, bitter, and divisive debate" and thereby have risked a defeat which would have discredited the administration and turned the nation back to isolationism. Sherwood sadly agrees, saying, "He had no more tricks left. The hat from which he had pulled so many rabbits was empty. The President of the United States was now the creature of circumstance which must be shaped not by his own will or his own ingenuity but by the unpredictable determination of his enemies."

In part this was true, but these sympathetic historians fail to point out that Roosevelt was the prisoner of his own policies. He had told the nation time and time again that it was not necessary for the United States to enter the war. He had propounded the doctrine that America could achieve Hitler's downfall simply by giving all-out aid to England. He had repeatedly denied that his measures would lead the nation to war. In essence, he had foreclosed to himself the possibility of going directly to the people and bluntly stating that the United States must enter the war as the only way to guarantee the nation's security. All he could do was edge the country closer and closer, leaving the ultimate decision to Germany and Japan.

We will never know at what point Roosevelt decided in his own mind that it was essential that the United States enter the war. His own personal hatred of war was deep and genuine, and it was this conviction that set him apart from men like Stimson and Morgenthau, who decided that American participation was necessary as early as the spring of 1941. William Langer and Everett Gleason believe that Roosevelt realized by the fall of 1941 that there was no other way to defeat Hitler, but they conclude that, even so, he thought the American military contribution could be limited to naval and air support and not include the dispatch of an American army to the European battlefields.

It is quite possible that Roosevelt never fully committed himself to American involvement prior to Pearl Harbor. His hesitancy was not just a catering to isolationist strength but a reflection of his own inner uncertainty. Recognizing that Hitler threatened the security of the United States, he took a series of steps which brought the nation to the brink of war, but his own revulsion at the thought of plunging his country into the most devastating conflict in history held him back until the Japanese attack left him no choice.

Arthur M. Schlesinger, Jr.

 **NO**

The Man of the Century

After half a century it is hard to approach Franklin D. Roosevelt except through a minefield of clichés. Theories of FDR, running the gamut from artlessness to mystification, have long paraded before our eyes. There is his famous response to the newspaperman who asked him for his philosophy: "Philosophy? I am a Christian and a Democrat—that's all"; there is Robert E. Sherwood's equally famous warning about "Roosevelt's heavily forested interior"; and we weakly conclude that both things were probably true.

FDR's Presidency has commanded the attention of eminent historians at home and abroad for fifty years or more. Yet no consensus emerges, especially in the field of foreign affairs. Scholars at one time or another have portrayed him at every point across a broad spectrum: as an isolationist, as an internationalist, as an appeaser, as a warmonger, as an impulsive decision maker, as an incorrigible vacillator, as the savior of capitalism, as a closet socialist, as a Machiavellian intriguer plotting to embroil his country in foreign wars, as a Machiavellian intriguer avoiding war in order to let other nations bear the brunt of the fighting, as a gullible dreamer who thought he could charm Stalin into postwar collaboration and ended by selling Eastern Europe down the river into slavery, as a tight-fisted creditor sending Britain down the road toward bankruptcy as a crafty imperialist serving the interests of American capitalist hegemony, as a high-minded prophet whose vision shaped the world's future. Will the real FDR please stand up?

Two relatively recent books illustrate the chronically unsettled state of FDR historiography—and the continuing vitality of the FDR debate. In *Wind Over Sand* (*1988*) Frederick W. Marks III finds a presidential record marked by ignorance, superficiality, inconsistency, random prejudice, erratic impulse, a man out of his depth, not waving but drowning, practicing a diplomacy as insubstantial and fleeting as wind blowing over sand. In *The Juggler* (1991), Warren F. Kimball finds a record marked by intelligent understanding of world forces, astute maneuver, and a remarkable consistency of purpose, a farsighted statesman facing dilemmas that defied quick or easy solutions. One-third of each book is given over to endnotes and bibliography, which suggests that each portrait is based on meticulous research. Yet the two historians arrive at diametrically opposite conclusions.

So the debate goes on. Someone should write a book entitled *FDR: For and Against,* modeled on Pieter Geyl's *Napoleon: For and Against.* "It is impossible," the great Dutch historian observed, "that two historians, especially two historians living in different periods, should see any historical personality in the same light. The greater the political importance of a historical character, the more impossible this is." History, Geyl (rightly) concluded, is an "argument without end."

I suppose we must accept that human beings are in the last analysis beyond analysis. In the case of FDR, no one can be really sure what was going on in that affable, welcoming, reserved, elusive, teasing, spontaneous, calculating, cold, warm, humorous, devious, mendacious, manipulative, petty, magnanimous, superficially casual, ultimately decent, highly camouflaged, finally impenetrable mind. Still, if we can't as historians puzzle out what he *was,* we surely must as historians try to make sense out of what he *did.* If his personality escapes us, his policies must have some sort of pattern.

What Roosevelt wrote (or Sam Rosenman wrote for him) in the introduction to the first volume of his *Public Papers* about his record as governor of New York goes, I believe, for his foreign policy too: "Those who seek inconsistencies will find them. There were inconsistencies of methods, inconsistencies caused by ceaseless efforts to find ways to solve problems for the future as well as for the present. There were inconsistencies born of insufficient knowledge. There were inconsistencies springing from the need of experimentation. But through them all, I trust that there also will be found a consistency and continuity of broad purpose."

Now purpose can be very broad indeed. To say that a statesman is in favor of peace, freedom, and security does not narrow things down very much. Meaning resides in the details, and in FDR's case the details often contradict each other. If I may invoke still another cliché, FDR's foreign policy seems to fit Churchill's description of the Soviet Union: "a riddle wrapped in a mystery inside an enigma." However, we too often forget what Churchill said next: "But perhaps there is a key. That key is Russian national interest." German domination of Eastern Europe, Churchill continued, "would be contrary to the historic life-interests of Russia." Here, I suggest, may be the key to FDR, the figure in his carpet: his sense of the historic life-interests of the United States.

Of course, "national interest" narrows things down only a little. No one, except a utopian or a millennialist, is against the national interest. In a world of nation-states the assumption that governments will pursue their own interests gives order and predictability to international affairs. As George Washington said, "no nation is to be trusted farther than it is bound by [its] interest." The problem is the substance one pours into national interest. In our own time, for example, Lyndon Johnson and Dean Rusk thought our national interest required us to fight in Vietnam; William Fulbright, Walter Lippmann, Hans Morgenthau thought our national interest required us to pull out of Vietnam. The phrase by itself settles no arguments.

How did FDR conceive the historic life-interests of the United States? His conception emerged from his own long, if scattered, education in world affairs. It should not be forgotten that he arrived in the White House with an unusual amount of international experience. He was born into a cosmopolitan family. His father knew Europe well and as a young man had marched with Garibaldi. His elder half-brother had served in American legations in London and Vienna. His mother's family had been in the China trade; his mother herself had lived in Hong Kong as a little girl. As FDR reminded Henry Morgenthau in 1934, "I have a background of a little over a century in Chinese affairs."

FDR himself made his first trip to Europe at the age of three and went there every summer from his ninth to his fourteenth year. As a child he learned French and German. As a lifelong stamp collector he knew the world's geography and politics. By the time he was elected President, he had made thirteen trips across the Atlantic and had spent almost three years of his life in Europe. "I started . . . with a good deal of interest in foreign affairs," he told a press conference in 1939, "because both branches of my family have been mixed up in foreign affairs for a good many generations, the affairs of Europe and the affairs of the Far East."

Now much of his knowledge was social and superficial. Nor is international experience in any case a guarantee of international wisdom or even of continuing international concern. The other American politician of the time who rivaled FDR in exposure to the great world was, oddly, Herbert Hoover. Hoover was a mining engineer in Australia at twenty-three, a capitalist in the Chinese Empire at twenty-five, a promoter in the City of London at twenty-seven. In the years from his Stanford graduation to the Great War, he spent more time in the British Empire than he did in the United States. During and after the war he supervised relief activities in Belgium and in Eastern Europe. Keynes called him the only man to emerge from the Paris Peace Conference with an enhanced reputation.

Both Hoover and Roosevelt came of age when the United States was coming a world power. Both saw more of that world than most of their American contemporaries. But international experience led them to opposite conclusions. What Hoover saw abroad soured him on foreigners. He took away from Paris an indignant conviction of an impassable gap between his virtuous homeland and the European snake pit. Nearly twenty years passed before he could bring himself to set foot again on the despised continent. He loathed Europe and its nationalist passions and hatreds. "With a vicious rhythm," he said in 1940, "these malign forces seem to drive [European] nations like the Gadarene swine over the precipice of war." The less America had to do with so degenerate a place, the Quaker Hoover felt, the better.

The patrician Roosevelt was far more at home in the great world. Moreover, his political genealogy instilled in him the conviction that the United States must at last take its rightful place among the powers. In horse breeder's parlance, FDR was by Woodrow Wilson out of Theodore Roosevelt. These two remarkable Presidents taught FDR that the United States was irrevocably a world power and poured substance into his conception of America's historic life-interests.

FDR greatly admired TR, deserted the Democratic party to cast his first presidential vote for him, married his niece, and proudly succeeded in 1913 to the office TR had occupied fifteen years earlier, Assistant Secretary of the Navy. From TR and from that eminent friend of both Roosevelts, Admiral Mahan, young Roosevelt learned the strategic necessities of international relations. He learned how to distinguish between vital and peripheral interests. He learned why the national interest required the maintenance of balances of power in areas that, if controlled by a single power, could threaten the United States. He learned what the defense of vital interests might require in terms of ships and arms and men and production and resources. His experience in Wilson's Navy Department during the First World War consolidated these lessons.

But he also learned new things from Wilson, among them that it was not enough to send young men to die and kill because of the thrill of battle or because of war's morally redemptive qualities or even because of the need to restore the balance of power. The awful sacrifices of modern war demanded nobler objectives. The carnage on the Western Front converted FDR to Wilson's vision of a world beyond war, beyond national interest, beyond balances of power, a world not of secret diplomacy and antagonistic military alliances but of an organized common peace, founded on democracy, self-determination, and the collective restraint of aggression.

Theodore Roosevelt had taught FDR geopolitics. Woodrow Wilson now gave him a larger international purpose in which the principles of power had a strong but secondary role. FDR's two mentors detested each other. But they joined to construct the framework within which FDR, who cherished them both, approached foreign affairs for the rest of his life.

As the Democratic vice presidential candidate in 1920, he roamed the country pleading for the League of Nations. Throughout the twenties he warned against political isolationism and economic protectionism. America would commit a grievous wrong, he said, if it were "to go backwards towards an old Chinese Wall policy of isolationism." Trade wars, he said, were "symptoms of economic insanity." But such sentiments could not overcome the disillusion and disgust with which Americans in the 1920s contemplated world troubles. As President Hoover told the Italian foreign minister in 1931, the deterioration of Europe had led to such "despair . . . on the part of the ordinary American citizen [that] now he just wanted to keep out of the whole business."

Depression intensified the isolationist withdrawal. Against the national mood, the new President brought to the White House in 1933 an international outlook based, I would judge, on four principles. One was TR's commitment to the preservation of the balance of world power. Another was Wilson's vision of concerted international action to prevent or punish aggression. The third principle argued that lasting peace required the free flow of trade among nations. The fourth was that in a democracy foreign policy must rest on popular consent. In the isolationist climate of the 1930s, this fourth principle compromised and sometimes undermined the first three.

Diplomatic historians are occasionally tempted to overrate the amount of time Presidents spend in thinking about foreign policy. In fact, from Jackson to FDR, domestic affairs have always been, with a few fleeting exceptions—perhaps Polk, McKinley, Wilson—the presidential priority. This was powerfully the case at the start for FDR. Given the collapse of the economy and the anguish of unemployment, given the absence of obvious remedy and the consequent need for social experiment, the surprise is how much time and energy FDR did devote to foreign affairs in these early years.

He gave time to foreign policy because of his acute conviction that Germany and Japan were, or were about to be, on the rampage and that unchecked aggression would ultimately threaten vital interests of the United States. He packed the State Department and embassies abroad with unregenerate Wilsonians. When he appointed Cordell Hull Secretary, he knew what he was getting; his brain trusters, absorbed in problems at hand, had warned him against international folly. But there they were, Wilsonians all: Hull, Norman Davis, Sumner Welles, William Phillips, Francis B. Sayre, Walton Moore, Breckinridge Long, Josephus Daniels, W. E. Dodd, Robert W. Bingham, Claude Bowers, Joseph E. Davies. Isolationists like Raymond Moley did not last long at State.

⋅◉⋅

Roosevelt's early excursions into foreign policy were necessarily intermittent, however, and in his own rather distracting personal style. Economic diplomacy he confided to Hull, except when Hull's free-trade obsessions threatened New Deal recovery programs, as at the London Economic Conference of 1933. He liked, when he found the time, to handle the political side of things himself. He relished meetings with foreign leaders and found himself in advance of most of them in his forebodings about Germany and Japan. He invited his ambassadors, especially his political appointees, to write directly to him, and nearly all took advantage of the invitation.

His diplomatic style had its capricious aspects. FDR understood what admirals and generals were up to, and he understood the voice of prophetic statesmanship. But he never fully appreciated the professional diplomat and looked with some disdain on the career Foreign Service as made up of tea drinkers remote from the realities of American life. His approach to foreign policy, while firmly grounded in geopolitics and soaring easily into the higher idealism, always lacked something at the middle level.

At the heart of Roosevelt's style in foreign affairs was a certain incorrigible amateurism. His off-the-cuff improvisations, his airy tendency to throw out half-baked ideas, caused others to underrate his continuity of purpose and used to drive the British especially wild, as minutes scribbled on Foreign Office dispatches make abundantly clear. This amateurism had its good points. It could be a source of boldness and creativity in a field populated by cautious and conventional people. But it also encouraged superficiality and dilettantism.

The national mood, however, remained FDR's greatest problem. Any U.S. contribution to the deterrence of aggression depended on giving the government power to distinguish between aggressors and their victims. He asked Congress for this authority, first in cooperating with League of Nations sanctions in 1933, later in connection with American neutrality statutes. Fearing that aid to one side would eventually involve the nation in war, Congress regularly turned him down. By rejecting policies that would support victims against aggressors, Congress effectively nullified the ability of the United States to throw its weight in the scales against aggressors.

Roosevelt, regarding the New Deal as more vital for the moment than foreign policy and needing the support of isolationists for his domestic program, accepted what he could not change in congressional roll calls. But he did hope to change public opinion and began a long labor of popular education with his annual message in January 1936 and its condemnation of "autocratic institutions that beget slavery at home and aggression abroad."

It is evident that I am not persuaded by the school of historians that sees Roosevelt as embarked until 1940 on a mission of appeasement, designed to redress German grievances and lure the Nazi regime into a constructive role in a reordered Europe. The evidence provided by private conversations as well as by public pronouncements is far too consistent and too weighty to permit the theory that Roosevelt had illusions about coexistence with Hitler. Timing and maneuver were essential, and on occasion he tacked back and forth like the small-boat sailor that Gaddis Smith reminds us he was. Thus, before positioning the United States for entry into war, he wanted to make absolutely sure there was no prospect of negotiated peace: hence his interest in 1939–40 in people like James D. Mooney and William Rhodes Davis and hence the Sumner Welles mission. But his basic course seems pretty clear: one way or another to rid the world of Hitler.

I am even less persuaded by the school that sees Roosevelt as a President who rushed the nation to war because he feared German and Japanese economic competition. America "began to go to war against the Axis in the Western Hemisphere," the revisionist William Appleman Williams tells us, because Germany was invading U.S. markets in Latin America. The Open Door cult recognizes no geopolitical concerns in Washington about German bases in the Western Hemisphere. Oddly, the revisionists accept geopolitics as an O.K. motive for the Soviet Union but deny it to the

United States. In their view American foreign policy can never be aimed at strategic security but must forever be driven by the lust of American business for foreign markets.

⟡

In the United States, of course, as any student of American history knows, economic growth has been based primarily on the home market, not on foreign markets, and the preferred policy of American capitalists, even after 1920, when the United States became a creditor nation, was protection of the home market, not freedom of trade. Recall Fordney-McCumber and Smoot-Hawley. The preference of American business for high tariffs was equally true in depression. When FDR proposed his reciprocal trade agreements program in 1934, the American business community, instead of welcoming reciprocal trade as a way of penetrating foreign markets, denounced the whole idea. Senator Vandenberg even called the bill "Fascist in its philosophy, Fascist in its objectives." A grand total of two Republicans voted for reciprocal trade in the House, three in the Senate.

The "corporatism" thesis provides a more sophisticated version of the economic interpretation. No doubt we have become a society of large organizations, and no doubt an associational society generates a certain momentum toward coordination. But the idea that exporters, importers, Wall Street, Main Street, trade unionists, and farmers form a consensus on foreign policy and impose that consensus on the national government is hard to sustain.

It is particularly irrelevant to the Roosevelt period. If Roosevelt was the compliant instrument of capitalist expansion, as the Open Door ideologies claim, or of corporate hegemony, as the corporatism thesis implies, why did the leaders of American corporate capitalism oppose him so viciously? Business leaders vied with one another in their hatred of "that man in the White House." The family of J. P. Morgan used to warn visitors against mentioning Roosevelt's name lest fury raise Morgan's blood pressure to the danger point. When Averell Harriman, one of that rare breed, a pro-New Deal businessman, appeared on Wall Street, old friends cut him dead. The theory that Roosevelt pursued a foreign policy dictated by the same corporate crowd that fought him domestically and smeared him personally belongs, it seems to me, in the same library with the historiography of Oliver Stone.

⟡

What was at stake, as FDR saw it, was not corporate profits or Latin American markets but the security of the United States and the future of democracy. Basking as we do today in the glow of democratic triumph, we forget how desperate the democratic cause appeared half a century ago. The Great War had apparently proved that democracy could not produce peace; the Great Depression that it could not produce prosperity. By the 1930s contempt for democracy was widespread among elites and masses alike: contempt for parliamentary methods, for government by discussion, for freedoms of expression and opposition, for bourgeois individualism, for pragmatic muddling through. Discipline, order, efficiency, and all-encompassing ideology were the talismans of the day. Communism and fascism had their acute doctrinal differences, but their structural similarities—a single leader, a single party, a single body of infallible dogma, a single mass of obedient followers—meant that each in the end had more in common with the other than with democracy, as Hitler and Stalin acknowledged in August 1939.

The choice in the 1930s seemed bleak: either political democracy with economic chaos or economic planning with political tyranny. Roosevelt's distinctive contribution was to reject this either/or choice. The point of the New Deal was to chart and vindicate a middle way between laissez-faire and totalitarianism. When the biographer Emil Ludwig asked FDR to define his "political motive," Roosevelt replied, "My desire to obviate revolution. . . . I work in a contrary sense to Rome and Moscow."

Accepting renomination in 1936, FDR spoke of people under economic stress in other lands who had sold their heritage of freedom for the illusion of a living. "Only our success," he continued, "can stir their ancient hope. They begin to know that here in America we are waging a great and successful war. It is not alone a war against want and destitution and economic demoralization. It is more than that: it is a war for the survival of democracy. We are fighting to save a great and precious form of government for ourselves and for the world."

Many people around the world thought it a futile fight. Let us not underestimate the readiness by 1940 of Europeans, including leading politicians and intellectuals, to come to terms with a Hitler-dominated Europe. Even some Americans thought the downfall of democracy inevitable. As Nazi divisions stormed that spring across Scandinavia, the Low Countries, and France, the fainthearted saw totalitarianism, in the title of a poisonous little book published in the summer by Anne Morrow Lindbergh, a book that by December 1940 had rushed through seven American printings, as "the wave of the future." While her husband, the famous aviator, predicted Nazi victory and opposed American aid to Britain, the gentle Mrs. Lindbergh lamented "the beautiful things . . . lost in the dying of an age," saw totalitarianism as democracy's predestined successor, a "new, and perhaps even ultimately good, conception of humanity trying to come to birth," discounted the evils of Hitlerism and Stalinism as merely "scum on the wave of the future," and concluded that "the wave of the future is coming and there is no fighting it." For a while Mrs. Lindbergh seemed to be right. Fifty years ago there were only twelve democracies left on the planet.

Roosevelt, however, believed in fighting the wave of the future. He still labored under domestic constraints. The American people were predominantly against Hitler. But they were also, and for a while more strongly, against war. I believe that FDR himself, unlike the hawks of 1941—Stimson, Morgenthau, Hopkins, Ickes, Knox—was in no hurry to enter the European conflict. He remembered what Wilson had told him when he himself had been a young hawk a quarter-century before: that a President could commit no greater mistake than to take a divided country into war. He also no doubt wanted to minimize American casualties and to avoid breaking political promises. But probably by the autumn of 1941 FDR had finally come to believe that American participation was necessary if Hitler was to be beaten. An increasing number of Americans were reaching the same conclusion. Pearl Harbor in any case united the country, and Hitler then solved another of FDR's problems by declaring war on the United States.

We accepted war in 1941, as we had done in 1917, in part because, as Theodore Roosevelt had written in 1910, if Britain ever failed to preserve the European balance of power, "the United States would be obliged to get in . . . in order to restore the balance." But restoration of the balance of power did not seem in 1941, any more than it had in 1917, sufficient reason to send young men to kill and die. In 1941 FDR provided higher and nobler aims by resurrecting the Wilsonian vision in the Four Freedoms and the Atlantic Charter and by proceeding, while the war was on, to lay the foundations for the postwar reconstruction of the world along Wilsonian lines.

I assume that it will not be necessary to linger with a theory that had brief currency in the immediate postwar years, the theory that Roosevelt's great failing was his subordination of political to military objectives, shoving long-term considerations aside in the narrow interest of victory. FDR was in fact the most political of politicians, political in every reflex and to his fingertips—and just as political in war as he had been in peace. As a virtuoso politician he perfectly understood that there could be no better cloak for the pursuit of political objectives in wartime than the claim of total absorption in winning the war. He had plenty of political objectives all the same.

The war, he believed, would lead to historic transformations around the world. "Roosevelt," Harriman recalled, "enjoyed thinking aloud on the tremendous changes he saw ahead—the end of colonial empires and the rise of newly independent nations across the sweep of Africa and Asia." FDR told Churchill, "A new period has opened in the world's history, and you will have to adjust yourself to it." He tried to persuade the British to leave India and to stop the French from returning to Indochina, and he pressed the idea of UN trusteeships as the means of dismantling empires and preparing colonies for independence.

·◦·

Soviet Russia, he saw, would emerge as a major power. FDR has suffered much criticism in supposedly thinking he could charm Stalin into postwar collaboration. Perhaps FDR was not so naive after all in concentrating on Stalin. The Soviet dictator was hardly the helpless prisoner of Marxist-Leninist ideology. He saw himself not as a disciple of Marx and Lenin but as their fellow prophet. Only Stalin had the power to rewrite the Soviet approach to world affairs; after all, he had already rewritten Soviet ideology and Soviet history. FDR was surely right in seeing Stalin as the only lever capable of overturning the Leninist doctrine of irrevocable hostility between capitalism and communism. As Walter Lippmann once observed, Roosevelt was too cynical to think he could charm Stalin. "He distrusted everybody. What he thought he could do was to outwit Stalin, which is quite a different thing."

Roosevelt failed to save Eastern Europe from communism, but that could not have been achieved by diplomatic methods alone. With the Red Army in control of Eastern Europe and a war still to be won against Japan, there was not much the West could do to prevent Stalin's working his will in countries adjacent to the Soviet Union. But Roosevelt at Yalta persuaded Stalin to sign American-drafted Declarations on Liberated Europe and on Poland—declarations that laid down standards by which the world subsequently measured Stalin's behavior in Eastern Europe and found it wanting. And FDR had prepared a fallback position in case things went wrong: not only tests that, if Stalin failed to meet them, would justify a change in policy but also a great army, a network of overseas bases, plans for peacetime universal military training, and the Anglo-American monopoly of the atomic bomb.

In the longer run Roosevelt anticipated that time would bring a narrowing of differences between democratic and Communist societies. He once told Sumner Welles that marking American democracy as one hundred and Soviet communism as zero, the American system, as it moved away from laissez-faire, might eventually reach sixty, and the Soviet system, as it moved toward democracy, might eventually reach forty. The theory of convergence provoked much derision in the Cold War years. Perhaps it looks better now.

So perhaps does his idea of making China one of the Four Policemen of the peace. Churchill, with his scorn for "the pigtails," dismissed Roosevelt's insistence on China as the "Great American Illusion." But Roosevelt was not really deluded. As he said at Teheran, he wanted China there "not because he did not realize the weakness of China at present, but he was thinking farther into the future." At Malta he told Churchill that it would take "three generations of education and training . . . before China could become a serious factor." Today, two generations later, much rests on involving China in the global web of international institutions.

As for the United States, a great concern in the war years was that the country might revert to isolationism after the war just as it had done a quarter-century before—a vivid memory for FDR's generation. Contemplating Republican gains in the 1942 midterm election, Cordell Hull told Henry Wallace that the country was "going in exactly the same steps it followed in 1918." FDR himself said privately, "Anybody who thinks that isolationism is dead in this country is crazy."

He regarded American membership in a permanent international organization, in Charles Bohlen's words, as "the only device that could keep the United States from slipping back into isolationism." And true to the Wilsonian vision, he saw such an organization even more significantly as the only device that could keep the world from slipping back into war. He proposed the Declaration of the United Nations three weeks after Pearl Harbor, and by 1944 he was grappling with the problem that had defeated Wilson: how to reconcile peace enforcement by an international organization with the American Constitution. For international peace enforcement requires armed force ready to act swiftly on the command of the organization, while the Constitution requires (or, in better days, required) the consent of Congress before American troops can be sent into combat against a sovereign state. Roosevelt probably had confidence that the special agreements provided for in Article 43 of the UN Charter would strike a balance between the UN's need for prompt action and Congress's need to retain its war-making power and that the great-power veto would further protect American interests.

⌒◉⌒

He moved in other ways to accustom the American people to a larger international role—and at the same time to assure American predominance in the postwar world. By the end of 1944 he had sponsored a series of international conferences designed to plan vital aspects of the future. These conferences, held mostly at American initiative and dominated mostly by American agendas, offered the postwar blueprints for international organization (Dumbarton Oaks), for world finance, trade, and development (Bretton Woods), for food and agriculture (Hot Springs), for relief and rehabilitation (Washington), for civil aviation (Chicago). In his sweeping and sometimes grandiose asides, FDR envisaged plans for regional development with environmental protection in the Middle East andelsewhere, and his Office of the Coordinator for Inter-American Affairs pioneered economic and technical assistance to developing countries. Upon his death in 1945 FDR left an imaginative and comprehensive framework for American leadership in making a better world—an interesting achievement for a President who was supposed to subordinate political to military goals.

New times bring new perspectives. In the harsh light of the Cold War some of FDR's policies and expectations were condemned as naive or absurd or otherwise misguided. The end of the Cold War may cast those policies and expectations in a somewhat different light.

FDR's purpose, I take it, was to find ways to safeguard the historic life-interests of the Republic—national security at home and a democratic environment abroad—in a world undergoing vast and fundamental transformations. This required policies based on a grasp of the currents of history and directed to the protection of U.S. interests and to the promotion of democracy elsewhere. From the vantage point of 1994, FDR met this challenge fairly well.

Take a look at the Atlantic Charter fifty years after. Is not the world therein outlined by Roosevelt and Churchill at last coming to pass? Consider the goals of August 1941—"the right of all peoples to choose the form of government under which they will live," equal access "to the trade and to the raw materials of the world," "improved labor standards, economic advancement and social security," assurance that all "may live their lives in freedom from fear and want," relief from "the crushing burden of armaments," establishment of a community of nations. Is this not the agenda on which most nations today are at last agreed?

Does not most of the world now aspire to FDR's Four Freedoms? Has not what used to be the Soviet Union carried its movement toward the West even more rapidly than FDR dared contemplate? Has not China emerged as the "serious factor" FDR predicted? Did not the Yalta accords call for precisely the democratic freedoms to which Eastern Europe aspires today? Has not the UN, at last liberated by the end of the Cold War to pursue the goals of the founders, achieved new salience as the world's best hope for peace and cooperation?

Consider the world of 1994. It is manifestly not Adolf Hitler's world. The thousand-year Reich turned out to have a brief and bloody run of a dozen years. It is manifestly not Joseph Stalin's world. That world disintegrated before our eyes, rather like the Deacon's one-hoss shay. Nor is it Winston Churchill's world. Empire and its glories have long since vanished into the past.

ᴇ⁄ᴏ⁊ᴇ

The world we live in today is Franklin Roosevelt's world. Of the figures who, for good or for evil, bestrode the narrow world half a century ago, he would be the least surprised by the shape of things at the end of the century. Far more than the rest, he possessed what William James called a "sense of futurity." For all his manifold foibles, flaws, follies, and there was a sufficiency of all of those, FDR deserves supreme credit as the twentieth-century statesman who saw most deeply into the grand movements of history.

POSTSCRIPT

Was Franklin Roosevelt a Reluctant Internationalist?

Divine is a well-known diplomatic historian who has written numerous books on World War II diplomacy and military policies. Divine takes issue with many historians like Herbert Feis, Basil Rauch, and playwright Robert Sherwood, who believe that Roosevelt was a true internationalist. He makes the case that Roosevelt sincerely abhorred war and held strong isolationist views until the Munich crisis in September 1938.

But Divine may have underestimated the importance of politics in the presidential election year of 1940, when both candidates were strongly courting the isolationist vote in their campaigns. Roosevelt, in particular, was running for an unprecedented third term and was fearful that any hint that American soldiers may be sent to fight overseas could cost him the election.

Schlesinger portrays Roosevelt's diplomacy in a broader and more favorable light than Divine does. Admitting that no contemporary of Roosevelt, much less a historian, has been able to penetrate the mind of this very complex individual, Schlesinger nevertheless believes that of all the allied leaders, only Roosevelt saw the big picture before, during, and after World War II. Schlesinger believes that the world of today greatly resembles the vision projected by Roosevelt over 50 years ago. Fascism was eliminated from Italy, Germany, and Japan as a result of World War II. Communism collapsed in Eastern Europe and Russia in 1989. Countries all over the world struggle to achieve what Roosevelt and Churchill outlined when they signed the Atlantic Charter in the summer of 1941.

The bibliography on America's entrance into World War II is enormous and continues to grow. The best and most accessible short text and comprehensive bibliography is Justin D. Doeneke and John E. Wiltz, *From Isolation to War, 1931–1941*, 3d ed. (Harlan Davidson, 2003), a publication in *The American History Series*, which contains 30 volumes written by specialists summarizing the most recent scholarship and interpretations. See also J. Garry Clifford, "Both Ends of the Telescope: New Perspectives on FDR and American Entry into World War II," *Diplomatic History* (spring 1989) and two articles in Gerald K. Haines and J. Samuel Walker, eds., *American Foreign Relations: A Historiographical Review* (Greenwood Press, 1981): Ernest C. Bolt, Jr.'s "Isolation, Expansionism and Peace: American Foreign Policy Between the Wars" and Gerald K Haines's "Roads to War: United States Foreign Policy, 1931–1941."

Internet References . . .

The University of Michigan Library Digital Archive: *Brown v. Board of Education*

Created and maintained by the University of Michigan Library, Ann Arbor.

http://www.lib.umich.edu/exhibits/brownarchive/

Brown@50: Fulfilling the Promise

This site provides links to relevant court cases both north and south since *Plessy v. Ferguson* (1896) as well as journal articles.

http://www.brownat50.org/

Civil Rights: A Status Report

Kevin Hollaway is the author of this detailed history of black civil rights from the dicovery of the New World to the present.

http://www.earthlink.net/~civilrightsreport/

Cold War Hot Links

This page contains links to Web pages on the Cold War.

http://www.stmartin.edu/~dprice/cold.war.html

The History Place Presents: The Vietnam War

This page offers comprehensive timelines of U.S. involvement in the Vietnam conflict from 1945 to 1975, with quotes and analysis.

http://www.historyplace.com/unitedstates/vietnam

Vietnam: Yesterday and Today

This Web site has been created primarily for students and teachers interested in studying and teaching about the Vietnam War.

http://www.servercc.oakton.edu/~wittman/

Documents from the Women's Liberation Movement

This site focuses on the radical origins of the women's movement.

http://scriptorium.lib.duke.edu/wlm/

The National Women's History Project

This site provides numerous links to sites on women's history under such categories as The Women's Rights Movement, Politics, African-American Women, and Peace and War.

http://www.nwhp.org

UNIT 3

The Cold War and Beyond

*W*orld War II ended in 1945, but the peace that everyone had hoped for never came. By 1947 a "Cold War" between the Western powers and the Russians was in full swing. Three years later, American soldiers were fighting a hot war of "containment" against communist expansion in Korea. By 1968, President Lyndon Johnson had escalated America's participation in the Vietnam War and then tried to negotiate peace, which was accomplished by President Nixon in January 1973.

From 1950 to 1974, most white American families were economically well-off. Many veterans had attended college under the G.I. bill, moved to the suburbs and worked in white collar jobs. The nuclear family was frozen in a state described by one historian as "domestic containment." Ideally, Dad went to work, Mom stayed home, and the kids went to school. But fissures developed in the 1950s that affected African Americans who were segregated from the suburbs and most white collar jobs; women who questioned the role of stay-at-home mom; and children who felt alienated from the cultural values of their family. The first sign was the emergence of rock and roll and its white icon Elvis Presley. Was the music revolt the traditional acting out of children against their parents, or did it reflect a real change in values that would culminate in political protests and the establishment of a counterculture in the 1960s?

Did rock and roll reflect a real change in values and lead to the counterculture protests of the 1960s? Did the Brown decision, which outlawed "separate but equal" schools, pave the way for the elimination of a segregated society? Did the women's liberation movement destroy the traditional American family, or did it provide opportunities for women to become physicians, lawyers, and CEOs of large corporations? Finally did the industrialization of the economy of the 1970s destroy the blue collar working class New Deal Democrats and create a more affluent middle-class of Reagan Republican voters?

- Was President Truman Responsible for the Cold War?
- Was Rock and Roll Responsible for Dismantling America's Traditional Family, Sexual and Racial Customs in the 1950s and 1960s?
- Did the *Brown* Decision Fail to Desegregate and Improve the Status of African Americans?
- Was the Americanization of the War in Vietnam Inevitable?
- Has the Women's Movement of the 1970s Failed to Liberate American Women?
- Were the 1980s a Decade of Affluence for the Middle Class?

ISSUE 12

Was President Truman Responsible for the Cold War?

YES: Arnold A. Offner, from "Another Such Victory": President Truman, American Foreign Policy, and the Cold War, *Diplomatic History* (Spring 1999)

NO: John Lewis Gaddis, from *We Now Know: Rethinking Cold War History* (Oxford University Press, 1997)

ISSUE SUMMARY

YES: Arnold A. Offner argues that President Harry S. Truman was a parochial nationalist whose limited vision of foreign affairs precluded negotiations with the Russians over cold war issues.

NO: John Lewis Gaddis argues that after a half century of scholarship, Joseph Stalin was uncompromising and primarily responsible for the cold war.

Less than a month before the war ended in Europe the most powerful man in the world, President Franklin Delano Roosevelt, died suddenly from a brain embolism. A nervous, impetuous and an inexperienced Vice President Harry S. Truman became the president. Historians disagree whether Truman reversed Roosevelt's relationship with Stalin or whether the similarities in policy were negated by Truman's blunt negotiating style compared with FDR's suave, calm approach. But disagreements emerged over issues such as control over the atomic bomb (see Issue 1), Germany, Poland, and the economic reconstruction of Europe.

The question of Germany was paramount. During the war it was agreed that Germany would be temporarily divided into zones of occupation with the United States, Great Britain, and the newly liberated France controlling the Western half of Germany while the Russians were in charge of the Eastern half. Berlin, which was 90 miles inside of the Russian zone, would also be divided into zones of occupation. Arguments developed over boundaries, reparations and transfers of industrial equipment and agricultural foodstuffs between zones. In May, 1946, the Americans began treating the western zones as a separate economic unit because the Russians were transferring the food from their zone back to the Soviet Union. In September, 1946, Secretary of State James Byrnes announced that the Americans would continue to occupy their half of Germany indefinitely with military troops. By 1948, a separate democratic

West German government was established. The Russians protested by blocking ground access to the western zones of Berlin. But the Americans continued to supply the West Berliners with supplies through an airlift. After 10 months, because of the bad publicity, the Russians abandoned the Berlin blockade and created a separate communist East German government.

Roosevelt and Churchill had conceded Russian control over Eastern Europe during the World War II Conferences. The question was how much control. Stalin was not going to allow anti-Communist governments to be established in these countries. He had no understanding of how free elections were held. Consequently, when the cold war intensified in 1947 and 1948, Russian-dominated Communist governments were established in Hungary, Poland and Czechoslovakia.

In February 1946, Stalin delivered a major speech declaring the incompatibility of the two systems of Communism and Capitalism. The next month, Winston Churchill, now a retired politician, delivered his famous speech at a commencement in Fulton, Missouri, with the Truman administration's consent in which he complained about the "iron curtain" that Russia was imposing on Eastern Europe. At the same time, George Kennan, a bright multilinguist American diplomat who spent years in Germany and Russia and would become the head of Truman's policy planning staff, wrote a series of telegrams and articles which set the tone for the specific policies the Truman administration would undertake. Kennan had coined the phrase "containment," a word that would be used to describe America's foreign policy from Truman to the first President Bush. Containment would assume various meanings and would be extended to other areas of the globe besides Europe in ways Kennan claims were a misuse of what his original intentions were. Nevertheless the Truman administration took steps to stop further Russian expansionism.

In 1947, a series of steps were undertaken both to "contain" Russian expansionism and to rebuild the economies of Europe. On March 12, in an address before a Republican-controlled Congress, Truman argued in somewhat inflated rhetoric that "it must be the policy of the United States to support free peoples who are resisting attempted subjugation by armed minorities or by outside pressures." In the same speech in what became known as the "Truman Doctrine," the President requested and received $400 million economic and military assistance to Greece and Turkey. Almost as an afterthought, American military personnel were sent to oversee the reconstruction effort, a precedent that would later be used to send advisers to Vietnam.

In June 1947, Secretary of State George C. Marshall announced a plan to provide economic assistance to all European nations. This included the Soviet Union, who rejected the program and formed its own economic recovery group. In April 1948, Congress approved the creation of the Economic Cooperation Administration, the agency that would administer the program. The Marshall Plan would be remembered as America's most successful foreign aid program, where billion dollars were channeled to the western European nations. By 1950, industrial production had increased 64 percent since the end of the war, while the communist parties declined in membership and influence.

When did the cold war begin? Was it inevitable? Or should one side take most of the blame?

YES

Arnold A. Offner

"Another Such Victory": President Truman, American Foreign Policy, and the Cold War

As the twenty-first century nears, President Harry S. Truman's reputation stands high. This is especially true regarding his stewardship of foreign policy although, ironically, he entered the Oval Office in 1945 untutored in world affairs, and during his last year in the White House Republicans accused his administration of having surrendered fifteen countries and five hundred million people to communism and sending twenty thousand Americans to their "burial ground" in Korea. Near the end of his term, Truman's public "favorable" rating had plummeted to 23 percent.

Within a decade, however, historians rated Truman a "near great" president, crediting his administration with reconstructing Western Europe and Japan, resisting Soviet or Communist aggression from Greece to Korea, and forging collective security through NATO. In the 1970s the "plain speaking" Truman became a popular culture hero. Recently, biographers have depicted him as the allegory of American life, an ordinary man whose extraordinary character led him to triumph over adversity from childhood through the presidency, and even posited a symbiotic relationship between "His Odyssey" from Independence to the White House and America's rise to triumphant superpower status. Melvyn P. Leffler, in his *A Preponderance of Power,* has judged Truman to have been neither a naif nor an idealist but a realist who understood the uses of power and whose administration, despite serious, costly errors, prudently preserved America's national security against real or perceived Soviet threats.

Collapse of the Soviet Union and Europe's other Communist states, whose archives have confirmed Truman's belief in 1945 that their regimes governed largely by "clubs, pistols and concentration camps," has further raised the former president's standing. This has encouraged John Lewis Gaddis and others to shift their focus to Stalin's murderous domestic rule as the key determinant of Soviet foreign policy and the Cold War. As Gaddis has contended, Stalin was heir to Ivan the Terrible and Peter the Great, responsible for more state-sanctioned murders than Adolf Hitler, and treated world politics as an extension of domestic politics: a zero sum

From *Diplomatic History,* vol. 32, no. 2, Spring 1999. Copyright © 1999 by Society for Historians of American Foreign Relations. Reprinted by permission of Blackwell Publishing Ltd.

game in which his gaining security meant depriving all others of it. For Gaddis and others, that is largely the answer to the question of whether Stalin sought or caused the Cold War.

But as Walter LaFeber has said, to dismiss Stalin's policies as the work of a paranoid is greatly to oversimplify the Cold War. Indeed, historians of Stalin's era seem to be of the preponderant view that he pursued a cautious but brutal realpolitik. He aimed to restore Russia's 1941 boundaries, establish a sphere of influence in border states, provide security against a recovered Germany or Japan or hostile capitalist states, and gain compensation, notably reparations, for the ravages of war. Stalin calculated forces, recognized America's superior industrial and military power, put Soviet state interests ahead of Marxist-Leninist ideology, and pursued pragmatic or opportunistic policies in critical areas such as Germany, China, and Korea.

Thus, the time seems ripe, given our increased knowledge of Soviet policies, to reconsider President Truman's role in the Cold War. As Thomas G. Paterson has written, the president stands at the pinnacle of the diplomatic-military establishment, has great capacity to set the foreign policy agenda and to mold public opinion, and his importance, especially in Truman's case, cannot be denied. But contrary to prevailing views, I believe that his policymaking was shaped by his parochial and nationalistic heritage. This was reflected in his uncritical belief in the superiority of American values and political-economic interests and his conviction that the Soviet Union and communism were the root cause of international strife. Truman's parochialism also caused him to disregard contrary views, to engage in simplistic analogizing, and to show little ability to comprehend the basis for other nations' policies. Consequently, his foreign policy leadership intensified Soviet-American conflict, hastened the division of Europe, and brought tragic intervention in Asian civil wars.

In short, Truman lacked the qualities of the creative or great leader who, as James MacGregor Burns has written, must broaden the environment in which he and his citizenry operate and widen the channels in which choices are made and events flow. Truman, to the contrary, narrowed Americans' perception of their world political environment and the channels for policy choices and created a rigid framework in which the United States waged long-term, extremely costly global cold war. Indeed, before we celebrate America's victory in this contest we might recall that after King Pyrrhus's Greek forces defeated the Romans at the battle of Asculum in 280 B.C., he reflected that "another such victory, and we are undone."

II

Truman's parochialism and nationalism, and significant insecurity, were rooted in his background, despite his claim to have had a bucolic childhood of happy family, farm life, and Baptist religiosity. In fact, young Harry's poor eyesight, extended illness, and "sissy" piano playing alienated him from both his peers and his feisty father and fostered ambivalence in him toward powerful men. On the one hand, Truman deferred to "Boss" Thomas

Pendergast, his dishonest political benefactor, and to Secretaries of State George Marshall and Dean Acheson, whose manner and firm viewpoints he found reassuring. On the other hand, he denounced those whose style or ways of thinking were unfamiliar. This included the State Department's "striped pants boys," the military's "brass hats" and "prima donnas," political "fakirs" [sic] such as Teddy and Franklin Roosevelt, and "professional liberals." For Truman, Charles de Gaulle, Josef Stalin, Ernest Bevin, and Douglas MacArthur were each, at one time or another, a "son of a bitch."

Truman's need to demonstrate his authority underlay his upbraiding of both Soviet Foreign Minister Vyacheslav Molotov in April 1945 for Russia's alleged failure to keep its agreements and his secretary of state, James Byrnes, for allegedly exceeding his authority at the Moscow Conference of Foreign Ministers (CFM) that December. Truman naively likened Stalin to Pendergast, who, like Harry's father, always kept his word, but then took great umbrage at the thought that the Soviet leader had broken his word over Poland, Iran, or Germany. Truman also blamed MacArthur for misleading him at their Wake Island meeting in 1950 about Chinese intentions in the Korean War, but this was equally Truman self-deception.

Truman's self-tutelage in history derived largely from didactic biographies of "great men" and empires. This enhanced his vision of the globe but provided little sense of complexity or ambiguity and instilled exaggerated belief that current events had exact historical analogues that provided the key to contemporary policy. The new president was "amazed" that the Yalta accords were so "hazy" and fraught with "new meanings" at every reading, which probably contributed to his "lackluster" adherence to them. Shortly, Truman uncritically applied analogues about 1930s appeasement of Nazi Germany to diplomacy with the Soviet Union and crises in Iran, Greece, Turkey, and Korea.

Further, young Harry's Bible reading and church going did not inspire an abiding religiosity or system of morals so much as a conviction that the world was filled with "liars and hypocrites," terms he readily applied to his presidential critics, and a stern belief, as he wrote in 1945, that "punishment always followed transgression," a maxim that he applied to North Korea and the People's Republic of China (PRC).

Truman's early writings disdained non-Americans and minorities ("Chink doctor," "dago," "nigger," "Jew clerk," and "bohunks and Rooshans"), and in 1940 he proposed to deport "disloyal inhabitants." As president in 1945 he questioned the loyalty of "hyphenate" Americans, and in 1947 he signed Executive Order 9835, creating an unprecedented "loyalty" program that jettisoned basic legal procedural safeguards and virtually included a presumption of guilt.

Truman's command of men and bravery under fire in World War I were exemplary but not broadening. He deplored Europe's politics, mores, and food and sought only to return to "God's country." He intended never to revisit Europe: "I've nearly promised old Miss Liberty that she'll have to turn around to see me again," he wrote in 1918, and in 1945 he went reluctantly to Potsdam to his first and only European summit.

Nonetheless, Truman identified with Wilsonian internationalism, especially the League of Nations, and as a senator he supported President Franklin Roosevelt on the World Court, neutrality revision, rearmament, and Lend Lease for Britain and Russia. He rightfully said "I am no appeaser." But his internationalism reflected unquestioned faith in American moral superiority, and his foreign policy proposals largely comprised military preparedness. He was indifferent to the plight of Republican Spain and too quickly blamed international conflict on "outlaws," "savages," and "totalitarians." After Germany invaded the Soviet Union in 1941, he hastily remarked that they should be left to destroy one another—although he opposed Germany's winning—and he likened Russian leaders to "Hitler and Al Capone" and soon inveighed against the "twin blights—atheism and communism." Hence, while Truman supported the fledgling United Nations and the liberalization of world trade, the man who became president in April 1945 was less an incipient internationalist than a parochial nationalist given to excessive fear that appeasement, lack of preparedness, and enemies at home and abroad would thwart America's mission (the "Lord's will") to "win the peace" on its terms.

President Truman inherited an expedient wartime alliance that stood on shaky ground at Yalta in February 1945 and grew more strained over Soviet control in Romania and Poland and U.S. surrender talks with German officials at Bern that aroused Stalin's fears of a separate peace. Truman lamented that "they didn't tell me anything about what was going on." He also had to depend on advisers whose views ranged from Ambassador Averell Harriman's belief that it was time to halt the Russians' "barbarian invasion" of Europe to counsel from FDR emissaries Joseph Davies and Harry Hopkins to try to preserve long-term accord. Truman's desire to appear decisive by making quick decisions and his instinct to be "tough" spurred his belief that he could get "85 percent" from the Russians on important matters and that they could go along or "go to hell."

Initially, the president's abrupt style and conflicting advice produced inconsistent policy. His mid-April call for a "new" government in Poland and his "one-two to the jaw" interview with Molotov brought only a sharp reply from Stalin, after which the United States recognized a predominantly Communist Polish government. In May, Truman approved "getting tough" with the Russians by suddenly curtailing Lend Lease shipments, but Anglo-Soviet protests caused him to countermand the cutoffs. He then refused Prime Minister Winston Churchill's proposal to keep Anglo-American troops advanced beyond their agreed occupation zones to bargain in Germany and soon wrote that he was "anxious to keep all my engagements with the Russians because they are touchy and suspicious of us."

Still, Truman determined to have his way with the Russians, especially in Germany. Tutored in part by Secretary of War Henry L. Stimson, he embraced the emergent War-State Department position that Germany was key to the balance of power in Europe and required some reconstruction because a "poor house" standard of living there meant the same for Europe, and might cause a repeat of the tragic Treaty of Versailles history.

Truman replaced Roosevelt's reparations negotiator, Isador Lubin, with conservative oil entrepreneur Edwin Pauley, who brushed off both Soviet claims to Yalta's $20 billion in reparations and State Department estimates that Germany could pay $12–14 billion. Truman also said that when he met with Churchill and Stalin he wanted "all the bargaining power—all the cards in my hands, and the plan on Germany is one of them."

The other card was the atomic bomb, which inspired Truman and Byrnes to think that they could win their way in Europe and Asia. Byrnes told the president in April that the bomb might allow them to "dictate our terms" at the war's end and in May indicated his belief that it would make the Russians more "manageable." Stimson counseled Truman that America's industrial strength and unique weapon comprised a "royal straight flush and we mustn't be a fool about how we play it," that it would be "dominant" in any dispute with Russia over Manchuria, and a "weapon" or "master card" in America's hand in its "big stakes" diplomacy with the Russians.

The president readily analogized diplomacy with his poker playing and, as Martin J. Sherwin has shown, believed that use of his atomic "ace-in-the-hole" would allow him to wrest concessions from Stalin. Truman had incentive to delay a summit meeting until the bomb was ready and to take no steps to obviate its use. In late spring he passed over proposals to modify unconditional surrender that sought to induce Japan's quick capitulation, and he would not give the Japanese or Russians notice of the atomic bomb.

Truman set sail for Potsdam highly disposed to atomic diplomacy, albeit not "blackmail." His nationalist perspective shaped his thinking. He aimed to advance American interests only: "win, lose, or draw—and we must win." En route, he approved Pauley's policy to give "first charge" priority to German occupation and maintenance costs over reparations. "Santa Claus is dead," Truman wrote, and the United States would never again "pay reparations, feed the world, and get nothing for it but a nose thumbing." Further, after Stimson brought word on 16 July of the successful atomic test in New Mexico and urged an early warning and offer to retain the Emperor as means to induce Japan's rapid surrender, Truman and Byrnes refused. That ended the last, brief chance at atomic restraint.

After meeting Stalin on 17 July Truman wrote that he was unfazed by the Russian's "dynamite" agenda because "I have some dynamite too which I'm not exploding now." The following day he asserted that the "Japs will fold up" before Russia entered the Pacific war, specifically "when Manhattan appears over their homeland." Truman agreed with Byrnes that use of the bomb would permit them to "out-maneuver Stalin on China," that is, negate the Yalta concessions in Manchuria and guarantee that Russia would "not get in so much on the kill" of Japan or its occupation. Assured by 24 July that the bomb would be ready before Russia's entry, the president had to be persuaded even to hint to Stalin that he had a new weapon and afterward exulted in the mistaken belief that the Russian leader had not caught on to the bomb. Truman then hastened to issue the Potsdam Declaration without Soviet signature on 26 July and signed his "release when ready" order on the bombs on the 31st.

News of the bomb's power also greatly reinforced Truman's confidence to allow Byrnes to press European negotiations to impasse by refusing the Russians access to the Ruhr, rejecting even their low bid for $4 billion in industrial reparations, and withdrawing the Yalta accords. Convinced that the New Mexico atomic test would allow the United States to "control" events, Byrnes pushed his famous 30 July tripartite ultimatum on German zonal reparations, Poland's de facto control over its new western border (including Silesia) with Germany, and Italy's membership in the UN. "Mr. Stalin is stallin'," Truman wrote hours before the American-set deadline on 31 July, but that was useless because "I have an ace in the hole and another one showing," aces that he knew would soon fall upon Japan.

Truman won his hand, as Stalin acceded to zonal reparations. But Truman's victory was fraught with more long-term consequences than he envisioned. He had not only equated his desire to prevent use of taxpayer dollars to help sustain occupied Germany with the Russians' vital need for reparations but also given them reason to think, as Norman Naimark has written, that the Americans were deaf to their quest for a "paltry" $10 billion or less to compensate for Germany's having ravaged their nation. Further, America's insistence on zonal reparations would impede development of common economic policy for all of Germany and increase likelihood of its East-West division.

In addition, use of two atomic bombs on Hiroshima and Nagasaki—the second was not militarily necessary—showed that for Truman and Byrnes, the prospect of political gain in Europe and Asia precluded serious thought not to use the bombs. And this may have led the Russians to conclude that the bombs were directed against them, or their ability to achieve their strategic interests. But Stalin would not be pressured; he was determined to pursue a Russian atomic bomb.

Shortly, Truman backed Byrnes's "bomb in his pocket" diplomacy at the London CFM, which deadlocked over Russian control in Eastern Europe and American control in Japan. Truman told Byrnes to "stick to his guns" and tell the Russians "to go to hell." The president then agreed with "ultranationalist" advisers who opposed international atomic accord by drawing misleading analogies about interwar disarmament and "appeasement" and by insisting that America's technological-industrial genius assured permanent atomic supremacy. Truman held that America was the world's atomic "trustee"; that it had to preserve the bomb's "secret"; and that no nation would give up the "locks and bolts" necessary to protect its "house" from "outlaws." The atomic arms race was on, he said in the fall of 1945, and other nations had to "catch up on their own hook."

In the spring of 1946, Truman undercut the Dean Acheson-David Lilienthal plan for international control and development of atomic resources by appointing as chief negotiator Bernard Baruch, whose emphasis on close inspections, sanctions, no veto, and indefinite American atomic monopoly virtually assured Russian refusal. Despite Acheson's protests, Truman analogized that "if Harry Stimson had been backed up in Manchuria [in 1931] there would have been no war." And as deadlock neared in July 1946, the president told Baruch to "stand pat."

Ultimately the UN commission weighing the Baruch Plan approved it on 31 December 1946. But the prospect of a Soviet veto in the Security Council precluded its adoption. Admittedly, Stalin's belief that he could not deal with the United States on an equal basis until he had the bomb and Soviet insistence on retention of their veto power and national control of resources and facilities may have precluded atomic accord in 1946. Still, Baruch insisted that the United States could get its way because it had an atomic monopoly, and American military officials sought to preserve a nuclear monopoly as long as possible and to develop a strategy based on air power and atomic weapons. As David Holloway has written, neither Truman nor Stalin "saw the bomb as a common danger to the human race."

Meanwhile, Byrnes's diplomacy in Moscow in December 1945 had produced Yalta-style accords on a European peace treaty process, Russian predominance in Bulgaria and Romania and American primacy in China and Japan, and compromise over Korea, with Soviet disputes with Iran and Turkey set aside. But conservative critics cried "appeasement," and in his famous but disputed letter of 5 January 1946, an anxious president charged that Byrnes had kept him "completely in the dark"; denounced Russian "outrage[s]" in the Baltic, Germany, Poland, and Iran and intent to invade Turkey; and said that the Russians understood only an "iron fist" and "divisions" and that he was tired of "babying" them. In fact, Truman knew of most of Byrnes's positions; they had hardly "babied" Russia since Potsdam; and no Russian attack was imminent. The letter reflected Truman's new "get tough" policy, or personal cold war declaration, which, it must be emphasized, came six weeks before George Kennan's Long Telegram and Churchill's Iron Curtain speech.

Strong American protests in 1946 caused the Russians to withdraw their troops from Iran and their claims to joint defense of the Turkish Straits. In the latter case, Truman said he was ready to follow his policy of military response "to the end" to determine if Russia intended "world conquest." Once again he had taken an exaggerated, nationalist stance. No one expected a Russian military advance; America's action rested on its plans to integrate Turkey into its strategic planning and to use it as a base of operations against Russia in event of war. And in September Truman approved announcement of a Mediterranean command that led to the United States becoming the dominant naval power there by year's end.

Meanwhile, Truman ignored Secretary of Commerce Henry Wallace's lengthy memoranda during March–September 1946 that sought to promote economic ties with Russia and questioned America's atomic policies and global military expansiveness. The president then fired Wallace after he publicly challenged Byrnes's speech on 6 September in Stuttgart propounding West German reconstruction and continued American military presence there. The firing was reasonable, but not the rage at Wallace as "a real Commy" and at "parlor pinks and soprano-voiced men" as a "national danger" and "sabotage front" for Stalin.

Equally without reason was Truman's face value acceptance of White House special counsel Clark Clifford's "Russian Report" of September 1946 and accompanying "Last Will of Peter the Great." Clifford's report rested on a hasty compilation of apocalyptic projections of Soviet aim to conquer the world by military force and subversion, and he argued that the United States had to prepare for total war. He wrote in the "black and white" terms that he knew Truman would like and aimed to justify a vast global military upgrade and silence political critics on the left and right. Tsar Peter's will was an old forgery purporting to show that he had a similar design to conquer Eurasia. Truman may have found the report so "hot" that he confined it to his White House safe, but he believed the report and the will and soon was persisting that the governments of the czars, Stalin, and Hitler were all the same. Later he told a mild critic of American policy to read Tsar Peter's will to learn where Russian leaders got their "fixed ideas."

It was a short step, Clifford recalled, from the Russian Report to Truman's epochal request in March 1947 for military aid to Greece and Turkey to help "free peoples" fight totalitarianism. Truman vastly overstated the global-ideological aspects of Soviet-American conflict. Perhaps he sought to fire "the opening gun" to rouse the public and a fiscally conservative Republican Congress to national security expenditures. But he also said that this was "only the beginning" of the "U.S. going into European politics," that the Russians had broken every agreement since Potsdam and would now get only "one language" from him. He added in the fall of 1947 that "if Russia gets Greece and Turkey," it would get Italy and France, the iron curtain would extend to western Ireland, and the United States would have to "come home and prepare for war."

Truman's fears were excessive. Stalin never challenged the Truman Doctrine or Western primacy in Turkey, now under U.S. military tutelage, and Greece. He provided almost no aid to the Greek rebels and told Yugoslavia's leaders in early 1948 to halt their aid because the United States would never allow the Greek Communists to win and break Anglo-American control in the Mediterranean. When Marshal Josip Broz Tito balked, Stalin withdrew his advisers from Yugoslavia and expelled that nation from the Cominform. Tito finally closed his borders to the Greek rebels in July 1949.

Perhaps U.S. officials feared that Britain's retreat from Greece might allow Russia to penetrate the Mediterranean, or that if Greek Communists overthrew the reactionary Greek regime (Turkey was not threatened) they might align Athens with Moscow. Still, the Truman administration's costly policy never addressed the causes of Greece's civil war; instead, it substituted military "annihilation of the enemy for the reform of the social and economic conditions" that had brought civil war. Equally important, Truman's rhetorical division of the world into "free" versus "totalitarian" states, as Gaddis once said, created an "ideological straitjacket" for American foreign policy and an unfortunate model for later interventions, such as in Korea—"the Greece of the Far East," as Truman would say—and in French Indochina.

The Truman Doctrine led to the Marshall Plan in June 1947, but they were not "two halves of the same walnut," as Truman claimed. State Department officials who drew up the European Recovery Plan (ERP) differentiated it from what they viewed as his doctrine's implications for "economic and ultimately military warfare." The Soviets likened the Truman Doctrine to retail purchase of separate nations and the Marshall Plan to wholesale purchase of Europe.

The Soviet view was narrow, although initially they had interest in participating and perhaps even harbored dreams that the United States would proffer a generous Lend Lease-style arrangement. But as the British quickly saw, Soviet participation was precluded by American-imposed financial and economic controls and, as Michael J. Hogan has written, by the integrated, continental approach to aid rather than a nation-by-nation basis that would have benefited war-devastated Russia. Indeed, in direct talks in Paris, U.S. officials refused concessions, focused on resources to come from Russia and East Europe, and insisted on German contributions to the ERP ahead of reparations payments or a peace treaty—and then expressed widespread relief when the Soviets rejected the ERP for themselves and East Europe.

The Marshall Plan proved to be a very successful geostrategic venture. It helped to spur American-European trade and Western European recovery, bring France into camp with Germany and satisfy French economic and security claims, and revive western Germany industrially without unleashing the 1930s-style "German colossus" that Truman's aides feared. The Marshall Plan was also intended to contain the Soviets economically, forestall German-Soviet bilateral deals, and provide America with access to its allies' domestic and colonial resources. Finally, as the British said, the Truman administration sought an integrated Europe resembling the United States, "God's own country."

The Marshall Plan's excellent return on investment, however, may have cost far more than the $13 billion expended. "The world is definitely split in two," Undersecretary of State Robert Lovett said in August 1947, while Kennan forewarned that for defensive reasons the Soviets would "clamp down completely on Czechoslovakia" to strengthen their hold on Eastern Europe. Indeed, the most recent evidence indicates that Stalin viewed the Marshall Plan as a "watershed" event, signaling an American effort to predominate over all of Europe. This spurred the Soviets into a comprehensive strategy shift. They now rigged the elections in Hungary, proffered Andrei Zhdanov's "two camps" approach to world policy, created the Cominform, and blessed the Communist coup in Czechoslovakia in February 1948. Truman, in turn, concluded that the Western world confronted the same situation it had a decade earlier with Nazi Germany, and his bristling St. Patrick's Day speeches in March 1948 placed sole onus for the Cold War on the Soviet Union. Subsequently, Anglo-American talks at the Pentagon would culminate in NATO in April 1949.

Meanwhile, the U.S. decision to make western Germany the cornerstone of the ERP virtually precluded negotiations to reunify the country. In fact, when Secretary of State Marshall proposed during a CFM meeting in the spring of 1947 to offer current production reparations to the Russians to induce agreement to unify Germany, the president sternly refused. Marshall complained of lack of "elbow room" to negotiate. But Truman would not yield, and by the time of the next CFM in late 1947 the secretary showed no interest in Russian reparations or Ruhr access. Despite America's public position, Ambassador to Moscow Walter Bedell Smith wrote, "we really do not want nor intend to accept German unification on any terms that the Russians might agree to, even though they seemed to meet most of our requirements."

The Americans were by then onto their London Conference program to create a West German state and, as Stalin said in February 1948, "The West will make Western Germany their own, and we shall turn Eastern Germany into our own state." In June the Soviet dictator initiated the Berlin blockade to try to forestall the West's program, but Truman determined to "stay period." He believed that to withdraw from Berlin would seriously undermine U.S. influence in Europe and the ERP and destroy his presidential standing, and he remained determined to avert military confrontation.

But Truman saw no connection between the London program and the blockade, as Carolyn Eisenberg has written. Further, his belief that "there is nothing to negotiate" and accord with General Lucius Clay's view that to withdraw from Berlin meant "we have lost everything we are fighting for" exaggerated the intent of Stalin's maneuver and diminished even slim chances for compromise on Germany, including Kennan's "Plan A" for a unified, neutralized state with American and Soviet forces withdrawn to its periphery. As Marshall said in August 1948, there would be "no abandonment of our position" on West Germany.

Eventually, Truman and the airlift prevailed over Stalin, who gave in to a face-saving CFM in May 1949 that ended the blockade, with nothing else agreed. The new secretary of state, Acheson, said that the United States intended to create a West German government "come hell or high water" and that Germany could be unified only by consolidating the East into the West on the basis of its incipient Bonn Constitution. Likewise Truman said in June 1949 that he would not sacrifice West Germany's basic freedoms to gain "nominal political unity."

Long convinced that the United States was locked in "a struggle with the USSR for Germany," the president showed no interest when Stalin made his most comprehensive offer on 10 March 1952, proposing a Big Four meeting to draft a peace treaty for a united, neutral, defensively rearmed Germany free of foreign troops. Whether Stalin was seeking a settlement to reduce great power conflict over a divided Germany has been debated. His note came only after the United States and its allies were near contractual accord on West German sovereignty and Acheson had just negotiated his "grand slam" providing for German forces to enter a proposed European Defense Community (EDC) linked to NATO. Acheson held that Stalin had thrown a "golden apple" of discord over the iron curtain to forestall a sovereign, industrially strong, and rearmed West Germany joining an American-led alliance system.

Truman gave full sway to Acheson, who hesitated to reject Stalin's offer out of hand. But he insisted that the allies "drive ahead" with the German contractuals and EDC. He also got support from West German Chancellor Konrad Adenauer to shape uniform allied replies, with conditions, such as UN-supervised elections in all of Germany prior to negotiations and unified Germany's right to join any "defensive European community," that he knew Stalin would reject. Further, although Truman and Acheson had just coaxed Kennan to become ambassador to Moscow, they never asked his advice or gave him a policy clue despite meeting with him three times in April. This confirmed Kennan's view that "we had no interest in discussing the German problem with the Soviet Government in any manner whatsoever."

Stalin, meanwhile, told East German leaders in April 1952 that the West would never accept any proposal they made and that it was time to "organize your own state" and protect its border. The United States won the so-called battle of the notes, although exchanges continued. But the allies concluded the German contractuals and the EDC in late May. And when the French then reverted to proposing a four power meeting on Germany, Acheson said that four power control was long past. He then shaped the note so that it "puts onus on Sovs sufficiently to make it unlikely that Sovs will agree to mtg on terms proposed." He was right, and in September the note writing drew to its anticlimactic closure.

Prospect for accord based on Stalin's note was remote, but not just because Stalin wanted, as Vojtech Mastny has written, either a unified "pro-Soviet though not necessarily communist" Germany or a full-fledged East German satellite. Truman had no interest in a unified, neutral, or demilitarized Germany and now believed that a rearmed FRG was as vital to NATO as West Germany was to ERR German unity was possible only on the basis of West over East. Thus, Ambassador Kennan said after talking to U.S. officials linked to NATO in the fall of 1952 that they saw no reason to withdraw U.S. forces from Germany "at any time within the foreseeable future under any conceivable agreement with Russia." This meant that the "split of Germany and Europe" would continue. And it did, for the next forty years. . . .

⚜

No one leader or nation caused the Cold War. The Second World War generated inevitable Soviet-American conflict as two nations with entirely different political-economic systems confronted each other on two war-torn continents. The Truman administration would seek to fashion a world order friendly to American political and economic interests, to achieve maximum national security by preventing any nation from severing U.S. ties to its traditional allies and vital areas of trade and resources, and to avoid 1930s-style "appeasement." Truman creditably favored creation of the UN, fostered foreign aid and reconstruction, and wished to avert war, and, after he recognized his "overreach" in Korea, he sought to return to the status quo ante.

Nonetheless, from the Potsdam Conference through the Korean War, the president contributed significantly to the growing Cold War and militarization of American foreign policy. He assumed that America's economic-military-moral superiority assured that he could order the world on its terms, and he ascribed only dark motives to nations or leaders who resisted America's will. Monopoly control of the atomic bomb heightened this sense of righteous power and impelled his use of atomic bombs partly to outmaneuver the Russians in China and over Japan. Truman also drew confidence from the bombs that he could deny the Soviets any fixed sum of German reparations despite their feasibility, the Yalta accords, and the apparent disregard of Russia's claim to compensation for its wartime suffering. American-imposed zonal reparations policy only increased the East-West divide and diminished prospects to reunite Germany, although Stalin evidently remained open to the idea of a united and neutralized Germany until 1949 and conceivably as late as 1952. But Truman, as Marshall learned in the spring of 1947, had little interest in negotiating such an arrangement, and his administration's decision that year to make western Germany the cornerstone of the Marshall Plan and Western Europe's reconstruction virtually precluded German unification except by melding East into West. Formation of NATO and insistence that a unified Germany be free to join a Western military alliance reinforced division of Germany and Europe.

It is clear that Truman's insecurity with regard to diplomacy and world politics led him to seek to give the appearance of acting decisively and reinforced his penchant to view conflict in black and white terms and to divide nations into free or totalitarian societies. He shied from weighing the complexities of historic national conflicts and local or regional politics. Instead, he attributed nearly every diplomatic crisis or civil war—in Germany, Iran, Turkey, Greece, and Czechoslovakia–to Soviet machination and insisted that the Russians had broken every agreement and were bent on "world conquest." To determine his response he was quick to reach for an analogy, usually the failure of the Western powers to resist Germany and Japan in the 1930s, and to conclude that henceforth he would speak to the Russians in the only language that he thought they understood: "divisions." This style of leadership and diplomacy closed off both advocates and prospects for more patiently negotiated and more nuanced or creative courses of action.

Truman also viscerally loathed the Chinese Communists, could not comprehend Asian nationalism, demonized Asian opponents, and caused the United States to align itself with corrupt regimes. He was unable to view China's civil war apart from Soviet-American conflict. He brushed off criticism of America's intervention on behalf of the frightful GMD, refused to open channels of communication with the emergent PRC, and permitted the American-armed, Taiwan-based GMD to wage counterrevolutionary war against China's new government, whose sovereignty or legitimacy he never accepted. The Korean War then overtook his administration. The president decided to preserve South Korea's independence but set an unfortunate if not tragic precedent by refusing to seek formal congressional sanction for war. His decision to punish North Korea and implement "rollback," and his disdain for the PRC and its concerns before and after it entered the war, brought unnecessary, untold destruction and suffering to Asians and Americans and proved fatal to his presidency. Still, in his undelivered farewell address Truman insisted that "Russia was at the root" of every problem from Europe to Asia, and that "Trumanism" had saved countless countries from Soviet invasion and "knocked the socks off the communists" in Korea.

In conclusion, it seems clear that despite Truman's pride in his knowledge of the past, he lacked insight into the history unfolding around him. He often could not see beyond his immediate decision or visualize alternatives, and he seemed oblivious to the implications of his words or actions. More often than not he narrowed rather than broadened the options that he presented to the American citizenry, the environment of American politics, and the channels through which Cold War politics flowed. Throughout his presidency, Truman remained a parochial nationalist who lacked the leadership to move America away from conflict and toward detente. Instead, he promoted an ideology and politics of Cold War confrontation that became the modus operandi of successor administrations and the United States for the next two generations.

John Lewis Gaddis  **NO**

We Now Know:
Rethinking Cold War History

[Joseph] Stalin appears to have relished his role, along with [Franklin D.] Roosevelt and [Winston] Churchill, as one of the wartime Big Three. Such evidence as has surfaced from Soviet archives suggests that he received reassuring reports about Washington's intentions: "Roosevelt is more friendly to us than any other prominent American," Ambassador Litvinov commented in June 1943, "and it is quite obvious that he wishes to cooperate with us." Whoever was in the White House, Litvinov's successor Andrei Gromyko predicted a year later, the Soviet Union and the United States would "manage to find common issues for the solution of . . . problems emerging in the future and of interest to both countries." Even if Stalin's long-range thinking about security did clash with that of his Anglo-American allies, common military purposes provided the strongest possible inducements to smooth over such differences. It is worth asking why this *practice* of wartime cooperation did not become a *habit* that would extend into the postwar era.

The principal reason, it now appears, was Stalin's insistence on equating security with territory. Western diplomats had been surprised, upon arriving in Moscow soon after the German attack in the summer of 1941, to find the Soviet leader already demanding a postwar settlement that would retain what his pact with Hitler had yielded: the Baltic states, together with portions of Finland, Poland, and Romania. Stalin showed no sense of shame or even embarrassment about this, no awareness that the *methods* by which he had obtained these concessions could conceivably render them illegitimate in the eyes of anyone else. When it came to territorial aspirations, he made no distinction between adversaries and allies: what one had provided the other was expected to endorse. . . .

On the surface, this strategy succeeded. After strong initial objections, Roosevelt and Churchill did eventually acknowledge the Soviet Union's right to the expanded borders it claimed; they also made it clear that they would not oppose the installation of "friendly" governments in adjoining states. This meant accepting a Soviet sphere of influence from the Baltic to the Adriatic, a concession not easily reconciled with the Atlantic Charter. But the authors of that document saw no feasible way to avoid that outcome: military necessity required continued Soviet cooperation against the

Germans. Nor were they themselves prepared to relinquish spheres of influence in Western Europe and the Mediterranean, the Middle East, Latin America, and East Asia. Self-determination was a sufficiently malleable concept that each of the Big Three could have endorsed, without sleepless nights, what the Soviet government had said about the Atlantic Charter: "practical application of these principles will necessarily adapt itself to the circumstances, needs, and historic peculiarities of particular countries."

That, though, was precisely the problem. For unlike Stalin, Roosevelt and Churchill would have to defend their decisions before domestic constituencies. The *manner* in which Soviet influence expanded was therefore, for them, of no small significance. Stalin showed little understanding of this. Having no experience himself with democratic procedures, he dismissed requests that he respect democratic proprieties. "[S]ome propaganda work should be done," he advised Roosevelt at the Tehran conference after the president had hinted that the American public would welcome a plebiscite in the Baltic States. "It is all nonsense!" Stalin complained to [Soviet Foreign Minister V. M.] Molotov. "[Roosevelt] is their military leader and commander in chief. Who would dare object to him?" When at Yalta F.D.R. stressed the need for the first Polish election to be as pure as "Caesar's wife," Stalin responded with a joke: "They said that about her, but in fact she had her sins." Molotov warned his boss, on that occasion, that the Americans' insistence on free elections elsewhere in Eastern Europe was "going too far." "Don't worry," he recalls Stalin as replying, "work it out. We can deal with it in our own way later. The point is the correlation of forces."

The Soviet leader was, in one sense, right. Military strength would determine what happened in that part of the world, not the enunciation of lofty principles. But unilateral methods carried long-term costs Stalin did not foresee: the most significant of these was to ruin whatever prospects existed for a Soviet sphere of influence the East Europeans themselves might have accepted. This possibility was not as far-fetched as it would later seem. . . . [Stalin] would, after all, approve such a compromise as the basis for a permanent settlement with Finland. He would initially allow free elections in Hungary, Czechoslovakia, and the Soviet occupation zone in Germany. He may even have *anticipated an enthusiastic response* as he took over Eastern Europe. "He was, I think, surprised and hurt," [W. Averell] Harriman [one of Roosevelt's closest advisors] recalled, "when the Red Army was not welcomed in all the neighboring countries as an army of liberation." "We still had our hopes," [Nikita] Khrushchev remembered, that "after the catastrophe of World War II, Europe too might become Soviet. Everyone would take the path from capitalism to socialism." It could be that there was another form of romanticism at work here, quite apart from Stalin's affinity for fellow authoritarians: that he was unrealistic enough to expect ideological solidarity and gratitude for liberation to override old fears of Russian expansionism as well as remaining manifestations of nationalism among the Soviet Union's neighbors, perhaps as easily as he himself had overridden the latter—or so it then appeared—within the multinational empire that was the Soviet Union itself.

If the Red Army could have been welcomed in Poland and the rest of the countries it liberated with the same enthusiasm American, British, and Free French forces encountered when they landed in Italy and France in 1943 and 1944, then some kind of Czech–Finnish compromise might have been feasible. Whatever Stalin's expectations, though, this did not happen. That non-event, in turn, removed any possibility of a division of Europe all members of the Grand Alliance could have endorsed. It ensured that an American sphere of influence would arise there largely by consent, but that its Soviet counterpart could sustain itself only by coercion. The resulting asymmetry would account, more than anything else, for the origins, escalation, and ultimate outcome of the Cold War.

⋅⟨⊙⟩⋅

. . . It has long been clear that, in addition to having had an authoritarian vision, Stalin also had an imperial one, which he proceeded to implement in at least as single-minded a way [as the American]. No comparably influential builder of empire came close to wielding power for so long, or with such striking results, on the Western side.

It was, of course, a matter of some awkwardness that Stalin came out of a revolutionary movement that had vowed to smash, not just tsarist imperialism, but all forms of imperialism throughout the world. The Soviet leader constructed his own logic, though, and throughout his career he devoted a surprising amount of attention to showing how a revolution and an empire might coexist. . . .

Stalin's fusion of Marxist internationalism with tsarist imperialism could only reinforce his tendency, in place well before World War II, to equate the advance of world revolution with the expanding influence of the Soviet state. He applied that linkage quite impartially: a major benefit of the 1939 pact with Hitler had been that it regained territories lost as a result of the Bolshevik Revolution and the World War I settlement. But Stalin's conflation of imperialism with ideology also explains the importance he attached, following the German attack in 1941, to having his new Anglo-American allies confirm these arrangements. He had similar goals in East Asia when he insisted on bringing the Soviet Union back to the position Russia had occupied in Manchuria prior to the Russo-Japanese War: this he finally achieved at the 1945 Yalta Conference in return for promising to enter the war against Japan. "My task as minister of foreign affairs was to expand the borders of our Fatherland," Molotov recalled proudly many years later. "And it seems that Stalin and I coped with this task quite well." . . .

⋅⟨⊙⟩⋅

From the West's standpoint, the critical question was how far Moscow's influence would extend *beyond* whatever Soviet frontiers turned out to be at the end of the war. Stalin had suggested to Milovan Djilas that the Soviet Union would impose its own social system as far as its armies could reach, but he was also very cautious. Keenly aware of the military power the United States and its allies had accumulated, Stalin was determined to do nothing that might involve the USSR in another devastating war until it had recovered sufficiently to be certain of winning it. "I do not wish to begin the Third World War over the Trieste question," he explained to disappointed Yugoslavs, whom he ordered to evacuate that territory in June 1945. Five years later, he would justify his decision not to intervene in the Korean War on the grounds that "the Second World War ended not long ago, and we are not ready for the Third World War." Just how far the expansion of Soviet influence would proceed depended, therefore, upon a careful balancing of opportunities against risks. . . .

Who or what was it, though, that set the limits? Did Stalin have a fixed list of countries he thought it necessary to dominate? Was he prepared to stop in the face of resistance within those countries to "squeezing out the capitalist order"? Or would expansion cease only when confronted with opposition from the remaining capitalist states, so that further advances risked war at a time when the Soviet Union was ill-prepared for it?

Stalin had been very precise about where he wanted Soviet boundaries changed; he was much less so on how far Moscow's sphere of influence was to extend. He insisted on having "friendly" countries around the periphery of the USSR, but he failed to specify how many would have to meet this standard. He called during the war for dismembering Germany, but by the end of it was denying that he had ever done so: that country would be temporarily divided, he told leading German communists in June 1945, and they themselves would eventually bring about its reunification. He never gave up on the idea of an eventual world revolution, but he expected this to result—as his comments to the Germans suggested—from an expansion of influence emanating from the Soviet Union itself. "[F]or the Kremlin," a well-placed spymaster recalled, "the mission of communism was primarily to consolidate the might of the Soviet state. Only military strength and domination of the countries on our borders could ensure us a superpower role."

But Stalin provided no indication—surely because he himself did not know—of how rapidly, or under what circumstances, this process would take place. He was certainly prepared to stop in the face of resistance from the West: at no point was he willing to challenge the Americans or even the British where they made their interests clear. . . . He quickly backed down when confronted with Anglo-American objections to his ambitions in Iran in the spring of 1946, as he did later that year after demanding Soviet bases in the Turkish Straits. This pattern of advance followed by retreat had shown up in the purges of the 1930s, which Stalin halted when the external threat from Germany became too great to ignore, and it would reappear with the Berlin Blockade and the Korean War, both situations in which the Soviet Union would show great caution after provoking an unexpectedly strong American response.

What all of this suggests, though, is not that Stalin had limited ambitions, only that he had no timetable for achieving them. Molotov retrospectively confirmed this: "Our ideology stands for offensive operations when possible, and if not, we wait." Given this combination of appetite with aversion to risk, one cannot help but wonder what would have happened had the West tried containment earlier. To the extent that it bears partial responsibility for the coming of the Cold War, the historian Vojtech Mastny has argued, that responsibility lies in its failure to do just that. . . .

Stalin's policy, then, was one of imperial expansion and consolidation differing from that of earlier empires only in the determination with which he pursued it, in the instruments of coercion with which he maintained it, and in the ostensibly anti-imperial justifications he put forward in support of it. It is a testimony to his skill, if not to his morality, that he was able to achieve so many of his imperial ambitions at a time when the tides of history were running against the idea of imperial domination—as colonial offices in London, Paris, Lisbon, and The Hague were finding out—and when his own country was recovering from one of the most brutal invasions in recorded history. The fact that Stalin was able to *expand* his empire when others were contracting and while the Soviet Union was as weak as it was requires explanation. Why did opposition to this process, within and outside Europe, take so long to develop?

One reason was that the colossal sacrifices the Soviet Union had made during the war against the Axis had, in effect, "purified" its reputation: the USSR and its leader had "earned" the right to throw their weight around, or so it seemed. Western governments found it difficult to switch quickly from viewing the Soviet Union as a glorious wartime ally to portraying it as a new and dangerous adversary. President Harry S. Truman and his future Secretary of State Dean Acheson—neither of them sympathetic in the slightest to communism—nontheless tended to give the Soviet Union the benefit of the doubt well into the early postwar era. . . .

Resistance to Stalin's imperialism also developed slowly because Marxism-Leninism at the time had such widespread appeal. It is difficult now to recapture the admiration revolutionaries outside the Soviet Union felt for that country before they came to know it well. . . . Because the Bolsheviks themselves had overcome one empire and had made a career of condemning others, it would take decades for people who were struggling to overthrow British, French, Dutch, or Portuguese colonialism to see that there could also be such a thing as Soviet imperialism. European communists—notably the Yugoslavs—saw this much earlier, but even to most of them it had not been apparent at the end of the war.

Still another explanation for the initial lack of resistance to Soviet expansionism was the fact that its repressive character did not become immediately apparent to all who were subjected to it. . . .

One has the impression that Stalin and the Eastern Europeans got to know one another only gradually. The Kremlin leader was slow to recognize that Soviet authority would not be welcomed everywhere beyond Soviet borders; but as he did come to see this he became all the more determined to impose it everywhere. The Eastern Europeans were slow to recognize how confining incorporation within a Soviet sphere was going to be; but as they did come to see this they became all the more determined to resist it, even if only by withholding, in a passive but sullen manner, the consent any regime needs to establish itself by means other than coercion. Stalin's efforts to consolidate his empire therefore made it at once more repressive and less secure. Meanwhile, an alternative vision of postwar Europe was emerging from the other great empire that established itself in the wake of World War II, that of the United States, and this too gave Stalin grounds for concern. . . .

⚜

What is there new to say about the old question of responsibility for the Cold War? Who actually started it? Could it have been averted? Here I think the "new" history is bringing us back to an old answer: that *as long as Stalin was running the Soviet Union a cold war was unavoidable.*

History is always the product of determined and contingent events: it is up to historians to find the proper balance between them. The Cold War could hardly have happened if there had not been a United States and a Soviet Union, if both had not emerged victorious from World War II, if they had not had conflicting visions of how to organize the postwar world. But these long-term trends did not in themselves *ensure* such a contest, because there is always room for the unexpected to undo what might appear to be inevitable. *Nothing* is ever completely predetermined, as real triceratops and other dinosaurs discovered 65 million years ago when the most recent large asteroid or comet or whatever it was hit the earth and wiped them out.

Individuals, not asteroids, more often personify contingency in history. Who can specify in advance—or unravel afterwards—the particular intersection of genetics, environment, and culture that makes each person unique? Who can foresee what weird conjunctions of design and circumstance may cause a very few individuals to rise so high as to shape great events, and so come to the attention of historians? Such people may set their sights on getting to the top, but an assassin, or a bacillus, or even a carelessly driven taxicab can always be lurking along the way. How entire countries fall into the hands of malevolent geniuses like Hitler and Stalin remains as unfathomable in the "new" Cold War history as in the "old."

Once leaders like these do gain power, however, certain things become highly probable. It is only to be expected that in an authoritarian state the chief authoritarian's personality will weigh much more heavily than those of democratic leaders, who have to share power. And whether because of social alienation, technological innovation, or economic desperation, the first half of the twentieth century was particularly susceptible to great authoritarians and all that resulted from their ascendancy. It is hardly possible to imagine Nazi Germany or the world war it caused without Hitler. I find it increasingly difficult, given what we know now, to imagine the Soviet Union or the Cold War without Stalin.

For the more we learn, the less sense it makes to distinguish Stalin's foreign policies from his domestic practices or even his personal behavior. Scientists have shown the natural world to be filled with examples of what they call "self-similarity across scale": patterns that persist whether one views them microscopically, macroscopically, or anywhere in between. Stalin was like that: he functioned in much the same manner whether operating within the international system, within his alliances, within his country, within his party, within his personal entourage, or even within his family. The Soviet leader waged cold wars on all of these fronts. The Cold War we came to know was only one of many from *his* point of view.

Nor did Stalin's influence diminish as quickly as that of most dictators after their deaths. He built a *system* sufficiently durable to survive not only his own demise but his successors' fitful and half-hearted efforts at "de-Stalinization." They were themselves its creatures, and they continued to work within it because they knew no other method of governing. Not until [Mikhail] Gorbachev was a Soviet leader fully prepared to dismantle Stalin's structural legacy. It tells us a lot that as it disappeared, so too did the Cold War and ultimately the Soviet Union itself.

This argument by no means absolves the United States and its allies of a considerable responsibility for how the Cold War was fought—hardly a surprising conclusion since they in fact won it. Nor is it to deny the feckless stupidity with which the Americans fell into peripheral conflicts like Vietnam, or their exorbitant expenditures on unusable weaponry: these certainly caused the Cold War to cost much more in money and lives than it otherwise might have. Nor is it to claim moral superiority for western statesmen. None was as bad as Stalin—or Mao—but the Cold War left no leader uncorrupted: the wielding of great power, even in the best of times, rarely does.

It is the case, though, that if one applies the always useful test of counterfactual history—drop a key variable and speculate as to what difference this might have made—Stalin's centrality to the origins of the Cold War becomes quite clear. For all of their importance, one could have removed Roosevelt, Churchill, Truman, Bevin, Marshall, or Acheson, and a cold war would still have probably followed the world war. If one could have eliminated Stalin, alternative paths become quite conceivable. For with the possible exception of Mao, no twentieth-century leader imprinted himself upon his country as thoroughly and with such lasting effect as Stalin did. And given his personal propensity for cold wars—a tendency firmly rooted long before he had even heard of Harry Truman—once Stalin wound up at the top in Moscow and once it was clear his state would survive the war, then it looks equally clear that there was going to be a Cold War whatever the west did. Who then was responsible? The answer, I think, is authoritarianism in general, and Stalin in particular.

POSTSCRIPT

Was President Truman Responsible for the Cold War?

Offner takes issue with President Truman's recent biographers, Robert H. Ferrell, *Harry S. Truman: A Life* (University of Missouri Press, 1994), Alonzo L. Hamby, *Man of the People: A Life* of Harry S. Truman (Oxford, 1995) and especially David McCullough's bestseller, *Truman* (Simon & Schuster, 1992), all of whom rank Truman among the near-great presidents. All of the most recent polls of presidents place Truman among the ten greatest. Offner calls Truman a "parochial nationalist." His outlook on foreign policy was ethnocentric in spite of his command in combat in a Missouri national guard unit in World War One. He deplored Europe's politics, customs and food. In his early writings, he expressed disdain for "chinks," "dagos," "niggers," "Jew clerks," "bohunks" and "Rooshans."

Brash and impulsive in temperament, Offner accuses Truman of making rash and quick decisions to cover over his insecurities. Truman, he says, often relied on strong personalities such as Boss Tom Pendergast, who pushed Truman up the ladder of Missouri politics and General George Marshall and career diplomat Dean Acheson among others who helped formulate "the containment policy" in 1946 to prevent the Russians from imposing an iron curtain around all of Europe.

Offner also charges the Truman administration of practicing "Atomic diplomacy" at the end of the war, when we were the sole possessor of the A-bomb, to make the Russians more manageable in Europe. He also argues that the Truman doctrine, the Marshall plan, refusing to compromise on the German questions and the formation of the North Atlantic Treaty Organization (NATO) run roughshod over a country who suffered many more military losses and severe damage to its economy and physical infrastructure.

In his attempt to place most of the blame for the cold war on Truman, Offner overstates his case. He calls Truman a parochial nationalist, yet the former President, though not formerly educated, read widely biographies of great leaders and military history. He also, as Offner admits, performed heroically as an officer in a Missouri national guard unit in combat and as a United States Senator supported FDR's foreign policy "on the World Court, neutrality revision, rearmament and Lend Lease for Britain and Russian before America's Entrance into World War Two."

Offner also downplays the uncertainties facing American foreign policy at the end of the war. For example, FDR had hoped that a revised international organization such as the United Nations might succeed in preventing future world wars because it would be stronger and supported by the major powers than the failed League of Nations.

Offner plays up Truman's insecurities which was true, but then accuses him of making both rash decisions and relying on strong foreign policy advisers such as George Kennan, George Marshall, and Dean Acheson. But why wouldn't Truman be insecure? He was chosen as vice president in 1944 to replace the controversial Henry Wallace because he came from Missouri, a border state that made him acceptable to southern conservative democrats, yet with a voting record that supported FDR's New Deal liberal domestic programs.

When he became president after Roosevelt's sudden death on April 12, 1945, Truman knew very little of the intricacies of Roosevelt's agreements with Churchill and Stalin. In fact, both Henry Stimson, the Secretary of Defense and Senator James Byrnes both claim to have informed Truman about the "Manhattan Project's" development of atomic bombs which would be ready for use in the summer of 1945.

Professor John Gaddis accepts the fact that Truman was insecure. He also believes that for all of 1945 up to early 1946, the Truman administration was responding to the political and economic uncertainties of the post-World War Two environment. While the United States took the lead in creating the World Bank and the International Monetary Fund to supply money for rebuilding Europe's destroyed infrastructure, these institutions were woefully inadequate to the task. It was also unclear whether the United States was going to re-enter its own recession as had occurred at the end of the First World War which turned into the great depression of the 1930s.

Gaddis believes that the united States created its Western European empire by invitation through the implementation of the Truman Doctrine, the Marshall Plan, the rebuilding of West Germany and the formation of NATO. On the other hand, Russia created its empire by force. Starting in Romania in 1945 and in Poland and Hungary in 1947 and ending with the murder or suicide of the Masuryk government in Czechoslovakia in 1948, the Russians imposed totalitarian governments on its citizens.

Gaddis places most of the blame for the cold war on Stalin, an authoritarian imperialist who "equated world revolution with the expanding influence of the Soviet state." Truman was constrained by the democratic electoral system of checks and balances and a Republican-controlled Congress from 1946 to 1948. But Stalin had no such constraints. He purged all his real and potential revolutionary opponents in the 1930s and also the late 1940s and pursued foreign policy objectives as a romantic revolutionary. What limits did Stalin have? Gaddis said Stalin was precisely where he wanted Soviet boundaries changed but was imprecise about how far Moscow's sphere of influence would extend without confronting Western resistance.

In summary, if Gorbachev was the Soviet leader in 1945, there may have been alternate paths to the cold war. But with Stalin in charge, says Gaddis, "there was going to be a cold war whatever the West did."

Gaddis' interpretation goes too far in blaming most of the cold war on Stalin. He argues that new sources from the former USSR and the Eastern European countries demonstrate the control that Stalin exerted. But as Tony Judt points out, these sources are quite limited and they do not tell us about the operations of the Politburo and the twelve men who along with Stalin made decisions. See Tony Judt, "Why the Cold War Worked," *The New York Review of Books* (October 9, 1997) and "A Story Still to be Told," *The New York Review of Books* (March 23, 2006) for critical reviews of Gaddis' *We Now Know: Rethinking Cold War History* (Oxford University Press, 1997) and *The Cold War: A New History* (Penguin Press, 2005). The best critiques of Gaddis are three of his earlier books, *The United States and the Origins of the Cold War, 1941–1947* (Columbia University Press, 1972), *Russia, the Soviet Union and the United States: An Interpretative History,* 2nd ed. (McGraw Hill, 1990) and *Strategies of Containment: A Critical Appraisal of America's Postwar Foreign Policy* (Oxford, 1978).

The literature on the cold war is enormous. Students who wish to study the cold war in greater detail should consult *Containment: Documents on American Policy and Strategy, 1945–1950* edited by Thomas H. Etzold and John Lewis Gaddis (Columbia University Press, 1978). Another comprehensive work is Melvyn P. Leffler, *A Preponderance of Power: National Security, the Truman Administration, and the Cold War* (Stanford University Press, 1992). The two best readers to excerpt the various viewpoints on the cold war are Thomas G. Paterson and Robert J. McMahon, eds., *The Origins of the Cold War,* 3rd ed. (D. C. Heath, 1991) and Melvyn P. Leffler and David S. Painter, eds., *Origins of the Cold War: An International History* (Routledge, 1994). Finally David Reynolds has edited a series of essays in *The Origins of the Cold War: International Perspectives* (Yale University Press, 1994).

Bibliographies are contained in all the previous books. The most up-to-date is Melvin P. Leffler, "Cold War and Global Hegemony, 1945–1991," *OAH Magazine of History* (March 2005). Gaddis' argument with the revisionists is nicely summarized in Karen J. Winkler, "Scholars Refight the Cold War," *The Chronicle of Higher Education* (March 2, 1994), pp. 8–10.

ISSUE 13

Was Rock and Roll Responsible for Dismantling America's Traditional Family, Sexual, and Racial Customs in the 1950s and 1960s?

YES: Glenn C. Altschuler, from *All Shook Up: How Rock and Roll Changed America* (Oxford University Press, 2003)

NO: J. Ronald Oakley, from *God's Country: America in the Fifties* (Dembner Books, 1986, 1990)

ISSUE SUMMARY

YES: Professor Glenn C. Altschuler maintains that rock and roll's "switchblade" beat opened wide divisions in American society along the fault lines of family, sexuality, and race.

NO: Writer J. Ronald Oakley argues that although the lifestyles of youth departed from their parents, their basic ideas and attitudes were still the conservative ones that mirrored the conservativism of the affluent age in which they grew up.

$\mathbf{M}$ost Americans assume that rock and roll has dominated American popular music since the 1950s, but this is not true. The phrase "rhythm and blues" was coined by the first white rock and roll Cleveland disc jockey Alan Freed who, when he went national, was pushed by a lawsuit in 1954 to abandon the name of his show from "The Moondog House" to "Rock 'n Roll Party." A black euphemism for sexual intercourse, "rock 'n roll" had appeared as early as 1922 in a blues song and was constantly used by black singers into the early 1950s. It's not clear whether DJ Freed consciously made the name change to cultivate a broader audience, but that is precisely what happened. The phrase caught on, and Freed and station WINS secured a copyright for it.

Rock and roll was a fashion of rhythm and blues, black gospel, and country-western music. It combined black and white music, which explains why so many of the early rock singers came from the south and recorded their hit songs in New Orleans or Memphis. Between 1953 and 1955, the first true rockers—Fats Domino, Chuck Berry, and Little Richard—were African-American. Fats Domino came from New Orleans, sang from his piano, and sold over 65 million records between 1949 and 1960, including "Ain't That a Shame," "I'm Walking," and "Blueberry Hill." Even more influential because of his electric guitar riffs, body and leg gyrations, and songs full of wit and clever wordplay was Chuck Berry, whose lifestyle (he did two stints in prison) and songs ("Maybellene," "Johnny B. Good," and "Roll Over Beethoven") influenced two generations of rockers, including sixties British rock bands the Beatles and the Rolling Stones. Another rocker, Little Richard, known as "the Georgia Peach," became famous as much for his flamboyant style of dress with his towering hair and multicolored clothes that reflected a teasing sexuality. He created a string of hits—"Tutti Frutti," "Long Tall Sally," and "Good Golly Miss Molly"—which were recorded as cover records by white artists like Pat Boone. Best known today for his Geico commercial, Little Richard scared the hell out of the parents from white middle-class America.

More threatening to middle-class white American parents was Elvis Presley, the king of rock and roll, and the most influential pop icon in the history of America, but Elvis was not the inventor of rock and roll. His voice was average, and his songs (written by others) were often mediocre. But his rugged good looks and his sexy gyrations on the stage threw young girls into spasms. Most importantly, he was white. More than 30 years after his death, Elvis still defines the age of rock and roll. He continues to sell records, which number over a billion.

Presley was the first star to take advantage of the new teenage consumer market. By the middle 1950s there were 16.5 million teenagers, half in high school and the other half in college or the work force, who possessed a lot of disposable income, available via allowances or part-time jobs. Suburban teenagers had their own rooms replete with radios and record players. "By the end of 1957," says Professor Altschuler, "seventy-eight Elvis Presley items had grossed $55 million." Presley helped plug the products, making personal appearances in department stores. Fans could purchase shoes, skirts, blouses, T-shirts, sweaters, charm bracelets, handkerchiefs, purses, etc. inscribed "Sincerely Yours."

There is little argument that a new generation of teenagers had emerged in the fifties. Historians can trace the adolescent generations to the early twentieth century. The gap between parent and child always existed, but the new value system that set apart the two generations might have occurred earlier had the great depression and World War II not intervened. Television shows were geared to the very young and the parents. Radio had lost its nightly sitcoms to television and switched to news and music formats. Teenagers were tired of their parents' sentimental croon and swoon ballads that did not address their feelings. New DJs emerged, who played the rock and roll songs for teenagers who sat in their rooms pretending to do their homework.

How radical was rock and roll music? Was it responsible for the revolution in values that took place in the 1960s? In the first selection, Professor Glenn C. Altschuler argues that "rock 'n roll" deepened the divide between the generations, helped teenagers differentiate themselves from others, transformed popular culture in the United States, and rattled the reticent by pushing sexuality into the public arena. But writer J. Ronald Oakley disagrees. "Although their lifestyle had departed from the conventions of their elders," Oakley believes "their basic ideas and attitudes were still the conservative ones that mirrored the conservativism of the affluent age in which they grew up."

YES

Glenn C. Altschuler

"All Shook Up": Popular Music and American Culture, 1945–1955

Rock 'n' Roll Fight Hospitalizes Youth, the *New York Times* announced on April 15, 1957. In a fracas between white and black boys and girls following a rock 'n' roll show attended by ten thousand fans, fifteen-year-old Kenneth Myers of Medford, Massachusetts, was stabbed and thrown onto the tracks at a subway station. Myers missed touching a live rail by inches and scrambled back onto the platform seconds before a train sped into the station. "The Negro youths were responsible for it," police lieutenant Francis Gannon told reporters. "The fight was senseless . . . but we expect difficulty every time a rock 'n' roll show comes in."

For two years the *Times* printed dozens of articles linking destructive activities at, outside, or in the aftermath of concerts to "the beat and the booze" or the music alone. Public interest in rock 'n' roll was so great, *Times* editors even viewed the absence of a riot as newsworthy. "Rock 'n' Rollers Collect Calmly," readers learned, following a concert at the Paramount Theater in New York City. The journalist attributed the good order on this occasion and several others that year to the police, who arrived early and in force, as many as three hundred strong, some of them on horseback, to set up wooden barriers along the sidewalk, separate the crowd from passersby on Times Square, and then station themselves in the aisles and at the rear of the theater to keep the audience "under surveillance." During the performances, the fans "cheered, shrieked, applauded, and jumped up and down." A few dancers were escorted back to their seats, and the police ordered several excited fans who stood up to sit down. But no one had to be removed or arrested for "obstreperous" behavior. The implication was clear: teenage rock 'n' rollers should not be left on their own.

Reports of riotous behavior convinced many public officials to ban live rock 'n' roll shows. After frenzied fans in San Jose, California, "routed" seventy-three policemen, neighboring Santa Cruz refused permits for concerts in public buildings. Mayor Bernard Berry and two commissioners in Jersey City, New Jersey, decided not to allow Bill Haley and the Comets to perform in the municipally owned Roosevelt Stadium. Following several fistfights at a dance attended by 2,700 teenagers that were broken up by

From *All Shook Up: How Rock and Roll Changed America*, (Oxford University Press, 2003), pp. 3–4, 6–8, 10–18, 19–34. Copyright © 2003 by Glenn C. Altschuler. Reprinted by permission of Oxford University Press, Ltd.

twelve police officers, the city council of Asbury Park, New Jersey, ruled that "swing and blues harmonies" would no longer be permitted. . . .

In the mass media, however, alarmists drowned out apologists. That pop singers would not like the competition might be expected, but their condemnations of rock 'n' roll were especially venomous. It "smells phony and false," said Frank Sinatra, at whose feet bobby-soxers had swooned and shrieked in the 1940s. "It is sung, played, and written for the most part by cretinous goons, and by means of its almost imbecilic reiteration and sly, lewd, in plain fact dirty, lyrics it manages to be the martial music of every side-burned delinquent on the face of the earth." Therapists weighed in as well. *Time* magazine informed readers that psychologists believed that teenagers embraced rock 'n' roll because of a deep-seated, abnormal need to belong. Allegiances to favorite performers, *Time* warned, "bear passing resemblance to Hitler's mass meetings." The *New York Times* provided a platform to psychiatrist Francis Braceland, who had a similar view. Branding rock 'n' roll "a cannibalistic and tribalistic" form of music that appealed to the insecurity and rebelliousness of youth, he thought it all the more dangerous because it was "a communicable disease."

A few went further, declaring the music of teenagers a tool in a conspiracy to ruin the morals of a generation of Americans. In their best-seller *U.S.A. Confidential*, journalists Jack Lait and Lee Mortimer linked juvenile delinquency "with tom-toms and hot jive and ritualistic orgies of erotic dancing, weed-smoking and mass mania, with African jungle background. Many music shops purvey dope; assignations are made in them. White girls are recruited for colored lovers. . . .We know that many platter-spinners are hopheads. Many others are Reds, left-wingers, or hecklers of social convention. . . . Through disc jockeys, kids get to know colored and other musicians; they frequent places the radio oracles plug, which is done with design . . . to hook juves [juveniles] and guarantee a new generation subservient to the Mafia."

Rock 'n' roll generated sound and fury. What, if anything, did it signify? The rise of rock 'n' roll and the reception of it, in fact, can tell us a lot about the culture and values of the United States in the 1950s. According to historian James Gilbert, there was a struggle throughout the decade "over the uses of popular culture to determine who would speak, to what audience, and for what purpose." At the center of that struggle, rock 'n' roll unsettled a nation that had been "living in an 'age of anxiety'" since 1945.

The Cold War produced numerous foreign crises—the Berlin Airlift and the Korean War among them. A fear of internal subversion by Communists, stoked by the often irresponsible charges of Senator Joseph McCarthy, resulted in loyalty oaths, blacklists, and a more general suppression of dissent. In a national poll conducted in 1954, more than 50 percent of Americans agreed that all known Communists should be jailed; 58 percent favored finding and punishing all Communists, "even if some innocent people should be hurt"; and a whopping 78 percent thought reporting to the FBI neighbors or acquaintances they suspected of being Communists a good idea. Coinciding with the Cold War, of course, was the nuclear age, and the possibility of a war that would obliterate the human race. The construction of fallout shelters, and instructions to schoolchildren about how to survive an atomic attack ("Fall instantly face down, elbows out, forehead on arms, eyes shut . . . duck and cover"), probably alarmed as much as they reassured.

The family seemed as vulnerable as the nation to internal subversion in the 1950s. "Not even the Communist conspiracy," U.S. Senator Robert Hendrickson asserted, "could devise a more effective way to demoralize, confuse, and destroy" the United States than the behavior of apathetic, absent, or permissive parents. Americans worried about working moms, emasculated dads, and especially about a growing army of teenage terrors, poised to seize control of the house, lock, stock, and living room. These fears, Gilbert has shown, crystallized in a decade-long crusade against juvenile delinquency, replete with dozens of congressional hearings and hundreds of pieces of legislation to regulate youth culture.

Finally, a principled and persistent civil rights movement demanded in the 1950s that the commitment to equal rights for African Americans no longer be deferred. With the Supreme Court decision in *Brown v. Board of Education*, the Montgomery, Alabama, Bus Boycott, and the use of federal troops to escort black students into heretofore all-white Little Rock Central High School in Arkansas, a revolution in race relations was well under way. Americans in the North as well as the South were not at all sure where it was headed.

Rock 'n' roll entered indirectly into Cold War controversies, but in helping young Americans construct social identities, it did provide a discourse through which they could examine and contest the meanings adults ascribed to family, sexuality, and race. That discourse was not always verbal. Rock 'n' roll moved audiences as much with the body language of performers and the beat of the music as with its lyrics, perhaps more. When rock 'n' roll tries to criticize something, critic Greil Marcus believes, "it becomes hopelessly self-righteous and stupid." When the music is most exciting, "when the guitar is fighting for space in the clatter while voices yelp and wail as one man finishes another's lines or spins it off in a new direction—the lyrics are blind baggage, and they emerge only in snatches." Without a consistent or coherent critique, and never fully free from an attachment to traditional 1950s values, rock 'n' roll nonetheless provided a fresh perspective, celebrating leisure, romance, and sex, deriding deferred gratification and men in gray flannel suits stationed at their office desks, and delighting in the separate world of the teenager.

According to media commentator Jeff Greenfield, by unleashing a perception that young bodies were "Joy Machines," rock 'n' roll set off "the first tremors along the Generational Fault," paving the way for the 1960s. "Nothing we see in the Counterculture," Greenfield claims, "not the clothes, the hair, the sexuality, the drugs, the rejection of reason, the resort to symbols and magic—none of it is separable from the coming to power in the 1950s of rock and roll music. Brewed in the hidden corners of black American cities, its rhythms infected white Americans, seducing them out of the kind of temperate bobby-sox passions out of which Andy

Hardy films are spun. Rock and roll was elemental, savage, dripping with sex; it was just as our parents feared." . . .

The Zeitgeist was evident on the new mass medium, television. Installed in nearly two-thirds of American households by 1955, television spread the gospel of prosperity, barely acknowledging the existence of poverty or conflict. Whether dramas were set in the Old West of Marshal Matt Dillon or the courtroom of Perry Mason, viewers had no difficulty distinguishing right from wrong or the good guys from the bad guys. In the end, justice was always done. Situation comedies, the reigning genre of the 1950s, presented a lily-white, suburban United States, full of happy housewives like June Cleaver, fathers like Jim Anderson, who knew best, and cute kids like the Beaver, whose biggest dilemma was the size of his allowance. TV commercials suggested that every viewer could easily afford the most modern appliance and the latest model automobile. When African Americans appeared on the small screen, they played chauffeurs, maids, and janitors or sang and danced. The small screen, then, was mainstream. Another America might be glimpsed occasionally on an Edward R. Murrow documentary, or *Playhouse 90*, or the Army-McCarthy hearings, but with the nightly network news limited to fifteen minutes, television rarely left viewers uncertain or scared.

In the early '50s, popular music sent similar messages. Bing Crosby and Perry Como sang soothing, romantic ballads, while the orchestras of Mantovani, Hugo Winterhalter, Percy Faith, and George Cates created mood music for middle-of-the-road mid-lifers, who hummed and sang along in elevators and dental offices. Seeking to create a calm, warm environment for men and women who made love with the lights out, pop singers, according to Arnold Shaw, adhered to the following precepts: "Don't sing out—croon, hum, reflect, daydream. Wish on a star, wink at the moon, laze in the sun. . . . Accentuate the positive, eliminate the negative. . . . DO stick with Mister In-Between." Popular black singers—Nat King Cole and Johnny Mathis—harmonized with white tastes, in style, sound, and lyrics. As late as 1955, the top five on the pop charts were "Unchained Melody," "The Ballad of Davy Crockett," "Cherry Pink and Apple-Blossom White," "The Yellow Rose of Texas," and "Melody of Love." Those who knew physical activity began after "I give my heart to you . . ." did not want to talk about it.

Another sound, however, was available. Before it was supplanted by rock 'n' roll, rhythm and blues provided a dress rehearsal on a smaller stage for the agitation that reached the *New York Times* in the second half of the decade. After World War II, the industry substituted rhythm and blues for the harsher-sounding "race records" as the term for recordings by black artists that were not gospel or jazz. But R&B also emerged as a distinctive musical genre, drawing on the rich musical traditions of African Americans, including the blues' narratives of turbulent emotions, and the jubilation, steady beat, hand clapping, and call and response of gospel. Rhythm and blues tended to be "good time music," with an emphatic dance rhythm. Its vocalists shouted, growled, or falsettoed over guitars and pianos, bass drums stressing a 2–4 beat, and a honking tenor saxophone. "Body music rather than head or heart music," according to Arnold Shaw, appealing to the flesh more than the spirit, rhythm and blues "embodied the fervor of gospel music, the throbbing vigor of boogie woogie, the jump beat of swing, and the gutsiness and sexuality of life in the black ghetto."

Three strains of rhythm and blues music appealed to that market. Louis Jordan was the premier exponent of "the jump blues." Born in Brinkley, arkansas in 1908, Jordan played alto sax with the bands of Louis Armstrong and Chick Webb before forming his own combo, the Tympany Five, in 1938. A showman in the tradition of Cab Calloway, Jordan cut records that for a decade kept him at or near the top of the "Harlem Hit Parade," *Billboard* magazine's title for its black charts. But Jordan's exuberant hits, unlike those of Calloway, the Mills Brothers, or Nat King Cole, drew on the manners, mores, and hazards of life in the ghetto.

Jordan's earthy themes, vernacular language, and humorous, amorous, and amused tone are evident in the titles of his songs: "The Chicks I Pick Are Slender, Tender, and Tall," "Is You Is or Is You Ain't Ma Baby?," "Reet, Petite, and Gone," "Beans and Cornbread," "Saturday Night Fish Fry," and "What's the Use of Gettin' Sober (When You Gonna Get Drunk Again)?" Urban blacks may have felt they were laughing, from a distance, at their lower-class, hayseed cousins. Or, as Shaw suggests, Jordan may have communicated to his audience that he was self-confident enough to laugh at himself.

More romantic and idealistic were the vocal or street-corner "doo-wop" groups, whose output resembled the standard juvenile fare of white pop music. These balladeers preferred the "preliminaries" and "hearts and kisses" to sweaty sex, in such songs as "Hopefully Yours" (the Larks), "I'm a Sentimental Fool" (the Marylanders), and "Golden Teardrops" (the Flamingoes). On occasion, as R&B historian Brian Ward suggests, the grain of the voices, the tone of the instruments, and the manipulation of harmonies and rhythms subverted the saccharine lyrics, hinting at "barely contained lust and sexual expectancy." The dominant theme of "doo-wop," though, was adolescent longing and loss.

The third and most controversial strain dominated and defined rhythm and blues. It appealed to urban blacks who had fled from deference and demeaning employment in the South but remained powerless to control key aspects of their lives. Perhaps in compensation, R&B "shouters" proclaimed—and sometimes parodied—their independence and sexual potency with a pounding beat and lyrics that could be vulgar, raunchy, and misogynist. "Let me bang your box," shouted the Toppers; "Her machine is full of suds . . . it will cost you 30 cents a pound," proclaimed the Five Royales. One of the most talented of the shouters was Nebraska native Wynonie Harris, a tall, dapper, handsome man who billed himself as the "hard-drinkin', hard-lovin', hard-shoutin' Mr. Blues." Harris's biggest hit, "Good Rockin' Tonight," recorded in 1947, was vintage jump blues, but he made a career bellowing songs about sex. Telling readers of *Tan* magazine that "deep down in their hearts" black women "wanted a hellion, a rascal," Harris sang of "cheatin' women" and men who were better off satisfying their needs with a mechanical "Lovin' Machine" in songs like "I Want My Fanny Brown" and "I Like My Baby's Pudding." Harris's idol and sometime partner in duets, Big Joe Turner, also found love "nothin' but a lot of misery," but in the macho tradition of R&B shouters, he refused to whine: "Turn off the water works," he tells his woman. "That don't move me no mo'."

Shouters made good use of a new instrument, the electric guitar. The first mass-produced, solid-body electric guitar, the Fender Esquire, became available in 1950. By eliminating the diaphragm top of the acoustic guitar, Leo Fender helped musicians amplify each string cleanly, without feedback. Electricity, argues music historian Michael Lydon, provided "that intensity that made non-believers call it noisy when played low, but made believers know it had to be played loud." In the hands of a master, like bluesman Aaron "T-Bone" Walker, the electric guitar could also be a stage prop, held behind the head when he did the splits, and a phallic symbol, pressed against the body or pointed provocatively at the audience.

In the '40s and early '50s, rhythm and blues fought its way onto the radio and records. As the Federal Communications Commission sifted through a backlog of applications for new radio stations at the end of World War II, white entrepreneurs founded independent stations aimed at urban African Americans, who in the aggregate had considerable disposable income—and nearly all of whom owned radios. In late 1948 and early 1949, WDIA in Memphis abandoned white pop to become the first radio station in the United States to program entirely for blacks, putting former school-teacher Nat D. Williams on the air as its first black announcer. Its ratings began to climb. Within a few years, 70 percent of the African-Americans in Memphis turned to the station at some time during the day. When thousands in the mid-South joined them, national advertisers flocked to WDIA. Stations throughout the country began to expand "Negro appeal programming." In 1949, WWEZ in New Orleans hired a black DJ, Vernon Winslow ("Doctor Daddy-O"), for "Jivin' with Jax"; that same year, WEDR in Birmingham, Alabama, went all black, and WERD in Atlanta became black owned and operated. Farther west, in Flagstaff, Arizona, KGPH began to feature R&B in 1952. By the mid-'50s, twenty-one stations in the country were "all black"; according to a "Buyer's Guide" survey, more than six hundred stations in thirty-nine states, including WWRL in New York City, WWDC in Washington, D.C., and WDAS in Philadelphia, aired "Negro-slanted" shows. In 1953, *Variety* noted that the "strong upsurge in R&B" provided employment for black disc jockeys, with some five hundred of them "spotted on stations in every city where there is a sizable colored population."

The dramatic shift toward television as the entertainment medium of choice for white adults helped convince executives to reorient radio toward young people's music, and particularly R&B. The kids stayed with radio throughout the '50s, as transistors replaced large, heat-generating vacuum tubes, and cheap portable radios and car radios became available. By 1959, 156 million radios were in working order in the United States, three times the number of TV sets.

As R&B found a niche on radio, independent record producers established R&B labels. The major companies—Capitol, Columbia,
Decca, Mercury, MGM, and RCA—stuck with pop music, leaving R&B
to the "indies." The latter could compete because after 1948 they could
acquire high-quality, low-cost recording equipment. Because producers
paid composers and performers as little as $10 and a case of whiskey per
song (Bo Diddley once referred to R&B as "Ripoffs and Bullshit"), they
could break even with sales of only 1,500 units. Between 1948 and 1954,
a thousand "indies" went into business. Unlike the majors, whose offices
were in New York City, independents spread across the country. Founded
by former jukebox operators, nightclub owners, music journalists, and
record manufacturers, only some of whom (like Ahmet Ertegun and Jerry
Wexler of Atlantic) knew a lot about music and almost all of whom were
white, independent producers grossed $15 million in 1952, much of it
on R&B. "I looked for an area neglected by the majors," confessed Art
Rupe, founder of Specialty Records in Los Angeles, "and in essence took
the crumbs off the table in the record industry."

Bottom-line businessmen, independent producers, and radio station
operators often exploited R&B artists, but many of them recognized and
endorsed the role that the music industry was playing in the struggle for
civil rights. Following World War II, which was in no small measure a war
against racism, some progress had been made. When he broke the color
barrier in baseball in 1947 Jackie Robinson had, in essence, put the nation
on notice that the days of segregation were numbered. A year later, by
executive order, President Harry Truman ended the practice in the army. But
the hard battles had yet to be fought, let alone won. The laws in southern
states separating the races in schools, buses, trains, and public swimming
pools and bathrooms had been upheld by the U.S. Supreme Court in a
decision, *Plessy v. Ferguson* (1896), that was still in force. Many southerners
remained implacably racist. "The Negro is different," insisted Ross Barnett,
governor of Mississippi, "because God made him different to punish him.
His fore-head slants back. His nose is different. His legs are different, and his
color is sure different." Such attitudes made it impossible in 1955 to convict
the murderers of black teenager Emmett Till, whose crime was daring to
converse with (and perhaps whistle at) a young white woman. Race mixing
of any kind, according to Barnett, was unnatural and unthinkable: "We will
not drink from the cup of genocide."

In the North, racial antipathy was often muted but no less real.
Discrimination in employment in the public and private sectors was
pervasive, and African Americans often had to take the most menial jobs.
While segregation was not legal in any northern state, the races remained
largely separate, with many white neighborhoods implacably opposed to
black renters or owners of apartments or houses. The migration of blacks
to the North made the situation more volatile. In 1951, Harvey Clark, a
graduate of Fisk University, moved his family's furniture into an apartment
they had leased in Cicero, Illinois. When the Clarks' van arrived, the police
intervened and an officer struck him, advising the veteran of World War II

to leave the area "or you'll get a bullet through you." When Clark persisted, four thousand whites trashed the apartment building, destroying furniture and plumbing while the police were "out of town." As the NAACP tried to raise funds to replace the Clarks' furniture, a grand jury investigated, only to return an indictment against an NAACP lawyer, the owner of the apartment, her lawyer, and the rental agent, for conspiring to reduce property values by causing "depreciation in the market selling price." Months later a federal grand jury did indict police and city officials for violating the civil rights of the Clarks, but even then three of the seven defendants were acquitted. Occurring in one of the most "southern" of northern cities, the Cicero riot was hardly a typical occurrence in the 1950s, but it served as a graphic reminder that "the Negro problem" was a national problem.

The music business could not solve the problem, of course, but because it depended so heavily on African-American writers and performers, civil rights advocates pressed record producers and radio station owners to promote integration—and practice what they preached. In his monthly column on rhythm and blues in the music industry publication *Cash Box*, Sam Evans pushed for the employment of more African Americans in all phases of the business. When NBC's San Francisco outlet KNBC hired Wallace Ray in May 1952, Evans detected a "fast growing trend." A qualified black, he suggested, is always available to fill the job: "In short course we expect to find a fair and equal representation, racially speaking, in the record manufacturing and distribution biz." Ernie and George Leaner became the agents for OKeh Records, a division of Columbia, in seven midwestern states, Evans informed readers a few months later, not because they "are Negroes, or because they are fat or skinny, or because they are tall or short. But just because the boys are good sound businessmen and know how to run a record distributing company." Evans took an entire column to sum up racial progress in the jukebox, recording, radio, and television businesses. "We have seen supposedly insurmountable barriers broken down," he claimed. In addition to "Negro talent" onstage, "many industry companies, and allied branches, are today employing young Negro people in positions of responsibility and trust. The day when the Negro was automatically delegated to the broom department is a thing of the past. Now we see typists, accountants, bookkeepers, receptionists, road managers, traveling representatives, A&R [artist and repertoire] men, publicity men, publishers, staff radio announcers, staff radio engineers, plus many other jobs, and all drawn from the huge Negro labor market." With praise came a plea that all applicants for employment be judged "only by personal qualifications rather than by skin pigmentation." In the next decade, as high schools and colleges turned out thousands of educated African-American men and women, Evans predicted, the clarion call would be "Give us jobs, and we will win the Freedom."

Even if the music industry did not discriminate in hiring—and Evans's account was far too sanguine—its most important role was not behind the scenes. Mitch Miller, A&R man for Columbia Records and, it would turn out, no friend of rock 'n' roll, suggested that as whites listened to

African-American music and cheered performers on the stage, they struck a blow for racial understanding and harmony. Since jazz and the blues reached relatively few whites, R&B probably had the greatest impact. "By their newfound attachment to rhythm and blues," Miller wrote, "young people might also be protesting the Southern tradition of not having anything to do with colored people. There is a steady—and healthy—breaking down of color barriers in the United States; perhaps the rhythm and blues rage—I am only theorizing—is another expression of it."

In the short run, at least, Miller proved to be too sanguine, too. White teenagers were listening, but as they did a furor erupted over R&B. Good enough for blacks, apparently, the music seemed downright dangerous as it crossed the color line.

Actually buying R&B records required some effort. Most music stores in white neighborhoods did not stock them. Until 1954, New Yorkers usually went to 125th Street to buy best-selling R&B platters. Neither the stores on Broadway nor any Madison Avenue shop carried them. On radio, rhythm and blues got airtime primarily on small, independent stations, and even then, Sam Evans reported, "in the very early hours of the morning or late at night."

In pursuit of R&B, however, white teenagers proved to be resolute and resourceful. At the Dolphin Record Store, located in an African-American neighborhood in Los Angeles, about 40 percent of the customers for rhythm and blues in 1952 were white. There, and in other stores in ethnic neighborhoods, in addition to R&B, the stock included the multicultural musical fare produced in the city. In 1948, for example, "Pachuco Boogie," a song blending Mexican speech patterns with African-American scat singing and blues harmonies, sold two million copies.

Whites habituated black nightclubs throughout the country as well. Although some clubs, fearing trouble from the authorities, restricted them to "white spectator tickets," forbidding them to dance or even sit down, "the whites kept on coming," Chuck Berry remembered. . . .

The vast majority of R&B fans remained orderly, obedient, and buttoned down, but rhythm and blues did release inhibitions and reduce respect for authority in enough teenagers to give credibility to charges that the music promoted licentious behavior. "The first time I ever saw a guy put his hand down a girl's pants was at the Paramount," explained a white fan of Chuck Berry. As a teenager in Granite City, Illinois, Bonnie Bramlett went to the Harlem Club in East St. Louis, even though she knew it "was definitely the wrong neighborhood for white girls." She and her friends had a wonderful time, "sneakin' and smokin' and drinkin' and doin' damn near everything."

By 1954, *Cash Box* was reporting that as R&B records received greater airplay, "the complaints are pouring in from parents." Unless record companies stopped producing all "suggestive and risque" songs, the publication predicted, adults would prohibit their children from purchasing any R&B records, and the goose that had been laying golden eggs would perish.

The call for self-regulation did not go unheeded. After 1954, R&B records were less raspy and raunchy, with more of the "sweet stylings" of vocal groups like Frankie Lymon and the Teenagers ("Why Do Fools Fall in Love?") and Little Anthony and the Imperials ("Tears on My Pillow"). By then, however, the battleground had shifted: rock 'n' roll had gotten its name.

Alan Freed is generally credited with using the phrase to describe rhythm and blues. Born in Windber, Pennsylvania, just south of Johnstown, in 1921, Freed got his first experience with radio broadcasting when he was a student at Ohio State. A successful disc jockey in Akron, he moved to Cleveland in 1950, first to introduce movies on WXEL-TV, and then as the host of "Request Review" on WJW radio. Freed learned about rhythm and blues from Leo Mintz, the owner of Record Rendezvous, located near Cleveland's black ghetto, and began to showcase R&B music on his show. Billing himself as "Alan Freed, King of the Moondoggers," the DJ rang a cowbell, banged a telephone book, and bellowed a Negro-inflected patter into the microphone as he spun the platters. Freed had a "teenager's mind funneled into 50,000 watts," wrote Clark Whelton of the *New York Times*. He "jumped into radio like a stripper into Swan Lake," giving listeners the musical equivalent of a front-row seat for the San Francisco earthquake: "Freed knocked down the buildings you hated and turned the rest into dance floors."

Black and white listeners, in the city and the suburbs, responded enthusiastically to the music and Freed's showmanship and sincerity. "The Moondog House" became the hottest show in town. With a national reputation, Freed in 1953 took on the management of the Moonglows and the Coronets, organized a concert tour. "The Biggest Rhythm and Blues Show," that opened in Revere, Massachusetts, and closed in New Orleans, and reached an agreement with WNJR to rebroadcast "The Moondog House" in Newark, New Jersey. So great was Freed's perceived power that after he became the first white DJ in Cleveland to play "Crying in the Chapel," by the Orioles, he got the credit for the thirty thousand records of the song sold in the city the next day! In 1954 Freed moved to WINS and soon became the dominant nighttime personality on radio in New York City.

In November, he faced a crisis. Thomas Louis Hardin, a blind street musician, composer, and beggar, who set up shop outside Carnegie Hall, decked out in shabby Viking garb, playing triangular drums he called trimbas, claimed that he had used the name "Moondog" for many years. Charging that Freed had "infringed" on his name, Hardin sued. When it turned out that Freed had played Hardin's recording of "Moondog Symphony" on his program, Judge Carroll Walter awarded Hardin $5,700 and forbade Freed from using the name "Moondog."

Initially "very angry and shocked," Freed quickly decided to change the name of his show to "Rock 'n' Roll Party." He had, in fact, occasionally used the phrase in Cleveland to describe his program, though he did not apply it specifically to the music he played. A black euphemism for sexual intercourse, "rock 'n' roll" had appeared in a song title as early as 1922, when blues singer Trixie Smith recorded "My Daddy Rocks Me (With One Steady Roll)." In 1931, Duke Ellington cut "Rockin' Rhythm," and three years later the Boswell Sisters sang "Rock and Roll." After Wynonie Harris's hit "Good Rockin' Tonight," in 1948 so many songs mentioned rock or rockin' that *Billboard* complained Connie Jordan's "I'm Gonna Rock" was the "umpteenth variation" on Harris's title. In 1952, a Rockin' Records Company did a brisk business in Los Angeles.

"Rock 'n' roll," then, was not, as Freed later claimed, an "inspirational flash" that came to him as a "colorful and dynamic" description of the "rolling, surging beat of the music." Nor did he use the phrase to eliminate the racial stigma of "rhythm and blues." Whether or not Freed consciously sought "to cultivate a broader audience" for the music—that is precisely what happened. With a sale of forty thousand records in the late '40s an R&B hit might reach the Top Ten; a rock 'n' roll smash would sell over a million.

As it entered popular discourse, rock 'n' roll was a social construction and not a musical conception. It was, by and large, what DJs and record producers and performers said it was. In any event, the phrase caught on, and Freed and WINS secured a copyright for it. Louis Jordan might complain, with considerable justification, that "rock 'n' roll was just a white imitation, a white adaptation of Negro rhythm and blues." What's in a name? Alan Freed's choice allowed fans to affirm—without having to think about it—that rock 'n' roll was a distinctive, not a derivative, musical form.

A few months before Freed started plugging his radio "Rock 'n' Roll Party," *Billboard* magazine welcomed a "potent new chanter who can sock over a tune for either the country or the R&B markets. . . . A strong new talent." By 1955, he would be hailed as a rock 'n' roll sensation.

Elvis Aron Presley was born in 1935 in Tupelo, Mississippi. His father, Vernon, a drifter, worked sporadically as a farmer or truck driver; Gladys, his mother, kept the family together. She lavished love on her only child (a twin brother, Jessie Garon, was stillborn). In 1948, when Vernon got a job in a paint factory, the Presleys moved to Memphis. As a teenager, Elvis developed the unique and self-contradictory combination of rebelliousness and adherence to conventional values he would exhibit throughout his life—and bequeath to rock 'n' roll. At Humes High School, he joined ROTC, the Biology Club, the English Club, the History Club, and the Spanish Club. With his family, he attended the Pentecostal Assembly of God. He enjoyed the music of Bing Crosby, Perry Como, Eddie Fisher, and Dean Martin. At the same time, Elvis imagined himself the hero of comic books and movies and contrived to let everyone know he was different. He let his sideburns grow long and got kicked off the high school football team for refusing to cut his hair. He bought clothes at Lansky's on Beale Street, a store patronized by blacks, dressed often in his favorite colors, pink and black, and kept his shirt collar up in back and his hair pomaded in a wave. Elvis later remembered that when his classmates saw him walking down the street, they yelled, "Hot dang, let's get him, he's a squirrel, get him, he just come down outta the trees."

A misfit and an outcast, Elvis was, in essence, a southern juvenile delinquent. Journalist Stanley Booth has described the type, "lounging on the hot concrete of a gas station on a Saturday afternoon, stopping for a second on the sidewalk as if they were looking for someone who was looking for a fight. You could even see their sullen faces, with a toughness lanky enough to just miss being delicate, looking back at you out of old photographs of the Confederate Army. . . . All outcasts with their contemporary costumes of duck-ass haircuts, greasy Levi's, motorcycle boots, T-shirts for day and black leather jackets for evening wear. Even their unfashionably long sideburns (Elvis' were furry) expressed contempt for the American Dream they were too poor to be part of." And yet, Booth concludes, Elvis was an especially daring delinquent, unwilling to become a mechanic, housepainter, bus driver, or cop, as so many "hoods" did. With volcanic ambition, he aspired to become a singer, and a star.

Elvis taught himself chord progressions on the guitar his mother gave him, as he listened to WDIA or the phonograph. A regular at Ellis Auditorium's All-Night Gospel Singings, he was mesmerized by the amplitude of some spirituals and the delicacy of others. Although his parents disapproved, Elvis kept listening to blues men Big Bill Broonzy and Arthur Crudup. African-American music, Greil Marcus speculates, gave him more excitement than he could get from the "twangs and laments" of country music. It provided "a beat, sex, celebration, the stunning nuances of the blues and the roar of horns and electric guitars."

After he graduated from Humes, Elvis drove a truck and worked as a machinist and as an usher at the movies. He gave his paycheck to Gladys Presley but kept enough money for his clothes and accessories. In 1953, he appeared with his beat-up guitar in the office of Sun Studios in Memphis. He wanted to make a record to surprise his mother, he said, but "if you know anyone that wants a singer . . ." "Who do you sound like?" the receptionist asked. "I don't sound like nobody." Elvis recorded two Ink Spots songs, "My Happiness" and "That's When Your Heartaches Begin," with Sam Phillips, the owner of Sun, listening from the control room. The receptionist wrote down next to his name "Good ballad singer," and Presley left, with an acetate and an inkling that he was about to be discovered. He reappeared in January and cut another record. But Sam Phillips did not yet recognize that his ship had just come in.

A native of Florence, Alabama, Phillips had dropped out of school to begin working in radio, as an engineer and disc jockey. He came to Memphis in 1945, joining WREC, the CBS affiliate, to set up national hookups of big band music from the Skyway at the Peabody Hotel. Phillips found the pop songs he played dreadfully dull: "It seemed to me that the Negroes were the only ones who had any freshness left in their music; and there was no place in the South they could go to record." He told just about everyone he met that he was looking for "Negroes with field mud on their boots and patches in their overalls . . . battered instruments and unfettered techniques." In 1950 Phillips opened a small office, recording bar mitzvahs and political speeches to defray the expenses of making demos of new artists and sending them to independent producers around the country. Within a short time, he sold recordings of Howlin' Wolf and B. B.

King to Chess in Chicago and Modern Records in Los Angeles. He retained his job at WREC, until he could no longer abide snide coworkers asking him "whether he had been hanging around those niggers." By 1953, Sun Studios was promoting and distributing as well as producing, out of a two-person office. Rufus Thomas's "Bear Cat" was the studio's first success; "Feeling Good," by Little Junior Parker, and "Just Walkin' in the Rain," by the Prisonaires, were in the can. Sun's label, an orange, yellow, and black image of a rooster crowing and the sun rising, looked to a new day, and to an open door for African-American artists.

Sam Phillips's commitment to rhythm and blues never wavered; throughout his career he sought out and recorded black singers. He also realized that in the South, and in the North as well, whites were uneasy about listening to black music. In the '50s, as one jukebox operator noted, putting a "black blues record on a honky tonk machine" in a white establishment was a mistake, "because somebody would go over there and play it, just for devilment, and the whole place would explode." So Phillips kept his eyes open for white country boys who could sing the blues. Marion Keisker, Phillips's colleague at Sun, remembers him saying over and over, "If I could find a white man who had the Negro sound and the Negro feel, I could make a billion dollars."

In the summer of 1954, Phillips received a demo of a song called "Without You" from a black performer he did not know. For some reason, he thought the polite young man with the sideburns should record it. At the Sun Studio, Elvis tried and tried but failed to find the ballad's essence. Phillips persevered, asking the youngster to practice with Scotty Moore, a twenty-two-year-old guitarist. After several rehearsals, Presley and Moore returned, with stand-up bass player Bill Black, and played "I Love You Because," a country ballad. This session, too, went badly. Out of anxiety, or perhaps absent-mindedly, Elvis picked up his guitar to strum and sing "That's All Right," a blues song recorded by Arthur Crudup in 1946. Moore and Black joined in, and suddenly Sam Phillips stuck his head out of the control booth and asked them to play it again. He felt "like someone stuck me in the rear end with a brand new super-sharp pitchfork." It sounds pretty good, he said, but "what is it? I mean, who, who you going to give it [i.e., sell it] to?" Elvis did not have the ragged tone, irregular rhythms, and intonation most blues singers used, but he had found something. Instinctively, Greil Marcus argues, he had turned Crudup's lament for a lost love into a "satisfied declaration of independence. . . . His girl may have left him but nothing she can do can dent the pleasure that radiates from his heart. It's the blues, but free of all worry, all sin; a simple joy with no price to pay." When the trio finished the song, Phillips, by now very excited, realized that if he was to get a record out in a hurry he needed something for the flip side. Within a few days, Presley, Moore, and Black recorded the hillbilly classic "Blue Moon of Kentucky." Here, too, Elvis produced a distinctive tone and sound, transforming a country classic into that hybrid of country and R&B that became known as "rockabilly."

Even before he chose "Blue Moon of Kentucky," Sam Phillips played the acetate for his friend Dewey Phillips, by then at WHBQ, but still the "man with the platinum ear." As they listened, Sam wondered "where you going to go with this, it's not black, it's not white, it's not pop, it's not country." He was delighted when Dewey offered to play the songs on his show. As if by magic, most of Memphis seemed to be listening. When Dewey Phillips played "That's All Right," the switchboard lit up with requests that he play it again—and again and again. Dewey complied, then called the Presley home and asked Gladys to get Elvis, who was out at the movies, to the station for an interview. Within minutes the singer arrived, "shaking all over." Dewey told him to cool it and make sure to say "nothing dirty." During the brief chat, Dewey got Elvis to say that he had been a student at (all-white) Humes High School: "I wanted to get that out, because a lot of people listening had thought he was colored."

On July 19, 1954, Sun released Elvis Presley's first record. An instant hit in Memphis, it had to overcome initial resistance elsewhere in the South, because disc jockeys did not know how to categorize it. Some DJs told Phillips that Elvis was so "country he shouldn't be played after five A.M."; others said flatly he was too black for their tastes. If he played the record, T. Tommy Cutrer, the top country DJ in Shreveport, Louisiana, told Phillips, his white country audience would "run me out of town." In Houston, Paul Berlin, who was still getting mileage spinning the platters of Tennessee Ernie Ford and Patti Page, said, "Sam, your music is just so ragged, I just can't handle it right now. Maybe later on." Even in Tupelo, Elvis's hometown, Ernest Bowen, the sales manager at WELO, told him the record was "a bunch of crap."

When Phillips prevailed, and disc jockeys played the record, listeners couldn't get enough of it. And they liked "Blue Moon of Kentucky" every bit as much as "That's All Right." A scout for RCA asked Sam Morrison, a record dealer in Knoxville, "It's just a normal rhythm and blues record, isn't it?" No, it isn't, Morrison replied, "it's selling to a country audience." Just then, according to Morrison, a man with "more hair growing out of his ears and nose than on his head" entered the store and in an easy Tennessee drawl said, "By granny, I want that record." By mid-August the record was number 3 on *Billboard* magazine's regional country and western best-sellers.

By then, Elvis was a performer as well as a singer. After a shaky debut in front of a "pure redneck" crowd at the Bon Air Club in Memphis, he backed up Slim Whitman at a hillbilly hoedown in an outdoor amphitheater in Overton Park. Elvis approached the mike, with legs quivering and lips contorted into what looked like a sneer. "We were all scared to death," Scotty Moore recalled, "and Elvis, instead of just standing flat-footed and tapping his foot, well, he was kind of jiggling. . . . Plus I think with those old loose britches that we wore—they weren't pegged, they had lots of material and pleated fronts—you shook your leg, and it made it look like all hell was going on under there. During the instrumental parts he would back off from the mike and be playing and shaking, and the crowd would just go wild, but he thought they were actually making fun of him." By the encore, Elvis knew that the image he had projected, whether by accident or not, with his eyes shut and his legs shaking, was arousing the audience: "I did a little more, and the more I did, the wilder they went."

Elvis was something new under the Sun. Although he did not invent "rockabilly," he introduced it to tens of thousands of teenagers. With loose rhythms, no saxophone or chorus, rockabilly was a "personal, confiding, confessing" sound, as Charlie Gillett has defined it, with instrumentalists responding "more violently to inflections in the singer's voice, shifting into double-time for a few bars to blend with a sudden acceleration in the vocalist's tempo." After Elvis's meteoric rise, Sam Phillips signed other rockabilly singers, including Carl Perkins, Roy Orbison, Johnny Cash, and Jerry Lee Lewis.

Beyond his musical style, Elvis embodied some of the characteristics of his "low-down" social class and of many fellow teenagers. Angry at a world that had excluded him, yet eager for recognition and status, Elvis could be arrogant and prideful—and also emotionally vulnerable, inse-cure, and deferential. No one has captured Elvis's "authentic multiplicity" better than Greil Marcus, who imagines the singer introducing himself as a "house rocker, a boy steeped in mother love, a true son of the church, a matinee idol who's only kidding, a man with too many rough edges for anyone ever to smooth away," a balladeer yearning to settle affairs, a rock 'n' roller apt to "break away at any time."

By instinct more than design, Elvis contributed to the agitation about race relations during the 1950s. In public, and in the South, he acknowl-edged his indebtedness to the music of African Americans. "The colored folks been singing and playing it [rock 'n' roll] just like I'm doing now, man, for more years than I know," he told the *Charlotte Observer* in 1956. "They played it like that in the shanties and in their juke joints and nobody paid it no mind until I goosed it up. I got it from them. Down in Tupelo, Mississippi, I used to hear Arthur Crudup bang his box the way I do now and I said that if I ever got to the place where I could feel all old Arthur felt, I'd be a music man like nobody ever saw." Sam Phillips believed that Elvis was without prejudice and that "sneaking around through" his music, but clearly discernible to his fans, was an "almost subversive" identification with and empathy for blacks. Phillips's claim that he and Elvis "went out into this no man's land" and "knocked the shit out of the color line" should be dismissed as retrospective fantasy. He was, perhaps, closer to the mark in asserting that, with respect to race, "we hit things a little bit, don't you think?"

As Alan Freed provided a name, and Elvis an icon, Bill Haley gave rock 'n' roll its anthem. In almost all respects, Haley was an improbable '50s teen idol. Born in Highland Park, Michigan, in 1925, he received his first guitar at age seven and began to play hillbilly music, taking as his models country singer Hank Williams and cowboy star Gene Autry. Billed as the "Ramblin' Yodeler," Haley toiled in obscurity for years, perform-ing at fairs, auction barns, and amusement parks in Delaware, Indiana, and Pennsylvania, decked out in cowboy boots and hat. In the late '40s, he formed his own band, first named the Four Aces of Western Swing, then the Saddlemen. Thwarted by the limited appeal of country music in the region, Haley began to experiment with rhythm and blues. In 1951, the Saddlemen recorded "Rocket 88," a stomping R&B song about an Oldsmobile. A year later came "Rock the Joint," a loud and lively jump blues hit, which sold well in Philadelphia and New Jersey. Haley was now ready to exchange his boots and hat for a Scotch plaid jacket or a tuxedo, shave his sideburns, and rename the Saddlemen "Bill Haley and the Comets." Composed of six or seven men, playing stringed instruments, drums, and a saxophone, with Haley as guitarist and lead singer, the Comets played driving and danceable music. Haley's own composition, "Crazy, Man, Crazy," reached the *Billboard*'s Top Twenty. The tune had a pop beat, *The Cash Box* reported; the lyrics "lend themselves to R&B treatment, and the instrumentalization is hillbilly."

Signed by a major national label, Decca, Haley and the Comets recorded "(We're Gonna) Rock Around the Clock" early in 1954. Bursting with energy, the song used a snare drum to produce a heavy backbeat and featured an electric guitar solo. After just one week on *Billboard's* pop charts, at number 23, it faded. Late that year, however, with "Shake, Rattle, and Roll," a "cover" of Joe Turner's R&B song, with sanitized lyrics, Haley had a huge hit, selling more than a million copies. In his version, Haley copied the basic R&B beat but did not use many other musical effects—the loosely pronounced words, complex and harmonious backing, the slurred "bluesy" notes. He added guitar work and his own thumping, shouting delivery. The success of this song, and the emergence of rock 'n' roll, convinced Hollywood producers to use "Rock Around the Clock" in the film *Blackboard Jungle*.

As the opening credits of *Blackboard Jungle* rolled across the screen, the soundtrack blared "One, two, three o'clock, four o'clock ROCK." An asphalt schoolyard appeared on the screen, visible through a chain-link fence, and students danced, with a few toughs hovering in the background, a saxophone and electric guitar blaring on. For two minutes and ten seconds, "Rock Around the Clock" issued a clarion call to students to break out of jail and have fun. Whereas *Rebel Without a Cause* and *The Wild Ones* belied their themes of youth rebellion with big band sound tracks, *Blackboard Jungle* found music appropriate to its melodramatic ad campaign: "A drama of teenage terror! They turned a school into a jungle." "It was the loudest sound kids ever heard at that time," Frank Zappa remembered. Bill Haley "was playing the Teenage National Anthem and he was LOUD. I was jumping up and down. *Blackboard Jungle*, not even considering that it had the old people winning in the end, represented a strange act of endorsement of the teenage cause."

Despite a conclusion designed to reassure, with an alliance between a young black student, played by Sidney Poitier, and the teacher, played by Glenn Ford, *Blackboard Jungle* (and, by implication, "Rock Around the Clock") suggested that generational conflict was endemic in American culture. In an unforgettable scene, the class fidgeted as a teacher at North Manual High tried to connect with them by playing his favorite jazz records.

When the sound track countered with *their* music, the youths erupted, tossing his 78s across the room, then shattering them, as the hapless teacher dissolved in tears. As they watched the movie, observers noted, some teenagers sang along, danced in the aisles, and slashed their seats. *Blackboard Jungle*, music critic Lillian Roxon has written, had a "special, secret defiant meaning for teenagers only." It suggested to them that "they might be a force to be reckoned with, in numbers alone. If there could be one song, there could be others; there could be a whole world of songs, and then, a whole world." The movie reinforced the association between rock 'n' roll and anarchy in the minds of anxious adults. *Blackboard Jungle, Time* magazine opined, undermined the American way of life, giving aid and comfort to Communists. If it were not withdrawn, predicted Clare Booth Luce, U.S. ambassador to Italy, the film would "cause the greatest scandal in motion picture history." "No matter what the outcome of the film," Senator Estes Kefauver's committee on juvenile delinquency concluded, a substantial number of teenagers would identify with Artie West, the sadistic teenager in *Blackboard Jungle*, who assaults Glenn Ford's young and pretty wife. "It was unfortunate," no less an authority than Alan Freed acknowledged, that Haley's song about having a good time had been used "in that hoodlum-infested movie," which "seemed to associate rock 'n' rollers with delinquents."

Blackboard Jungle was denounced by teachers' organizations, the Daughters of the American Revolution, the American Legion, and the Girl Scouts. Banned in Memphis until MGM threatened an injunction, the film played in several cities with the sound track turned off during the opening and closing credits. Despite—and perhaps because of—these denunciations, *Blackboard Jungle* was a sensational hit. And, with a second chance, "Rock Around the Clock" climbed to the top of the charts. By the end of 1955, two million records had been sold, and by the end of the decade the song was gaining on Bing Crosby's "White Christmas" as the best-selling single in history. Bill Haley did not quite know what had hit him. Thirty years old in 1955, chunky, blind in one eye, with chipmunk cheeks and a spit curl plastered on his forehead, Haley found it difficult to compete with younger, sexier performers. Although he went on to make a short feature film, *Rock Around the Clock*, with Freed, in 1956, and had another gold record, "See You Later, Alligator," Haley seemed out of touch with the culture of rock 'n' roll. "He didn't even know what to call it, for the love of Christ," snorts critic Nick Tosches, citing Haley's comment that the Comets used country and western instruments to play rhythm and blues, "and the result is pop music." Haley was no rebel against the dominant values of the 1950s. While the Comets were on the road, he instituted bed checks and prohibited drinking and dating by members of the band. In 1957, the group recorded "Apple Blossom Time"; a year later, "Ida, Sweet as Apple Cider."

Although Bill Haley was unable to take full advantage of it, rock 'n' roll had emerged as a mass culture phenomenon. At the end of 1956, 68 percent of the music played by disc jockeys was rock 'n' roll, an increase of two-thirds over the previous year. By December 1957 virtually every position on *Billboard's* Top Ten was occupied by a rock 'n' roller. "Whatever emotional and psychological factors there are behind its acceptance," *Cash Box* editors asserted, "whatever spark it may have touched off in a teenager's makeup, the one fact that remains certain is that youngsters today find what they are looking for in the way of music in Rock 'n' Roll. It seems futile to try to deny this fact or pretend that it is a temporary thing."

As Carl Perkins's "Blue Suede Shoes" and Elvis Presley's "Heartbreak Hotel" surged to the top of the pop, rhythm and blues, and country charts, *The Cash Box* exulted that rock 'n' roll was affecting "the lives of everyone in our country." Rock 'n' roll, the editors believed, provided evidence of and served as an impetus for greater cultural harmony and homogenization in the United States. "Greater mobility and more dynamic means of communication," they explained, "have brought the taste and mode of living of people in various areas of our country to the attention and knowledge of those in other areas." In a banner headline, they predicted that "Rock and Roll May Be the Great Unifying Force!"

They were wrong. Although rock 'n' roll was a commodity, produced and distributed by a profit-making industry, and therefore subject to co-optation by the dominant culture, it continued to resist and unsettle "mainstream" values. For African Americans, rock 'n' roll was a mixed blessing. At times a force for integration and racial respect, rock 'n' roll was also an act of theft that in supplanting rhythm and blues deprived blacks of appropriate acknowledgment, rhetorical and financial, of their contributions to American culture. Rock 'n' roll deepened the divide between the generations, helped teenagers differentiate themselves from others, transformed popular culture in the United States, and rattled the reticent by pushing sexuality into the public arena. Anything but a "great unifying force," rock 'n' roll kept many Americans in the 1950s off balance, on guard, and uncertain about their families and the future of their country.

God's Country: America in the Fifties

Generation in a Spotlight

As the 1950s opened, America's adolescents were basically a conservative, unrebellious lot. Although the word *teenager* had come into widespread circulation in the 1940s to describe this distinct age group mired in the limbo between puberty and adulthood, the teenagers of the early fifties had not yet developed a distinct subculture. They had few rights and little money of their own, wore basically the same kind of clothing their parents wore, watched the same television shows, went to the same movies, used the same slang, and listened to the same romantic music sung by Perry Combo, Frank Sinatra, and other middle-aged or nearly middle-aged artists. Their idols were Joe DiMaggio, General MacArthur, and other prominent members of the older generation. In spite of what they learned from older kids and from the underground pornography that circulated on school playgrounds, they were amazingly naive about sex, believing well into their high school years that French kissing could cause pregnancy or that the douche, coitus interruptus, and chance could effectively prevent it. Heavy petting was the limit for most couples, and for those who went "all the way" there were often strong guilt feelings and, for the girl at least, the risk of a bad reputation. Rebellion against authority, insofar as it occurred, consisted primarily of harmless pranks against unpopular adult neighbors or teachers, occasional vandalism (especially on Halloween night), smoking cigarettes or drinking beer, and the decades-old practice of mooning. Although most families had the inevitable clashes of opinion between parents and offspring, there were few signs of a "generation gap" or of rebellion against the conventions of the adult world.

But all of this began to change in the early fifties, and by the middle of the decade the appearance of a distinct youth subculture was causing parents and the media to agonize over the scandalous behavior and rebellious nature of the nation's young people. The causes of the emergence of this subculture are not hard to find. One was the demographic revolution of the postwar years that was increasing the influence of the young by producing so many of them in such a short period of time. Another was the affluence of the period, an affluence shared with the young through allowances from their parents or through part-time jobs. As teenagers acquired their own money, they were able to pursue their own life-style, and now American business and advertisers geared up to promote and exploit a gigantic youth consumer market featuring products designed especially for them. Then there were the effects of progressive education and Spockian child-rearing practices, for while neither was quite as permissive or indulgent toward the young as the critics claimed, they did emphasize the treatment of adolescents as unique people who should be given the freedom to develop their own personality and talents. Another factor was television and movies, which had the power to raise up new fads, new heroes, and new values and to spread them to young people from New York to Los Angeles. And finally, there was rock 'n' roll, which grew from several strains in American music and emerged at mid-decade as the theme song of the youth rebellion and as a major molder and reflector of their values.

One of the earliest landmarks in the history of the youth rebellion came in 1951 with the publication of J. D. Salinger's *The Catcher in the Rye*. Infinitely more complex than most of its young readers or older detractors perceived, this novel featured the actions and thoughts of one Holden Caulfield, a sixteen-year-old veteran of several private schools, who roams around New York City in his own private rebellion from home and school. In colloquial language laced with obscenities absent from most novels of the day, Holden tells the reader of his rejection of the phoniness and corruption of the adult world, of how parents, teachers, ministers, actors, nightclub pianists and singers, old grads, and others lie to themselves and to the young about what the world is really like. *The Catcher in the Rye* was popular throughout the fifties with high school and college students, for while young people might not understand all that Salinger was trying to say, they did identify with his cynical rejection of the adult world and adult values. The book was made even more popular by the attempts of school boards, libraries, and state legislatures to ban it. It was one of the first books, if not the first, to perceive the existence of a generation gap in the supposedly happy, family-oriented society of the early 1950s.

Still another sign of the changes occurring in the nation's youth was the rise of juvenile delinquency. Between 1948 and 1953 the number of juveniles brought into court and charged with crimes increased by 45 percent, and it was estimated that for every juvenile criminal brought into court there were at least five who had not been caught. It was especially disturbing that juvenile crimes were committed by organized gangs that roamed—and seemed to control—the streets of many of the larger cities. Street gangs had existed before in American history, but in the fifties they were larger, more violent, and more widespread than ever before. Thanks to modern communications, they tended to dress alike, to use the same jargon, and share the same values all across the country. And they were not just in America—they appeared in England (Teddy Boys), Sweden

("Skinn-Nuttar" or leather jackets), and other industrial countries across the globe. The youth rebellion, including the criminal fringe that made up part of it, was international.

Learning about these gangs in their newspapers and weekly magazines, Americans were horrified by what they read and by how often they read it. It seemed that hardly a week went by without the occurrence of shocking crimes committed by teenagers or even younger children who did not seem to know the difference between good and bad—or worse, deliberately chose the bad over the good. Sporting colorful names like Dragons, Cobras, Rovers, and Jesters, they carried all kinds of weapons— zip guns, pistols, rifles, knives, chains, shotguns, brass knuckles, broken bottles, razors, lead pipes, molotov cocktails, machetes, and lye and other chemicals. They drank alcoholic beverages, smoked reefers, took heroin and other drugs, had their own twisted code of honor, and organized well-planned attacks on other gangs or innocent victims. They also had their own jargon, borrowed from the criminal underworld and spoken by gangs from coast to coast: *dig, duke, gig, jap, jazz, rumble, turf, cool, chick, pusher, reefer,* and hundreds of other slang terms.

To a nation accustomed to believing in the essential goodness of its young people, the behavior of these delinquent gangs was puzzling and frightening. They seemed to pursue violence for the pure joy of violence and to delight in sadistic actions toward other gangs or innocent victims. They engaged in shootings, stabbings, individual and gang rapes, sense-less beatings, and unspeakable tortures. They extorted "protection" money from frightened merchants, sprayed crowds in streets or restaurants or subways with rifle fire, doused people with gasoline and set them ablaze, firebombed bars and nightclubs, stole automobiles, vandalized apartments and public buildings, and fought vicious gang wars over girls or invasion of turf or to avenge some real or imagined slight. They often terrorized and vandalized schools and assaulted teachers and students, leading the *New York Daily News* in 1954 to describe "rowdyism, riot, and revolt," as the new three Rs in New York's public schools.

It was particularly disturbing that these young hoodlums often showed no remorse for their actions, recounting with delight to police or social workers the details of a rape, murder, or torture in which they had been involved. One eighteen-year-old who had participated in the torture and murder of an innocent young man in a public park told police that "last night was a supreme adventure for me. Describing his role in the killing of another gang member, one young man told police that "he was laying on the ground looking up at us. I kicked him on the jaw or someplace; then I kicked him in the stomach. That was the least I could do, was kick 'im. In another incident a gang member described his part in a stabbing by saying: "I stabbed him with a bread knife. You know, I was drunk, so I just stabbed him. [Laughs] He was screaming like a dog.

The rise of juvenile delinquency, and especially its organized forms in the street gangs of the major cities, caused agonizing soul-searching among anxious parents, school authorities, psychologists, and other experts on adolescent and criminal behavior. Parents of delinquents anxiously asked, "What did we do wrong?" and many admitted to school, police, and court authorities that they could not control their children. The experts came up with a whole range of explanations of juvenile criminality, blaming it on poverty, slum conditions, permissive parents, lack of religious and moral training, television, movies, comic books, racism, parents who were too busy working or pursuing their own pleasures to rear their children properly, the high divorce rate with the resulting broken homes, anxiety over the draft, and decline of parental discipline and control. Early in the decade most authorities tended to blame it on the problems of poverty and slum living, but as the decade wore on, it became very clear that many of the delinquents were from middle- and upper-class families that provided a good environment for their children. So then it was blamed on society or on simple "thrill seeking" by bored, pampered, and jaded youths. As the problem worsened, many were inclined to agree with Baltimore psychologist Robert Linder, who claimed that the young people of the day were suffering from a form of collective mental illness. "The youth of the world today," he told a Los Angeles audience in 1954, "is touched with madness, literally sick with an aberrant condition of mind formerly confined to a few distressed souls but now epidemic over the earth."

Whatever the causes of juvenile delinquency, and they were certainly multiple and complex, it was obvious that delinquent and criminal acts by individual adolescents and organized gangs were increasing every year and were making the streets of many large cities dangerous for law-abiding citizens. And while many people thought of the problem as one that plagued primarily the slums of the big cities of the Northeast or California, it soon became clear that it was spreading to large cities all across the country, to the new suburbs, to the rural areas which were so accessible now to middle-class teenagers with automobiles, and to the South, which had often prided itself on not having the problems of the big northern cities. In 1954 *New York Times* education editor Benjamin Fine wrote a much-discussed book on the problem, *1,000,000 Delinquents*, which correctly predicted that during the next year 1 million adolescents would get into serious trouble that would bring them into the courtroom. In that same year *Newsweek* published an article entitled "Our Vicious Young Hoodlums: Is There Any Hope?" By now, many people thought that there was none and found themselves in the unusual position of being afraid of their own children.

By the midfifties Americans had become so saturated with stories of juvenile delinquency that there was a tendency among many to stereotype all teenagers as bad, especially if they adopted the clothing, ducktail haircuts, or language of gangs. But the truth was that few teenagers were juvenile delinquents or gang members, very few used drugs (except for alcohol), and very few ever got into trouble with the police. And many teenagers resented the stereotyped image the adult world had of them. As one seventeen-year-old high school girl said in 1955, "I've never set a fire, robbed a gas station, or beaten a defenseless old man. In fact, I don't even know anyone who has. . . . I wish someone would think of the 95% of us who *aren't* delinquents. Because we're here, too." The young woman was correct, of course, for most teenagers were not delinquents. But they were changing in ways that were disturbing even the parents of "good" teens, and one of the major causes of these changes was the rise of a new musical form, rock 'n' roll. . . .

Born in the small town of Fairmount, Indiana, on February 8, 1931, James Dean led a life much like that of the troubled youth he later came to portray in his movies. His mother died when he was nine, and he was reared on the farm of his aunt and uncle with only brief glimpses of his father. A confused adolescent, he went to California after his graduation from high school, attended Santa Monica City College and UCLA, and played some small parts in movies before going back to New York to study acting in 1951. In 1954 he came back to Hollywood as an admirer of Marlon Brando, motorcycles, and fast cars. He quickly earned a reputation as a lazy, undisciplined, ill-mannered star who often stayed out all night long and then showed up on the set too tired to do good work. His first major film, *East of Eden* (1955), brought him instant fame through his portrayal of the sensitive son suffering from the fear that his father does not love him, but his rise as a teenage idol came later in the year through his performance as a misunderstood and rebellious teenager in *Rebel Without a Cause.* Costarring Natalie Wood and Sal Mineo, the film was released to the theaters in the fall of 1955, only two weeks after Dean's tragic death in a high-speed wreck between his Porsche and a Ford on a lonely California highway. By the time the just-completed *Giant* was released, in November of 1956, an astonishing cult had sprung up around the young star and his death, so senseless, at the age of twenty-four.

The legends that grew up around James Dean were the greatest since the death of Rudolph Valentino. Young people saw Dean as the embodiment of their restlessness, confusion, and rejections, as a rebel fighting, like them, against the rules and conformity the adult world was trying to impose upon them. But while Valentino and most other movie legends had appealed as sex symbols. Dean appealed to an age group—to young males and females between fourteen and twenty-four. Young males saw him as a symbol of their own rebellious and troubled nature, while young girls saw him as an attractive, sensual male who needed mothering as much as sexual love. Although Dean was a good actor with great promise, his acting reputation was exaggerated beyond all reality by the myths and legends that shrouded his life and acting career after his premature death.

Within a few weeks after Dean's death, Warner Brothers was swamped with hundreds of letters. Their number rose to 3,000 a month by January of 1956 and to 7,000 a month by July, some with money enclosed for a picture of the dead star. The fan magazines played the Dean legend for all it was worth, publishing thousands of pictures and stories. In these magazines and across the national teenage grapevine, the rumors flew: that he was not really dead, that he had been so disfigured from the wreck that he had gone into hiding or been sent to a sanatorium, that he was just a vegetable in a secret hospital room known only to his close friends, that he had talked to some of his fans from beyond his grave, and that his tomb in Fairmount, Indiana, had been emptied by grave robbers or by Dean's own miraculous resurrection. Several records appeared—"Tribute to James Dean," "The Ballad of James Dean," "His Name Was Dean." "The Story of James Dean," "Jimmy Jimmy," and "We'll Never Forget You." Dozens of biographies and other literary tributes were rushed to the market, along with the inevitable movie, *The James Dean Story*. When the wreckage of his car was put on display in Los Angeles, over 800,000 people paid to view it. The adulation swept teens all across America and even in Europe. In England, a young man legally changed his name to James Dean, copied his clothing and mannerisms, went to America twice to visit the real Dean's family and grave, and claimed to have seen *Rebel Without a Cause* over 400 times. As *Look* magazine observed, the subject of this almost psychopathic adulation was "a 24-year old who did not live long enough to find out what he had done and was in too much of a hurry to find out who he was."

Along with *The Wild One*, a 1954 film starring Marlon Brando as the leader of a motorcycle gang, *The Blackboard Jungle* and the films of James Dean helped to spawn a series of films aimed specifically at young people. In addition to the films of Elvis Presley and other teen idols, the second half of the fifties saw a spate of second-rate rock movies—*Rock Around the Clock, Don't Knock the Rock, Rock Pretty Baby, Rock Around the World,* and *Let's Rock*—and a series of shallow, trashy movies about young people and delinquency, such as *Girls in Prison, Eighteen and Anxious, Reform School Girl, Hot Rod Rumble,* and *High School Confidential*. For better or worse—mostly worse—teenagers were getting their own movies as well as their own music.

In 1955 teenagers had their music, their movies, their idols—dead and alive—but as yet they had no one who combined all three of these and served as a focal point for their growing consciousness as a subculture. But he was waiting in the wings, for in that year a young performer with a regional reputation was making records and gaining a wide following among teenagers, especially young girls, with live performances in southern cities that were often punctuated by desperate attempts by the police to prevent these screaming fans from rushing the stage to tear off his clothes. He was a James Dean fan, who had seen *Rebel Without a Cause* several times, could recite the script by heart, and had been wearing tight pants, leather jackets, and a ducktail haircut with long sideburns for several years. In 1956 he would burst on the national entertainment stage and proceed to become one of the most popular and influential musical performers of all time, rivaling Rudy Vallee, Bing Crosby, Frank Sinatra, and other singers before him. His name was Elvis Presley, and he was destined to claim the title of King of Rock 'n' Roll. . . .

Record sales soared with the coming of rock 'n' roll. Aided by the affluence of the time, the invention of the 45 rpm and 33⅓ rpm records, and the introduction of high fidelity, record sales had steadily climbed from 109 million in 1945 to 189 million in 1950 and to 219 million in

1953, then with the arrival of rock 'n' roll rose to 277 million in 1955 and to 600 million in 1960. In 1956 alone, RCA Victor sold over 13.5 million Elvis Presley singles and 3.75 million Presley albums. By 1957, the new 45s and 33⅓s had driven the 78s out of production. Teenagers bought most of the inexpensive and convenient 45s and most of the long-playing rock 'n' roll albums, whereas adults bought most of the long-playing albums of traditional popular music, jazz, and classical music. While in 1950 the average record buyer was likely to be in his early twenties, by 1958, 70 percent of all the records sold in the United States were purchased by teenagers. Most of the popular singles were purchased by girls between the ages of thirteen and nineteen, the group most receptive, as one critic said, to "little wide-eyed wishes for ideal love and perfect lovers, little songs of frustration at not finding them." Thanks to these revolutions in the musical world, record sales, which had stood at only $7.5 million in 1940, had risen to a healthy $521 million in 1960.

Why was rock 'n' roll so popular? One of the reasons, of course, was that it was written and performed by young people and was centered upon what was important to them: love, going steady, jealousy, high school, sex, dancing, clothing, automobiles, and all the other joys and problems of being young. The lyrics were just as silly, sentimental, and idealistic as the music of the crooners of the first half of the decade, but it was written just for the young and the singing styles, beat, electrical amplification, and volume of the music was much more dynamic than that of the earlier period. Teens were attracted to its celebration of sexuality, expressed in the more explicit lyrics, driving tempo, movements of the rock 'n' roll performers, and in new dances at high school hops and private parties. Perhaps Jeff Greenfield, a member of this first generation of rock 'n' roll fans, expressed it best in his *No Peace, No Place.* "Each night, sprawled on my bed on Manhattan's Upper West Side, I would listen to the world that Alan Freed created. To a twelve- or thirteen-year-old, it was a world of unbearable sexuality and celebration: a world of citizens under sixteen, in a constant state of joy or sweet sorrow. . . . New to sexual sensations, driven by the impulses that every new adolescent generation knows, we were the first to have a music rooted in uncoated sexuality." And very importantly, rock 'n' roll gave young people a sense of cohesion, of unity, all across the nation. It was *their* music, written for them and for them only, about their world, a world that adults could not share and did not understand. As such, it was one of the major harbingers of the generation gap.

It was not long after teenagers acquired their own music and movies that they also acquired their own television show. *American Bandstand* began as a local television show in Philadelphia in 1952, and in August of 1957 it premiered as a network show on ABC over sixty-seven stations across the country, from 3:00 to 4:30 in the afternoon, with twenty-six-year-old Dick Clark as the host. The first network show featured songs by Jerry Lee Lewis, the Coasters, and other top rock 'n' roll artists, and guest star Billy Williams singing "I'm Gonna Sit Right Down and Write Myself a Letter." Some of the early reviews of the show were not complimentary. According to *Billboard*, "The bulk of the ninety minutes was devoted to colorless juveniles trudging through early American dances like the Lindy and the Box Step to recorded tunes of the day. If this is the wholesome answer to the 'detractors' of rock 'n' roll, bring on the rotating pelvises." But by the end of 1958 the show was reaching over 20 million viewers over 105 stations, and had spawned dozens of imitations on local stations. This was a show about teens, and its consistent high rating and longevity proved that they liked it, regardless of what adults said about it.

American Bandstand had a great influence on popular music and on America's teenagers. Clark's good looks, neat clothing, and civilized manner helped reassure American parents that rock 'n' roll was not a barbarian invasion that was turning the young into juvenile delinquents. All the dancers on the show in the fifties were white, adhered to a strict dress code (coats and ties for boys, dresses and skirts and blouses for girls, and no jeans, T-shirts, or tight sweaters), and followed a strict language code that even prohibited the use of the term "going steady." One of Clark's most embarrassing moments on the show came when a young girl told him that the pin she was wearing was a "virgin pin." Stars with unsavory reputations were not allowed on the show, so when the news of Jerry Lee Lewis's marriage to his thirteen-year-old cousin broke, Clark joined other disc jockeys and promotors across the country in canceling all future appearances of the pioneer rock 'n' roll star. The show also featured the biggest stars of the day and helped launch the careers of Connie Francis, Fabian, Frankie Avalon, and several other singers. The new dances performed on the show—such as "the stroll," "the shake," and "the walk"—were soon copied all across the country. Teenagers everywhere also imitated the slang and the dress of this very influential show and brought the records its regulars danced to. The success of this dance show brought popularity and wealth to its host, who freely admitted that "I dance very poorly," yet became a millionaire by the age of thirty.

The rise of rock 'n' roll, teen movies, teen television shows, and teen magazines helped create the teen idol. Many of the idols were singers, like Elvis Presley, Rick Nelson, Frankie Avalon, Bobby Darin, Fabian, Pat Boone, Connie Francis, and Annette Funicello. Others were movie or television actors, like James Dean and Marlon Brando, though of course many of the singers also went on to movie careers which might be called, at best, undistinguished. Most of the idols were teenagers themselves or in their twenties, and it is important to note here that while earlier generations had tended to create idols much older than themselves—like Bing Crosby, Perry Como, and Clark Gable—the teenagers of the late fifties made idols of people from their own generation. And although clean-cut starts like Ricky Nelson or Frankie Avalon were chosen as idols, many young people also idolized Brando and Dean, who seemed so much like them in their agonizing over the problems of life. The inclination of the young to idolize those who portrayed problem youth was puzzling and disturbing to parents who wanted their children to grow up to be clean-cut, middle-class kids who went to church, obeyed their parents and other authorities, drank nothing harder than a soft drink, had no sexual experience before marriage, saved and studied for college, hung around soda shops rather than pool rooms, and after college went into a respectable career with a good income and a secure future. In short, they wanted their children to be like Pat Boone.

Born in Jacksonville, Florida, in 1934, Boone rose to fame while still a college student by winning first place on Ted Mack's *Original Amateur Hour* and *Arthur Godfrey's Talent Scouts* in 1954. He became a regular on Godfrey's morning show, and then began a career as a singer, movie star (*Bernadine* and *April Love*, both in 1957), and television star with his own show (*Pat Boone Chevy Showroom*). Many of his recordings were covers of original black songs like "Tutti-Frutti" and "Ain't That a Shame," and traditional romantic tunes such as "Friendly Persuasion," "April Love," and "Love Letters in the Sand." Boone was an all-American boy, a dedicated Christian and family man who had not been spoiled by his success, although at the age of twenty-four he was already popular and wealthy, earning $750,000 annually. He had an attractive wife, four pretty daughters, a baccalaureate degree from Columbia University, a love of milk and ice cream, and a severe distaste for strong drink, tobacco, and anything else immoral. He attracted wide publicity in 1958 when he refused to kiss Shirley Jones in the movie *April Love*, saying that "I've always been taught that when you get married, you forget about kissing other women." However, after talking it over with his wife, he agreed to do the kissing scene, although "she would prefer to keep that part of our lives solely to ourselves." This old-fashioned wholesomeness enabled him to hit the best-seller list in 1958 with *Twist Twelve and Twenty,* a moral and social guide for teenagers that reflected Boone's conservative view of sex and his deeply religious outlook on life. Some teenagers found Boone hopelessly "square," but many others admired his moral rectitude. He was immensely popular in the fifties, perhaps second only to Elvis.

In spite of the existence of clean-cut white performers like Pat Boone, much of the adult world was against the new rock 'n' roll. Many musicians and music critics condemned it on musical grounds, disliking its primitive beat, electrical amplification, witless and repetitive lyrics, loudness, and screams. But most adults opposed it for other reasons. Many objected to its suggestive lyrics and claimed that it fomented rebellion against parents and other authorities, bred immorality, inflamed teenagers to riot, and was unchristian and unpatriotic. They agreed with Frank Sinatra, who called it "the martial music of every sideburned delinquent on the face of the earth." Others objected to its racial background and content, even claiming, as many southerners did, that rock 'n' roll was a plot jointly sponsored by the Kremlin and the NAACP, and that rock musicians and disc jockeys were dope addicts, communists, integrationists, atheists, and sex fiends. To many whites, North and South, it was "nigger music," and as such was designed to tear down the barriers of segregation and bring about sexual promiscuity, intermarriage, and a decline in the morals of young whites.

The fears of parents and other adults were fed by the isolated incidents of rioting that accompanied rock 'n' roll concerts in Boston, Washington, D.C., and several other cities. As a result of these headline-getting events, rock 'n' roll concerts were banned in many cities or else accompanied by heavy police security and strict regulations as to what the performers could do or say on stage. In many cities, city councils and other local groups also tried to ban rock 'n' roll from record stores or jukeboxes. In San Antonio, Texas, the city council even went so far as to ban the music from the jukeboxes of public swimming pools, claiming that it "attracted undesirable elements given to practicing their gyrations in abbreviated bathing suits." A disc jockey in Buffalo was fired when he played an Elvis Presley record, and across the country disc jockeys were similarly punished for playing the new music or were pressured into boycotting it. Some disc jockeys broke rock 'n' roll records on the air, while radio station WLEV in Erie, Pennsylvania, loaded over 7,000 rock 'n' roll records into a rented hearse and led a funeral procession to Erie Harbor, where the records were "buried at sea." Ministers preached against it, claiming, like the Rev. John Carroll in Boston, that the music corrupted young people and that "rock and roll inflames and excites youth like jungle tom-toms readying warriors for battle," and many churches held public burnings of rock 'n' roll records. Some were even willing to resort to the ugliest kinds of violence to try to stem the advance of rock music. On April 23, 1956, in Birmingham, Alabama, where the White Citizens' Council had succeeded in removing all rock 'n' roll records from jukeboxes, five men connected with the council rushed the stage of the city auditorium and assaulted black ballad singer Nat King Cole, who was badly bruised before the police stopped the attack.

The debate over rock 'n' roll continued through the end of the decade, carried on in the press, over radio and television, in teachers' meetings, pulpits, and city council meeting rooms. By 1960 the debate had begun to die down, with parents coming to see that the music was not going to fade away, that it had not made delinquents of their children, and that all the other dire predictions had not come to pass, either. Some even began to admit grudgingly that they liked some of it, though they wished that it were not played so loudly. Some of the older professional musicians had also come to defend it—Benny Goodman, Sammy Kaye, Paul Whiteman, and Duke Ellington had kind words for the new music from the very beginning, and Whiteman and Kaye publicly recalled that most new musical forms, including their own swing music, had been condemned when it first appeared. And in the May 1959 issue of *Harper's*, critic Arnold Shaw noted that "perhaps it should be added (although it should be self-evident) that just as hot jazz of the twenties (then anathema to our grandparents) did not destroy our parents, and swing (anathema to our parents) did not destroy us, it is quite unlikely that rock 'n' roll will destroy our children."

The spectacular rise of rock 'n' roll should not obscure the fact that the older music continued to thrive. In 1957, when rock 'n' roll claimed seven of the top ten records of the year, the number one song was "Tammy," recorded by both Debbie Reynolds and the Ames Brothers, and Perry Como remained a favorite of young and old throughout the decade. In a 1956 poll by *Woman's Home Companion*, teenage boys and girls chose Como as the best male vocalist, with Presley, Boone, and Sinatra trailing behind. Johnny Mathis, Paul Anka, Pat Boone, Bobby Darin, the Everly Brothers, and many other teen idols also continued to sing fairly traditional love songs, and in the late fifties, building on a tradition established early in the decade by the Weavers, the Kingston Trio brought a revival of folk music to college students with a touch of rock and protest in songs like "Tom Dooley," "Tijuana Jail," and "A Worried Man," paving the way for the folk music explosion in the early 1960s. Rock music dominated from 1956 to 1960, but it did not completely push the older music aside.

In addition to obtaining their own music, movies, television shows, and idols, teenagers of the fifties also acquired their own fashions, and here they followed the trend toward casual dress that was characterizing the rest of society. The favorite dress of high school boys was denim jeans with rolled-up cuffs, sport shirts, baggy pegged pants, pleated rogue trousers with a white side stripe, slacks with buckles in the back, V-neck sweaters, button-down striped shirts, blazers, white bucks, and loafers. In 1955 they also joined older males on college campuses and executive offices in the pink revolution, donning pink shirts, pink striped or polka dot ties, and colonel string ties. Hair styles ranged from the popular flat top or crew cut to the Apache or ducktail (banned at some high schools). "Greasers" of course shunned the Ivy League and pink attire as too effeminate, sticking to their T-shirts (often with sleeves rolled up to hold a cigarette pack), jeans, leather jackets, and ducktails. For girls, the fashions ranged from rolled-up jeans to casual blouses or men's shirts, full dresses with crinolines, skirts and sweaters, blazers, occasional experiments with the tube dress and sack dress and other disasters foisted upon older women by fashion designers, short shorts (with rolled-up cuffs) that got progressively shorter as the decade wore on, two-piece bathing suits (few were bold enough to wear the bikini, imported from France in the late forties), brown and white saddle shoes and loafers, and hair styles from the poodle to the ponytail. Couples who were going steady wore one another's class rings, identification tags, and necklaces or bracelets, and often adopted a unisex look by wearing matching sweaters, blazers, and shirts.

Like the generations before them, the teenagers of the fifties also had their slang. Much of it was concerned, of course, with the great passion of teens, cars. Cars were *wheels*, tires were *skins*, racing from a standing start was called a *drag*, the bumper was *nerf-bar*, a special kind of exhaust system was called *duals*, and a car specially modified for more engine power was a *hot rod* or *souped up car* or *bomb*. A drive-in movie was a *passion pit*, anything or anyone considered dull was a *drag,* and a really dull person was a *square* or a *nosebleed*. An admirable or poised individual or anything worthy of admiration or approval was *cool* or *neat* or *smooth*, someone who panicked or lost his *cool* was accused of *clutching*, and people admonished not to worry were told to *hang loose*. Teenagers also borrowed lingo from the jazz and beatnik world, such as *dig, hip, cat, bread,* and *chick*. A cutting, sarcastic laugh at someone's bad joke was expressed by a *hardeeharhar*. And teenagers also shared the jargon of the rest of society—*big deal, the royal screw or royal shaft, up the creek without a paddle, forty lashes with a wet noodle, wild, wicked, crazy, classy, horny, BMOC, looking for action, bad news, out to lunch, gross, fink, loser, creep, dumb cluck, doing the deed, going all the way, or coming across*. Many of these colloquialisms were borrowed from earlier generations, sometimes with modifications in meaning, while some had been regionalisms that now became national through the great homogenizing power of television.

By the mid-1950s there were 16.5 million teenagers in the United States. About half of them were crowding the nation's secondary schools, while the rest had entered college or the work world. Wherever they were, they had become, as Gereon Zimmerman would write in *Look* magazine, a "Generation in a Searchlight," a constant subject of media attention and a constant source of anxiety for their parents and the rest of the adult world. As Zimmerman observed, "No other generation has had so such attention, so much admonition, so many statistics."

Zimmerman might also have added that no other young generation had had so much money. One of the most revolutionary aspects of the teenage generation was its effects on the American economy, for by the midfifties teenagers made up a very lucrative consumer market for American manufacturers. By mid-decade teenagers of this affluent era were viewing as necessities goods that their parents, reared during the depression, still saw as luxuries, such as automobiles, televisions, record players, cameras, and the like. By the midfifties, teenagers were buying 43 percent of all records, 44 percent of all cameras, 39 percent of all new radios, 9 percent of all new cars, and 53 percent of movie tickets. By 1959, the amount of money spent on teenagers by themselves and by their parents had reached the staggering total of $10 billion a year. Teenagers were spending around $75 million annually on single popular records, $40 million on lipstick, $25 million on deodorant, $9 million on home permanents, and over $837 million on school clothes for teenage girls. Many teenagers had their own charge accounts at local stores and charge cards issued especially for them, such as Starlet Charge Account, Campus Deb Account, and the 14 to 21 Club. Like their parents, teenagers were being led by the affluence and advertising of the age to desire an ever-increasing diet of consumer goods and services and to buy them even if they had to charge them against future earnings.

Many adults had a distorted image of this affluent young generation, focusing too much on its delinquency, rock 'n' roll, unconventional hair styles and clothing, and dating and sexual practices. Only a very small percentage were delinquents or problem-ridden adolescents. Most were reasonably well-groomed, well-behaved, and active in school and extracurricular functions. Most were interested in sports, automobiles, movies, rock 'n' roll, dating, dancing, hobbies, radio, and television. Their major worries were the typical problems of youth in an affluent age: problems with their parents, their popularity with other teens, their looks and complexions, proper dating behavior, sex, first dates, first kisses, love, bad breath, body odors, posture, body build, friends, schoolwork, college, future careers, money, religion, and the draft.

These teenagers that parents worried so much about were remarkably conservative. Survey after survey of young people in the fifties found that over half of them—and sometimes even larger percentages—believed that censorship of printed materials and movies was justified, that politics was beyond their understanding and was just a dirty game, that most people did not have the ability to make important decisions about what was good for them, that masturbation was shameful and perhaps harmful, that women should not hold public office, and that the theory of evolution was suspect and even dangerous. Like their parents, they were also very religious as a group, tending to believe in the divine inspiration of the Bible, heaven and hell, and a God who answered the prayers of the faithful. They were suspicious of radical groups and were willing to deny them the right to assemble in meetings and to disseminate their ideas, and they saw nothing wrong with denying accused criminals basic constitutional rights, such as the right to know their accuser, to be free from unreasonable search or seizure of their property, or to refuse to testify against themselves. Teenagers were also very conformist: They were very concerned about what their friends thought of their dress, behavior, and ideas, and they tried very hard to be part of the group and not be labeled an oddball or individualist. In short, in this age of corporation man, the country also had corporation teen.

Most teens were also conservative in their approach to dating, sex, and marriage. Religious views, social and peer pressure, and fear of pregnancy all combined to create this conservatism and to ensure that most teens kept their virginity until marriage or at least until the early college years, though heavy petting was certainly prevalent among couples who were engaged or "going steady," a practice reflecting society's emphasis on monogamy. These conservative attitudes toward sexual behavior were reinforced by the authorities teenagers looked to for guidance—parents, teachers, ministers, advice to the lovelorn columnists like Dear Abby and Ann Landers (both of whom began their columns in the midfifties), and books on teenage etiquette by Allen Ludden, Pat Boone, and *Seventeen* magazine. In his book for young men, *Plain Talk for Men Under 21,* Ludden devoted an entire chapter to such things as "That Good Night Kiss"—discussing whether to, how to, and the significance of it if you did. And in the very popular *The Seventeen Book of Young Living* (1957), Enid Haupt, the editor and publisher of *Seventeen* magazine, advised young girls to "keep your first and all your romances on a beyond reproach level" and to save themselves for the one right man in their lives. Acknowledging that "it isn't easy to say no to a persuasive and charming boy," she offered one answer for all potentially compromising situations: "'No, please take me home. Now.'"

The conservatism of the young would continue over into the college-age population, where it would remain entrenched for the rest of the fifties. The decade witnessed a boom in higher education, as rising prosperity. G.I. benefits, increasing governmental and private financial aid, fear of the draft, and a growing cultural emphasis on higher education all contributed to a great increase in the number of college students, faculty, programs, and buildings. The boom occurred at all levels—undergraduate, graduate, professional, and in the burgeoning junior- and community-college movement. The number of students, which had stood at 1.5 million in 1940 and 2.3 million in 1950, steadily rose in the decade and reached 3.6 million in 1960, and while the population of the country grew by 8 percent in the decade, the college population grew by 40 percent. By the end of the decade, almost 40 percent of the eighteen-to-twenty-one-year-old age group was attending some institution of higher education.

The conservatism of the college students of the 1950s led them to be called the Silent Generation. Why was it so silent? One of the most important reasons was that it mirrored the conservatism of the society at large, a society caught up in the materialistic and Cold War mentality of the decade. Like their elders, students were seeking the good life rather than the examined one, and as the Great Fear spread to the campuses, many were afraid of acquiring a radical reputation that might jeopardize their scholarships and their future careers in private industry, government service, or the military. Many were veterans, and their military experience, especially for those who had served in Korea, had tended to confirm their conservatism. Many others were in college in order to evade or at least defer the draft, and did not want to do or say anything that might endanger their deferred status. And finally, most students were white and drawn from the middle and upper-middle classes of society. The doors of higher education were still closed to most minority groups and to the economically and socially disadvantaged—groups who might have brought questioning or even radical attitudes into the field of higher education had they been part of it. It is not surprising then that most college students were hardworking, conservative, and career-oriented, truly deserving of their Silent Generation label.

The conservatism of the college generation prevailed throughout the decade. In a study of the college generation in 1951, *Time* magazine noted that "the most startling thing about the younger generation is its silence. . . . It does not issue manifestoes, make speeches, or carry posters." Most students, *Time* found, were worried about the Korean War and its effects on their plans for careers and marriage, but they pushed these fears into the background and concentrated on earning good grades and landing a good job. They were serious and hardworking, in rebellion against nothing, and had no real heroes or villains. Born during the depression years, they were primarily interested in a good job and security, and they did not want to do or say anything that would jeopardize these goals. "Today's generation," *Time* concluded, "either through fear, passivity, or conviction, is ready to conform."

Soon after the end of the Korean War, *Newsweek* studied college students in seven institutions, and its findings were little different from those of *Time* two years before. In "U.S. Campus Kids of 1953: Unkiddable and Unbeatable," *Newsweek* reported that students were hardworking, ambitious conformists who looked forward to secure jobs and a happy married life. Going steady was more popular then ever before, a sign of the period's emphasis on marriage and of young people's desire for the security that a going-steady relationship brought. Most students, *Newsweek* found, were not very interested in politics or international affairs, and they avoided being linked with unpopular causes. One Vassar girl told the magazine, "We're a cautious generation. We aren't buying any ideas we're not sure of." Another said that "you want to be popular, so naturally you don't express any screwy ideas. To be popular you have to conform." And a Princeton senior said that "the world doesn't owe me a living—but it owes me a job." *Newsweek* also saw a renewed interest in religion, as reflected in increasing enrollments in religion courses and frequent "religious emphasis weeks." The magazine found much to admire in the hardworking materialistic class of 1953, although it did concede that "they might seem dull in comparison with less troubled eras."

Similar collegiate characteristics were reported in a 1955 study by David Riesman, who found that students were ambitious, very sure of what they wanted to do, but also very unadventurous—they wanted secure positions in big companies and were already concerned about retirement plans. As one Princeton senior saw it, "Why struggle on my own, when I can enjoy the big psychological income of being a member of a big outfit?" Most males had already decided that they wanted middle-management jobs—they did not want to rise to the presidential or vice-presidential level because that would require too much drive, take time away from their family life and leisure time, and force them to live in a big city. Most had already decided upon the kind of girl they would marry, how many kids they would have, and which civic clubs and other organizations they would join—and they would be joiners, for they liked the gregarious life and knew it would help their careers. They wanted educated wives who would be intellectually stimulating, yet they wanted them to be dutiful and obedient and to stay at home and raise the kids. Many said they wanted as many as four or five kids, because they felt that a large family would bring happiness, security, contentment. One Harvard senior said that "I'd like six kids. I don't know why I say that—it seems like a minimum production goal." They did not know or care much about politics, but they did like Ike and said that they would probably be Republicans because corporation life dictated that they should be.

These attitudes still seemed to prevail in 1957, when *The Nation* surveyed college and university professors about what their students were reading and thinking. Most reported that their students still read the standard authors—Hemingway, Wolfe, Lawrence, Orwell, Huxley, Faulkner, and Steinbeck—but shied away from fiction or nonfiction that dealt with economic, social, or political protest. One professor lamented that "the only young novelist I have heard praised vociferously is J. D. Salinger, for his discovery of childhood," and complained that "when a liberal and speculative voice is heard in the classroom, it is more likely than not to be the professor's, despite whatever caution the years may have taught him." The director of the Writing Program at Stanford University claimed that students were "hard to smoke out. Sometimes a professor is baited into protest by the rows and circles of their closed, watchful, apparently apathetic faces, and says in effect, 'My God, *feel* something! Get enthusiastic about something, plunge, go boom, look alive!'" A Yale English professor complained that "the present campus indifference to either politics or reform or rebellion is monumental." And most agreed with a University of Michigan professor's claim that to the student of 1957, "college has ceased to be a brightly lighted stage where he discovers who he is. It is rather a processing-chamber where, with touching submissiveness, he accepts the remarks of lecturers and the hard sentences of textbooks as directives that will lead him to a job."

What did the members of the Silent Generation do when they were not studying, planning what company they intended to find a safe niche in, deciding what kind of mate they would marry or how many kids they would have, or planning for retirement? They played sports, drank beer, ate pizzas and hamburgers, went to football games and movies, participated in panty raids, dated, dreamed of the opposite sex, read novels and magazines, watched television, and listened to recordings of jazz, classical music, or the popular crooners of the day. For most, the hottest issues on campus were what to do about a losing football coach or who should be elected homecoming queen or student body president. Both sexes wore conservative preppy clothes, and at many coeducational institutions women were forbidden to wear jeans or shorts to class. Those who could afford to joined one of the fast-growing number of fraternities or sororities in order to party, find identity and security, and form friendships that might later be useful in the business world they hoped to enter after graduation. College students were, indeed, an unrebellious lot.

By the late fifties America's teenagers had acquired a distinct subculture of their own. They had their own money, music, movies, television shows, idols, clothing, and slang. In contrast to previous generations, they were more affluent, better educated, talked more openly about sex, had greater mobility through the widespread ownership of automobiles by their parents or themselves, demanded and received more personal freedom, had more conflicts with their parents, and were the subject of more media and parental concern. But they were not yet in rebellion, for although their life-style had departed from the conventions of their elders, their basic ideas and attitudes were still the conservative ones that mirrored the conservatism of the affluent age in which they grew up.

Still, their parents were worried. As *Look* magazine reported in 1958 in an article entitled "What Parents Say About Teenagers," "many parents are in a state of confusion or despair about their teenagers. And they don't exactly know what to do about it. They would like to sit down with their children and talk over their mutual problems, but often this desire is thwarted by the teenagers themselves." The much-heralded generation gap was coming into view. In the next decade, when the junior high and senior high school students of the fifties crowded the colleges, marched in civil rights demonstrations, protested the Vietnam War, and engaged in unconventional sexual and drug practices, it would take on the temper of a revolution.

POSTSCRIPT

Was Rock and Roll Responsible for Dismantling America's Traditional Family, Sexual, and Racial Customs in the 1950s and 1960s?

Between 1958 and 1963, rock and roll as a distinct form of music nearly disappeared. There were several reasons for this. First were the congressional investigations of 1959–1961 into payoffs to DJs to push certain records on their shows. "Payola" ruined the careers of a number of rock DJs, including Alan Freed, the original rock DJ, who lost his two major jobs in New York, was hounded by the IRS for back taxes, and succumbed to alcoholism in 1965. But Dick Clark of "American Bandstand" fame, was protected by the music establishment even though he became a multimillionaire with interests in a number of record companies whose songs he featured on his own show.

Second, payola McCarthyism receded in the early sixties as a result of rock and roll being fused into the mainstream of American popular music. Religious preachers appeared less worried about rock's perversion of the country's sexual moral values, southerners lost the fear of rock's racial mongrelization, and American parents no longer associated rock music with subversives, communists, and other radicals. How could they, when Elvis Presley cut his hair, was drafted into the army, and sang ballads and religious songs that were often integrated into his two dozen forgettable movies? By the time Presley's manager finished reshaping the King's image, Elvis looked more like Pat Boone, a clean-cut handsome wide-toothed singer who "covered" Little Richard's songs for white audiences in the early rock period. At the same time, Dick Clark turned his Philadelphia-based show, "American Bandstand," into an afternoon phenomenon that featured well-groomed teenagers dancing to the latest songs.

In 1963, serious rock was replaced by folk music. Greenwich Village, in the heart of downtown New York City, was its epicenter, Bob Dylan was its creator by writing new folk songs instead of retreading old ones, and the group Peter, Paul, and Mary popularized the music into commercial success. At the same time, folk music became anthems for the civil rights and anti-war protest movements.

Meanwhile, a sixties rock revival came from two sources. First was the British invasion, symbolized by the arrival of the Beatles in 1963, followed by other groups, such as the Rolling Stones, who traced their roots to the early guitar riffs of Chuck Berry. Having come from working-class backgrounds in Liverpool, the Beatles grew up in an environment that challenged authority and poked fun at some of the hypocrisy of middle-class values. Their later songs influenced the protest movements in the United States.

A second source of revival for protest rock music came from the counterculture movement in San Francisco. Bands such as the Grateful Dead and Jefferson Airplane brought "underground" rock to the forefront. Soon, even the Beatles were imitating the San Francisco underground with their classic album, "Sgt. Pepper's Lonely Hearts Club Band," a style that, according to one writer, combined "a peculiar blend of radical political rhetoric, of allusions to the drug culture, and of the excited sense of imminent, apocalyptic liberation."

Two events in 1969 symbolized the high and low points of sixties rock. In August, 500,000 people converged on a farm in upstate New York for a three-day rock festival. Woodstock became a legendary symbol. There was scant political protest. Music was the common bond that united people sitting in the rain-filled mud, sharing food and drugs while drowning out the fears of participating in an endless war. In December, all the good will of Woodstock was destroyed at a free Rolling Stones concert in Altamont, California. Four people died, one of whom was clubbed, stabbed, and kicked to death by the Hell's Angels, hired as body guards for the Stones on the advice of the Grateful Dead.

Would the sixties "new left" and counterculture movements have taken place without the emergence of rock and roll in the 1950s? Did rock help to reshape America's values, or was it all one big commercial hustle?

The two best overviews of the early history of rock and roll are Glenn C. Altschuler, *All Shook Up: How Rock and Roll Changed America* (Oxford University Press, 2003) and James Miller, *Flowers in the Dustbin: The Rise of Rock and Roll, 1947–1977* (Simon & Schuster, 1999). Four excellent overviews of the 1950s are Douglas T. Miller and Marion Nowak, *The Fifties: The Way We Really Were* (Doubleday, 1975), J. Ronald Oakley, *God's Country: America in the Fifties* (Dembner Books, 1985–1990); David Halberstam, *The Fifties* (Villard, 1993) and William L. O'Neill, *American High: The Years of Confidence, 1945–1960* (Simon & Schuster, 1986). Earlier, O'Neill wrote *Coming Apart: An Informal History of the 1960s* (Times Books, 1971), a classic treatment of the 1960s replete with vignettes that still hold up. David Marcus examines the impact of the 1950s and 1960s upon present-day politics and pop culture in *Happy Days and Wonder Years: The Fifties and Sixties in Contemporary Cultural Politics* (Rutgers University Press, 2004). Between 2000 and 2005, Greenhaven Press has published three readers with great selections on *The 1950s, The 1960s,* and *The 1960s: Examining Pop Culture.*

ISSUE 14

Did the *Brown* Decision Fail to Desegregate and Improve the Status of African Americans?

YES: Peter Irons, from *Jim Crow's Children: The Broken Promise of the Brown Decision* (Viking Press, 2002)

NO: Richard Kluger, from *Simple Justice: The History of Brown v. Board of Education and Black America's Struggle for Equality* (Alfred A. Knopf, 2004)

ISSUE SUMMARY

YES: Peter Irons argues that, despite evidence that integration improves the status of African Americans, the school integration prescribed by the *Brown* decision was never seriously tried, with the consequence that major gaps between white and black achievement persist and contribute to many of the social problems confronting African Americans today.

NO: Richard Kluger concludes that fifty years after the *Brown* decision, African Americans are better educated, better housed, and better employed than they were before 1954 in large part because the Supreme Court's ruling spawned the modern civil rights movement that culminated in the Civil Rights Act of 1964, the 1965 Voting Rights Act, and many programs of Lyndon Johnson's Great Society that were designed to improve the status of African Americans.

O n May 17, 1954, the United States Supreme Court announced the results of its deliberation in the cases of *Brown v. Board of Education of Topeka et al.* In a unanimous decision engineered by new Chief Justice Earl Warren, the Court paved the way for the collapse of a legally supported racial segregation system that had dominated black-white relations in the United States. This landmark ruling also represented a victory for the National Association for the Advancement of Colored People (NAACP), the nation's leading civil rights organization.

The Court's decision created a generally celebratory atmosphere throughout the nation's African American communities, despite the fact that many blacks remained concerned about the ultimate impact the end of Jim Crow schools would have on those black educators who had derived their professional livelihoods from the separate educational systems in the South. Most, however, saw the case as a vital step in finally eliminating separate and unequal facilities throughout the country. In contrast, the *Brown* decision sent shock waves through the white South, and even as local school board representatives publicly announced that they would comply with the Court's ruling, back-channel efforts were quickly underway to block biracial schools. Unintentionally aided by the Supreme Court's refusal to establish a definite time frame by which desegregation of public schools should take place, many white southerners interpreted the Court's dictum to act "with all deliberate speed" to mean "never." Claiming that they were only protecting ancient regional mores from the intrusive arm of the federal government, these individuals followed the lead of a group of over 100 southern Congressmen who signed "The Southern Manifesto," which charged the Warren Court with abuse of power and pledged resistance to the enforcement of *Brown*. In the face of this program of "massive resistance," brief episodes of school integration, such as in Little Rock, Arkansas, in 1957, proved to be the exceptions to the rule, and by 1964 only 2 percent of the African American students in the South attended integrated schools. Not until the Supreme Court invalidated "freedom of choice" plans in the South and endorsed busing as an instrument of desegregation did the *Brown* decision have much impact. By 1972, some 37 percent of all African American students in the states of the former Confederacy were attending majority white schools; this figure peaked in 1988 at 43 percent. Busing, however, was a highly controversial remedy that generated resistance for the first time in the North, especially in Boston, which was ravaged by riots and racial violence.

Since the 1990s, the Supreme Court has seemed to turn away from the model set by the Warren Court and made it easier for school districts to avoid desegregation orders already in place. Similarly, the Court has stymied many affirmative action plans designed by universities and professional schools to diversify their student populations. In addition, some African American leaders have begun working to re-establish strong schools for their children within black neighborhoods rather than relying upon instruction at predominately white schools. As a result, "resegregation" is a term that has emerged to describe the reality of the nation's educational system in the early twenty-first century.

The selections that follow summarize the results of desegregation since 1954 and assess the legacy of *Brown* for African Americans and the nation as a whole. In the first essay, Peter Irons concludes that despite evidence that integration works, it was never seriously tried in much of the country. Consequently, a gap remains between blacks and whites. The Court's ruling in *Brown*, says Irons, remains unfulfilled.

In the second essay, Richard Kluger offers a more optimistic appraisal. In an updated version of his definitive study *Simple Justice* first published in 1976, Kluger contends that with the aid of the *Brown* decision, desegregation proceeded at a relatively rapid pace, despite southern defiance, and set the stage for key civil rights successes that continue to benefit the African American community.

YES

Peter Irons

Jim Crow's Children: The Broken Promise of the *Brown* Decision

Linda Brown was eight years old and in the third grade at Monroe Elementary School in Topeka, Kansas, when the case bearing her name was filed on February 28, 1951. This two-story brick building had thirteen classrooms and served black students from kindergarten through eighth grade. Directly across the street from the school was a playground area, where the older students played softball. Younger children used smaller playgrounds on the north and south ends of the building.

Today, the Monroe school has been transformed into a museum, where visitors can troop through the renovated classrooms, look at photo displays, and watch a video about the history of the *Brown* case. The weed-covered playground across from the school has been spruced up, and friendly, helpful guides from the National Park Service are ready to answer questions about the school and the historic case that challenged the segregation imposed on Linda Brown and other black children in Topeka's elementary schools. One question, however, lies beyond their ability to answer. Have things improved for Topeka's black students in the years since the Supreme Court decided in 1954 that Jim Crow schools violated the Constitution? One person with an answer to that question is Linda Brown, who still lives in Topeka and whose children and grandchildren attended integrated schools. "Sometimes I wonder if we really did the children and the nation a favor by taking this case to the Supreme Court," she told a reporter in 1994, who visited Topeka on the fortieth anniversary of the *Brown* decision. "I knew it was the right thing for my father and others to do then," she said. "But after nearly forty years, we find the court's ruling remains unfulfilled." . . .

One salient fact underscores [the] discussion of Jim Crow education over the past two centuries: there has not been a single year in American history in which at least half of the nations black children attended schools that were largely white. To be sure, pushing school integration past this "halfway" point was never the goal of the civil rights lawyers and activists who labored for so long to end the system of de jure segregation that separated black and white students in southern and order states. Their goal was simply to make sure that school assignments were no longer based solely on race. At the same time, however, many of these lawyers and activists pursued the larger, more ambitious goal of using the courts to achieve the maximum possible racial mixture of students. They urged the courts to order school boards and officials to employ a variety of means—including busing and "metropolitan" desegregation plans—that would overcome the entrenched de facto segregation of residential areas and their neighborhood schools. The failure of those efforts, after the political backlash that ended the short-lived period of "forced busing," cannot be entirely blamed on the Supreme Court and the decisions that ended judicial supervision of school districts that had achieved "unitary" status. Yet, the Court quite clearly yielded to political pressure, and reflected in its decisions the increasingly conservative mood of the American public, which has endorsed school integration in numerous public opinion polls but has balked at concrete plans to implement that policy in their own cities and neighborhoods. It is fair to conclude that school integration has failed, or—put more honestly—was never seriously tried.

The failure of integration over the past half-century, after the imposition by law during the previous century of inferior Jim Crow schools on the vast majority of black children, adds force to the statement of Justice John Marshall Harlan in 1896 that whites constituted the dominant race "in prestige, in achievements, in education, in wealth and in power." The historic and persisting gap between blacks and white—measured by any part of Harlan's yardstick—is largely the consequence of generations of Jim Crow education. This single factor lies at the root of the problems that afflict or touch virtually every member of America's urban black population of some 25 million people: higher rates of crime, domestic violence, drug and alcohol abuse, teen pregnancy, low-wage jobs, unemployment, infant mortality, lowered life expectancy, and many other indices of social pathology. Singling out one factor to explain a multitude of complex social problems may appear simplistic and reductionist. But there is no denying that the system of Jim Crow schooling has given millions of America's black residents inferior education as children, has consigned them to unskilled jobs as adults, and has made it difficult to escape the urban ghettos into which rural migrants were confined by poverty and white hostility.

There is also no denying that many blacks have overcome the legacy of Jim Crow education and have joined a growing black middle class. The numbers of black doctors, lawyers, engineers, managers, and other professionals have increased since the adoption of "affirmative action" plans by colleges, corporations, and government agencies. But, much like school integration imposed through busing, affirmative action plans imposed through racial "preferences" have produced their own political backlash; federal judges have struck down such programs at the University of Texas and other schools, and the Supreme Court has rejected minority "set-aside" plans designed to channel more public funds to minority-owned firms. Even the modest gains in black education and employment have been slowed, and in some cases reversed, as the economic boom of the 1990s has gone bust and given way to recession and retrenchment in recent years.

One measure of the damaging impact of school resegregation on black students can be found in the report issued in August 2001 of the federally funded National Assessment of Educational Progress on tests of math skills of students in the fourth, eighth, and twelfth grades. On the positive side, the NEAP report showed that the math scores of fourth- and eighth-graders had improved since 1990. Disturbingly, the scores of high school seniors, which had risen slightly during the past decade, dropped sharply between 1996 and 2000. Broken down by race, the NEAP figures show a huge performance gap between black and white students at every grade level. For example, the number of white eighth-graders who scored at the "proficient" or "advanced" levels in math grew from 19 percent in 1990 to 34 percent in 2000, while only 5 percent of blacks scored at those levels in both years. Educational experts attributed the decline in twelfth-grade scores of black students to the substandard schools which most attend. Ann Wilkens of the Educational Trust, a nonprofit organization that works to improve urban schools, stressed the impact of poor math skills on the job prospects of black students. Back in the 1950s, "people could go to work in factories with basic skills," she said. "But in the 1990s, you're seeing a growing gap between the races in the ability to participate at the high levels of society."

Studies like the NEAP report, and similar measures of academic performance on the SAT test, provide growing evidence that the increasing resegregation of American public schools is threatening to turn the "growing gap" between black and white students into a racial chasm. The failure of school integration, largely a consequence of the broken promise of the *Brown* decision, becomes an even more bitter pill to swallow in light of the clear evidence that integration works. More precisely, attending school with substantial numbers of white students improves the academic performance of black children. This reflects, of course, the advantages that majority-white schools have in terms of better-trained, more experienced, and more highly paid teachers, with access to better laboratory and library resources, a wider range of courses, particularly the Advanced Placement courses that challenge students and prepare them for college-level work, and a greater number and variety of extracurricular activities.

In his 2001 report, *Schools More Separate*, Gary Orfield of the Harvard Civil Rights Project summed up the demonstrated benefits of integrated schools for black students. Orfield cited "evidence that students from desegregated educational experiences benefit in terms of college going, employment, and living in integrated settings as adults." Black students who attend integrated high schools, and who then graduate from integrated colleges and universities, make up the majority of black professionals. Orfield and his colleague, Dean Whitla, released a study in 1999 on *Diversity and Legal Education*, which focused on elite laws schools and reported that "almost all of the black and Latino students who made it into those schools came from integrated educational backgrounds."

Integrated education has benefits that go beyond academic performance. A report by Michael Kurleander and John Yun of the Harvard Civil

Rights Project in 2000 compiled surveys of students, concluding that "both white and minority students in integrated school districts tend to report by large majorities that they have learned to study and work together and that they are highly confident about their ability to work in such settings as adults. Students report that they have learned a lot about the other group's background and feel confident about the ability to discuss even controversial racial issues across racial lines." These studies illustrate the truth of Thurgood Marshall's statement, during his argument before the Supreme Court of the Little Rock school case in 1958. "Education is not the teaching of the three R's. Education is the teaching of the overall citizenship, to learn to live together with fellow citizens," Marshall told the justices.

Many people, liberals and conservatives alike, believe that the Supreme Court ended the Jim Crow system with its historic *Brown* decision in 1954. Those who profess this belief also claim that black students, now able to compete with whites on a level playing field, have only themselves to blame for doing poorly in school and failing to achieve the test scores required for admission to prestigious colleges. These advocates of "blaming the victim" fail to recognize any connection between the social and economic problems that burden the black ghetto population, and the Jim Crow educational system that has created and perpetuates the urban black underclass. After all, they argue, more than two generations of blacks have gone to schools that are no longer segregated by race, and are protected from discrimination in finding jobs and places to live by federal and state civil rights laws. Consequently, those blacks who can't find decent jobs, and who live in decaying urban ghettos, cannot blame the Jim Crow schools of past generations for their problems. Nor can they blame the Supreme Court for deciding that "resegregation" based on residential housing patterns is not something that federal judges can remedy, and for allowing the number of one-race schools to increase every year.

In my opinion, those who argue that courts have no further responsibility to remedy the damaging effects of Jim Crow schooling on America's black population are either naive or callous. To assume that two generations of "desegregation" can erase the educational harm of the preceding five or six generations is simply wrong. Studies of the continuing impact of yesterday's Jim Crow schools on today's black children are persuasive. The best compilation of these studies, *The Black-White Test Score Gap*, edited in 1998 by Christopher Jencks and Meredith Phillips, argues that grandparents "pass along their advantages and disadvantages to parents, who then pass them along to the next generation of children." Pushed back several generations, this commonsense observation has a cumulative and highly damaging effect, given the very low educational levels of blacks during the century before the *Brown* decision. Even when black families match whites in years of schooling and income, "it can take more than one generation for successful families to adopt the 'middle-class' parenting practices that seem most likely to increase children's cognitive skills." Jencks and Phillips conclude that "it could take several generations before reductions in socioeconomic inequality produce their full benefits" in higher school performance by black children.

A paradox emerges from these studies. If the past effects of Jim Crow schooling have such harmful consequences on today's black students, what benefits would they obtain from greater "reintegration" of schools? Many black leaders and educators have given up on the ideal of integration and now press for improving the quality of the one-race schools that most urban black children attend. "At this political moment, integration of the schools has been an abysmal failure," Doris Y. Wilkinson wrote in 1996. A leading black sociologist at the University of Kentucky, Wilkinson argues that the "benefits gained from obligatory school integration do not outweigh the immeasurable cultural and psychological losses." These losses include the black school as a community center and resource, the leadership training of black students in their own teams, clubs, and activities, and the close involvement of black parents in their children's education. "What has been neglected in integration history" since the *Brown* decision, Wilkinson claims, "has been a rational assessment of the emotional, motivational, learning, and community impact of abolishing the black school on poor and working-class African American children."

Another black sociologist, Leslie Innis of Florida State University, was herself a "desegregation pioneer" in the 1960s. Her study of other blacks who were among the first to attend formerly white schools shows that "the pioneers generally feel they have paid too high an emotional and psychological price for what they now perceive as too little change in the "whole system of race relations." The pioneers "do not seem to have fared any better in terms of objective social status criteria such as education, occupation, and income than their peers who went to segregated schools," writes Innis. She asserts that a "deepening dissatisfaction with the educational system has created feelings of alienation and anger" among many blacks. "These feelings have generated a call for new educational policies to be considered. Among these new policies are schools that are racially separate but equal in all important aspects—buildings, facilities, books, and personnel."

Given the growing chorus of black educators and activists who have literally given up on integration, would it not be more helpful to the millions of black children who now attend virtually all-black schools to abandon the futile efforts to achieve racial balance through busing and other means of moving children from their neighborhood schools? In place of these policies, for which there currently exists hardly any political clout, why not campaign for better-trained and better-paid teachers in urban schools, new buildings, more computers and science labs, and more rigorous standards in language and math skills? These are, in fact, the proposals to improve American schools that are currently fashionable. Other plans—giving vouchers for private school tuition to children from "failing" public schools, creating more "magnet" schools with specialized programs, expanding the Teacher Corps of highly motivated college graduates—have gained influential sponsors in Congress and state governments.

However laudable their goals, these and other "school reform" pro-posals have two major drawbacks. First, they do not address the serious problems of the "total environment" of the urban ghettos in which close to half of all black children live. This is the environment with high crime rates, low income, few cultural resources, and very high rates—more than 70 percent in most big cities—of female-headed households in which single mothers have little time or energy to help their children with homework, and most often are barely literate themselves. However good their schools and teachers, black children from this environment come to school with obstacles to effective learning that few white children must overcome.

The second drawback of current school reform proposals is that they rely largely on standardized testing to measure results. One consequence of " teaching to the test" is that school officials pressure teachers to rely on old-fashioned methods of rote learning, the mainstay of Jim Crow schools before the *Brown* decision. Creativity, curiosity, and critical thinking are stifled, and the pressure on teachers in largely black and Hispanic schools to raise test scores and avoid "failing" grades for their schools becomes intense. *The New York Times* reported in June 2001 that many fourth-grade teachers in the city's schools, the grade in which testing begins, are re-questing transfers to other grades, to escape the "test pressure" that forces them to use a lockstep curriculum.

If the current push for school reforms that will not change the unbal-anced racial composition of most schools means that integration has failed, is there any point in assigning the blame for this failure? We can point the finger at individuals and institutions: Justice Felix Frankfurter's insist-ence on the "all deliberate speed" formula in the second *Brown* decision; President Dwight Eisenhower's failure to speak out in support of court or-ders; the "war on the Constitution" waged by Governor Orval Faubus and other southern politicians; the Supreme Court's refusal to allow school buses to cross district lines in the *Milliken* case; and the Court's explicit approval of "one-race" schools in decisions that ended judicial oversight of desegregation orders. In a broader sense, however, the blame rests with the "dominant race" in America. Whites created the institution of slavery; whites fashioned the Jim Crow system that replaced slavery with segrega-tion; whites spat on black children, threw rocks at buses, and shut down entire school districts to avoid integration; and white parents abandoned the cities when neighborhoods and schools passed the "tipping point" and became too black for comfort.

This is not an indictment of a race, merely an acknowledgment of reality. Many whites took part in the abolitionist crusade, fought and died in the Civil War to end slavery, campaigned to end the Jim Crow system, and kept their children in public schools that had become largely black. Most white Americans, in fact, profess their belief in school integration; two-thirds of those polled in 1994 agreed that integration has "improved the quality of education for blacks," and two-fifths said the same for white students. Belief in an ideal and support for its implementation, however, are not the same. Substantially more than two-thirds of whites oppose busing for "racial balance" in the schools, and most say they would move out of their present neighborhood if it became more than 20 percent black. The phenomenon of "white flight" shows that many people have put their attitudes into action.

Perhaps we should accept the reality that Jim Crow schools are here to stay, and make the best of the situation. Kenneth W. Jenkins, who headed the NAACP chapter in Yonkers, New York, was removed from that post by the national organization in 1996 for questioning the protracted litigation to integrate his city's segregated schools. "This thing is not working," he said. "I support integration, but I don't think integration is the goal. The goal is quality education." Even a dedicated NAACP lawyer, Ted Shaw, voiced his frustration at the futility of litigation to integrate urban schools. "You're beating your head up against the wall until it's bloody. At some point you have to ask, 'Should I continue to beat up against this wall?' To ask that question is not a terrible thing."

Perhaps the best person to answer Jenkins and Shaw, and others who share their frustration—white and black alike—is Thurgood Marshall, who put his whole life into struggling against the Jim Crow system. It is worth repeating here the words he wrote in 1974, dissenting in the *Milliken* case: " Desegregation is not and was never expected to be an easy task. Racial attitudes ingrained in our Nation's childhood and adolescence are not quickly thrown aside in its middle years." Marshall concluded: "In the short run, it may seem to be the easiest course to allow our great metropolitan areas to be divided up each into two cities—one white, the other black—but it is a course, I predict, our people will ultimately regret."

Visible Man: Fifty Years After *Brown*

Exorcism is rarely a pretty spectacle. It is frequently marked by violent spasms and protracted trauma, and so it has been over the five decades since *Brown* launched the nation's effort to rid itself of the consuming demons of racism. The Supreme Court's ruling may be visualized as the cresting wave of a tidal movement resulting from the great economic earthquake of 1929. Not until then had American society seriously acknowledged that its most sacred obligation went beyond the protection of property and capital to its citizens' needs for daily subsistence. People were no longer to be viewed as an infinitely disposable market commodity. The New Deal of Franklin Roosevelt became the first national program since the end of Reconstruction in the South in 1876 to treat black Americans as recognizably human. Worldwide conflicts with fascism and communism added to the country's consciousness that its African Americans had not been precisely the beneficiaries of the social order; a system that inflicted so much pain and hardship was understood by many to be in urgent need of repair—if only the signal were given. It was in this receptive soil that Chief Justice Warren and his eight robed brethren planted the seed of *Brown v. Board of Education of Topeka, Kansas.*

At a stroke the Court had erased the most flagrant remaining insignia of slavery. No longer could the African American be relegated to the status of official pariah. No longer could whites look right through him as if he were, in the title words of Ralph Ellison's soon-to-become-classic 1952 novel, an "Invisible Man."

The mass movement spawned by *Brown* was unmistakably under way within six months of the Court's issuing its open-ended implementation decree. It began in the Deep South, in Montgomery, Alabama, when a fortythree-year-old seamstress and active NAACP member named Rosa Parks refused to surrender her seat to a white passenger and move to the back of a city bus as the local ordinances required. Within days, thanks to the leadership of Martin Luther King, Jr., Mrs. Parks's pastor, all blacks were refusing to ride Montgomery's buses in a massive display of resentment over the continuing humiliation of Jim Crow. With dignity, courage, and resolve that was capturing the nation's attention, Montgomery's African Americans made their boycott stick for more than a year. By the end of it,

Excerpts from *Simple Justice: The History of Brown v. Board of Education and Black America's Struggle for Equality,* (Alfred A. Knopf, 1975) pp. 754–759, 780–782, 786–789. Copyright © 1975 by Richard Kluger. Reprinted by permission of Random House Inc.

the Supreme Court had struck down segregation laws in public transportation just as it had in public education.

Over the next dozen years the Warren Court would hand down decision after decision that followed the path *Brown* had opened. Segregation was outlawed in public parks and recreation areas, on or at all transportation facilities (waiting rooms and lunch counters as well as the carriers themselves), in libraries and courtrooms and the facilities of all public buildings, and in hotels, restaurants, and other enterprises accommodating the public. It was declared unlawful to list on a ballot the race of a candidate for public office. Black witnesses could no longer be addressed by their first names in Southern courtrooms. Sexual relations between consenting blacks and whites were removed from the criminal decalogue, and in 1967, with scarcely a murmur of objection in the land, the high court ruled that state laws forbidding the rite most hateful to the cracker mentality—the joining of white and black in holy matrimony—were unconstitutional. Within that same dozen years the Court issued historic rulings in two other areas of critical importance to African Americans. The sweeping "one man, one vote" decisions of *Baker v. Carr* in 1962 and *Reynolds v. Sims* in 1964 mandated massive legislature reapportionment that resulted in significantly increased representation of urban areas where blacks were concentrated. In the criminal justice realm, the Court markedly improved the ability of accused criminals to defend themselves; *Miranda v. Arizona, Escobedo v. Illinois*, and *Gideon v. Wainwright* were the landmark cases.

Once ordered by the Court, desegregation proceeded at a relatively rapid pace in most categories. Streetcars and eating places and amusement parks were, after all, settings for transient commingling of the races; schools, though, were something else. There the interracial contact would last six to eight hours a day, and was from interaction with one another as much as immersion in their lesson book that schoolchildren were acculturated. So it was the schoolhouse that became the arena for the South's fiercest show of hostility to desegregation. The most rabid elements in the region pledged "massive resistance" to the command and were abetted in that resolve by the so-called Southern Manifesto issued in the spring of 1956 by 101 U.S. Senators and members of the House of Representatives, a politically potent assemblage who termed *Brown* "a clear abuse of judicial power" that had substituted the Justices' "personal, political, and social ideas for the established law of the land."

The popular and amiable President of the United States, Dwight D. Eisenhower, might reasonably have been expected to place the prestige of his august office behind the Supreme Court's monumental ruling. Yet this soldier of formidable rectitude never did so, except in the most offhand way. Declining to say whether he agreed with the *Brown* decision, Ike lamely remarked, "I think it makes no difference whether or not I endorse it. The Constitution is as the Supreme Court interprets it, and I must conform to that and do my very best to see that it is carried out in this country." It might have been carried out far sooner and less bruisingly if the President had urged the country to obey *Brown*, not just because it was a ruling of the nation's ultimate court but because it was right. For him to stand above the battle was to lend aid and comfort to the forces of resistance. "If Mr. Eisenhower had come through," recalled former Justice Tom Clark after he had retired from the bench, "it would have changed things a lot."

Thus unchallenged by the executive and legislative branches of the federal government, the South succeeded for ten years in largely evading and defying the Supreme Court's directive to end racial separation in public schools. Only a trickle of black students was allowed to enter the white schools of Old Dixie, and even then this small brave band often had to endure menacing taunts and the spittle of die-hard white supremacists. A decade after *Brown*, not even one in fifty African American pupils was attending classes with whites in the eleven states with the largest proportion of black residents. Meanwhile, the rest of the nation looked on not overly concerned, preferring to see the South's stalling tactics as a regional problem and turning a blind eye to the depth and virulence of their own uncodified racism and the *de facto* segregation in their urban ghettos.

John F. Kennedy became the first U.S. President to commit his administration, if belatedly and somewhat reluctantly, to broad action to improve the condition of black America. That burden no longer rested, as it had since *Brown* was promulgated, almost entirely upon the Supreme Court and the rest of the federal judiciary. Government protection was extended to freedom riders who risked their necks to protest the continuing disenfranchisement of Southern blacks and other inequities in the old fire-breathing bastions of Jim Crow. The Justice Department pushed the Interstate Commerce Commission to issue a blanket order ending segregation at all rail, air, and bus facilities, and its enforcement was rapid. The government initiated suits to force recalcitrant school districts to desegregate, and the pace of the process now quickened: 31 districts in 1961, 46 districts in 1962, 166 districts in 1963. All branches of the federal government were urged to step up their hiring of blacks, and federally funded contractors were similarly pushed. But because Democrat Kennedy hesitated to cross swords with the powerful Southern wing of his party, fearing that a clash would scuttle the rest of his legislative program, he delayed for more than two years before signing an executive order prohibiting discrimination in all housing that received direct federal subsidies and in the much broader sector of the home-building market financed by government-guaranteed mortgages. . . .

[F]ive months and three days before he was slain, Kennedy ended his fragile working relationship with the entrenched Southern bloc on Capitol Hill and sent Congress the most sweeping civil-rights law proposed in nearly a century. The bill bore this heading: "An act to enforce the constitutional right to vote, to confer jurisdiction upon the district courts of the United States to provide injunctive relief against discrimination in public accommodations, to authorize the Attorney General to institute suits to protect constitutional rights in public facilities and public education, to extend the Commission on Civil Rights, to prevent discrimination in federally assisted programs, to establish a Commission on Equal Employment Opportunity, and for other purposes." And to oversee this disestablishment of racism, the Justice Department would be empowered to go to court in the name of black Americans who could ill afford the time, energy, and cost of suing sovereign states and their subdivisions whose laws and policies effectively frustrated the desegregation process. . . .

During Lyndon Johnson's first months in the White House, Malcolm X demeaned him as "a Southern cracker—that's all he is." Perhaps black leaders feared that the new President would prove the reincarnation of the last man named Johnson to occupy the White House; he, too, was a Southerner succeeding a murdered friend of the blacks. But Lyndon, born poor in the bleak west Texas hill country and never forgetting his hardscrabble origins, was not Andrew; he was, rather, a consummate practitioner of legislative deal-making, whose glad-handing could turn bone-crushing if need be. His expansive rhetoric and carrot-and-stick enticements drew together liberal and moderate lawmakers of both parties and fashioned a program that advanced the rights of African Americans far beyond what Kennedy, for all his good intentions, could probably ever have accomplished. The Senate passed the 1964 Civil Rights Act a year to the day after Kennedy sent it to Congress.

Over the next ten years, with inconstant degrees of enthusiasm, the federal government put the 1964 rights bill to a great deal of use. And having outflanked the Dixiecrat power base in the Senate, where he had presided so ably as majority leader, Johnson kept pushing civil-rights measures through Congress during his remaining five years in the Oval Office. In 1965 the Voting Rights Act restricted "tests and devices" used to foil and intimidate would-be black voters and assigned federal registrars and observers to bolster the voter-recruitment efforts of civil-rights workers in the field. Within a decade the number of blacks on Southern voting rolls was triple the total on the day the Kennedy-Johnson administration had taken office. Before long, Congress was responding to LBJ's fervent requests by passing the Elementary and Secondary Education Act, providing unprecedented federal funds to help local school districts—and, in the process, arming Washington with a weighty financial club to enforce compliance with the desegregation orders of the federal courts. The widely welcomed education bill was part of a proliferating series of imaginative new federal programs aimed at declaring war on poverty and ignorance throughout the nation. Together—aid to schools, Model Cities, the Office of Economic Opportunity, Head Start, VISTA, the Fair Housing Act, legal services for the poor, consumer protection laws, and Medicare to tend the ailing elderly— the President labeled them stepping-stones to a Great Society, one that would benefit no sector of its people more than black Americans. . . .

Among African Americans who were to enjoy such a reward was fifty-nine-year-old Thurgood Marshall, the emblematic "Mr. Civil Rights," as the press had dubbed him. In 1967, after Marshall had served as a U.S. Circuit Court judge and the nation's Solicitor General, Johnson nominated him to the Supreme Court, the arena where he had so often appeared to advance the rights of his race. After a bloc of Southern Senators took a final turn at tormenting him by holding up his nomination for months, Marshall was confirmed as the ninety-sixth man to sit on the nation's highest tribunal—and its first African American. He would remain there for twenty-five years, and while never its brightest light and often ailing, he proved an unflinching protector of the civil rights and civil liberties of all Americans. . . .

✦

Scanning the half-century since *Brown* was handed down from the white marble temple of justice close by the nation's Capitol, what can we say with confidence about the transforming effect of the event on the national psyche and the condition of African Americans in particular?

At the least, we can say it brought to an end more than three centuries of an officially sanctioned mind-set embracing white supremacy and excusing a massive and often pitiless oppression. At long last a roster of magnanimous Justices had been moved to instruct the country that such beliefs and the resulting conduct were unconscionable and intolerable under the law. But delegitimizing the racist caste system could not magically remake the chastened former master class into overnight paragons of decency, eager to extend to their darker ex-captives full and equal access to their shared society's bounty. The lash, though, had been cast away for good. To gain their due, black Americans soon discovered, they would have to go on the march, under the banner of lawful entitlement, and not wait to be gifted with the nation's long withheld kindness. En route, they now felt licensed to vent a rage they had so long repressed for fear of swift reprisal. Their march did not proceed without its perils—or rewards.

By almost every measurable standard, African Americans as a group were significantly better off in 2004 than they had been in 1954. They were better educated and housed, more gainfully employed in more demanding jobs, more self-confident and highly regarded by their white countrymen, and had made undemable contributions to the mainstream culture. No one any longer questioned that jazz and blues were art. The black presence was ubiquitous, even where blacks were not there in person. Its impact had become detectable in nearly every aspect of Americans' daily lives: how they talk, dress, eat, play, fix their hair, sing their national anthem, even how they shake hands. Black artists were no longer a sub-category, catering only or mainly to black audiences. Black athletes dominated their fields. Every U.S. Cabinet now included one or two African Americans; the Supreme Court likewise had an all-but-obligatory black seat; the Congressional Black Caucus, at times numbering more than forty members, was a formidable voting bloc in legislative decision-making; the "Old Dominion" of Virginia had elected a black governor, and almost every major American city had at one time or another chosen a black mayor. Even in the corporate world, still a mostly white preserve, black executives were emerging, though generally in the lower echelons. The nation's biggest stock brokerage firm and the largest entertainment conglomerate chose African Americans as their CEO. . . .

For all these heartening signs of far greater black prominence and white acceptance in American daily life, there was no denying that mixed with the good news were too many remnants of an aching disparity between the races that time and good intentions had not cured.

⌒

Why haven't African Americans progressed further toward equality of both opportunity and attainment? Why hasn't the nation achieved true racial integration?

One plausible explanation is that the American fondness for quick fixes and ready expedients does not compute in a realm with so many complex emotional variables. The evolution of human habits and attitudes takes time, and while the United States has not yet fully solved its most intractable social dilemma, neither has it shied away altogether. But some on both sides of the color line remain convinced that further measures to encourage interracial bonding will prove fruitless. There are many whites who believe that America has done enough to redress black grievances by substantially correcting its formerly prejudicial laws, thinking, and conduct. For those blacks willing to try earnestly to overcome their acknowledged historic disadvantages, these whites say, the way upward is open, so that African Americans should no longer be indulged as perpetual invalids, and the groans of the self-pitying among them should fall on deaf ears. In stark contrast, a substantial segment of black Americans believe—or have been persuaded—that white hatred toward them runs so deep in the American ethos that it will never yield more ground than it is forced to. And no one, they note, is forcing it. Indeed, the opposite seems to be true: instead of structured social initiatives, there have been retreats and rollbacks by mean-spirited government policymakers, so that for far too many blacks there has been little or no progress.

Such polarizing views, not without some truth to them, miss the larger picture.

The uniqueness of the African American experience cannot be fully grasped by white Americans without an understanding that for many, if not for most, blacks, their color—of whatever hue—has been and remains the indelible, shaping, and often ruling factor in their existence. Their skin cannot be shed. It is a daily reminder of the cumulative and all too frequently sorry history of their race in America. However much improved their status or however loud the proclamations by white America that racial equality is in the offing, the suspicion lingers among blacks, along with so many bitter memories, that they can never measure up and will always be seen in whites' hurtful eyes as water-bearers, tap dancers, and clowning inferiors. It is a suspicion steeped in the reality that white America has never said forthrightly that it is sorry for the enormity of the pain both physical and spiritual long inflicted on its black people—or faced up to the effort and cost truly required to undo the remnants of that atrocity.

"A society that places so much premium on 'getting ahead,'" wrote Andrew Hacker in *Two Nations*, "cannot afford to spare much compassion for those who fall behind." Hacker got it half right. It is not that America cannot do so; it *will not* do so—or, at any rate, has not yet seriously considered the matter. By the governments it has put in place and the leaders it has chosen since *Brown*, the nation has not acted in good faith—except for a short season all but forgotten now—to better educate, house, and employ those whom it had long abused. Halfhearted (or less) seemed good enough: witness the rapidity with which the "war on poverty" was shut down before it could be granted time to take hold. Why make sacrifices in the form of tax dollars, job set-asides, and "affirmative action" and thereby elevate African Americans into fully competitive rivals for society's material rewards? It made better economic sense to keep them disadvantaged in a Darwinian world where the fittest prevail.

Consider housing. Conspired against by laws, customs, crass real-estate agents, profiteering landlords, redlining bankers, merciless federal mortgage insurers, and thoughtless urban renewal planners, most black Americans who broke free from the white-supremacist South found themselves systematically penned into urban slums and their children isolated in one-race schools. When *Brown* finally ordered the gates unlocked and fair-housing laws were passed to encourage a black diaspora, few whites cheered; their property values might suffer. When busing was introduced as the only practicable method of integrating inner-city pupils, white objectors took to the hills by the legion, and soon few of them were left to integrate with. A generation later, segregation was returning to many areas. Fair-housing laws, meanwhile, were being honored far more in the breach than the practice. Yet African America persevered, a sizable black middle class emerged, and interracial communities have gradually become a spreading phenomenon. Still, no politician who reads his or her polling numbers seriously calls for a domestic Marshall Plan that could put an end to derelict black neighborhoods where so many remain mired in misery. Americans simply seem more dedicated to exploring outer space than to saving their inner cities; we lavish our wealth on outsized vehicles and state-of-the-art weaponry rather than on improving young minds or caring for the public health. The race issue has come to be regarded not as fertile ground for progressive policymakers but a burial ground for political activists of the stripe who once believed that government could lift the destitute, hound the predatory, and serve the common good. Now the liberating impulse has been largely co-opted by the political right, devoted to freeing private enterprise from allegedly incessant government meddling. The result has been an extreme maldistribution of the nation's wealth that outrages remarkably few Americans. Only an unpredictable wind shift toward altruism seems likely to power a new national consensus that identifies government as neither enemy nor savior but as a useful tool when put prudently to the task. As long as those put in charge of it profess to hate it, government cannot be the prime mover in the pursuit of justice.

If white America may be faulted for having too strictly rationed its generosity toward the black community within it, what may be ventured about the role of African America in assessing why, for all the statistical evidence of progress, the racial gulf still seems so obstinately wide?

Like its white counterpart, black America has never been a monolithic unit, its attitudes varying with history, geography, degree of assimilation, and even skin pigmentation. And with the steady expansion of the black middle class, new fissures have riddled African Americans' racial solidarity; the embittered poor are less forgiving toward their perceived oppressors than the newly prospering are. But regardless of their station in life, stagnant or evolving, the nation's blacks have understandably been haunted by twin fears: (1) Does the rest of America really accept them as equally human members of society, no longer a subspecies? (2) Has their escape from flagrant oppression taken them to the point where they can vie with confidence to achieve their individual potential? Neither is a rhetorical question.

Deep skepticism about the answer to the first question has fed the temptation among African Americans to blame many of their frustrations and disappointments on an intractable racism that some insist has scarcely abated. "Victimology is today nothing less than a keystone of cultural blackness," contends John McWhorter. The time is at hand, he argues, for blacks to address their failures and stop turning for solace to a defiantly separate—and distancing—cultural identity. Certainly there has always been a running debate within the African American community, as inside all ethnic groups, over the extent to which blacks can and should conform their conduct—their speech, dress, appearance, tastes—to white norms in order to win acceptance and advancement and yet not lose the essence of their beings. Expanded opportunities in the post-*Brown* age have intensified this concern. But to view, for example, the quest for academic excellence or entrepreneurial expertise as "acting white" and thus a denial of one's own core identity is to answer white flight with black flight. Why should a proudly practiced African American subculture be thought of as fatally diminished by flowing into the mainstream instead of being regarded as a powerful tributary that adds great life force to the national current?

Sadly, the rewards of interracial and transcultural blending have been spurned by many younger African Americans in the nation's high schools and colleges, precisely where the future is taking shape. Mingling with white classmates is often taken—whether out of long-smoldering resentment, fear of being rejected or patronized, or for some other phobic cause—as a denial of one's African American roots, while white students, detecting only a large threatening chip on their black schoolmates' shoulders and failing to perceive it as an expression of natural cultural affinities or a confession of insecurity, have often responded inhospitably, adding to the rancorous standoff. Nor have adult overseers helped matters. Administrators at many white-majority universities, in the misguided belief they were insulating their campuses against racial tension, have accomplished the opposite by setting aside blacksonly dormitories, or parts thereof, to accommodate

African American students who wish to segregate themselves. But what sort of lesson has been taught by such invitations to group avoidance in settings where young people migrate to be stimulated by new ideas and to gain understanding through exposure to fresh cultural influences?

A far more telling lesson was offered on the op-ed page of *The New York Times* on the first Fourth of July of the third millennium of the Christian Era by black scholar Roger Wilkins, nephew of the longtime executive secretary of the NAACP, Roy Wilkins. Without naming her, Wilkins took issue with the in-your-face remark by acclaimed black novelist Toni Morrison that she had never in her life felt like an American. "Well, I have—all my life," wrote Wilkins, stressing that he had never felt himself less of an American because he stemmed from slaves "who in their stolen lives built so much of this country." Having begun his education before *Brown* in a segregated one-room schoolhouse in Missouri, Wilkins conceded that black living conditions in the United States remained far from satisfactory, "but the change has nevertheless been so dramatic that my belief in American possibilities remains profound." At the end he held out hope for renewed citizen action "harnessed to our founding ideas to improve American life and even to transform some American hearts."

Genuine social justice has been an oft-announced but rarely pursued ambition throughout history and probably was never achieved by any enduring society or civilization. Within the recent past the world has witnessed the collapse of Soviet-style Marxism, whose ideology enshrined an egalitarian state of selfless citizens—never mind that they were ruthlessly lorded over by a council of privileged cutthroats. The mission of defining, creating, and sustaining a truly just society on a thronged planet, manifestly unfair from its creation, is rendered almost insuperably difficult for a people like ours, a vast, clamorous, polyglot and polychromatic, beaverishly purposeful multitude, without its match on earth. Good-hearted but grasping, earnest yet impatient, easily distractable, and prone to trade its avowed humanitarian principles for triumphalism, America is a colossus of contradictions. For a certainty, justice of any type cannot materialize in such an untidy place without the binding up of its constituent elements. And that is unlikely ever to occur unless and until Americans of every variety acknowledge that what separates them is small change when counted against all they hold in common. Possessing soul is not a uniquely black or white state of grace, any more than owning a white or black skin, or a beige, olive, sallow, or ruddy one is a mark of either superiority or disgrace. A precept, let us admit in candor but with hope, that is more easily stated than lived.

POSTSCRIPT

Did the *Brown* Decision Fail to Desegregate and Improve the Status of African Americans?

The fiftieth anniversary of the Supreme Court's ruling in *Brown* has generated numerous appraisals of the decision's legacy. In Brown v. Board of Education: *Caste, Culture, and the Constitution* (University Press of Kansas, 2003), law professors Robert J. Cottrol, Raymond T. Diamond, and Leland B. Ware emphasize that beyond attacking the "separate but equal" doctrine, *Brown* offered the American people a view of the beneficial role that an activist judiciary could play in resolving some of the nation's most difficult social problems. Derrick Bell is far less sanguine about the ability of the courts to challenge white dominance in *Silent Covenants*: Brown v. Board of Education *and the Unfulfilled Hopes for Racial Reform* (Oxford University Press, 2004). Charles T. Clotfelter, in *After* Brown: *The Rise and Retreat of School Desegregation* (Princeton University Press, 2004), recognizes the incomplete nature of school desegregation but describes the interracial contact derived from the Court's ruling as having a transformative impact on intergroup relations that has benefited both African Americans and whites. Charles J. Ogletree Jr., *All Deliberate Speed: Reflections on the First Half-Century of* Brown v. Board of Education (W. W. Norton, 2004) argues that the promises of integrated public education and full racial equality were undermined by the Supreme Court's refusal to set a specific date by which segregation must end. Albert L. Samuels, *Is Separate Unequal? Black Colleges and the Challenge to Desegregation* (University Press of Kansas, 2004) examines the impact of the *Brown* decision on historically black colleges and universities (HBCUs). For an excellent summary of the *Brown* case and its legacy, see Waldo Martin, Brown v. Board of Education: *A Brief History With Documents* (Bedford/St. Martin's Press, 1998) and James T. Patterson, Brown v. Board of Education: *A Civil Rights Milestone and Its Troubled Legacy* (Oxford University Press, 2001). Both the *Journal of Southern History* (May 2004) and the *Journal of American History* (June 2004) commemorated the fiftieth anniversary of the *Brown* decision with scholarly retrospectives by distinguished historians.

Regardless of how one assesses the impact of *Brown*, many scholars, including Kluger, view the decision as the starting point for the civil rights movement. Michael Klarman's *From Jim Crow to Civil Rights: The Supreme Court and the Struggle for Racial Equality* (Oxford University Press, 2004) challenges this assessment by concluding that *de jure* segregation would have been eliminated fairly quickly even without the Court's supportive verdict in 1954. In recent years, historians of the civil rights movement have argued that the struggle for African American equality began much earlier in the twentieth century and laid the groundwork for the successes of the 1950s and 1960s. *"We Return Fighting": The Civil Rights Movement in the Jazz Age* (Northeastern University Press, 2001) focuses on the role of the NAACP in the post–World War I era. Patricia Sullivan, *Days of Hope: Race and Democracy in the New Deal Era* (University of North Carolina Press, 1996) makes a case for the 1930s and 1940s as the true watershed for civil rights activity, while Richard Dalfiume, "The 'Forgotten Years' of the Negro Revolution," *Journal of American History* (June 1968) and John Dittmer, *Local People: The Struggle for Civil Rights in Mississippi* (University of Illinois Press, 1994) make a strong case for the Second World War as the stimulus for civil rights successes in the Cold War era.

The literature on the civil rights movement is extensive. August Meier, Elliott Rudwick, and Francis L. Broderick, eds., *Black Protest Thought in the Twentieth Century* (2d. ed.; Bobbs-Merrill, 1971) presents a collection of documents that places the activities of the 1950s and 1960s in a larger framework. The reflections of many of the participants of the movement are included in Howell Raines, *My Soul Is Rested: The Story of the Civil Rights Movement in the Deep South* (G. P. Putnam, 1977). Students should also consult Aldon D. Morris, *The Origins of the Civil Rights Movement: Black Communities Organizing for Change* (Free Press, 1984). August Meier's contemporary assessment, "On the Role of Martin Luther King," *Crisis* (1965), in many ways remains the most insightful analysis of King's leadership. More detailed studies include David L. Lewis, *King: A Critical Biography* (Praeger, 1970); Stephen B. Oates, *Let the Trumpet Sound: The Life of Martin Luther King, Jr.* (Harper and Row, 1982); and David J. Garrow's Pulitzer Prize–winning *Bearing the Cross: Martin Luther King, Jr., and the Southern Christian Leadership Conference* (William Morrow, 1986). Taylor Branch's *Parting the Waters: America in the King Years, 1954–63* (Simon & Schuster, 1988), which won the Pulitzer Prize, and *Pillar of Fire: America in the King Years, 1963–1968* (Simon & Schuster, 1998) are beautifully written narratives. Finally, the texture of the civil rights movement is captured brilliantly in Henry Hampton's documentary series "Eyes on the Prize."

A critical assessment of the legacy of the civil rights movement is presented in two books by political scientist Robert C. Smith: *We Have No Leaders: African Americans in the Post–Civil Rights Era* (State University of New York Press, 1994) and *Racism in the Post–Civil Rights Era: Now You See It, Now You Don't* (State University of New York Press, 1996).

ISSUE 15

Was the Americanization of the War in Vietnam Inevitable?

YES: Brian VanDeMark, from *Into the Quagmire: Lyndon Johnson and the Escalation of the Vietnam War* (Oxford University Press, 1991)

NO: H. R. McMaster, from *Dereliction of Duty: Lyndon Johnson, Robert McNamara, the Joint Chiefs of Staff, and the Lies That Led to Vietnam* (HarperCollins, 1997)

ISSUE SUMMARY

YES: Professor of history Brian VanDeMark argues that President Lyndon Johnson failed to question the viability of increasing U.S. involvement in the Vietnam War because he was a prisoner of America's global containment policy and because he did not want his opponents to accuse him of being soft on communism or endanger support for his Great Society reforms.

NO: H. R. McMaster, an active-duty army tanker, maintains that the Vietnam disaster was not inevitable but a uniquely human failure whose responsibility was shared by President Johnson and his principal military and civilian advisers.

$\mathbf{A}$t the end of World War II, imperialism was coming to a close in Asia. Japan's defeat spelled the end of its control over China, Korea, and the countries of Southeast Asia. Attempts by the European nations to reestablish their empires were doomed. Anti-imperialist movements emerged all over Asia and Africa, often producing chaos.

The United States faced a dilemma. America was a nation conceived in revolution and was sympathetic to the struggles of Third World nations. But the United States was afraid that many of the revolutionary leaders were Communists who would place their countries under the control of the expanding empire of the Soviet Union. By the late 1940s the Truman administration decided that it was necessary to stop the spread of communism. The policy that resulted was known as containment.

Vietnam provided a test of the containment doctrine in Asia. Vietnam had been a French protectorate from 1885 until Japan took control of it during

World War II. Shortly before the war ended, the Japanese gave Vietnam its independence, but the French were determined to reestablish their influence in the area. Conflicts emerged between the French-led nationalist forces of South Vietnam and the Communist-dominated provisional government of the Democratic Republic of Vietnam (DRV), which was established in Hanoi in August 1945. Ho Chi Minh was the president of the DRV. An avowed Communist since the 1920s, Ho had also become the major nationalist figure in Vietnam. As the leader of the anti-imperialist movement against French and Japanese colonialism for over 30 years, Ho managed to tie together the communist and nationalist movements in Vietnam.

A full-scale war broke out in 1946 between the communist government of North Vietnam and the French-dominated country of South Vietnam. After the Communists defeated the French at the battle of Dien Bien Phu in May 1954, the latter decided to pull out. At the Geneva Conference that summer, Vietnam was divided at the 17th parallel, pending elections.

The United States became directly involved in Vietnam after the French withdrew. In 1955 the Republican president Dwight D. Eisenhower refused to recognize the Geneva Accord but supported the establishment of the South Vietnamese government. In 1956 South Vietnam's leader, Ngo Dinh Diem, with U.S. approval, refused to hold elections, which would have provided a unified government for Vietnam in accordance with the Geneva Agreement. The Communists in the north responded by again taking up the armed struggle. The war continued for another 19 years.

Both President Eisenhower and his successor, John F. Kennedy, were anxious to prevent South Vietnam from being taken over by the Communists, so economic assistance and military aid were provided. Kennedy's successor, Lyndon B. Johnson, changed the character of American policy in Vietnam by escalating the air war and increasing the number of ground forces from 21,000 in 1965 to a full fighting force of 550,000 at its peak in 1968.

The next president, Richard Nixon, adopted a new policy of "Vietnamization" of the war. Military aid to South Vietnam was increased to ensure the defeat of the Communists. At the same time, American troops were gradually withdrawn from Vietnam. South Vietnamese president Thieu recognized the weakness of his own position without the support of U.S. troops. He reluctantly signed the Paris Accords in January 1973 only after being told by Secretary of State Henry Kissinger that the United States would sign them alone. Once U.S. soldiers were withdrawn, Thieu's regime was doomed. In spring 1975 a full-scale war broke out, and the South Vietnamese government collapsed.

In the following selection, Brian VanDeMark argues that President Johnson failed to question the viability of increasing U.S. involvement in Vietnam because he was a prisoner of America's global containment policy and he did not want his opponents to accuse him of being soft on communism. In the second selection, H. R. McMaster argues that the Vietnam disaster was not inevitable but a uniquely human failure whose responsibility was shared by Johnson and his civilian and military advisers.

YES

Brian VanDeMark

Into the Quagmire

Vietnam divided America more deeply and painfully than any event since the Civil War. It split political leaders and ordinary people alike in profound and lasting ways. Whatever the conflicting judgments about this controversial war—and there are many—Vietnam undeniably stands as the greatest tragedy of twentieth-century U.S. foreign relations.

America's involvement in Vietnam has, as a result, attracted much critical-scrutiny, frequently addressed to the question, "Who was guilty?"— "Who led the United States into this tragedy?" A more enlightening question, it seems, is "How and why did this tragedy occur?" The study of Vietnam should be a search for explanation and understanding, rather than for scapegoats.

Focusing on one important period in this long and complicated story—the brief but critical months from November 1964 to July 1965, when America crossed the threshold from limited to large-scale war in Vietnam—helps to answer that question. For the crucial decisions of this period resulted from the interplay of longstanding ideological attitudes, diplomatic assumptions and political pressures with decisive contemporaneous events in America and Vietnam.

Victory in World War II produced a sea change in America's perception of its role in world affairs. Political leaders of both parties embraced a sweepingly new vision of the United States as the defender against the perceived threat of monolithic communist expansion everywhere in the world. This vision of American power and purpose, shaped at the start of the Cold War, grew increasingly rigid over the years. By 1964–1965, it had become an iron-bound and unshakable dogma, a received faith which policymakers unquestionably accepted—even though the circumstances which had fostered its creation had changed dramatically amid diffused authority and power among communist states and nationalist upheaval in the colonial world.

Policymakers' blind devotion to this static Cold War vision led America into misfortune in Vietnam. Lacking the critical perspective and sensibility to reappraise basic tenets of U.S. foreign policy in the light of changed events and local circumstances, policymakers failed to perceive

Vietnamese realities accurately and thus to gauge American interests in the area prudently. Policymakers, as a consequence, misread an indigenous, communist-led nationalist movement as part of a larger, centrally directed challenge to world order and stability; tied American fortunes to a non-communist regime of slim popular legitimacy and effectiveness; and intervened militarily in the region far out of proportion to U.S. security requirements.

An arrogant and stubborn faith in America's power to shape the course of foreign events compounded the dangers sown by ideological rigidity. Policymakers in 1964–1965 shared a common postwar conviction that the United States not only should, but could, control political conditions in South Vietnam, as elsewhere throughout much of the world. This conviction had led Washington to intervene progressively deeper in South Vietnamese affairs over the years. And when—despite Washington's increasing exertions—Saigon's political situation declined precipitously during 1964–1965, this conviction prompted policymakers to escalate the war against Hanoi, in the belief that America could stimulate political order in South Vietnam through the application of military force against North Vietnam.

Domestic political pressures exerted an equally powerful, if less obvious, influence over the course of U.S. involvement in Vietnam. The fall of China in 1949 and the ugly McCarthyism it aroused embittered American foreign policy for a generation. By crippling President Truman's political fortunes, it taught his Democratic successors, John Kennedy and Lyndon Johnson [LBJ], a strong and sobering lesson: that another "loss" to communism in East Asia risked renewed and devastating attacks from the right. This fear of reawakened McCarthyism remained a paramount concern as policymakers pondered what course to follow as conditions in South Vietnam deteriorated rapidly in 1964–1965.

_◦◉◦_

Enduring traditions of ideological rigidity, diplomatic arrogance, and political vulnerability heavily influenced the way policymakers approached decisions in Vietnam in 1964–1965. Understanding the decisions of this period fully, however, also requires close attention to contemporary developments in America and South Vietnam. These years marked a tumultuous time in both countries, which affected the course of events in subtle but significant ways.

Policymakers in 1964–1965 lived in a period of extraordinary domestic political upheaval sparked by the civil rights movement. It is difficult to overstate the impact of this upheaval on American politics in the mid-1960s. During 1964–1965, the United States—particularly the American South—experienced profound and long overdue change in the economic, political, and social rights of blacks. This change, consciously embraced by the liberal administration of Lyndon Johnson, engendered sharp political hostility among conservative southern whites and their deputies in Congress—hostility which the politically astute Johnson sensed could spill over into the realm of foreign affairs, where angry civil rights opponents could exact their revenge should LBJ stumble and "lose" a crumbling South Vietnam. This danger, reinforced by the memory of McCarthyism, stirred deep political fears in Johnson, together with an abiding aversion to failure in Vietnam.

LBJ feared defeat in South Vietnam, but he craved success and glory at home. A forceful, driving President of boundless ambition, Johnson sought to harness the political momentum created by the civil rights movement to enact a far-reaching domestic reform agenda under the rubric of the Great Society. LBJ would achieve the greatness he sought by leading America toward justice and opportunity for all its citizens, through his historic legislative program.

Johnson's domestic aspirations fundamentally conflicted with his uneasy involvement in Vietnam. An experienced and perceptive politician, LBJ knew his domestic reforms required the sustained focus and cooperation of Congress. He also knew a larger war in Vietnam jeopardized these reforms by drawing away political attention and economic resources. America's increasing military intervention in 1964–1965 cast this tension between Vietnam and the Great Society into sharp relief.

Johnson saw his predicament clearly. But he failed to resolve it for fear that acknowledging the growing extent and cost of the war would thwart his domestic reforms, while pursuing a course of withdrawal risked political ruin. LBJ, instead, chose to obscure the magnitude of his dilemma by obscuring America's deepening involvement as South Vietnam began to fail. That grave compromise of candor opened the way to Johnson's eventual downfall.

Events in South Vietnam during 1964–1965 proved equally fateful. A historically weak and divided land, South Vietnam's deeply rooted ethnic, political, and religious turmoil intensified sharply in the winter of 1964–1965. This mounting turmoil, combined with increased communist military attacks, pushed Saigon to the brink of political collapse.

South Vietnam's accelerating crisis alarmed American policymakers, driving them to deepen U.S. involvement considerably in an effort to arrest Saigon's political failure. Abandoning the concept of stability in the South *before* escalation against the North, policymakers now embraced the concept of stability *through* escalation, in the desperate hope that military action against Hanoi would prompt a stubbornly elusive political order in Saigon.

This shift triggered swift and ominous consequences scarcely anticipated by its architects. Policymakers soon confronted intense military, political, and bureaucratic pressures to widen the war. Unsettled by these largely unforeseen pressures, policymakers reacted confusedly and defensively. Rational men, they struggled to control increasingly irrational forces. But their reaction only clouded their attention to basic assumptions and ultimate costs as the war rapidly spun out of control in the spring and summer of 1965. In their desperation to make Vietnam policy work amid this rising tide of war pressures, they thus failed ever to question whether it could work—or at what ultimate price. Their failure recalls the warning of a prescient political scientist, who years before had cautioned against those policymakers with "an infinite capacity for making ends of [their] means."

The decisions of 1964–1965 bespeak a larger and deeper failure as well. Throughout this period—as, indeed, throughout the course of America's Vietnam involvement—U.S. policymakers strove principally to create a viable noncommunist regime in South Vietnam. For many years and at great effort and cost, Washington had endeavored to achieve political stability and competence in Saigon. Despite these efforts, South Vietnam's political disarray persisted and deepened, until, in 1965, America intervened with massive military force to avert its total collapse.

Few policymakers in 1964–1965 paused to mull this telling fact, to ponder its implications about Saigon's viability as a political entity. The failure to reexamine this and other fundamental premises of U.S. policy—chief among them Vietnam's importance to American national interests and Washington's ability to forge political order through military power—proved a costly and tragic lapse of statesmanship. . . .

⋅◦◉◦⋅

The legacy of Vietnam, like the war itself, remains a difficult and painful subject for Americans. As passions subside and time bestows greater perspective, Americans still struggle to understand Vietnam's meaning and lessons for the country. They still wonder how the United States found itself ensnared in an ambiguous, costly, and divisive war, and how it can avoid repeating such an ordeal in the future.

The experience of Lyndon Johnson and his advisers during the decisive years 1964–1965 offers much insight into those questions. For their decisions, which fundamentally transformed U.S. participation in the war, both reflected and defined much of the larger history of America's Vietnam involvement.

Their decisions may also, one hopes, yield kernels of wisdom for the future; the past, after all, can teach us lessons. But history's lessons, as Vietnam showed, are themselves dependent on each generation's knowledge and understanding of the past. So it proved for 1960s policymakers, whose ignorance and misperception of Southeast Asian history, culture, and politics pulled America progressively deeper into the war. LBJ, [Secretary of State Dean] Rusk, [Robert] McNamara, [McGeorge] Bundy, [Ambassador Maxwell] Taylor—most of their generation, in fact—mistakenly viewed Vietnam through the simplistic ideological prism of the Cold War. They perceived a deeply complex and ambiguous regional struggle as a grave challenge to world order and stability, fomented by communist China acting through its local surrogate, North Vietnam.

This perception, given their mixture of memories—the West's capitulation to Hitler at Munich, Stalin's postwar truculence, Mao's belligerent rhetoric—appears altogether understandable in retrospect. But it also proved deeply flawed and oblivious to abiding historical realities. Constrained by their memories and ideology, American policymakers neglected the subtle but enduring force of nationalism in Southeast Asia. Powerful and decisive currents—the deep and historic tension between Vietnam and China; regional friction among the Indochinese states of Vietnam, Laos, and Cambodia; and, above all, Hanoi's fanatical will to unification—went unnoticed or unweighed because they failed to fit Washington's worldview. Although it is true, as Secretary of State Rusk once said, that "one cannot escape one's experience," Rusk and his fellow policymakers seriously erred by falling uncritical prisoners of their experience.

Another shared experience plagued 1960s policymakers like a ghost: the ominous specter of McCarthyism. This frightful political memory haunted LBJ and his Democratic colleagues like a barely suppressed demon in the national psyche. Barely ten years removed from the traumatic "loss" of China and its devastating domestic repercussions, Johnson and his advisers remembered its consequences vividly and shuddered at a similar fate in Vietnam. They talked about this only privately, but then with genuine and palpable fear. Defense Secretary McNamara, in a guarded moment, confided to a newsman in the spring of 1965 that U.S. disengagement from South Vietnam threatened "a disastrous political fight that could . . . freeze American political debate and even affect political freedom."

Such fears resonated deeply in policymakers' minds. Nothing, it seemed, could be worse than the "loss" of Vietnam—not even an intensifying stalemate secured at increasing military and political risk. For a President determined to fulfill liberalism's postwar agenda, Truman's ordeal in China seemed a powerfully forbidding lesson. It hung over LBJ in Vietnam like a dark shadow he could not shake, an agony he would not repeat.

McCarthyism's long shadow into the mid-1960s underscores a persistent and troubling phenomenon of postwar American politics: the peculiar vulnerability besetting liberal Presidents thrust into the maelstrom of world politics. In America's postwar political climate—dominated by the culture of anti-communism—Democratic leaders from Truman to Kennedy to Johnson remained acutely sensitive to the domestic repercussions of foreign policy failure. This fear of rightwing reaction sharply inhibited liberals like LBJ, narrowing what they considered their range of politically acceptable options, while diminishing their willingness to disengage from untenable foreign commitments. Thus, when Johnson did confront the bitter choice between defeat in Vietnam and fighting a major, inconclusive war, he reluctantly chose the second because he could not tolerate the domestic consequences of the first. Committed to fulfilling the Great Society, fearful of resurgent McCarthyism, and afraid that disengagement meant sacrificing the former to the latter, LBJ perceived least political danger in holding on.

But if Johnson resigned never to "lose" South Vietnam, he also resigned never to sacrifice his cherished Great Society in the process. LBJ's determination, however understandable, nonetheless led him deliberately and seriously to obscure the nature and cost of America's deepening involvement in the war during 1964–1965. This decision bought Johnson the short-term political maneuverability he wanted, but at a costly long-term political price. As LBJ's credibility on the war subsequently eroded, public confidence in his leadership slowly but irretrievably evaporated. And this, more than any other factor, is what finally drove Johnson from the White House.

It also tarnished the presidency and damaged popular faith in American government for more than a decade. Trapped between deeply conflicting pressures, LBJ never shared his dilemma with the public. Johnson would not, or felt he dare not, trust his problems with the American people. LBJ's decision, however human, tragically undermined the reciprocal faith between President and public indispensable to effective governance in a democracy. Just as tragically, it fostered a pattern of presidential behavior which led his successor, Richard Nixon, to eventual ruin amid even greater popular political alienation.

Time slowly healed most of these wounds to the American political process, while reconfirming the fundamental importance of presidential credibility in a democracy. Johnson's Vietnam travail underscored the necessity of public trust and support to presidential success. Without them, as LBJ painfully discovered, Presidents are doomed to disaster.

Johnson, in retrospect, might have handled his domestic dilemma more forthrightly. An equally serious dilemma, however, remained always beyond his—or Washington's—power to mend: the root problem of political disarray in South Vietnam. The perennial absence of stable and responsive government in Saigon troubled Washington policymakers profoundly; they understood, only too well, its pivotal importance to the war effort and to the social and economic reforms essential to the country's survival. Over and over again, American officials stressed the necessity of political cooperation to their embattled South Vietnamese allies. But to no avail. As one top American in Saigon later lamented, "[Y]ou could tell them all 'you've got to get together [and stop] this haggling and fighting among yourselves,' but how do you make them do it?" he said. "How do you make them do it?"

Washington, alas, could not. As Ambassador Taylor conceded early in the war, "[You] cannot order good government. You can't get it by fiat." This stubborn but telling truth eventually came to haunt Taylor and others. South Vietnam never marshaled the political will necessary to create an effective and enduring government; it never produced leaders addressing the aspirations and thus attracting the allegiance of the South Vietnamese people. Increasing levels of U.S. troops and firepower, moreover, never offset this fundamental debility. America, as a consequence, built its massive military effort on a foundation of political quicksand.

The causes of this elemental flaw lay deeply imbedded in the social and political history of the region. Neither before nor after 1954 was South Vietnam ever really a nation in spirit. Divided by profound ethnic and religious cleavages dating back centuries and perpetuated under French colonial rule, the people of South Vietnam never developed a common political identity. Instead, political factionalism and rivalry always held sway. The result: a chronic and fatal political disorder.

Saigon's fundamental weakness bore anguished witness to the limits of U.S. power. South Vietnam's shortcomings taught a proud and mighty nation that it could not save a people in spite of themselves—that American power, in the last analysis, offered no viable substitute for indigenous political resolve. Without this basic ingredient, as Saigon's turbulent history demonstrated, Washington's most dedicated and strenuous efforts will prove extremely vulnerable, if not futile.

This is not a happy or popular lesson. But it is a wise and prudent one, attuned to the imperfect realities of an imperfect world. One of America's sagest diplomats, George Kennan, understood and articulated this lesson well when he observed: "When it comes to helping people to resist Communist pressures, . . . no assistance . . . can be effective unless the people themselves have a very high degree of determination and a willingness to help themselves. The moment they begin to place the bulk of the burden on us," Kennan warned, "the whole situation is lost." This, tragically, is precisely what befell America in South Vietnam during 1964–1965. Hereafter, as perhaps always before—*external* U.S. economic, military, and political support provided the vital elements of stability and strength in South Vietnam. Without that *external* support, as events following America's long-delayed withdrawal in 1973 showed, South Vietnam's government quickly failed.

Washington's effort to forge political order through military power spawned another tragedy as well. It ignited unexpected pressures which quickly overwhelmed U.S. policymakers, and pulled them ever deeper into the war. LBJ and his advisers began bombing North Vietnam in early 1965 in a desperate attempt to spur political resolve in South Vietnam. But their effort boomeranged wildly. Rather than stabilizing the situation, it instead unleashed forces that soon put Johnson at the mercy of circumstances, a hostage to the war's accelerating momentum. LBJ, as a result, began steering with an ever looser hand. By the summer of 1965, President Johnson found himself not the controller of events but largely controlled by them. He had lost the political leader's "continual struggle," in the words of Henry Kissinger, "to rescue an element of choice from the pressure of circumstance."

LBJ's experience speaks powerfully across the years. With each Vietnam decision, Johnson's vulnerability to military pressure and bureaucratic momentum intensified sharply. Each step generated demands for another, even bigger step—which LBJ found increasingly difficult to resist. His predicament confirmed George Ball's admonition that war is a fiercely unpredictable force, often generating its own inexorable momentum.

Johnson sensed this danger almost intuitively. He quickly grasped the dilemma and difficulties confronting him in Vietnam. But LBJ lacked the inner strength—the security and self-confidence—to overrule the counsel of his inherited advisers.

Most of those advisers, on the other hand—especially McGeorge Bundy and Robert McNamara—failed to anticipate such perils. Imbued with an overweening faith in their ability to "manage" crises and "control" escalation, Bundy and McNamara, along with Maxwell Taylor, first pushed military action against the North as a lever to force political improvement in the South. But bombing did not rectify Saigon's political problems; it only exacerbated them, while igniting turbulent military pressures that rapidly overwhelmed these advisers' confident calculations.

These advisers' preoccupation with technique, with the application of power, characterized much of America's approach to the Vietnam War. Bundy and McNamara epitomized a postwar generation confident in the exercise and efficacy of U.S. power. Despite the dark and troubled history of European intervention in Indochina, these men stubbornly refused to equate America's situation in the mid-1960s to France's earlier ordeal. To them, the United States possessed limitless ability, wisdom, and virtue; it would therefore prevail where other western powers had failed.

This arrogance born of power led policymakers to ignore manifest dangers, to persist in the face of ever darkening circumstances. Like figures in Greek tragedy, pride compelled these supremely confident men further into disaster. They succumbed to the affliction common to great powers throughout the ages—the dangerous "self-esteem engendered by power," as the political philosopher Hans Morgenthau once wrote, "which equates power and virtue, [and] in the process loses all sense of moral and political proportion."

Tradition, as well as personality, nurtured such thinking. For in many ways, America's military intervention in Vietnam represented the logical fulfillment of a policy and outlook axiomatically accepted by U.S. policymakers for nearly two decades—the doctrine of global containment. Fashioned at the outset of the Cold War, global containment extended American interests and obligations across vast new areas of the world in defense against perceived monolithic communist expansion. It remained the lodestar of America foreign policy, moreover, even as the constellation of international forces shifted dramatically amid diffused authority and power among communist states and nationalist upheaval in the post-colonial world.

Vietnam exposed the limitations and contradictions of this static doctrine in a world of flux. It also revealed the dangers and flaws of an undiscriminating, universalist policy which perceptive critics of global containment, such as the eminent journalist Walter Lippmann, had anticipated from the beginning. As Lippmann warned about global containment in 1947:

> Satellite states and puppet governments are not good material out of which to construct unassailable barriers [for American defense]. A diplomatic war conducted as this policy demands, that is to say conducted indirectly, means that we must stake our own security and the peace of the world upon satellites, puppets, clients, agents about whom we can know very little. Frequently they will act for their own reasons, and on their own judgments, presenting us with accomplished facts that we did not intend, and with crises for which we are unready. The "unassailable barriers" will present us with an unending series of insoluble dilemmas. We shall have either to disown our puppets, which would be tantamount to appeasement and defeat and loss of face, or must support them at an incalculable cost. . . .

Here lay the heart of America's Vietnam troubles. Driven by unquestioning allegiance to an ossified and extravagant doctrine, Washington officials plunged deeply into a struggle which itself dramatized the changed realities and complexities of the postwar world. Their action teaches both the importance of re-examining premises as circumstances change and the costly consequences of failing to recognize and adapt to them.

Vietnam represented a failure not just of American foreign policy but also of American statesmanship. For once drawn into the war, LBJ and his advisers quickly sensed Vietnam's immense difficulties and dangers—Saigon's congenital political problems, the war's spiraling military costs, the remote likelihood of victory—and plunged in deeper nonetheless. In their determination to preserve America's international credibility and protect their domestic political standing, they continued down an ever costlier path.

That path proved a distressing, multifaceted paradox. Fearing injury to the perception of American power, diminished faith in U.S. resolve, and a conservative political firestorm, policymakers rigidly pursued a course which ultimately injured the substance of American power by consuming exorbitant lives and resources, shook allied confidence in U.S. strategic judgment, and shattered liberalism's political unity and vigor by polarizing and paralyzing American society.

Herein lies Vietnam's most painful but pressing lesson. Statesmanship requires judgment, sensibility, and, above all, wisdom in foreign affairs—the wisdom to calculate national interests prudently and to balance commitments with effective power. It requires that most difficult task of political leaders: "to distinguish between what is desireable and what is possible, . . . between what is desireable and what is essential."

This is important in peace; it is indispensable in war. As the great tutor of statesmen, Carl von Clausewitz, wrote, "Since war is not an act of senseless passion but is controlled by its political object, the value of this object must determine the sacrifices to be made for it in *magnitude* and also in *duration*. Once the expenditure of effort exceeds the value of the political object," Clausewitz admonished, "the object must be renounced. . . ." His maxim, in hindsight, seems painfully relevant to a war which, as even America's military commander in Vietnam, General William Westmoreland, concluded, "the vital security of the United States was not and possibly could not be clearly demonstrated and understood. . . ."

LBJ and his advisers failed to heed this fundamental principle of statesmanship. They failed to weigh American costs in Vietnam against Vietnam's relative importance to American national interests and its effect on overall American power. Compelled by events in Vietnam and, especially, coercive political pressures at home, they deepened an unsound, peripheral commitment and pursued manifestly unpromising and immensely costly objectives. Their failure of statesmanship, then, proved a failure of judgment and, above all, of proportion.

Dereliction of Duty

T he Americanization of the Vietnam War between 1963 and 1965 was the product of an unusual interaction of personalities and circumstances. The escalation of U.S. military intervention grew out of a complicated chain of events and a complex web of decisions that slowly transformed the conflict in Vietnam into an American war.

Much of the literature on Vietnam has argued that the "Cold War mentality" put such pressure on President Johnson that the Americanization of the war was inevitable. The imperative to contain Communism was an important factor in Vietnam policy, but neither American entry into the war nor the manner in which the war was conducted was inevitable. The United States went to war in Vietnam in a manner unique in American history. Vietnam was not forced on the United States by a tidal wave of Cold War ideology. It slunk in on cat's feet.

Between November 1963 and July 1965, LBJ made the critical decisions that took the United States into war almost without realizing it. The decisions, and the way in which he made them, profoundly affected the way the United States fought in Vietnam. Although impersonal forces, such as the ideological imperative of containing Communism, the bureaucratic structure, and institutional priorities, influenced the president's Vietnam decisions, those decisions depended primarily on his character, his motivations, and his relationships with his principal advisers.

❦

Most investigations of how the United States entered the war have devoted little attention to the crucial developments which shaped LBJ's approach to Vietnam and set conditions for a gradual intervention. The first of several "turning points" in the American escalation comprised the near-contemporaneous assassinations of Ngo Dinh Diem and John F. Kennedy. The legacy of the Kennedy administration included an expanded commitment to South Vietnam as an "experiment" in countering Communist insurgencies and a deep distrust of the military that manifested itself in the appointment of officers who would prove supportive of the administration's policies. After November 1963 the United States confronted what in many ways was a new war in South Vietnam. Having deposed the government of Ngo Dinh Diem and his brother Nhu, and having supported actions that led to their deaths, Washington assumed responsibility for the new South Vietnamese leaders. Intensified Viet Cong activity added impetus to U.S. deliberations, leading Johnson and his advisers to conclude that the situation in South Vietnam demanded action beyond military advice and support. Next, in the spring of 1964, the Johnson administration adopted graduated pressure as its strategic concept for the Vietnam War. Rooted in Maxwell Taylor's national security strategy of flexible response, graduated pressure evolved over the next year, becoming the blueprint for the deepening American commitment to maintaining South Vietnam's independence. Then, in August 1964, in response to the Gulf of Tonkin incident, the United States crossed the threshold of direct American military action against North Vietnam.

The Gulf of Tonkin resolution gave the president carte blanche for escalating the war. During the ostensibly benign "holding period" from September 1964 to February 1965, LBJ was preoccupied with his domestic political agenda, and McNamara built consensus behind graduated pressure. In early 1965 the president raised U.S. intervention to a higher level again, deciding on February 9 to begin a systematic program of limited air strikes on targets in North Vietnam and, on February 26, to commit U.S. ground forces to the South. Last, in March 1965, he quietly gave U.S. ground forces the mission of "killing Viet Cong." That series of decisions, none in itself tantamount to a clearly discernable decision to go to war, nevertheless transformed America's commitment in Vietnam.

⚬⟨◈⟩⚬

Viewed together, those decisions might create the impression of a deliberate determination on the part of the Johnson administration to go to war. On the contrary, the president did not want to go to war in Vietnam and was not planning to do so. Indeed, as early as May 1964, LBJ seemed to realize that an American war in Vietnam would be a costly failure. He confided to McGeorge Bundy, ". . . looks like to me that we're getting into another Korea. It just worries the hell out of me. I don't see what we can ever hope to get out of this." It was, Johnson observed, "the biggest damn mess that I ever saw. . . . It's damn easy to get into a war, but . . . it's going to be harder to ever extricate yourself if you get in." Despite his recognition that the situation in Vietnam demanded that he consider alternative courses of action and make a difficult decision, LBJ sought to avoid or to postpone indefinitely an explicit choice between war and disengagement from South Vietnam. In the ensuing months, however, each decision he made moved the United States closer to war, although he seemed not to recognize that fact.

The president's fixation on short-term political goals, combined with his character and the personalities of his principal civilian and military advisers, rendered the administration incapable of dealing adequately with the complexities of the situation in Vietnam. LBJ's advisory system was structured to achieve consensus and to prevent potentially damaging leaks. Profoundly insecure and distrustful of anyone but his closest civilian advisers, the president viewed the JCS [Joint Chiefs of Staff] with suspicion. When the situation in Vietnam seemed to demand military action, Johnson did not turn to his military advisers to determine how to solve the problem. He turned instead to his civilian advisers to determine how to postpone a decision. The relationship between the president, the secretary of defense, and the Joint Chiefs led to the curious situation in which the nation went to war without the benefit of effective military advice from the organization having the statutory responsibility to be the nation's "principal military advisers."

What Johnson feared most in 1964 was losing his chance to win the presidency in his own right. He saw Vietnam principally as a danger to that goal. After the election, he feared that an American military response to the deteriorating situation in Vietnam would jeopardize chances that his Great Society would pass through Congress. The Great Society was to be Lyndon Johnson's great domestic political legacy, and he could not tolerate the risk of its failure. McNamara would help the president first protect his electoral chances and then pass the Great Society by offering a strategy for Vietnam that appeared cheap and could be conducted with minimal public and congressional attention. McNamara's strategy of graduated pressure permitted Johnson to pursue his objective of not losing the war in Vietnam while postponing the "day of reckoning" and keeping the whole question out of public debate all the while.

McNamara was confident in his ability to satisfy the president's needs. He believed fervently that nuclear weapons and the Cold War international political environment had made traditional military experience and thinking not only irrelevant, but often dangerous for contemporary policy. Accordingly, McNamara, along with systems analysts and other civilian members of his own department and the Department of State, developed his own strategy for Vietnam. Bolstered by what he regarded as a personal triumph during the Cuban missile crisis, McNamara drew heavily on that experience and applied it to Vietnam. Based on the assumption that carefully controlled and sharply limited military actions were reversible, and therefore could be carried out at minimal risk and cost, graduated pressure allowed McNamara and Johnson to avoid confronting many of the possible consequences of military action.

Johnson and McNamara succeeded in creating the illusion that the decisions to attack North Vietnam were alternatives to war rather than war itself. Graduated pressure defined military action as a form of communication, the object of which was to affect the enemy's calculation of interests and dissuade him from a particular activity. Because the favored means of communication (bombing fixed installations and economic targets) were not appropriate for the mobile forces of the Viet Cong, who lacked an infrastructure and whose strength in the South was political as well as military, McNamara and his colleagues pointed to the infiltration of men and supplies into South Vietnam as proof that the source and center of the enemy's power in Vietnam lay north of the seventeenth parallel, and specifically in Hanoi. Their definition of the enemy's Source of strength was derived from that strategy rather than from a critical examination of the full reality in South Vietnam—and turned out to be inaccurate.

Graduated pressure was fundamentally flawed in other ways. The strategy ignored the uncertainty of war and the unpredictable psychology of an activity that involves killing, death, and destruction. To the North Vietnamese, military action, involving as it did attacks on their forces and bombing of their territory, was not simply a means of communication. Human sacrifices in war evoke strong emotions, creating a dynamic that defies systems analysis quantification. Once the United States crossed the threshold of war against North Vietnam with covert raids and the Gulf of Tonkin "reprisals," the future course of events depended not only on decisions made in Washington but also on enemy responses and actions that were unpredictable. McNamara, however, viewed the war as another business management problem that, he assumed, would ultimately succumb to his reasoned judgment and others' rational calculations. He and his assistants thought that they could predict with great precision what amount of force applied in Vietnam would achieve the results they desired and they believed that they could control that force with great precision from halfway around the world. There were compelling contemporaneous arguments that graduated pressure would not affect Hanoi's will sufficiently to convince the North to desist from its support of the South, and that such a strategy would probably lead to an escalation of the war. Others expressed doubts about the utility of attacking North Vietnam by air to win a conflict in South Vietnam. Nevertheless, McNamara refused to consider the consequences of his recommendations and forged ahead oblivious of the human and psychological complexities of war.

⁌☞⁍

Despite their recognition that graduated pressure was fundamentally flawed, the JCS were unable to articulate effectively either their objections or alternatives. Interservice rivalry was a significant impediment. Although differing perspectives were understandable given the Chiefs' long experience in their own services and their need to protect the interests of their services, the president's principal military advisers were obligated by law to render their best advice. The Chiefs' failure to do so, and their willingness to present single-service remedies to a complex military problem, prevented them from developing a comprehensive estimate of the situation or from thinking effectively about strategy.

When it became clear to the Chiefs that they were to have little influence on the policy-making process, they failed to confront the president with their objections to McNamara's approach to the war. Instead they attempted to work within that strategy in order to remove over time the limitations to further action. Unable to develop a strategic alternative to graduated pressure, the Chiefs became fixated on means by which the war could be conducted and pressed for an escalation of the war by degrees. They hoped that graduated pressure would evolve over time into a fundamentally different strategy, more in keeping with their belief in the necessity of greater force and its more resolute application. In so doing, they gave tacit approval to graduated pressure during the critical period in which the president escalated the war. They did not recommend the total force they believed would ultimately be required in Vietnam and accepted a strategy they knew would lead to a large but inadequate commitment of troops, for an extended period of time, with little hope for success.

⋘❀⋙

McNamara and Lyndon Johnson were far from disappointed with the joint Chiefs' failings. Because his priorities were domestic, Johnson had little use for military advice that recommended actions inconsistent with those priorities. McNamara and his assistants in the Department of Defense, on the other hand, were arrogant. They disparaged military advice because they thought that their intelligence and analytical methods could compensate for their lack of military experience and education. Indeed military experience seemed to them a liability because military officers took too narrow a view and based their advice on antiquated notions of war. Geopolitical and technological changes of the last fifteen years, they believed, had rendered advice based on military experience irrelevant and, in fact, dangerous. McNamara's disregard for military experience and for history left him to draw principally on his staff in the Department of Defense and led him to conclude that his only real experience with the planning and direction of military force, the Cuban missile crisis, was the most relevant analogy to Vietnam.

While they slowly deepened American military involvement in Vietnam, Johnson and McNamara pushed the Chiefs further away from the decision-making process. There was no meaningful structure through which the Chiefs could voice their views—even the chairman was not a reliable conduit. NSC meetings were strictly *pro forma* affairs in which the president endeavored to build consensus for decisions already made. Johnson continued Kennedy's practice of meeting with small groups of his most trusted advisers. Indeed he made his most important decisions at the Tuesday lunch meetings in which Rusk, McGeorge Bundy, and McNamara were the only regular participants. The president and McNamara shifted responsibility for real planning away from the JCS to ad hoc committees composed principally of civilian analysts and attorneys, whose main goal was to obtain a consensus consistent with the president's pursuit of the middle ground between disengagement and war. The products of those efforts carried the undeserved credibility of proposals that had been agreed on by all departments and were therefore hard to oppose. McNamara and Johnson endeavored to get the advice they wanted by placing conditions and qualifications on questions that they asked the Chiefs. When the Chiefs' advice was not consistent with his own recommendations, McNamara, with the aid of the chairman of the Joint Chiefs of Staff, lied in meetings of the National Security Council about the Chiefs' views.

Rather than advice McNamara and Johnson extracted from the JCS acquiescence and silent support for decisions already made. Even as they relegated the Chiefs to a peripheral position in the policy-making process, they were careful to preserve the facade of consultation to prevent the JCS from opposing the administration's policies either openly or behind the scenes. As American involvement in the war escalated, Johnson's vulnerability to disaffected senior military officers increased because he was purposely deceiving the Congress and the public about the nature of the American military effort in Vietnam. The president and the secretary of defense deliberately obscured the nature of decisions made and left undefined the limits that they envisioned on the use of force. They indicated to the Chiefs that they would take actions that they never intended to pursue. McNamara and his assistants, who considered communication the purpose of military action, kept the nature of their objective from the JCS, who viewed "winning" as the only viable goal in war. Finally, Johnson appealed directly to them, referring to himself as the "coach" and them as "his team." To dampen their calls for further action, Lyndon Johnson attempted to generate sympathy from the JCS for the great pressures that he was feeling from those who opposed escalation.

The ultimate test of the Chiefs' loyalty came in July 1965. The administration's lies to the American public had grown in magnitude as the American military effort in Vietnam escalated. The president's plan of deception depended on tacit approval or silence from the JCS. LBJ had misrepresented the mission of U.S. ground forces in Vietnam, distorted the views of the Chiefs to lend credibility to his decision against mobilization, grossly understated the numbers of troops General Westmoreland had requested, and lied to the Congress about the monetary cost of actions already approved and of those awaiting final decision. The Chiefs did not disappoint the president. In the days before the president made his duplicitous public announcement concerning Westmoreland's request, the Chiefs, with the exception of commandant of the Marine Corps Greene, withheld from congressmen their estimates of the amount of force that would be needed in Vietnam. As he had during the Gulf of Tonkin hearings, Wheeler lent his support to the president's deception of Congress. The "five silent men" on the Joint Chiefs made possible the way the United States went to war in Vietnam.

❧⚙❧

Several factors kept the Chiefs from challenging the president's subterfuges. The professional code of the military officer prohibits him or her from engaging in political activity. Actions that could have undermined the administration's credibility and derailed its Vietnam policy could not have been undertaken lightly. The Chiefs felt loyalty to their commander in chief. The Truman-MacArthur controversy during the Korean War had warned the Chiefs about the dangers of overstepping the bounds of civilian control. Loyalty to their services also weighed against opposing the president and the secretary of defense. Harold Johnson, for example, decided against resignation because he thought he had to remain in office to protect the Army's interests as best he could. Admiral McDonald and Marine Corps Commandant Greene compromised their views on Vietnam in exchange for concessions to their respective services. Greene achieved a dramatic expansion of the Marine Corps, and McDonald ensured that the Navy retained control of Pacific Command. None of the Chiefs had sworn an oath to his service, however. They had all sworn, rather, to "support and defend the Constitution of the United States."

General Greene recalled that direct requests by congressmen for his assessment put him in a difficult situation. The president was lying, and he expected the Chiefs to lie as well or, at least, to withhold the whole truth. Although the president should not have placed the Chiefs in that position, the flag officers should not have tolerated it when he had.

Because the Constitution locates civilian control of the military in Congress as well as in the executive branch, the Chiefs could not have been justified in deceiving the peoples' representatives about Vietnam. Wheeler in particular allowed his duty to the president to overwhelm his obligations under the Constitution. As cadets are taught at the United States Military Academy, the JCS relationship with the Congress is challenging and demands that military officers possess a strong character and keen intellect. While the Chiefs must present Congress with their best advice based on their professional experience and education, they must be careful not to undermine their credibility by crossing the line between advice and advocacy of service interests.

Maxwell Taylor had a profound influence on the nature of the civil-military relationship during the escalation of American involvement in Vietnam. In contrast to Army Chief of Staff George C. Marshall, who, at the start of World War II, recognized the need for the JCS to suppress service parochialism to provide advice consistent with national interests, Taylor exacerbated service differences to help McNamara and Johnson keep the Chiefs divided and, thus, marginal to the policy process. Taylor recommended men for appointment to the JCS who were less likely than their predecessors to challenge the direction of the administration's military policy, even when they knew that that policy was fundamentally flawed. Taylor's behavior is perhaps best explained by his close personal friendship with the Kennedy family; McNamara; and, later, Johnson. In contrast again to Marshall, who thought it important to keep a professional distance from President Franklin Roosevelt, Taylor abandoned an earlier view similar to Marshall's in favor of a belief that the JCS and the president should enjoy "an intimate, easy relationship, born of friendship and mutual regard."

The way in which the United States went to war in the period between November 1963 and July 1965 had, not surprisingly, a profound influence on the conduct of the war and on its outcome. Because Vietnam policy decisions were made based on domestic political expediency, and because the president was intent on forging a consensus position behind what he believed was a middle policy, the administration deliberately avoided clarifying its policy objectives and postponed discussing the level of force that the president was willing to commit to the effort. Indeed, because the president was seeking domestic political consensus, members of the administration believed that ambiguity in the objectives for fighting in Vietnam was a strength rather than a weakness. Determined to prevent dissent from the JCS, the administration concealed its development of "fall-back" objectives.

Over time the maintenance of U.S. credibility quietly supplanted the stated policy objective of a free and independent South Vietnam. The principal civilian planners had determined that to guarantee American credibility, it was not necessary to win in Vietnam. That conclusion, combined with the belief that the use of force was merely another form of diplomatic communication, directed the military effort in the South at achieving stalemate rather than victory. Those charged with planning the war believed that it would be possible to preserve American credibility even if the United States armed forces withdrew from the South, after a show of force against the North and in the South in which American forces were "bloodied." After the United States became committed to war, however, and more American soldiers, airmen, and Marines had died in the conflict, it would become impossible simply to disengage and declare America's credibility intact, a fact that should have been foreseen. The Chiefs sensed the shift in objectives, but did not challenge directly the views of civilian planners in that connection. McNamara and Johnson recognized that, once committed to war, the JCS would not agree to an objective other than imposing a solution on the enemy consistent with U.S. interests. The JCS deliberately avoided clarifying the objective as well. As a result, when the United States went to war, the JCS pursued objectives different from those of the president. When the Chiefs requested permission to apply force consistent with their conception of U.S. objectives, the president and McNamara, based on their goals and domestic political constraints, rejected JCS requests, or granted them only in part. The result was that the JCS and McNamara became fixated on the means rather than on the ends, and on the manner in which the war was conducted instead of a military strategy that could connect military actions to achievable policy goals.

Because forthright communication between top civilian and military officials in the Johnson administration was never developed, there was no reconciliation of McNamara's intention to limit the American military effort sharply and the Chiefs' assessment that the United States could not possibly win under such conditions. If they had attempted to reconcile those positions, they could not have helped but recognize the futility of the American war effort.

The Joint Chiefs of Staff became accomplices in the president's deception and focused on a tactical task, killing the enemy. General Westmoreland's "strategy" of attrition in South Vietnam, was, in essence, the absence of a strategy. The result was military activity (bombing North Vietnam and killing the enemy in South Vietnam) that did not aim to achieve a dearly defined objective. It was unclear how quantitative measures by which McNamara interpreted the success and failure of the use of military force were contributing to an end of the war. As American casualties mounted and the futility of the strategy became apparent, the American public lost faith in the effort. The Chiefs did not request the number of troops they believed necessary to impose a military solution in South Vietnam until after the Tet offensive in 1968. By that time, however, the president was besieged by opposition to the war and was unable even to consider the request. LBJ, who had gone to such great lengths to ensure a crushing defeat over Barry Goldwater in 1964, declared that he was withdrawing from the race for his party's presidential nomination.

Johnson thought that he would be able to control the U.S. involvement in Vietnam. That belief, based on the strategy of graduated pressure and McNamara's confident assurances, proved in dramatic fashion to be false. If the president was surprised by the consequences of his decisions between November 1963 and July 1965, he should not have been so. He had disregarded the advice he did not want to hear in favor of a policy based on the pursuit of his own political fortunes and his beloved domestic programs.

❧◉☙

The war in Vietnam was not lost in the field, nor was it lost on the front pages of the *New York Times* or on the college campuses. It was lost in Washington, D.C., even before Americans assumed sole responsibility for the fighting in 1965 and before they realized the country was at war; indeed, even before the first American units were deployed. The disaster in Vietnam was not the result of impersonal forces but a uniquely human failure, the responsibility for which was shared by President Johnson and his principal military and civilian advisers. The failings were many and reinforcing: arrogance, weakness, lying in the pursuit of self-interest, and, above all, the abdication of responsibility to the American people.

POSTSCRIPT

Was the Americanization of the War in Vietnam Inevitable?

The book from which VanDeMark's selection was excerpted is a detailed study of the circumstances surrounding the decisions that President Lyndon Johnson made to increase America's presence in Vietnam via the bombing raids of North Vietnam in February 1965 and the introduction of ground troops the following July. VanDeMark agrees with McMaster that Johnson did not consult the Joint Chiefs of Staff about the wisdom of the policy of escalating the war. In fact, Johnson's decisions of "graduated pressure" were made in increments by the civilian advisers surrounding Secretary of Defense Robert McNamara. The policy, if it can be called such, was to prevent the National Liberation Front and its Viet Cong army from taking over South Vietnam. Each service branch fought its own war without coordinating with one another or with the government of South Vietnam. In VanDeMark's view, U.S. intervention was doomed to failure because South Vietnam was an artificial and very corrupt nation-state created by the French and later supported by the Americans. It was unfortunate that the nationalist revolution was tied up with the Communists led by Ho Chi Minh, who had been fighting French colonialism and Japanese imperialism since the 1920s—unlike Korea and Malaysia, which had alternative, noncommunist, nationalist movements.

Why did Johnson plunge "into the quagmire"? For one thing, Johnson remembered how previous Democratic presidents Franklin D. Roosevelt and Harry S. Truman had been charged with being soft on communism and accused of losing Eastern Europe to the Russians after the Second World War and China to the Communists in the Chinese Civil War in 1949. In addition, both presidents were charged by Senator Joseph McCarthy and others of harboring Communists in U.S. government agencies. If Johnson was tough in Vietnam, he could stop communist aggression. At the same time, he could ensure that his Great Society social programs of Medicare and job retraining, as well as the impending civil rights legislation, would be passed by Congress.

As an army officer who fought in the Persian Gulf War, McMaster offers a unique perspective on the decision-making processes used by government policymakers. McMaster spares no one in his critique of what he considers the flawed Vietnam policy of "graduated pressure." He says that McNamara, bolstered by the success of America during the Cuban Missile Crisis, believed that the traditional methods of fighting wars were obsolete. Johnson believed in McNamara's approach, and the president's own need for consensus in the decision-making process kept the Joint Chiefs of Staff out of the loop.

Unlike other military historians, who generally absolve the military from responsibility for the strategy employed during the war, McMaster argues that the Joint Chiefs of Staff were responsible for not standing up to Johnson and telling him that his military strategy was seriously flawed. McMaster's views are not as new as some reviewers of his book seem to think. Bruce Palmer, Jr., in *The Twenty-Five Year War: America's Military Role in Vietnam* (University Press of Kentucky, 1984), and Harry G. Summers, Jr., in *On Strategy: A Critical Analysis of the Vietnam War* (Presidio Press, 1982), also see a flawed strategy of war. Summers argues that Johnson should have asked Congress for a declaration of war and fought a conventional war against North Vietnam.

One scholar has claimed that over 7,000 books about the Vietnam War have been published. The starting point for the current issue is Lloyd Gardner and Ted Gittinger, eds., *Vietnam: The Early Decisions* (University of Texas Press, 1997). See also Larry Berman, *Planning a Tragedy: The Americanization of the War in Vietnam* (W. W. Norton, 1982) and *Lyndon Johnson's War* (W.W. Norton, 1989); David Halberstam, *The Best and the Brightest* (Random House, 1972); and Lloyd C. Gardner, *Pay Any Price: Lyndon Johnson and the Wars for Vietnam* (Ivan Dee, 1995). Primary sources can be found in the U.S. Department of State's two-volume *Foreign Relations of the United States, 1964–1968: Vietnam* (Government Printing Office, 1996) and in the relevant sections of one of the most useful collections of primary sources and essays, *Major Problems in the History of the Vietnam War*, 2d ed., by Robert J. McMahon (Houghton Mifflin, 2000).

The bureaucratic perspective can be found in a series of essays by George C. Herring entitled *LBJ and Vietnam: A Different Kind of War* (University of Texas Press, 1995). Herring is also the author of the widely used text *America's Longest War: The United States and Vietnam* (Alfred A. Knopf, 1986). A brilliant article often found in anthologies is by historian and former policymaker James Thompson, "How Could Vietnam Happen: An Autopsy," *The Atlantic Monthly* (April 1968). An interesting comparison of the 1954 Dien Bien Phu and 1965 U.S. escalation decisions is Fred I. Greenstein and John P. Burke, "The Dynamics of Presidential Reality Testing: Evidence From Two Vietnam Decisions," *Political Science Quarterly* (Winter 1989–1990). A nice review essay on Vietnam's impact on today's military thinking is Michael C. Desch's "Wounded Warriors and the Lessons of Vietnam," *Orbis* (Summer 1998).

ISSUE 16

Has the Women's Movement of the 1970s Failed to Liberate American Women?

YES: F. Carolyn Graglia, from *Domestic Tranquility: A Brief Against Feminism* (Spence, 1998)

NO: Sara M. Evans, from "American Women in the Twentieth Century," in Harvard Sitkoff, ed., *Perspectives on Modern America: Making Sense of the Twentieth Century* (Oxford University Press, 2001)

ISSUE SUMMARY

YES: Writer and lecturer F. Carolyn Graglia argues that women should stay at home and practice the values of "true motherhood" because contemporary feminists have discredited marriage, devalued traditional homemaking, and encouraged sexual promiscuity.

NO: According to Professor Sara M. Evans, despite class, racial, religious, ethnic, and regional differences, women in America experienced major transformations in their private and public lives in the twentieth century.

In 1961, President John F. Kennedy established the Commission on the Status of Women to examine "the prejudice and outmoded customs that act as barriers to the full realization of women's basic rights." Two years later, Betty Friedan, a closet leftist from suburban Rockland County, New York, wrote about the growing malaise of the suburban housewife in her best-seller *The Feminist Mystique* (W.W. Norton, 1963).

The roots of Friedan's "feminine mystique" go back much earlier than the post–World War II "baby boom" generation of suburban America. Women historians have traced the origins of the modern family to the early nineteenth century. As the nation became more stable politically, the roles of men, women, and children became segmented in ways that still exist today. Dad went to work, the kids went to school, and Mom stayed home. Women's magazines, gift books, and the religious literature of the period ascribed to these women a role that Professor Barbara Welter has called the "Cult of True Womanhood." She describes the ideal woman as upholding four virtues—piety, purity, submissiveness, and domesticity.

In nineteenth-century America, most middle-class white women stayed home. Those who entered the workforce as teachers or became reformers were usually extending the values of the Cult of True Womanhood to the outside world. This was true of the women reformers in the Second Great Awakening and the peace, temperance, and abolitionist movements before the Civil War. The first real challenge to the traditional values system occurred when a handful of women showed up at Seneca Falls, New York, in 1848 to sign the Women's Declaration of Rights.

It soon became clear that if they were going to pass reform laws, women would have to obtain the right to vote. After an intense struggle, the Nineteenth Amendment was ratified on August 26, 1920. Once the women's movement obtained the vote, there was no agreement on future goals. The problems of the Great Depression and World War II overrode women's issues.

World War II brought about major changes for working women. Six million women entered the labor force for the first time, *many* of whom were married. "The proportion of women in the labor force," writes Lois Banner, "increased from 25 percent in 1940 to 36 percent in 1945. This increase was greater than that of the previous four decades combined." Many women moved into high-paying, traditionally men's jobs as policewomen, firefighters, and precision tool-makers. Steel and auto companies that converted over to wartime production made sure that lighter tools were made for women to use on the assembly lines. The federal government also erected federal childcare facilities.

When the war ended in 1945, many of these women lost their nontraditional jobs. The federal day-care program was eliminated, and the government told women to go home even though a 1944 study by the Women's Bureau concluded that 80 percent of working women wanted to continue in their jobs after the war.

Most history texts emphasize that women did return home, moved to the suburbs, and created a baby boom generation, which reversed the downward size of families in the years from 1946 to 1964. What is lost in this description is the fact that after 1947 the number of working women again began to rise, reaching 31 percent in 1951. Twenty-two years later, at the height of the women's liberation movement, it reached 42 percent.

When Friedan wrote *The Feminine Mystique* in 1963, both working-class and middle-class college-educated women experienced discrimination in the marketplace. When women worked, they were expected to become teachers, nurses, secretaries, and airline stewardesses—the lowest-paying jobs in the workforce. In the turbulent 1960s, this situation was no longer accepted.

In the following selection, F. Carolyn Graglia defends the traditional role of women in contemporary America. Women, she contends, should stay at home and practice the values of "true womanhood." Contemporary feminists, she argues, have devalued traditional homemaking, encouraged sexual promiscuity, and discredited marriage as a career for women. In the second selection, Sara M. Evans argues that in spite of class, racial, religious, ethnic, and regional differences, women in America experienced major transformations in their private and public lives in the twentieth century.

YES

F. Carolyn Graglia

Domestic Tranquility

Introduction

Since the late 1960s, feminists have very successfully waged war against the traditional family, in which husbands are the principal breadwinners and wives are primarily homemakers. This war's immediate purpose has been to undermine the homemaker's position within both her family and society in order to drive her into the work force. Its long-term goal is to create a society in which women behave as much like men as possible, devoting as much time and energy to the pursuit of a career as men do, so that women will eventually hold equal political and economic power with men. . . .

Feminists have used a variety of methods to achieve their goal. They have promoted a sexual revolution that encouraged women to mimic male sexual promiscuity. They have supported the enactment of no-fault divorce laws that have undermined housewives' social and economic security. And they obtained the application of affirmative action requirements to women as a class, gaining educational and job preferences for women and undermining the ability of men who are victimized by this discrimination to function as family breadwinners.

A crucial weapon in feminism's arsenal has been the status degradation of the housewife's role. From the journalistic attacks of Betty Friedan and Gloria Steinem to Jessie Bernard's sociological writings, all branches of feminism are united in the conviction that a woman can find identity and fulfillment only in a career. The housewife, feminists agree, was properly characterized by Simone de Beauvoir and Betty Friedan as a "parasite," a being something less than human, living her life without using her adult capabilities or intelligence, and lacking any real purpose in devoting herself to children, husband, and home.

Operating on the twin assumptions that equality means sameness (that is, men and women cannot be equals unless they do the same things) and that most differences between the sexes are culturally imposed, contemporary feminism has undertaken its own cultural impositions. Revealing their totalitarian belief that they know best how others should live and their totalitarian willingness to force others to conform to their dogma, feminists have sought to modify our social institutions in order to create an androgynous society in which male and female roles are as identical as possible. The results of the feminist juggernaut now engulf us. By almost all indicia of well-being, the institution of the American family has become significantly less healthy than it was thirty years ago.

Certainly, feminism is not alone responsible for our families' sufferings. As Charles Murray details in *Losing Ground,* President Lyndon Johnson's Great Society programs, for example, have often hurt families, particularly black families, and these programs were supported by a large constituency beyond the women's movement. What distinguishes the women's movement, however, is the fact that, despite the pro-family motives it sometimes ascribes to itself, it has actively sought the traditional family's destruction. In its avowed aims and the programs it promotes, the movement has adopted Kate Millett's goal, set forth in her *Sexual Politics,* in which she endorses Friedrich Engels's conclusion that "the family, as that term is presently understood, must go"; "a kind fate," she remarks, in "view of the institution's history." This goal has never changed: feminists view traditional nuclear families as inconsistent with feminism's commitment to women's independence and sexual freedom.

Emerging as a revitalized movement in the 1960s, feminism reflected women's social discontent, which had arisen in response to the decline of the male breadwinner ethic and to the perception—heralded in Philip Wylie's 1940s castigation of the evil "mom"—that Western society does not value highly the roles of wife and mother. Women's dissatisfactions, nevertheless, have often been aggravated rather than alleviated by the feminist reaction. To mitigate their discontent, feminists argued, women should pattern their lives after men's, engaging in casual sexual intercourse on the same terms as sexually predatory males and making the same career commitments as men. In pursuit of these objectives, feminists have fought unceasingly for the ready availability of legal abortion and consistently derogated both motherhood and the worth of full-time homemakers. Feminism's sexual teachings have been less consistent, ranging from its early and enthusiastic embrace of the sexual revolution to a significant backlash against female sexual promiscuity, which has led some feminists to urge women to abandon heterosexual sexual intercourse altogether.

Contemporary feminism has been remarkably successful in bringing about the institutionalization in our society of the two beliefs underlying its offensive: denial of the social worth of traditional homemakers and rejection of traditional sexual morality. The consequences have been pernicious and enduring. General societal assent to these beliefs has profoundly distorted men's perceptions of their relationships with and obligations to women, women's perceptions of their own needs, and the way in which women make decisions about their lives.

Traditional Homemaking Devalued

The first prong of contemporary feminism's offensive has been to convince society that a woman's full-time commitment to cultivating her marriage and rearing her children is an unworthy endeavor. Women, assert feminists, should treat marriage and children as relatively independent appendages to their life of full-time involvement in the workplace. To live what feminists assure her is the only life worthy of respect, a woman must devote the vast bulk of her time and energy to market production, at the expense of marriage and children. Children, she is told, are better cared for by surrogates, and marriage, as these feminists perceive it, neither deserves nor requires much attention; indeed, the very idea of a woman's "cultivating" her marriage seems ludicrous. Thus spurred on by the women's movement, many women have sought to become male clones.

But some feminists have appeared to modify the feminist message; voices—supposedly of moderation—have argued that women really are different from men. In this they are surely right: there are fundamental differences between the average man and woman, and it is appropriate to take account of these differences when making decisions both in our individual lives and with respect to social issues. Yet the new feminist voices have not conceded that acknowledged differences between the sexes are grounds for reexamining women's flight from home into workplace. Instead, these new voices have argued only that these differences require modification of the terms under which women undertake to reconstruct their lives in accordance with the blueprint designed by so-called early radicals. The edifice erected by radical feminism is to remain intact, subject only to some redecorating. The foundation of this edifice is still the destruction of the traditional family. Feminism has acquiesced in women's desire to bear children (an activity some of the early radicals discouraged). But it continues steadfast in its assumption that, after some period of maternity leave, daily care of those children is properly the domain of institutions and paid employees. The yearnings manifested in women's palpable desire for children should largely be sated, the new voices tell us, by the act of serving as a birth canal and then spending so-called quality time with the child before and after a full day's work.

Any mother, in this view, may happily consign to surrogates most of the remaining aspects of her role, assured that doing so will impose no hardship or loss on either mother or child. To those women whose natures make them less suited to striving in the workplace than concentrating on husband, children, and home, this feminist diktat denies the happiness and contentment they could have found within the domestic arena. In the world formed by contemporary feminism, these women will have status and respect only if they force themselves to take up roles in the workplace they suspect are not most deserving of their attention. Relegated to the periphery of their lives are the home and personal relationships with husband and children that they sense merit their central concern.

Inherent in the feminist argument is an extraordinary contradiction. Feminists deny, on the one hand, that the dimension of female sexuality which engenders women's yearning for children can also make it appropriate and satisfying for a woman to devote herself to domestic endeavors and provide her children's full-time care. On the other hand, they plead the fact of sexual difference to justify campaigns to modify workplaces in order to correct the effects of male influence and alleged biases. Only after such modifications, claim feminists, can women's nurturing attributes and other female qualities be adequately expressed in and truly influence the workplace. Manifestations of these female qualities, feminists argue, should and can occur in the workplace once it has been modified to blunt the substantial impact of male aggression and competitiveness and take account of women's special requirements.

Having launched its movement claiming the right of women—a right allegedly denied them previously—to enter the workplace on an *equal* basis with men, feminism then escalated its demands by arguing that female differences require numerous changes in the workplace. Women, in this view, are insufficiently feminine to find satisfaction in rearing their own children but too feminine to compete on an equal basis with men. Thus, having taken women out of their homes and settled them in the workplace, feminists have sought to reconstruct workplaces to create "feminist playpens" that are conducive to female qualities of sensitivity, caring, and empathy. Through this exercise in self-contradiction, contemporary feminism has endeavored to remove the woman from her home and role of providing daily care to her children—the quintessential place and activity for most effectively expressing her feminine, nurturing attributes.

The qualities that are the most likely to make women good mothers are thus redeployed away from their children and into workplaces that must be restructured to accommodate them. The irony is twofold. Children—the ones who could benefit most from the attentions of those mothers who do possess these womanly qualities—are deprived of those attentions and left only with the hope of finding adequate replacement for their loss. Moreover, the occupations in which these qualities are now to find expression either do not require them for optimal job performance (often they are not conducive to professional success) or were long ago recognized as women's occupations—as in the field of nursing, for example—in which nurturing abilities do enhance job performance.

Traditional Sexual Morality Traduced

The second prong of contemporary feminism's offensive has been to encourage women to ape male sexual patterns and engage in promiscuous sexual intercourse as freely as men. Initially, feminists were among the most dedicated supporters of the sexual revolution, viewing female participation in casual sexual activity as an unmistakable declaration of female equality with males. The women in our society who acted upon the teachings of feminist sexual revolutionaries have suffered greatly. They are victims of the highest abortion rate in the Western world. More than one in five Americans is now infected with a viral sexually transmitted disease which at best can be controlled but not cured and is often chronic. Sexually transmitted diseases, both viral and bacterial, disproportionately affect women because, showing fewer symptoms, they often go untreated for a longer time. These diseases also lead to pelvic infections that cause infertility in 100,000 to 150,000 women each year.

The sexual revolution feminists have promoted rests on an assumption that an act of sexual intercourse involves nothing but a pleasurable physical sensation, possessing no symbolic meaning and no moral dimension. This is an understanding of sexuality that bears more than a slight resemblance to sex as depicted in pornography: physical sexual acts without emotional involvement. In addition to the physical harm caused by increased sexual promiscuity, the denial that sexual intercourse has symbolic importance within a framework of moral accountability corrupts the nature of the sex act. Such denial necessarily makes sexual intercourse a trivial event, compromising the act's ability to fulfill its most important function after procreation. This function is to bridge the gap between males and females who often seem separated by so many differences, both biological and emotional, that they feel scarcely capable of understanding or communicating with each other.

Because of the urgency of sexual desire, especially in the male, it is through sexual contact that men and women can most easily come together. Defining the nature of sexual intercourse in terms informed by its procreative potentialities makes the act a spiritually meaningful event of overwhelming importance. A sexual encounter so defined is imbued with the significance conferred by its connection with a promise of immortality through procreation, whether that connection is a present possibility, a remembrance of children already borne, or simply an acknowledgment of the reality and truth of the promise. Such a sex act can serve as the physical meeting ground on which, by accepting and affirming each other through their bodies' physical unity, men and women can begin to construct an enduring emotional unity. The sexual encounter cannot perform its function when it is viewed as a trivial event of moral indifference with no purpose or meaning other than producing a physical sensation through the friction of bodily parts.

The feminist sexual perspective deprives the sex act of the spiritual meaningfulness that can make it the binding force upon which man and woman can construct a lasting marital relationship. The morally indifferent sexuality championed by the sexual revolution substitutes the sex without emotions that characterizes pornography for the sex of a committed, loving relationship that satisfies women's longing for romance and connection. But this is not the only damage to relationships between men and women that follows from feminism's determination to promote an androgynous society by convincing men and women that they are virtually fungible. Sexual equivalency, feminists believe, requires that women not only engage in casual sexual intercourse as freely as men, but also that women mimic male behavior by becoming equally assertive in initiating sexual encounters and in their activity throughout the encounter. With this sexual prescription, feminists mock the essence of conjugal sexuality that is at the foundation of traditional marriage.

Marriage as a Woman's Career Discredited

Even academic feminists who are considered "moderates" endorse doctrines most inimical to the homemaker. Thus, Professor Elizabeth Fox-Genovese, regarded as a moderate in Women's Studies, tells us that marriage can no longer be a viable career for women. But if marriage cannot be a woman's career, then despite feminist avowals of favoring choice in this matter, home-making cannot be a woman's goal, and surrogate child-rearing must be her child's destiny. Contrary to feminist claims, society's barriers are not strung tightly to inhibit women's career choices. Because of feminism's very success-ful efforts, society encourages women to pursue careers, while stigmatizing and preventing their devotion to child-rearing and domesticity.

It was precisely upon the conclusion that marriage cannot be a viable career for women that *Time* magazine rested its Fall 1990 special issue on "Women: The Road Ahead," a survey of contemporary women's lives. While noting that the "cozy, limited roles of the past are still clearly re-membered, sometimes fondly," during the past thirty years "all that was orthodox has become negotiable." One thing negotiated away has been the economic security of the homemaker, and *Time* advised young women that "the job of full-time homemaker may be the riskiest profession to choose" because "the advent of no-fault and equitable-distribution divorce laws" reflect, in the words of one judge, the fact that "[s]ociety no longer believes that a husband should support his wife."

No-fault divorce laws did not, however, result from an edict of the gods or some force of nature, but from sustained political efforts, particularly by the feminist movement. As a cornerstone of their drive to make women exchange home for workplace, and thereby secure their independence from men, the availability of no-fault divorce (like the availability of abortion) was sacrosanct to the movement. *Time* shed crocodile tears for displaced home-makers, for it made clear that women must canter down the road ahead with the spur of no-fault divorce urging them into the workplace. Of all *Time*'s recommendations for ameliorating women's lot, divorce reform—the most crying need in our country today—was not among them. Whatever hardships may be endured by women who would resist a divorce, *Time*'s allegiance, like that of most feminists, is clearly to the divorce-seekers who, it was pleased to note, will not be hindered in their pursuit of self-realization by the barriers to divorce that their own mothers had faced.

These barriers to divorce which had impeded their own parents, how-ever, had usually benefited these young women by helping to preserve their parents' marriage. A five-year study of children in divorcing families disclosed that "the overwhelming majority preferred the unhappy mar-riage to the divorce," and many of them, "despite the unhappiness of their parents, were in fact relatively happy and considered their situa-tion neither better nor worse than that of other families around them." A follow-up study after ten years demonstrated that children experienced the trauma of their parents' divorce as more serious and long-lasting than any researchers had anticipated. *Time* so readily acquiesced in the disadvantaging of homemakers and the disruption of children's lives be-cause the feminist ideological parameters within which it operates have excluded marriage as a *proper* career choice. Removing the obstacles to making it a *viable* choice would, therefore, be an undesirable subversion of feminist goals.

That *Time* would have women trot forward on life's journey constrained by the blinders of feminist ideology is evident from its failure to question any feminist notion, no matter how silly, or to explore solutions incompatible with the ideology's script. One of the silliest notions *Time* left unexamined was that young women want "good careers, good marriages and two or three kids, and they don't want the children to be raised by strangers." The supposed realism of this expectation lay in the new woman's attitude that "I don't want to work 70 hours a week, but I want to be vice president, and *you* have to change." But even if thirty hours were cut from that seventy-hour workweek, the new woman would still be working the normal full-time week, her children would still be raised by surrogates, and the norm would continue to be the feminist version of child-rearing that *Time* itself described unflatteringly as "less a preoccupation than an improvisation."

The illusion that a woman can achieve career success without sacrificing the daily personal care of her children—and except among the very wealthy, most of her leisure as well—went unquestioned by *Time*. It did note, however, the dissatisfaction expressed by Eastern European and Russian women who had experienced as a matter of government policy the same liberation from home and children that our feminists have undertaken to bestow upon Western women. In what *Time* described as "a curious reversal of Western feminism's emphasis on careers for women," the new female leaders of Eastern Europe would like "to reverse the communist diktat that all women have to work." Women have "dreamed," said the Polish Minister of Culture and Arts, "of reaching the point where we have the choice to stay home" that communism had taken away. But blinded by its feminist bias, *Time* could only find it "curious" that women would choose to stay at home; apparently beyond the pale of respectability was any argument that it would serve Western women's interest to retain the choice that contemporary feminism—filling in the West the role of communism in the East—has sought to deny them.

Now was its feminist bias shaken by the attitudes of Japanese women, most of whom, *Time* noted, reject "equality" with men, choosing to cease work after the birth of a first child and later resuming a part-time career or pursuing hobbies or community work. The picture painted was that of the 1950s American suburban housewife reviled by Betty Friedan, except that the American has enjoyed a higher standard of living (particularly a much larger home) than has the Japanese. In Japan, *Time* observed, being "a housewife is nothing to be ashamed of." Dishonoring the housewife's role was a goal, it might have added, that Japanese feminists can, in time, accomplish if they emulate their American counterparts.

Japanese wives have broad responsibilities, commented *Time,* because most husbands leave their salaries and children entirely in wives' hands; freed from drudgery by modern appliances, housewives can "pursue their interests in a carefree manner, while men have to worry about supporting their wives and children." Typically, a Japanese wife controls household finances, giving her husband a cash allowance, the size of which, apparently, dissatisfies one-half of the men. Acknowledging that Japanese wives take the leadership in most homes, one husband observed that "[t]hings go best when the husband is swimming in the palm of his wife's hand." A home is well-managed, said one wife, "if you make your men feel that they're in control when they are in front of others, while in reality you're in control." It seems like a good arrangement to me.

Instead of inquiring whether a similar carefree existence might appeal to some American women, *Time* looked forward to the day when marriage would no longer be a career for Japanese women, as their men took over household and child-rearing chores, enabling wives to join husbands in the workplace. It was noted, however, that a major impediment to this goal, which would have to be corrected, was the fact that Japanese day-care centers usually run for only eight hours a day. Thus, *Time* made clear that its overriding concern was simply promoting the presence of women in the work force. This presence is seen as a good *per se,* without any *pro forma* talk about the economic necessity of a second income and without any question raised as to whether it is in children's interest to spend any amount of time—much less in excess of eight hours a day—in communal care. . . .

The Awakened Brünnhilde

. . . Those who would defend anti-feminist traditionalism today are like heretics fighting a regnant Inquisition. To become a homemaker, a woman may need the courage of a heretic. This is one reason that the defense of traditional women is often grounded in religious teachings, for the heretic's courage usually rests on faith. The source of courage I offer is the conviction, based on my own experience, that contemporary feminism's stereotypical caricature of the housewife did not reflect reality when Friedan popularized it, does not reflect reality today, and need not govern reality.

Feminists claimed a woman can find identity and fulfillment only in a career; they are wrong. They claimed a woman can, in that popular expression, "have it all"; they are wrong—she can have only some. The experience of being a mother at home is a different experience from being a full-time market producer who is also a mother. A woman can have one or the other experience, but not both at the same time. Combining a career with motherhood requires a woman to compromise by diminishing her commitment and exertions with respect to one role or the other, or usually, to both. Rarely, if ever, can a woman adequately perform in a full-time career if she diminishes her commitment to it sufficiently to replicate the experience of being a mother at home.

Women were *never* told they could *not* choose to make the compromises required to combine these roles; within the memory of all living today there were always some women who did so choose. But by successfully degrading the housewife's role, contemporary feminism undertook to force this choice upon all women. I declined to make the compromises necessary to combine a career with motherhood because I did not want to become like Andrea Dworkin's spiritual virgin. I did not want to keep my being intact, as Dworkin puts it, so that I could continue to pursue career success. Such pursuit would have required me to hold too much of myself aloof from husband and children: the invisible "wedge-shaped core of darkness" that Virginia Woolf described as being oneself would have to be too large, and not enough of me would have been left over for them.

I feared that if I cultivated that "wedge-shaped core of darkness" within myself enough to maintain a successful career, I would be consumed by that career, and that thus desiccated, too little of me would remain to flesh out my roles as wife and mother. Giving most of myself to the market seemed less appropriate and attractive than reserving myself for my family. Reinforcing this decision was my experience that when a woman lives too much in her mind, she finds it increasingly difficult to live through her body. Her nurturing ties to her children become attenuated; her physical relationship with her husband becomes hollow and perfunctory. Certainly in my case, Dr. James C. Neely spoke the truth in *Gender: The Myth of Equality:* "With too much emphasis on intellect, a woman becomes 'too into her head' to function in a sexual, motherly way, destroying by the process of thought the process of feeling her sexuality."

Virginia Woolf never compromised her market achievements with motherhood; nor did the Brontë sisters, Jane Austen, or George Eliot. Nor did Helen Frankenthaler who, at the time she was acknowledged to be the most prominent living female artist, said in an interview: "We all make different compromises. And, no, I don't regret not having children. Given my painting, children could have suffered. A mother must make her children come first: young children are helpless. Well, paintings are objects but they're also helpless." I agree with her; that is precisely how I felt about the briefs I wrote for clients. Those briefs were, to me, like helpless children; in writing them, I first learned the meaning of complete devotion. I stopped writing them because I believed they would have been masters too jealous of my husband and my children.

Society never rebuked these women for refusing to compromise their literary and artistic achievements. Neither should it rebuke other kinds of women for refusing to compromise their own artistry of motherhood and domesticity. Some women may agree that the reality I depict rings truer to them than the feminist depiction. This conviction may help them find the courage of a heretic. Some others, both men and women, may see enough truth in the reality I depict that they will come to regret society's acquiescence in the status degradation of the housewife. They may then accept the currently unfashionable notion that society should respect and support women who adopt the anti-feminist perspective.

It is in society's interest to begin to pull apart the double-bind web spun by feminism and so order itself as not to inhibit any woman who *could* be an awakened Brünnhilde. Delighted and contented women will certainly do less harm—and probably more good—to society than frenzied and despairing ones. This is not to suggest that society should interfere with a woman's decision to follow the feminist script and adopt any form of spiritual virginity that suits her. But neither should society continue to validate destruction of the women's pact by the contemporary feminists who sought to make us all follow their script. We should now begin to dismantle our regime that discourages and disadvantages the traditional woman who rejects feminist spiritual virginity and seeks instead the very different delight and contentment that she believes best suits her.

Sara M. Evans

 **NO**

American Women in the Twentieth Century

In 1900, our foremothers predicted that the twentieth century would be the "century of the child." It might be more accurate, however, to call it the "century of women." Among the many dramatic changes in American society, it is hard to find an example more striking than the changes in women's lives on every level.

At the beginning of the twentieth century, women were challenging the confines of an ideology that relegated them to the private realm of domesticity. Despite the reality that thousands of women could be found in factories, offices, and fields—not to mention in a wide variety of political and reform activities—those ideas still held powerful sway both in law and in dominant notions of propriety. Over the course of the twentieth century, however, women in America emerged fully (though still not equally) into all aspects of public life—politics, labor force participation, professions, mass media, and popular culture. As they did so, they experienced a transformation in the fundamental parameters of their private lives as well—marriage, family, fertility, and sexuality. In complex ways, women transformed the landscapes of both public and private life so that at century's end we are left with a deeply puzzling conundrum about just what we mean by the terms *public* and *private*.

Women, of course, are part of every other social group. Deeply divided by race, class, religion, ethnicity, and region, they don't always identify with one another, and as a result women's collective identity—their sense of solidarity as women—has waxed and waned. Twice in this century, however, there has been a massive wave of activism focused on women's rights. We can trace the surges of change in women's status that accompanied each of these, one at the beginning and another near the end of the century.

Changes in women's lives were certainly driven by large structural forces such as the emergence of the postindustrial service economy, rising levels of education, and the exigencies of two world wars. Yet they have also been due to women's own self-organized activism in two great waves and in numerous ripples in between. In some instances women fought for the right to participate in public life. In other instances, already present in public spaces, they struggled for equity. As a result of these struggles, American political and public life has undergone a series of fundamental transformations. Not only are women in different places at the end of the century then they were at the beginning, but also all Americans enter a new century shaped by the complexities of women's journey.

1900—Dawn of the Twentieth Century

At the beginning of the twentieth century, women's lives were defined primarily by their marital status, linked to race and class. If we take a snapshot (understanding that we are capturing a moment in a dynamic process of change), the normative adult woman—both statistically and in the images that pervaded popular culture—was married, middle class, and white. On average, women lived to 48.3 years; they married around age 22 and bore approximately four children. The vast majority of households consisted of male-headed married couples and their children.

In 1900 women's legal standing was fundamentally governed by their marital status. They had very few rights.

- A married woman had no separate legal identity from that of her husband.
- She had no right to control of her reproduction (even conveying information about contraception, for example, was illegal); and no right to sue or be sued, since she had no separate standing in court.
- She had no right to own property in her own name or to pursue a career of her choice.
- Women could not vote, serve on juries, or hold public office. According to the Supreme Court, Women were not "persons" under the Fourteenth Amendment to the Constitution that guarantees equal protection under the law.

These realities reflected an underlying ideology about women and men that allocated the public realms of work and politics to men and defined the proper place of women in society as fundamentally domestic. Confined to the realm of the home, women's duty to society lay in raising virtuous sons (future citizens) and dutiful daughters (future mothers). Over the course of the nineteenth century, however, women had pushed at the boundaries of their domestic assignment, both by choice and by necessity. They invented forms of politics outside the electoral arena by forming voluntary associations and building institutions in response to unmet social needs. In the 1830s, when women like Sarah and Angelina Grimké began to speak publicly against slavery, the mere appearance of a woman as a public speaker was considered scandalous. By 1900, however, women appeared in all manner of public settings, setting the stage for change in the twentieth century.

Signs of Change

A closer look at women's status in 1900 reveals trends that signal imminent change particularly in the areas of education, labor force participation, and sexuality. The coexistence of new possibilities alongside ongoing restrictions and discrimination laid the groundwork for challenges to the norms of female subordination.

Education   Women in 1900 had achieved a high degree of literacy. In fact, more girls than boys actually graduated from high school, probably because boys had access to many jobs that did not require significant education. When it came to higher education, however, women were seriously disadvantaged. They were overtly excluded from most professional education: only about 5 percent of medical students were women, and women's exclusion from legal education shows up in the fact that in 1920 only 1.4 percent of lawyers in the United States were female.

It is crucial to note, however, that in 1900 women constituted about 30 percent of students in colleges and universities, including schools for the growing female professions of nursing, teaching, librarianship, and social work. In the long run, this was a potent mix, as thousands of middle-class women embraced the opportunity to pursue higher education, which in turn generated new expectations. Education was a crucial force in creating the key leadership as well as a highly skilled constituency for the feminist mobilizations at either end of the century.

Labor Force Participation   In 1900, though wage labor was defined as a fundamentally male prerogative, women could be found in many parts of the labor force. Women's work outside the home, however, was framed by their marital status and overt discrimination based on race as well as sex.

- Approximately one in five women worked outside the home, a figure that was sharply distinguished by race: 41 percent nonwhite; 17 percent white.
- The average working woman was single and under age 25.
- Only 11 percent of married women worked outside the home (up to 15% by 1940), though the proportion among black women (26%) was considerably higher because discrimination against black men made it much harder for blacks to secure a livable income from a single wage.
- Available occupations were sharply limited. Most women who worked for wages served as domestics, farm laborers, unskilled factory operatives, or teachers. In fact, one in three women employed in nonagricultural pursuits worked in domestic service.
- Some new female-dominated professions, such as nursing, social work, and librarianship, were emerging. In addition, the feminization of clerical work, linked to the new technology of the typewriter and the record-keeping needs of growing corporate bureaucracies, signaled a dramatic trend that made the "working girl" increasingly respectable. By 1920 the proportion of women engaged in clerical work (25.6%) had surpassed the number in manufacturing (23.8), domestic service (18.2%), and agriculture (12.9%).

Sexuality and the Body   Late Victorians presumed (if they thought about it at all) that female sexuality should be confined entirely to marriage. Compared with today, there was very little premarital sex, and women were understood not to have much in the way of sexual desire. It was illegal to transmit information about contraception, though women clearly conveyed it anyway through networks of rumor and gossip. Within the dominant middle class even the simplest acknowledgments of female sexuality were suppressed into euphemism and other forms of denial. Body parts could not be named in polite company, so chicken "legs" and "breast," for example, became "dark meat" and "white meat." Female attire covered women's bodies with clothing that revealed some shape but very little skin.

Yet, as the twentieth century dawned with its emerging consumer culture, sexuality could no longer be so easily contained. Popular culture included vaudeville, dance halls, and a growing variety of public amusements (such as the brand-new movie theaters). In the past, women who frequented such places risked having a "bad reputation." Yet the growing popularity of public amusements within the "respectable middle class" was beginning to challenge such perceptions.

Women's bodies were also finding new visibility in athletics. In the wildly popular arenas of public competition such as baseball and boxing, athletics were virtually synonymous with masculinity. And yet women were beginning to play lawn tennis, field hockey, and gymnastics. Some even rode bicycles.

Race, Class, and Gender Ideals   Within the gender ideology of the urban middle class that emerged over the course of the nineteenth century, the "good woman" (and her antithesis) took on distinct characteristics associated with race and class. "Good" (white, Protestant, middle class) women embodied private virtues. They were chaste, domestic, pious, and submissive. "Bad" women were "low class"—immigrants, racial minorities—presumed to be promiscuous, bad mothers, and improper housewives largely on the basis of their presence in previously male-only public spaces (factories, saloons, dance halls). Such perceptions multiplied in the case of southern black women subjected to a regime of racial/sexual domination that included the constant threat of rape and the public humiliations of segregation. Yet, the denigration of lower-class and minority women on the basis of their presence in public was getting harder to sustain as growing numbers of supposedly "respectable" women showed up in the same, or similar, spaces.

The First Wave

This brief sketch of women's condition at the beginning of the century points to several forces for change that would bear fruit in the first few decades. The growth in women's education, their move into a wide variety of reform efforts as well as professions, laid the groundwork for a massive suffrage movement that demanded the most basic right of citizenship for women. The claim of citizenship was in many ways a deeply radical challenge to the ideology of separate spheres for men and women. It asserted the right of the individual woman to stand in direct relation to the state rather than to be represented through the participation of her husband or father. The growing power of the women's suffrage movement rested both on women's collective conscious-ness, born in female associations, and on increased individualism among women in an urbanizing industrializing economy.

While a small but crucial number of upper-middle-class women attended college, where they developed a transformed awareness of their own potential as women both individually and collectively, working-class immigrant and African-American women experienced both individualism and collectivity in very different ways. Forced to work outside the home in the least-skilled, low-est paying jobs, both they and their employers presumed that women's labor force participation was temporary. Unions objected to their presence and blocked them from apprenticeship and access to skilled jobs. Despite these obstacles, when wage-earning women organized their own unions, often in alliance with middle-class reformers, they exhibited awesome courage and militancy. In the garment district of New York, for example, the "uprising of the twenty thousand" in 1909 confounded the garment industry and led to a new kind of industrial unionism.

By 1910, middle-class white reformers had formed increasingly effective alliances with black and working-class women around the issue of women's suffrage. The massive mobilization of American women in the decade before the Nineteenth Amendment was ratified in 1920 included rallies of thou-sands of "working girls" and the organization of numerous African-American women's suffrage clubs. Shared exclusion from the individual right of civic participation symbolized their common womanhood. Following their vic-tory, leaders of the National American Woman Suffrage Association joyfully dismantled their organization and reassembled as the newly formed League of Women Voters. Their new task, as they defined it, was to train women to exercise their individual citizenship rights.

Such a reorientation seemed congruent with the popular culture of the 1920s, which emphasized individual pleasures along with individual rights. The development of a consumer economy, emphasizing pleasure and using sexuality to sell, offered women other paths out of submissive domesticity and into more assertive forms of individualism, paths that did not require solidarity, indeed undermined it. The female subculture that relied on a singular definition of "woman" eroded. Female reform ef-forts remained a powerful force in American politics—laying much of the groundwork for the emergence of a welfare state—but a broad-based move-ment for women's rights no longer existed after 1920. The pace of change in areas like education and labor force participation also reached a plateau and remained relatively unchanged for several decades after 1920. Modern women were individuals. And "feminism" became an epithet.

The loss of female solidarity meant that women's organizations in subsequent decades drew on narrow constituencies with very different priorities. Professional women, lonely pioneers in many fields, felt the continuing sting of discrimination and sought to eradicate the last ves-tiges of legal discrimination with an Equal Rights Amendment (ERA). The National Women's Party, one of the leading organizations in the struggle, first proposed the ERA in 1923 for the vote. But they were opposed by former allies, social reformers who feared that the protections for working women, which they had won during the Progressive era, would be lost. Though fiercely opposed to the ERA, reformers continued to advocate a stronger role for government in responding to social welfare. Many of them—with leaders like Eleanor Roosevelt—assumed key positions in the 1930s and shaped the political agenda known as the New Deal. In particular, their influence on the Social Security Act laid the foundations of the welfare state. Even among female reformers, however, alliances across racial lines remained rare and fraught with difficulty. As the progressive female reform tradition shaped an emergent welfare state, African-American voices remained muted, the needs of working women with children unaddressed.

The Second Wave

By mid-century the conditions for another surge of activism were under way. During the Second World War women joined the labor force in unprecedented numbers. Most significant, perhaps, married women and women over age 35 became normative among working women by 1950. Yet cold war culture, in the aftermath of World War II, reasserted traditional gender roles. The effort to contain women within the confines of the "feminine mystique" (as Betty Friedan later labeled this ideology), however, obscured but did not prevent rising activism among different constituencies of women. Under the cover of popular images of domesticity, women were rapidly changing their patterns of labor force and civic participation, initiating social movements for civil rights and world peace, and flooding into institutions of higher education.

The President's Commission on the Status of Women, established in 1961, put women's issues back on the national political agenda by recruiting a network of powerful women to develop a set of shared goals. They issued a report in 1963, the same year that Friedan published The Feminine Mystique. That report documented in meticulous detail the ongoing realities of discrimination in employment and in wages, numerous legal disabilities such as married women's lack of access to credit, and the growing problems of working mothers without adequate child care. In 1964, Title VII of the Civil Rights Act gave women their most powerful legal weapon against employment discrimination. An opponent of civil rights introduced Title VII, and many members of Congress treated it as a joke. But Title VII passed because the small number of women then in Congress fiercely and effectively defended the need to prohibit discrimination on the basis of "sex" as well as race, religion, and national origin.

The second wave emerged simultaneously among professional women and a younger cohort of social activists. Professionals, with the leadership of women in labor unions, government leaders, and intellectuals like Friedan, created the National Organization for Women (NOW) in 1966 to demand enforcement of laws like Title VII. A second branch of feminist activism emerged from younger women in the civil rights movement and the student new left. Civil rights offered a model of activism, an egalitarian and visionary language, an opportunity to develop political skills, and role models of courageous female leaders. Young women broke away in 1967 to form consciousness-raising groups and build on the legacy of the movements that had trained them.

The slogan, "the personal is political," became the ideological pivot of the second wave of American feminism. It drove a variety of challenges to gendered relations of power, whether embodied in public policy or in the most intimate personal relationships. The force of this direct assault on the public/private dichotomy has left deep marks on American politics, American society, and the feminist movement itself. Issues like domestic violence, child care, abortion, and sexual harassment have become central to the American political agenda, exposing deep divisions in American society that are not easily subject to the give-and-take compromises of political horse-trading.

From 1968 to 1975, the "Women's Liberation Movement," using the techniques of consciousness-raising in small groups, grew explosively. The synergy between different branches of feminist activism made the 1970s a very dynamic era. Feminist policymakers dubbed the years 1968 to 1975 "the golden years" because of their success in courtrooms and legislatures. These included the Equal Rights Amendment, which passed Congress in 1972 and went to the states; the 1973 Supreme Court decision legalizing abortion (*Roe* v. *Wade*); Title IX of the Higher Education Act, which opened intercollegiate athletics to women; the Women's Equity Education Act; and the Equal Credit Opportunity Act.

Women formed caucuses and organizations in most professional associations and in the labor movement. By the mid-1970s there were feminist organizations representing a broad range of racial groups as well— African-American women, Chicanas and Hispanic women, Asian-American women, Native American women. Women also built new organizations among clerical workers to challenge the devaluation and limited opportunities of traditional women's work.

With their new strength, women challenged barriers to the professions (law, medicine), to ordination within mainstream Protestant and Jewish denominations, and to the full range of traditionally male blue-collar occupations, from carpenters to firefighters and police. They filed thousands of complaints of discrimination, mounted hundreds of lawsuits, and also built thousands of new institutions—day-care centers, shelters for battered women, bookstores, coffeehouses, and many others. The new feminism drew on women's stories to rethink the most intimate personal aspects of womanhood including abortion rights, sexual autonomy, rape, domestic violence, and lesbian rights.

The second wave of feminism also changed the American language both through its own publications (of which there were hundreds, the largest of them being *Ms.*, first published in 1972) and through pressure on commercial publishing houses and mass media. New words entered the American lexicon—"Ms.," "firefighter," "sexism"—while uses of the generic masculine (mankind, brotherhood, policeman) suddenly seemed exclusive. In Women's Studies programs, which grew rapidly in the early 1970s, young scholars rethought the paradigms of their disciplines and initiated new branches of knowledge.

The second wave provoked a strong reaction, of course, revealing not only male hostility but also deep fissures among women themselves. Antifeminism became a strong political force by the late 1970s with the mobilization of Phyllis Schlafley's Stop-ERA and antiabortion forces. In the face of widespread cultural anxiety about equality for women and changing gender roles, the Equal Rights Amendment stalled after 1975 and went down to defeat in 1982 despite an extension of the deadline for ratification. Antifeminism drew on the insecurities of a declining economy in the wake of the Vietnam War and on the growing political power of the New Right which made cultural issues (abortion, the ERA, "family values," and homophobia) central. The 1980s, framed by the hostile political climate of the Reagan administration, nourished a growing backlash against feminism in the media, the popular culture, and public policy. As public spending shifted away from social programs and toward the military, female poverty increased sharply. The Reagan boom after 1983 did not touch the poorest, disproportionately female and racial minority, segments of the population.

At the same time, the 1980s witnessed the continued growth of women's presence in positions of public authority: Supreme Court justice, astronaut, arctic explorer, military officer, truck driver, carpenter, Olympic star, bishop, rabbi. Mainstream religious denominations began to rewrite liturgies and hymn books to make them more "inclusive." Despite regular announcements of the "death" of feminism, it would be more accurate to say that in the 1980s feminism entered the mainstream with new levels of community activism, sophisticated political fundraisers like EMILY's List, and broad political alliances on issues like comparable worth. Experimental "counterinstitutions" started in the 1970s (battered women's shelters, health clinics, bookstores, etc.) survived by adopting more institutionalized procedures, professionalized staff, and state funding. Women's Studies took on the trappings of an academic discipline.

Feminism was broad, diffuse, and of many minds in the 1980s. Legal and cultural issues grew more complex. Feminist theorists wrestled with the realities of differences such as race, class, age, and sexual preference, asking themselves whether the category "woman" could withstand such an analysis. The multifaceted activities that embraced the label "feminist"—policy activism, research think tanks, literary theory, music, art, spirituality—signaled the fact that the women's movement had lost some cohesiveness.

The testimony of Anita Hill during the 1991 hearings on the nomination of Clarence Thomas to the Supreme Court, however, catalyzed a new round of national conversation, complicated by the deep fissures of race and sex. The sight of a genteel black woman being grilled by a committee of white men who made light of this "sexual harassment crap" mobilized thousands of women to run for office and contribute to campaigns. In 1992 an unprecedented number of women were elected to public office.

2000—Dawn of a New Millennium

If we return to our original categories to describe women's situation at the end of the twentieth century, the contrast with 1900 could hardly be more dramatic. The average woman now can expect to live 79.7 years (65% longer than her great-grandmother in 1900), marry at age 24.5, and bear only about two children (if any at all). There are now decades in women's lives—both before and after the years of childbearing and child care—which earlier generations never experienced. As a result of the second wave of women's rights activism in the final decades of the twentieth century, in politics and law, labor force participation, education, and sexuality women live in a truly different world. Yet, in each instance equity remains an elusive goal, suggesting the need for continued and revitalized activism in the twenty-first century.

Politics and Law

No longer defined by their marital status, women enjoy virtually the full range of formal legal rights. In addition to winning the right to vote in 1920, they achieved equal pay (for the same work) in 1963 and guarantees against discrimination in housing and employment in 1964 (Title VII of the Civil Rights Act). Since 1970 women have won the right to a separate legal identity; privacy rights regarding reproduction and bodily integrity; and rights to sue for discrimination in employment, to work when pregnant, to equal education, and to equal access to athletics. Whole new bodies of law have developed since the 1970s on issues like domestic violence and sexual harassment. Nonetheless, the failure of the Equal Rights Amendment (ERA) in 1982 means that women still have no constitutional guarantee of equality.

In the last twenty-five years we have also seen a dramatic growth in the numbers of female elected officials. In 1997 there were 60 women in Congress (11.2%)—14 of them women of color; 81 statewide executive officials (25%); 1,597 state legislators (21.5%); and 203 mayors of cities with population over 30,000 (20.6%). There are two women on the Supreme Court, 30 female circuit court judges (18.6%), and 107 female district court judges (17.2%).

Education

At the end of the twentieth century, 88 percent of young women ages 25 to 34 are high-school graduates. The transformations in primary and secondary education for girls cannot be captured in graduation numbers, however. They also reside in the admission of girls to shop and other vocational classes (and boys to cooking and sewing courses), in girls' participation in athletics, in curricula that—at least sometimes—emphasize women's achievements in the past, and in school counselors who no longer singlemindedly socialize girls for domesticity and/or nonskilled stereotypically female jobs.

In the arena of higher education women are closing in on equity. Today, 54 percent of all bachelor of arts degrees go to women; 25 percent of women aged 25 to 34 are college graduates. Most striking, the proportion of women in professional schools is now between 36 and 43 percent. The revolution of the late twenteeth century is evident in these figures, as most of the change occurred in the last three decades. Compare current numbers with those of 1960, when the proportion of women in law school was 2 percent (today 43%); medicine 6 percent (today 38%); MBA programs 4 percent (today 36%); Ph.D. programs 11 percent (today 39%), and dentistry 1 percent (today 38%).

Labor Force Participation

In stark contrast to a century ago, more than 61 percent of all women are in the labor force, including two-thirds of women with preschoolers and three-fourths of women with school-age children. Though African-American women continue to work at a higher rate than average (76% overall), the gap is clearly shrinking as the patterns that they pioneered are becoming the norm. With overt discrimination now outlawed, women practice virtually every occupation on the spectrum from blue collar to professional.

Yet alongside change, older patterns persist. Women remain concentrated in female-dominated, low-paid service occupations despite their presence in many professions and in traditionally male blue-collar occupations such as construction or truck driving. Although the exceptions are highly visible (tracked in the popular media frequently as interesting and unusual phenomena), 70 percent of women work either in the services industry (health and education) or in wholesale or retail trade. Women's median weekly earnings are still only 75 percent those of men—though there has been a dramatic gain since 1970 when they were 62.2 percent. (Note, however, that this change represents a combined gain for women of 17% and a 3% decline for men.)

Sexuality, Fertility, and Marriage

The late twentieth century has witnessed a sharp increase in single motherhood even as overall fertility has declined. One birth in three is to an unmarried woman; in 1970, that proportion was only one in ten. Sixty-nine percent of children live with two parents; 23.5 percent with mother only (for African Americans this is 52%).

Some of this single parenthood is due to divorce, something that was relatively rare in 1900 and today affects nearly one in every two marriages. The divorce rate seems to have peaked in 1980, however, and has declined somewhat since that time (in 1980 there were 5.2 divorces/1,000 population; today there are 4.4). Single motherhood is not the source of shame that it was in 1900, but it remains highly correlated with poverty.

If female sexuality was suppressed in 1900 (even though incompletely), at the end of the century sexual references and images saturate

American culture. It was not until the 1930s that birth control became legal in most states. In 1961 the birth control pill introduced the possibility of radically separating sexual experience from the likelihood of procreation. Then in 1973, the Supreme Court's Roe v. Wade decision legalized abortion. Today, premarital sex is common, even normative. According to the Alan Guttmacher Institute, in the early 1990s 56 percent of women and 73 percent of men had sex by age 18.

As dramatic, homosexuality has become an open subject of public discourse, and lesbians—once completely hidden, even to one another—are creating new public spaces and organizations, fields of intellectual inquiry and theory, and families that rely on voluntary ties in the absence of any legal sanction. Lesbians have been a major constituency and source of leadership in the second feminist wave. Twenty years of visibility, however, is just a beginning. American society remains deeply, and emotionally, divided on the issue of homosexuality. Opposition to gay rights marks a key issue for the religious right, and open violence against lesbians and gay men continues.

Race and Class

The second wave grew directly from and modeled itself on the civil rights movement in the 1950s and 1960s. That movement, itself, relied heavily on the grass-roots (if relatively invisible) leadership of African-American women. In the last decades of the century, the voices of minority women have become increasingly distinct and powerful. Diversity among women, as in the society at large, has taken on new dimensions with a surge of immigration since the 1960s from Southeast Asia, East Africa, Central America, and other parts of the Third World. Predictions based on immigration and fertility suggest that by the middle of the next century whites will be only half the U.S. population. Women of color will become the new norm. Women remain deeply divided on racial grounds, but race is no longer defined as black and white.

Challenges to traditional conceptions of gender have also shaken the previous consensus on what constitutes a "good woman" (except perhaps to the right-wing traditionalists who still hold to a set of ideals quite similar to those that dominated American culture a century ago). Yet discomfort with women's move into public life is still widespread, and race and class stigmas remain. The massive growth of a welfare system whose clients are disproportionately women and children combines racial and gender stereotypes to create a new category of "bad women": single, minority, poor mothers. And wherever women appear in previously male-dominated environments, they remain suspect. In particular, the sharply polarized emotional response to Hillary Rodham Clinton during her time as first lady illustrates the undercurrent of anger at powerful, professional women. Radio talk shows have filled thousands of hours with hosts and callers venting their hostility toward this woman who, in their view, did not stay "in her place." But, of course, that is the open question at century's end: just what is "woman's place"?

Conclusion

This brief discussion of women in the twentieth century does not trace a smooth arc from the beginning of the century to the end. It is not simply about "progress" toward "equality." But it is, indeed, about a kind of sea change with unanticipated consequences and with dramatic acceleration in the last thirty years.

In the nineteenth century women created much of what today we call civil society. In the twentieth century they used that layer of society—which lies between formal governmental structures and private familial life—in an amazing variety of ways to reshape the landscape of American life. Virtually all of the public spaces previously presumed to belong properly to men—paid labor, higher education, electoral politics and public office, athletics—now incorporate a large and visible proportion of women. This theme of participation in public life, and the concomitant politicization of issues previously considered personal, runs through the entire century.

Such spectacular shifts have clearly been driven by large structural forces: the emergence of a postindustrial service economy, rising levels of education, two cataclysmic world wars, global power and national wealth on a level never imagined, changing patterns of marriage, fertility, and longevity. Yet the most dramatic changes can clearly be traced in equal measure to two large waves of women's activism.

The suffrage movement, by the 1910s, involved hundreds of thousands of women, branching out both tactically with the use of massive public parades and street corner speeches (females occupying public, political spaces) and in composition as it reached out to working women, immigrants, and minorities. That movement won for women the fundamental right of citizenship, the right to vote. And the Progressive movement on which it built laid the groundwork and provided many key players for the subsequent emergence of the welfare state. The impact of the second wave shows up in the astonishing acceleration of change in the last three decades of the century.

Each of these waves continued to surge forward in the decades after cresting. But each was also followed by a period in which the multiplicity of women's voices reasserted itself along with debates over the real meaning of equality. And each left much work undone for subsequent generations that face new issues and new dilemmas.

In the twenty-first century women will have choices that have never before been available, but they will not be easy. The twentieth century challenged our very definitions of male and female. Many of the signs of manhood and womanhood no longer function effectively. Work is no longer a manly prerogative and responsibility. Families are no longer constituted around a male breadwinner, a wife, and their children. More often they are two-income households (same or different sexes) or single-parent households. Large numbers of single men and women live alone. Yet "family values" have become a political code for attacks on welfare mothers, homosexuals, and nontraditional families (which, in fact, far outnumbered traditional ones). In the absence of significant societal or governmental support for women's traditional responsibilities, women assume a double burden. They participate in the labor force almost to the same degree as men, and yet work outside the home is still organized as though workers had wives to take care of household work, child care, and the myriad details of private life. Work outside the home makes few accommodations to the demands and priorities of family life.

The pioneering work of the twentieth century—as women made their way into hostile, male-dominated public spaces—remains unfinished. Most of the barriers have been broken at least once. But equity remains a distant goal. Achieving that goal is complicated by the fact that for the moment women are not a highly unified group. The contemporary struggles within feminism to deal with the differences among women are the essential precursor to any future social movement that claims to speak for women as a group. The very meanings of masculinity and femininity and their multiple cultural and symbolic references are now overtly contested throughout the popular culture.

Another legacy of the feminist movement that proclaimed that "the personal is political" is an unresolved ambiguity about just where the boundary between the personal and the political properly lies, and the dilemmas resulting from politicizing private life. At the end of the century, Americans faced a constitutional crisis rooted in the strange career of personal politics. For an entire year virtually everyone in the United States was riveted by the scandal concerning President Clinton, Monica Lewinsky, Kenneth Starr, and the American Congress. Behaviors that once would have been considered purely private (and gone unremarked by political reporters, for example) became the basis for impeachment. Who defended the distinction between public and private and who assaulted it? The tables seem to have turned with a vengeance as the right wing pried into intimate details about the president's sexual activities in a consensual relationship while the liberals (including feminist leaders) protested. The politicization of private life is indeed a double-edged sword. This should be no surprise, as conservative backlash since the 1970s has evidanced a clear willingness to use the power of the state to enforce its vision of proper private relationships on issues such as abortion, homosexuality, divorce, prayer in the schools, and the content of textbooks.

The recent history of feminism calls to our attention a number of dimensions in this crisis that should not go unnoticed. First, there have always been many members of society (racial and sexual minorities, welfare recipients, and women, to name only the most obvious) whose private behaviors have been scrutinized and regulated by those in power. By forcing these issues into public debate and evolving laws that might protect such groups (for example laws against sexual harassment) feminists have also removed the cover of silence that protected powerful men from public scrutiny for their private behaviors. That such laws were subsequently used in a campaign to unseat a president whose election was directly due to the votes of politically mobilized women resonates with irony.

Women's solidarity has waxed and waned across the twentieth century. It will certainly continue to do so in the twenty-first. The next wave of feminist activism will no doubt take a shape we cannot envision, just as no one at the dawn of the twentieth century could have imagined the battles that awaited them. That there will be another wave, however, is a safe prediction, given the unfinished agendas of the last century and the still unforeseen contradictions that future changes will create. The next wave will shape the new century.

Bibliography

William H. Chafe, *The American Woman: Her Changing Social, Economic, and Political Roles, 1920–1970* (New York: Oxford University Press, 1972), laid the groundwork for subsequent studies of twentieth-century women. Peter Filene examines the implications of changing definitions of womanliness and manliness on both sexes in *Him/Her Self: Sex Roles in Modern America*, 2nd ed. (Baltimore: Johns Hopkins University Press, 1986). Sara M. Evans, *Born for Liberty: A History of Women in America*, 2nd ed. (New York: Free Press, 1996) provides a general overview of women in American history.

The "first wave" of women's rights activism in the twentieth century is chronicled by Nancy F. Cott, *The Grounding of Modern Feminism* (New Haven, Conn.: Yale University Press, 1987), and Mari Jo Buhle and Paul Buhle, eds., *The Concise History of Woman Suffrage: Selections from the Classic Work of Stanton, Anthony, Gage, and Harper* (Urbana: University of Illinois Press, 1978). On women's role in the New Deal see Susan Ware, *Beyond Suffrage: Women in the New Deal* (Cambridge, Mass.: Harvard University Press, 1981). The critical eras of the 1940s and the cold war are examined in Susan Hartmann, *The Homefront and Beyond: American Women in the 1940s* (Boston: Twayne Publishers, 1982) and Elaine Tyler May, *Homeward Bound: American Families in the Cold War Era* (New York: Basic Books, 1988). There is a growing literature on the "second wave" of feminism. Some starting points would be Sara Evans, *Personal Politics: The Roots of Women's Liberation in the Civil Rights Movement and the New Left* (New York: Vintage, 1980); Alice Echols, *Daring to Be Bad: Radical Feminism in America, 1967–1975* (Minneapolis: University of Minnesota Press, 1989); and Donald Mathews and Jane De Hart, *Sex, Gender, and the Politics of ERA* (New York: Oxford University Press, 1990).

For more depth on the history of sexuality see John D'Emilio and Estelle B. Freedman, *Intimate Matters: A History of Sexuality in America* (New York: Harper & Row, 1988); on education see Barbara Solomon, *In the Company of Educated Women: A History of Women and Higher Education in America* (New Haven, Conn.: Yale University Press, 1985); on women in the labor force see Julia Blackwelder, *Now Hiring: The Feminization of Work in the United States: 1900–1995* (College Station: Texas A&M University Press, 1997. Some excellent starting points on racial minority and immigrant ethnic women include Vicki L. Ruíz, *From Out of the Shadows: Mexican Women in Twentieth-Century America* (New York: Oxford University Press,

1999); on African-American women see Jacqueline Jones, *Labor of Love, Labor of Sorrow: Black Women, Work, and the Family from Slavery to the Present* (New York: Basic Books, 1985), and on Chinese women Judy Yung, *Unbound Feet: A Social History of Chinese Women in San Francisco* (Barkeley: University of California Press, 1995); Donna Gabaccia, *From the Other Side: Women, Gender, and Immigrant Life in the U.S., 1920–1990* (Bloomington: Indiana University Press, 1994),

For the most recent descriptions of women's status in all aspects of American life, see the series sponsored by the Women's Research and Education Institute in Washington, D.C., *The American Woman* (New York: W. W. Norton). This series has been updated biannually from its inception in 1987.

POSTSCRIPT

Has the Women's Movement of the 1970s Failed to Liberate American Women?

F. Carolyn Graglia's critique of contemporary feminism is a throwback to women of the late nineteenth and early twentieth century who opposed the women social workers and suffragettes who entered the man's world. Her book is a modern restatement of Barbara Welter's classic and widely reprinted article, "The Cult of True Womanhood," *American Quarterly* (Summer 1996).

Graglia argues that contemporary feminism ignores women's primary role in raising the children and preserving the moral character of the family. She blames contemporary feminism along with the Great Society's social programs for promoting a sexual revolution that has destroyed the American family by fostering sexually transmitted diseases and a high divorce rate.

Historian Sara M. Evans takes a long-range view of the women's liberation movement. By comparing the political, legal, and domestic situation of women in 1900 with today, Evans charts the successes and failures that were achieved by the two waves of feminist protest movements in the twentieth century.

At the beginning of the twentieth century, a number of middle-class women from elite colleges in the northeast were in the vanguard of a number of progressive reform movements—temperance, anti-prostitution, child labor, and settlement houses. Working in tandem with the daughters of first-generation immigrants employed in the garment industry, the early feminists realized that laws affecting women could be passed only if women had the right to vote. The suffragettes overcame the arguments of male and female antisuffragists who associated women voters with divorce, promiscuity, and neglect of children and husbands with the ratification of the Nineteenth Amendment in 1920.

The women's movement stalled between the two wars for a variety of reasons: Women pursued their own individual freedom in a consumer-oriented society in the 1920s, and the Great Depression of the 1930s placed the economic survival of the nation at the forefront. But the Second World War had long-range effects on women. Minorities—African Americans and Hispanics—worked for over 3 years in factory jobs traditionally reserved for white males at high wages. So did married white females, often in their thirties. Although the majority of these women returned to the home or took more traditional low-paying "women's" jobs after the war, the consciousness of the changing role of women during the Second World War would reappear during the 1960s.

Evans points out the two streams that formed the women's liberation movement from the mid-1960s. First were the professional women like Betty Freidan, who created the National Organization for Women (NOW) in 1966, who worked with women leaders in labor unions, government, and consciousness-raising groups to demand enforcement of Title VII of the 1965 Civil Rights Act, which banned discrimination in employment and wages. A second wing of feminist activists came from the civil rights and anti-war new left protest groups from the elite universities. Many of these women felt like second-class citizens in these movements and decided they had their own issues that they had to deal with.

Evans dubbed the years 1968 to 1975 "the golden years" because of the following successes: "Passage of the Equal Rights Amendment in Congress in 1972; the 1973 Supreme Court decision (*Roe* v. *Wade*) legalizing abortion; Title IX of the Higher Education Act which opened intercollegiate athletics to women; the Women's Equity Education Act; and the Equal Credit Opportunity Act."

Evans points out that the women's movement suffered a "backlash" in the 1980s as America became much more conservative. The new right blamed the increases in divorce, single parenthood, out-of-wedlock births, abortions, and open homosexuality on the cultural values of the 1960s. But by the beginning of the twenty-first century, middle-class women made substantial gains in the professions compared with 1960: Law school today 43 percent, 1960 2 percent; medicine today 38 percent, 1960 6 percent; MBA programs today 35 percent, 1960 4 percent; dentistry today 38 percent, 1960 1 percent; and Ph.D. programs today 39 percent, 1960 11 percent. Working-class women, however, have been much less successful in breaking into traditional blue collar jobs such as truck driving and construction.

Both the antifeminist Graglia and to a much less extent the pro-feminist Evans have been critiqued by moderate feminists like Elizabeth Fox-Genovese and Cathy Young, who contend that contemporary feminists have not spoken to the concerns of married women, especially women from poor to lower-middle-class families who must work in order to help support the family. Fox-Genovese's *Feminism Is Not the Story of My Life: How Today's Feminist Elite Have Lost Touch With the Real Concerns of Women* (Doubleday, 1996) is peppered with interviews of white, African American, and Hispanic Americans of different classes and gives a more complex picture of the problems women face today. Young, author of *Cease Fire! Why Women and Men Must Join Forces to Achieve True Equality* (Free Press, 1999), asserts that Graglia denies the real discrimination women faced in the job market in the 1950s. Furthermore, Graglia's critique of the sexual revolution is an attempt to restore a view of female sexuality as essentially submissive.

In 1998 Harvard University Press reprinted Betty Friedan's two later books—*The Second Stage* and *It Changed My Life*, both with new introductions with suggestions for the twenty-first century—which are critical of some of the directions that the women's movement took.

Important books and articles by activists with a historical perspective include Sara Evans, *Personal Politics: The Roots of Women's Liberation in the Civil Rights Movement and the New Left* (Vintage, 1979). This book is nicely summarized in "Sources of the Second Wave: The Rebirth of Feminism," in Alexander Bloom, ed., *Long Time Gone: Sixties America Then and Now* (Oxford, 2001). For a general overview of women's history, see Evans, *Born for Liberty: A History of Women in America*, 2nd ed. (Free Press, 1996), and Roger Adelson's "*Interview with Sara Margaret Evans*," *The Historian* (vol. 63, Fall 2000); Donna Gabaccia, *From the Other Side: Women, Gender and Immigrant Life in the U.S., 1920–1990* (Indiana University Press, 1994); and John D'Emilio and Estelle B. Freedman, *Intimate Matters: A History of Sexuality in America* (Harper & Row, 1988).

Review essays from various journals reflect the continuous battle over the importance of the women's movement. The neo-conservative magazine *Commentary* is constantly critical of feminism. See Elizabeth Kristol, "The Sexual Revolution" (April 1996) and Elizabeth Powers, "Back to Basics" (March 1999). Also critical is Daphne Patai, "Will the Real Feminists in Academe Stand Up," *The Chronicle of Higher Education* (October 6, 2000 pp. B6–9). Sympathetic to the movement is Christine Stansell, "Girlie Interrupted: The Generational Progress of Feminism," *The New Republic* (January 15, 2001); Andrew Hacker, "How Are Women Doing," *The New York Review of Books* (Fall 2000). See also Jo Freeman, "The Women's Liberation Movement: Its Origins, Structure, Activities, and Ideas," in Jo Freeman, ed., *Women: A Feminist Perspective*, 3rd ed. (Mayfield, 1984); Estelle B. Freedman, *No Turning Back: The History of Feminism and the Future of Women* (Balantine, 2001); and Susan Brownmiller, *In Our Time: Memoir of a Revolution* (Dial Press, 2000).

The best starting point is Ruth Rosen, *The World Split Open: How the Modern Woman's Movement Changed America* (Viking, 2000), written by a former Berkley activist for her students who were born in the 1980s.

Books that deal with the impact of the movement on specific groups include Johnnetta B. Cole and Beverly Gray-Sheftall, *Gender Talk: The Struggle for Women's Equality in African American Communities* (Balantine, 2003); Jacqueline Jones, *Labor of Love, Labor of Sorrow: Black Women, Work, and the Family from Slavery to the Present* (Basic Books, 1985); Vicki L. Ruiz, *From out of the Shadows: Mexican Women in Twentieth-Century Books* (April 11, 2002); and Kim France's review of Phyllis Chesler, *Letters to a Young Feminist* (Four Walls Eight Windows, 1998) in *The New York Times Book Review* (April 26, 1998 pp. 10–11).

ISSUE 17

Were the 1980s a Decade of Affluence for the Middle Class?

YES: J. David Woodard, from *The America That Reagan Built* (Praeger, 2006)

NO: Thomas Byrne Edsall, from "The Changing Shape of Power: A Realignment in Public Policy," in Steve Fraser and Gary Gerstle, *The Rise and Fall of the New Deal Order, 1930–1980* (Princeton University Press, 1980)

ISSUE SUMMARY

YES: According to Professor J. David Woodard, supply-side economics unleashed a wave of entrepreneurial and technological innovation that transformed the economy and restored America's confidence in the Golden Age from 1983 to 1992.

NO: Political journalist Thomas B. Edsall argues that the Reagan revolution brought about a policy realignment that reversed the New Deal and redistributed political power and economic wealth to the top 20 percent of Americans.

In 1939, after 6 years of the New Deal, unemployment in the United States remained at an unacceptably high rate of 17 percent. World War II bailed America out of the Great Depression. When 20 million workers entered the armed forces, married American women, along with African-American and Hispanic males and females, filled the void in the higher-paying factory jobs. Everyone not only made money but poured it into war bonds and traditional savings accounts. Government and business cemented their relationship with "cost plus" profits for the defense industries.

By the end of 1945, Americans had stashed away $134 billion in cash, savings accounts, and government securities. This pent-up demand meant there would be no depression akin to the end of World War I or the 1930s. Following initial shortages before industry completed its conversion to peacetime production, Americans engaged in the greatest spending spree in the country's history. Liberals and conservatives from both political parties had developed a consensus on foreign and domestic policies.

The president's Council of Economic Advisers was composed of Keynesians, who believed that government spending could increase employment even if it meant that budget deficits would be temporarily created. For nearly 25 years, they used fiscal and monetary tools to manipulate the economy so that inflation would remain low while employment would reach close to its maximum capacity.

Around 1968, the consensus surrounding domestic and foreign policy broke down for three reasons: (1) the Vietnam imbroglio, (2) the oil crises of 1974 and 1979, and (3) the decline of the smokestack industries.

Lyndon Johnson's presidency was ruined by the Vietnam War. He believed that he could escalate the war and his Great Society programs at the same time. His successor, Richard Nixon, attempted to solve the Vietnam dilemma by bringing the American troops home and letting Asians fight Asians. The process of withdrawal was slow and costly. Also expensive were many of the Great Society programs, such as Social Security, Aid to Families with Dependent Children, environmental legislation, and school desegregation, which Nixon continued to uphold. In August 1971, Nixon acknowledged that he had become a Keynesian when he imposed a 90-day wage and price control freeze and took the international dollar off the gold standard and allowed it to float. With these bold moves, Nixon hoped to stop the dollar from declining in value. He was also faced with a recession that included both high unemployment and high inflation. "Stagflation" resulted, leading to the demise of Keynesian economics.

In early 1974, shortly before Nixon was forced to resign from office, the major oil-producing nation of the world—primarily in the Middle East—agreed to curb oil productions and raise oil prices. The OPEC cartel, protesting the pro-Israeli policies of the Western nations, brought these countries to their knees. In the United States, gasoline went from $0.40 to $2.00 per gallon in a matter of days. In the early 1980s, President Jimmy Carter implored the nation to conserve energy, but he appeared helpless as the unemployment rate approached double digits and as the Federal Reserve Board raised interest rates to 18 percent in a desperate attempt to stem inflation.

The Reagan administration introduced a new economic philosophy: supply-side economics. Its proponents, led by economists Martin Anderson and Arthur Laffer, believed that if taxes were cut and spending on frivolous social programs were reduced—even while military spending increases—businesses will use the excess money to expand. More jobs would result, consumers would increase spending, and the multiplying effect would be a period of sustained growth and prosperity. Did it work?

Professor J. David Woodward answers this question with an arousing yes. Supply-side economics, he says in the first essay, unleashed a wave of entrepreneurial and technological innovation that transformed the economy and restored America's confidence in the Golden Age from 1983 to 1992. But political journalist Thomas B. Edsall disagrees with this analysis. Yes, there was prosperity in the 1980s, but only for a few groups. The Reagan revolution, he says, brought about a policy realignment as well as a political one that redistributed political and economic wealth to the top 20 percent of Americans.

A Rising Tide

The Reagan Revolution, as the times came to be called, followed the economic growth in real income from 1983 through the end of the president's second term in 1988, to the recession that concluded the Bush presidency in 1992. During this time the gross domestic product (GDP) doubled. In the expansion through the two Reagan terms, "real-after-tax income per person rose by 15.5 percent, [and] the real median income of families, before taxes, went up 12.5 percent." Measured in constant 1990 dollars, the percentage of families earning between $15,000 and $50,000 fell by 5 points, and the percentage earning more than $50,000 in constant dollars rose by 5 points. Millions of families moved up the ladder from the lower class to the middle class. America had gone from "stagflation" and the highest prices in thirty years to galloping capitalism, and everyday citizens were investing in the stock market.

The middle-class market sought the deposits of ordinary savers and young people just beginning to accumulate assets. Wall Street had previously ignored these customers, but now it sought them out. Prudential-Bache, an aggressive firm, was quoted in *Barron's* as saying it "sees its clients as the $40,000-a-year young professional on the fast track." As the market expanded, more individuals placed their money in funds to balance risk and profit. Suddenly the stock market report was of interest to everyone.

Stockbrokers assured investors that their money was safe, but in late 1987 they discovered the real meaning of risk. The market was doing quite well for the first nine months of the year; it was up more than 30 percent and reaching unprecedented heights. Then, in the days between October 14 and October 19, the market fell off a cliff. On October 19, subsequently known as "Black Monday," the Dow Jones Industrial Average plummeted 508 points, losing 22.6 percent of its total value. This was the greatest loss Wall Street had ever suffered on a single day, even worse than the crash of 1929. It took two years for the Dow to recover completely; not until September of 1989 did it regain all the value it lost in the 1987 crash.

One important lesson came out of the crash: investors who sold took a bath. Those who held on and continued a disciplined and systematic program received rewards. The American economy continued as the greatest wealth producer the world had ever seen. The consequence of all this was a standard of living beyond the comprehension of the rest

From chapter 4 of *The America That Built Reagan,* (Praeger, 2006) pp. 63–77. Copyright © 2006 by J. David Woodard. Reprinted by permission of Greenwood Publishing Group, Inc.

of the world, and a cause for envy by peer nations. While $200,000 was enough to make the top 1 percent of American income in 1980, a family might need well over $300,000 to be in that category a decade later. The Congressional Budget Office estimated that it would take more than $550,000 to be in the top 1 percent in 1992. No sooner had a survivor of the 1970s comprehended what was happening than he became obsolete. Reagan's supply-side ideas unleashed a wave of entrepreneurial and technological innovation that transformed the economy and restored the country's self-confidence. Economic prosperity had been the impossible dream of youth, and now it was everywhere.

The vast majority of the population experienced substantial gains in real income and wealth. With millions of people earning more money, much higher incomes were required to make it to the top 5 percent, or the top 1 percent of the nation's income bracket. At the time, the rising tide of economic prosperity lifted at least 90 percent of the American family boats. For those who lived through it, the 1983–1992 period would be remembered as an uncomplicated golden time, mourned as lost, and remembered as cloudless.

The spending began at home, where people purchased new homes and remodeled older ones. Declining interest rates made mortgages affordable, and the number of single-family homes expanded each year from 1980 to 1988. Consumers also had more cars to drive as the two-income, two-car family became the norm. From 1980 to 1988, the number of new car models increased by half, the most popular being the minivans for suburban families. Lower air fares and discount packages allowed passengers to travel to previously unheard-of places, and the number of people flying overseas rose by 40 percent during the 1980s.

Much of this expense for the new lifestyle was charged to credit cards. Americans took three-, four-, and five-day trips and the amount of credit card debt more than doubled. Specialty chain stores like the Gap, Limited, and Banana Republic targeted upscale, professional customers who wanted to take advantage of their new standing and credit to add the latest styles to their wardrobes. Shopping malls proliferated in suburban settings, and the consumption ethic gave birth to Wal-Mart, destined in the next decade to become the nation's largest company. While American life was becoming more affluent, it was also becoming more complex.

Of course there were critics, and for them the era was never that splendid; it was derided for its inbred conformity, flatulent excesses, and materialistic binges. The "me" decade of the 1970s turned into the "my" decade of the 1980s. The faultfinders saw the surge of abundance as a joyless vulgarity. In 1987, filmmaker Oliver Stone released the movie *Wall Street*. The story involved a young stockbroker, Bud Fox, who becomes involved with his hero, Gordon Gekko, an extremely successful, but corrupt, stock trader. In the most memorable scene of the movie. Gekko makes a speech to the shareholders of a company he was planning to take over. Stone used the scene to give Gekko, and by extension corporate America at the time, the characteristic trait of economic success.

Gekko: Teldar Paper, Mr. Cromwell, Teldar Paper has 33 different vice presidents, each making over 200 thousand dollars a year. Now, I have spent the last two months analyzing what all these guys do, and I still can't figure it out. One thing I do know is that our paper company lost 110 million dollars last year, and I'll bet that half of that was spent in all the paperwork going back and forth between all these vice presidents.

The new law of evolution in corporate America seems to be survival of the unfittest. Well, in my book you either do it right or you get eliminated.

In the last seven deals that I've been involved with, there were 2.5 million stockholders who had made a pretax profit of 12 billion dollars. Thank you.

I am not a destroyer of companies. I am a liberator of them!

The point is, ladies and gentlemen, is that greed—for lack of a better word—is good.

Greed is right.

Greed works.

Greed clarifies, cuts through, and captures the essence of the evolutionary spirit.

Greed in all its forms—greed for life, for money, for love, knowledge—has marked the upward surge of mankind.

And greed—you mark my words—will not only save Teldar Paper, but that other malfunctioning corporation called the USA.

Thank you very much.

The same theme was addressed in literature. In 1990, one of America's foremost writers, Tom Wolfe, released a blockbuster bestseller entitled *The Bonfire of the Vanities.* The book dealt with what Wolfe called the "big, rich slices of contemporary life," in this case the heady materialism of the 1980s. The plot followed the life of Sherman McCoy, a prodigiously successful bond trader at a prestigious Wall Street firm. One night Sherman, accompanied by his mistress, fatally injures a black man in a car accident. As a result of this accident, all the ennui of metropolitan life, race relations, instant affluence and gratification, and the class structure of the city afflict the lead character.

As a member of the new ruling class, Sherman McCoy and other bond traders were allied with opportunistic politicians in speculative excesses. Sherman was supremely confident that he would escape his fate. The 1980s were critiqued as the epitome of American decline and the triumph of finance capitalism spurred by Wall Street bond and stock manipulators, like McCoy's employer, Eugene Lopwitz. Sherman McCoy had to pay for his greed and irresponsibility; he lost his job, his wife and his child, his mistress, his home, and his class standing. But in the end he lied to escape prosecution, and got even with every institution—the courts, the media, and the economic system—which were also built on a foundation of lies.

American capitalism, and its excesses, had long been a topic of intellectual and literary criticism. Theodore Dreiser wrote the novel *An American*

Tragedy in 1925 as a critique of business practices at the time. The story followed a bellboy who sets out to gain success and fame, only to slip into murder and death by execution. Dreiser declared that the materialistic society was as much to blame as the murderer himself. What was new in the *Bonfire* plot was that the perpetrators escaped capture and conviction. In the new world people could be evil and—if they had enough money—bear no consequences for their actions.

During the 1980s, the power and influence of American corporations expanded to exorbitant heights. General Motors had revenues greater than 90 percent of the world's nations. The Reagan administration eased restrictions on the stock market and on antitrust laws so some of the more massive corporate takeovers in American history happened in the decade. The largest one was between R. J. Reynolds, the tobacco company, and Nabisco, the maker of cookies, crackers, and cereals, for $24.9 billion.

Other companies were taken over in what was known as a leveraged buyout, where investors joined forces with the managers of a company to buy it. The funds came from the managers themselves, but most were borrowed. The money for takeovers was raised through the sale of so-called junk bonds. Junk bonds were high-risk investments by securities rating agencies, such as Standard and Poor's and Moody's, marked as such because they had a potential for higher yield and failure. If the people who bought the bonds were successful in the takeover, then they were handsomely rewarded; but if they failed, then there was the possibility that the bonds would not be repaid.

Companies with low debt loads were attractive targets for leveraged buyouts, which meant that successful businessmen found themselves the object of "corporate raiders." Benjamin Franklin's age-old virtues of thrift and frugality resulted in business success, so much so that the entrepreneurial founders lost control of their companies. Sometimes, to prevent these unwanted effects, recently acquired companies bought back their stock at higher than market prices—in effect, paying raiders to go away. The practice was known as "green-mail," for its resemblance to blackmail. More than $12 billion in greenmail was paid by corporations such as Texaco, Warner, and Quaker State in the first few months of 1984.

The business of mergers required dozens of brokers, lawyers, and bankers. A new class of business people known as "young, urban professionals," or "yuppies," emerged as experts in the takeover game. They were stereotyped as college-educated men and women, who dressed well, lived in expensive apartments, drove expensive cars, exercised in gyms, and worked twelve-hour days. "An MBA (Masters of Business Administration), a condo and a BMW" became the mantra of the age. One woman interviewed on television unabashedly declared, "I aspire to materialism." "Big spender" became a term of approbation. A writer at the time described it this way: "People saw money as power . . . [they went to] 'power lunches' while wearing fashionable 'power suits' . . . designer fashions bloated egos and fattened the cash registers of swank stores." The spenders were living on credit and buying on margin, but they did not seem to mind. Spending and mergers were fueling the boom, and any tendency to go slow was seen as alarming.

Leveraged buyouts were risky, but legal, transactions. As in any business, a few successful corporate raiders operated outside the law. On May 12, 1986, Dennis Levine, who had made $12.6 million on insider-trading deals, implicated two well-known Wall Street traders: Michael Milken and Ivan Boesky. Both men were charged with violations of federal securities law. Boesky agreed to pay $100 million in forfeitures and penalties, and Michael Milken admitted to six felonies and agreed to pay $600 million in fines. The amount of the fines was staggering, but more revealing was the corporate raider lifestyle the investigations uncovered. In the early 1980s Milken was reportedly making $550 million a year.

Overall, the freeing of the market for corporate control had important benefits for women in the workforce. College-educated women moved into fields like business, engineering, medicine, and law. "The result was that women as a whole, whose average earnings had been 58 percent of those of men in 1979, earned 68 percent ten years later." Professional women began moving into managerial positions where they soon faced the problem of how to combine motherhood and career. In the 1980s work itself was changing. The computer and instant communication enabled more people to work at home, and women soon learned that part-time, or maternity leave, arrangements allowed them to close the income gap with their male counterparts.

The boom arose from numerous springs: the new government economic philosophy, technological innovation, an altered world economy, and a changing labor market. The latter trend would have political consequences well into the next century. For example, immigration had a dramatic influence on the labor pool and the expansion of entry-level jobs. In the 1970s, 4.5 million immigrants were legally admitted into the country, and many more came illegally. In the 1980s legal immigration swelled to 7.4 million, with additional millions of illegal entrants. The vast majority of immigrants from Central and South America, who made up about half the total, had considerably lower levels of schooling than native-born Americans. Their presence resulted in higher wages for college graduates and depressed wages for those who had lower levels of schooling.

The immigration trends caused increases in wage and income inequality, because of the demand for skilled labor due to technological changes and new trade patterns. Sophisticated new technologies flourished in the aerospace, defense, electronics, and computer industries. Sprawling scientific complexes raised the standard of living for millions of Americans. Research funds for technology, or R & D (research and development), which were practically insignificant in the 1950s, amounted to an estimated $100 billion a year at the end of the 1980s. Americans were making money with their minds, and not on the assembly line.

Little of this was new. Sociologist Daniel Bell wrote in 1973 that there was a natural progression from a traditional society, based on agriculture, to an industrial one based on manufacturing. Then there was a subsequent transition from an industrial to a postindustrial society, which culminated in a service economy. This progression to a postindustrial society occurred when the emphasis on the production of goods was overtaken by a service economy. The postindustrial society meant an extension of scientific rationality into the economic, social, and political spheres. By the late 1970s only 13 percent of American workers were involved in the manufacture of goods, whereas a full 60 percent were engaged in the production of information. The new "knowledge society" was run by university-trained employers. In this society technical skill was the base of power, and education the means of access to power. Individuals who exercised authority through technical competence, called "technocrats," dominated society.

The birth years of the postindustrial society were in the 1950s, but it came to fruition in the 1980s. The 1950s saw great technological developments such as the atomic bomb and the digital computer, but the character of knowledge itself began to change thirty years later. Workers had to be taught how to think, not how to do routine tasks. Change was so prevalent that knowledge of any specific task was quickly washed away by a new wave of innovation. Theoretical knowledge of abstract principles was central in the postindustrial society, and the key organization of the future was the university, along with think tanks and research centers.

During the 1980s the academy itself was changing. The number of professors at American universities in 1980 was four times what it was in 1960. As faculties grew, so too did the specialization of their disciplines. Student enrollments in fields like business, computer science, engineering, and mathematics soared, while the liberal arts and social sciences lost out in comparison. It was the age of the computer chip, which made everything smaller and faster.

Universities were only the tip of the iceberg of culture producers that included not only the creators of the new society, but also its transmitters. Labor in the postindustrial context involved those in journalism, publishing, magazines, broadcast media, theater, and museums and anyone who was involved in the influence and reception of serious cultural products. The growth of cultural output was a fact in the knowledge industry. Consider what happened to those Daniel Bell called "the cultural mass" of art producers. New York had only a handful of galleries in 1945, and no more than a score of known artists; by the 1980s the city had some 680 galleries and more than 150,000 artists. Add to these artists producers of books, printers, serious music recordings, writers, editors, movie makers, musicians, and so forth and the size of just one part of the mass culture was exposed.

Bell argued that the postindustrial society would change politics, as well as culture and economics. In his view, government would increasingly become instrumental in the management of the economy; less control would be left to market forces. Instead of relying on the invisible hand, Bell saw that the postindustrial society would work toward directing and engineering society. He could not have been more wrong. The spirit of the 1980s was against the command decision views of Daniel Bell.

Conservatives had long denounced Keynesian economics as a fraud, and expanding government as a threat, but their ideas were unpopular in the period of post-World War II prosperity. When liberalism's troubles began to mount in the 1970s, free market alternatives re-emerged.

Milton and Rose Friedman effectively rebutted the government as manager thesis, and replaced it with the free market-rational actor model. Their book, *Free to Choose*, was as clear an exposition of free market economics as anything since Adam Smith, and it showed how good intentions in Washington often had deplorable results in practice. Friedman made conservative economic ideas available and attractive to the mass public. To quote their thesis on the power of a free market idea: "If an exchange between two parties is voluntary, it will not take place unless both believe that they will benefit from it," or "the price system is the mechanism that performs this task without central direction, without requiring people to speak to one another or like one another." This was the book that explained how freedom had been eroded, and prosperity undermined, by the runaway spending and growth of government in Washington. *Free to Choose* was very influential on the thinking of Ronald Reagan and millions of ordinary Americans.

As strange as it may seem, by the 1980s the modern postindustrial society was itself becoming old fashioned. The period after World War II was characterized by three things: (1) the power of reason over ignorance, (2) the power of order over disorder, and (3) the power of science over superstition. These features were regarded as universal values, and were inculcated into the fabric of American culture. They were also the basis for Ronald Reagan's view of the world. His time with General Electric convinced him that American technology was second to none, and he wedded that faith to the national experience. After he left office he said, "There are no such things as limits to growth, because there are no limits on the human capacity for intelligence, imagination and wonder."

In the decade of the 1980s, the faith in reason, order, and the power of science, so dear to Reagan, was coming in for criticism. The command and control center for the criticism was the universities, the very postindustrial leaders Daniel Bell had identified years earlier. Much of Reagan's initial political success in his California gubernatorial race was based on criticism of antagonistic college students and their teachers, and his belief that America was a nation of technological might that outproduced and advanced knowledge to win a rightful place on the world stage. For example, Reagan regularly recalled American production in World War II, and his belief that the nation was a "bastion of freedom," and "a city set on a hill."

The problem was that universities were questioning everything Reagan said and stood for. The best known of these criticisms was labeled as deconstruction, a French import that questioned rationality and definitions. Deconstruction held that written words could never have fixed meanings, and, as a result, any text revealed ambiguities, contradictions, hidden meanings, and repressive political relationships. The modern world, according to these new thinkers, had expanded industrial capitalism and scientific thinking, but it also brought the world Auschwitz, the possibility of nuclear war, the horrors of Nazism and Stalinism, neocolonialism, racism, and world hunger. The critics believed that modernism had run its course, and society had entered a new age—the age of postmodernism.

Postmodernism is a complicated term because the concept appears in a wide variety of disciplines and areas of study, including art, architecture, music, film, literature, fashion, and technology. In general, postmodernism rejects the uncritical acceptance of the power of reason, order, and science. According to postmodernists, the assumption that there is such a thing as objective truth is at base a modern fallacy. For them there is no linear progress in society, no ideal social order, and no standardization of knowledge. Instead the world was a picture of fragmentation, indeterminacy, and chaos. Postmodernists held that culture should affirm this fragmented reality, and consider order to be only provisional and varying from person to person.

The contrast between modern and postmodern is seen in a comparison of professions. In several of them, such as medicine, law, and engineering, mastery of a specific body of knowledge and the application of an intrinsic logic led to something known as progress. When a doctor diagnosed and treated a disease, or when an engineer designed a bridge, their work assumed a rational understanding of the world and a logical means of dealing with it. In short, these professions presupposed an objective order in existence. Different medical doctors, using the same objective science and trained in a standard methodology, could examine the same patient and arrive at an identical diagnosis and course of treatment. They exemplify modernism.

A host of new professions arose by the 1980s that had no universally recognized body of knowledge, and no generally accepted methods, although they invoked the jargon of science. The social sciences were shining examples of new postmodern professions. For example, someone in need of "mental health" could be treated by a Freudian, a Jungian, a humanist, or a behaviorist. A political scientist could be a behaviorist, a formal theorist, one trained in classical political thought, or an area specialist with no training other than language skills, and then there were those who believed politics could not be a science. The philosophies behind the psychological analysis and the political analysis were incompatible, and the methodologies conflicted and were oftentimes incomplete and sometimes untested. They exemplify postmodern professions.

The conflict between modern and postmodern surfaced in Reagan's appointment of William Bennett as chairman of the National Endowment for the Humanities. Bennett had a Ph.D. in philosophy from the University of Texas and a law degree from Harvard. He was a conservative academic who spoke movingly about the threat deconstruction and postmodernism posed to the teaching of the Western classics. "We must give greater attention to a sound common curriculum emphasizing English, history, geography, math, and science . . . [and] we have to understand why these subjects were thrown out or weakened in the cultural deconstruction of our schools of the last twenty-five years." The very thing Bennett warned against was taking place at one of America's premier universities. The curriculum of Stanford became an issue in 1988, when the faculty voted to reform the Western Civilization course away from a "European-Western and male bias." The revision became an issue for discussion not only on college campuses, but also in newspapers and television talk shows across the country.

The education debate was part of a national one on the modernist/postmodernist divide. The society had not moved beyond modernity; there were still plenty of people who thought America was the hope of the world and believed in its technological future as well. But there were others who had their doubts, and they delighted in the period of transition. The character of the change was seen in the new pop culture.

The baby boomers, usually defined as those born between 1946 and 1964, left the world a legacy of rock and roll. In the 1980s "rock became a reference point for a splintered culture." The most important outlet for 1980s music was MTV, or Music Television, that began broadcasting on August 1, 1981. It brought music videos into American homes, and criticism of the dominant modern culture to a new generation. Some immediately saw that the new medium, which exulted in "fast cuts, slow motion, and artsy black-and-white photography—all selling sex and violence—defined the visual style of the decade, spreading to movies, prime time series, advertising and magazines."

The end of the peace and love generation of music came on December 8, 1980, when John Lennon was shot seven times outside the Dakota, an apartment building where he lived in New York City. Lennon's murder, by twenty-five-year-old Mark David Chapman, was made more horrifying because the assassin was a self-confessed fan. The paranoid fear by pop starts of their audiences was epitomized in Lennon's death, which was a prelude to the era's approaching fragmentation and cult of personality.

Michael Jackson was the most important pop rock star of the decade. When Jackson recorded *Off the Wall* with Quincy Jones as producer in 1979, it sold 6 million copies. That achievement made it the best-selling album ever recorded by an African American. His next album, *Thriller*, entered the Billboard Top Ten on January 3, 1983, where it stayed for seventy-eight weeks, remaining at number one for thirty-seven weeks. At the end of the decade, *Thriller* had sold over 40 million copies, making it the best-selling record album of all time.

By the mid-1980s, African American artists dominated the Top Ten music list. Lionel Richie, Tina Turner, Rick James, Billy Ocean, and Stevie Wonder all had number one hits in 1984. The most flamboyant artist of the time was Prince Rogers Nelson, whose shocking lyrics on the album *Dirty Mind* (1980) led Tipper Gore to form the Parents Music Resource Center in 1984 to protest sexually explicit lyrics. That protest would eventually result in "Parental Advisory" labels on album covers. Prince's flamboyant style led to questions about his personal life, especially if he was gay or bisexual. His response was classically postmodern: "Who cares?"

The popularity of rock music, and musicians, became a global experience in the 1980s. Renowned rock figures embarked on world tours, and the performances were experienced through enormous video screens and television broadcasts. Technology blurred the distinction between live events and reproduced videos and recordings. "From rock music to tourism to television and even education, advertising imperatives and consumer demand are no longer for goods, but for experiences." A rock music concert became the ultimate postmodern experience, proof with manufactured reality that all claims to truth—and even truth itself—were socially constructed.

In July 1985, one of the biggest events in rock history, the Live Aid concert, was held simultaneously in London and Philadelphia. The concert was attended by 160,000 fans while another 1.5 billion watched it on television or listened on the radio in 130 countries. The two simultaneous all-day concerts involved pretty much anybody who was anybody in the rock-and-roll world, and Phil Collins caught the supersonic Concord to play in both cities on two different continents. Hundreds of thousands of people raised their voices together to end the show by singing, "We are the World." The Live Aid concert raised over $80 million in foreign aid that went to seven African nations: Ethiopia, Mozambique, Chad, Burkina Faso, Niger, Mali, and Sudan.

MTV opened opportunities for women to flaunt their personality and sexuality on the screen in ways, and at an age, their parents could never have imagined. Tina Turner, Cyndi Lauper, and Madonna Ciccone emerged as singing, sexual icons of the time. The latter's album *Like a Virgin* created a stir when she took the woman-as-sex-object ploy to new public heights. She found herself singing to prepubescent audiences dressed in layered gypsy blouses, bangled necklaces, and an exposed midriff. In true postmodern style, Madonna changed her public image many times, going from dance queen to "boy toy," to the "Material Girl," to trashy on-stage exhibitionist. Each time, she influenced popular fashion and the style of pop music.

Rock music was becoming an index of cultural capital, and a telltale revelation of social change. Older Americans, who had invented the youth culture, stood by speechless as their children adopted rebellious fashions at increasingly younger ages. Girls as young as eleven or twelve found themselves on the cover of beauty magazines. A 1989 article in the *New York Times* described a new marketing drive of cosmetics for little girls, six years old, "painted to the hilt." Preadolescent dieting was rampant in the fourth and fifth grades, and in a survey of schoolgirls in San Francisco, more than half described themselves as overweight, while only 15 percent were so by medical standards.

American adolescence in the 1980s was prolonged, enjoyed, and catered to by a host of advertisers offering instant gratification. None of this was new, but the scale of the assault was unprecedented. The television suggested a morality far different from what most Americans were used to. Little girls wore leg warmers and wanted to be like Jennifer Beals, the dancing heroine in *Flashdance*. Patrick Swayze crossed the line from courtship to seduction in *Dirty Dancing*. The top movie in 1986 was *Top Gun* starring Tom Cruise as Lt. Pete "Maverick" Mitchell, a U.S. Navy fighter pilot who seduces his flight instructor. At some time every kid saw, or played with, a *Ghostbuster* product. The 1984 science fiction comedy starred three parapsychologists who were fired from New York University and started up their own business investigating and eliminating ghosts.

The 1980s were a time when the "Cola Wars" between Coke and Pepsi reached new heights—or lows, depending on your perspective. Coke was losing market share to its competitor, so on April 23, 1985, "New Coke," a sweeter variant on the original, was released with great fanfare, By the middle of June, people were saying "no" to New Coke. The reaction was nationwide, with the recent product called "furniture polish" and "sewer water." Within weeks "Coke Classic" returned to the market, and the company stock jumped 36 percent. Only in America could a marketing disaster turn into company profit. For entertainment, Americans fooled with Rubik's Cube, a plastic square with its surface subdivided so that each face consisted of nine squares. Rotation of each face allowed the smaller cubes to be arranged in different ways. The challenge, undertaken by millions of addicts, was to return the cube from any given state to its original array with each face consisting of nine squares of the same color.

Kids still rode bicycles around the neighborhood, swam in local pools, and used little CB radios to talk to each other. Schools were discussing twelve-month sessions, but summer for most was still from Memorial Day to Labor Day. They did not yet have 100 channels to flip through on television, or cell phones to flip open, email, or instant messengers. If they wanted to visit with friends they still went home and gave them a call.

Television aired a number of shows with black stars, the most successful of which was the *Bill Cosby Show*. It was the top-rated show of the decade, and showed African Americans as economically successful, middle-class professionals. *Miami Vice* made a star of Don Johnson. *The Golden Girls* made its premier in 1985 and featured stars well into their fifties and sixties. The best night on television from 1984 to 1986 was Thursday, when *The Cosby Show, Family Ties, Cheers, Night Court,* and *Hill Street Blues* dominated. *St. Elsewhere,* along with shows like *Hill Street Blues, L.A. Law,* and *Thirtysomething* were a result of demographic programming at a time when cable television was experiencing spectacular growth. The shows earned comparatively low ratings, but were kept on the air because they delivered highly desirable audiences of young affluent viewers whom advertisers wanted to reach. In 1987, a fourth network, Fox, went on the air to compete with CBS, NBC, and ABC. Before the end of the decade, 90 percent of American homes were able to tune into Fox.

Talk shows flooded onto the airways in the 1980s. David Letterman got his start in 1982, and by 1989 Oprah Winfrey, Geraldo Rivera, Sally Jessey Raphael, Pat Sajak, Arsenio Hall, and Larry King hosted popular shows. The Reagan appointees on the Federal Communications Commission (FCC) revolutionized broadcasting when they voted to abolish the agency's long-standing fairness doctrine, which required broadcasters to provide a balanced presentation of public issues. With FM radio stations given over to rock and country music, older, more conservative listeners turned to AM radio, where right-wing hosts like Rush Limbaugh, Pat Buchanan, and G. Gordon Liddy entertained them with criticisms of women, liberals, Democrats, and environmentalists.

In the burgeoning suburbs, kids collected and traded Garbage Pail Kids, and had to have as many Cabbage Patch Kids as possible. They wore Swatch watches and Izod shirts, and spent time in shopping malls where they found their every need: music stores, clothing stores, fast food courts, movie theaters, and all their friends. On their first kiss they heard "Take Your Breath Away" on the radio, they danced like an Egyptian, and they did the "moonwalk," The Challenger explosion was broadcast live, and a viewer never heard a curse word used on television.

The combination of technological change and more consumer outlets led to a growth in pornography. Cheap video technology allowed the industry to grow to an estimated $7 billion in 1984, as three-quarters of the nation's video stores carried the tapes for rental. In May of 1985, Attorney General Ed Meese appointed a commission to study the effects of pornography and suggest ways to control it. The recommendations had little effect because the individualistic ethic of the time valued choice and consumption over any standard of government control of cultural morality.

For most Americans, the return of economic prosperity was tacit proof that an improvement of black and white relations was imminent. An expanding economy meant gains for everyone. Discussions of race revolved around the place of affirmative action, but the nation was occasionally treated to sensational stories of scandal, and introduced to new leaders. In November 1987, a black teenager covered in dog excrement with racial slurs written on her body was discovered crawling in the garbage of a town south of Poughkeepsie, New York. The girl, Tawana Brawley, was soon represented by the Reverend Al Sharpton of New York City and two lawyers. Sharpton had no congregation, but did have a reputation as a community activist and spokesman for dissident causes. Brawley claimed to have been abducted by several white men who held her for four days and repeatedly raped her while in captivity. The Sharpton team turned the sensational incident into a national media feeding frenzy.

Before the press, Sharpton claimed that Brawley was the victim of a racist judicial system, and the legal team recommended she not cooperate with the police conducting the investigation. Eventually, Tawana Brawley's story fell apart, and an official examination found that she had never been assaulted and had smeared the excrement and written the epithets herself. Once the truth came out, the two lawyers were subject to legal discipline, but Al Sharpton suffered no repercussions and continued his race-baiting activities. He ran for the New York Senate seat in 1992 and 1994, for mayor of New York City in 1997, and for the Democratic presidential nomination in 2004. Throughout his career he never apologized or explained his activities in the Tawana Brawley case.

The Brawley case showed the power of the new mass media. The "age of publicity," as Louis Kronenberger called it, began in the 1920s when flagpole sitting and goldfish swallowing became ways to get attention. Conspicuous ballyhoo became fashionable after World War II, when couples took their marriage vows on carnival carousels and spent their honeymoons in department store windows. As television grew, so too did the Barnum spirit. World records were set for domino toppling, frankfurter eating, and kazoo playing, and all of it was seen on television. The problem was that no one could predict what was likely to become news or why it would occupy public attention or for how long. More importantly, fame in America not only lasted for just fifteen minutes; it often left devastating results in its wake.

In October of 1987 the country fixated on the rescue of "Baby Jessica" McClure, who fell down an eight-inch-wide, twenty-two-foot-deep hole in her backyard in Midland, Texas. For the next fifty-eight hours the country watched spellbound as rescuers left jobs and worked nonstop to save the baby. On the evening of October 16, paramedics Steve Forbes and Robert O'Donnell wriggled into a passageway drilled through rock to save "Baby Jessica."

When it was over, the gifts sent to her would provide a million-dollar trust fund. Twenty years later, hardened West Texas roughnecks would wipe tears from their cheeks as they talked about the rescue and the media coverage it inspired. The child's parents, Chip and Cissy McClure, subsequently divorced, and one of the rescuers, Robert O'Donnell, killed himself in 1995. His brother, Ricky, said O'Donnell's life fell apart because of the stress of the rescue. In the new media age fame was fleeting and suffocating at the same time.

In 1941 Henry Luce wrote an article for *Life* magazine entitled "The American Century." Luce was the most powerful and innovative mass communications person of his era, and the purpose of his essay was twofold: (1) to urge American involvement in World War II, and (2) to put forth the idea that the American principles of democracy and free enterprise would eventually come to dominate the world. The idea of American preeminence was dangerous in the eyes of some, but the basis of the piece bespoke what most people acknowledged whether they liked Luce's formulation or not.

"We have some things in this country which are infinitely precious and especially American," wrote Luce, "a love of freedom, a feeling for the equality of opportunity, a tradition of self-reliance and independence." Forty-two years later, the editors of *Time* magazine, the sister publication to *Life,* updated Luce's vision with an essay entitled "What Really Mattered." In the essay the *Time* editors evaluated the meaning of America and what values were most precious to its citizens in 1983. They concluded the fundamental idea America represented was freedom, but it was different from what Luce had in mind: "America was merely free: it was freed unshackled. . . . To be free was to be modern: to be modern was to take chances. . . . The American Century was to be the century of unleashing."

During the 1980s the limits of freedom were explored in the political, social, and personal realm. In the 1930s, scientists freed the atom, and fifty years later doctors were trying to free the body from its genetic dictates. Could organ transplants, sex change operations, and genetic manipulation make us immortal? Could the nation be free of superstition, so that Americans could indulge their passions for personal peace and affluence? Freedom was one of the prime conditions of postmodernity, and the cultural preoccupation with it a prelude for change. The advent of a global communications system meant that the world was coming together at one level, and falling apart at another. At the end of the decade the United States was the world's only superpower, yet it would be held captive by countries with only a fraction of its political power, but united by television to worldwide religious followers across the globe.

Postmodernism came of age in this climate in the decade of the 1980s. The election and re-election of ex-actor Ronald Reagan put a new gloss on the possibility of politics shaped by images alone. The convictions of the president were a throwback to an earlier time, but his style of image politics, carefully crafted and orchestrated for mass consumption, was of a newer era. The world was changing, and the older language of genres and forms was becoming obsolete.

Thomas Byrne Edsall  **NO**

The Changing Shape of Power:
A Realignment in Public Policy

The past twenty years in America have been marked by two central political developments. The first is the continuing erosion of the political representation of the economic interests of those in the bottom half of the income distribution. The second is the growing dominance of the political process by a network of elites that includes fund-raisers, the leadership of interest groups, specialists in the technology and manipulation of elections, and an army of Washington lobbyists and law firms—elites that augment and often overshadow political officeholders and the candidates for office themselves.

This shift in the balance of power has not been accompanied by realignment of the electorate, although the shape and relative strength of the Republican and Democratic Parties have changed dramatically.

Twice during the past twenty years, the Republican party has had the opportunity to gain majority status: in the early 1970s, and again after the 1980 election. The first opportunity emerged when the fragile Democratic coalition was fractured by the independent presidential bid of Alabama governor George G. Wallace in 1968. The Democratic party then amplified its own vulnerability four years later with the nomination of Sen. George S. McGovern, Democrat of South Dakota, whose candidacy alienated a spectrum of traditional Democrats from Detroit to Atlanta. This potential Republican opportunity crumbled, however, when the web of scandals known as Watergate produced across-the-board setbacks for the GOP in campaigns ranging from city council contests to the presidency in the elections of 1974 and 1976.

The period from 1978 to 1981 offered even more fertile terrain for the Republican party. Not only had Democratic loyalties dating back to the depression of the 1930s been further weakened during the presidency of Jimmy Carter, with the emergence of simultaneous inflation and high unemployment, but the candidacy of Ronald Reagan provided the Republican party with its first substantial opportunity to heal the fissures that had relegated the GOP to minority status for two generations. In Reagan, the party long identified with the rich found a leader equipped to bridge divisions between the country club and the fundamentalist church, between

From *The Rise and Fall of the New Deal Order, 1930–1980,* by Steve Fraser, pp. 269–279, 281–289. © 1989 Princeton University Press. Reprinted by permission.

the executives of the Fortune 500 and the membership of the National Rifle Association. Just as Watergate halted Republican momentum in the early 1970s, however, the severe recession of 1981–82 put the brakes on what had the earmarks of a potential Republican takeover, for the first time since 1954, of both branches of Congress. In the first two years of the Reagan administration, the Republican party captured the Senate by a six-vote margin and, with a gain of thirty-two House seats, acquired de facto control of the House in an alliance with southern Democratic conservatives. The recession, however, resulted in the return of twenty-six House seats to the Democrats in 1982, and with those seats went the chance to establish Republican dominance of the federal government.

As the two parties have gained and lost strength, the underlying alteration of the balance of political power over the past decade has continued in a shift of power among the rich, the poor, and the middle class; among blacks and whites; among regions in the country; and among such major competitors for the federal dollar as the defense and social services sectors.

The past twenty years have, in effect, produced a policy realignment in the absence of a political realignment. The major beneficiaries of this policy realignment are the affluent, while those in the bottom half of the income distribution, particularly those whose lives are the most economically marginal, have reaped the fewest rewards or have experienced declines in their standard of living.

A major factor contributing to this development is the decline of political parties: In the United States, as well as in most democratic countries, parties perform the function of representing major interests and classes. As parties erode, the groups that suffer most are those with the fewest resources to protect themselves. In other words, the continued collapse of the broad representation role of political parties in the United States has direct consequences for the distribution of income.

As the role of parties in mobilizing voters has declined, much of the control over both election strategy and issue selection—key functions in defining the national agenda—has shifted to a small, often interlocking, network of campaign specialists, fund-raisers, and lobbyists. While this element of politics is among the most difficult to quantify, there are some rough measures. For example, there are approximately thirty Republican and Democratic consultants and pollsters, almost all based in Washington, who at this writing are the principal strategists in almost every presidential and competitive Senate race, in addition to playing significant roles in gubernatorial, House, and local referenda contests.

At another level, the years from 1974 to 1984 show a steady growth in the financial dependence of House and Senate candidates on political action committees (PACS), vehicles through which money is transferred from organized interest groups to elected officeholders. In that decade, the PAC share of the total cost of House campaigns went from 17 percent to 36 percent, while individual contributions fell from 73 percent to 47 percent, with the remainder coming from parties, loan, and other sources. For

House Democratic incumbents, 1984 marked the first year in which PACS were the single most important source of cash; they provided 47 percent of the total, compared with 45 percent from individuals.

This shift has, in turn, magnified the influence of a group of lobbyists who organize Washington fund-raisers for House and Senate incumbents, among whom are Thomas Hale Boggs, Jr., whose clients include the Trial Lawyers Association, the Chicago Board of Options Exchange, and Chrysler; Edward H. Forgotson, whose clients include Enserch Corp., the Hospital Corp. of America, and the Texas Oil and Gas Corp.; Robert J. Keefe, whose clients include Westinghouse and the American Medical Association; and J. D. Williams, whose clients include General Electric Co. and the National Realty Committee. The Washington consulting-lobbying firm of Black, Manafort, Stone, Kelly and Atwater provides perhaps the best example of the range of political and special interests one firm can represent. In 1987, one partner, Charles Black, managed the presidential bid of Rep. Jack Kemp (R—N.Y.); another, Lee Atwater, managed the campaign of Vice-President George Bush; and a third, Peter Kelly, was a principal fund-raiser for the campaign of Sen. Albert Gore (D—Tenn.). At the same time, the firm's clients have included the Dominican Republic, the anti-Communist insurgency in Angola run by Jonas Savimbi, Salomon Brothers, the government of Barbados, the Natural Gas Supply Association, and, briefly, the Marcos government in the Philippines. In addition, the firm has served as principal political consultant to the Senate campaigns of Phil Gramm (R—Tex.), Jesse Helms (R—N.C), and Paula Hawkins (formerly R—Fla.).

A few general indicators of the scope of lobbying and political party bureaucracies point to the sizable influence small elites can exercise over public policy. In 1986, there were almost 10,000 people employed as registered Washington lobbyists, with 3,500 of these serving as officers of 1,800 trade and professional organizations, including labor unions; another 1,300 were employed by individual corporations, and approximately 1,000 represented organizations ranging from the National Right to Life Association to the Sierra Club. The six major political party committees headquartered in Washington now employ roughly 1,200 people. The creation and expansion of such ideological think tanks as the Heritage Foundation, the Center for National policy, the Urban Institute, the American Enterprise Institute, the Cato Institute, and the Hoover Institution have established whole networks of influential public policy entrepreneurs specializing in media relations and in targeted position papers. Within a general framework of increasingly monopolized American mass media—both print and electronic—the growth of the Gannett and Los Angeles Times—Mirror chains are examples of an ever greater concentration of power within the media, just as the acquisition of NBC by General Electric has functioned to submerge a major network within the larger goals of the nation's sixth biggest corporation. Staffers acquiring expertise and influence on Capitol Hill, in the executive branch, and throughout the regulatory apparatus routinely travel to the private sector—and sometimes back again—through the so-called revolving door. In effect, an entire class of public and private specialists in the determination of government policy and political strategy has been created—a process replicated in miniature at the state level.

The rise to authority of elites independent of the electorate at large, empowered to make decisions without taking into direct account the economic interests of voters, is part of a much larger shift in the balance of power involving changed voting patterns, the decline of organized labor, a restructuring of the employment marketplace, and a transformed system of political competition. This power shift, in turn, has produced a policy realignment most apparent in the alteration of both the *pre-tax* distribution of income and the *after-tax* distribution of income. In both cases, the distribution has become increasingly regressive. The alteration of the pretax distribution of income is the subject of a broad debate in which there are those, particularly critics on the left, who argue that growing regressivity emerges from government policies encouraging weakened union representation and a proliferation of low-wage service industry jobs. On the other side, more conservative analysts contend that changes in the pre-tax distribution result from natural alterations of the marketplace and the workplace, as the United States adjusts to a changing economic and demographic environment. The figures in table 1, derived from Census Bureau data, indicate changes in the distribution of pretax household income from 1980 through 1985, the most recent year for which data from the census is available.

The data clearly show a growing disparity in the distribution of income. Of the five quintiles, all but those in the top 20 percent have seen their share of household income decline. In addition, most of the gains of

Table 1

Shares of Pre-Tax Household Income, by Income Distribution

	Year	
Income group	1980 (%)	1985 (%)
Quintile[a]		
Bottom	4.1	3.9
Second	10.2	9.7
Third	16.8	16.3
Fourth	24.8	24.4
Top	44.2	45.7
Top 5%	16.5	17.6

Sources: Bureau of the Census, *Estimating After-Tax Money Income Distribution,* Series P-23, no. 126, issued August 1983; and ibid., *Household After-Tax Income: 198S,* Series P-23, no. 151, issued June 1987.

[a] A quintile is a block of 20% of the population.

Table 2

Shares of After-Tax Household Income, by Income Distribution

Income group	Year	
	1980 (%)	1985 (%)
Quintile[a]		
Bottom	4.9	4.6
Second	11.6	11.0
Third	17.9	17.2
Fourth	25.1	24.7
Top	40.6	42.6
Top 5%	14.1	15.5

Sources: Bureau of the Census, *Estimating After-Tax Money Income Distribution,* Series P-23, no. 126, issued August 1983; and ibid., *Household After-Tax Income: 1985,* Series P-23, no. 151, issued June 1987.

[a] A quintile is a block of 20% of the population.

the top 20 percent have, in fact, been concentrated in the top 5 percent of the income distribution. The gain of 1.1 percent for the top 5 percent translates into a total of $38.8 billion (in 1987 dollars) more for this segment of the population than if the income distribution had remained constant after 1980. These regressive trends were, moreover, intensified by the tax policies enacted between 1980 and 1985, as demonstrated in table 2, based on Census Bureau data.

What had been a $38.8 billion improvement in the status of the top 5 percent in pre-tax income over these six years becomes a $49.5 billion gain in after-tax income, while the bottom 80 percent of the population saw larger losses in its share of after-tax income between 1980 and 1985 than it had seen in the case of pre-tax income. These findings are even more sharply delineated in a November 1987 study by the Congressional Budget Office showing that from 1977 to 1988, 70 percent of the population experienced very modest increases in after-tax income or, for those in the bottom 40 percent, net drops, when changes over that period in the federal income tax, the Social Security tax, corporate tax, and excise taxes are taken into account. In contrast, those in the seventy-first to ninetieth percentiles experienced a modest improvement, and those in the top 10 percent significantly improved their standard of living. For those at the very top, the gains have been enormous. Table 3, developed from Congressional Budget Office data, shows that distribution.

What these tables point to is a major redistribution of economic power in the private marketplace and of political power in the public

Table 3

Changes in Estimated Average After-Tax Family Income, by Income Distribution (In 1987 Dollars)

Income group	1977 average income ($)	1988 average income ($)	Percentage change (+ or −)	Dollar change (+ or −)
Decile[a]				
First (poor)	3,528	3,157	−10.5	−371
Second	7,084	6,990	−1.3	−94
Third	10,740	10,614	−1.2	−126
Fourth	14,323	14,266	−0.4	−57
Fifth	18,043	18,076	+0.2	+33
Sixth	22,009	22,259	+1.1	+250
Seventh	26,240	27,038	+3.0	+798
Eighth	31,568	33,282	+5.4	+1,718
Ninth	39,236	42,323	+7.9	+3,087
Tenth (rich)	70,459	89,793	+27.4	+19,324
Top 5%	90,756	124,651	+37.3	+33,895
Top 1%	174,498	303,900	+74.2	+129,402
All groups	22,184	26,494	+9.6	+2,310

Sources: Congressional Budget Offices, *The Changing Distribution of Federal Taxes: 1975–1990,* October 1987.

[a]A decile is a block of 1096 of the population.

sector, which, in turn, has been reflected in very concrete terms in family income patterns. One of the major characteristics, then, of the post–New Deal period in American politics has been a reversal of the progressive redistribution of income that underlay the policies of the administrations of Franklin Roosevelt and Harry Truman.

In the competition between the defense and social welfare sectors, the outcome of a parallel, although more recent, shift in the balance of power can be seen in the years from 1980 through 1987. During this period, the share of the federal budget going to national defense grew from 22.7 percent in 1980 to 28.4 percent in 1987. At the same time, the share of federal dollars collectively going to education, training, employment, social services, health, income security, and housing dropped from 25.5 percent in 1980 to 18.3 percent in 1987.

In many respects, these policy changes reflect the rising strength of the Republican party. In terms of tax policy and the balance of spending between defense and social programs, the Republican party under Ronald Reagan has been the driving force pushing the country to the right. During the past ten years, the Republican party has made substantial gains in the competition for the allegiance of voters, gaining near parity by 1987, reducing what had been a 20- to 25-point Democratic advantage in terms of self-identification to a six- or seven-point edge.

The income distribution trends and the shifts in budget priorities began, however, before the Republican party took over the presidency and the U.S. Senate in 1980. The emergence of a vital, competitive Republican party is less cause of the changed balance of power in the country than a reflection of the underlying forces at work in the post-New Deal phase of American politics.

Together, these forces—which include the deterioration of organized labor, the continued presence of divisive racial conflict, the shift from manufacturing to service industries, the slowing rates of economic growth, the threat of international competition to domestic production, the replacement of political organization with political technology, and the growing class-skew of voter turnout—have severely undermined the capacity of those in the bottom half of the income distribution to form an effective political coalition.

In tracing the erosion of the left wing of the Democratic party in the United States, it is difficult to overestimate the importance of the collapse of the labor movement. In 1970, the continuing growth in the number of labor union members came to a halt. Unions represented 20.7 million workers that year, or 27.9 percent of the nonagricultural work force. Through 1980, the number of workers represented by unions remained roughly the same, dropping slightly to 20.1 million employees by 1980. At the same time, however, the total work force had grown, so that the percentage of workers who were represented by unions fell to 23 percent in 1980. With the election of Ronald Reagan, however, the decline of organized labor began to accelerate sharply, a process encouraged by Reagan's firing of 11,500 striking PATCO air traffic controllers, and by the appointment of pro-management officials to the National Labor Relations Board and to the Department of Labor. From 1980 to 1986, not only did the share of the work force represented by unions drop from 23 percent to 17.5 percent, but the number of workers in unions began to fall precipitously for the first time in fifty years, dropping by 3.1 million men and women, from 20.1 million to 17 million, in 1986. During the first half of the 1980s, almost all the decline in union membership was among whites employed in private industry.

The decline of organized labor dovetailed with a continuing shift from traditional manufacturing, mining, and construction employment to work in the technology and service industries. From 1970 to 1986, the number of jobs in goods-producing industries, which lend themselves to unionization, grew only from 23.8 million to 24.9 million, while employment in the service industries, which are much more resistant to labor organizing, shot up from 47.3 million to 75.2 million.

The difficulties of organized labor were compounded by the unexpected decision on the part of many of the major corporations in the early 1970s to abandon what had been a form of tacit détente between labor and management, in which Fortune 500 companies kept labor peace through agreements amounting to a form of profit sharing by means of automatic cost-of-living pay hikes. Faced with growing competition from foreign producers—in 1968, car imports exceeded exports for the first time in the nation's history, an unmistakable signal that domestic producers of all goods faced serious foreign competition—major American companies dropped the fundamentally cordial relations that had characterized the largest part of postwar union negotiations. Catching the leaders of organized labor entirely unprepared, these corporations adopted a tough, adversarial approach regarding both pay and fringe benefits, willing to break union shops and to relocate facilities either abroad or in nonunion communities in the South and Southwest.

The decline of organized labor was particularly damaging to the Democratic party because unions represent one of the few remaining institutional links between working-class voters and the Democratic party. The decline of political parties has resulted in the end of the clubhouse tie between the party of Franklin Delano Roosevelt and the blue-collar voters of row- and tract-house neighborhoods throughout the Northeast and Midwest. In addition, it is among these white, blue-collar workers that the racial conflicts within the Democratic party have been the most divisive. Interviews with whites in Dearborn, Michigan, the west-side suburbs of Birmingham, Chicago, Atlanta, and New Orleans—all communities that have suffered major industrial layoffs and that are either part of or adjoin cities now run by Democratic black mayors—reveal voters who are disenchanted with the unions that failed to protect their jobs, and with a local Democratic party no longer controlled by whites. Race, which previously severed the tie between the white South and the Democratic party, has, in cities with black mayors, served to produce white Republican voting, not only for president but for local offices that once were unchallenged Democratic bastions.

These developments, in the 1970s, contributed significantly to the creation of a vacuum of power within the Democratic party, allowing the party to be taken over, in part, by its most articulate and procedurally sophisticated wing: affluent, liberal reformers. This faction capitalized first on the public outcry against police violence at the Chicago presidential convention in 1968, and then on the Watergate scandals in the mid-1970s, to force priority consideration of a series of reforms involving campaign finance, the presidential nominating process, the congressional seniority system, the congressional code of ethics—and an expansion of the federal role in regulating the environment, through creation of the Environmental Protection Agency and new water- and air-pollution standards.

The strength of this wing of the Democratic party subsided during the 1980s, although its leverage within the party has been institutionalized through the creation of a host of primaries and caucuses in the presidential selection process, giving disproportionate influence to middle- and upper-middle-class voters and interests in a party that claims to represent the nation's working and lower-middle classes. The turnout in primaries and in caucuses is skewed in favor of the affluent and upper-middle class. In addition, these delegate selection processes have been contributing factors in the acceleration of the decline of political organizations in working-class communities.

The Democratic agenda set in the 1970s by the reform wing of the party was, however, more important for what it omitted and neglected than for what was included. The ascendancy of the reformers took place just when the fissures within the Democratic party had become most apparent. In 1968, 9.9 million mostly Democratic voters turned to George C. Wallace, the segregationist-populist governor of Alabama, and they strayed off the Democratic reservation in 1972 when Nixon beat McGovern by a margin of 47.2 million votes to 29.2 million. The cultural and ideological gulf that had steadily widened between these voters and the wings of the Democratic party supporting the antiwar movement, gay rights, women's rights, and civil rights had reached such proportions in the early and mid 1970s that rapprochement between warring factions was difficult, if not impossible.

The rise to prominence within the Democratic party of a well-to-do liberal-reform wing worked in other ways to compound the divisions in the party Relatively comfortable in their own lives, reformers failed to recognize the growing pressure of marginal tax rates on working- and lower-middle-class voters. The progressive rate system of the federal income tax remained effectively unchanged from the early 1950s through the 1970s, so that the series of sharply rising marginal tax rates that had originally been designed to affect only the upper-middle class and rich, began to directly impinge on regular Democratic voters whose wages had been forced up by inflation. By neglecting to adjust the marginal rate system to account for inflation, in combination with repeated raising of the highly regressive Social Security tax, Democrats effectively encouraged the tax revolt of the 1970s which, in turn, provided a critically important source of support to the conservative movement and to the rise of the Republican party. . . .

On the Republican side, the same developments that debilitated the Democratic coalition served to strengthen ascendant constituencies of the Right. For a brief period in the late 1970s and early 1980s, the constituencies and interests underpinning the Republican party had the potential to establish a new conservative majority in the electorate. The tax revolt, the rise of the religious right, the mobilization of much of the business community in support of the Republican party, renewed public support for defense spending, the political-financial mobilization of the affluent, and the development of a conservative economic theory promising growth through lower taxes—all combined to empower the political right to a degree unprecedented since the 1920s.

Proposed tax cuts provided an essential common ground for the right-of-center coalition that provided the core of the Reagan revolution. The combination of corporate tax reductions and individual tax cuts embodied in the 1981 tax bill served to unify a divided business community by providing a shared legislative goal, to strengthen the commitment of the affluent to the Republican party, and to attract white working- and lower-middle-class former Democrats who had seen their paychecks eaten away by inflation-driven higher marginal rates. The tax cut theme was adopted as a central element of the speeches of such religious-right figures as the Rev. Jerry Falwell of the Moral Majority, Ed McAteer of the Religious Roundtable, and the Rev. Marion G. (Pat) Robertson of the Christian Broadcast Network. . . .

This growing political tilt in favor of the affluent is further reflected in voting turnout patterns over the past twenty years. During this period, the class-skewing of voting in favor of the affluent has grown significantly. In the presidential election year of 1964, the self-reported turnout among members of professions associated with the middle and upper classes was 83.2 percent, compared with 66.1 percent among those employed in manual jobs, including skilled crafts, a difference of 17.1 points; by 1980, the spread between the two had grown to 25 points, 73 percent to 48 percent. In the off-year election of 1966, the percentage-point spread in terms of voter turnout between middle-to-upper-class job holders and those employed in manual jobs was 18.1 percent; by 1978, this had grown to a 23.8-percent spread. While overall turnout has been declining, the drop has been most severe among those in the bottom third of the income distribution.

For the Republican party, these turnout trends were a political bonanza, accentuated by trends in the correlation between income and both voting and partisan commitment. Through the 1950s, 1960s, and into the early 1970s, the sharp class divisions that characterized the depression-era New Deal coalition structure gave way to diffuse voting patterns with relatively little correlation between income and allegiance to the Democratic or Republican party. By 1980 and 1982, with the election of Reagan and then the enactment of the budget and tax bills of 1981, the correlation between income and voting began to reemerge with a vengeance. By 1982, the single most important determinant of probable voting, aside from membership in either the Republican or Democratic party, became income, with the Democratic margin steadily declining as one moved up the ladder. . . .

In other words, the Reagan years polarized the electorate along sharp income lines. While income made almost no difference in the partisan loyalties of 90 percent of the population in 1956, by 1984 income became one of the sharpest dividing lines between Democrats and Republicans. In 1956, the very poor were only 5 percentage points more likely to be Democratic than the upper-middle class, and 40 points more likely than the affluent top 10 percent of the income distribution. By 1984, however, the spread between the poor and the upper-middle class reached 36 points, and between the poor and affluent, 69 points. . . .

These figures accurately describe an electorate polarized by income, but what they mask are the effects of black and white voter participation on the figures. The civil rights movement, and civil rights legislation enacted in the 1960s, enfranchised millions of blacks who, in 1956, were barred from voting. During the twenty-eight years from 1956 to 1984, roughly 4.2 million blacks entered the electorate. During the same period, blacks' allegiance to the Democratic party, which in 1956 held their loyalty by a 34-percentage-point edge, increased to provide an overwhelming 72-percentage-point Democratic edge in 1984. This infusion of black Democratic support sharply increased the low-income tilt of the party: in 1984, the median family income for whites was $28,674, while for blacks it was $15,982.

The Reagan revolution was, at its core, a revolution led by the affluent. The class polarization of voters . . . cut across the country, but nowhere were the trends stronger than in the South, where a realignment in miniature took place among the white elite. In the 1950s, Democratic allegiance in the South was strongest among the most well-to-do whites, for whom the Democratic party was the vehicle for maintaining the pre-civil rights social structure of the Confederate states. These voters gave the Democratic party their support by a 5 to 1 margin, higher than that of any other income group in the South. By the 1980s, in the aftermath of a civil rights movement supported by the Democratic party, these same voters had become the most Republican in the South. "The class cleavage had reversed itself," John R. Petrocik, of UCLA, noted. Whites, particularly white men, have become increasingly Republican as blacks have become the most consistent source of Democratic votes. In the five presidential elections from 1968 to 1984, only one Democrat, Jimmy Carter, received more than 40 percent of the white vote, and by 1984, white, male Protestants voted for Reagan over Mondale by a margin of 74 to 26.

The Reagan revolution would, however, have been a political failure if it had not gained extensive support from voters outside the upper-middle class. In addition to the deep inroads made in previously Democratic working-class communities in northern urban areas, perhaps the single most important source of new support for the Republican party has been the religious Right.

In a far shorter period, voters identifying themselves as born-again Christians radically shifted their voting in presidential elections. Between 1976 and 1984, these voters went from casting a 56-to-44 margin for the Democratic candidate, Jimmy Carter, to one of the highest levels of support of any group for the reelection of President Reagan in 1984: 81 to 19, according to *New York Times*/CBS exit polls. This shift represents, in effect, a gain of eight million voters for the GOP.

As a political resource, support among born-again Christians represents not only a loyal core of voters, but a growing core. In contrast with such mainline churches as the United Methodist Church, the United Church of Christ, and the United Presbyterians, which experienced membership losses from 1970 to 1980, the fundamentalist, evangelical, and charismatic churches have seen their congregations grow at an explosive rate: the Southern Baptist Convention by 16 percent, the Assemblies of God by 70 percent, and Seventh Day Adventists by 36 percent.

The Republican party has, in turn, been the major beneficiary of an internal power struggle taking place within the Southern Baptist Convention, now the largest Protestant denomination. During a ten-year fight, the denomination has been taken over by its conservative wing, believers in the "absolute inerrancy" of the Bible. This wing of the denomination, in turn, has been a leading force within the broader religious Right, as such pastors as Adrian Rogers, James T. Draper, Jr., and Charles F. Stanley—all outspoken conservatives—have won the denomination's presidency. The move to the right has been reflected in the ranks of the denomination, producing what amounts to a realignment of the ministry of the Southern Baptist Convention. James L. Guth, of Furman University, found that in just three years, surveys of Southern Baptist ministers showed a remarkable shift from a strong majority in 1981 favoring the Democratic party 41 to 29, to nearly 70 percent in 1984 favoring the GOP, 66 to 26.

The growth of Republican strength is not, however, confined to evangelical and charismatic Christians, and the party appears to be developing a much broader religious base as part of its core constituency. In one of the most interesting recent analyses of voting trends, Frederick T. Steeper, of Market Opinion Research, and John Petrocik, of UCLA, have found that since 1976, one of the sharpest partisan cleavages emerging among white voters in the electorate is between those who attend church regularly and those who never go to church. This represents a major change from past findings. In the period from 1952 to 1960, there was no statistical difference between the Democratic and Republican loyalties of white churchgoers and nonchurchgoers. By the elections of 1972 and 1976, a modest difference began to appear, with non-churchgoers 7 percentage points more likely to be Democrats than regular churchgoers. By 1986, however, the spread had grown to a striking 35-point difference, with regular churchgoers identifying themselves as Republicans by a 22-point margin, and with nonchurchgoers identifying themselves as Democrats by a 13-point edge. The partisan spread between churchgoers and nonchurchgoers was most extreme among white Northern Protestants (51 points) and Catholics (52 points). These findings dovetail with studies showing that the memberships of such Establishment, nonevangelical denominations as the Methodists, Episcopalians, Lutherans, and Presbyterians were significantly more supportive of the election of Ronald Reagan than the electorate at large. . . .

Cumulatively, developments over the past twenty years—the deterioration of the labor movement; economically polarized partisanship; the skewing of turnout patterns by income; stagnation of the median family income; the rising importance of political money; the emergence of a Republican core composed of the well-to-do and the religious; the globalization of the economy; and competition from foreign producers—have combined to disperse constituencies and groups seeking to push the country to the left, and to consolidate those on the right. The consequences of that shift are most readily seen in the figures in table 3, which show that 80 percent of the population has experienced a net loss in after-tax income between 1977 and 1988, while the top 5 percent has seen average family income grow by $26,134, and the top 1 percent, by $117,222.

In the long run the prospects are for the maintenance of a strong, conservative Republican party, continuing to set the national agenda on basic distributional issues, no matter which party holds the White House. Barring a major economic catastrophe, or a large-scale international conflict, the basic shift from manufacturing to service industry jobs is likely to continue to undermine the political left in this country, not only for the reasons outlined earlier in this essay, but also by weakening economically—and therefore politically—those in the bottom 40 percent of the income distribution.

In the thirty-year period spanning 1949 to 1979, the number of manufacturing jobs grew by an average of three million a decade, from 17.6 million in 1949, to 20.4 million in 1959, to 24.4 million in 1969, and finally to a high of 26.5 million in 1979. This growth in no way kept pace with the increase in service industry jobs, which shot up from 26.2 million in 1949 to 63.4 million in 1979, but the continuing, if modest, manufacturing expansion provided a partial cushion in an economy going through a major restructuring—a restructuring involving the loss of 950,000 jobs in steel and other metals industries, automobiles, food production, and textiles from 1972 to 1986. From 1979 to 1986, however, the absolute number of manufacturing jobs began to decline, dropping from 26.5 million to 24.9 million, a loss of 1.6 million jobs.

These employment shifts have been particularly damaging to blacks and Hispanics. From 1970 to 1984, in major northern cities, there has been a massive decline in the number of jobs requiring relatively little education—the kind of jobs that provide entry into the employment marketplace for the poor—and a sharp increase in the number of jobs requiring at least some higher education: "Demographic and employment trends have produced a serious mismatch between the skills of inner-city blacks and the opportunities available to them . . . substantial job losses have occurred in the very industries in which urban minorities have the greatest access, and substantial employment gains have occurred in the higher-education-requisite industries that are beyond the reach of most minority workers," according to William Julius Wilson, of the University of Chicago (see table 4).

While blacks and Hispanics will, at least for the time being, disproportionately bear the burden of this shift in job requirements, the altered structure of the marketplace will work to the disadvantage of the poorly educated of all races. In 1985, there were 30.6 million whites over the age of twenty-five without a high school education—five times the number of blacks without high school degrees (5.9 million) and seven times the number of poorly educated Hispanics (4.4 million). These job market trends will intensify throughout the rest of this century. According to estimates by the Department of Labor, 21.4 million jobs will be created

Table 4

Changes in the Combined Number of Jobs, by Employee Education Level, in New York, Philadelphia, Boston, Baltimore, St. Louis, Atlanta, Houston, Denver, and San Francisco, 1970 and 1984

	Number of Jobs		
Mean level of employee education	1970	1984	Change, 1970–84
Less than high school	3,068,000	2,385,000	−683,000
Some higher education	2,023,000	2,745,000	+722,000

Sources: Computed from William Julius Wilson, *The Truly Disadvantaged: The Inner City, the Underclass, and Public Policy* (Chicago: University of Chicago Press, 1987), table 2.6, p. 40. The table, in turn, is taken from John D. Kasarda, "The Regional and Urban Redistribution of People and Jobs in the U.S." (Paper presented to the National Research Council Committee on National Urban Policy, National Academy of Sciences, 1986).

between 1986 and the year 2000, all of which will be in service industries or government, as losses in traditional goods manufacturing industries are unlikely to be fully offset by gains in the technology manufacturing sector. In terms of educational requirements, there will be a significant increase in the proportion of jobs requiring at least one year of college education, no change in the proportion of jobs requiring a high school degree, and a sharp decline in the percentage of jobs requiring no high school education.

In effect, trends in the job market through the next ten years will in all likelihood exacerbate the regressive distribution of income that has taken place over the past decade. Under American democracy, those who are unemployed or marginally employed are weakest politically. The decline of traditional political organizations and unions has made significantly more difficult the political mobilization of the working poor, the working class, and the legions of white-collar workers making from $10,000 to $25,000 a year—a universe roughly containing 24.6 million white households, 3.4 million black households, and 2 million Hispanic households. Within this group, providing a political voice becomes even more difficult for those workers with poor educations who have been dispersed from manufacturing employment into cycles of marginal work. While most of those who have lost manufacturing jobs have found full-time employment, such workers have, in the main, seen wages fall and fringe benefits, often including medical coverage, decline or disappear, leaving them even further outside of the American mainstream and even less well equipped to ensure adequate educational levels for their children. When combined with the declining voter turnout rates associated with falling income, these workers have fallen into what amounts to a new political underclass.

The major forces at work in the last two decades of the post-New Deal period are, then, cumulatively functioning to weaken the influence and power of those in the bottom half of the income distribution, while strengthening the authority of those in the upper half, and particularly the authority of those at elite levels. Trends in political competition and pressures in the private marketplace have combined to create a whipsaw action, reversing New Deal policies that empowered the labor movement and reduced disparities between rich and poor. Recent forces, both in the marketplace and in the political arena, have not produced a realignment of the electorate, but, in terms of outcomes, there has been a realignment in public policy—with few forces, short of a downturn in the business cycle, working against the continuing development of a political and economic system in which the dominant pressures will be toward increased regressively in the distribution of money and in the ability to influence the outcome of political decisions.

POSTSCRIPT

Were the 1980s a Decade of Affluence for the Middle Class?

Professor J. David Woodard takes a broader view of the 1980s. He notes with approval the increased participation of the middle class in the stock market. He also points out the risks taken by the new investors who saw a 22 percent dip in the market in mid-October 1987. While disapproving of the insider trading tactics that landed multimillionaire Wall Street dealers Michael Milken and Ivan Boesky in jail, Woodard approves of the free-market rational actor model espoused by Milton and Rose Friedman in their book *Free to Choose* (Avon Books, 1985), which "effectively" rebutted the government-as-manager thesis.

While Woodard argues that "a rising tide" raised the income level of 90 percent of Americans, he does not counter the statistical arguments of Edsall, who believes the boat leaked for those blue collar urban whites and minorities who found themselves in the poverty and lower middle class. Woodard admits that inequalities existed between "the knowledge practitioners" who controlled the new economy and the non-educated blue collar worker who saw their well-paid union protected jobs in steel, automobile and the oil industry disappear, victims of automation or outsourced to foreign countries.

Woodard is somewhat critical of the movie industry, which dispensed anti-capitalist movies such as *Wall Street* and *Bonfire of the Vanities*. He also shows a mild distaste for the non-rational "deconstructionist" views of the social science and humanities at America's elite universities. He also sees MTV as an opportunity to flaunt the sexuality of rock and roll music, now dominated by African-American artists, in ways previously denied to earlier rock pioneers like Elvis Presley whose gyrating pelvis was not shown on the Ed Sullivan Sunday-night variety show in 1956. Ironically, Woodard views President Ronald Reagan as both a premodern and postmodern figure. While his convictions were of an earlier time, "his style of image politics, [were] carefully crafted and orchestrated for mass consumption." Two books that explain the rise of the post–World War II conservative movement in which Reagan became the major player are Lee Edwards' sympathetic *The Conservative Revolution: The Movement That Remade America* (Free Press, 1999) and Godfrey Hodgson's more critical *The World Turned Right Side Up: A History of the Conservative Ascendancy in America* (Houghton Mifflin, 1996). Gregory L. Schneider's essay on "Conservatives and the Reagan Presidency," in Richard S. Conley, ed., *Reassessing the Reagan Presidency* (University Press of America, 2003) is a sympathetic objective account with a full bibliography.

Written nearly two decades ago, political journalist Thomas B. Edsall's analysis on the changing landscape of political and economic power in the 1970s and 1980s remains the same in 2007. Political parties have declined in influence. Members of Congress continue receiving the bulk of their money from economic interest groups and political action committees (PACs). Reforms in the 1970s and 2004 have not significantly changed their influence. Presidential candidates and presidential office holders continue to operate their campaign and policy operations independent of Congress.

Edsall believes that the Republican party attained power because of the defection of the white male working class, both in the South and the North. He argues that the Wallace third-party movement in 1968 and 1972 capitalized on the civil rights and women's movement, which led to affirmative action jobs for women and minorities in areas previously held by white males. The erosion of well-paid union jobs in steel, coal, automobiles, and clothing manufacturing to foreign countries also contributed to the income decline of the noncollege educated white male, who had to settle for low-wage jobs in the service industries.

Edsall's major thesis is that in the 1980s, a policy rather than a political realignment was led by the upper middle and upper classes, whose tax reform bills in the 1980s caused a redistribution of income to these classes. This view is supported by Frederick Strobel, a former senior business economist at the Federal Reserve, Bank of Atlanta, in *Upward Dreams, Downward Mobility: The Economic Decline of the American Middle Class* (Rowman & Littlefield, 1993).

The reasons that Strobel gives for the economic decline include an increased supply of workers (baby boomers, housewives, and immigrants), a decline in union membership, a strong dollar, an open import dollar that destroyed many U.S. manufacturing jobs, corporate merger mania, declining government jobs, energy inflation, high interest rates, and the corporate escape for federal, state, and local taxes.

Unexpected criticism also comes from President Reagan's own director of the Office of Management and Budget, David A. Stockman. His *Triumph of Politics: Why the Revolution Failed* (Harper & Row, 1986) details the "ideological hubris" that surrounded Reagan's advisers, who, in conjunction with a spendthrift Congress beholden to outside interest groups, ran up massive budget deficits by implementing a theory known as supply-side economics. More critical from the left are a series of academic articles in *Understanding America's Economic Decline*, edited by Michael A. Bernstein and David E. Adler (Cambridge University Press, 1994). Also critical are the writings of Kevin Phillips, especially *The Politics of Rich and Poor: Wealth and the American Electorate in the Reagan Afermath* (Random House, 1990) and Joseph J. Hogan, "Reaganomics and Economic Policy," in Dilys M. Hill et-al., eds., *The Reagan Presidency: An Incomplete Revolution?* (St. Martin's Press, 1990), which argues, "while constantly disavowing government interventionism and proclaiming the virtues of a free market economy, the Reagan administration continually pursued economic expansionist policies based upon massive government deficits, periods of maintained monetary expansionism and unprecedented high levels of international borrowing."

For dissenting views that support supply-side economics as the key policy leading to America's economy since the early 1980s, see almost any issue of *Commentary, The National Review, The Weekly Standard, Barron's,* and editorial pages of *The Wall Street Journal.* For example, see "The Real Reagan Record," *The National Review* (August 31, 1992, pp. 25–62); in particular, the essays by Alan Reynolds in "Upstarts and Downstarts," who asserts that all income groups experienced significant gains in income during the 1980s; and Paul Craig Roberts, "What Everyone 'Knows' about Reaganomics," *Commentary* (February 1991), which is critical of the Keynesian explanation for the economic downturn in the early 1990s.

Two books that fully support Reagan's positive contribution to the prosperity of the 1980s (in addition to Woodard) are John Ehrman, *The Eighties: America in the Age of Reagan* (Yale University Press, 2005) and Cato Institute economist Richard B. McKenzie, *What Went Right in the 1980s* (Pacific Research Institute for Public Policy, 1994). Karl Zinsmeister, "Summing Up the Reagan Era," *Wilson Quarterly* (Winter 1990) is similar to Woodard and Ehrman in its interpretation.

James D. Torr, editor, provides balanced treatments in *Ronald Reagan* (Thomson Gale, 2001) and *The 1980s: America's Decades* (Greenhaven Press, 2000). The two most recent and important collection of essays by historians and political scientists are Richard S. Conley, ed., *Reassuring the Reagan Presidency* (University Press of America, 2003) and W. Eliot Brownlee and Hugh David Graham, eds., *The Reagan Presidency: Pragmatic Conservatism and Legacies* (University Press of Kansas, 2003), which lives up to its title. In the essay on taxation, authors Brownlee and C. Eugene Steuerle argue that Reagan's commitment to the extreme version of the Laffer curve came in 1977, two or three years earlier than the version given by David Stockman, just before his victory in the 1980 New Hampshire primaries where supposedly Laffer drew his famous curve on a dinner napkin. The two authors claim that Reagan had been reading economist Jude Wanniski's *Wall Street Journal* editorials supporting Laffer's ideas. Finally worth consulting for the worldwide perspective is Bruce J. Schulman, "The Reagan Revolution in International Perspective: Conservative Assaults on the Welfare State across the Industrialized World in the 1980s," in Richard Steven Conley, ed., *Reassessing the Reagan Presidency.* For Reagan's impact on the 2008 presidential race, see Karen Tumulty, "How the Right Went Wrong: What Would Ronnie Do? And Why the Republican Candidates Need to Reclaim the Reagan Legacy," *Time* (March 26, 2007).

Contributors to This Volume

EDITORS

LARRY MADARAS is a professor of history emeritus at Howard Community College in Columbia, Maryland. He received a B.A. from the College of Holy Cross in 1959 and an M.A. and a Ph.D. from New York University in 1961 and 1964, respectively. He has also taught at Spring Hill College, the University of South Alabama, and the University of Maryland at College Park. He has been a Fulbright Fellow and has held two fellowships from the National Endowment for the Humanities. He is the author of dozens of journal articles and book reviews.

JAMES M. SoRELLE is a professor of history and former chair of the Department of History at Baylor University in Waco, Texas. He received a B.A. and M.A. from the University of Houston in 1972 and 1974, respectively, and a Ph.D. from Kent State University in 1980. In addition to introductory courses in United States and world history, he teaches advanced undergraduate classes in African American history, the American civil rights movement, and the 1960s, as well as a graduate seminar on the civil rights movement. His scholarly articles have appeared in the *Houston Review, Southwestern Historical Quarterly,* and *Black Dixie: Essays in Afro-Texan History and Culture in Houston* (Texas A&M University Press, 1992), edited by Howard Beeth and Cary D. Wintz. He also has contributed entries to *The New Handbook of Texas, The Oxford Companion to Politics of the World, Encyclopedia of African American Culture and History,* the *Encyclopedia of the Confederacy,* and the *Encyclopedia of African American History.*

AUTHORS

GLENN C. ALTSCHULER is Thomas and Dorothy Litwin Professor of American Studies and Dean of the School of Continuing Education and Summer Sessions at Cornell University. He is the author of several books on American history and popular culture, including *Changing Channels: America in TV Guide*.

RICHARD M. ABRAMS is a professor of history at the University of California, Berkeley, where he has been teaching since 1961. He has been a Fulbright professor in both London and Moscow and has taught and lectured in many countries throughout the world, including China, Austria, Norway, Italy, Japan, Germany, and Australia. He has published numerous articles in history, business, and law journals, and he is the editor of *The Shaping of Twentieth Century America; Interpretative Essays*, 2nd ed. (Little, Brown, 1971) and the author of *The Burdens of Progress* (Scott, Foresman, 1978). His most recent book is *America Transformed: Sixty Years of Revolutionary Change, 1941–2001* (Cambridge University Press, 2006).

THOMAS A. BAILEY (1902–1983) was a distinguished professor of history at Stanford University for over fifty years. He wrote many books and articles for both professional and general readers. His text on *A Diplomatic History of the American People* was issued in ten editions between 1940 and 1980, and was one of the great successes in textbook publishing.

GARY DEAN BEST is a professor of history at the University of Hawaii in Hilo, Hawaii. He is a former fellow of the American Historical Association and of the National Endowment for the Humanities, and he was a Fulbright scholar in Japan from 1974 to 1975. His publications include *The Nickel and Dime Decade: American Popular Culture During the 1930s* (Praeger, 1933).

ROGER BILES is a professor in and chair of the history department at East Carolina University in Greenville, North Carolina. He is the author of *The South and the New Deal* (University Press of Kentucky, 1994) and *Richard J. Daly: Politics, Race, and the Governing of Chicago* (Northern Illinois Press, 1994).

JOHN C. BURNHAM teaches the history of American science at the Ohio State University and is the author of *Lester Frank Ward in American Thought and Psychoanalysis and American Medicine*.

WILLIAM G. CARLETON (1903–1982) was professor emeritus at the University of Florida and author of the widely used textbook on *The Revolution in American Foreign Policy*.

DAVID T. COURTRIGHT has written numerous articles on United States' western history and is a Professor of History at the University of North Florida. He is the author of *Single Men and Social Disorder from the Frontier to the Inner City* (Harvard University Press, 1996).

CARL N. DEGLER is the Margaret Byrne Professor Emeritus of American History at Stanford University in Stanford, California. He is a member of the editorial board for the Plantation Society, and he is a member and former president of the American History Society and the Organization of American Historians. His book *Neither Black nor White: Slavery and Race Relations in Brazil and the United States* (University of Wisconsin Press, 1972) won the 1972 Pulitzer Prize for history.

ROBERT A. DIVINE is a professor of history at the University of Texas at Austin. He has written several books, including *Eisenhower and the Cold War* (Oxford University Press, 1981) and *Since 1945: Politics and Diplomacy in Recent American History,* 3rd ed. (Alfred A. Knopf, 1985).

ROBERT R. DYKSTRA is professor of history and public policy at the State University of New York, Albany. A specialist in nineteenth-century American social and political history, he is the author of two books on the trans-Mississippi West, most recently *Bright Radical Star: Black Freedom and White Supremacy on the Hawkeye Frontier* (Cambridge: Harvard University Press, 1993). He is currently engaged in a long-term project on black-family demography in post-Civil War Virginia.

THOMAS B. EDSALL is a widely respected political journalist who has written numerous books and articles for *The New Republic, The Atlantic, The Washington Post,* and *The New York Times.*

SARA M. EVANS is Distinguished McKnight University Professor of History at the University of Minnesota, where she has taught women's history since 1976. She is the author of several books including *Personal Politics: The Roots of Women's Liberation in the Civil Rights Movement and the New Left* (1979) and *Born for Liberty: A History of Women in America,* 2nd ed., (1997). Born in a Methodist parsonage in South Carolina, she was a student activist in the civil rights and antiwar movements in North Carolina and has been an active feminist since 1967.

JOHN LEWIS GADDIS is the Robert A. Lovett Professor of History at Yale University in New Haven, Connecticut. He has also been Distinguished Professor of History at Ohio University, where he founded the Contemporary History Institute, and he has held visiting appointments at the United States Naval War College, the University of Helsinki, Princeton University, and Oxford University. He is the author of many books, including *We Now Know: Rethinking Cold War History* (Oxford University Press, 1997).

OSCAR HANDLIN was the Carl M. Loeb Professor of History at Harvard University in Cambridge, Massachusetts, where he has been teaching since 1941. A Pulitzer Prize–winning historian, he has written or edited more than 100 books, including *Liberty in Expansion* (Harper & Row, 1989), which he coauthored with Lilian Handlin, and *The Distortion of America,* 2nd ed. (Transaction Publishers, 1996).

PETER IRONS is a well-known civil rights lawyer and scholar. He is a professor of political science and director of the Earl Warren Bill of Rights Project at the University of California, San Diego.

RICHARD KLUGER began a career in journalism at *The Wall Street Journal*, and was a writer for *Forbes* magazine and then the *New York Post* before becoming a literary editor of the *New York Herald Tribune*. In book publishing, he served as executive editor at Simon and Schuster and editor in chief at Atheneum. In addition to his three books of social history, he has written six novels.

DAVID E. KYVIG is a professor of history at Northern Illinois University. He was awarded the Bancroft Prize for his work *Explicit and Authentic Acts: Amending the U.S. Constitution, 1776–1995*.

ARTHUR S. LINK was a professor at Princeton University. He is the editor-in-chief of the Woodrow Wilson papers and the author of the definitive multi-volume biography of President Wilson.

RICHARD L. McCORMICK is president of Rutgers University in New Brunswick, New Jersey. He received his Ph.D. in history from Yale University in 1976, and he is the author of *The Party Period and Public Policy: American Politics from the Age of Jackson to the Progressive Era* (Oxford University Press, 1986).

H. R. McMASTER graduated from the U.S. Military Academy at West Point in 1984. Since then, he has held numerous command and staff positions in the military, and during the Persian Gulf War he commanded Eagle Troop 2 Armored Cavalry Regiment in combat. He is the author of *A Distant Thunder* (Harper Collins, 1997). He is currently a Senior Researcher at the Institute for Advanced Studies.

WILLIAM H. McNEILL, Robert A. Millikan Distinguished Service Professor at the University of Chicago, was president of the American Historical Association in 1985. The essay in this volume is his presidential address. He has written more than twenty books of which the most important is *The Rise of the West: A History of the Human Community* (1963). He received his Ph.D. from Cornell University, after studying under Carl Becker and Edward Fox. His next literary enterprise will be a biography of Arnold J. Toynbee.

ROBERT J. NORRELL holds the Bernadotte Schmitt Chair of Excellence in the history department at the University of Tennessee, Knoxville. He is the author of *Reaping the Whirlwind: The Civil Rights Movement in Tuskegee* (1985) and *The House I Live In: Race in the American Century* (Oxford University Press, 2005).

J. RONALD OAKLEY was a professor of history at Davidson County Community College in Greensboro, North Carolina.

ARNOLD A. OFFNER is Cornelia F. Hugel Professor of History and head of the history department at Lafayette College. He is the author of *American Appeasement: United States Foreign Policy and Germany, 1933–1938* (1969) and *Origins of the Second World War: American Foreign Policy and World Politics, 1917–1941* (1975) and with Theodore A. Wilson co-edited *Victory in Europe, 1945: The Allied Triumph over Germany and the Origins of the*

Cold War (1999). He has recently completed a book-length study of President Harry S. Truman and the origins of the Cold War.

ARTHUR M. SCHLESINGER, JR. (1917–2008) was the Albert Schweitzer Professor Emeritus of the Humanities at the City University of New York and the author of prize-wining books on Presidents Andrew Jackson, Franklin Roosevelt, and John F. Kennedy. His publications include *The Cycles of American History* (Houghton Mifflin, 1986) and *History of American Lif*e (Simon & Schuster, 1996).

DONALD SPIVEY is professor of history and Cooper Fellow in the history department at the University of Miami. He received his Ph.D. from the University of California, Davis (1976). He is the editor of *Sport in America: New Historical Perspective*s (Greenwood Press, 1985) and the author of *The Politics of Miseducation: The Booker Washington Institute of Liberia, 1929–1984* (University Press of Kentucky, 1996). He is currently working on a biography of Leroy "Satchel" Paige.

JOHN C. TEAFORD is a professor of history at Purdue University in West Lafayette, Indiana. His publications include *Post-Suburbia: Government and Politics in the Edge Citie*s (Johns Hopkins University Press, 1996) and *Cities of the Heartland: The Rise and Fall of the Industrial Midwes*t (Indiana University Press, 1994).

BRIAN VANDEMARK teaches history at the United States Naval Academy at Annapolis. He served as research assistant on Clark Clifford's autobiography, *Counsel to the President: A Memoir* (Random House, 1991) and as collaborator on former secretary of defense Robert S. McNamara's Vietnam memoir, *In Retrospect: The Tragedy and Lessons of Vietnam* (Times Books, 1995).

J. DAVID WOODARD is a professor of history and political science at the University of South Carolina and is the author of a number of books and articles about the modern conservative movement.

MARK WYMAN is professor of history at Illinois State University and the author of *Round-Trip to America: the Immigrant Returns to Europe, 1880–193*0 (Cornell University Press, 1993).

decisively

apparent

integration

indispensable

null previous

ratify

aggressor

FDR returned to A...

material

Villain &.L

63

352 - 432 5277